BUSINESS DATABASE SYSTEMS

Visit the *Business Database Systems* Companion Website at **www.pearsoned.co.uk/connolly** to find valuable **student** learning material including:

- Lecture slides
- An implementation of the *StayHome Online Rentals* database system in Microsoft Access®
- An SQL script for each common data model described in Appendix I to create the corresponding set of base tables for the database system
- An SQL script to create an implementation of the *Perfect Pets* database system

PEARSON
Education

BUSINESS DATABASE SYSTEMS

Thomas Connolly
School of Computing
University of the West of Scotland

Carolyn Begg
School of Computing
University of the West of Scotland

Richard Holowczak
Department of Statistics and Computer Information Systems
Zicklin School of Business, Baruch College
City University of New York

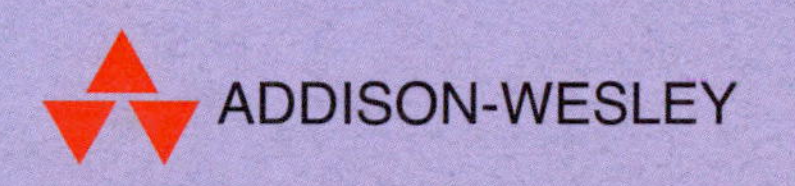

An imprint of Pearson Education
Harlow, England • London • New York • Boston • San Francisco • Toronto • Sydney • Singapore • Hong Kong
Tokyo • Seoul • Taipei • New Delhi • Cape Town • Madrid • Mexico City • Amsterdam • Munich • Paris • Milan

Pearson Education Limited
Edinburgh Gate
Harlow
Essex CM20 2JE
England

and Associated Companies throughout the world

Visit us on the World Wide Web at:
www.pearsoned.co.uk

First published 2008

ISBN 978-1-4058-7437-3

British Library Cataloguing-in-Publication Data
A catalogue record for this book is available from the British Library

Library of Congress Cataloging-in-Publication Data
Connolly, Thomas.
Business database systems / Thomas Connolly, Carolyn Begg, Richard Holowczak.
p. cm.
Includes bibliographical references and index.
ISBN 978-1-4058-7437-3 (pbk.)
1. Business—Databases. 2. Database management. 3. Database design. 4. Management information systems. I. Begg, Carolyn E. II. Holowczak, Richard. III. Title.
HF5548.2.C623 2008
005.74—dc22

2008013992

10 9 8 7 6 5 4 3 2 1
12 11 10 09 08

Typeset in 10/12 pt Times by 35
Printed and bound by Rotolito Lombarda, Italy

The publisher's policy is to use paper manufactured from sustainable forests.

Dedication

T.C.: To Sheena, Kathryn, Michael and Stephen will all my love.

C.B.: To my Mother for her endless support and encouragement

R.H.: To Yvette, Christopher and Ethan for all of their love and support.

Brief contents

Contents

Supporting resources

Visit **www.pearsoned.co.uk/connolly** to find valuable online resources.

Companion Website for students

- Lecture slides
- An implementation of the *StayHome Online Rentals* database system in Microsoft Access®
- An SQL script for each common data model described in Appendix I to create the corresponding set of base tables for the database system
- An SQL script to create an implementation of the *Perfect Pets* database system

For instructors

- Editable lecture slides in Microsoft PowerPoint®
- Teaching suggestions
- Solutions to all review questions and exercises
- Sample examination questions with model solutions
- Additional case studies and assignments with solutions

Also: The regularly maintained Companion Website provides the following features:

- Search tool to help locate specific items of content
- E-mail results and profile tools to send results of quizzes to instructors
- Online help and support to assist with website usage and troubleshooting

For more information please contact your local Pearson Education sales representative or visit **www.pearsoned.co.uk/connolly**

Guided Tour

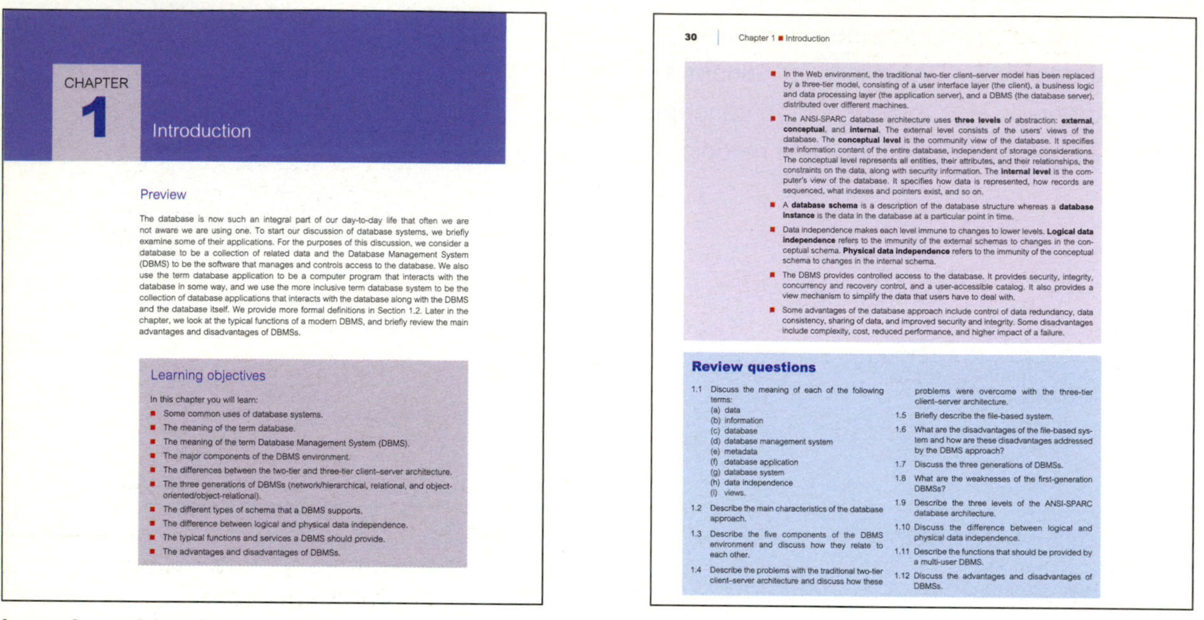

CHAPTER 1

Introduction

Preview

The database is now such an integral part of our day-to-day life that often we are not aware we are using one. To start our discussion of database systems, we briefly examine some of their applications. For the purposes of this discussion, we consider a database to be a collection of related data and the Database Management System (DBMS) to be the software that manages and controls access to the database. We also use the term database application to be a computer program that interacts with the database in some way, and we use the more inclusive term database system to be the collection of database applications that interacts with the database along with the DBMS and the database itself. We provide more formal definitions in Section 1.2. Later in the chapter, we look at the typical functions of a modern DBMS, and briefly review the main advantages and disadvantages of DBMSs.

Learning objectives

In this chapter you will learn:

- Some common uses of database systems.
- The meaning of the term database.
- The meaning of the term Database Management System (DBMS).
- The major components of the DBMS environment.
- The differences between the two-tier and three-tier client-server architecture.
- The three generations of DBMSs (network/hierarchical, relational, and object-oriented/object-relational).
- The different types of schema that a DBMS supports.
- The difference between logical and physical data independence.
- The typical functions and services a DBMS should provide.
- The advantages and disadvantages of DBMSs.

Learning objectives outline the key topics covered in each chapter.

30 | Chapter 1 ■ Introduction

- In the Web environment, the traditional two-tier client–server model has been replaced by a three-tier model, consisting of a user interface layer (the client), a business logic and data processing layer (the application server), and a DBMS (the database server), distributed over different machines.
- The ANSI-SPARC database architecture uses **three levels** of abstraction: **external**, **conceptual**, and **internal**. The external level consists of the users' views of the database. The **conceptual level** is the community view of the database. It specifies the information content of the entire database, independent of storage considerations. The conceptual level represents all entities, their attributes, and their relationships, the constraints on the data, along with security information. The **internal level** is the computer's view of the database. It specifies how data is represented, how records are sequenced, what indexes and pointers exist, and so on.
- A **database schema** is a description of the database structure whereas a **database instance** is the data in the database at a particular point in time.
- Data independence makes each level immune to changes to lower levels. **Logical data independence** refers to the immunity of the external schemas to changes in the conceptual schema. **Physical data independence** refers to the immunity of the conceptual schema to changes in the internal schema.
- The DBMS provides controlled access to the database. It provides security, integrity, concurrency and recovery control, and a user-accessible catalog. It also provides a view mechanism to simplify the data that users have to deal with.
- Some advantages of the database approach include control of data redundancy, data consistency, sharing of data, and improved security and integrity. Some disadvantages include complexity, cost, reduced performance, and higher impact of a failure.

Review questions

1.1 Discuss the meaning of each of the following terms:
(a) data
(b) information
(c) database
(d) database management system
(e) metadata
(f) database application
(g) database system
(h) data independence
(i) views.

1.2 Describe the main characteristics of the database approach.

1.3 Describe the five components of the DBMS environment and discuss how they relate to each other.

1.4 Describe the problems with the traditional two-tier client–server architecture and discuss how these problems were overcome with the three-tier client–server architecture.

1.5 Briefly describe the file-based system.

1.6 What are the disadvantages of the file-based system and how are these disadvantages addressed by the DBMS approach?

1.7 Discuss the three generations of DBMSs.

1.8 What are the weaknesses of the first-generation DBMSs?

1.9 Describe the three levels of the ANSI-SPARC database architecture.

1.10 Discuss the difference between logical and physical data independence.

1.11 Describe the functions that should be provided by a multi-user DBMS.

1.12 Discuss the advantages and disadvantages of DBMSs.

Review questions help you to test your understanding of the concepts covered in the chapter you've just read.

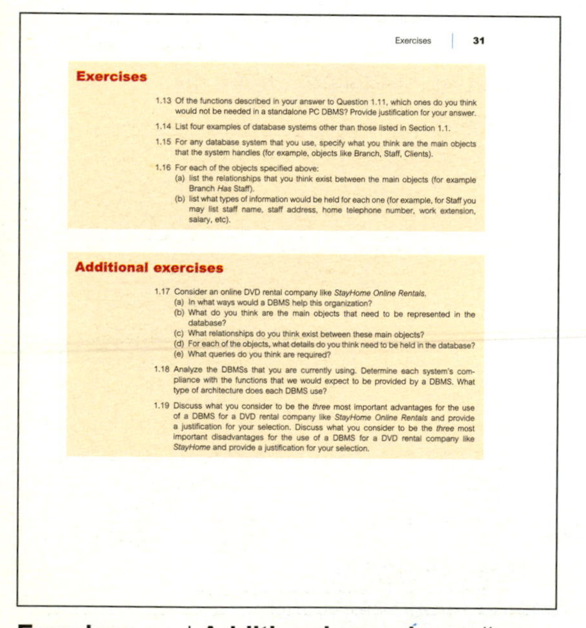

Exercises | 31

Exercises

1.13 Of the functions described in your answer to Question 1.11, which ones do you think would not be needed in a standalone PC DBMS? Provide justification for your answer.

1.14 List four examples of database systems other than those listed in Section 1.1.

1.15 For any database system that you use, specify what you think are the main objects that the system handles (for example, objects like Branch, Staff, Clients).

1.16 For each of the objects specified above:
(a) list the relationships that you think exist between the main objects (for example Branch *Has* Staff).
(b) list what types of information would be held for each one (for example, for Staff you may list staff name, staff address, home telephone number, work extension, salary, etc).

Additional exercises

1.17 Consider an online DVD rental company like *StayHome Online Rentals*.
(a) In what ways would a DBMS help this organization?
(b) What do you think are the main objects that need to be represented in the database?
(c) What relationships do you think exist between these main objects?
(d) For each of the objects, what details do you think need to be held in the database?
(e) What queries do you think are required?

1.18 Analyze the DBMSs that you are currently using. Determine each system's compliance with the functions that we would expect to be provided by a DBMS. What type of architecture does each DBMS use?

1.19 Discuss what you consider to be the *three* most important advantages for the use of a DBMS for a DVD rental company like *StayHome Online Rentals* and provide a justification for your selection. Discuss what you consider to be the *three* most important disadvantages for the use of a DBMS for a DVD rental company like *StayHome* and provide a justification for your selection.

Exercises and **Additional exercises** allow you to try your hand in 'real-world' scenarios and so develop a solid working knowledge.

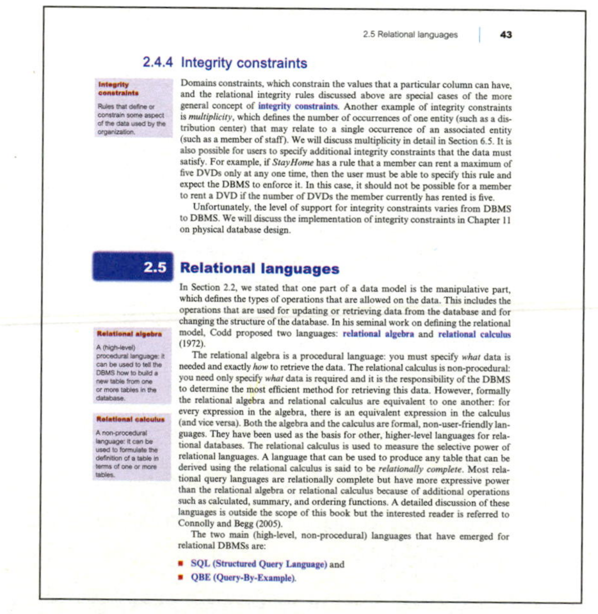

2.5 Relational languages | 43

2.4.4 Integrity constraints

Integrity constraints — Rules that define or constrain some aspect of the data used by the organization.

Domains constraints, which constrain the values that a particular column can have, and the relational integrity rules discussed above are special cases of the more general concept of **integrity constraints**. Another example of integrity constraints is *multiplicity*, which defines the number of occurrences of one entity (such as a distribution center) that may relate to a single occurrence of an associated entity (such as a member of staff). We will discuss multiplicity in detail in Section 6.5. It is also possible for users to specify additional integrity constraints that the data must satisfy. For example, if *StayHome* has a rule that a member can rent a maximum of five DVDs only at any one time, then the user must be able to specify this rule and expect the DBMS to enforce it. In this case, it should not be possible for a member to rent a DVD if the number of DVDs the member currently has rented is five.

Unfortunately, the level of support for integrity constraints varies from DBMS to DBMS. We will discuss the implementation of integrity constraints in Chapter 11 on physical database design.

2.5 Relational languages

In Section 2.2, we stated that one part of a data model is the manipulative part, which defines the types of operations that are allowed on the data. This includes the operations that are used for updating or retrieving data from the database and for changing the structure of the database. In his seminal work on defining the relational model, Codd proposed two languages: **relational algebra** and **relational calculus** (1972).

Relational algebra — A (high-level) procedural language: it can be used to tell the DBMS how to build a new table from one or more tables in the database.

Relational calculus — A non-procedural language: it can be used to formulate the definition of a table in terms of one or more tables.

The relational algebra is a procedural language: you must specify *what* data is needed and exactly *how* to retrieve the data. The relational calculus is non-procedural: you need only specify *what* data is required and it is the responsibility of the DBMS to determine the most efficient method for retrieving this data. However, formally the relational algebra and relational calculus are equivalent to one another: for every expression in the algebra, there is an equivalent expression in the calculus (and vice versa). Both the algebra and the calculus are formal, non-user-friendly languages. They have been used as the basis for other, higher-level languages for relational databases. The relational calculus is used to measure the selective power of relational languages. A language that can be used to produce any table that can be derived using the relational calculus is said to be *relationally complete*. Most relational query languages are relationally complete but have more expressive power than the relational algebra or relational calculus because of additional operations such as calculated, summary, and ordering functions. A detailed discussion of these languages is outside the scope of this book but the interested reader is referred to Connolly and Begg (2005).

The two main (high-level, non-procedural) languages that have emerged for relational DBMSs are:

- **SQL (Structured Query Language)** and
- **QBE (Query-By-Example).**

Key terms are highlighted and many are defined in the margin when they are first introduced in the text.

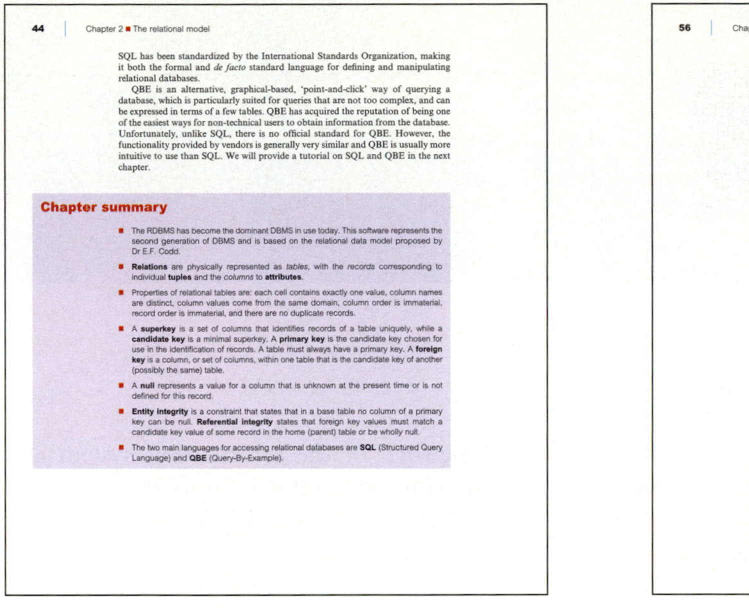

44 | Chapter 2 ■ The relational model

SQL has been standardized by the International Standards Organization, making it both the formal and *de facto* standard language for defining and manipulating relational databases.

QBE is an alternative, graphical-based, 'point-and-click' way of querying a database, which is particularly suited for queries that are not too complex, and can be expressed in terms of a few tables. QBE has acquired the reputation of being one of the easiest ways for non-technical users to obtain information from the database. Unfortunately, unlike SQL, there is no official standard for QBE. However, the functionality provided by vendors is generally very similar and QBE is usually more intuitive to use than SQL. We will provide a tutorial on SQL and QBE in the next chapter.

Chapter summary

- The RDBMS has become the dominant DBMS in use today. This software represents the second generation of DBMS and is based on the relational data model proposed by Dr E.F. Codd.
- **Relations** are physically represented as *tables*, with the *records* corresponding to individual **tuples** and the *columns* to **attributes**.
- Properties of relational tables are: each cell contains exactly one value, column names are distinct, column values come from the same domain, column order is immaterial, record order is immaterial, and there are no duplicate records.
- A **superkey** is a set of columns that identifies records of a table uniquely, while a **candidate key** is a minimal superkey. A **primary key** is the candidate key chosen for use in the identification of records. A table must always have a primary key. A **foreign key** is a column, or set of columns, within one table that is the candidate key of another (possibly the same) table.
- A **null** represents a value for a column that is unknown at the present time or is not defined for this record.
- **Entity integrity** is a constraint that states that in a base table no column of a primary key can be null. **Referential integrity** states that foreign key values must match a candidate key value of some record in the home (parent) table or be wholly null.
- The two main languages for accessing relational databases are **SQL** (Structured Query Language) and **QBE** (Query-By-Example).

Chapter summaries recap the most important points you should take from each chapter.

56 | Chapter 3 ■ SQL and QBE

Query 3.8 Pattern match search condition (LIKE/NOT LIKE)

List all staff whose first name is 'Sally'.

Note SQL has two special pattern-matching symbols:

% the percent character represents any sequence of zero or more characters (*wildcard*);

_ an underscore character represents any single character.

All other characters in the pattern represent themselves. For example:

- `name` **LIKE** 'S%' means the first character must be S, but the rest of the string can be anything.
- `name` **LIKE** 'S_ _ _ _' means that there must be exactly five characters in the string, the first of which must be an S.
- `name` **LIKE** '%S' means any sequence of characters, of length at least 1, with the last character an S.
- `name` **LIKE** '%Sally%' means a sequence of characters of any length containing Sally.
- `name` **NOT LIKE** 'S%' means the first character cannot be an S.

If the search string can include the pattern-matching character itself, we can use an escape character to represent the pattern-matching character. For example, to check for the string '15%,' we can use the predicate:

LIKE '15#%' **ESCAPE** '#'

Using the pattern-matching search condition of SQL, we can find all staff whose first name is 'Sally' using the following query:

```
SELECT staffNo, name, position, salary
FROM Staff
WHERE name LIKE 'Sally%';
```

The result table is shown in Table 3.8.

Table 3.8 Result table of Query 3.8

staffNo	name	position	salary
S0003	Sally Adams	Assistant	30000
S2250	Sally Stern	Manager	48000

Note Some RDBMSs, such as Microsoft Office Access, use the wildcard characters * and ? instead of % and _.

Highlighted **Notes** and **Tips** feature throughout, giving you useful additional information.

3.2 Data manipulation | 59

These functions operate on a single column of a table and return a single value. COUNT, MIN, and MAX apply to both numeric and non-numeric fields, but SUM and AVG may be used on numeric fields only. Apart from COUNT(*), each function eliminates nulls first and operates only on the remaining non-null values. COUNT(*) is a special use of COUNT, which counts all the rows of a table, regardless of whether nulls or duplicate values occur.

If we want to eliminate duplicates before the function is applied, we use the keyword DISTINCT before the column name in the function. DISTINCT has no effect with the MIN and MAX functions. However, it may have an effect on the result of SUM or AVG, so consideration must be given to whether duplicates should be included or excluded in the computation. In addition, DISTINCT can be specified only once in a query.

Key point It is important to note that an aggregate function can be used only in the SELECT list and in the HAVING clause. It is incorrect to use it elsewhere. If the SELECT list includes an aggregate function and no GROUP BY clause is being used to group data together, then no item in the SELECT list can include any reference to a column unless that column is the argument to an aggregate function. We discuss the HAVING and GROUP BY clauses in Section 3.2.5. For example, the following query is illegal:

```
SELECT staffNo, COUNT(salary)
FROM Staff;
```

because the query does not have a GROUP BY clause and the column `staffNo` in the SELECT list is used outside an aggregate function.

Query 3.11 Use of COUNT and SUM

List the total number of staff with a salary greater than $40 000 and the sum of their salaries.

```
SELECT COUNT(staffNo) AS totalStaff, SUM(salary) AS totalSalary
FROM Staff
WHERE salary > 40000;
```

The WHERE clause is the same as in Query 3.5. However, in this case, we apply the COUNT function to count the number of rows satisfying the WHERE clause and we apply the SUM function to add together the salaries in these rows. The result table is shown in Table 3.11.

Table 3.11 Result table of Query 3.11

totalStaff	totalSalary
4	189000

Key points indicate the crucial details you'll need to remember in order to build/manage databases successfully.

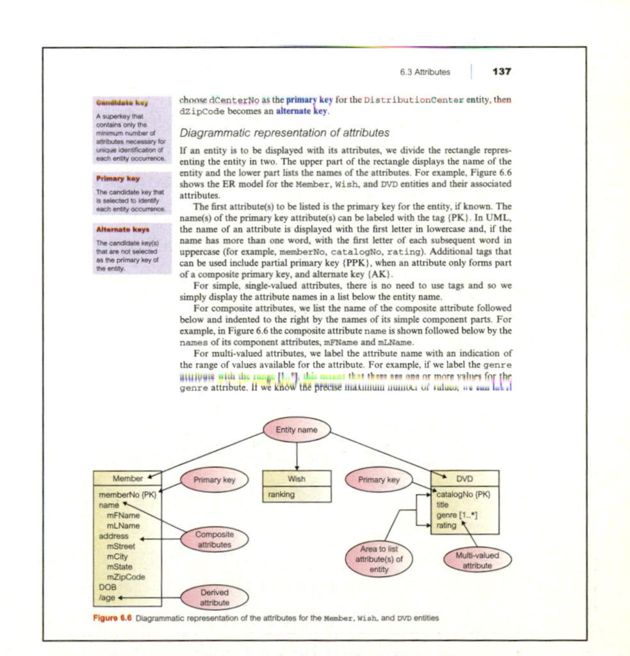

6.3 Attributes | 137

Candidate key
A superkey that contains only the minimum number of attributes necessary for unique identification of each entity occurrence.

Primary key
The candidate key that is selected to identify each entity occurrence.

Alternate keys
The candidate key(s) that are not selected as the primary key of the entity.

choose `dCenterNo` as the **primary key** for the `DistributionCenter` entity, then `dZipCode` becomes an **alternate key**.

Diagrammatic representation of attributes

If an entity is to be displayed with its attributes, we divide the rectangle representing the entity in two. The upper part of the rectangle displays the name of the entity and the lower part lists the names of the attributes. For example, Figure 6.6 shows the ER model for the `Member`, `Wish`, and `DVD` entities and their associated attributes.

The first attribute(s) to be listed is the primary key for the entity, if known. The name(s) of the primary key attribute(s) can be labeled with the tag {PK}. In UML, the name of an attribute is displayed with the first letter in lowercase and, if the name has more than one word, with the first letter of each subsequent word in uppercase (for example, `memberNo`, `catalogNo`, `rating`). Additional tags that can be used include partial primary key {PPK}, when an attribute only forms part of a composite primary key, and alternate key {AK}.

For simple, single-valued attributes, there is no need to use tags and so we simply display the attribute names in a list below the entity name.

For composite attributes, we list the name of the composite attribute followed below and indented to the right by the names of its simple component parts. For example, in Figure 6.6 the composite attribute `name` is shown followed below by the names of its component attributes, `mFName` and `mLName`.

For multi-valued attributes, we label the attribute name with an indication of the range of values available for the attribute. For example, if we label the `genre` attribute with the range [1..*], this means that there are one or more values for the `genre` attribute. If we know the precise maximum number of values, we can label

Figure 6.6 Diagrammatic representation of the attributes for the `Member`, `Wish`, and `DVD` entities

The industry standard **Unified Modelling Language** diagramming style is used throughout.

Preface

Background

The database is now the underlying framework of the information system and has fundamentally changed the way many companies and individuals work. The developments in this technology over the last few years have produced database systems that are more powerful and more intuitive to use, and some users are creating databases and applications without the necessary knowledge to produce an effective and efficient system. Looking at the literature, we found many excellent books that examine a part of the database system development lifecycle. However, we found very few that covered analysis, design, and implementation and described the development process in a simple-to-understand way that could be used by both business and business IT readers.

Our original concept therefore was to provide a book for the academic and business community that explained as clearly as possible how to analyze, design, and implement a database. This would cover both simple databases consisting of a few tables to large databases containing tens to hundreds of tables. During the initial reviews that we carried out, it became clear that the book would also be useful for the academic community and provide a very simple and clear presentation of a database design methodology that would complement a more extensive recommended textbook, such as our own book *Database System, Fourth Edition*. With the help of our reviewers and readers, we have extended our previous work, *Database Solutions, Second Edition*, to provide a more up-to-date integrated case study and added new chapters to cover advanced database systems and applications.

A methodology for understanding database design

The methodology we present in this book for relational database management systems (DBMSs) – the predominant system for business applications at present – has been tried and tested over the years in both industrial and academic environments. The methodology is divided into three phases:

- a conceptual database design phase, in which we develop a model of the **data** used in an organization independent of *all* physical considerations;

- a logical database design phase, in which we develop a model of the data used in an organization based on a specific data model (in our case, the relational data model), but independent of a particular DBMS and other physical considerations;
- a physical database design phase, in which we decide how we are going to realize the implementation in the target DBMS, such as Microsoft Access, Microsoft SQL Server, Oracle, DB2, or Informix.

We present each phase as a series of simple-to-follow steps. For the inexperienced designer, we expect that the steps will be followed in the order described, and guidelines are provided throughout to help with this process. For the experienced designer, the methodology can be less prescriptive, acting more as a framework or checklist.

To help use the methodology and understand the important issues, we provide a comprehensive worked example that is integrated throughout the book based on an online DVD rental company called *StayHome Online Rentals*. To reinforce the methodology we also provide a second case study based on a veterinary clinic called *PerfectPets* that we use in the Exercises at the end of most chapters.

Common data models

As well as providing readers with additional experience of designing databases, Appendix I provides many common data models that may be useful to you in your professional work. In fact, it has been estimated that one third of a data model consists of common constructs that are applicable to most companies and the remaining two thirds are either industry-specific or company-specific. Thus, most database design work consists of recreating constructs that have already been produced many times before in other companies. The models featured may not represent a company exactly, but they may provide a starting point from which a more suitable data model can be developed that matches the company's specific requirements. Some of the models we provide cover the following common business areas:

- Customer Order Entry
- Inventory Control
- Asset Management
- Project Management
- Course Management
- Human Resource Management
- Payroll Management.

UML (Unified Modeling Language)

Increasingly, companies are standardizing the way in which they model data by selecting a particular approach to data modeling and using it throughout their database development projects. A popular high-level data model used in logical database design, and the one we use in this book, is based on the concepts of the Entity–Relationship (ER) model. Currently there is no standard notation for an ER model. Most books that cover database design for relational DBMSs tend to use one of two conventional notations:

- Chen's notation, consisting of rectangles representing entities and diamonds representing relationships, with lines linking the rectangles and diamonds;
- Crow's Feet notation, again consisting of rectangles representing entities and lines between entities representing relationships, with a crow's foot at the end of a line representing a one-to-many relationship.

Both notations are well supported by current CASE tools. However, they can be quite cumbersome to use and a bit difficult to explain. Following an extensive questionnaire carried out on our behalf by Pearson Education, there was a general consensus that the favored notation for teaching database systems would become the object-oriented modeling language called **UML (Unified Modeling Language)**. UML is a notation that combines elements from the three major strands of object-oriented design: Rumbaugh's OMT modeling, Booch's Object-Oriented Analysis and Design, and Jacobson's Objectory.

There are three primary reasons for adopting UML:

(1) It is now an industry standard and has been adopted by the Object Management Group (OMG) as the standard notation for object methods.

(2) It is arguably clearer and easier to use. We have used both Chen's and Crow's Feet notation but made the transition to UML in 1999 and have found it much easier to use to teach modeling concepts. The feedback we received from the two editions of the previous version of this book, *Database Solutions*, was fully supportive of the UML notation.

(3) UML is now being adopted within academia for teaching object-oriented analysis and design (OOAD), and using UML for teaching in database courses provides more synergy.

Therefore, in this book we have adopted a simplified version of the **class** diagram notation from UML. We believe you will find this notation easier to understand and use.

Showing how to implement a design

We believe it is important to show you how to convert a database design into a physical implementation. In this book, we show how to implement the first case study (the online DVD rental company called *StayHome Online Rentals*) in the Microsoft Office Access 2007 DBMS.

Who should read this book?

We have tried to write this book in a self-contained way. The exception to this is physical database design, where you need to have a good understanding of how the target DBMS operates. Our intended audience is anyone who needs to develop a database, including but not limited to the following:

- information modelers and database designers;
- database application designers and implementers;
- database practitioners;
- data and database administrators;
- Information Systems, Business IT, and Computing Science professors specializing in database design;
- database students – undergraduate, advanced undergraduate, and graduate;
- anyone wishing to design and develop a database system.

Structure of this book

We have divided the book into four parts and a set of appendices.

- Part I – Background. We provide an introduction to DBMSs, the relational model, and a tutorial-style chapter on SQL and QBE in Chapters 1, 2, and 3. To avoid complexity in this part of the book, we consider only the SQL Data Manipulation Language (DML) statements in Chapter 3 and cover the main Data Definition Language (DDL) statements and the programming language aspects of SQL in Appendix E. We also provide an overview of the database system development lifecycle in Chapter 4.
- Part II – Database Analysis and Design Techniques. We discuss techniques for database analysis in Chapter 5 and show how to use some of these techniques to analyze the requirements for the online DVD rental company *StayHome Online Rentals*. We show how to draw Entity–Relationship diagrams using UML in Chapter 6, advanced ER techniques in Chapter 7, and how to apply the rules of normalization in Chapter 8. ER models and normalization are important techniques that are used in the database design methodology we describe in Part III.
- Part III – Database Design Methodology. In this part of the book we describe and illustrate a step-by-step approach for database design. In Step 1, presented in Chapter 9, we discuss conceptual data modeling and create a conceptual model for the DVD rental company *StayHome*. In Step 2, presented in Chapter 10, we discuss logical data modeling and map the ER model to a set of database tables. In Chapter 11 we discuss physical database design, and show how to design a set of base tables for the target DBMS. In this chapter we also show how to choose file organizations and indexes, how to design the user views and security mechanisms that will protect the data from unauthorized access, when and how to introduce controlled redundancy to achieve improved performance, and finally how to monitor and tune the operational system.
- Part IV – Current and Emerging Trends. In this part of the book, we examine a number of current and emerging trends in Database Management, covering:

Database Administration and Security (Chapter 12), Professional, Legal, and Ethical Issues in Database Management (Chapter 13), Transaction Management (Chapter 14), eCommerce and Database Systems (Chapter 15), Distributed and Mobile DBMSs (Chapter 16), object-oriented DBMSs (OODBMSs) and object-relational DBMSs (ORDBMSs) in Chapter 17, and Data Warehousing, Online Analytical Processing (OLAP), and Data Mining (Chapter 18).

- Appendices. Appendix A provides a further user view for the *StayHome Online Rentals* case study to demonstrate an extension to the basic logical database design methodology for database systems with multiple user views, which are managed using the view integration approach. Appendix B provides a second case study based on a veterinary clinic called *PerfectPets*, which we use in the Exercises at the end of many chapters. Appendix C examines the two main alternative ER notations: Chen's notation and the Crow's Feet notation. Appendix D provides a summary of the methodology as a quick reference guide. Appendix E presents some advanced SQL material covering the SQL DDL statements and elements of the SQL programming language, such as cursors, stored procedures and functions, and database triggers. Appendices F and G provide guidelines for choosing indexes and when to consider denormalization to help with Step 4.3 and Step 7 of the physical database design methodology presented in Part III. Appendix H provides an introduction to the main object-oriented concepts for those readers who are unfamiliar with them. Finally, Appendix I provides a set of15 common data models.

The logical organization of the book and the suggested paths through it are illustrated in Figure P.1.

Pedagogy

To make the book as readable as possible, we have adopted the following style and structure:

- A set of objectives for each chapter, clearly highlighted at the start of the chapter.
- A summary at the end of each chapter covering the main points introduced.
- Review Questions and Exercises at the end of most chapters.
- Each important concept that is introduced is clearly defined and highlighted by placing the definition in a box.
- A series of notes and tips – you will see these throughout the book with an adjacent icon to highlight them.
- Diagrams are used liberally throughout to support and clarify concepts.
- A very practical orientation. Each chapter contains many worked examples to illustrate the points covered.
- A Glossary at the end of the book, which you may find useful as a quick reference guide.

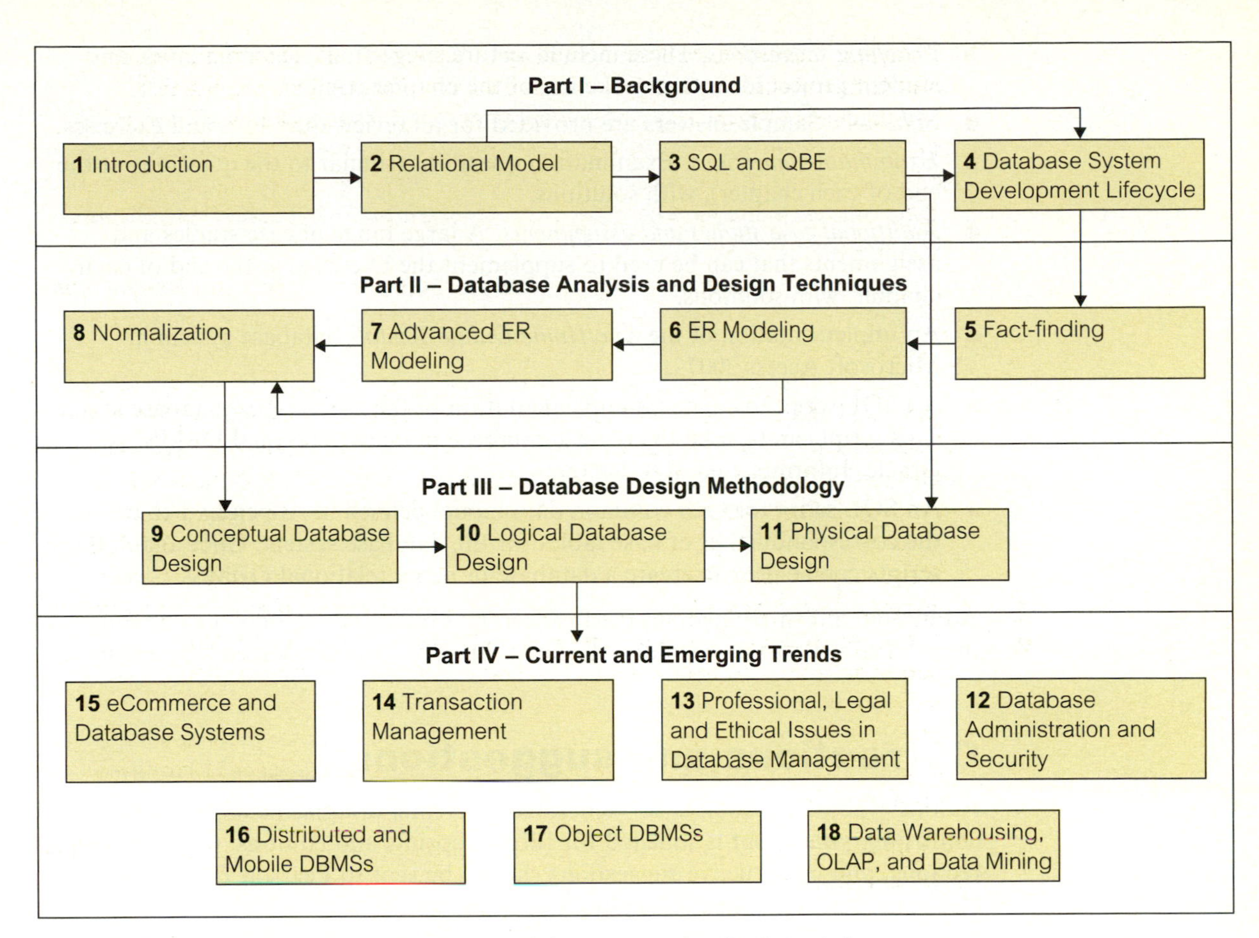

Figure P.1 Logical organization of the book and the suggested paths through it

Business schools that are (or aspire to be) accredited by the Association to Advance Collegiate Schools of Business (AACSB) can make immediate use of the chapter objectives to form clear and concise learning objectives mandated by the 2005 AACSB re-accreditation requirements.

Accompanying Instructor's Guide and Companion Website

A comprehensive supplement containing numerous instructional resources is available for this textbook, upon request to Pearson Education. The accompanying Instructor's Guide includes:

- *Transparency masters* (created using PowerPoint). Containing the main points from each chapter, enlarged illustrations, and tables from the text, these are provided to help the instructor associate lectures and class discussion to the material in the textbook.

- *Teaching suggestions*. These include lecture suggestions, teaching hints, and student project ideas that make use of the chapter content.
- *Solutions*. Sample answers are provided for all review questions and exercises.
- *Examination questions*. Examination questions (similar to the questions at the end of each chapter), with solutions.
- *Additional case studies and assignments*. A large range of case studies and assignments that can be used to supplement the Exercises at the end of each chapter, with solutions.
- An implementation of the *StayHome Online Rentals* database system in Microsoft Access 2007.
- An SQL script to create an implementation of the *PerfectPets* database system. This script can be used to create a database in many relational DBMSs, such as Oracle, Informix, and SQL Server.
- An SQL script for each common data model defined in Appendix I to create the corresponding set of base tables for the database system. Once again, these scripts can be used to create a database in many relational DBMSs.

Additional information about the Instructor's Guide and the book can be found on the Addison Wesley Longman web site at: **http://www.pearsoned.co.uk/connolly**

Corrections and suggestions

As this type of textbook is so vulnerable to errors, disagreements, omissions, and confusion, your input is solicited for future reprints and editions. Comments, corrections, and constructive suggestions should be sent to Pearson Education, or by electronic mail to: **thomas.connolly@uws.ac.uk**

Acknowledgements

This book is the outcome of many years of work by the authors in industry, research, and academia. It is therefore difficult to name all the people who have directly or indirectly helped us in our efforts; an idea here and there may have appeared insignificant at the time but may have had a significant causal effect. For those people we are about to omit, we apologize now. However, special thanks and apologies must first go to our families, who over the years have been neglected, even ignored, while we have been writing our books.

We would first like to thank Simon Plumtree, Owne Knight, our editor, and Joe Vella, our desk editor. We should also like to thank the reviewers of this book, who contributed their comments, suggestions, and advice. In particular, we would like to mention those who took part in the Reviewer Panel listed below:

Kakoli Bandyopadhyay, Lamar University
Dr. Gary Baram, Temple University
Paul Beckman, San Francisco State University
Hossein Besharatian, Strayer University

Linus Bukauskas, Aalborg University
Wingyan Chung, The University of Texas at El Paso
Michael Cole, Rutgers University
Ian Davey-Wilson, Oxford Brookes
Peter Dearnley, University of East Anglia
Lucia Dettori, DePaul University
Nenad Jukic, Loyola University, Chicago
Dawn Jutla, St. Mary's University
Simon Harper, University of Manchester
Robert Hofkin, Goldey-Beacom College
Ralf Klamma, RWTH Aachen
William Lankford, University of West Georgia
Chang Liu, Northern Illinois University
Martha Malaty, Orange Coast College
John Mendonca, Purdue University
Brian Mennecke, Iowa State University
Barry L. Myers, Nazarene University
Kjetil Nørvåg, Norwegian University of Science and Technology
Mike Papazoglou, Tilburg University
Sudha Ram, University of Arizona
Arijit Sengupta, Wright State University
Gerald Stock, Canterbury
Tony Stockman, Queen Mary University, London
Stuart A. Varden, Pace University
John Warren, University of Texas at San Antonio
Robert C. Whale, CTU Online

Thomas M. Connolly
Carolyn E. Begg
Richard Holowczak
Spring 2008

PART I Background

In this part of the book, we introduce you to what constitutes a database system and how this tool can bring great benefits to any organization that chooses to use one. In fact, database systems are now so common and form such an integral part of our day-to-day life that often we are not aware we are using one. The focus of Chapter 1 is to give you a good overview of all the important aspects of database systems. Some of the aspects of databases introduced in this first chapter will be covered in more detail in later chapters.

There are many ways that **data** can be represented and organized in a database system; however, at this time the most popular data model for database systems is called the **relational data model**. To emphasize the importance of this topic to your understanding of databases, this topic is covered in detail in Chapter 2. The relational data model is associated with an equally popular language called **Structured Query Language (SQL)**, and the nature and important aspects of this language are covered in Chapter 3. Also included in this chapter is an introduction to an alternative way to access a relational database using **Query-By-Example (QBE)**.

Evidence of the popularity of the relational data model and SQL is shown by the large number of commercially available database system products that use this model, such as Microsoft Office Access, Microsoft SQL Server, and Oracle Database Management Systems (DBMSs). Aspects of these relational database products are discussed throughout this book and therefore it is important that you understand the topics covered in Chapters 2 and 3 to fully appreciate how these systems do the job of managing data.

Relational database systems have been popular for such a long time that there are now many commercial products to choose from. However, choosing the correct DBMS for your needs is only part of the story in building the correct database system. In the final chapter of this part of the book you are introduced to the **Database System Development Lifecycle (DSDL)**, and it is this lifecycle that takes you through the steps necessary to ensure the correct design, effective creation, and efficient management of the required database system. With the ability to purchase mature DBMS products, the emphasis has shifted from the development of data management software to how the Database System Development Lifecycle can support your customization of the product to suit your needs.

CHAPTER

1 Introduction

Preview

The database is now such an integral part of our day-to-day life that often we are not aware we are using one. To start our discussion of database systems, we briefly examine some of their applications. For the purposes of this discussion, we consider a database to be a collection of related data and the Database Management System (DBMS) to be the software that manages and controls access to the database. We also use the term database application to be a computer program that interacts with the database in some way, and we use the more inclusive term database system to be the collection of database applications that interacts with the database along with the DBMS and the database itself. We provide more formal definitions in Section 1.2. Later in the chapter, we look at the typical functions of a modern DBMS, and briefly review the main advantages and disadvantages of DBMSs.

Learning objectives

In this chapter you will learn:

- Some common uses of database systems.
- The meaning of the term database.
- The meaning of the term Database Management System (DBMS).
- The major components of the DBMS environment.
- The differences between the two-tier and three-tier client–server architecture.
- The three generations of DBMSs (network/hierarchical, relational, and object-oriented/object-relational).
- The different types of schema that a DBMS supports.
- The difference between logical and physical data independence.
- The typical functions and services a DBMS should provide.
- The advantages and disadvantages of DBMSs.

1.1 Examples of the use of database systems

Purchases from the supermarket

When you purchase goods from your local supermarket, it is likely that a database is accessed. The checkout assistant uses a bar code reader to scan each of your purchases. This is linked to a database application that uses the bar code to find the price of the item from a product database. The application then reduces the number of such items in stock and displays the price on the cash register. If the reorder level falls below a specified threshold, the database system may automatically place an order to replenish that item.

Purchases using your credit card

When you purchase goods using your credit card, the cashier normally checks that you have sufficient credit left to make the purchase. This check may be carried out by telephone or it may be done automatically by a card reader linked to a computer system. In either case, there is a database somewhere that contains information about the purchases that you have made using your credit card. To check your credit, there is a database application that uses your credit card number to check that the price of the goods you wish to buy, together with the sum of the purchases you have already made this month, is within your credit limit. When the purchase is confirmed, the details of your purchase are added to this database. The database application also accesses the database to check that the credit card is not on the list of stolen or lost cards before authorizing the purchase. There are other database applications to send out monthly statements to each cardholder and to credit accounts when payment is received.

Booking a holiday travel agent

When you make inquiries about a holiday, the travel agent may access several databases containing vacation and flight details. When you book your holiday, the database system has to make all the necessary booking arrangements. In this case, the system has to ensure that two different agents do not book the same holiday or overbook the seats on the flight. For example, if there is only one seat left on the flight from London to New York and two agents try to reserve the last seat at the same time, the system has to recognize this situation, allow one booking to proceed, and inform the other agent that there are now no seats available. The travel agent may have another, usually separate, database for invoicing.

Using the local library

Whenever you visit your local library, there is probably a database containing details of the books in the library, details of the readers, reservations, and so on. There will be a computerized **index** that allows readers to find a book based on its title, or its authors, or its subject area, or its ISBN. The database system handles reservations to allow a reader to reserve a book and to be informed by post or email when the book is available. The system also sends out reminders to borrowers who have failed to return books by the due date. Typically, the system will have a bar code reader, similar to that used by the supermarket described earlier, which is used to keep track of books coming in and going out of the library.

Renting a DVD

When you wish to rent a DVD from a DVD rental company, you will probably find that the company maintains a database consisting of the DVD titles that it stocks, details on the copies it has for each title, which copies are available for rent and which copies are currently on loan, details of its members (the renters) and which DVDs they are currently renting and date they are to be returned. The company can use this information to monitor stock usage and predict buying trends based on historic rental data. The database may even store more detailed information on each DVD, such as its actors, a brief storyline, and perhaps an image of the DVD cover. Figure 1.1 shows some sample data for such a company.

Using the Internet

Many of the sites on the Internet are driven by database applications. For example, you may visit an online bookstore, such as Amazon.com, that allows you to browse and buy books. The bookstore allows you to browse books in different categories, such as computing or management, or it may allow you to browse books by author name. In either case, there is a database on the organization's **Web server** that consists of book details, availability, shipping information, stock levels, and on-order information. Book details include book titles, ISBNs, authors, prices, sales histories,

DVD

catalogNo	title	genre	rating
207132	Casino Royale	Action	PG-13
902355	Harry Potter and the GOF	Children	PG
330553	Lord of the Rings III	Action	PG-13
781132	Shrek 2	Children	PG
445624	Mission Impossible III	Action	PG-13
634817	War of the Worlds	Sci-Fi	PG-13

Actor

actorNo	actorName
A1002	Judi Dench
A3006	Elijah Wood
A2019	Tom Cruise
A7525	Ian McKellen
A4343	Mike Myers
A8401	Daniel Radcliffe

DVDActor

actorNo	catalogNo	character
A1002	207132	M
A3006	330553	Frodo Baggins
A2019	445624	Ethan Hunt
A2019	634817	Ray Ferrier
A7525	330553	Gandalf
A4343	781132	Shrek
A8401	902355	Harry Potter

Figure 1.1 Sample data for a DVD rental company

publishers, reviews, and in-depth descriptions. The database allows books to be cross-referenced – for example, a book may be listed under several categories, such as computing, programming languages, bestsellers, and recommended titles. The cross-referencing also allows Amazon to give you information on other books that are typically ordered along with the title you are interested in.

These are only a few of the applications for database systems, and you will no doubt be aware of many others. Although we take many of these applications for granted, behind them lies some highly complex technology. At the center of this technology is the database itself. For the system to support the applications that the end-users want, in an efficient a manner as possible, requires a suitably structured database. Producing this structure is known as **database design**, and it is this important activity that we are going to concentrate on in this book. Whether the database you wish to build is small, or large like the ones above, database design is a fundamental issue, and the methodology presented in this book will help you build the database correctly in a structured way. Having a well-designed database will allow you to produce a system that satisfies the users' requirements and, at the same time, provides acceptable performance.

1.2 Database approach

In this section, we provide a more formal definition of the terms *database, Database Management System*, and *database application* than we gave at the start of the last section. To help understand the discussions that follow, we first briefly examine the difference between data and information.

1.2.1 Data and information

Data

Raw (unprocessed) facts that have some relevancy to an individual or organization.

Consider the following **data**:

Ann Peters 1 Casino Royale

Without further structure these pieces of data appearing together have no meaning to us. We can deduce that 'Ann Peters' is an individual and that 'Casino Royale' is the name of an Ian Fleming book as well as the name of a film, but thereafter, the '1' could represent many things. However, consider Figure 1.2. We can now see that Ann Peters has something to do with a DVD rental company called *StayHome Online Rentals*[1] (she is probably a member) and that the '1' and 'Casino Royale' represent data relating to her DVD rental wish list. Having imposed a structure, we have transformed this raw data into **information** – something that has some meaning to us.

Information

Data that has been processed or given some structure that brings meaning to an individual or organization.

Another way to transform data into something that has meaning is to process the data, for example, using some statistical technique or graphically. Figure 1.3(a) shows some data, which we may be able to deduce is some form of quarterly data.

[1] *Stayhome* is used throughout this book and described in detail in Chapter 5.

Figure 1.2 Transforming data into information by imposing a structure on the data

However, by representing the data graphically and adding some labels, as illustrated in Figure 1.3(b), we transform the data into information, something that is now meaningful to us. This distinction between data and information is not universal and you may find the terms used interchangeably.

1.2.2 The database

Database

A shared collection of logically related data (and a description of this data), designed to meet the information needs of an organization.

Let us examine the definition of a **database** in detail to understand this concept fully.

(1) The database is a single, possibly large, repository of data that can be used simultaneously by many departments and users. All data that is required by these users is integrated with a minimum amount of duplication. Importantly, the database is normally not owned by any one department or user but is a shared corporate resource. Figure 1.4 shows two tables in the *StayHome Online Rentals* database that store data on distribution centers and staff.

(2) As well as holding the organization's operational data, the database holds a description of this data. For this reason, a database is also defined as *a self-describing collection of integrated records*. The description of the data, that is the **metadata** – the 'data about data,' is known as the **system catalog** or **data**

	2006				2007			
	Q1	Q2	Q3	Q4	Q1	Q2	Q3	Q4
D001-Portland	5000	10000	15000	20000	25000	26000	28000	30000
D002-Seattle	5000	10000	15000	18000	20000	23000	26000	29000
D003-New York	6000	20000	30000	32000	35000	26000	28000	31000
D004-San Francisco	6000	20000	25000	30000	32000	34000	40000	41000

(a)

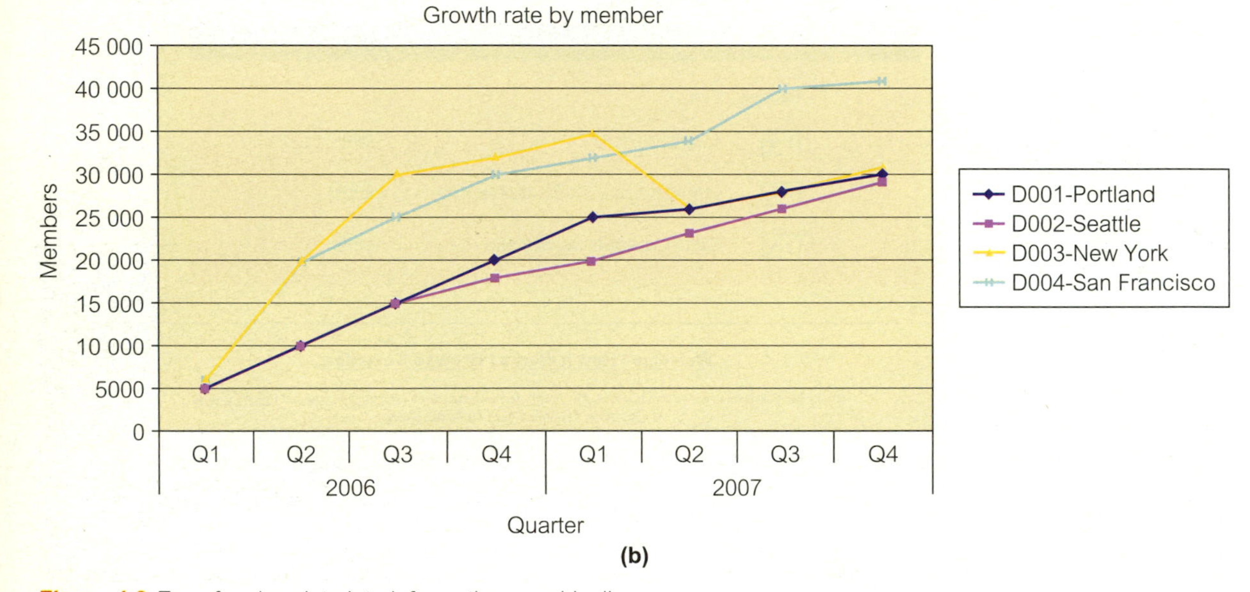

(b)

Figure 1.3 Transforming data into information graphically

dictionary. It is the self-describing nature of a database that provides what is known as **data independence**. This means that if new data structures are added to the database or existing structures in the database are modified, then the database applications that use the database are unaffected, provided they do not directly depend upon what has been modified. For example, if we add a new column to a record or create a new table, existing database applications are unaffected by this change. However, if we remove a column from a table that a database application uses, then that application program is affected by this change and must be modified accordingly.

(3) The final term in the definition of a database that we should explain is 'logically related.' When we analyze the organization's information needs, we attempt to identify the important objects that need to be represented in the database and the *logical relationships* between these objects. The methodology we will present for database design in Chapters 9–11 will provide guidelines for identifying these important objects and their logical relationships.

DCenter No	Street	City	State	Zip Code	Manager
D001	8 Jefferson Way	Portland	OR	97201	Tom Daniels
D002	City Center Plaza	Seattle	WA	98122	Mary Martinez
D003	14 - 8th Avenue	New York	NY	10012	Art Peters
D004	2 W. El Camino	San Francisco	CA	94087	Sally Stern

(a)

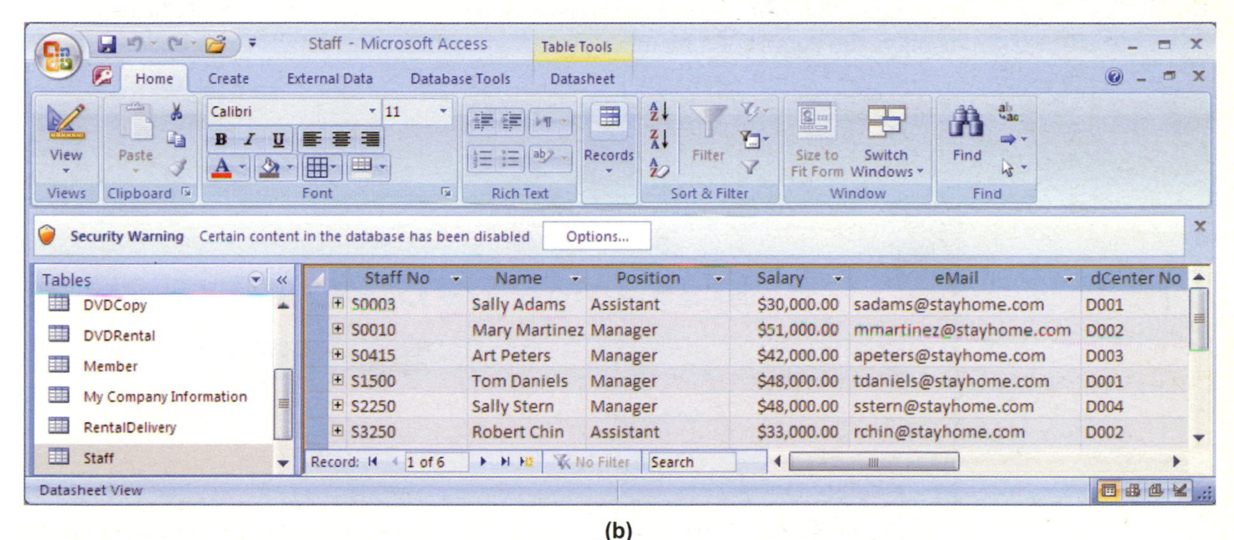

Staff No	Name	Position	Salary	eMail	dCenter No
S0003	Sally Adams	Assistant	$30,000.00	sadams@stayhome.com	D001
S0010	Mary Martinez	Manager	$51,000.00	mmartinez@stayhome.com	D002
S0415	Art Peters	Manager	$42,000.00	apeters@stayhome.com	D003
S1500	Tom Daniels	Manager	$48,000.00	tdaniels@stayhome.com	D001
S2250	Sally Stern	Manager	$48,000.00	sstern@stayhome.com	D004
S3250	Robert Chin	Assistant	$33,000.00	rchin@stayhome.com	D002

(b)

Figure 1.4 Tables in the *StayHome Online Rentals* database that stores data on: (a) distribution centers; (b) staff

1.2.3 The Database Management System (DBMS)

DBMS

A software system that enables users to define, create, and maintain the database, and provides controlled access to this database.

The **DBMS** is the software that interacts with the users, database applications, and the database. Among other things, the DBMS allows users to insert, update, delete, and retrieve data from the database. Having a central repository for all data and the data descriptions allows the DBMS to provide a general inquiry facility to this data, called a *query language*. The provision of a query language (such as SQL) alleviates the problems with earlier systems where the user has to work with a fixed set of queries or where there is a proliferation of database applications, giving major software management problems. We discuss the typical functions and services of a

DBMS in Section 1.6. Some people use the term DBMS more generically to include functions and tools to help users develop database applications.

> **Note** The Structured Query Language (SQL – pronounced 'S-Q-L' or sometimes 'See-Quel') is the main query language for relational DBMSs, such as Microsoft Access, Microsoft SQL Server, DB2, and Oracle. We provide an extensive tutorial on SQL in Chapter 3 and Appendix E.

1.2.4 Database applications

Database application

A computer program that interacts with the database by issuing an appropriate request (typically one or more SQL statements) to the DBMS.

Users interact with the database through a number of **database applications** that are used to create and maintain the database and to generate information. These programs can be conventional batch applications or, more typically nowadays, online applications. The database applications may be written in a third-generation programming language such as C++ or Java, or in some higher-level fourth-generation language. Figure 1.5 shows a (web-based) *StayHome* database application that displays the details of a member of staff and allows the details to be updated.

Figure 1.5 *StayHome* database application to display and update a member of staff's details

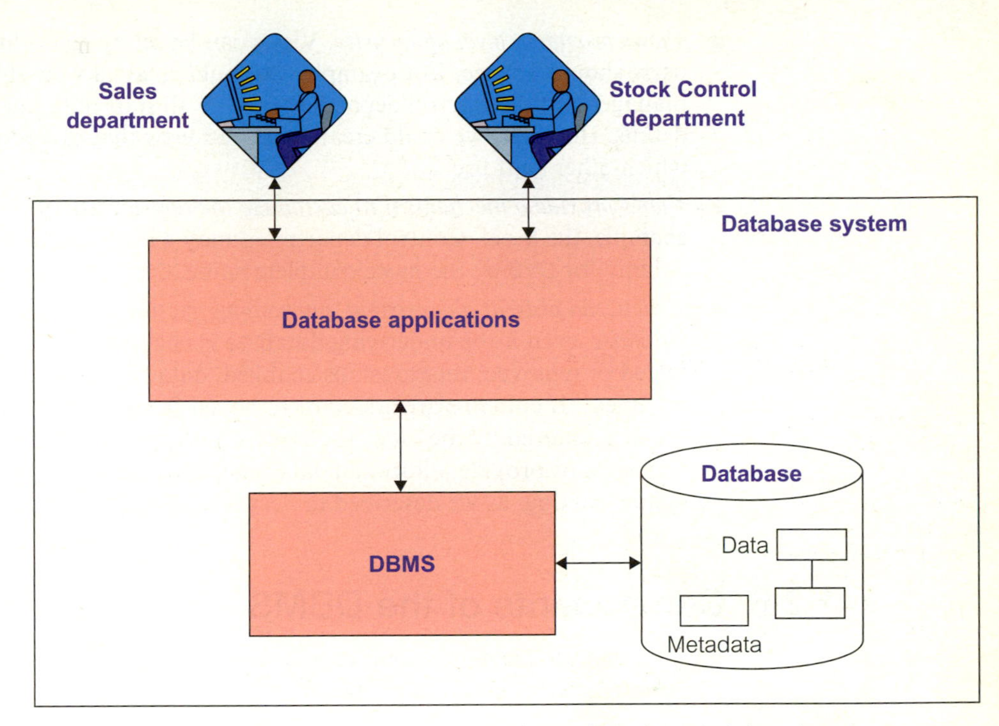

Figure 1.6 The database approach showing sales and stock control departments accessing database through database applications and DBMS

Database system

The collection of database applications that interacts with the database along with the DBMS and the database itself.

Figure 1.6 illustrates the database approach. It shows the Sales and Stock Control departments using their application programs to access the database through the DBMS. Each set of departmental database applications handles data entry, data maintenance, and the generation of reports. The physical structure and storage of the data are managed by the DBMS.

For completeness, we also have the definition of the **database system**.

1.2.5 Views

View

A *virtual table* that does not necessarily exist in the database but is generated by the DBMS from the underlying base tables whenever it is accessed.

With the functionality described above, the DBMS is an extremely powerful tool. However, as end-users are not too interested in how complex or easy a task is for the system, it could be argued that the DBMS has made things more complex because users may now see more data than they actually need or want to do their job. In recognition of this problem, a DBMS provides another facility known as a *view mechanism*, which allows each user to have his or her own customized view of the database, where a view is some subset of the database.

A **view** is usually defined as a query that operates on the base tables to produce another *virtual table*. As well as reducing complexity by letting users see the data in the way they want to see it, views have several other benefits:

- *Views provide a level of security*. Views can be set up to exclude data that some users should not see. For example, we could create a view that allows a center manager and the Payroll department to see all staff data, including salary details. However, we could create a second view that excludes salary details, which other staff use.
- *Views provide a mechanism to customize the appearance of the database*. For example, the Stock Control department may wish to call the `catalogNo` column for `DVD` by the more complete name, `Catalog Number`.
- *A view can present a consistent, unchanging picture of the structure of the database*, even if the underlying database is changed (for example, columns added or removed, relationships changed, data files split, restructured, or renamed). If columns are added or removed from a table, and these columns are not required by the view, the view is not affected by this change. Thus, a view helps provide additional data independence to that provided by the system catalog, as we described in Section 1.2.2.

1.2.6 Components of the DBMS environment

We can identify five major components in the DBMS environment: hardware, software, data, procedures, and people:

(1) *Hardware*: The computer system(s) that the database system runs on. This can range from a single PC, to a single mainframe, to a network of computers.

(2) *Software*: The DBMS software and the database applications, together with the operating system, including network software if the DBMS is being used over a network.

(3) *Data*: The data acts as a bridge between the hardware and software components and the human components. As we have already said, the database contains both the *operational data* (the data for the day-to-day running of the business) and the metadata.

(4) *Procedures*: The instructions and rules that govern the design and use of the database. These may include instructions on how to log on to the DBMS, make backup copies of the database, and handle hardware or software failures.

(5) *People*: This includes the business analysts, database designers, data administrators (DAs), database administrators (DBAs), application programmers, and end-users.

1.2.7 DBMS architectures

Before the advent of the Web, generally a DBMS would be divided into two parts:

- a **client** program that handles the main business and data processing logic and interfaces with the user;
- a **server** program (sometimes called the **DBMS engine**) that manages and controls access to the database.

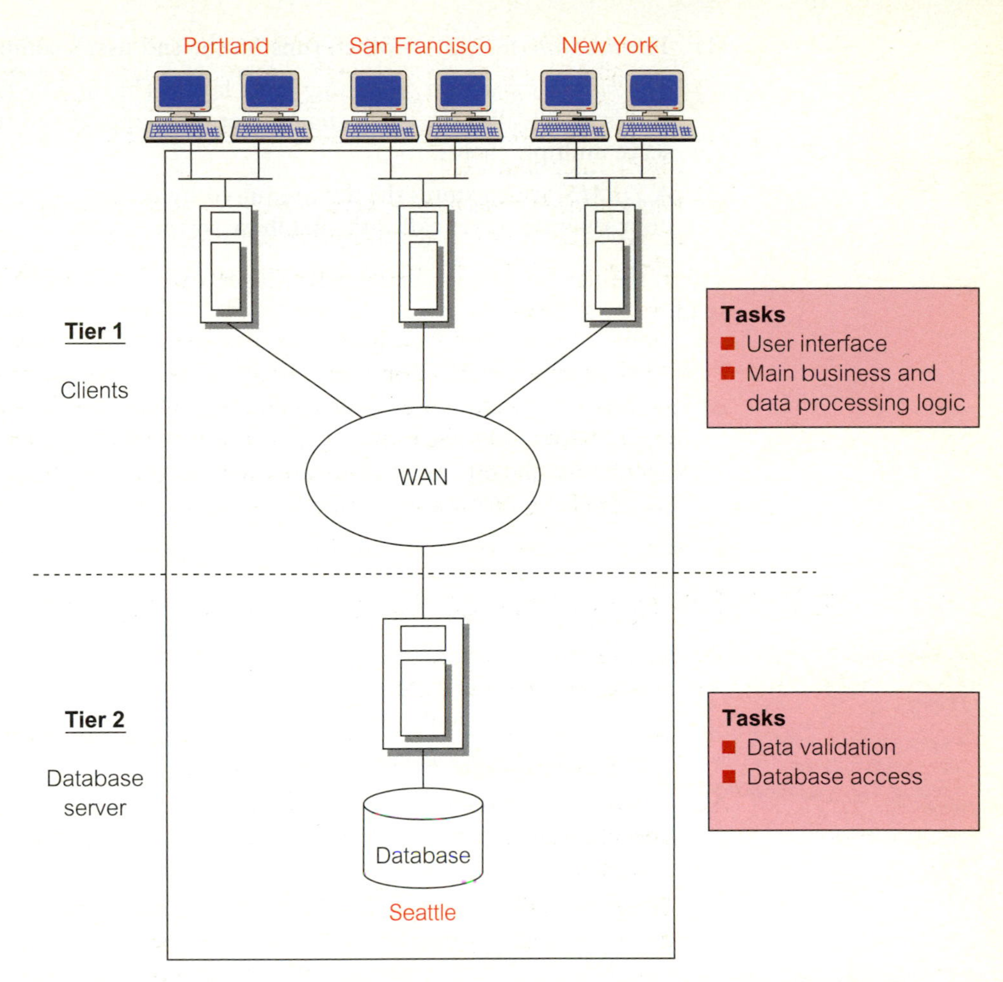

Figure 1.7 Simplified two-tier client–server configuration for *StayHome Online Rentals*

This is known as a **(two-tier) client–server architecture**. Figure 1.7 illustrates a possible client–server architecture for *StayHome Online Rentals* that has four distribution centers in America. It shows a centralized database and server located at the company's headquarters in Seattle and a number of clients located at the other centers connected to the Seattle server by a Wide Area Network (WAN).

In the mid-1990s, as applications became more complex and potentially could be deployed to hundreds or thousands of end-users, the client side of this architecture gave rise to two problems:

- a **'fat' client**, requiring considerable resources on the client's computer to run effectively (resources include disk space, RAM, and CPU power);
- a significant client-side administration overhead.

By 1995, a new variation of the traditional two-tier client–server model appeared to overcome these problems, called the **three-tier client–server architecture**. This new architecture proposed three layers, each potentially running on a different platform:

(1) The *user interface* layer, which runs on the end-user's computer (the *client*).

(2) The *business and data processing logic* layer. This middle tier runs on a server and is often called the **application server**. One application server is designed to serve multiple clients.

(3) A *DBMS*, which stores the data required by the middle tier. This tier may run on a separate server called the **database server**.

The three-tier design has many advantages over the traditional two-tier design, such as:

- a **'thin' client**, which requires less expensive hardware;
- simplified application maintenance, as a result of centralizing the business logic for many end-users into a single application server. This eliminates the concerns of software distribution that are problematic in the traditional two-tier client–server architecture;
- added modularity, which makes it easier to modify or replace one tier without affecting the other tiers;
- improved scalability and easier load balancing, again as a result of separating the core business logic from the database functions. For example, a **Transaction Processing Monitor (TPM)** can be used to reduce the number of connections to the database server and additional application servers can be added to distribute application processing.

Transaction Processing Monitor (TPM)

A program that controls data transfer between clients and servers in order to provide a consistent environment for Online Transaction Processing (OLTP).

An additional advantage is that the three-tier architecture maps quite naturally to the Web environment, with a **Web browser** acting as the 'thin' client, and a Web server acting as the application server. The three-tier client–server architecture is illustrated in Figure 1.8.

1.3 Database design

Until now, we have taken it for granted that there is a structure to the data in the database. But how do we get this structure? The answer is quite simple: the structure of the database is determined during **database design**. However, carrying out database design can be extremely complex. To produce a system that will satisfy the organization's information needs requires a data-driven approach, which means we think of the data first and the applications second. For the system to be acceptable to the end-users, database design is crucial. A poorly designed database will generate errors that may lead to bad decisions being made, with potentially serious repercussions for the organization. Yet a well-designed database produces a system that provides the correct information for the decision-making process to succeed, in an efficient way.

We devote several chapters to the presentation of a complete methodology for database design (see Chapters 9–11). We present it as a series of simple-to-follow steps, with guidelines provided throughout. In these chapters we use the case study

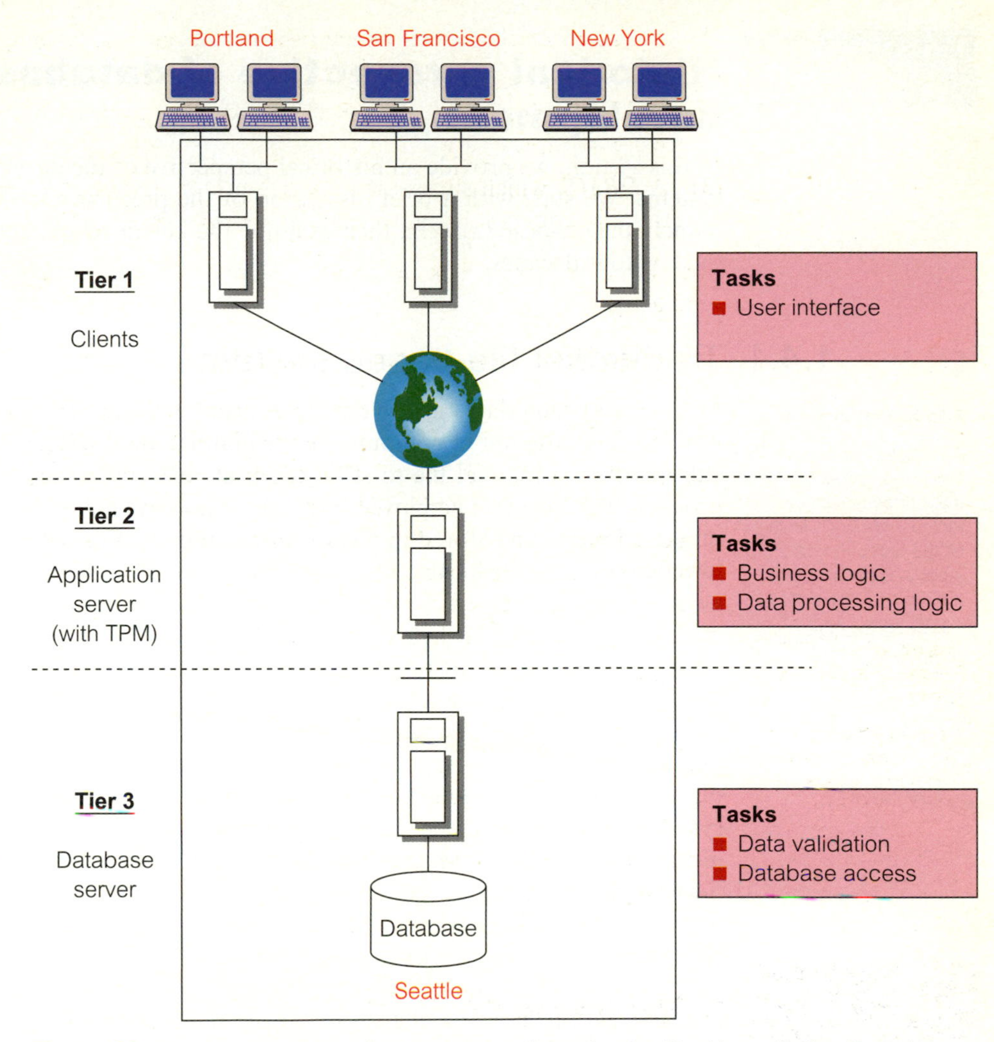

Figure 1.8 Simplified three-tier client–server configuration for *StayHome Online Rentals*

on *StayHome Online Rentals* (see Chapter 5 and Appendix A). We also provide a second case study, that we refer to in Exercises at the end of various chapters, based on a private healthcare practice for domestic pets called *PerfectPets* (see Appendix B). Unfortunately, database design methodologies are not very popular, which may be a major cause of failure in the development of database systems. Due to the lack of structured approaches to database design, the time and resources required for a database project are typically underestimated, the databases developed are inadequate or inefficient in meeting the demands of users, documentation is limited, and maintenance is difficult. We hope the methodology presented in this book will help change this attitude.

1.4 Historical perspective of database system development

In this section, we provide an historical perspective of the development of database systems. We start with a brief discussion of the precursor to the database system, namely the *file-based system*, then examine the key developments in databases over the last four decades.

1.4.1 Traditional file-based systems

File-based system

A collection of application programs that performs services for the end-users, such as the production of reports. Each program defines and manages its own data.

File-based systems date back to the 1960s prior to the development of databases and were an early attempt to computerize the manual filing system. Many organizations still maintain a manual file to store external correspondence relating to a project, product, task, client, or employee. Typically, they have many such files and, for safety, they are labeled and stored in one or more cabinets. For security, the cabinets may have locks or may be located in secure areas. To look something up in such a system, we start from the first entry and search until we find what we want. Alternatively, we may have an index that helps locate what we want more quickly. For example, we may have divisions in the filing system or separate folders for different types of item that are in some way *logically related.*

The manual filing system is a perfectly satisfactory solution while the number of items remains small. It even works quite adequately when there are large numbers of items and we have only to store and retrieve them. However, the manual filing system breaks down when we have to cross-reference or process the information in the files. For example, consider the amount of effort that a member of staff at *StayHome* would expend looking through 100 000 DVD records searching for DVD titles that star 'Mike Myers,' or 1 million rental records searching for all the DVDs that the member 'Don Nelson' rented between January and December 2006.

The timely production of reports such as these is critical to the successful operation of organizations nowadays. In some areas, there is a legal requirement to produce detailed monthly, quarterly, and annual reports. Clearly, the manual system is totally inadequate for this type of work. The file-based system was developed in response to the needs of industry for more efficient data access. However, rather than create a centralized repository for the organization's operational data, a decentralized approach was taken and each department, usually with the support of Data Processing (DP) staff, stored and controlled its own data.

Figure 1.9 illustrates a potential scenario for *StayHome Online Rentals* using a file-based system. The figure shows two departments: Member Services, which deals with sending DVDs to members, and Stock Control, which monitors the DVDs going out and coming back in.

The file-based approach has a number of disadvantages compared with the DBMS approach:

- *Data dependence*. It can be seen from Figure 1.9 that each department has its own application programs, each with their own file handling routines and, significantly, with the underlying file structure definitions embedded within

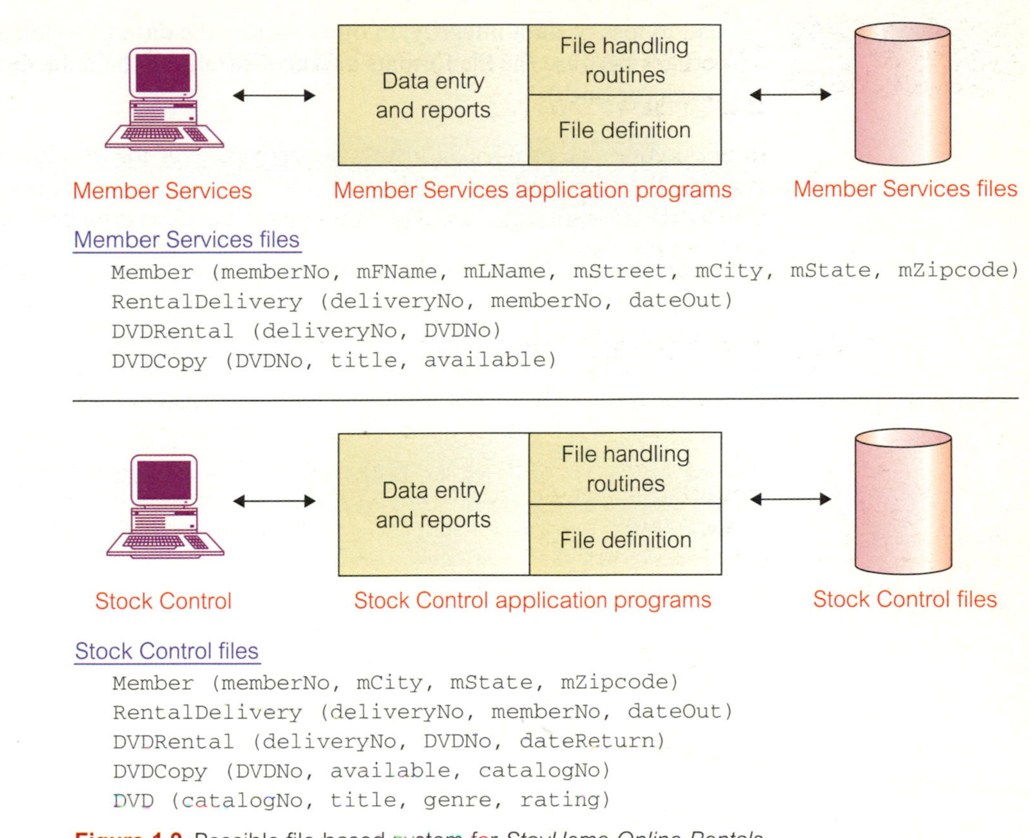

Figure 1.9 Possible file-based system for *StayHome Online Rentals*

them. This means that changes to an existing structure are difficult, requiring a change and rebuild of all the application programs that access the file. It also usually involves the writing of a throw-away piece of software that converts the file from the old structure to the new structure and modifying the structure of the content of each record accordingly. Clearly, this could be very time-consuming and subject to error. This characteristic of file-based systems is known as **program–data dependence**.

> **Note** This is unlike the DBMS approach where the file-handling software exists only once (within the DBMS server) and the file definitions (the metadata) are stored in the system catalog rather than within the database applications or even within the DBMS server.

- *Duplication of data.* It can be seen quite clearly from Figure 1.9 that there is a significant amount of duplication of data in these departments, and this is generally true of file-based systems. Uncontrolled duplication of data is undesirable for several reasons. Duplication is wasteful – it costs time and money to enter the data more than once. Furthermore, it takes up additional storage space, again with associated costs. Often, the duplication of data can be avoided by sharing data files. Perhaps more important, duplication can lead to loss of data integrity; in other words, the data is no longer consistent, perhaps because the file formats are inconsistent or the data values do not match (or both).

Note This is unlike the DBMS approach where the database is designed to remove all unnecessary duplication.

- *Separation and isolation of data*. When data is isolated in separate files, it is more difficult to access data that should be available. For some reports the application developer must synchronize the processing of two or more files to ensure the correct data is extracted, which can be difficult, particularly if the file formats of the matching data are inconsistent.

Note Again, this is unlike the DBMS approach where the database is designed to integrate all the operational data together and to define the format of data consistently throughout.

- *Fixed queries/proliferation of application programs*. End-users found file-based systems to be a great improvement over manual systems and, as a result, requested new or modified queries and reports. However, file-based systems are very dependent upon the application developer, who has to write any programs that are required. This caused two things to happen. In some cases, the type of query or report that could be produced was fixed; there was no facility for asking unplanned (that is, spur-of-the-moment or *ad hoc*) queries. In other cases, there was a proliferation of files and application programs. This put enormous pressure on the DP department, resulting in programs that were inadequate or inefficient in meeting the demands of the users, documentation that was limited, and maintenance that was difficult. Often, certain types of functionality were omitted or limited, such as security and integrity; recovery, in the event of a hardware or software failure; shared access to allow more than one user to access data at the same time.

Note The DBMS provides extensive query and report generation facilities that can be used by both naïve and experienced end-users. At the same time, as we discuss in Section 1.6, the DBMS provides a number of centralized services such as security and integrity, concurrency, and recovery.

- *Limited data sharing*. Due to the fact that each department has its own set of files, data sharing is limited. Not only can this be frustrating for management trying to get a complete picture of how the organization is performing at any moment in time but it can also result in loss of potential information that becomes apparent only with access to all operational data.

Note Again, this is unlike the DBMS approach where the operational data is integrated together and stored so that it can be accessed and shared by all authorized users.

1.4.2 DBMS development

There was never a time when the file-based system ceased and the database approach began. In fact, the file-based system is still in existence today in specific areas. It has been suggested that the DBMS has its roots in the 1960s' Apollo moon-landing project, at a time when there was no system available that would be able to handle and manage the vast amounts of information that the project would generate. In the mid-1960s, two competing DBMSs emerged. The first was IMS (Information Management System) from IBM that stored records based on an inverted tree structure, which allowed the use of serial storage devices, most notably magnetic tape, that was a market requirement at that time. This became known as a **hierarchical DBMS**. Although one of the earliest commercial DBMSs, IMS is still the main hierarchical DBMS used by most large mainframe installations.

The second was IDS (Integrated Data Store) from General Electric, which was developed partly to address the need to represent more complex data relationships than could be modeled with hierarchical structures, and partly to impose a database standard. This became known as a **network DBMS**. In such systems, data is represented as a collection of *records* and one-to-many relationships are represented as *sets* (one owner, many members). A record may be an owner in any number of sets and a member in any number of sets. A network DBMS supports **navigational access**: a program maintains a current position and navigates from one record to another by following the relationships in which the record participates. It also allows records to be located through key values. Although not essential, network systems generally implement set relationships by means of pointers that directly address the location of a record on disk. This gives excellent retrieval performance at the expense of operations such as database loading and reorganization. The most popular network DBMS is now Computer Associates' IDMS/R.

The hierarchical and network approaches represented the **first-generation** of DBMSs. These two approaches have some fundamental disadvantages:

- complex programs have to be written to answer even simple queries based on navigational record-at-a-time access;
- there is minimal data independence so that applications are not protected from changes to data formats;
- there is no widely accepted theoretical foundation.

In 1970, E. F. Codd of the IBM Research Laboratory produced his highly influential paper on the relational data model. This paper was very timely and addressed the disadvantages of the former approaches. The data model is relatively simple and represents all data in the form of tables. Many experimental relational DBMSs were implemented thereafter, with the first commercial products appearing in the late 1970s and early 1980s. A key development during this period was SQL, a standard language for querying a relational database. Relational DBMSs, such as Oracle, Microsoft SQL Server, and IBM DB2, are now the dominant database technology and represent a multi-billion-dollar industry. Relational DBMSs are referred to as *second-generation* DBMSs. We will discuss the relational data model in Chapter 2 and provide a tutorial on SQL in Chapter 3 and Appendix E.

However, the relational model is not without its failings – in particular, its limited modeling capabilities. There has been significant research carried out since then attempting to address this problem. In 1976, Chen presented the entity–relationship (ER) model, which is now a widely accepted technique for database design and the basis for the methodology presented in Chapters 9 and 10 of this book. The attempts to provide a data model that represents the 'real world' more closely have been loosely classified as **semantic data modeling**.

In response to the increasing complexity of database applications, during the 1990s two 'new' systems emerged: the **Object-Oriented DBMS (OODBMS)** and the **Object-Relational DBMS (ORDBMS)**. However, unlike previous models, the actual composition of these models is not clear. This evolution represents **third-generation** DBMSs, which we will discuss in detail in Chapter 17. The 1990s also saw the rise of the Internet, the three-tier client–server architecture, and the demand to allow corporate databases to be integrated with Web applications. The late 1990s saw the development of XML (eXtensible Markup Language), which has had a profound effect on many aspects of IT, including database integration, graphical interfaces, embedded systems, distributed systems, and database systems. We will discuss Web–database integration and XML in Chapter 15.

Specialized DBMSs have also been created, such as **data warehouses**, which can store data drawn from several data sources, possibly maintained by different operating units of an organization. Such systems provide comprehensive data analysis facilities to allow strategic decisions to be made based on, for example, historical trends. All the major DBMS vendors provide data warehousing solutions. We will discuss data warehouses in Chapter 18. Another example is the **enterprise resource planning (ERP) system**, an application layer built on top of a DBMS, which integrates all the business functions of an organization, such as manufacturing, sales, finance, marketing, shipping, invoicing, and human resources. Popular ERP systems are SAP R/3 from SAP and PeopleSoft from Oracle. Figure 1.10 provides a summary of historical development of database systems.

1.5 Three-level ANSI-SPARC architecture

An early proposal for a standard terminology and general architecture for database systems was produced in 1971 by the DBTG (Data Base Task Group) appointed by the Conference on Data Systems and Languages (CODASYL). The DBTG recognized the need for a two-level approach with a system view called the **schema** and user views called **subschemas**. The American National Standards Institute (ANSI) Standards Planning and Requirements Committee (SPARC) produced a similar terminology and architecture in 1975. ANSI-SPARC recognized the need for a three-level approach with a system catalog. Although the ANSI-SPARC model did not become a standard, it still provides a basis for understanding some of the functionality of a DBMS.

The ANSI-SPARC model identified three distinct levels at which data items can be described: an **external level**, a **conceptual level**, and an **internal level**, as depicted in Figure 1.11. The way users perceive the data is called the external level. The way the DBMS and the operating system perceive the data is the internal level, where the

Timeframe	Development	Comments
1960s (onwards)	File-based systems	Precursor to the database system. Decentralized approach: each department stored and controlled its own data.
Mid-1960s	Hierarchical and network data models	Represent first-generation DBMSs. Main hierarchical system is IMS from IBM and the main network system is IDMS/R from Computer Associates. Lacked data independence and required complex programs to be developed to process the data.
1970	Relational model proposed	Publication of E. F. Codd's seminal paper 'A relational model of data for large shared data banks' that addresses the weaknesses of first-generation systems.
1970s	Prototype RDBMSs developed	During this period two main prototypes emerged: the INGRES project at the University of California at Berkeley (started 1970) and the System R project at IBM's San José Research Laboratory in California (started 1974), which led to the development of SQL.
1976	ER model proposed	Publication of Chen's paper 'The Entity–Relationship model – Toward a unified view of data'. ER modeling becomes a significant component in methodologies for database design.
1979	Commercial RDBMSs appear	Commercial RDBMSs like Oracle, INGRES, and DB2 appear. These represent the second generation of DBMSs.
1987	ISO SQL standard	SQL is standardized by ISO (International Standards Organization). There are subsequent releases of the standard in 1989, 1992 (SQL2), 1999 (SQL:1999), and 2003 (SQL:2003).
1990s	OODBMSs and ORDBMSs appear	This period sees initially the emergence of OODBMSs and latterly ORDBMSs (Oracle 8 with object features released in 1997).
1990s	Data warehousing systems appear	This period also see releases from the major DBMS vendors of data warehousing systems and thereafter data mining products.
Mid-1990s	Web-database integration	First Internet database applications appear. DBMS vendors and third-party vendors recognize the significance of the Internet and support Web-database integration.
1998	XML	XML 1.0 ratified by the W3C. XML becomes integrated with DBMS products and native XML databases are developed.

Figure 1.10 Historical development of database systems

data is actually stored. The conceptual level provides both the *mapping* and the desired *independence* between the external and internal levels.

The objective of this 'three-level architecture' is to separate each user's view of the database from the way it is physically represented. There are several reasons why this separation is desirable:

- Each user should be able to access the same data, but have a different customized view of the data, as we discussed above for views in Section 1.2.5.

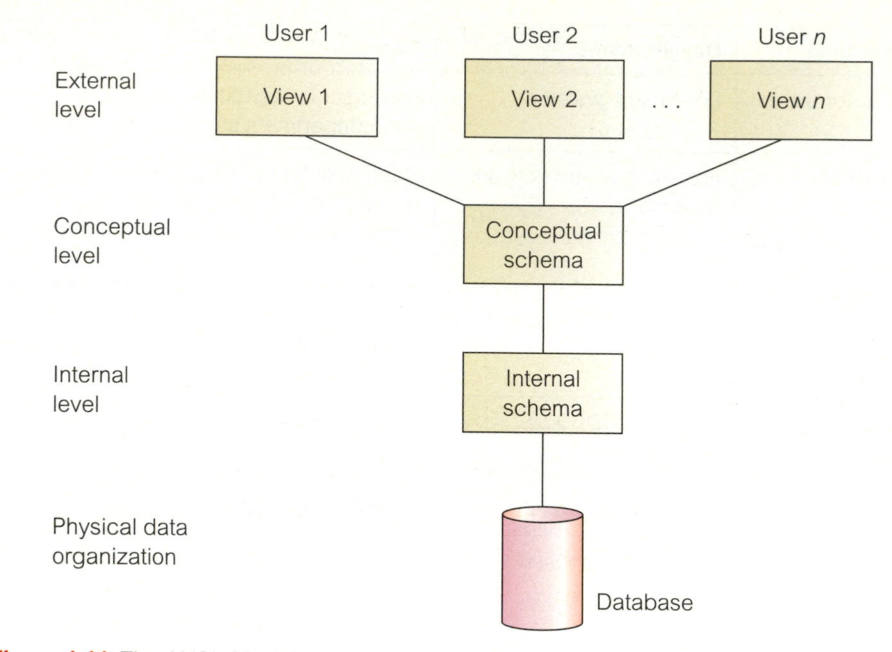

Figure 1.11 The ANSI–SPARC three-level architecture

- Users should not have to deal directly with physical database storage details, such as file structures or indexing.
- The Database Administrator (DBA) should be able to change the database storage structures without affecting the users' views.
- The internal structure of the database should be unaffected by changes to the physical aspects of storage, such as moving to a new storage device.
- The DBA should be able to change the conceptual structure of the database without affecting all users.

1.5.1 External level

External level

The users' view of the database. This level describes that part of the database that is relevant to each user.

The **external level** consists of a number of different external views of the database. Each user has a view of the 'real world' represented in a form that is familiar for that user. The external view includes only those entities, attributes, and relationships that the user is interested in. Other entities, attributes, or relationships that are not of interest may be represented in the database, but the user will be unaware of them.

In addition, different views may have different representations of the same data. For example, one user may view dates in the form (day, month, year), while another may view dates as (year, month, day). Some views might include derived or calculated data, data not actually stored in the database as such but created when needed. For example, in the *StayHome Online Rentals* case study, we may wish to view the age of a member of staff. However, it is unlikely that ages would be stored, as this data would have to be updated on a daily basis. Instead, the member of staff's date of birth would be stored and age would be calculated by the DBMS when it was referenced.

1.5.2 Conceptual level

Conceptual level

The community view of the database. This level describes *what* data is stored in the database and the relationships among the data.

The middle level in the three-level architecture is the **conceptual level**. This level contains the logical structure of the entire database as seen by the DBA. It is a complete view of the data requirements of the organization that is independent of any storage considerations. The conceptual level represents:

- all entities, their attributes, and their relationships;
- the constraints on the data;
- semantic information about the data;
- security information.

The conceptual level supports each external view, in that any data available to a user must be contained in, or derivable from, the conceptual level. However, this level must not contain any storage-dependent details. For instance, the description of an entity should contain only data types of attributes (for example, integer, float, character) and their length (such as the maximum number of digits or characters), but not any storage considerations, such as the number of bytes occupied.

1.5.3 Internal level

Internal level

The physical representation of the database on the computer. This level describes *how* the data is stored in the database.

The **internal level** covers the physical implementation of the database to achieve optimal runtime performance and storage space utilization. It covers the data structures and **file organizations** used to store data on storage devices. It interfaces with the operating system **access methods** (file management techniques for storing and retrieving data records) to place the data on the storage devices, build the indexes, retrieve the data, and so on.

Below the internal level there is a **physical level** that may be managed by the operating system under the direction of the DBMS. Some DBMSs take advantage of many of the operating system access methods, while others use only the most basic ones and create their own file organizations. The physical level below the DBMS consists of items only the operating system knows, such as exactly how the sequencing is implemented and whether the fields of internal records are stored as contiguous bytes on the disk.

1.5.4 Schemas and instances

The overall description of the database is called the **database schema**. There are three different types of schema in the database and these are defined according to the levels of **abstraction** of the three-level architecture, as illustrated in Figure 1.12.

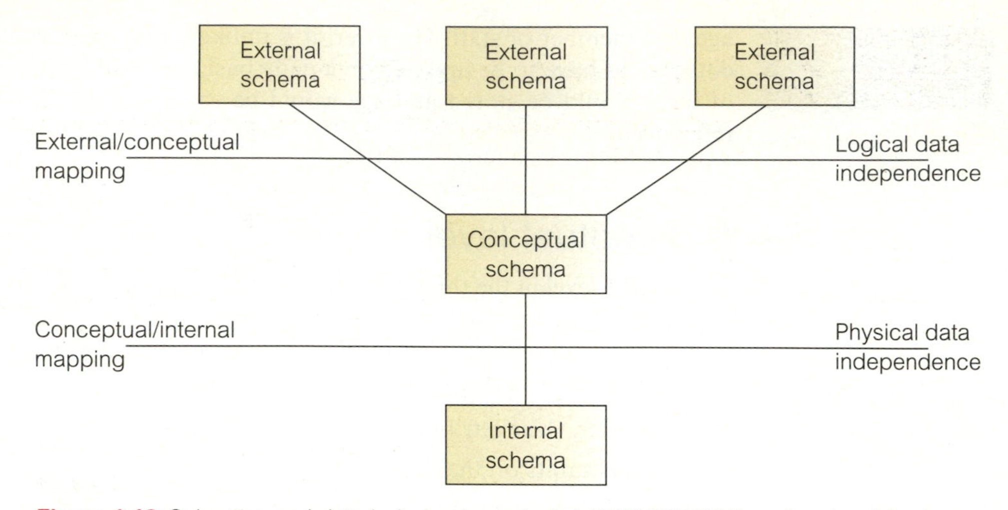

Figure 1.12 Schemas and data independence in the ANSI-SPARC three-level architecture

While there is an **external schema** for each user view of the database, there is only one **conceptual schema** and one **internal schema** per database.

It is important to distinguish between the description of the database and the database itself. The description of the database is the *database schema*. The schema is specified during the database design process and is not expected to change frequently. However, the actual data in the database may change frequently; for example, it changes every time we insert details of a new member of staff or a new DVD. The data in the database at any particular point in time is called a **database instance**. Therefore, many database instances can correspond to the same database schema.

1.5.5 Data independence

Logical data independence

Refers to the immunity of the external schemas to changes in the conceptual schema.

Physical data independence

Refers to the immunity of the conceptual schema to changes in the internal schema.

A major objective for the three-level architecture is to provide **data independence**, which means that upper levels are unaffected by changes to lower levels. There are two kinds: **logical data independence** and **physical data independence**.

Changes to the conceptual schema, such as the addition or removal of new entities, attributes, or relationships, should be possible without having to change existing external schema or having to rewrite database applications. Clearly, the users for whom the changes have been made need to be aware of them, but what is important is that other users should not be.

Changes to the internal schema, such as using different file organizations or modifying indexes, should be possible without having to change the conceptual or external schemas. From the users' point of view, the only effect that may be noticed is a change in performance. In fact, deterioration in performance is the most common reason for internal schema changes. Figure 1.12 illustrates where each type of data independence occurs in relation to the three-level architecture.

1.6 Functions of a DBMS

In this section, we look briefly at the functions and services we would expect a full-scale DBMS to provide nowadays.

Data storage, retrieval, and update

This is the fundamental function of a DBMS. From our earlier discussion, clearly in providing this functionality the DBMS should hide the internal physical implementation details (such as file organizations) from the user.

A user-accessible catalog

A key feature of a DBMS is the provision of an integrated **system catalog** to hold data about the structure of the database, users, applications, and so on. The catalog is expected to be accessible to users as well as to the DBMS. The amount of information and the way the information is used vary with the DBMS. Typically, the system catalog stores:

- names, types, and sizes of data items;
- integrity constraints on the data;
- names of authorized users who have access to the data.

Transaction support

Transaction

An action, or series of actions, carried out by a single user or database application that accesses or changes the contents of the database.

For example, some simple **transactions** for the *StayHome Online Rentals* company might be to add a new member of staff to the database, to update the salary of a particular member of staff, or to delete a member from the register. A more complicated example might be to delete a manager from the database *and* to reassign the distribution center that he or she managed to another member of staff. In this case, there is more than one change to be made to the database. If the transaction fails during execution, perhaps because of a computer crash, the database will be in an *inconsistent* state: some changes will have been made and others not (for example, a distribution center is not allocated a new manager). Consequently, the changes that have been made will have to be undone to return the database to a consistent state.

To overcome this, a DBMS should provide a mechanism that will ensure that either all the updates corresponding to a given transaction are made or that none of them is made.

Concurrency control services

One major objective in using a DBMS is to enable many users to access shared data concurrently; this is known as **concurrency control**. Concurrent access is relatively easy if all users are only reading data, as there is no way that they can interfere with one another. However, when two or more users are accessing the database simultaneously and at least one of them is updating data, there may be interference that can result in inconsistencies. For example, consider two transactions – T_1 and T_2 – that are executing concurrently, as illustrated in Figure 1.13.

Time	T_1	T_1	bal_x
t_1		begin_transaction	100
t_2	begin transaction	read(bal_x)	100
t_3	read(bal_x)	$bal_x = bal_x + 100$	100
t_4	$bal_x = bal_x - 10$	write(bal_x)	200
t_5	write(bal_x)	commit	90
t_6	commit		90

Figure 1.13 The lost update problem

T_2 is withdrawing \$10 from a *StayHome* member's account (with a balance, bal_x, currently \$100) and T_1 is crediting \$100 to the same account. If these transactions were executed one after the other with no interleaving of operations, the final balance would be \$190 regardless of which was performed first. Transactions T_1 and T_2 start at nearly the same time and both read the balance as \$100. T_2 increases bal_x by \$100 to \$200 and stores the update in the database. Meanwhile, transaction T_1 decreases its copy of bal_x by \$10 to \$90 and stores this value in the database, overwriting the previous update and thereby 'losing' \$100.

When multiple users are accessing the database, the DBMS must ensure that interference like this cannot occur.

Recovery services

When discussing transaction support, we mentioned that if the transaction fails then the database has to be returned to a consistent state; this is known as **recovery control**. This may be the result of a system crash, media failure, a hardware or software error causing the DBMS to stop, or it may be the result of the user detecting an error during the transaction and aborting the transaction before it completes. In all these cases, the DBMS must provide a mechanism to recover the database to a consistent state.

Authorization services

It is not difficult to envisage instances where we would want to protect some of the data stored in the database from being seen by all users. For example, we may want only distribution center managers and the Payroll department to see salary-related information for staff and prevent all other users from seeing this data. Additionally, we may want to protect the database from unauthorized access. The term **security** refers to the protection of the database against unauthorized access, either intentional or accidental. We expect the DBMS to provide mechanisms to ensure the data is secure.

Support for data communication

Most users access the database from terminals. Sometimes, these terminals are connected directly to the computer hosting the DBMS. In other cases, the terminals are at remote locations and communicate with the computer hosting the DBMS over a network. In either case, the DBMS must be capable of integrating with networking/ communication software. Even DBMSs for PCs should be capable of being run on a local area network (LAN) so that one centralized database can be established for users to share, rather than having a series of disparate databases, one for each user.

Integrity services

Database integrity refers to the correctness and consistency of stored data. It can be considered as another type of database protection. While it is related to security, it has wider implications; integrity is concerned with the quality of data itself. Integrity is usually expressed in terms of **constraints**, which are consistency rules that the database is not permitted to violate. For example, we may specify a constraint that no member of *StayHome* can rent more than five DVDs at the one time. Here, we want the DBMS to check when we assign a DVD to a member that this limit is not being exceeded and to prevent the rental from occurring if the limit has been reached.

Services to promote data independence

Data independence is normally achieved through a view mechanism, as we discussed in Section 1.2.5. There are usually several types of changes that can be made to the physical characteristics of the database without affecting the views, such as using different file organizations or modifying indexes. This is called *physical data independence*. However, complete *logical data independence* is more difficult to achieve. The addition of a new table or column can usually be accommodated, but not their removal. In some systems, any type of change to a table's structure is prohibited.

Utility services

Utility programs help the DBA to manage the database effectively. Some examples of utilities are:

- import facilities, to load the database from flat files, and export facilities, to unload the database to flat files;
- monitoring facilities, to monitor database usage and operation.

Note The above discussion is general. The actual level of functionality offered by a DBMS differs from product to product. For example, a DBMS for a PC may not support concurrent shared access, and it may provide only limited security, integrity, and recovery control. However, modern, large, multi-user DBMS products offer all the above functions and much more. Modern systems are extremely complex pieces of software consisting of millions of lines of code, with documentation comprising many volumes.

The above discussion is intentionally brief but should be sufficient to provide a general overview of DBMS functionality. We expand on some of these services in later chapters.

1.7 Advantages and disadvantages of the database approach

The database approach has a number of distinct advantages, such as the following:

- *Control of* ***data redundancy***. The database approach eliminates redundancy where possible. However, it does not eliminate redundancy entirely, but controls the amount of redundancy inherent in the database. For example, it is normally necessary to duplicate key data items to model relationships between data, and sometimes it is desirable to duplicate some data items to improve performance. The reasons for controlled duplication will become clearer when you read the chapters on database design.
- *Data consistency*. By eliminating or controlling redundancy, we are reducing the risk of inconsistencies occurring. If a data item is stored only once in the database, any update to its value has to be performed only once and the new value is immediately available to all users. If a data item is stored more than once and the system is aware of this, the system can ensure that all copies of the data are kept consistent. Unfortunately, many of today's DBMSs do not automatically ensure this type of consistency.
- *Sharing of data*. In the file-based approach, files are typically owned by the people or departments that use them. Yet the database belongs to the entire organization and can be shared by all authorized users. In this way, more users share more of the data. Furthermore, new applications can build on the existing data in the database and add only data that is not currently stored, rather than having to define all data requirements again. The new applications can also rely on the functions provided by the DBMS, such as data definition and manipulation, and concurrency and recovery control, rather than having to provide these functions themselves.
- *Improved data integrity*. As we have already noted, database integrity is usually expressed in terms of *constraints*, which are consistency rules that the database is not permitted to violate. Constraints may apply to data within a single record or they may apply to relationships between records. Again, data integration allows users to define, and the DBMS to enforce, integrity constraints.
- *Improved maintenance through data independence*. Since a DBMS separates the data descriptions from the applications, it helps make applications immune to changes in the data descriptions. This is known as *data independence* and its provision simplifies database application maintenance.

Other advantages include improved security, improved data accessibility and responsiveness, increased productivity, increased concurrency, and improved backup and recovery services. There are, however, some disadvantages of the database approach, such as the following:

- *Complexity*. As we have already mentioned, a DBMS is an extremely complex piece of software, and all users (database designers and developers, DBAs, and end-users) must understand the DBMS's functionality to take full advantage of it.

- *Cost of DBMS*. The cost of DBMSs varies significantly, depending on the environment and functionality provided. For example, a single-user DBMS for a PC may cost only $100. However, a large mainframe multi-user DBMS servicing hundreds of users can be extremely expensive, perhaps $100 000 to $1 million. There is also the recurrent annual maintenance cost, which is typically a percentage of the list price.
- *Cost of conversion*. In some situations, the cost of the DBMS and any extra hardware may be insignificant compared with the cost of converting existing applications to run on the new DBMS and hardware. This cost also includes the cost of training staff to use these new systems, and possibly the employment of specialist staff to help with the conversion and running of the system. This cost is one of the main reasons why some companies feel tied to their current systems and cannot switch to more modern database technology. The term **legacy system** is sometimes used to refer to an older, and usually inferior, system (such as file-based, hierarchical, or network systems).
- *Performance*. Typically, a file-based system is written for a specific application, such as invoicing. As a result, performance is generally very good. However, a DBMS is written to be more general, to cater for many applications rather than just one. The effect is that some applications may not run as fast using a DBMS as they did before.
- *Higher impact of a failure*. The centralization of resources increases the vulnerability of the system. Since all users and applications rely on the availability of the DBMS, the failure of any component can bring operations to a complete halt until the failure is repaired.

Chapter summary

- A **database** is a shared collection of logically related data (and a description of this data), designed to meet the information needs of a organization. A **DBMS** is a software system that enables users to define, create, and maintain the database, and also provides controlled access to this database. A **database application** is a computer program that interacts with the database by issuing an appropriate request (typically an SQL statement) to the DBMS. The more inclusive term **database system** is used to define a collection of application programs that interacts with the database along with the DBMS and database itself.
- All access to the database is through the DBMS. The DBMS provides facilities that allow users to define the database and to insert, update, delete, and retrieve data from the database.
- The DBMS environment consists of hardware (the computer), software (the DBMS, operating system, and applications programs), data, procedures, and people. The people include database administrators (DBAs), database designers, application programmers, and end-users.

- In the Web environment, the traditional two-tier client–server model has been replaced by a three-tier model, consisting of a user interface layer (the client), a business logic and data processing layer (the application server), and a DBMS (the database server), distributed over different machines.
- The ANSI-SPARC database architecture uses **three levels** of abstraction: **external**, **conceptual**, and **internal**. The external level consists of the users' views of the database. The **conceptual level** is the community view of the database. It specifies the information content of the entire database, independent of storage considerations. The conceptual level represents all entities, their attributes, and their relationships, the constraints on the data, along with security information. The **internal level** is the computer's view of the database. It specifies how data is represented, how records are sequenced, what indexes and pointers exist, and so on.
- A **database schema** is a description of the database structure whereas a **database instance** is the data in the database at a particular point in time.
- Data independence makes each level immune to changes to lower levels. **Logical data independence** refers to the immunity of the external schemas to changes in the conceptual schema. **Physical data independence** refers to the immunity of the conceptual schema to changes in the internal schema.
- The DBMS provides controlled access to the database. It provides security, integrity, concurrency and recovery control, and a user-accessible catalog. It also provides a view mechanism to simplify the data that users have to deal with.
- Some advantages of the database approach include control of data redundancy, data consistency, sharing of data, and improved security and integrity. Some disadvantages include complexity, cost, reduced performance, and higher impact of a failure.

Review questions

1.1 Discuss the meaning of each of the following terms:
   (a) data
   (b) information
   (c) database
   (d) database management system
   (e) metadata
   (f) database application
   (g) database system
   (h) data independence
   (i) views.

1.2 Describe the main characteristics of the database approach.

1.3 Describe the five components of the DBMS environment and discuss how they relate to each other.

1.4 Describe the problems with the traditional two-tier client–server architecture and discuss how these problems were overcome with the three-tier client–server architecture.

1.5 Briefly describe the file-based system.

1.6 What are the disadvantages of the file-based system and how are these disadvantages addressed by the DBMS approach?

1.7 Discuss the three generations of DBMSs.

1.8 What are the weaknesses of the first-generation DBMSs?

1.9 Describe the three levels of the ANSI-SPARC database architecture.

1.10 Discuss the difference between logical and physical data independence.

1.11 Describe the functions that should be provided by a multi-user DBMS.

1.12 Discuss the advantages and disadvantages of DBMSs.

Exercises

1.13 Of the functions described in your answer to Question 1.11, which ones do you think would not be needed in a standalone PC DBMS? Provide justification for your answer.

1.14 List four examples of database systems other than those listed in Section 1.1.

1.15 For any database system that you use, specify what you think are the main objects that the system handles (for example, objects like Branch, Staff, Clients).

1.16 For each of the objects specified above:
- (a) list the relationships that you think exist between the main objects (for example Branch *Has* Staff).
- (b) list what types of information would be held for each one (for example, for Staff you may list staff name, staff address, home telephone number, work extension, salary, etc).

Additional exercises

1.17 Consider an online DVD rental company like *StayHome Online Rentals*.
- (a) In what ways would a DBMS help this organization?
- (b) What do you think are the main objects that need to be represented in the database?
- (c) What relationships do you think exist between these main objects?
- (d) For each of the objects, what details do you think need to be held in the database?
- (e) What queries do you think are required?

1.18 Analyze the DBMSs that you are currently using. Determine each system's compliance with the functions that we would expect to be provided by a DBMS. What type of architecture does each DBMS use?

1.19 Discuss what you consider to be the *three* most important advantages for the use of a DBMS for a DVD rental company like *StayHome Online Rentals* and provide a justification for your selection. Discuss what you consider to be the *three* most important disadvantages for the use of a DBMS for a DVD rental company like *StayHome* and provide a justification for your selection.

CHAPTER

2 The relational model

Preview

The **Relational Database Management System** (often called **RDBMS** for short) has become the dominant DBMS in use today, with estimated sales of between approximately US$6 billion and US$10 billion per year (US$25 billion with application development tools sales included). The RDBMS represents the second generation of DBMS (the network and hierarchical DBMSs formed the first generation) and is based on the relational data model proposed by Dr E. F. Codd in 1970. In the relational model, all data is logically structured within *relations* (tables). A great strength of the relational model is this simple, logical structure. Because of its market dominance, the design methodology we present in this book is based on the relational data model. In this chapter, we discuss the basic principles of the relational data model and in the next chapter we examine the main relational languages: SQL (Structured Query Language) and QBE (Query-By-Example). We start with a brief history of the relational model and then examine what a data model is before discussing the key concepts of the relational model.

Learning objectives

In this chapter you will learn:

- The history of the relational data model.
- What a data model is and its uses.
- The terminology of the relational model.
- How tables are used to represent data.
- The properties of database relations.
- How to identify candidate, primary, alternate, and foreign keys.
- The meaning of entity integrity and referential integrity.
- That SQL and QBE are the two most widely used relational languages.

2.1 Brief history of the relational model

The relational model was first proposed by Dr E. F. Codd in the seminal paper 'A relational model of data for large shared data banks' (1970). This paper is now generally accepted as a landmark in database systems. The relational model's objectives were specified as follows:

- To allow a high degree of data independence. Application programs must not be affected by modifications to the internal data representation, particularly by the changes of file organizations, record orderings, and access paths.
- To provide substantial grounds for dealing with data semantics, consistency, and redundancy problems. In particular, Codd's paper introduced the concept of *normalized* relations, that is, relations that have no repeating groups. (The process of normalization will be discussed in Chapter 8.)
- To enable the expansion of set-oriented data manipulation languages.

Although interest in the relational model came from several directions, the most significant research may be attributed to two main projects with rather different perspectives. The first of these, at IBM's San José Research Laboratory in California, was the prototype relational DBMS, System R, which was developed during the late 1970s (Astrahan *et al.*, 1976). This project was designed to prove the practicality of the relational model by providing an implementation of its data structures and operations. In particular, the System R project led to two major developments:

- the development of a structured query language called SQL (pronounced 'S-Q-L' or sometimes 'See-Quel'), which has since become the formal International Standards Organization and the *de facto* standard language of relational DBMSs;
- the production of various commercial relational DBMS products during the 1980s: for example, DB2 and SQL/DS from IBM and Oracle from Oracle Corporation.

Commercial systems based on the relational model started to appear in the late 1970s and early 1980s. Now there are several hundred relational DBMSs for both mainframe and PC environments, even though many do not strictly adhere to the definition of the relational model. Examples of PC-based relational DBMSs are Office Access and Visual FoxPro from Microsoft, and InterBase and JDataStore from Borland. Examples of multi-user DBMSs are Microsoft SQL Server, Oracle, and DB2 from IBM.

Due to the popularity of the relational model, many non-relational systems now provide a relational user interface, irrespective of the underlying model. Computer Associates' IDMS, the principal network DBMS, has become Advantage CA-IDMS, supporting a relational view of data. Other mainframe DBMSs that support some relational features are Computer Corporation of America's Model 204 and Software AG's ADABAS.

Some extensions to the relational model have also been proposed to capture more closely the meaning of data (for example, Codd, 1979), to support object-oriented concepts (for example, Stonebraker and Rowe, 1986) and to support deductive capabilities (for example, Gardarin and Valduriez, 1989). We discuss some of these extensions in Chapter 17.

2.2 What is a data model?

A model is a representation of 'real world' objects and events, and their associations. It concentrates on the essential, inherent aspects of an organization and ignores the accidental properties. A **data model** attempts to represent the data requirements of the organization, or the part of the organization, that we wish to model. It should provide the basic concepts and notations that will allow database designers and end-users to unambiguously and accurately communicate their understanding of the organizational data. A data model can be thought of as comprising three components:

Data model

An integrated collection of concepts for describing data, relationships between data, and constraints on the data used by an organization.

(1) *a structural part*, consisting of a set of rules that defines how the database is to be constructed;
(2) *a manipulative part*, defining the types of operations (transactions) that are allowed on the data (this includes the operations that are used for updating or retrieving data and for changing the structure of the database);
(3) possibly *a set of integrity rules*, which ensures that the data is accurate.

The purpose of a data model is to represent data and to make the data understandable. If it does this, then it can be used to design a database. In the remainder of this chapter, we examine one such data model: the **relational data model**.

2.3 Terminology

The relational model is based on the mathematical concept of a **relation**, which is physically represented as a **table**. Codd, a trained mathematician, used terminology taken from mathematics, including set theory and predicate logic. In this section, we explain the terminology and structural concepts of the relational model. In Section 2.4, we discuss the integrity rules for the model and in Section 2.5 we examine the manipulative part of the model.

2.3.1 Relational data structure

There are five main structural components in the relational data model, namely relation, attribute, tuple, domain, and relational database.

Relation	A table with columns and rows
Attribute	A named column of a relation
Tuple	A row of a relation
Domain	The set of allowable values for one or more attributes
Relational database	A collection of normalized tables

In the relational model, we use **relations** to hold information about the objects that we want to represent in the database. We represent a relation as a **table** in which the table rows correspond to individual **tuples** and the table columns correspond to **attributes**. Attributes can appear in any order and the relation will still be the same relation, and therefore convey the same meaning.

For example, in the *StayHome Online Rentals* company, the information on distribution centers is represented by the `DistributionCenter` relation, with columns for attributes `dCenterNo` (the distribution center number), `dStreet`, `dCity`, `dState`, `dZipCode`, and `mgrStaffNo` (the staff number corresponding to the manager of the distribution center). Similarly, the information on staff is represented by the `Staff` relation, with columns for attributes `staffNo` (the staff number), `name`, `position`, `salary`, `eMail`, and `dCenterNo` (the number of the distribution center the staff member works at). Figure 2.1 shows instances of the `DistributionCenter` and `Staff` relations. As you can see from this figure, a column contains values for a single attribute; for example, the `dCenterNo` column contains only numbers of distribution centers. In the `Staff` relation, each row (tuple) contains six values, one for each attribute. As with attributes, tuples can appear in any order and the relation will still be the same relation, and therefore convey the same meaning.

Domains are an important feature of the relational model. Every attribute in a relational database is associated with a domain. Domains may be distinct for each attribute, or two or more attributes may be associated with the same

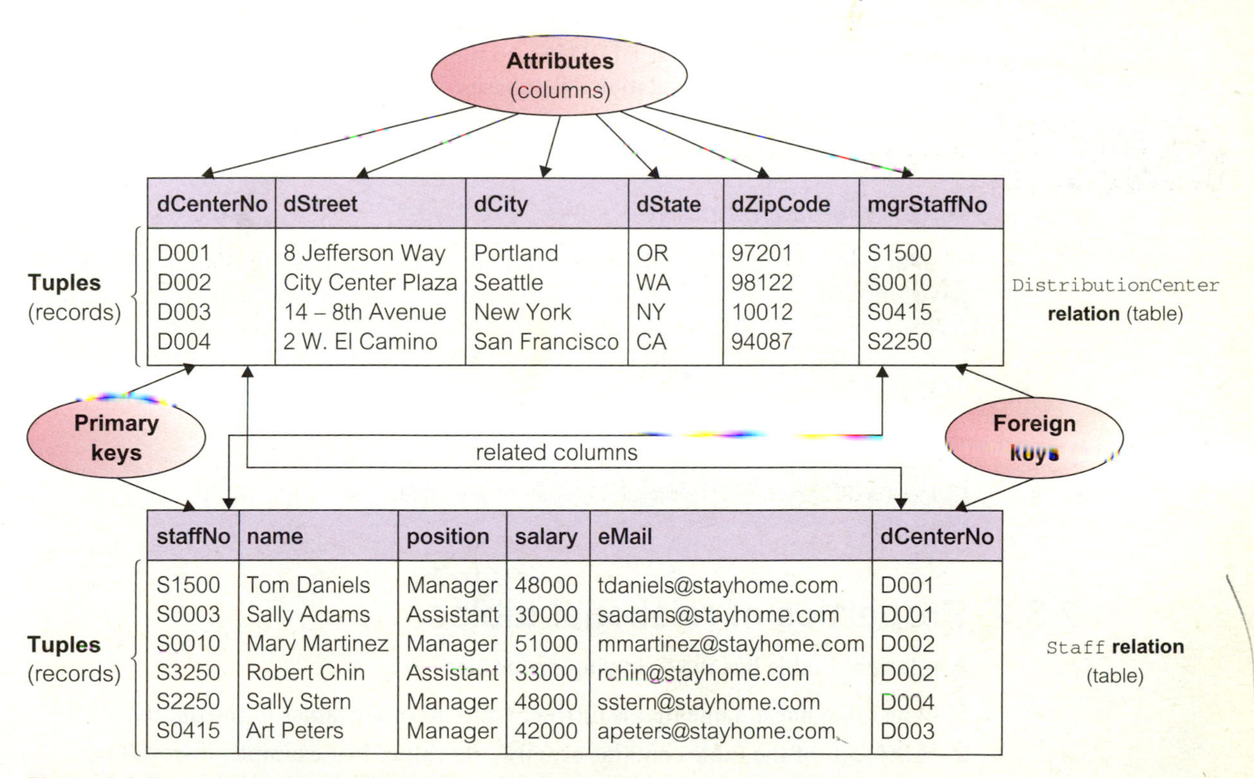

dCenterNo	dStreet	dCity	dState	dZipCode	mgrStaffNo
D001	8 Jefferson Way	Portland	OR	97201	S1500
D002	City Center Plaza	Seattle	WA	98122	S0010
D003	14 – 8th Avenue	New York	NY	10012	S0415
D004	2 W. El Camino	San Francisco	CA	94087	S2250

staffNo	name	position	salary	eMail	dCenterNo
S1500	Tom Daniels	Manager	48000	tdaniels@stayhome.com	D001
S0003	Sally Adams	Assistant	30000	sadams@stayhome.com	D001
S0010	Mary Martinez	Manager	51000	mmartinez@stayhome.com	D002
S3250	Robert Chin	Assistant	33000	rchin@stayhome.com	D002
S2250	Sally Stern	Manager	48000	sstern@stayhome.com	D004
S0415	Art Peters	Manager	42000	apeters@stayhome.com	D003

Figure 2.1 Example instances of the `DistributionCenter` and `Staff` relations

Attribute	Domain name	Meaning	Domain definition
dCenterNo	DCenter_Numbers	Set of all possible distribution center numbers.	Character: size 4, range D001 – D999
dStreet	Street_Names	Set of all possible street names.	Character: size 60
staffNo	Staff_Numbers	Set of all possible staff numbers.	Character: size 5, range S0001 – S9999
position	Staff_Positions	Set of all possible staff positions.	Manager or Assistant
salary	Staff_Salaries	Possible values of staff salaries.	Monetary: 8 digits, range $10 000.00 – $100 000.00

Figure 2.2 Domains for some attributes of the `DistributionCenter` and `Staff` relations

domain. Figure 2.2 shows the domains for some of the attributes of the `DistributionCenter` and `Staff` relations.

Key point At any given time, typically there will be values in a domain that do not currently appear as values in the corresponding attribute. In other words, a domain describes *possible* values for an attribute.

The domain concept is important because it allows us to define the meaning and source of values that attributes can hold. As a result, more information is available to the system and it can (theoretically) reject operations that do not make sense. For example, it would not be sensible for us to compare a staff number with a distribution center, even though the domain definitions for both these attributes are character strings. Unfortunately, most RDBMSs do not currently support domains.

Finally, we note that a **relational database** consists of tables that are appropriately structured. The appropriateness is obtained through the process of **normalization**, which we will discuss in Chapter 8.

Alternative terminology

The terminology for the relational model can be quite confusing. In this chapter, we have introduced two sets of terms: (relation, attribute, tuple) and (table, column, record), as shown in Figure 2.1. Other terms that you may encounter are **file** for table, row for record, and **field** for column. You may also find various combinations of these terms, such as table, row, and field.

Note From now on, we will tend to drop the formal terms of relation, tuple, and attribute, and instead use the more frequently used terms table, column, and record.

2.3.2 Properties of relational tables

A relational table has the following properties:

- The table has a name that is distinct from all other tables in the database.
- Each cell of the table contains exactly one value. For example, it would be wrong to store several telephone numbers for a single distribution center in a

single cell. In other words, tables do not contain repeating groups of data. A relational table that satisfies this property is said to be *normalized* or in *first normal form*.

- Each column has a distinct name.
- The values of a column are all from the same domain.
- The order of columns has no significance. In other words, provided a column name is moved along with the column values, we can interchange columns.
- Each record is distinct; there are no duplicate records.
- The order of records has no significance, theoretically. However, in practice, the order may affect the efficiency of accessing records, as we will see in Chapter 11 on physical database design.

2.3.3 Relational keys

As we have just stated, each record in a table must be unique. This means that we need to be able to identify a column or combination of columns (called *relational keys*) that provide uniqueness. In this section, we explain the terminology used for relational keys.

Superkey

A column, or set of columns, that uniquely identifies a record within a table.

Since a **superkey** may contain additional columns that are not necessary for unique identification, we are interested in identifying superkeys that contain only the *minimum number* of columns necessary for unique identification.

Candidate key

A superkey that contains only the minimum number of columns necessary for unique identification.

A **candidate key** for a table has two properties:

- *Uniqueness.* In each record, the value of the candidate key uniquely identifies that record.
- *Irreducibility.* No proper subset of the candidate key has the uniqueness property.

Consider the `Staff` table shown in Figure 2.1. For a given value of `position`, we would expect to be able to determine several staff with the same position (for example, there are four Managers). This column, therefore, cannot be selected as a candidate key. On the other hand, since *StayHome Online Rentals* allocates each member of staff a unique staff number, then for a given value of the staff number, `staffNo`, we can determine at most one record, so that `staffNo` is a candidate key. Similarly, as no two members of staff can have the same email address, `eMail` is also a candidate key for the `Staff` table.

The candidate key for a table may be made up from more than one column. Consider, for example, a table called `Wish`, which represents the ranked list of DVDs that a member would like to view. The table comprises a member number (`memberNo`), a DVD catalog number (`catalogNo`), and the ranking that the member has assigned to this DVD (`ranking`), as shown in Figure 2.3. For a given member number, `memberNo`, there may be several different DVDs the member wishes to view. Similarly, for a given DVD catalog number, `catalogNo`, there may be several members who wish to view this DVD. Therefore, `memberNo` by itself or `catalogNo` by itself cannot be selected as a candidate key. However, the combination of `memberNo` and `catalogNo` identifies at most one record (as does `memberNo` and `ranking`). When a key consists of more than one column, we call it a **composite key**.

Wish

memberNo	catalogNo	ranking
M250178	330553	1
M250178	634817	2
M166884	207132	1
M166884	330553	2
M166884	634817	3

Figure 2.3 An example instance of the `Wish` table

Key point

Be careful not to look at sample data and try to deduce the candidate key(s), unless you are certain the sample is representative of the data that will be stored in the table. Generally, an instance of a table cannot be used to prove that a column or combination of columns is a candidate key. The fact that there are no duplicates for the values that appear at a particular moment in time does not guarantee that duplicates are not possible. However, the presence of duplicates in an instance can be used to show that some column combination is not a candidate key. Identifying a candidate key requires that you know the 'real world' meaning of the column(s) involved so that you can decide whether duplicates are possible. Only by using this semantic information can you be certain that a column combination is a candidate key.

For example, from the data presented in Figure 2.1, you may think that a suitable candidate key for the `Staff` table would be `name`, the employee's name. However, although there is only a single value of Tom Daniels in this table just now, a new member of staff with the same name could join the company, which would therefore prevent the choice of `name` as a candidate key.

Primary key

The candidate key that is selected to identify records uniquely within the table.

Since a table has no duplicate records, it is always possible to uniquely identify each record. This means that a table always has a **primary key**. In the worst case, the entire set of columns could serve as the primary key, but usually some smaller subset is sufficient to distinguish the records. The candidate keys that are not selected to be the primary key are called **alternate keys**. For the `Staff` table, if we choose `staffNo` as the primary key, `eMail` would then be an alternate key. For the `Wish` table, if we choose (`memberNo`, `catalogNo`) as the primary key, (`memberNo`, `ranking`) would then be an alternate key.

Foreign key

A column, or set of columns, within one table that matches the candidate key of some (possibly the same) table.

When a column appears in more than one table, its appearance usually represents a relationship between records of the two tables. For example, in Figure 2.1 the inclusion of `dCenterNo` in both the `DistributionCenter` and `Staff` tables is quite deliberate and links distribution centers to the details of staff working there. In the `DistributionCenter` table, `dCenterNo` is the primary key. However, in the `Staff` table the `dCenterNo` column exists to match staff to the distribution center they work in. In the `Staff` table, `dCenterNo` is a **foreign key**. We say that the column `dCenterNo` in the `Staff` table *targets* or *references* the primary key column `dCenterNo` in the *home* table, `DistributionCenter`. In this situation, the `Staff` table is also known as the *child* table and the `DistributionCenter` table as the *parent* table.

In the same way, the column `mgrStaffNo` in the `DistributionCenter` table *targets* the primary key column `staffNo` in the *home* table, `Staff`. In the `DistributionCenter` table the `mgrStaffNo` column exists as a foreign key to match staff to the distribution center they manage. Note in this case that we have chosen to give the foreign key column, `mgrStaffNo`, a slightly different name to the corresponding primary key column name, `staffNo`, to more accurately reflect what the foreign key column represents.

> **Note** You may recall from Chapter 1 that one of the advantages of the DBMS approach was control of data redundancy. This is an example of 'controlled redundancy' – these common columns, namely primary key and foreign key(s), play an important role in modeling relationships, as we will see in later chapters.

2.3.4 Representing relational databases

A relational database consists of one or more tables. The common convention for representing a description of a relational database is to give the name of each table, followed by the column names in parentheses. Normally, the primary key is underlined. The description of the relational database for the *StayHome Online Rentals* company is:

```
DistributionCenter   (dCenterNo, dStreet, dCity, dState,
                     dZipCode, mgrStaffNo)
Staff                (staffNo, name, position, salary,
                     eMail, dCenterNo)
DVD                  (catalogNo, title, genre, rating)
Actor                (actorNo, actorName)
DVDActor             (actorNo, catalogNo, character)
Member               (memberNo, mFName, mLName, mStreet,
                     mCity, mState, mZipCode, mEMail,
                     mPword, mTypeNo, dCenterNo)
MembershipType       (mTypeNo, mTypeDesc, maxRentals,
                     monthlyCharge)
Wish                 (memberNo, catalogNo, ranking)
RentalDelivery       (deliveryNo, memberNo, dateOut)
DVDRental            (deliveryNo, DVDNo, dateReturn)
DVDCopy              (DVDNo, available, catalogNo, dCenterNo)
```

Figure 2.4 shows an instance of the *StayHome Online Rentals* database.

2.4 Relational integrity

In the previous section, we discussed the structural part of the relational data model. As we mentioned in Section 2.2, a data model has two other parts: a manipulative part, defining the types of operations that are allowed on the data, and a set of integrity rules, which ensures that the data is accurate. In this section, we discuss the relational integrity rules, and in the following section we discuss the main relational manipulation languages.

DistributionCenter

dCenterNo	dStreet	dCity	dState	dZipCode	mgrStaffNo
D001	8 Jefferson Way	Portland	OR	97201	S1500
D002	City Center Plaza	Seattle	WA	98122	S0010
D003	14 – 8th Avenue	New York	NY	10012	S0415
D004	2 W. El Camino	San Francisco	CA	94087	S2250

Staff

staffNo	name	position	salary	eMail	dCenterNo
S1500	Tom Daniels	Manager	48000	tdaniels@stayhome.com	D001
S0003	Sally Adams	Assistant	30000	sadams@stayhome.com	D001
S0010	Mary Martinez	Manager	51000	mmartinez@stayhome.com	D002
S3250	Robert Chin	Assistant	33000	rchin@stayhome.com	D002
S2250	Sally Stern	Manager	48000	sstern@stayhome.com	D004
S0415	Art Peters	Manager	42000	apeters@stayhome.com	D003

DVD

catalogNo	title	genre	rating
207132	Casino Royale	Action	PG-13
902355	Harry Potter and the GOF	Children	PG
330553	Lord of the Rings III	Action	PG-13
781132	Shrek 2	Children	PG
445624	Mission Impossible III	Action	PG-13
634817	War of the Worlds	Sci-Fi	PG-13

Actor

actorNo	actorName
A1002	Judi Dench
A3006	Elijah Wood
A2019	Tom Cruise
A7525	Ian McKellen
A4343	Mike Myers
A8401	Daniel Radcliffe

DVDActor

actorNo	catalogNo	character
A1002	207132	M
A3006	330553	Frodo Baggins
A2019	445624	Ethan Hunt
A2019	634817	Ray Ferrier
A7525	330553	Gandalf
A4343	781132	Shrek
A8401	902355	Harry Potter

Figure 2.4 An example instance of the *StayHome Online Rentals* database

Since every column has an associated domain (see Section 2.3.1), there are constraints (called *domain constraints*) in the form of restrictions on the set of values allowed for the columns of tables. In addition, there are two important integrity rules, which are constraints or restrictions that apply to all instances of the database. The two principal rules for the relational model are known as **entity integrity** and **referential integrity**. Before defining these terms, you need to first understand the concept of nulls.

Member

memberNo	mFName	mLName	mStreet	mCity	mState	mZipCode	mEMail	mPword	mTypeNo	dCenterNo
M250178	Bob	Adams	57 – 11th Avenue	Seattle	WA	98105	badams@yahoo.com	*******	MT2	D002
M166884	Ann	Peters	89 Redmond Rd	Portland	OR	97117	apeters@hotmail.com	******	MT3	D001
M115656	Serena	Parker	2 W. Capital Way	Portland	OR	97201	sparker@port.edu	******	MT1	D001
M284354	Don	Nelson	123 Suffolk Lane	Seattle	WA	98117	dnelson1@msoft.com	******	MT1	D002

MembershipType

mTypeNo	mTypeDesc	maxRentals	monthlyCharge
MT1	5-at-a-time	5	$14.99
MT2	3-at-a-time	3	$11.99
MT3	1-at-a-time	1	$9.99

Wish

memberNo	catalogNo	ranking
M250178	330553	1
M250178	634817	2
M166884	207132	1
M166884	330553	2
M166884	634817	3

RentalDelivery

deliveryNo	memberNo	dateOut
R75346191	M284354	4-Feb-06
R75346282	M284354	4-Feb-06
R66825673	M115656	5-Feb-06
R66818964	M115656	2-Feb-06

DVDRental

deliveryNo	DVDNo	dateReturn
R75346191	24545663	6-Feb-06
R75346282	24343196	6-Feb-06
R66825673	19900422	7-Feb-06
R66818964	17864331	

DVDCopy

DVDNo	available	catalogNo	dCenterNo
19900422	Y	207132	D001
24545663	Y	207132	D002
17864331	N	634817	D001
24343196	Y	634817	D002

Figure 2.4 *(Cont'd)*

2.4.1 Nulls

Null

Represents a value for a column that is currently unknown or is not applicable for this record.

A **null** can be taken to mean 'unknown.' It can also mean that a value is not applicable to a particular record, or it could just mean that no value has yet been supplied. Nulls are a way to deal with incomplete or exceptional data. However, a null is not the same as a zero numeric value or a text string filled with spaces; zeros and spaces are values, but a null represents the absence of a value. Therefore, nulls should be treated differently from other values.

For example, assume that it is possible for a distribution center to be temporarily without a manager, perhaps because the manager has recently left and a new manager has not yet been appointed. In this case, the value for the corresponding mgrStaffNo column would be undefined. Without nulls, it becomes necessary to introduce false data to represent this state or to add additional columns that may not be meaningful to the user. In this example, we may try to represent the absence of a manager with the value 'None at present.' Alternatively, we may add a new column 'currentManager?' to the DistributionCenter table, which contains a value Y (Yes) if there is a manager, and N (No) otherwise. Both these approaches can be confusing to anyone using the database.

Having defined nulls, we are now in a position to define the two relational integrity rules.

2.4.2 Entity integrity

The first integrity rule applies to the primary keys of base tables.

Key point

A **base table** is a named table whose records are physically stored in the database. This is in contrast to a view, which we mentioned in Section 1.2.5. A view is a 'virtual table' that does not actually exist in the database but is generated by the DBMS from the underlying base tables whenever it is accessed.

Entity integrity

In a base table, no column of a primary key can be null.

From an earlier definition, we know that a primary key is a minimal identifier that is used to identify records uniquely. This means that no subset of the primary key is sufficient to provide unique identification of records. If we allow a null for any part of a primary key, we are implying that not all the columns are needed to distinguish between records, which contradicts the definition of the primary key. For example, as dCenterNo is the primary key of the DistributionCenter table, we are not able to insert a record into the DistributionCenter table with a null for the dCenterNo column. For the Wish table the primary key is the combination of the memberNo and catalogNo columns. In this case, we are not able to insert a record into the Wish table with a null in either the memberNo column or the catalogNo column.

2.4.3 Referential integrity

Referential integrity

If a foreign key exists in a table, either the foreign key value must match a candidate key value of some record in its home table or the foreign key value must be wholly null.

The second integrity rule applies to foreign keys.

In Figure 2.1, mgrStaffNo in the DistributionCenter table is a foreign key targeting the staffNo column in the home (parent) table, Staff. It should not be possible to create a distribution center record with manager staff number S9999, for example, unless there is already a record for staff member S9999 in the Staff table. However, if it were possible for a center not to always have a manager, for example to allow for the situation where a distribution center has been set up but has not yet been assigned a manager (or an existing distribution center temporarily has no manager while the one who left is being replaced), then we should be able to create a new distribution center record with a null in the mgrStaffNo column.

2.4.4 Integrity constraints

Integrity constraints

Rules that define or constrain some aspect of the data used by the organization.

Domains constraints, which constrain the values that a particular column can have, and the relational integrity rules discussed above are special cases of the more general concept of **integrity constraints**. Another example of integrity constraints is *multiplicity*, which defines the number of occurrences of one entity (such as a distribution center) that may relate to a single occurrence of an associated entity (such as a member of staff). We will discuss multiplicity in detail in Section 6.5. It is also possible for users to specify additional integrity constraints that the data must satisfy. For example, if *StayHome* has a rule that a member can rent a maximum of five DVDs only at any one time, then the user must be able to specify this rule and expect the DBMS to enforce it. In this case, it should not be possible for a member to rent a DVD if the number of DVDs the member currently has rented is five.

Unfortunately, the level of support for integrity constraints varies from DBMS to DBMS. We will discuss the implementation of integrity constraints in Chapter 11 on physical database design.

2.5 Relational languages

Relational algebra

A (high-level) procedural language: it can be used to tell the DBMS how to build a new table from one or more tables in the database.

Relational calculus

A non-procedural language: it can be used to formulate the definition of a table in terms of one or more tables.

In Section 2.2, we stated that one part of a data model is the manipulative part, which defines the types of operations that are allowed on the data. This includes the operations that are used for updating or retrieving data from the database and for changing the structure of the database. In his seminal work on defining the relational model, Codd proposed two languages: **relational algebra** and **relational calculus** (1972).

The relational algebra is a procedural language: you must specify *what* data is needed and exactly *how* to retrieve the data. The relational calculus is non-procedural: you need only specify *what* data is required and it is the responsibility of the DBMS to determine the most efficient method for retrieving this data. However, formally the relational algebra and relational calculus are equivalent to one another: for every expression in the algebra, there is an equivalent expression in the calculus (and vice versa). Both the algebra and the calculus are formal, non-user-friendly languages. They have been used as the basis for other, higher-level languages for relational databases. The relational calculus is used to measure the selective power of relational languages. A language that can be used to produce any table that can be derived using the relational calculus is said to be *relationally complete*. Most relational query languages are relationally complete but have more expressive power than the relational algebra or relational calculus because of additional operations such as calculated, summary, and ordering functions. A detailed discussion of these languages is outside the scope of this book but the interested reader is referred to Connolly and Begg (2005).

The two main (high-level, non-procedural) languages that have emerged for relational DBMSs are:

- **SQL (Structured Query Language)** and
- **QBE (Query-By-Example)**.

SQL has been standardized by the International Standards Organization, making it both the formal and *de facto* standard language for defining and manipulating relational databases.

QBE is an alternative, graphical-based, 'point-and-click' way of querying a database, which is particularly suited for queries that are not too complex, and can be expressed in terms of a few tables. QBE has acquired the reputation of being one of the easiest ways for non-technical users to obtain information from the database. Unfortunately, unlike SQL, there is no official standard for QBE. However, the functionality provided by vendors is generally very similar and QBE is usually more intuitive to use than SQL. We will provide a tutorial on SQL and QBE in the next chapter.

Chapter summary

- The RDBMS has become the dominant DBMS in use today. This software represents the second generation of DBMS and is based on the relational data model proposed by Dr E.F. Codd.
- **Relations** are physically represented as *tables*, with the *records* corresponding to individual **tuples** and the *columns* to **attributes**.
- Properties of relational tables are: each cell contains exactly one value, column names are distinct, column values come from the same domain, column order is immaterial, record order is immaterial, and there are no duplicate records.
- A **superkey** is a set of columns that identifies records of a table uniquely, while a **candidate key** is a minimal superkey. A **primary key** is the candidate key chosen for use in the identification of records. A table must always have a primary key. A **foreign key** is a column, or set of columns, within one table that is the candidate key of another (possibly the same) table.
- A **null** represents a value for a column that is unknown at the present time or is not defined for this record.
- **Entity integrity** is a constraint that states that in a base table no column of a primary key can be null. **Referential integrity** states that foreign key values must match a candidate key value of some record in the home (parent) table or be wholly null.
- The two main languages for accessing relational databases are **SQL** (Structured Query Language) and **QBE** (Query-By-Example).

Review questions

2.1 Discuss each of the following concepts in the context of the relational data model:
(a) relation
(b) attribute
(c) domain
(d) tuple
(e) relational database.

2.2 Discuss the properties of a relational table. Give examples to illustrate your answer.

2.3 Discuss the relationship between the candidate keys and the primary key of a table.

2.4 Explain what is meant by a foreign key.

2.5 How do foreign keys of tables relate to candidate keys? Give examples to illustrate your answer.

2.6 What does a null represent?

2.7 What is a base table?

2.8 Define the two principal integrity rules for the relational model. Discuss why it is desirable to enforce these rules.

2.9 What are integrity constraints? Give examples to illustrate your answer.

2.10 Discuss the difference between procedural and non-procedural query languages.

Exercises

driverID	dFName	dLName
D456	Jane	Watt
D666	Karen	Black
D957	Steven	Smith
D344	Tom	Jones

clientID	cFName	cLName	cAddress
C034	Anne	Way	111 Storrie Road, Paisley
C089	Mark	Fields	120 Lady Lane, Paisley
C019	Anne	Brown	13 Renfrew Road, Paisley
C039	Karen	Way	34 High Street, Paisley

jobID	pickupDateTime	driverID	clientID
1001	25/07/06.10.00	D456	C034
1102	29/07/06.10.00	D456	C034
1203	30/07/06.11.00	D344	C034
1334	2/08/06.13.00	D666	C089
1455	2/08/06.13.00	D957	C019
1676	25/08/06.10.00	D344	C037

Figure 2.5 An example instance of the *FastCabs* taxi service

2.11 Consider the data in Figure 2.5 and assume that the data is representative of the data stored in these tables.
(a) Suggest a name for each table.
(b) Identify domains for the columns.
(c) Identify the candidate keys, primary keys, and alternate keys of each table.
(d) Identify any foreign keys.
(e) Under what conditions is `pickupDateTime` an atomic value?
(f) Suggest some integrity constraints for the tables.

2.12 Are the relational integrity rules being maintained? If not, suggest how the data should be modified to ensure relational integrity.

CHAPTER

3 SQL and QBE

Preview

In the previous chapter, we introduced the relational data model and noted that the two main languages that have emerged for relational DBMSs are:

- SQL (Structured Query Language)
- QBE (Query-By-Example).

QBE is essentially a graphical front-end to SQL that provides a potentially simpler method of querying relational databases than SQL. However, QBE converts the query expressed graphically into a corresponding SQL statement that is then run on the database. In this chapter, we examine both these languages, although we concentrate primarily on SQL because of its importance. In Appendix E, we will discuss some of the more advanced elements of SQL, including how to create tables and views, the SQL programming language, stored procedures, and triggers.

Learning objectives

In this chapter you will learn:

- The purpose and importance of SQL, the main language for querying relational databases.
- How to retrieve data from the database using the SELECT statement.
- How to insert data into the database using the INSERT statement.
- How to update data in the database using the UPDATE statement.
- How to delete data from the database using the DELETE statement.
- About an alternative language for querying relational databases called QBE.

3.1 Structured Query Language (SQL)

SQL is the most widely used commercial relational database language, designed to be used by professionals and non-professionals alike. It was originally developed in the SEQUEL and System R projects at IBM's research laboratory in San José between 1974 and 1977. Today, many people still pronounce SQL as 'See-Quel', although the official pronunciation is 'S-Q-L'. Starting with Oracle in the late 1970s, there have been many commercial RDBMSs based on SQL, and with an ANSI and ISO standard it is now the *de facto* language for defining and manipulating relational databases.

The main characteristics of SQL are:

- It is relatively easy to learn.
- It is a non-procedural language: you specify *what* information you require, rather than *how* to get it. In other words, SQL does not require you to specify the access methods to the data.
- Like most modern languages, SQL is essentially free-format, which means that parts of statements do not have to be typed at particular locations on the screen.
- The command structure consists of standard English words such as SELECT, INSERT, UPDATE, and DELETE.
- It can be implemented by a range of users including DBAs, management personnel, application programmers, and many other types of end-users.

SQL is an important language for a number of reasons:

- SQL is the first and, so far, only standard database language to gain wide acceptance. Nearly every major current vendor provides database products based on SQL or with an SQL interface, and most are represented on at least one of the standard-making bodies.
- There is a huge investment in the SQL language both by vendors and by users. It has become part of application architectures such as IBM's Systems Application Architecture (SAA), and is the strategic choice of many large and influential organizations, for example the X/OPEN consortium for UNIX standards.
- SQL has also become a Federal Information Processing Standard (FIPS), to which conformance is required for all sales of DBMSs to the US Government.
- SQL is used in other standards, and even influences the development of other standards as a definitional tool (for example, the ISO Remote Data Access (RDA) standard).

Before we go through some examples of SQL, we first examine the objectives of SQL.

3.1.1 Objectives of SQL

Ideally, a database language should allow a user to:

- create the database and table structures;
- perform basic data management tasks, such as the insertion, modification, and deletion of data from the tables;
- perform both simple and complex queries.

In addition, a database language must perform these tasks with minimal user effort, and its command structure and syntax must be relatively easy to learn. Finally, it must be portable: that is, it must conform to some recognized standard so that we can use the same command structure and syntax when we move from one DBMS to another. SQL is intended to satisfy these requirements.

SQL is an example of a *transform-oriented language*, or a language designed to transform input tables into required output tables. The ISO SQL standard has two major components:

- a **Data Definition Language (DDL)** for defining the database structure and controlling access to the data;
- a **Data Manipulation Language (DML)** for retrieving and updating data.

Until the release of the ISO SQL standard in 1999 (colloquially known as SQL:1999 or SQL3), SQL contained only these definitional and manipulative commands; it did not contain flow-of-control commands, such as IF . . . THEN . . . ELSE, GO TO, or DO . . . WHILE. These had to be implemented using a programming or job-control language, or interactively by the end-users. Due to this initial lack of *computational completeness*, SQL was used in two ways. The first way was to use SQL *interactively* by entering the statements at a terminal. The second way was to *embed* SQL statements in a procedural language. In this book, we consider only interactive SQL; for details on embedded SQL the interested reader is referred to Connolly and Begg (2005).

Note SQL conformance: SQL:2006 has a set of features called Core SQL that a vendor must implement to claim conformance with the SQL:2006 standard. Many of the remaining features are divided into **packages**; for example, there are packages for object features and Online Analytical Processing (OLAP). Vendors tend to implement additional features, although this does affect portability.

3.1.2 Terminology

The ISO SQL standard does not use the formal terms of relations, attributes, and tuples; instead it uses the terms **tables**, **columns**, and **rows**. In our presentation of SQL we mostly use the ISO terminology. It should also be noted that SQL does not adhere strictly to the definition of the relational model described in Chapter 2. For example, SQL allows the table produced as the result of the SELECT operation to contain duplicate rows, it imposes an ordering on the columns, and it allows the user to order the rows of a table.

3.1.3 Writing SQL commands

An SQL statement consists of reserved words and user-defined words. Reserved words are a fixed part of the SQL language and have a fixed meaning; they must be spelt *exactly* as required and cannot be split across lines. User-defined words are made up by the user (according to certain syntax rules), and represent the names of various database objects such as tables, columns, views, indexes, and so on. Throughout this chapter, we use uppercase letters to represent reserved words.

Most components of an SQL statement are *case insensitive*, which means that letters can be typed in either upper or lower case. The one important exception to this rule is that literal character data must be typed *exactly* as it appears in the database. For example, if we store a person's surname as 'SMITH' and then search for it using the string 'Smith,' the row will not be found. The words in a statement are also built according to a set of syntax rules. Although the standard does not require it, many dialects of SQL require the use of a statement terminator to mark the end of each SQL statement (usually the semicolon ';' is used).

Literals

Before we discuss the SQL DML statements, it is necessary to understand the concept of **literals**. Literals are **constants** that are used in SQL statements. There are different forms of literals for every data type supported by SQL. However, for simplicity, we can distinguish between literals that are enclosed in single quotes and those that are not. All non-numeric data values must be enclosed in single quotes; all numeric data values must *not* be enclosed in single quotes. For example, we could use literals to insert data into a table:

```
INSERT INTO  MembershipType (mTypeNo, mTypeDesc, maxRentals,
             monthlyCharge)
VALUES       ('MT1', '5-at-a-time', 5, 14.99);
```

The value in columns `maxRentals` and `monthlyCharge` are integer and decimal literals, respectively; they are not enclosed in single quotes. The other two columns are character strings and the values are enclosed in single quotes.

3.2 Data manipulation

In this section, we look at the SQL DML statements, namely:

- SELECT — to query data in the database;
- INSERT — to insert data into a table;
- UPDATE — to update data in a table;
- DELETE — to delete data from a table.

Due to the complexity of the SELECT statement and the relative simplicity of the other DML statements, we devote most of this section to the SELECT statement and its various formats. We begin by considering simple queries, and successively add more complexity to show how more complicated queries that use sorting, grouping, aggregates, and also queries on multiple tables, can be generated. Thereafter, we consider the INSERT, UPDATE, and DELETE statements.

We illustrate the SQL statements using part of the instance of the *StayHome Online Rentals* case study shown in Figure 2.4.

3.2.1 Simple queries

The purpose of the SELECT statement is to retrieve and display data from one or more database tables. It is an extremely powerful command and it is also the most frequently used SQL command. The SELECT statement has the following general form:

```
SELECT      [DISTINCT | ALL] {* | [columnExpression [AS newName]]
            [,...]}
FROM        TableName [alias] [,...]
[WHERE      condition]
[GROUP BY   columnList] [HAVING condition]
[ORDER BY   columnList]
```

- `columnExpression` represents a column name or an expression;
- `newName` is a name you can give the column as a display heading;
- `TableName` is the name of an existing database table or view that you have access to;
- `alias` is an optional abbreviation for `TableName`.

We have used the following extended form of the Backus Naur Form (BNF) notation to define the SELECT statement:

- a vertical bar (|) indicates a *choice* among alternatives; for example, after the SELECT clause we can add the DISTINCT or ALL keyword;
- curly braces indicate a *required element*; for example, in the SELECT clause we have to specify either * (which means all columns) or a column expression;
- square brackets indicate an *optional element*; for example, the WHERE clause is an optional clause;
- an ellipsis [. . .] is used to indicate *optional repetition* of an item zero or more times; for example, in the SELECT clause after specifying one column expression, we can specify a number of other column expressions.

Key point

The sequence of processing in a SELECT statement is:

FROM	specifies the table or tables to be used;
WHERE	filters the rows subject to some condition;
GROUP BY	forms groups of rows with the same column value;
HAVING	filters the groups subject to some condition;
SELECT	specifies which columns are to appear in the output;
ORDER BY	specifies the order of the output.

The order of the clauses in the SELECT statement *cannot* be changed. However, the only two mandatory clauses are the first two: SELECT and FROM; the remainder are optional. Every SELECT statement produces a query result table consisting of one or more columns and zero or more rows.

Query 3.1 Retrieve all columns, all rows

List the full details of all DVDs.

Since there are no restrictions specified in the query (that is, we want to list all rows in the DVD table), no WHERE clause is required. We can express this query as:

```
SELECT catalogNo, title, genre, rating
FROM DVD;
```

When you want to list all columns of a table, you can use an asterisk (*) in place of the column names. Therefore, the above query can be expressed more succinctly as:

```
SELECT *
FROM DVD;
```

The result table in either case is shown in Table 3.1.

Table 3.1 Result table for Query 3.1

catalogNo	title	genre	rating
207132	Casino Royale	Action	PG-13
902355	Harry Potter and the GOF	Children	PG
330553	Lord of the Rings III	Action	PG-13
781132	Shrek 2	Children	PG
445624	Mission Impossible III	Action	PG-13
634817	War of the Worlds	Sci-Fi	PG-13

Query 3.2 Retrieve specific columns, all rows

List the catalog number, title, and genre of all DVDs.

Once again, there are no restrictions specified in the query and so no WHERE clause is required. However, we wish to list only a subset of the columns, which we express as:

```
SELECT catalogNo, title, genre
FROM DVD;
```

The result table is shown in Table 3.2. Note that, unless specified, the rows in the result table may not be sorted. We describe how to sort the rows of a result table in the next section.

Table 3.2 Result table for Query 3.2

catalogNo	title	genre
207132	Casino Royale	Action
902355	Harry Potter and the GOF	Children
330553	Lord of the Rings III	Action
781132	Shrek 2	Children
445624	Mission Impossible III	Action
634817	War of the Worlds	Sci-Fi

Query 3.3 Use of DISTINCT

List all DVD genres.

```
SELECT genre
FROM DVD;
```

The result table is shown in Table 3.3(a). Note that there are several duplicate values (by default, SELECT does not eliminate duplicate values). To eliminate duplicates, we use the DISTINCT keyword and by rewriting the above query as:

```
SELECT DISTINCT genre
FROM DVD;
```

we obtain the result table shown in Table 3.3(b).

Table 3.3(a) Result table for Query 3.3 with duplicates

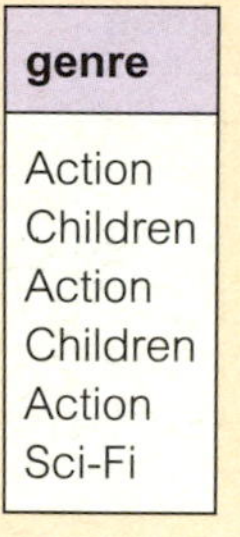

genre
Action
Children
Action
Children
Action
Sci-Fi

Table 3.3(b) Result table for Query 3.3 with duplicates eliminated

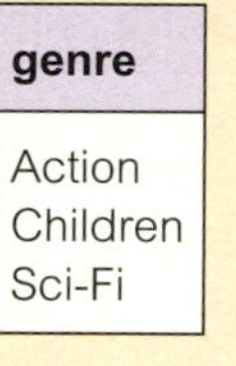

genre
Action
Children
Sci-Fi

Query 3.4 Calculated fields

List the monthly salary for all staff, showing the staff number, name, position, and monthly salary.

```
SELECT staffNo, name, position, salary/12
FROM Staff;
```

The `Staff` table contains annual salary details rather than monthly salary details. However, we can obtain the monthly salary by simply dividing the annual salary by 12, giving the result table shown in Table 3.4.

This is an example of the use of a *calculated field* (sometimes called a *computed* or *derived field*). In general, to use a calculated field, you specify an SQL expression in the SELECT list. An SQL expression can involve addition, subtraction, multiplication, and division, and you can use parentheses to build complex expressions. You can use more than one table column in a calculated column; however, the columns referenced in an arithmetic expression must be of a numeric type.

Table 3.4 Result table of Query 3.4

staffNo	name	position	col4
S1500	Tom Daniels	Manager	4000
S0003	Sally Adams	Assistant	2500
S0010	Mary Martinez	Manager	4250
S3250	Robert Chin	Assistant	2750
S2250	Sally Stern	Manager	4000
S0415	Art Peters	Manager	3500

The fourth column of this result table has been displayed as `col4`. Normally, a column in the result table takes its name from the corresponding column of the database table from which it has been retrieved. However, in this case SQL does not know how to label the column. Some systems give the column a name corresponding to its position in the table (for example, `col4`); some may leave the column name blank or use the expression entered in the SELECT list. The SQL standard allows the column to be named using an **AS** clause. In the previous example, we could have written:

```
SELECT staffNo, name, position, salary/12 AS monthlySalary
FROM Staff;
```

In this case, the column heading in the result table would be `monthlySalary` rather than `col4`.

3.2.2 Row selection (WHERE clause)

The above examples show the use of the SELECT statement to retrieve all rows from a table. However, we often need to restrict the rows that are retrieved. This can be achieved with the **WHERE** clause, which consists of the keyword WHERE followed by a search condition that specifies the rows to be retrieved. The five basic search conditions (or *predicates* using the ISO terminology) are as follows:

- *Comparison:* compare the value of one expression to the value of another expression;
- *Range:* test whether the value of an expression falls within a specified range of values;
- *Set membership:* test whether the value of an expression equals one of a set of values;
- *Pattern match:* test whether a string matches a specified pattern;
- *Null:* test whether a column has a null (unknown) value (see Section 2.3.1).

We now present examples of these types of search conditions.

Query 3.5 Comparison search condition

List all staff with a salary greater than $40 000.

```
SELECT staffNo, name, position, salary
FROM Staff
WHERE salary > 40000;
```

In this query, we have to restrict the rows in the `Staff` table to those where the value in the `salary` column is greater than $40 000. To do this, we specify a WHERE clause with the condition (*predicate*) 'salary > 40000'. The result table is shown in Table 3.5.

Table 3.5 Result table for Query 3.5

staffNo	name	position	salary
S1500	Tom Daniels	Manager	48000
S0010	Mary Martinez	Manager	51000
S2250	Sally Stern	Manager	48000
S0415	Art Peters	Manager	42000

Note In SQL, the following simple comparison operators are available:

=	equals	<>	is not equal to
<	is less than	<=	is less than or equal to
>	is greater than	>=	is greater than or equal to

More complex predicates can be generated using the logical operators **AND**, **OR**, and **NOT**, with parentheses (if needed or desired) to show the order of evaluation. The rules for evaluating a conditional expression are:

- an expression is evaluated left to right;
- subexpressions in brackets are evaluated first;
- NOTs are evaluated before ANDs and ORs;
- ANDs are evaluated before ORs.

The use of parentheses is always recommended to remove any possible ambiguities.

Query 3.6 Range search condition (BETWEEN/NOT BETWEEN)

List all staff with a salary between $45 000 and $50 000.

```
SELECT staffNo, name, position, salary
FROM Staff
WHERE salary >= 45000 AND salary <= 50000;
```

In this query, we use the logical operator AND in the WHERE clause to find the rows in the `Staff` table where the value in the `salary` column is between $45 000 and

Table 3.6 Result table for Query 3.6

staffNo	name	position	salary
S1500	Tom Daniels	Manager	48000
S2250	Sally Stern	Manager	48000

$50 000. The result table is shown in Table 3.6. SQL also provides the range test **BETWEEN** to test whether a data value lies between a pair of specified values. We could rewrite the previous query as:

```
SELECT staffNo, name, position, salary
FROM Staff
WHERE salary BETWEEN 45000 AND 50000;
```

The BETWEEN test includes the endpoints of the range, so any members of staff with a salary of $45 000 or $50 000 would be included in the result. There is also a negated version of the range test (**NOT BETWEEN**) that checks for values outside the range. The BETWEEN test does not add much to the expressive power of SQL because, as we have seen, it can be expressed equally well using two comparison tests.

Query 3.7 Set membership search condition (IN/NOT IN)

List all DVDs in the Sci-Fi or Children genre.

```
SELECT catalogNo, title, genre
FROM DVD
WHERE genre = 'Sci-Fi' OR genre = 'Children';
```

As in the previous example, we can express this query using a compound search condition in the WHERE clause. The result table is shown in Table 3.7. However, SQL also provides the set membership keyword **IN** to test whether a value matches one of a list of values. We can rewrite this query using the IN test as:

```
SELECT catalogNo, title, genre
FROM DVD
WHERE genre IN ('Sci-Fi', 'Children');
```

There is a negated version (**NOT IN**) that can be used to check for data values that do not lie in a specific list of values. Like BETWEEN, the IN test does not add much to the expressive power of SQL. However, the IN test provides a more efficient way of expressing the search condition, particularly if the set contains many values.

Table 3.7 Result table for Query 3.7

catalogNo	title	genre
902355	Harry Potter and the GOF	Children
781132	Shrek 2	Children
634817	War of the Worlds	Sci-Fi

Query 3.8 Pattern match search condition (LIKE/NOT LIKE)

List all staff whose first name is 'Sally'.

Note SQL has two special pattern-matching symbols:

% the percent character represents any sequence of zero or more characters (*wildcard*);

_ an underscore character represents any single character.

All other characters in the pattern represent themselves. For example:

- name **LIKE** 'S%' means the first character must be S, but the rest of the string can be anything.
- name **LIKE** 'S_ _ _ _' means that there must be exactly five characters in the string, the first of which must be an S.
- name **LIKE** '%S' means any sequence of characters, of length at least 1, with the last character an S.
- name **LIKE** '%Sally%' means a sequence of characters of any length containing Sally.
- name **NOT LIKE** 'S%' means the first character cannot be an S.

If the search string can include the pattern-matching character itself, we can use an escape character to represent the pattern-matching character. For example, to check for the string '15%,' we can use the predicate:

LIKE '15#%' **ESCAPE** '#'

Using the pattern-matching search condition of SQL, we can find all staff whose first name is 'Sally' using the following query:

```
SELECT staffNo, name, position, salary
FROM Staff
WHERE name LIKE 'Sally%';
```

The result table is shown in Table 3.8.

Table 3.8 Result table of Query 3.8

staffNo	name	position	salary
S0003	Sally Adams	Assistant	30000
S2250	Sally Stern	Manager	48000

Note Some RDBMSs, such as Microsoft Office Access, use the wildcard characters * and ? instead of % and _.

Query 3.9 NULL search condition (IS NULL/IS NOT NULL)

List the rentals that have no return date specified.

The DVDRental table has a column dateReturn representing the return date for the rental. You may think that we can find such rentals using the following search condition:

```
WHERE (dateReturn = ' ' OR dateReturn = 0)
```

However, neither of these conditions would work. A null dateReturn is considered to have an unknown value, so we cannot test whether it is equal or not equal to another value (see Section 2.4.1). If we tried to execute the SELECT statement using either of these compound conditions, we would get an empty result table. Instead, we have to test for null explicitly using the special keyword IS NULL:

```
SELECT deliveryNo, DVDNo
FROM DVDRental
WHERE dateReturn IS NULL;
```

The result table is shown in Table 3.9. The negated version (IS NOT NULL) can be used to test for values that are not null.

Table 3.9 Result table for Query 3.9

deliveryNo	DVDNo
R66818964	17864331

3.2.3 Sorting results (ORDER BY clause)

In general, the rows of an SQL query result table are not arranged in any particular order (although some DBMSs may use a default ordering, for example based on a primary key). However, we can ensure that the results of a query are sorted using the **ORDER BY** clause in the SELECT statement. The ORDER BY clause consists of a list of **column names** that the result is to be sorted on, separated by commas. The ORDER BY clause allows the retrieved rows to be ordered in ascending (**ASC**) or descending (**DESC**) order on any column or combination of columns, regardless of whether that column appears in the result. However, some dialects of SQL insist that the ORDER BY elements appear in the SELECT list. In either case, the ORDER BY clause must always be the last clause of the SELECT statement.

Query 3.10 Sorting results

List all DVDs, sorted in descending order of genre.

```
SELECT *
FROM DVD
ORDER BY genre DESC;
```

Table 3.10(a) Result table for Query 3.10 with ordering on `genre`

catalogNo	title	genre	rating
634817	War of the Worlds	Sci-Fi	PG-13
902355	Harry Potter and the GOF	Children	PG
781132	Shrek 2	Children	PG
207132	Casino Royale	Action	PG-13
330553	Lord of the Rings III	Action	PG-13
445624	Mission Impossible III	Action	PG-13

Table 3.10(b) Result table for Query 3.10 with ordering on `genre` and `catalogNo`

catalogNo	title	genre	rating
634817	War of the Worlds	Sci-Fi	PG-13
781132	Shrek 2	Children	PG
902355	Harry Potter and the GOF	Children	PG
207132	Casino Royale	Action	PG-13
330553	Lord of the Rings III	Action	PG-13
445624	Mission Impossible III	Action	PG-13

This is similar to Query 3.1 with the added requirement that the result table is to be sorted on the values in the `genre` column. This is achieved by adding the ORDER BY clause to the end of the SELECT statement, specifying `genre` as the column to be sorted, and DESC to indicate that the order is to be descending. In this case, we get the result table shown in Table 3.10(a).

As we have a number of values in the `genre` column that are the same, we may want to order the result first by `genre` (the major sort key) and second in ascending order of `catalogNo` (the minor sort key). In this case, the ORDER BY clause would be:

ORDER BY genre **DESC**, catalogNo **ASC**;

The result table for this alternative ordering is shown in Table 3.10(b).

3.2.4 Using the SQL aggregate functions

The ISO standard defines five aggregate functions:

COUNT Returns the number of values in a specified column.

SUM Returns the sum of the values in a specified column.

AVG Returns the average of the values in a specified column.

MIN Returns the minimum value in a specified column.

MAX Returns the maximum value in a specified column.

These functions operate on a single column of a table and return a single value. COUNT, MIN, and MAX apply to both numeric and non-numeric fields, but SUM and AVG may be used on numeric fields only. Apart from COUNT(*), each function eliminates nulls first and operates only on the remaining non-null values. COUNT(*) is a special use of COUNT, which counts all the rows of a table, regardless of whether nulls or duplicate values occur.

If we want to eliminate duplicates before the function is applied, we use the keyword DISTINCT before the column name in the function. DISTINCT has no effect with the MIN and MAX functions. However, it may have an effect on the result of SUM or AVG, so consideration must be given to whether duplicates should be included or excluded in the computation. In addition, DISTINCT can be specified only once in a query.

Key point

It is important to note that an aggregate function can be used only in the SELECT list and in the HAVING clause. It is incorrect to use it elsewhere. If the SELECT list includes an aggregate function and no GROUP BY clause is being used to group data together, then no item in the SELECT list can include any reference to a column unless that column is the argument to an aggregate function. We discuss the HAVING and GROUP BY clauses in Section 3.2.5. For example, the following query is illegal:

```
SELECT staffNo, COUNT(salary)
FROM Staff;
```

because the query does not have a GROUP BY clause and the column `staffNo` in the SELECT list is used outside an aggregate function.

Query 3.11 Use of COUNT and SUM

List the total number of staff with a salary greater than $40 000 and the sum of their salaries.

```
SELECT COUNT(staffNo) AS totalStaff, SUM(salary) AS totalSalary
FROM Staff
WHERE salary > 40000;
```

The WHERE clause is the same as in Query 3.5. However, in this case, we apply the COUNT function to count the number of rows satisfying the WHERE clause and we apply the SUM function to add together the salaries in these rows. The result table is shown in Table 3.11.

Table 3.11 Result table of Query 3.11

totalStaff	totalSalary
4	189000

Query 3.12 Use of MIN, MAX, and AVG

List the minimum, maximum, and average staff salary.

```
SELECT MIN(salary) AS minSalary, MAX(salary) AS maxSalary,
AVG(salary) AS avgSalary
FROM Staff;
```

In this query, we wish to consider all staff rows and therefore do not require a WHERE clause. The required values can be calculated using the MIN, MAX, and AVG functions. The result table is shown in Table 3.12.

Table 3.12 Result table of Query 3.12

minSalary	maxSalary	avgSalary
30000	51000	42000

3.2.5 Grouping results (GROUP BY clause)

The above summary queries are similar to the totals at the bottom of a report; they condense all the detailed data in the report into a single summary row of data. However, it is often useful to have subtotals in reports. We can use the **GROUP BY** clause of the SELECT statement to do this. A query that includes the GROUP BY clause is called a grouped query, because it groups the data from the SELECT table(s) and produces a single summary row for each group. The columns named in the GROUP BY clause are called the grouping columns. The ISO standard requires the SELECT clause and the GROUP BY clause to be closely integrated. When GROUP BY is used, each item in the SELECT list must be single-valued per group. Further, the SELECT clause may contain only:

- column names;
- aggregate functions;
- constants;
- an expression involving combinations of the above.

All column names in the SELECT list must appear in the GROUP BY clause unless the name is used only in an aggregate function. The contrary is not true: there may be column names in the GROUP BY clause that do not appear in the SELECT list. When the WHERE clause is used with GROUP BY, the WHERE clause is applied first, then groups are formed from the remaining rows that satisfy the search condition.

Key point The ISO standard considers two nulls to be equal for purposes of the GROUP BY clause. If two rows have nulls in the same grouping columns and identical values in all the non-null grouping columns, they are combined into the same group.

Query 3.13 Use of GROUP BY

Find the number of staff working in each distribution center and the sum of their salaries.

```
SELECT dCenterNo, COUNT(staffNo) AS totalStaff, SUM(salary)
AS totalSalary
FROM Staff
GROUP BY dCenterNo
ORDER BY dCenterNo;
```

It is not necessary to include the column names `staffNo` and `salary` in the GROUP BY list because they appear only in the SELECT list within aggregate functions. However, `dCenterNo` is not associated with an aggregate function and so must appear in the GROUP BY list. The result table is shown in Table 3.13.

Table 3.13 Result table for Query 3.13

dCenterNo	totalStaff	totalSalary
D001	2	78000
D002	2	84000
D003	1	42000
D004	1	48000

Conceptually, SQL performs the query as follows:

1. SQL divides the staff into groups according to their respective distribution center numbers. Within each group, all staff have the same distribution center number. In this example, we get four groups:

dCenterNo	staffNo	salary
D001	S1500	48000
D001	S0003	30000
D002	S0010	51000
D002	S3250	33000
D003	S0415	42000
D004	S2250	48000

COUNT(staffNo)	SUM(salary)
2	78000
2	84000
1	42000
1	48000

2. For each group, SQL computes the number of staff members and calculates the sum of the values in the `salary` column to get the total of their salaries. SQL generates a single summary row in the query result for each group.
3. Finally, the result is sorted in ascending order of distribution center number, `dCenterNo`.

Restricting groupings (HAVING clause)

The **HAVING** clause is designed for use with the GROUP BY clause to restrict the groups that appear in the final result table. Although similar in syntax, HAVING and WHERE serve different purposes. The WHERE clause filters individual rows going into the final result table, whereas HAVING filters groups going into the final result table. The ISO standard requires that column names used in the HAVING clause must also appear in the GROUP BY list or be contained within an aggregate function. In practice, the search condition in the HAVING clause always includes at least one aggregate function, otherwise the search condition could be moved to the WHERE clause and applied to individual rows. (Remember that aggregate functions cannot be used in the WHERE clause.)

The HAVING clause is not a necessary part of SQL – any query expressed using a HAVING clause can always be rewritten without the HAVING clause.

Query 3.14 Use of HAVING

For each distribution center with more than one member of staff, find the number of staff working in each of the centers and the sum of their salaries.

```
SELECT dCenterNo, COUNT(staffNo) AS totalStaff, SUM(salary)
AS totalSalary
FROM Staff
GROUP BY dCenterNo
HAVING COUNT(staffNo) > 1
ORDER BY dCenterNo;
```

This is similar to the previous example with the additional restriction that we want to consider only those groups (that is, distribution centers) with more than one member of staff. This restriction applies to the groups and so the HAVING clause is used. The result table is shown in Table 3.14.

Table 3.14 Result table of Query 3.14

dCenterNo	totalStaff	totalSalary
D001	2	78000
D002	2	84000

3.2.6 Subselects

In this section, we examine the use of a complete SELECT statement embedded within another SELECT statement. The results of this *inner* SELECT statement (or *subselect*) are used in the *outer* statement to help determine the contents of the final result. A subselect can be used in the WHERE and HAVING clauses of an outer SELECT statement, where it is called a *subquery* or *nested query*. Subselects may also appear in the FROM clause and in the INSERT, UPDATE, and DELETE statements (see Section 3.2.9).

Query 3.15 Using a subquery

Find the staff who work in the center at '8 Jefferson Way'.

```
SELECT staffNo, name, position
FROM Staff
WHERE dCenterNo = (SELECT dCenterNo
                   FROM DistributionCenter
                   WHERE dStreet = '8 Jefferson Way');
```

The inner SELECT statement (SELECT dCenterNo FROM DistributionCenter . . .) finds the number of the distribution center that has the street name '8 Jefferson Way' (there will be only one such distribution center, so this is an example of a scalar subquery). Having obtained this distribution center number, the outer SELECT statement then retrieves the details of all staff who work at this center. In other words, the inner SELECT returns a result table containing a single value 'D001', corresponding to the center at '8 Jefferson Way', and the outer SELECT becomes:

```
SELECT staffNo, name, position
FROM Staff
WHERE dCenterNo = 'D001';
```

The result table is shown in Table 3.15.

Table 3.15 Result table of Query 3.15

staffNo	name	position
S1500	Tom Daniels	Manager
S0003	Sally Adams	Assistant

We can think of the subquery as producing a temporary table with results that can be accessed and used by the outer statement. A subquery can be used immediately following a relational operator (that is =, <, >, <=, >=, < >) in a WHERE clause or a HAVING clause. The subquery itself is always enclosed in parentheses.

Key point

If the result of the inner query can result in more than one row, then you must use the set membership test IN rather than the equality test ('='). For example, if we wish to find staff who work at a center in Washington (WA) or New York (NY), the WHERE clause would become:

```
WHERE dCenterNo IN (SELECT dCenterNo FROM DistributionCenter
                    WHERE dState = 'WA' OR dState = 'NY');
```

Query 3.16 Using a subquery with an aggregate function

List all staff whose salary is greater than the average salary.

```
SELECT staffNo, name, position
FROM Staff
WHERE salary > (SELECT AVG(salary)
                FROM Staff);
```

Recall from Section 3.2.4 that an aggregate function can be used only in the SELECT list and in the HAVING clause. It would be incorrect to write 'WHERE salary > AVG(salary)'. Instead, we use a subquery to find the average salary, and then use the outer SELECT statement to find those staff with a salary greater than this average. In other words, the subquery returns the average salary as $42 000. The outer query is reduced then to:

```
SELECT staffNo, name, position
FROM Staff
WHERE salary > 42000;
```

The result table is shown in Table 3.16 (note, the record corresponding to Art Peters is not included because the salary is exactly $42 000, not greater than $42 000).

Table 3.16 Result table of Query 3.16

staffNo	name	position
S1500	Tom Daniels	Manager
S0010	Mary Martinez	Manager
S2250	Sally Stern	Manager

Key points

The following rules apply to subqueries:

(1) The ORDER BY clause may not be used in a subquery (although it may be used in the outermost SELECT statement).

(2) The subquery SELECT list must consist of a single column name or expression (except for subqueries that use the keyword EXISTS – see Section 3.2.8).

(3) By default, column names in a subquery refer to the table name in the FROM clause of the subquery. It is possible to refer to a table in a FROM clause of an outer query by qualifying the column name (see below).

(4) When a subquery is one of the two operands involved in a comparison, the subquery must appear on the right-hand side of the comparison. For example, it would be incorrect to express the previous example as:

```
SELECT staffNo, name, position
FROM Staff
WHERE (SELECT AVG(salary)) < salary;
```

because the subquery appears on the left-hand side of the comparison with salary.

3.2.7 Multi-table queries

All the examples we have considered so far have a major limitation: the columns that are to appear in the result table must all come from a single table. In many cases, this is not sufficient. To combine columns from several tables into a result table, we need to use a **join** operation. The SQL join operation combines information from two tables by forming pairs of related rows from the two tables. The row pairs that make up the joined table are those where the matching columns in each of the two tables have the same value.

If you need to obtain information from more than one table, the choice is between using a subquery and using a join. If the final result table is to contain columns from different tables, then you must use a join. To perform a join, you simply include more than one table name in the FROM clause, using a comma as a separator, and typically include a WHERE clause to specify the join column(s). It is also possible to use an `alias` for a table named in the FROM clause. In this case, the alias is separated from the table name with a space. An alias can be used to qualify a column name whenever there is ambiguity regarding the source of the column name. It can also be used as a shorthand notation for the table name. If an alias is provided it can be used anywhere in place of the table name.

Query 3.17 Simple join

List all actors and the characters they have played in DVDs.

```
SELECT a.actorNo, actorName, character
FROM Actor a, DVDActor da
WHERE a.actorNo = da.actorNo;
```

We want to display details from both the `Actor` table and the `DVDActor` table, so we have to use a join. The SELECT clause lists the columns to be displayed. To obtain the required rows, we include those rows from both tables that have identical values in the `actorNo` columns, using the search condition (`a.actorNo = da.actorNo`), as illustrated in Figure 3.1. We call these two columns the matching columns for the two tables. The result table is shown in Table 3.17.

Table 3.17 Result table of Query 3.17

actorNo	actorName	character
A1002	Judi Dench	M
A3006	Elijah Wood	Frodo Baggins
A2019	Tom Cruise	Ethan Hunt
A2019	Tom Cruise	Ray Ferrier
A7525	Ian McKellen	Gandalf
A4343	Mike Myers	Shrek
A8401	Daniel Radcliffe	Harry Potter

Key point It is necessary to qualify the actor number, `actorNo`, in the SELECT list: `actorNo` could come from either table, and we have to indicate which one. (We could equally well have chosen the `actorNo` column from the `DVDActor` table.) The qualification is achieved by prefixing the column name with the appropriate table name (or its alias). In this case, we have used `a` as the alias for the `Actor` table.

Actor

actorNo	actorName
A1002	Judi Dench
A3006	Elijah Wood
A2019	Tom Cruise
A7525	Ian McKellen
A4343	Mike Myers
A8401	Daniel Radcliffe

DVDActor

actorNo	catalogNo	character
A1002	207132	M
A3006	330553	Frodo Baggins
A2019	445624	Ethan Hunt
A2019	634817	Ray Ferrier
A7525	330553	Gandalf
A4343	781132	Shrek
A8401	902355	Harry Potter

Matching `actorNo` values

Figure 3.1 Matching the rows of the `Actor` and `DVDActor` tables based on common `actorNo` values

The most common multi-table queries involve two tables that have a one-to-many (1:*) relationship (see Section 6.5.2). The previous query involving actors and characters is an example of such a query. Each actor can have one or more characters. In Section 2.3.3, we described how candidate keys and foreign keys model relationships in a relational database. To use a relationship in an SQL query, we specify a search condition that compares one of the candidate keys (normally the primary key) and the corresponding foreign key. In Query 3.17, we compared the primary key in the `Actor` table, `a.actorNo`, with one of the foreign keys in the `DVDActor` table, `da.actorNo`.

The SQL standard provides the following alternative ways to specify this join:

```
FROM Actor a JOIN DVDActor da ON a.actorNo = da.actorNo;

FROM Actor JOIN DVDActor USING actorNo;

FROM Actor NATURAL JOIN DVDActor;
```

In each case, the FROM clause replaces the original FROM and WHERE clauses. However, the first alternative produces a table with two identical `actorNo` columns; the remaining two produce a table with a single `actorNo` column.

Query 3.18 Three table join

List all actors and the characters they have played in DVDs, along with the DVD's title.

```
SELECT a.actorNo, actorName, character, title
FROM Actor a, DVDActor da, DVD d
WHERE a.actorNo = da.actorNo AND
      da.catalogNo = d.catalogNo;
```

In this example, we want to display details from the `Actor`, `DVDActor`, and `DVD` tables, so we have to use a join. The SELECT clause lists the columns to be displayed. To obtain the required rows, we need to join the tables based on the various matching columns (that is, the primary keys/foreign keys), as shown below:

```
Actor       (actorNo, actorName)
               ↓
DVDActor    (actorNo, catalogNo, character)
               ↓
DVD         (catalogNo, title, genre, rating)
```

The result table is shown in Table 3.18.

Table 3.18 Result table of Query 3.18

actorNo	actorName	character	title
A1002	Judi Dench	M	Casino Royale
A3006	Elijah Wood	Frodo Baggins	Lord of the Rings III
A2019	Tom Cruise	Ethan Hunt	Mission Impossible III
A2019	Tom Cruise	Ray Ferrier	War of the Worlds
A7525	Ian McKellen	Gandalf	Lord of the Rings III
A4343	Mike Myers	Shrek	Shrek 2
A8401	Daniel Radcliffe	Harry Potter	Harry Potter and the GOF

3.2.8 EXISTS and NOT EXISTS

The keywords **EXISTS** and **NOT EXISTS** are designed for use only with subqueries. They produce a simple true/false result. EXISTS is true if and only if there exists at least one row in the result table returned by the subquery; it is false if the subquery returns an empty result table. NOT EXISTS is the opposite of EXISTS. Since EXISTS and NOT EXISTS check only for the existence or non-existence of rows in the subquery result table, the subquery can contain any number of columns. For simplicity, it is common for subqueries following one of these keywords to be of the form:

(SELECT * FROM . . .)

Query 3.19 Query using EXISTS

Find all staff who work in a Washington distribution center.

```
SELECT staffNo, name, position
FROM Staff s
WHERE EXISTS (SELECT *
              FROM DistributionCenter d
              WHERE s.dCenterNo = d.dCenterNo AND dState = 'WA');
```

This query could be rephrased as 'Find all staff such that there exists a `DistributionCenter` row containing their distribution center number, `dCenterNo`, and the `dState` equal to WA.' The test for inclusion is the existence of such a row. If it exists, the subquery evaluates to true. The result table is shown in Table 3.19.

Table 3.19 Result table of Query 3.19

staffNo	name	position
S0010	Mary Martinez	Manager
S3250	Robert Chin	Assistant

3.2.9 INSERT, UPDATE, and DELETE statements

SQL is a complete data manipulation language that can be used for modifying the data in the database as well as querying the database. The commands for modifying the database are not as complex as the SELECT statement. In this section, we describe the three SQL statements that are available to modify the contents of the tables in the database:

- INSERT adds new rows of data to a table;
- UPDATE modifies existing data in a table;
- DELETE removes rows of data from a table.

Insert statement

The general format of the INSERT statement is:

```
INSERT INTO TableName [(columnList)]
VALUES (dataValueList)
```

`TableName` is the name of a base table and `columnList` represents a list of one or more column names separated by commas. The `columnList` is optional; if omitted, SQL assumes a list of all columns in their original CREATE TABLE order (see Appendix E.1). If specified, then any column that is omitted from the list must have been declared as a NULL column or a default value specified when the table was created. The *`dataValueList`* must match the `columnList` as follows:

- the number of items in each list must be the same;
- there must be a direct correspondence in the position of items in the two lists, so that the first item in *dataValueList* applies to the first item in columnList, the second item in *dataValueList* applies to the second item in columnList, and so on;
- the data type of each item in *dataValueList* must be compatible with the data type of the corresponding column.

Query 3.20 Insert a row into a table

Insert a row into the DVD table.

```
INSERT INTO DVD
VALUES ('207132', 'Casino Royale', 'Action' 'PG-13');
```

In this particular example, we have supplied values for all columns in the order the columns were specified when the table was created (so we can omit the list of column names).

Update statement

The format of the UPDATE statement is:

```
UPDATE TableName
SET columnName1 = dataValue1 [, columnName2 = dataValue2...]
[WHERE searchCondition]
```

The SET clause specifies the names of one or more columns that are to be updated. The WHERE clause is optional; if omitted, the named columns are updated for *all rows* in the table. If a WHERE clause is specified, only those rows that satisfy the specified *searchCondition* are updated.

Query 3.21 Update rows in a table

Update the salary for all Managers with a 2% bonus.

```
UPDATE Staff
SET salary = salary * 1.02
WHERE position = 'Manager';
```

Delete statement

The format of the DELETE statement is:

```
DELETE FROM TableName
[WHERE searchCondition]
```

As with the UPDATE statement, the WHERE clause is optional; if omitted, `all rows` are deleted from the table. If a WHERE clause is specified, only those rows that satisfy the specified `searchCondition` are deleted.

Query 3.22 Delete rows in a table

Delete rental DVDs for catalog number 634817.

```
DELETE FROM DVDCopy
WHERE catalogNo = '634817';
```

3.3 Query-By-Example (QBE)

QBE is an alternative, graphical-based, 'point-and-click' way of querying the database. QBE has acquired the reputation of being one of the easiest ways for non-technical users to obtain information from a database. QBE provides a visual means for querying the data through the use of templates. Querying the database is achieved by illustrating the query to be answered. The screen display is used instead of typing the SQL statement; however, you must indicate the columns that you want to see and specify data values that you want to use to restrict the query. Languages like QBE can be a highly productive way to interactively query or update the database.

Like SQL, QBE was developed at IBM (in fact, QBE is an IBM trademark) but a number of other vendors, including Microsoft, sell QBE-like interfaces. Often vendors provide both SQL and QBE facilities, with QBE serving as a more intuitive interface for simple queries and the full power of SQL available for more complex queries.

Once you have read this section, you will see that the QBE version of the queries is usually more straightforward. For illustrative purposes, we use Microsoft Office Access 2007 and for each example we show the equivalent SQL statement for comparison. Note, in the following examples we use the terminology of Microsoft Office Access, which uses the term 'field' in place of column.

Query 3.1 (Revisited) Retrieve all columns, all rows

List the full details of all DVDs.

The QBE grid for this query is shown in Figure 3.2(a). In the top part of the QBE grid, we display the table(s) that we wish to query. For each table displayed, Microsoft Office Access shows the list of fields in that particular table. We can then drag the fields we wish to see in the result table to the Field row in the bottom part of the QBE grid. In this particular example, we wish to display all rows of the DVD table, so we drag the '*' field from the top part of the grid to the Field row. By default, Microsoft Office Access will tick the corresponding cell of the Show row to indicate that these fields are to be displayed in the result table.

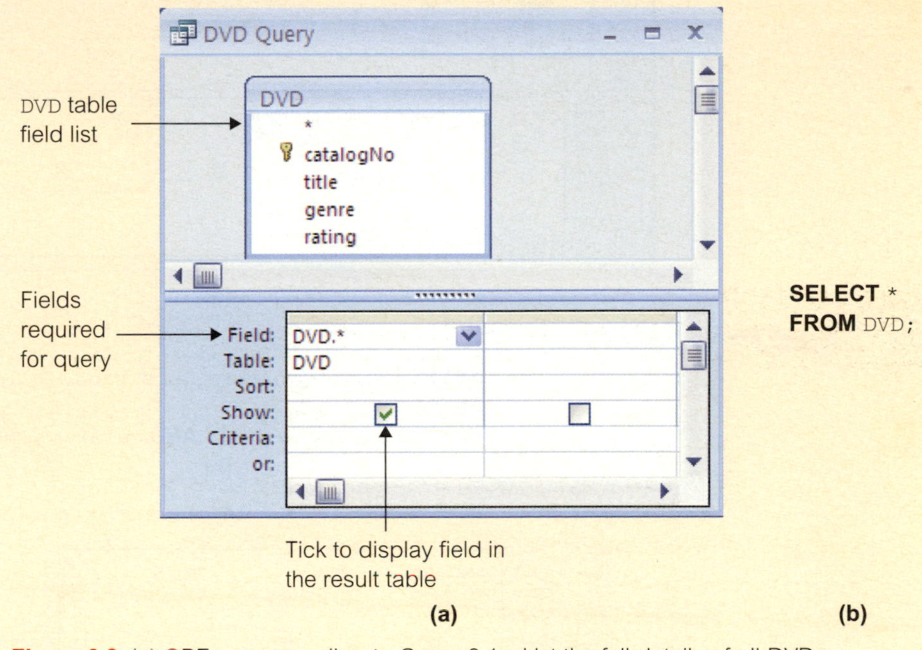

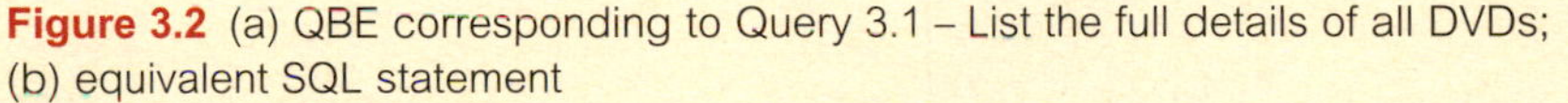

Figure 3.2 (a) QBE corresponding to Query 3.1 – List the full details of all DVDs; (b) equivalent SQL statement

Query 3.6 (Revisited) Range search condition (BETWEEN/NOT BETWEEN)

List all staff with a salary between $45 000 and $50 000.

The QBE grid for this query is shown in Figure 3.3(a). In this example, we show the `Staff` table in the top part of the QBE grid and then drag the relevant fields to the Field row in the bottom part of the grid. In this particular case, we also have to specify the criteria to restrict the rows that will appear in the result table. The criteria is 'salary >=45000 AND salary <= 50000', so under the `salary` column we enter the criteria '>=45000 AND <= 50000'.

Note If the criteria involved an OR condition, each part of the criteria would be entered on different rows, as illustrated in Figure 3.3(c) for the criteria (genre = 'Sci-Fi' OR genre = 'Children').

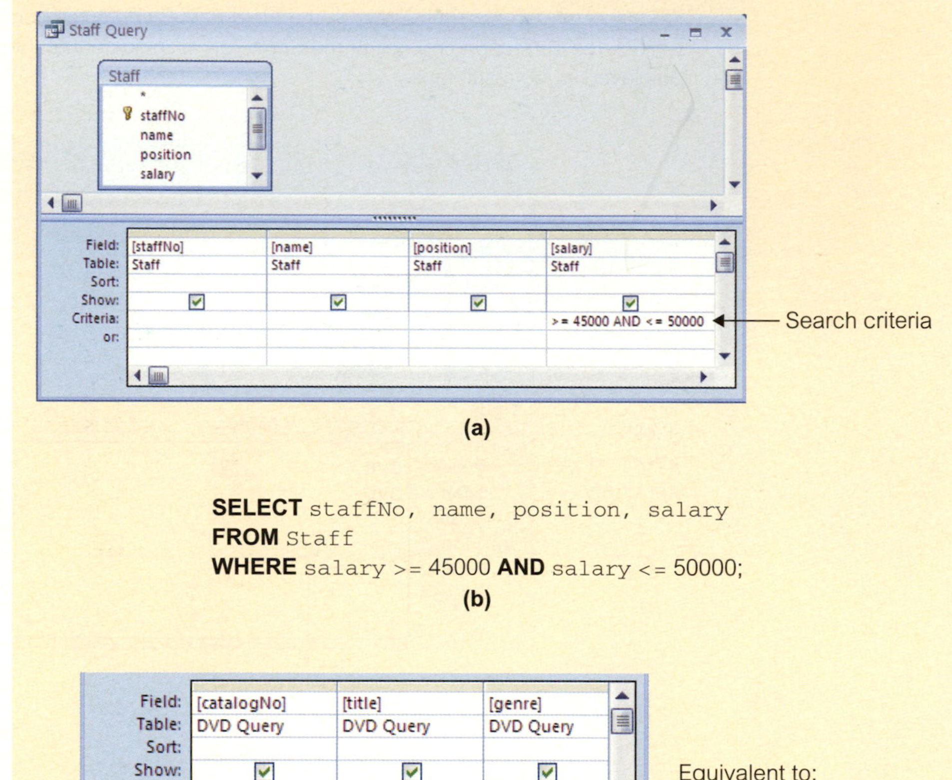

(a)

```
SELECT staffNo, name, position, salary
FROM Staff
WHERE salary >= 45000 AND salary <= 50000;
```

(b)

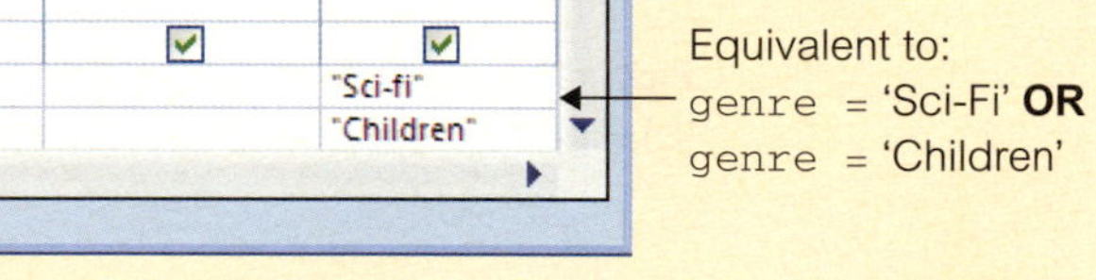

(c)

Figure 3.3 (a) QBE corresponding to Query 3.6 – List all staff with a salary between $45 000 and $50 000; (b) equivalent SQL statement; (c) example of how a criteria involving an OR condition would be entered

Query 3.10 (Revisited) Sorting results

List all DVDs sorted in descending order of genre.

The QBE grid for this query is shown in Figure 3.4(a). In this particular example, we wish to sort the result table in descending order of genre, which we achieve by selecting Descending from the drop-down list in the Sort cell for the `genre` field. Note in this case that the `genre` field has not been ticked to be shown because the field has already been included in the result table via the use of '*' in the first Field cell.

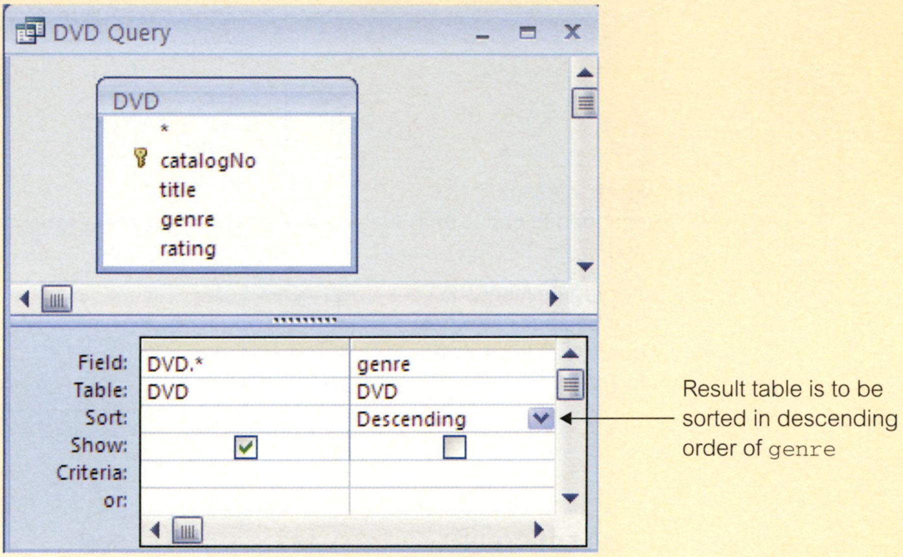

DVD Query

DVD
*
catalogNo
title
genre
rating

Field:	DVD.*	genre
Table:	DVD	DVD
Sort:		Descending
Show:	☑	☐
Criteria:		
or:		

Result table is to be sorted in descending order of genre

(a)

```
SELECT *
FROM DVD
ORDER BY genre DESC;
```

(b)

Figure 3.4 (a) QBE corresponding to Query 3.10 – List all DVDs sorted in descending order of genre; (b) equivalent SQL statement

Query 3.11 (Revisited) Use of COUNT and SUM

List the total number of staff with a salary greater than $40 000 and the sum of their salaries.

The QBE grid for this query is shown in Figure 3.5(a). In this example, we wish to calculate the total number of staff and the sum of their salaries for a subset of staff (those with a salary greater than $40 000). To do this, we use the aggregate functions COUNT and SUM, which are accessed by changing the query type to *Totals*. This results in the display of an additional row called *Total* in the QBE grid with all fields that have been selected automatically set to GROUP BY. However, using the drop-down list we can change the Total row for the staffNo field to COUNT and for the salary field to SUM. To make the output more meaningful, we change the name of the field headings in the resulting output to totalStaff and totalSalary, respectively. The condition '>40000' is entered into the Criteria cell for the salary field.

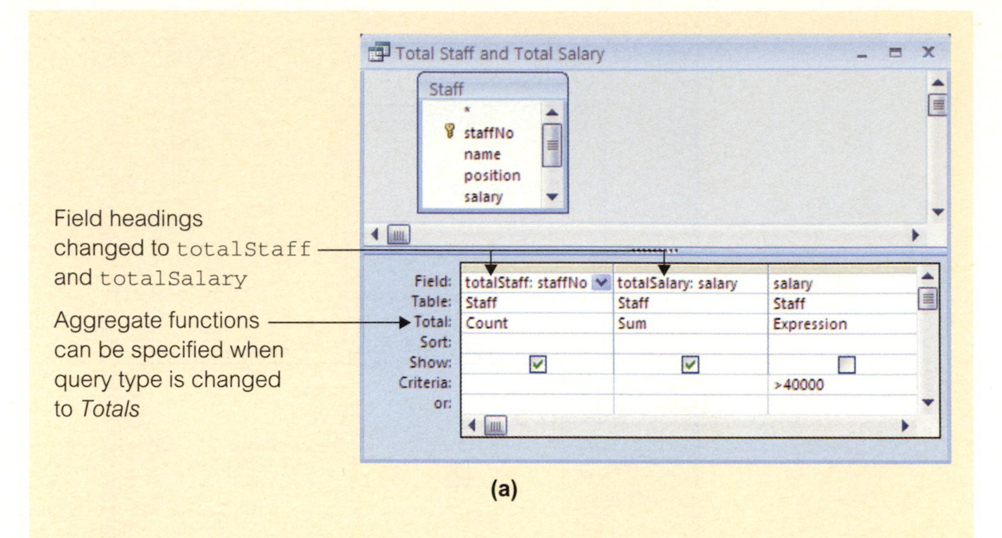

(a)

```
SELECT COUNT(staffNo) AS totalStaff, SUM(salary) AS totalSalary
FROM Staff
WHERE salary > 40000;
```

(b)

Figure 3.5 (a) QBE corresponding to Query 3.11 – List the total number of staff with a salary greater than $40 000 and the sum of their salaries; (b) equivalent SQL statement

Query 3.14 (Revisited) Use of HAVING

For each distribution center with more than one member of staff, find the number of staff working in each of the centers and the sum of their salaries.

The QBE grid for this query is shown in Figure 3.6(a). As with the previous query, we change the query type to *Totals* and use the COUNT and SUM functions to calculate the required totals. However, in this particular example, we need to group the information based on the distribution center number (we are looking for totals for each center), so the Total cell for the `dCenterNo` field has to be set to GROUP BY. Again, to make the output more meaningful, we change the name of the field headings to `totalStaff` and `totalSalary`, respectively. As we only wish to output this information for those centers with more than one member of staff, we enter the criteria '>1' for the COUNT(`staffNo`) field.

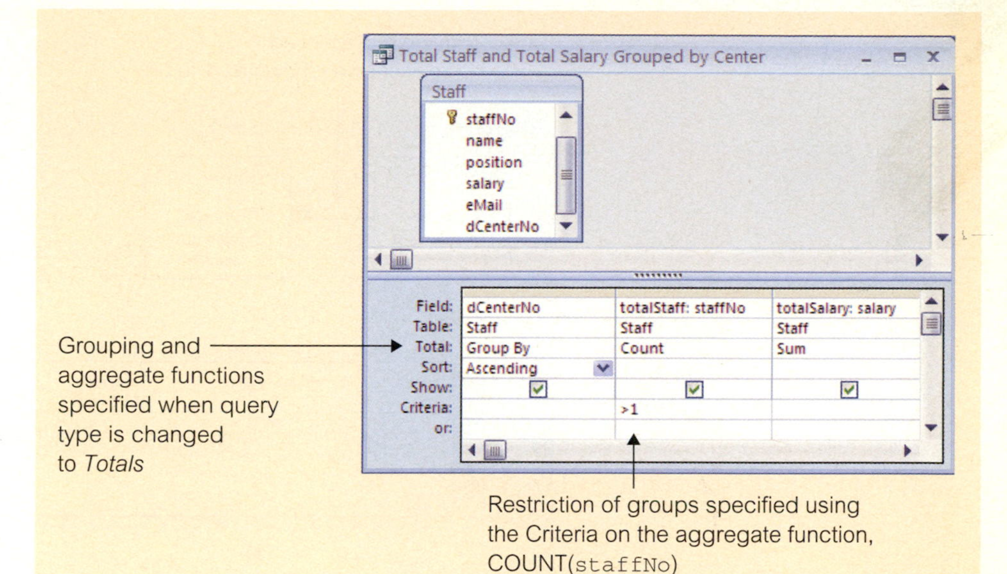


```
SELECT dCenterNo, COUNT(staffNo) AS totalStaff, SUM(salary)
AS totalSalary
FROM Staff
GROUP BY dCenterNo
HAVING COUNT(staffNo) > 1
ORDER BY dCenterNo;
```

(b)

Figure 3.6 (a) QBE corresponding to Query 3.14 – For each distribution center with more than one member of staff, find the number of staff working in each of the centers and the sum of their salaries; (b) equivalent SQL statement

Query 3.17 (Revisited) Simple join

List all actors and the characters they have played in DVDs.

The QBE grid for this query is shown in Figure 3.7(a). In the top part of the QBE grid, we display the tables that we wish to query, in this case the `Actor` and `DVDActor` tables. As before, we drag the columns we wish to be included in the output to the bottom part of the grid.

Note In the SQL query we have to specify how to join the `Actor` and `DVDActor` tables. However, QBE does this automatically for us provided the relationships have been established, making QBE significantly easier to use than SQL in this respect.

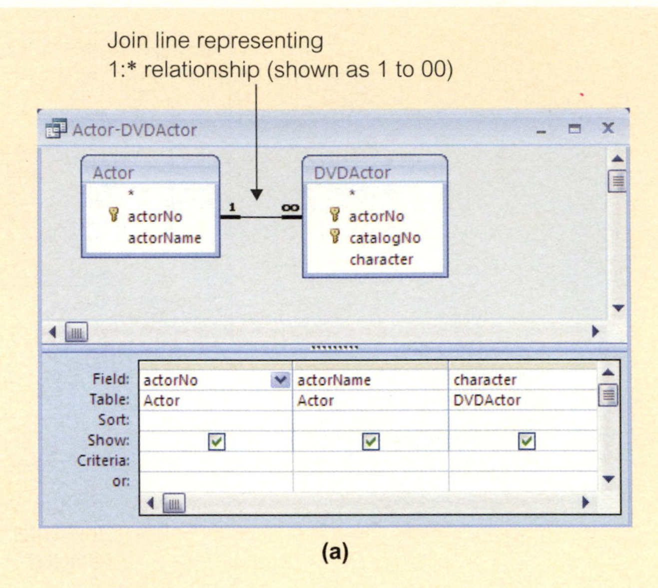

(a)

```
SELECT a.actorNo, actorName, character
FROM Actor a, DVDActor da
WHERE a.actorNo = da.actorNo;
```

(b)

Figure 3.7 (a) QBE corresponding to Query 3.17 – List all actors and the characters they have played in DVDs; (b) equivalent SQL statement

Query 3.18 (Revisited) Three table join

List all actors and the characters they have played in DVDs, along with the DVD's title.

The QBE grid for this query is shown in Figure 3.8(a). In the top part of the QBE grid, we display the three tables that we wish to query. As before, we drag the columns we wish to be included in the output to the bottom part of the grid. If the appropriate relationships have been established, QBE will automatically join the three tables on the join columns indicated in the top part of the grid.

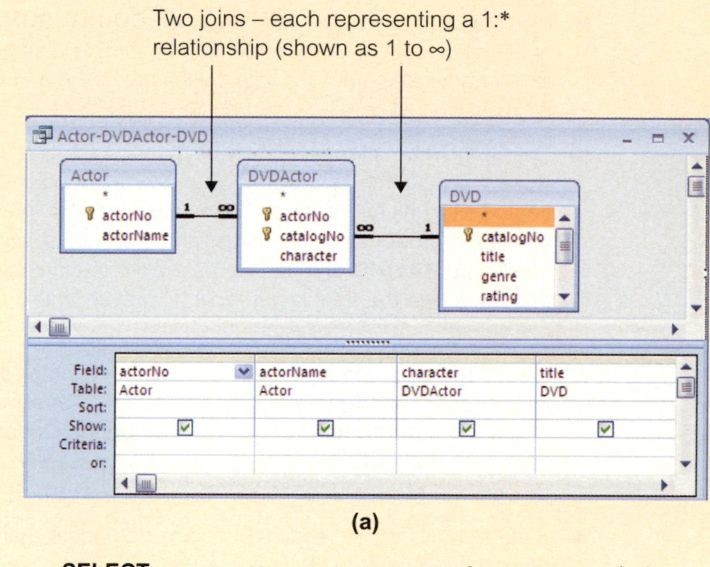

(a)

```
SELECT a.actorNo, actorName, character, title
FROM Actor a, DVDActor da, DVD d
WHERE a.actorNo = da.actorNo AND
      da.catalogNo = d.catalogNo;
```

(b)

Figure 3.8 (a) QBE corresponding to Query 3.18 – List all actors and the characters they have played in DVDs along with the DVD's title; (b) equivalent SQL statement

Chapter summary

- **SQL** is a non-procedural language consisting of standard English words such as SELECT, INSERT and DELETE that can be used by professionals and non-professionals alike. It is both the formal and *de facto* standard language for defining and manipulating relational databases.
- The **SELECT** statement is the most important statement in the language and is used to express a query. Every SELECT statement produces a query result table consisting of one or more columns and zero or more rows.
- The **SELECT clause** identifies the columns and/or calculated data to appear in the result table. All column names that appear in the SELECT clause must have their corresponding tables or views listed in the FROM clause.
- The **WHERE clause** selects rows to be included in the result table by applying a search condition to the rows of the named table(s). The **ORDER BY clause** allows the result table to be sorted on the values in one or more columns. Each column can be sorted in ascending or descending order. If specified, the ORDER BY clause must be the last clause in the SELECT statement.

- SQL supports five aggregate functions (**COUNT**, **SUM**, **AVG**, **MIN**, and **MAX**) that take an entire column as an argument and compute a single value as the result. It is illegal to mix aggregate functions with column names in a SELECT clause, unless the GROUP BY clause is used.
- The **GROUP BY clause** allows summary information to be included in the result table. Rows that have the same value for one or more columns can be grouped together and treated as a unit for using the aggregate functions. In this case, the aggregate functions take each group as an argument and compute a single value for each group as the result. The **HAVING clause** acts as a WHERE clause for groups, restricting the groups that appear in the final result table. However, unlike the WHERE clause, the HAVING clause can include aggregate functions.
- A **subselect** is a complete SELECT statement embedded in another query. A subselect may appear within the WHERE or HAVING clauses of an outer SELECT statement, where it is called a **subquery** or **nested query**. Conceptually, a subquery produces a temporary table whose contents can be accessed by the outer query. A subquery can be embedded in another subquery.
- If the columns of the result table come from more than one table, a **join** must be used by specifying more than one table in the FROM clause and typically including a WHERE clause to specify the join column(s).
- As well as SELECT, the SQL DML includes the **INSERT** statement to insert a single row of data into a named table or to insert an arbitrary number of rows from another table using a **subselect**; the **UPDATE** statement to update one or more values in a specified column or columns of a named table; the **DELETE** statement to delete one or more rows from a named table.
- QBE is an alternative, graphical-based, 'point-and-click' way of querying a database. QBE has acquired the reputation of being one of the easiest ways for non-technical users to obtain information from a database.

Review questions

3.1 What are the two major components of SQL and what function do they serve?

3.2 Explain the function of each of the clauses in the SELECT statement.

3.3 What restrictions are imposed on the clauses in the SELECT statement?

3.4 What restrictions apply to the use of the aggregate functions within the SELECT statement?

3.5 How do nulls affect the aggregate functions?

3.6 Explain how the GROUP BY clause works.

3.7 What is the difference between the WHERE and HAVING clauses?

3.8 What is the difference between a subquery and a join?

3.9 Under what circumstances would you not be able to use a subquery?

3.10 What is QBE and what is the relationship between QBE and SQL?

Exercises

The following tables form part of a database held in a relational DBMS:

Hotel (hotelNo, hotelName, city)

Room (roomNo, hotelNo, type, price)

Booking (hotelNo, guestNo, dateFrom, dateTo, roomNo)

Guest (guestNo, guestName, guestAddress)

where Hotel contains hotel details and hotelNo is the primary key;

Room contains room details for each hotel and (hotelNo, roomNo) forms the primary key;

Booking contains details of bookings and (hotelNo, guestNo, dateFrom) forms the primary key;

Guest contains guest details and guestNo is the primary key.

Create tables

3.11 Using the facilities of a relational DBMS you have access to (or using the CREATE TABLE statement discussed in Appendix E), create each of the above tables (create primary keys and foreign keys, where appropriate).

Now answer questions 3.12 to 3.33 using SQL.

Populating tables

3.12 Insert rows into each of these tables.

3.13 Update the price of all rooms by 5%.

Simple queries

3.14 List full details of all hotels.

3.15 List full details of all hotels in Washington.

3.16 List the names and addresses of all guests with addresses in Washington, alphabetically ordered by name.

3.17 List all double or family rooms with a price below $40.00 per night, in ascending order of price.

3.18 List the bookings for which no dateTo has been specified.

Aggregate functions

3.19 How many hotels are there?

3.20 What is the average price of a room?

3.21 What is the total revenue per night from all double rooms?

3.22 How many different guests have made bookings for August 2006?

Subqueries and joins

3.23 List the price and type of all rooms at the Hilton Hotel.

3.24 List all guests currently staying at the Hilton Hotel.

3.25 List the details of all rooms at the Hilton Hotel, including the name of the guest staying in the room if a room is occupied.

3.26 What is the total income from bookings for the Hilton Hotel today?

3.27 List the rooms that are unoccupied at the Hilton Hotel today.

3.28 What is the lost income from unoccupied rooms at the Hilton Hotel?

Grouping

3.29 List the number of rooms in each hotel.

3.30 List the number of rooms in each hotel in Washington.

3.31 What is the average number of bookings for each hotel in August 2006?

3.32 What is the most commonly booked room type for each hotel in Washington?

3.33 What is the lost income from unoccupied rooms at each hotel today?

QBE

3.34 Repeat exercises 3.14 to 3.33 using QBE.

Additional exercises

Case study – *Wellmeadows Hospital*

The following tables form part of a database held in a relational DBMS:

```
Patient     (patientNo, patientName, patientAddress,
            patientDateOfBirth)
Ward        (wardNo, wardName, wardType, noOfBeds)
Contains    (patientNo, wardNo, admissionDate)
Drug        (drugNo, drugName, costPerUnit)
Prescribed (patientNo, drugNo, startDate, unitsPerDay, finishDate)
```

where `Patient` contains patient details and `patientNo` is the primary key;

`Ward` contains hospital ward details and `wardNo` is the primary key;

`Contains` details the assignment of patients to wards and (`patientNo`, `wardNo`) forms the primary key;

`Drug` contains details of drugs administered to patients and `drugNo` is the primary key;

`Prescribed` details the assignment of drugs to patients and (`patientNo`, `drugNo`, `startDate`) forms the primary key.

Create tables

3.35 Using the facilities of a relational DBMS you have access to (or using the CREATE TABLE statement discussed in Appendix E), create each of the above tables (create primary keys and foreign keys, where appropriate).

Now answer questions 3.36 to 3.45 using SQL.

Populating tables

3.36 Insert rows into each of these tables.

3.37 Update the cost per unit of all drugs by 2%.

Queries

3.38 List all the patients' details, alphabetically by name.

3.39 List all the patients in the 'Surgical' ward.

3.40 List all the patients admitted today.

3.41 Find the names of all the patients being prescribed 'Morphine'.

3.42 What is the total cost of morphine supplied to a patient called 'John Smith'?

3.43 What is the maximum, minimum, and average number of beds in a ward? Create appropriate column headings for the results table.

3.44 For each ward that admitted more than 10 patients today, list the ward number, ward type, and number of beds in each ward.

3.45 List the numbers and names of all patients and the `drugNo` and number of units of their medication. The list should also include the details of patients who are not prescribed medication.

3.46 Repeat exercises 3.38 to 3.45 using QBE.

Case study – *Flights Database*

The following tables form part of a database held in a relational DBMS:

```
Employee  (empNo, empName, empSalary, empPosition)
Aircraft  (aircraftNo, acName, acModel, acFlyingRange)
Flight    (flightNo, fromAirport, toAirport, flightDistance,
           departTime, arriveTime)
Certified (empNo, aircraftNo)
```

where `Employee` contains details of all employees (pilots and non-pilots) and `empNo` is the key.

`Aircraft` contains details of aircraft and `aircraftNo` is the primary key.

`Flight` contains details of the flights and `flightNo` is the primary key.

`Certified` contains details of the staff who are certified to fly an aircraft and (`empNo`, `aircraftNo`) forms the primary key.

Create tables

3.47 Using the facilities of a relational DBMS you have access to (or using the CREATE TABLE statement discussed in Appendix E), create each of the above tables (create primary keys and foreign keys, where appropriate).

Now answer questions 3.48 to 3.57 using SQL.

Populating tables

3.48 Insert rows into each of these tables.

3.49 Update the salary of all managers by 3%.

Queries

3.50 List all Boeing aircraft.

3.51 List all Boeing 737 aircraft.

3.52 List the employee numbers of pilots certified for Boeing aircraft.

3.53 List the names of pilots certified for Boeing aircraft.

3.54 List the aircraft that can fly nonstop from London to New York (`acFlyingRange > flightDistance`).

3.55 List the employee numbers of employees who have the highest salary.

3.56 List the employee numbers of employees who have the second highest salary.

3.57 List the employee numbers of employees who are certified for exactly three aircraft.

3.58 Repeat exercises 3.50 to 3.57 using QBE.

General

3.59 From an SQL user's perspective, does the relational model provide logical and physical data independence?

CHAPTER

4 The database system development lifecycle

Preview

This chapter begins by explaining why there is a need for a structured approach to developing software applications. We introduce an example of such an approach, called the information systems lifecycle, and discuss the relationship between an information system and the database that supports it. We then focus on the database and introduce an example of a structured approach to developing database systems, called the database system development lifecycle. Finally, we take you through the stages that make up the database system development lifecycle (DSDLC).

Learning objectives

In this chapter you will learn:

- How problems associated with software development led to the software crisis.
- How the software crisis led to a structured approach to software development called the information systems lifecycle.
- About the relationship between the information systems lifecycle and the database system development lifecycle.
- The stages of the database system development lifecycle.
- The activities associated with each stage of the database system development lifecycle.

4.1 The software crisis

You are probably already aware that over the past few decades there has been a dramatic rise in the number of software applications being developed, ranging from small, relatively simple applications consisting of a few lines of code, to large, complex applications consisting of millions of lines of code. Once developed, many of these applications proved to be demanding, requiring constant maintenance. This maintenance involved correcting faults, implementing new user requirements, and modifying the software to run on new or upgraded platforms. With so much software around to support, the effort spent on maintenance began to absorb resources at an alarming rate. As a result, many major software projects were late, over budget, and the software produced was unreliable, difficult to maintain, and performed poorly. This led to what has become known as the 'software crisis.' Although this term was first used in the late 1960s, more than 40 years later the crisis is still with us. As a result, some people now refer to the software crisis as the 'software depression.' As an indication of the software crisis, a study carried out in the UK by OASIG, a special interest group concerned with the organizational aspects of IT, reached the following conclusions (OASIG, 1996):

- 80–90 per cent of systems do not meet their performance goals.
- About 80 per cent are delivered late and over budget.
- Around 40 per cent of developments fail or are abandoned.
- Under 40 per cent fully address training and skills requirements.
- Under 25 per cent properly integrate business and technology objectives.
- Just 10–20 per cent meet all their success criteria.

There are several major reasons for the failure of software projects, including:

- lack of a complete requirements specification;
- lack of an appropriate development methodology;
- poor decomposition of design into manageable components.

As a solution to these problems, a structured approach to the development of software was proposed and is commonly known as the information systems lifecycle (ISLC) or the software development lifecycle (SDLC).

4.2 The information systems lifecycle

Information system (IS)

The resources that enable the collection, management, control, and dissemination of data/information throughout an organization.

An **information system (IS)** not only collects, manages, and controls data used and generated by an organization but enables the transformation of the data into information. An information system also provides the infrastructure to facilitate the dissemination of information to those who make the decisions critical to the success of an organization. The essential component at the *heart* of an information system is the database that supports it.

Typically, the stages of the information systems lifecycle include planning, requirements collection and analysis, design (including database design), prototyping, implementation, testing, conversion, and operational maintenance. Of course, in this book we are interested in the development of the database component of an information system. As a database is a fundamental component of the larger organization-wide information system, the database system development lifecycle is inherently linked with the information systems lifecycle.

4.3 The database system development lifecycle

Database system development lifecycle (DSDLC)

An ordered list of stages that describe the appropriate techniques and tools to use in the development of a database system.

In this chapter, we describe the **database system development lifecycle (DSDLC)** for relational DBMSs. We discussed the relational data model in Chapter 2. An overview of the DSDLC is shown in Figure 4.1. Below the name of each stage is the section in this chapter that describes that stage. It is important to note that the stages of the database system development lifecycle are not strictly sequential, but involve some amount of repetition of previous stages through *feedback loops*. For example, problems encountered during database design may necessitate additional requirements for collection and analysis. As there are feedback loops between most stages, we show only some of the more obvious ones in Figure 4.1.

For small database systems with a small number of users, the lifecycle need not be very complex. However, when designing a medium to large database system with tens to thousands of users, using hundreds of queries and application programs, the lifecycle can become extremely complex.

4.4 Database planning

Database planning

The management activities that allow the stages of the database system development lifecycle to be realized as efficiently and effectively as possible.

A starting point for establishing a database project is the creation of a mission statement and mission objectives for the database system. The **mission statement** defines the major aims of the database system, while each **mission objective** identifies a particular task that the database must support. Of course, as with any project, part of the **database planning** process should also involve some estimation of the work to be done, the resources with which to do it, and the money to pay for it all.

As we have already noted, a database often forms part of a larger organization-wide information system and therefore any database project should be integrated with the organization's overall IS strategy.

planning → development of standards

Note Database planning may also include the development of standards that govern how data will be collected, how the format should be specified, what essential documentation will be needed, and how design and implementation should proceed. Standards can be very time-consuming to develop and maintain, requiring resources to set them up initially and to continue maintaining them. However, a well-designed set of standards provides a basis for training staff and measuring quality, and ensures that work conforms to a pattern, irrespective of staff skills and experience. Any legal or organizational requirements concerning the data should be documented, such as the stipulation that some types of data must be treated confidentially or kept for a specific period of time.

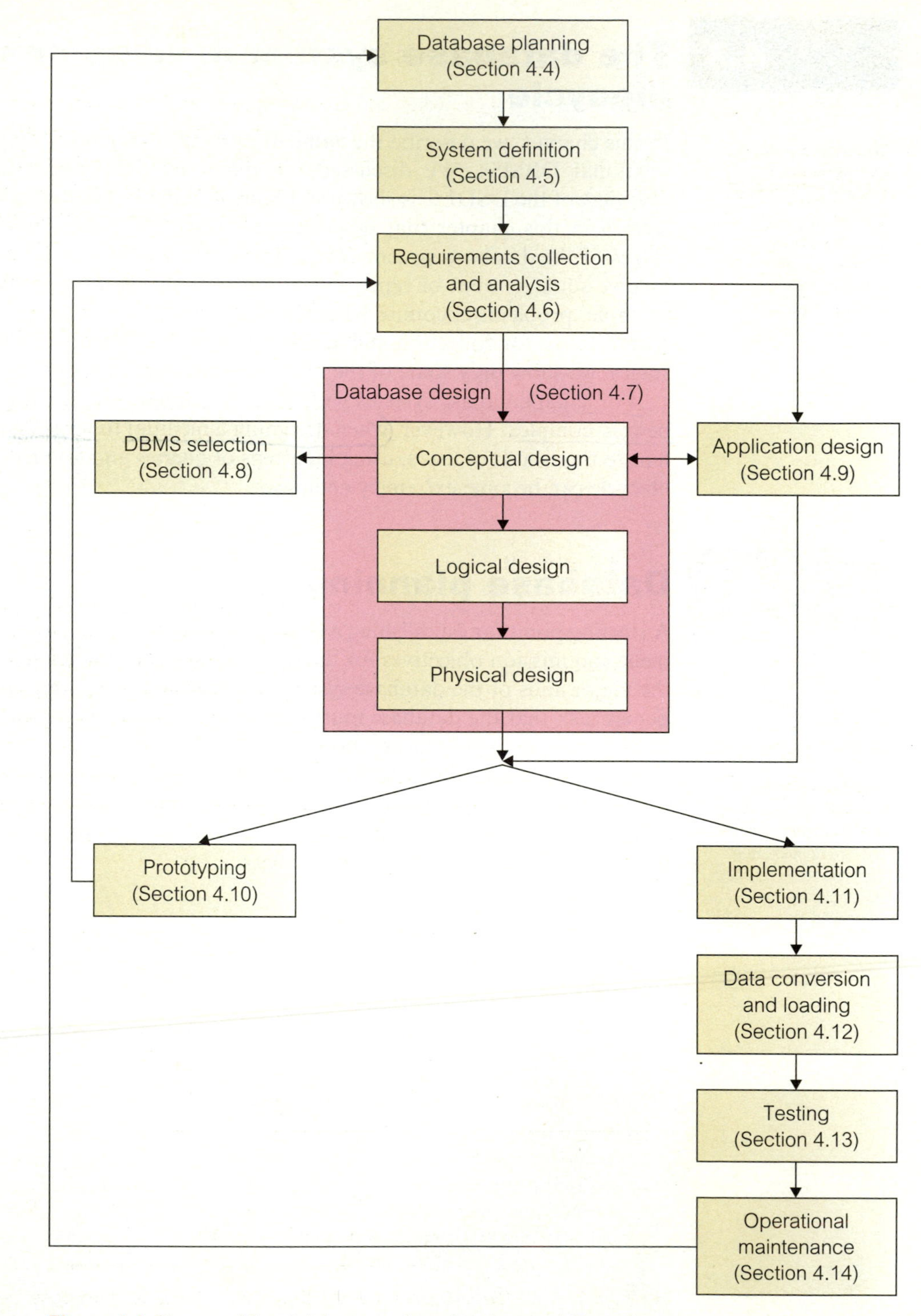

Figure 4.1 Stages of the database system development lifecycle

4.5 System definition

System definition

Defines the scope and boundary of the database system, including its major user views.

Before attempting to design a database system, it is essential that we first identify the scope and boundary of the system that we are investigating and how it interfaces with other parts of the organization's information system. Figure 4.2 shows an example of how to represent a system boundary using an *extended* version of the *StayHome Online Rentals* case study – the part of the case study described in Section 5.4 and used to demonstrate the development of a database system is highlighted. In other words, the boundary of the proposed database system includes only DVD rentals, Member services, and Staff. When defining the system boundary for a database system we include not only the current user views but also any known future user views.

Note An alternative way to represent a system boundary for the database system of the *StayHome Online Rentals* case study is shown in Figure 5.9.

4.5.1 User views

User view

Defines what is required of a database system from the perspective of a particular job (such as manager or supervisor) or business application area (such as marketing, personnel, or stock control).

A database system may have one or more **user views**. Identifying user views is an important aspect of developing a database system because it helps to ensure that no major users of the database are forgotten when developing the requirements for the new database system. User views are particularly helpful in the development of a relatively complex database system by allowing the requirements to be broken down into manageable pieces.

A user view defines what is required of a database system in terms of the data to be held and the transactions to be performed on the data (in other words, what the users will do with the data). The requirements of a user view may be specific to that

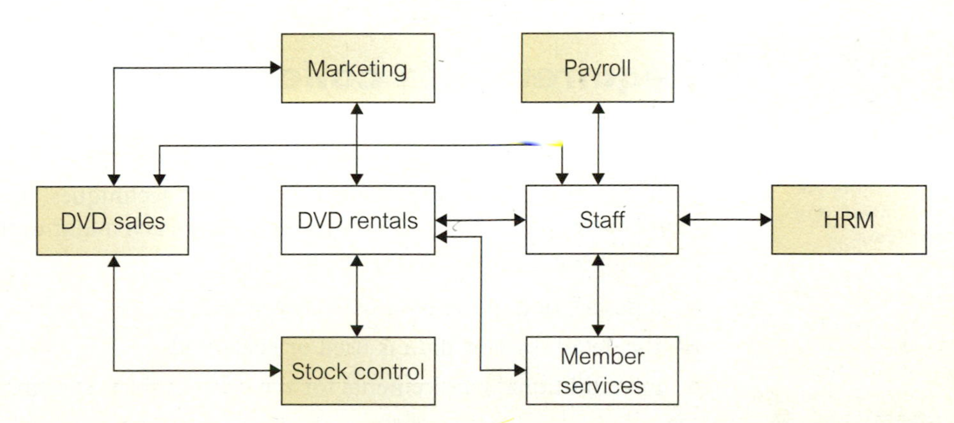

Figure 4.2 An *extended* version of the *StayHome Online Rentals* case study (the highlighted area identifies the part of the case study used to demonstrate the development of a database system in this book)

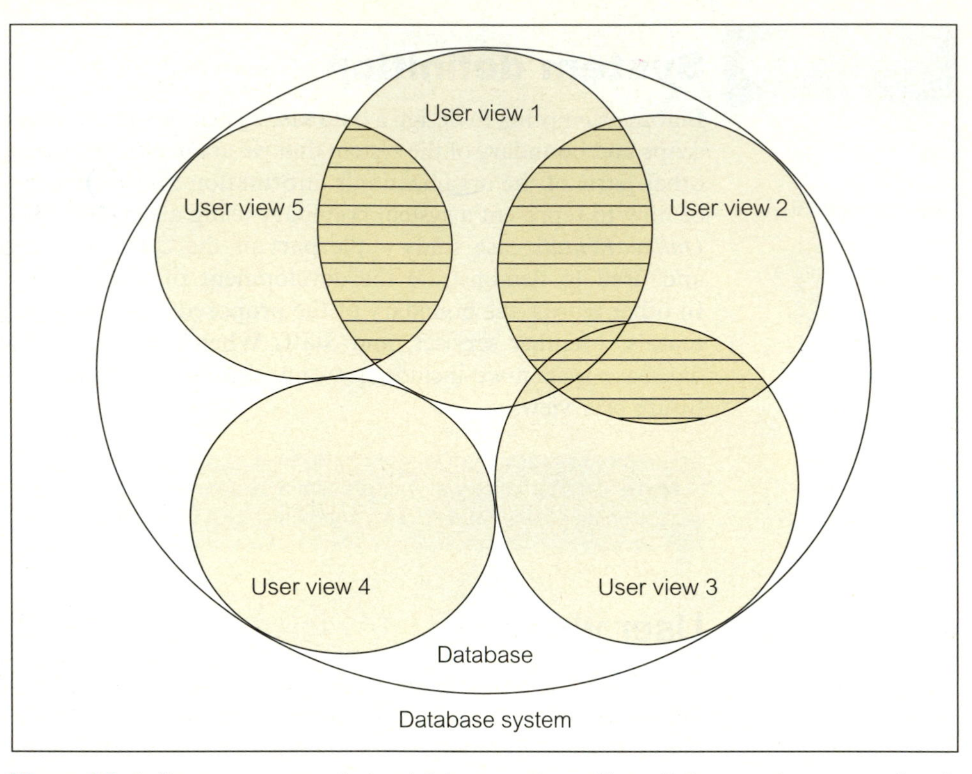

Figure 4.3 A diagram representing a database system with multiple user views: user view 4 is distinct; the others have some element of overlap

view or overlap with other user views. Figure 4.3 is a diagrammatic representation of a database system with multiple user views (denoted user view 1 to 5). Note that while user views 1, 2, 3 and 5 have overlapping requirements (shown as darker areas), user view 4 has distinct requirements.

4.6 Requirements collection and analysis

Requirements collection and analysis

The process of collecting and analyzing information about the organization to be supported by the database system, and using this information to identify the requirements for the new database system.

In this stage, we collect and analyze information about the organization, or the part of the organization, to be served by the database. There are many techniques for gathering this information, called fact-finding techniques, which we will discuss in detail in Chapter 5. We gather information for each major user view (that is, job role or business application area), including:

- a description of the data used or generated;
- the details of how data is used or generated;
- any additional requirements for the new database system.

We then analyze this information to identify the requirements (or features) to be included in the new database system. These requirements are described in documents collectively referred to as *requirements specifications* for the new database system.

Note Requirements collection and analysis is a preliminary stage to database design. The amount of data gathered depends on the nature of the problem and the policies of the organization. Identifying the required functionality for a database system is a critical activity, because systems with inadequate or incomplete functionality will annoy the users and may lead to rejection or underutilization of the system. However, excessive functionality can also be problematic as it can overcomplicate a system, making it difficult to implement, maintain, use, and learn.

Another important activity associated with this stage is deciding how to deal with the situation where there is more than one user view associated with the database system. There are three approaches to dealing with multiple user views:

- the centralized approach;
- the view integration approach;
- a combination of both approaches.

Centralized approach

Centralized approach

Requirements for each user view are merged into a single list of requirements for the new database system. A data model representing all user views is created during the database design stage.

The **centralized approach** involves collating the requirements for different user views into a single list of requirements. A data model representing all user views is created in the database design stage. A diagram representing the management of three user views using the centralized approach is shown in Figure 4.4. Generally, this approach is preferred when there is a significant overlap in requirements for each user view and the database system is not overly complex.

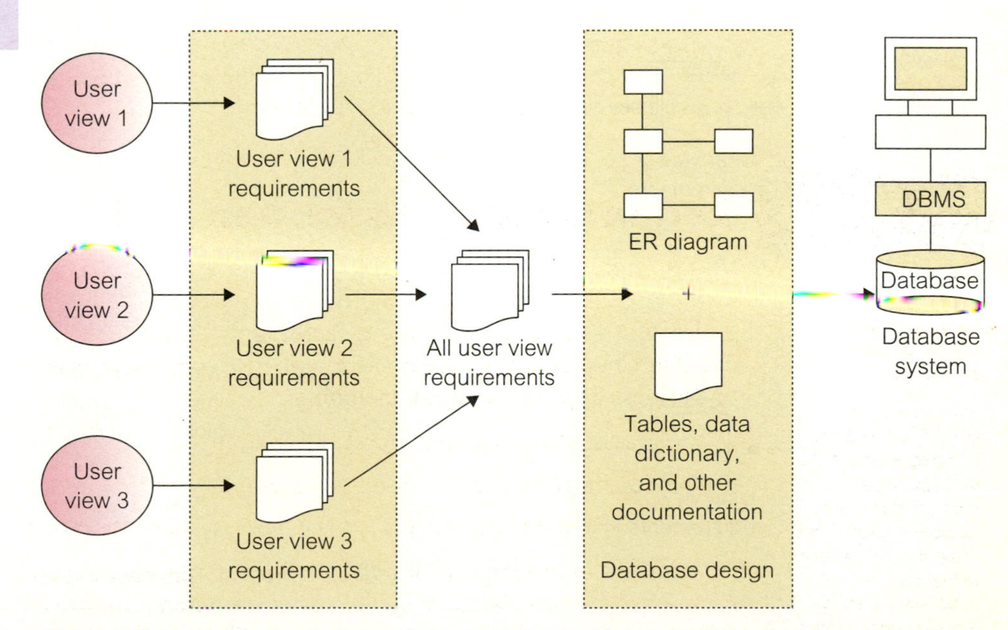

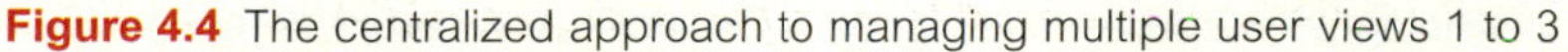
Figure 4.4 The centralized approach to managing multiple user views 1 to 3

View integration approach

View integration approach

The requirements for each user view remain as separate lists. Data models representing each user view are created and then merged later during the database design stage.

The **view integration approach** involves leaving the requirements for each user view as separate lists of requirements. We create data models representing each user view. A data model that represents a single user view is called a **local data model**. We then merge the local data models to create a **global data model** representing all user views of the organization. A diagram representing the management of three user views using the view integration approach is shown in Figure 4.5. Generally, this approach is preferred when there are significant differences between user views and the database system is sufficiently complex to justify dividing the work into more manageable parts.

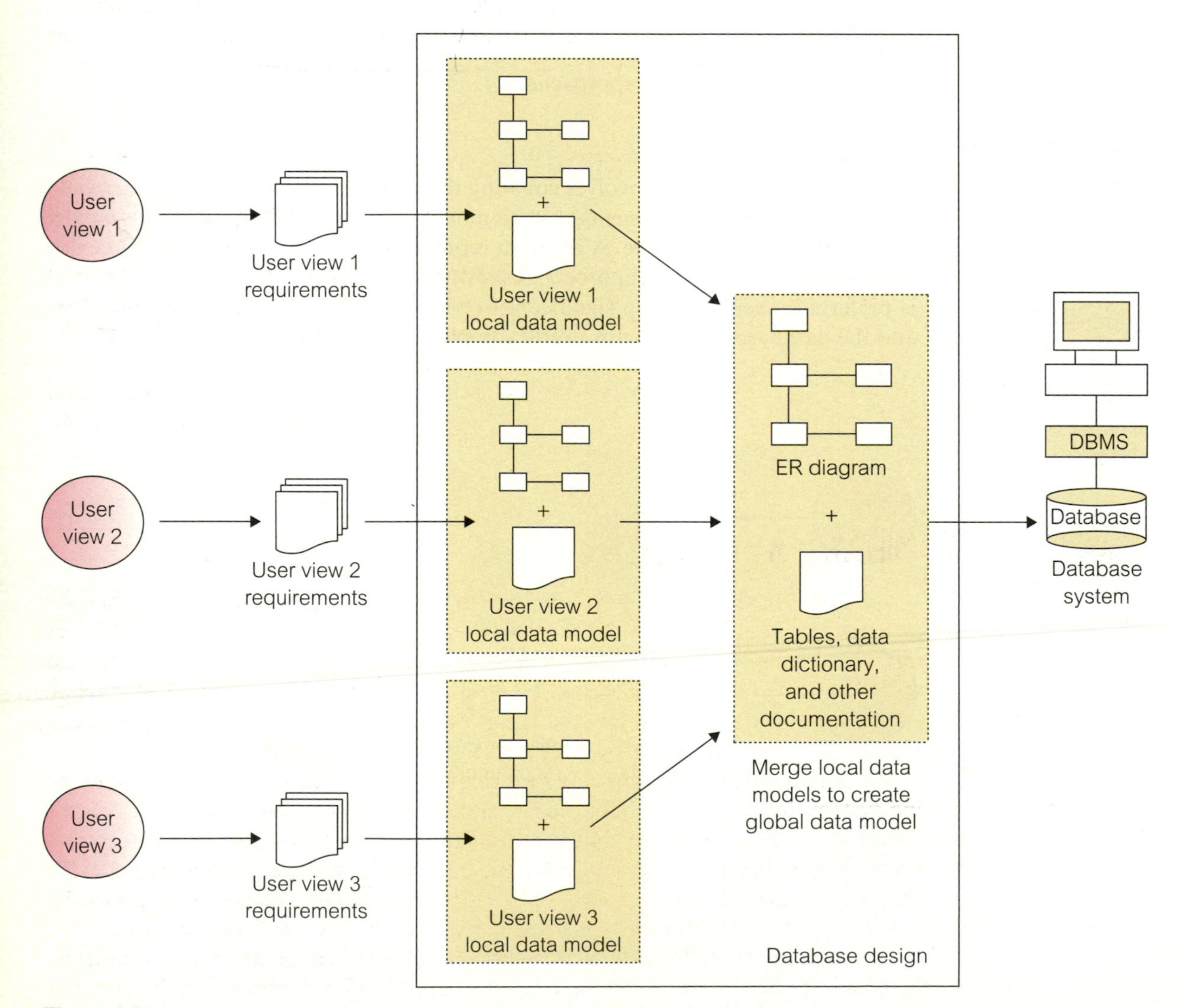

Figure 4.5 The view integration approach to managing multiple user views 1 to 3

> **Note** For some complex database systems it may be appropriate to use a combination of both the centralized and view integration approaches to managing multiple user views. For example, the requirements for two or more user views may be first merged using the centralized approach and then used to create a local data model. (Therefore in this situation the local data model represents not just a single user view but the number of user views merged using the centralized approach.) The local data models representing one or more user views are then merged using the view integration approach to form the global data model representing all user views.

We will discuss how to manage multiple user views in more detail in Section 5.4. The database design methodology described in Part III of this book will demonstrate how to build a database for the *StayHome Online Rentals* case study using the centralized approach. Guidelines for using the view integration approach are given in Appendix D in Step 2.6 of our database design methodology.

4.7 Database design

Database design

The process of creating a design that will support the organization's mission statement and mission objectives for the required database system.

Database design is made up of three main phases called conceptual, logical, and physical design. During conceptual database design, we try to identify the important objects that need to be represented in the database and the relationships between these objects. During logical database design, we represent the objects and their relationships as a set of tables. During physical database design, we decide how the tables are to be physically implemented in the target DBMS.

In Part III we will discuss the three phases of database design in more detail and present a step-by-step methodology for conceptual (Chapter 9), logical (Chapter 10), and physical database design (Chapter 11).

4.8 DBMS selection

DBMS selection

The selection of an appropriate DBMS to support the database system.

If no DBMS currently exists in the organization, an appropriate part of the lifecycle in which to make a **DBMS selection** is between the logical and physical database design phases. However, selection can be done at any time prior to logical design provided sufficient information is available regarding system requirements, such as networking, performance, ease of restructuring, security, and integrity constraints. We discussed integrity constraints in Section 2.4.4.

Although DBMS selection may be infrequent, as business needs expand or existing systems are replaced it may become necessary at times to evaluate new DBMS products. In such cases, the aim is to select a product that meets the current and future requirements of the organization, balanced against costs that include the purchase of the DBMS, any additional software/hardware required to support the database system, and the costs associated with changeover and staff training.

A simple approach to selection is to check off DBMS features against requirements. In selecting a new DBMS product, there is an opportunity to ensure that the selection process is well planned and that the system delivers real benefits to the organization.

Note Nowadays, the web is a good source of information and can be used to identify potential candidate DBMSs. Vendors' web sites can provide valuable information on DBMS products. As a starting point, consider a DBMS magazine's web site called DBMS ONLINE (available at www.intelligententerprise.com) for a comprehensive index of DBMS products.

4.9 Application design

Application design

The design of the user interface and the database application that use and process the database.

In Figure 4.1 we observed that database design and **application design** are parallel activities of the database system development lifecycle. In most cases, we cannot complete the application design until the design of the database itself has taken place. On the other hand, the database exists to support the applications, and so there must be a flow of information between application design and database design.

We must ensure that all the functionality stated in the requirements specifications is present in the application design for the database system. This involves designing the interaction between the user and the data, which we call *transaction design*. In addition to designing how the required functionality is to be achieved, we have to design an appropriate *user interface* to the database system.

4.9.1 Transaction design

Transaction

An action, or series of actions, carried out by a single user or database application that accesses or changes the content of the database.

Transactions represent 'real world' events such as the registering of a new member at an online DVD rental company, the recording of when a particular DVD is sent out and returned from a member, and the deletion of a record describing a copy of a DVD when it can no longer be rented out. These transactions have to be applied to the database to ensure that the database remains current with the 'real world' and to support the information needs of the users. There are three main types of transactions:

- retrieval transactions;
- update transactions;
- mixed transactions.

Retrieval transactions are used to retrieve data for display on the screen (or as a report) or as input into another transaction. For example, the operation to search for and display the details of a DVD (given the DVD number) is a retrieval transaction. *Update transactions* are used to insert new records, delete old records, or modify existing records in the database. For example, the operation to insert the details of a new DVD into the database is an update transaction. *Mixed transactions* involve both the retrieval and updating of data. For example, the operation to search for and display the details for a member of staff (given the staff number) and then update their salary is a mixed transaction.

The purpose of transaction design is to define and document the high-level characteristics of the transactions required on the database, including:

- data to be used by the transaction (for example, a member's email address);
- functional characteristics of the transaction (in other words, what the transaction will do, such as update a member's email address);
- output of the transaction (for example, the up-to-date email address appears on a form with all other personal details associated with the member);
- importance to the users (for example, an up-to-date email address is critical because it is used when a member logs on to the web site);
- expected rate of usage (for example, updating a member's email address should be infrequent so there will be a low rate of usage).

4.9.2 User interface design

In addition to designing how the required functionality is to be achieved, we have to design an appropriate user interface for the database system. This interface should present the required information in a *user-friendly* way. The importance of user interface design is sometimes ignored or left until late in the design stages. However, it should be recognized that the interface might be one of the most important components of the system. If it is easy to learn, simple to use, straightforward and forgiving, then users will be inclined to make good use of what information is presented. However, if the interface has none of these characteristics, the system will undoubtedly cause problems. For example, before implementing a form or report, it is essential that we first design the layout. Useful guidelines to follow when designing forms or reports are listed below (Shneiderman, 1992).

- meaningful title
- comprehensible instructions
- logical grouping and sequencing of fields
- visually appealing layout of the form/report
- familiar field labels
- consistent terminology and abbreviations
- consistent use of color
- visible space and boundaries for data-entry fields
- convenient cursor movement
- error correction for individual characters and entire fields
- error messages for unacceptable values
- optional fields marked clearly
- explanatory messages for fields
- completion signal.

4.10 Prototyping

At various points throughout the design process, we have the option to either fully implement the database system or to build a *prototype*.

A prototype is a working model that does not normally have all the required features or provide all the functionality of the final system. The purpose of developing a prototype database system is to allow users to identify the features of the system that work well, or are inadequate, and if possible to suggest improvements or even new features for the database system. In this way, we can greatly clarify the requirements and evaluate the feasibility of a particular system design. Prototypes should have the major advantage of being relatively inexpensive and quick to build.

Prototyping

Building a working model of a database system.

There are two **prototyping** strategies in common use today: requirements prototyping and evolutionary prototyping. *Requirements prototyping* uses a prototype to determine the requirements of a proposed database system and once the requirements are complete the prototype is discarded. While *evolutionary prototyping* is used for the same purposes, the important difference is that the prototype is not discarded but with further development becomes the working database system.

4.11 Implementation

Implementation

The physical realization of the database and application designs.

On completion of the design stages (which may or may not have involved prototyping), we are now in a position to implement the database and the database applications. The database **implementation** is achieved using the **Data Definition Language (DDL)** of the selected DBMS or a graphical user-interface (GUI), which provides the same functionality while hiding the low-level DDL statements. We describe the DDL of SQL (Structured Query Language) in Appendix E. The DDL statements are used to create the database structures and the empty database files. Any specified user views are also implemented at this stage.

The database applications are implemented using the preferred **third or fourth generation language (3GL or 4GL)**. Parts of these applications are the database transactions, which we implement using the **Data Manipulation Language (DML)** of the target DBMS, possibly embedded within a host programming language, such as Visual Basic (VB), VB.net, Python, Delphi, C, C++, C#, Java, COBOL, Fortran, Ada, or Pascal. We described the DML of SQL in Section 3.2. We also implement the other components of the application design such as menu screens, data entry forms, and reports. Again, the target DBMS may have its own fourth generation tools that allow rapid development of applications through the provision of non-procedural query languages, reports generators, forms generators, and application generators.

Security and integrity controls for the applications are also implemented. Some of these controls are implemented using the DDL, but others may need to be defined outside the DDL using, for example, the supplied DBMS tools or operating system controls.

4.12 Data conversion and loading

Data conversion and loading

Preparing any data (where applicable) into a form suitable for transferring into the new database.

Data conversion and loading is required only when a new database system is replacing an old system. Nowadays, it is common for a DBMS to have a utility that loads existing files into the new database. The utility usually requires the specification of the source file and the target database, and then automatically converts the data to the required format of the new database files. Whenever data conversion and loading are required, the process should be properly planned to ensure a smooth transition to full operation.

4.13 Testing

Testing

The process of running the database system with the intent of finding errors.

Before going live, the newly developed database system should be thoroughly *tested*. This is achieved using carefully planned test strategies and realistic data so that the entire testing process is methodically and rigorously carried out. Note that in our definition of testing we have not used the commonly held view that testing is the process of demonstrating that faults are not present. In fact, testing cannot show the absence of faults; it can show only that software faults are present. If testing is conducted successfully, it will uncover errors in the database applications and possibly the database structure. As a secondary benefit, testing demonstrates that the database and the application programs *appear* to be working according to their specification and that performance requirements *appear* to be satisfied. In addition, metrics collected from the testing stage provides a measure of software reliability and software quality.

As with database design, the users of the new system should be involved in the testing process. The ideal situation for system testing is to have a test database on a separate hardware system, but often this is not available. If real data is to be used, it is essential to have backups taken in case of error.

Testing should also cover usability of the database system. Ideally, an evaluation should be conducted against a usability specification. Examples of criteria that can be used to conduct the evaluation include (Sommerville, 2006):

- Learnability – how long does it take a new user to become productive with the system?
- Performance – how well does the system response match the user's work practice?
- Robustness – how tolerant is the system of user error?
- Recoverability – how good is the system at recovering from user errors?
- Adaptability – how closely is the system tied to a single model of work?

Some of these criteria may be evaluated in other stages of the lifecycle. After testing is complete, the database system is ready to be 'signed off' and handed over to the users.

4.14 Operational maintenance

Operational maintenance

The process of monitoring and maintaining the database system following installation.

In this stage, the database system moves into a **maintenance** stage, which involves the following activities:

- Monitoring the performance of the database system. If the performance falls below an acceptable level, the database may need to be tuned or reorganized.
- Maintaining and upgrading the database system (when required). New requirements are incorporated into the database system through the preceding stages of the lifecycle.

We will examine this stage in more detail in Chapter 11.

Chapter summary

- An **information system** is the resources that enable the collection, management, control, and dissemination of data/information throughout an organization.
- The **database** is a fundamental component of an **information system**. The lifecycle of an information system is inherently linked to the lifecycle of the database that supports it.
- The **database systems development lifecycle** (DSDLC) is an ordered list of stages that describe the appropriate techniques and tools to use in the development of a database system. The stages of the DSDLC include database planning, system definition, requirements collection and analysis, database design, DBMS selection (optional), application design, prototyping (optional), implementation, data conversion and loading, testing, and operational maintenance.
- **Database planning** is the management activities that allow the stages of the database system development lifecycle to be realized as efficiently and effectively as possible.
- **System definition** involves identifying the scope and boundaries of the database system, including its major user views. A user view can represent a job role or business application area.
- **Requirements collection and analysis** is the process of collecting and analyzing information about the organization that is to be supported by the database system, and using this information to identify the requirements for the new system.
- There are three main approaches to dealing with multiple user views, namely the centralized approach, the view integration approach, and a combination of both. The **centralized approach** involves collating the users' requirements for different user views into a single list of requirements. A data model representing all the user views is created during the database design stage. The **view integration approach** involves leaving the users' requirements for each user view as separate lists of requirements. Data models representing each user view are created and then merged at a later stage of database design.
- **Database design** is the process of creating a design that will support the organization's mission statement and mission objectives for the required database system. This stage includes three phases called conceptual, logical, and physical database design.

- The aim of **DBMS selection** is to select a system that meets the current and future requirements of the organization, balanced against costs that include the purchase of the DBMS product and any additional software/hardware, and the costs associated with changeover and training.
- **Application design** involves designing the user interface and the database applications that use and process the database. This stage involves two main activities: transaction design and user interface design.
- **Prototyping** involves building a working model of the database system, which allows the designers or users to visualize and evaluate the system.
- **Implementation** is the physical realization of the database and application designs.
- **Data conversion and loading** involves preparing any data (where applicable) into a form suitable for transferring into the new database.
- **Testing** is the process of executing the database system with the intent of finding errors.
- **Operational maintenance** is the process of monitoring and maintaining the system following installation.

Review questions

4.1 Describe what is meant by the term 'software crisis.'

4.2 Discuss the relationship between the information systems lifecycle and the database system development lifecycle.

4.3 Briefly describe the stages of the database system development lifecycle.

4.4 Describe the purpose of creating a mission statement and mission objectives for the required database during the database planning stage.

4.5 Discuss what a user view represents when designing a database system.

4.6 Compare and contrast the centralized approach and view integration approach to managing the design of a database system with multiple user views.

4.7 Describe the purpose of the database design stage and identify the three phases of this stage.

4.8 Explain why it is necessary to select the target DBMS before beginning the physical database design phase.

4.9 Discuss the two main activities associated with application design.

4.10 Describe the potential benefits of developing a prototype database system.

4.11 Discuss the main activities associated with the implementation stage.

4.12 Describe the purpose of the data conversion and loading stage.

4.13 Explain why software testing cannot show the absence of faults.

4.14 What are the main activities associated with operational maintenance stage?

PART II Database analysis and design techniques

In this part of the book, we describe techniques associated with database analysis (Chapter 5) and design (Chapters 6, 7, and 8) and introduce a case study concerning a DVD online rental company called the *StayHome Online Rentals* (Section 5.4), which is used throughout this book.

There are numerous approaches and techniques associated with database analysis. However, the goal is always the same and that is to identify and clearly describe the requirements for the new database system. We present a selection of the most commonly used database analysis techniques in Chapter 5 and then illustrate the use of these techniques using the *StayHome Online Rentals* case study. Database analysis is particularly important for the first three stages of the database systems development lifecycle (Chapter 4); namely database planning, systems definition, and requirements collection and analysis. It is critical that database analysis is done well as it is the information produced during each stage that is used to design and ultimately build the 'correct' database.

Following the chapter on database analysis we turn our attention to the core techniques associated with database design – entity–relationship (ER) modeling (Chapters 6 and 7) and normalization (Chapter 8). It requires two chapters to first introduce you to the basic concepts (Chapter 6) and then the enhanced concepts (Chapter 7) associated with ER modeling. You will see that ER modeling is a good technique for unambiguously representing the data to be stored in the database.

In the final chapter of this part of the book, we present an overview of an important database design technique called normalization (Chapter 8). We show you how this technique can be used to check the proposed structure for a given table. Normalization has the ability to identify errors in tables that, if not resolved, may cause problems when the table is implemented.

How and when to best use ER modeling and normalization is shown in the database design methodology presented in Part III of this book (Chapters 9, 10, and 11).

CHAPTER

5 Fact-finding

Preview

In Chapter 4, you learned about the stages of the database system development lifecycle. There are many occasions during these stages when it is critical that the necessary facts are captured to build the required database system. The necessary facts cover the organization and the users of the database system, including the terminology, problems, opportunities, constraints, requirements, and priorities. These facts are captured using fact-finding techniques. Fact-finding is the formal process of using techniques such as interviews and questionnaires to collect facts about systems, processes, requirements, and preferences.

In this chapter, we discuss when it is useful to use fact-finding techniques and what types of facts should be captured. We present an overview of how these facts are used to generate the main types of documentation used throughout the database system development lifecycle. We briefly describe the most commonly used fact-finding techniques and identify the advantages and disadvantages of each. We finally demonstrate how some of these techniques may be used during the earlier stages of the database system development lifecycle using *StayHome Online Rentals*. In Chapters 9, 10, and 11 we will use the *StayHome Online Rentals* case study to demonstrate a methodology for database design.

Learning objectives

In this chapter you will learn:

- When fact-finding techniques are used in the database system development lifecycle.
- The types of facts collected throughout the database system development lifecycle.
- The types of documentation produced throughout the database system development lifecycle.
- The most commonly used fact-finding techniques.
- How to use each fact-finding technique and the advantages and disadvantages of each.

- About a web-based DVD rental company called *StayHome Online Rentals*.
- How to use fact-finding techniques in the database planning, systems definition, and requirements collection and analysis stages of the database system development lifecycle.
- Examples of the types of documentation created in the database planning, systems definition, and requirements collection and analysis stages of the database system development lifecycle.

5.1 When are fact-finding techniques used?

There are many occasions for **fact-finding** during the database system development lifecycle. However, fact-finding is particularly crucial to the early stages of the lifecycle, including the database planning, system definition, and requirements collection and analysis stages. It is during these early stages that we learn about the terminology, problems, opportunities, constraints, requirements, and priorities of the organization and the users of the system. Fact-finding is also used during database design and the later stages of the lifecycle, but to a lesser extent. For example, during physical database design, fact-finding becomes technical as the developer attempts to learn more about the DBMS selected for the database system. During the final stage, operational maintenance, fact-finding is used to determine whether a system requires tuning to improve performance or needs further development to include new requirements.

Key point

It is important to have a rough estimate of how much time and effort is to be spent on fact-finding for a database project. Too much study too soon leads to *paralysis by analysis*. However, too little thought can result in an unnecessary waste of both time and money due to working on the wrong solution to the wrong problem.

5.2 What facts are collected?

Throughout the database system development lifecycle, we need to capture facts about the current and/or future system. Table 5.1 provides examples of the sorts of data captured and the documentation produced for each stage of the lifecycle. As we mentioned in Chapter 4, the stages of the database system development lifecycle are not strictly sequential but involve some amount of repetition of previous stages through feedback loops. This is also true for the data captured and the documentation produced at each stage. For example, problems encountered during database design may necessitate additional data capture on the requirements for the new system.

In Section 5.4, we will return to examine the first three stages of the database system development lifecycle, namely database planning, system definition, and requirements collection and analysis. For each stage, we demonstrate the process of

Table 5.1 Examples of the data captured and the documentation produced for each stage of the database system development lifecycle

Stage of database system development lifecycle	Examples of data captured	Examples of documentation produced
Database planning	Aims and objectives of database project	Mission statement and objectives of database system
System definition	Description of major user views (includes job roles and/or business application areas)	Definition of scope and boundary of database system; definition of user views to be supported
Requirements collection and analysis	Data requirements for user views and general requirements for the database system, including performance and security requirements	Users' requirements specifications (includes data dictionary, use case diagrams and descriptions) and systems specification
Database design	Users' responses to checking the conceptual, logical and physical database design; functionality provided by target DBMS	Conceptual/Logical database design (includes ER diagram(s), data dictionary, and description of tables) and physical database design (includes description of tables using target DBMS)
Application design	Users' responses to checking interface design	Application design (includes description of programs and user interface)
DBMS selection	Functionality provided by target DBMS	DBMS evaluation and recommendations
Prototyping	Users' responses to prototype	Modified users' requirements specifications and systems specification
Implementation	Functionality provided by target DBMS	
Data conversion and loading	Format of current data; data import capabilities of target DBMS	
Testing	Test results	Testing strategies used; analysis of test results
Operational maintenance	Performance testing results; new or changing user and system requirements	User manual; analysis of performance results; modified users' requirements and systems specification

collecting data using fact-finding techniques and the production of documentation for *StayHome Online Rentals*. However, we first present a review of the most commonly used fact-finding techniques.

5.3 Fact-finding techniques

It is common to use several fact-finding techniques during a single database project. There are five common fact-finding techniques:

- examining documentation;
- interviewing;

- observing the organization in operation;
- secondary research;
- questionnaires.

5.3.1 Examining documentation

Examining documentation can be useful when we are trying to gain some insight as to how the need for a database arose. We may also find that documentation can be helpful to provide information on the organization (or part of the organization) associated with the problem. If the problem relates to the current system there should be documentation associated with that system. Examining documents, forms, reports, and files associated with the current system, is a good way to quickly gain some understanding of the system. Examples of the types of documentation that should be examined are listed in Table 5.2.

The advantages and disadvantages of examining documentation as a fact-finding technique are listed in Table 5.3.

5.3.2 Interviewing

Interviewing is the most commonly used, and normally most useful, fact-finding technique. Interviewing allows information to be collected from individuals, face to

Table 5.2 Examples of types of documentation that should be examined

Purpose of documentation	Examples of useful sources
Describes problem and need for database	Internal memos, emails, and minutes of meetings
	Employee/customer complaints, and documents that describe the problem
	Performance reviews/reports
Describes organization (or part of organization) affected by problem	Organizational chart, mission statement, and company reports
	Objectives for the organization being studied
	Task/job descriptions
	Samples of manual forms and reports
	Samples of computerized forms and reports
	Completed forms/reports
Describes current system	Various types of flowcharts and diagrams
	Data dictionary
	Database system design
	Program documentation
	User/training manuals

Table 5.3 Advantages and disadvantages of examining documentation as a fact-finding technique

Advantages	Disadvantages
Provides background information on the company, problem area and current system(s)	Access to all useful company documents may not always be granted due to ethical, legal and/or business reasons
Allows a more focused approach to gathering requirements for new database system	Documents may be out dated, incomplete and/or inaccurate
	Amount of documentation to examine may be overwhelming
	Time-consuming and therefore may be impractical

face. There can be several objectives to using interviewing such as collecting facts, checking accuracy of facts, generating user interest and involvement, identifying requirements, and gathering ideas and opinions. However, using the interviewing technique requires good communication skills for dealing effectively with people who have different values, priorities, opinions, motivations, and personalities. As with other fact-finding techniques, interviewing is not always the best method for all situations. The advantages and disadvantages of using interviewing as a fact-finding technique are listed in Table 5.4.

There are two types of interviews, unstructured and structured. *Unstructured interviews* are conducted with only a general objective in mind and with few, if any, specific questions. The interviewer counts on the interviewee to provide a framework and direction to the interview. This type of interview frequently loses focus and for this reason it does not usually work well for database projects.

Table 5.4 Advantages and disadvantages of using interviewing as a fact-finding technique

Advantages	Disadvantages
Allows interviewee to respond freely and openly to questions	Very time-consuming and costly, and therefore may be impractical
Allows interviewee to feel involvement in project	Success is dependent on communication skills of interviewer
Allows interviewer to follow up on interesting comments made by interviewee	May gather conflicting requirements that may be difficult to resolve
Allows interviewer to adapt or re-word questions during interview	
Allows interviewer to observe interviewee's body language	
Current technologies such as video conferencing allow interviewing of employees working at remote sites	

In *structured interviews*, the interviewer has a specific set of questions to ask the interviewee. Depending on the interviewee's responses, the interviewer will direct additional questions to obtain clarification or expansion. *Open-ended questions* allow the interviewee to respond in any way that seems appropriate. An example of an open-ended question is: 'Why are you dissatisfied with the report on DVD rentals?' *Closed-ended questions* restrict answers to either specific choices or short, direct responses. An example of such a question might be: 'Are you receiving the report on DVD rentals on time?' or 'Does the report on DVD rentals contain accurate information?' Both questions require only a 'Yes' or 'No' response.

Key point To ensure a successful interview, select appropriate individuals to interview, prepare extensively for the interview, and conduct the interview in an efficient and effective manner.

5.3.3 Observing the organization in operation

Observation is one of the most effective fact-finding techniques that can be used to understand a system. With this technique, we can either participate in or watch a person perform activities to learn about the system. This technique is particularly useful when the validity of data collected through other methods is in question or when the complexity of certain aspects of the system prevents a clear explanation by the end-users.

As with the other fact-finding techniques, successful observation requires much preparation. To ensure that the observation is successful, we need to know as much about the individuals and the activity to be observed as possible. For example, when are the low, normal, and peak periods for the activity being observed and will the individuals be upset by having someone watch and record their actions? The advantages and disadvantages of using observation as a fact-finding technique are listed in Table 5.5.

Table 5.5 Advantages and disadvantages of using observation as a fact-finding technique

Advantages	Disadvantages
Allows the validity of facts and data to be checked	People may knowingly or unknowingly perform differently when being observed
Observer can see exactly what is being done	May miss observing tasks involving different levels of difficulty or volume normally experienced during that time period
Observer can identify what data is required to complete tasks and how accessible the sources of data are	Some tasks may not always be performed in the manner in which they are observed
Observer can also obtain data describing the physical environment of the task	May be impractical
Relatively inexpensive	
Observer can do work measurements such as time taken to complete particular tasks	

Table 5.6 Advantages and disadvantages of using secondary research as a fact-finding technique

Advantages	Disadvantages
Can save time if solution already exists Researcher can see how others have solved similar problems or met similar requirements Keeps researcher up to date with current developments Can provide useful background information to help inform the use of one or more of the other fact-finding techniques (such as questionnaires and interviews)	Can be time-consuming Requires access to appropriate sources of information May ultimately not help in solving a problem because the problem is not documented elsewhere

5.3.4 Secondary research

A useful fact-finding technique is to research the application and problem. Computer trade journals, reference books, and the Web are good sources of information. They can provide information on how others have solved similar problems, plus we can learn whether or not software packages exist to solve a similar problem. The advantages and disadvantages of using secondary research as a fact-finding technique are listed in Table 5.6.

5.3.5 Questionnaires

Another fact-finding technique is to conduct surveys through questionnaires. Questionnaires are special-purpose documents that allow facts to be gathered from a large number of people while maintaining some control over their responses. When dealing with a large audience, no other fact-finding technique can tabulate the same facts as efficiently. The advantages and disadvantages of using questionnaires as a fact-finding technique are listed in Table 5.7.

There are two formats for questionnaires, free-format and fixed-format. *Free-format questionnaires* offer the respondent greater freedom in providing answers. A question is asked and the respondent records the answer in the space provided after the question. Examples of free-format questions are: 'What reports do you currently receive and how are they used?' and 'Are there any problems with these reports? If so, please explain.' The problems with free-format questions are that the respondent's answers may prove difficult to tabulate and, in some cases, may not match the questions asked.

Fixed-format questionnaires contain questions that require specific responses from individuals. Given any question, the respondent must choose from the available answers. This makes the results much easier to tabulate. On the other hand, the respondent cannot provide additional information that might prove valuable. An example of a fixed-format question is: 'The current format of the report on the DVD

Table 5.7 Advantages and disadvantages of using questionnaires as a fact-finding technique

Advantages	Disadvantages
People can complete and return questionnaires at their convenience	Number of respondents can be low, possibly only 5–10 per cent (particularly if the postal service or email is used to deliver the questionnaires)
Relatively inexpensive way to gather data from a large number of people	Questionnaires may be returned incomplete, particularly if the questionnaire is long or overly complex
People more likely to provide the real facts because responses can be kept confidential	No opportunity to adapt or re-word questions that may have been misinterpreted
Responses can be tabulated and analyzed quickly	No opportunity to observe and analyze the respondent's body language
Can be delivered using various modes including person-to-person, postal service, and email	Can be time-consuming to prepare the questionnaire

rentals is ideal and should not be changed.' The respondent may be given the option to answer 'Yes' or 'No' to this question, or be given the option to answer from a range of responses, including 'Strongly agree', 'Agree', 'No opinion', 'Disagree', and 'Strongly disagree.'

5.4 The *StayHome Online Rentals* case study

In this section, we first describe the *StayHome Online Rentals* case study. We then use this case study to illustrate how to establish a database project in the early stages of the database system development lifecycle by going through the database planning, system definition, and requirements collection and analysis stages.

5.4.1 The *StayHome Online Rentals* case study – an overview

This case study describes a new web-based startup company called *StayHome Online Rentals*, which aims to provide an online DVD rental service. The Director of *StayHome Online Rentals*, Mary Martinez, plans to launch the company's web site within the next few months and hopes to attract more than 100 000 members within the first year of going live. The company will operate using four distribution centers spread throughout the US with the company's headquarters at the distribution center in Seattle.

The Director believes that members will be attracted to *StayHome Online Rentals* by providing a secure, efficient, and cost-effective online DVD rentals service. Members will interact with the company using an attractive, easy-to-use web site,

Figure 5.1 The home page for the *StayHome Online Rentals* web site

which will allow for the easy selection of DVDs for viewing at home. Members will receive and return DVDs back to the company by post. The home page for the *StayHome Online Rentals* web site is shown in Figure 5.1.

StayHome Online Rentals has recently recruited 20 staff. Each member of staff is assigned to work at one of the four distribution centers. Each distribution center has a Manager and several Assistants. The Manager is responsible for the day-to-day running of a given center. The Director of the company also acts as the Manager of the distribution center in Seattle. When a member of staff joins the company, the staff online registration form is used. Figure 5.2 shows a web page displaying the details of a new member of staff called Sally Adams.

StayHome Online Rentals intends to stock about 10 000 DVD titles. Each DVD title is uniquely identified using a catalog number. However, there are many copies of each DVD at each distribution center, and the individual copies are identified using the DVD number.

Before renting a DVD, a customer will be required to first join as a member of *StayHome Online Rentals*. To become a member, a customer will be requested to enter his or her details online. As well as providing personal details including an email address and postal address, the customer must provide a password. A member's email address and password will be requested whenever a member wishes to access

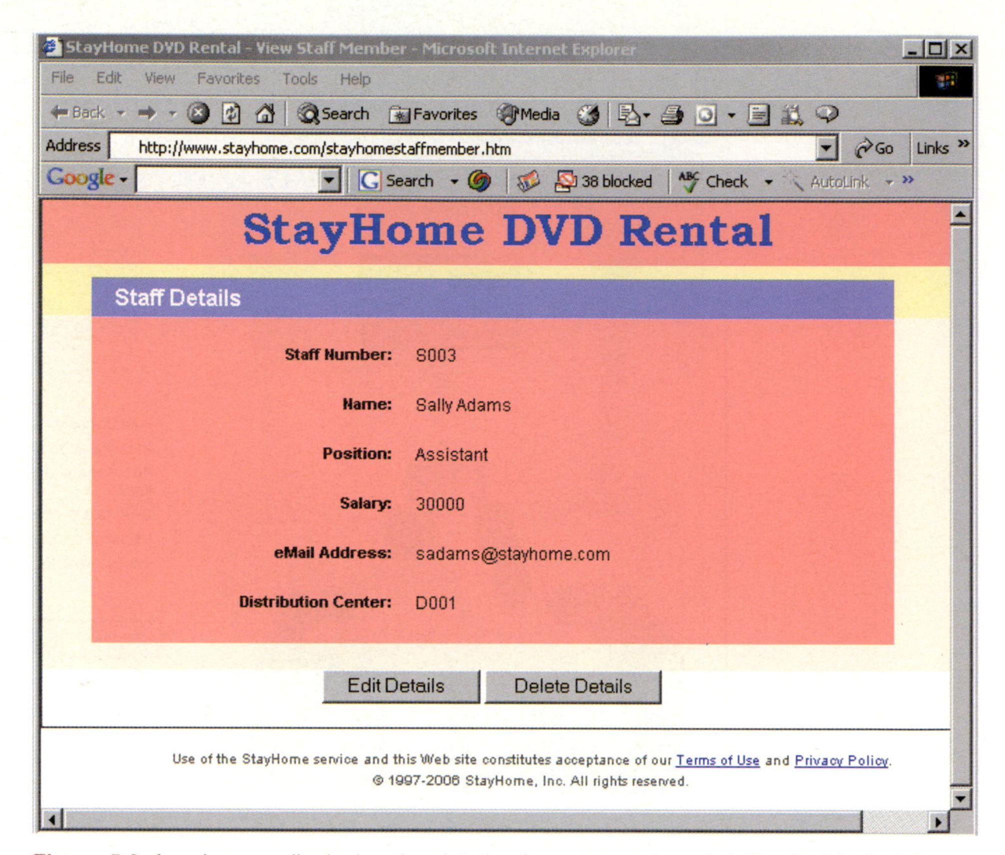

Figure 5.2 A web page displaying the details of a new member of staff called Sally Adams

his or her account with *StayHome Online Rentals*. Each member will receive and return DVDs to his or her nearest distribution center. The distribution center which supplies a member with DVDs will be allocated according to a member's postal address. Figure 5.3 shows the first of two web pages that a customer must complete to become a member of *StayHome Online Rentals*. Note that as *StayHome Online Rentals* has no members so far, the details for Don Nelson are fictitious.

As part of the registration process, a customer will select the type of DVD rental membership he or she wishes to hold with the company. *StayHome Online Rentals* has three types of memberships, which are dependent on the number of DVDs a member wishes to rent out at any one time. The memberships available are 1-at-a-time, 3-at-a-time, and 5-at-a-time, and each has a different monthly charge. Figure 5.4 shows the second of two web pages that a customer must complete to become a member of *StayHome Online Rentals*.

On completion of the online registration web pages, a new member will be requested to indicate which DVDs he or she wishes to view, up to a maximum of 25 DVDs. The selected DVDs will appear as a wish list of DVDs, ranked in order of member preference. To assist in the selection of DVDs that a members wishes to view, the *StayHome Online Rentals* web site will provide DVD search facilities including the ability to find a DVD based on its title, main actors, and genre.

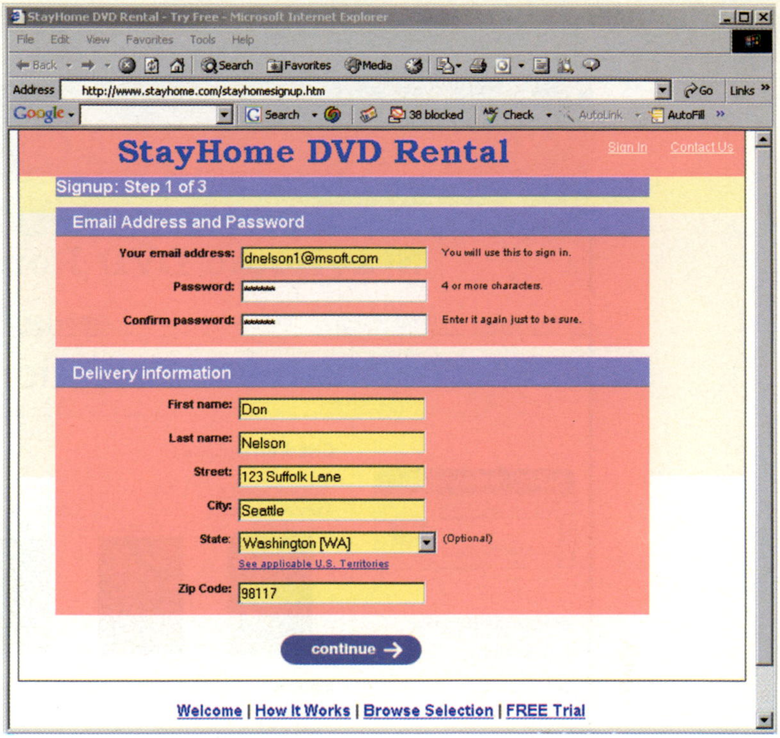

Figure 5.3 The first of two web pages that a customer must complete to become a member of *StayHome Online Rentals*

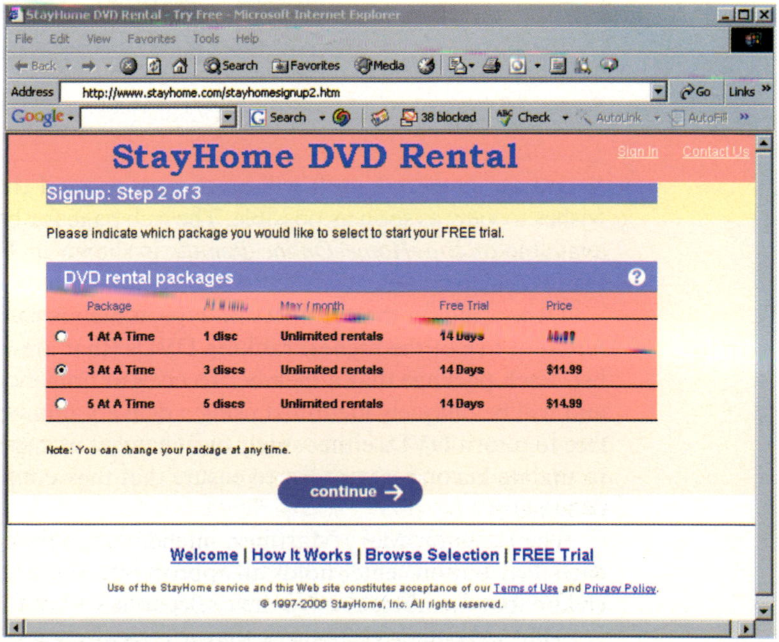

Figure 5.4 The second of two web pages that a customer must complete to become a member of *StayHome Online Rentals*

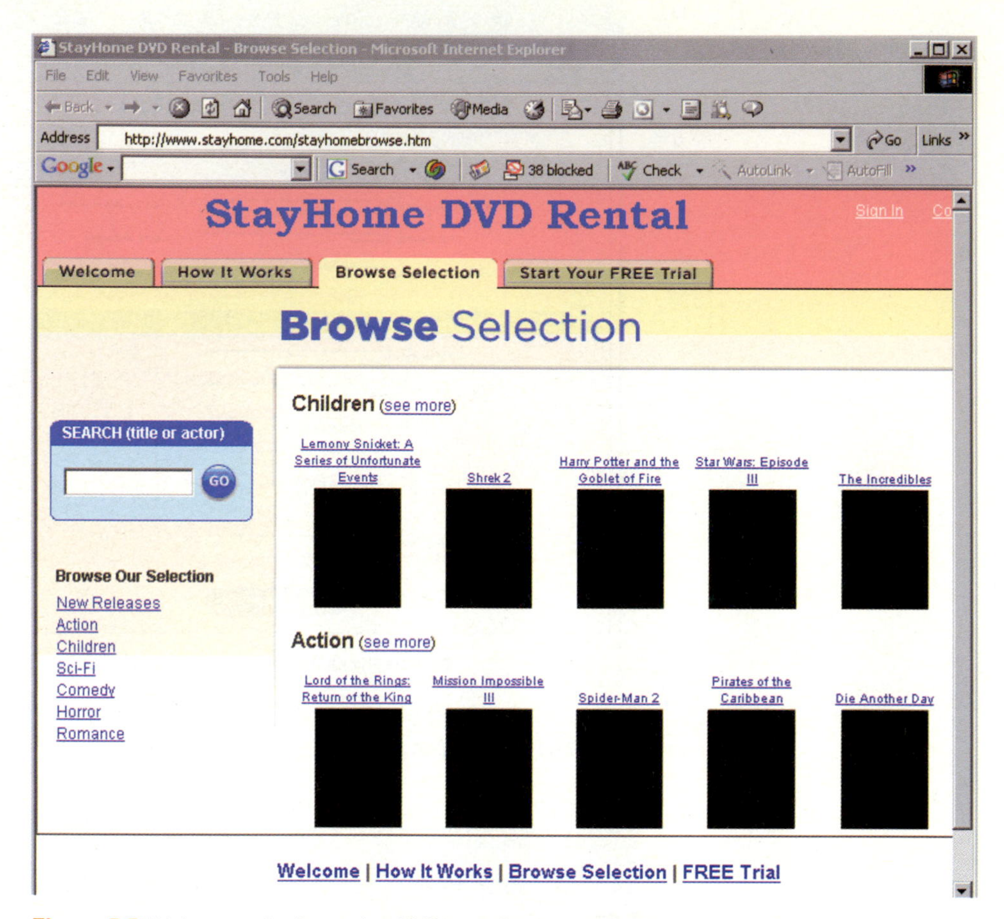

Figure 5.5 Web page for browsing DVDs available at *StayHome Online Rentals*

StayHome Online Rentals will always try to send the DVDs that a member most wishes to view as soon as possible. The web page for browsing the selection of DVDs available at *StayHome Online Rentals* is shown in Figure 5.5. An example of the DVDs that Ann Peters wishes to view is shown in Figure 5.6.

Depending on the membership type, a member will receive from one to a maximum of five of the highest ranking DVDs (that are available) from his or her wish list. Each package that a member receives at home will contain one or more DVDs and will be uniquely identified using a delivery number. However, a member will be free to return DVDs either singly or in batches at anytime. A member must continue to update his or her wish list to ensure that they continue to receive a new selection of DVDs.

The Director, Mary Martinez, intends to monitor member choice to ensure that each distribution center holds an appropriate number of the most popular DVDs to ensure that members receive their selections without unnecessary delay.

Mary Martinez recognizes that a critical component of the *StayHome Online Rentals* web site is the backend database system, which will manage the company's data. In the following sections, we demonstrate how the database system for

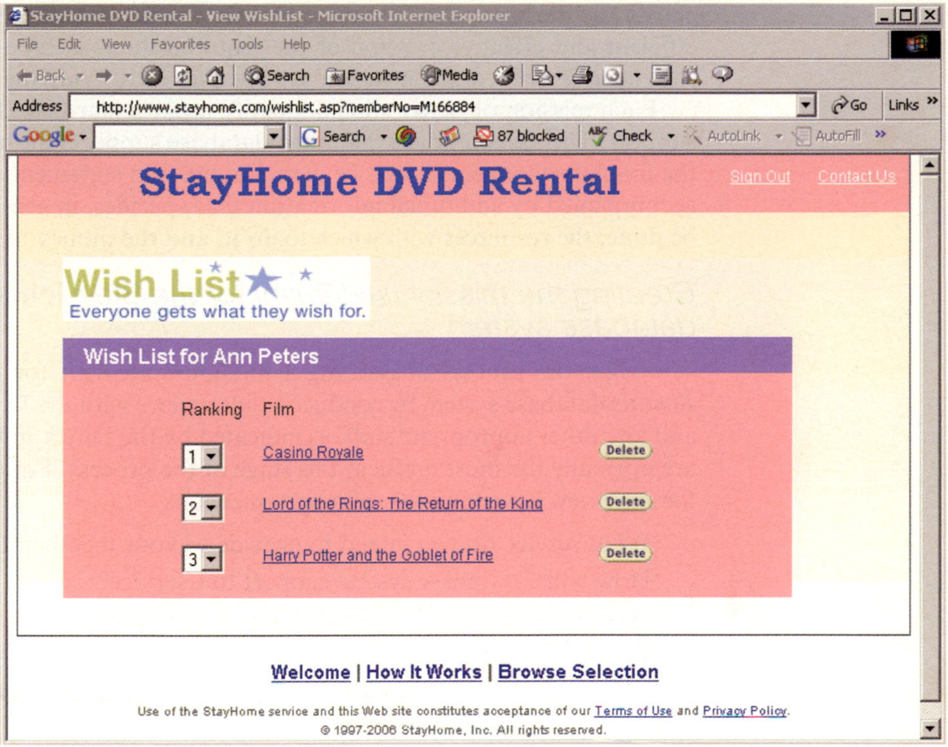
StayHome DVD Rental - View WishList - Microsoft Internet Explorer
File Edit View Favorites Tools Help
Back Search Favorites Media
Address http://www.stayhome.com/wishlist.asp?memberNo=M166884
Go Links
Google Search 87 blocked Check AutoLink AutoFill
StayHome DVD Rental
Sign Out Contact Us
Wish List
Everyone gets what they wish for.
Wish List for Ann Peters
Ranking Film
1 Casino Royale Delete
2 Lord of the Rings: The Return of the King Delete
3 Harry Potter and the Goblet of Fire Delete
Welcome | How It Works | Browse Selection
Use of the StayHome service and this Web site constitutes acceptance of our Terms of Use and Privacy Policy.
© 1997-2006 StayHome, Inc. All rights reserved.

Figure 5.6 An example of the DVDs that Ann Peters wishes to view

StayHome Online Rentals is established through the first three stages of the database systems lifecycle, namely database planning, systems definition, and requirements collection and analysis, which were described in the previous chapter.

> **Note** To simplify the *Stayhome Online Rentals* case study, a member's wish list will simply be used as an *aide-memoir* for staff and will not be directly connected to DVDs sent to members. However, the requirement to connect member wishes with actual DVD rentals is the subject of Exercises 9.11 and 10.7.

5.4.2 The *StayHome Online Rentals* case study – database planning

Database planning is the management of activities that allow the stages of the database system development lifecycle to be realized as efficiently and effectively as possible.

The first step in developing a database system is to clearly define the **mission statement** for the database project.

Those driving the database project within the organization (such as the director and/or owner) normally define the mission statement. A mission statement helps to clarify the purpose of the database project and provides a clearer path towards the efficient and effective creation of the required database system. Once the mission statement is defined, the next activity involves identifying the **mission objectives**.

Each mission objective should identify a particular task that the database must support. The assumption is that if the database supports the mission objectives then the mission statement should be met. The mission statement and objectives may be accompanied by additional information that specifies, in general terms, the work to be done, the resources with which to do it, and the money to pay for it all.

Creating the mission statement for the StayHome Online Rentals *database system*

We begin the process of creating a mission statement for the *StayHome Online Rentals* database system by conducting interviews with the Director of the company and any other appropriate staff, as indicated by the Director. Open-ended questions are normally the most useful at this stage of the process. For example, we may start the interview by asking the following questions:

'What service do you intend to provide to your members?'

'How will a database system support this service?'

'How important is the database system to the success of *StayHome Online Rentals*?'

Responses to these types of questions should help formulate the mission statement. For example, the mission statement for the *StayHome Online Rentals* database system is shown in Figure 5.7.

'The StayHome Online Rentals database system will manage the data captured through the web site and created at the distribution centers to help the company provide members with a secure, efficient, and cost effective online DVD rentals service that allows the easy selection and viewing of DVDs in their own home.'

Figure 5.7 Mission statement for the *StayHome Online Rentals* database system

When we have achieved a clear and unambiguous mission statement that the staff of *StayHome Online Rentals* agree with, we can move on to define the mission objectives.

Creating the mission objectives for the StayHome Online Rentals *database system*

The process of creating mission objectives involves conducting interviews with appropriate members of staff. Again, open-ended questions are normally the most useful at this stage of the process. To obtain the complete range of mission objectives, we interview various members of staff with different roles in *StayHome Online Rentals*. As this case study describes a new company with no members as yet, we must include questions to staff with the specific purpose of identifying the needs of this group of future users of the database. In other words, the mission objectives must also include the data requirements of members. For example, we may ask the following questions:

'What is your job description?'

'What kinds of tasks do you perform in a typical day?'

'What type of data do you input?'
'What type of data do you require to view?'
'What types of forms and/or reports do you use?'
'What types of data do you need to keep track of?'
'What service does your company provide to your members?'
'What type of data will members input?'
'What type of data will members require to view?'
'What types of forms and/or reports will members use?'
'What types of data will members need to keep track of?'

These questions (or similar) are put to the members of staff of *StayHome Online Rentals*. Of course, it may be necessary to adapt the questions as required depending on who is being interviewed. Responses to these types of questions should help formulate high-level mission objectives. For example, the mission objectives for the *StayHome Online Rentals* database are shown in Figure 5.8.

To maintain (enter, update, and delete) data on distribution centers
To maintain (enter, update, and delete) data on staff
To maintain (enter, update, and delete) data on DVDs
To maintain (enter, update, and delete) data on DVD copies
To maintain (enter, update, and delete) data on actors
To maintain (enter, update, and delete) data on member personal details
To maintain (enter, update, and delete) data on membership types
To maintain (enter, update, and delete) data on member wishes
To maintain (enter, update, and delete) data on rental deliveries

To perform searches on distribution centers
To perform searches on staff
To perform searches on DVDs
To perform searches on DVD copies
To perform searches on actors
To perform searches on member personal details
To perform searches on membership types
To perform searches on member wishes
To perform searches on rental deliveries

To track the status of DVD copies
To track the status of rental deliveries

To report on staff
To report on DVDs
To report on DVD copies
To report on actors
To report on member personal details
To report on member wishes
To report on rental deliveries

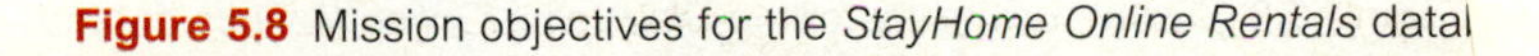

Figure 5.8 Mission objectives for the *StayHome Online Rentals* data

5.4.3 The *StayHome Online Rentals* case study – system definition

System definition

Defines the scope and boundary of the database system, including its major user views.

Defining the systems boundary for the StayHome Online Rentals *database system*

During this stage of the database system development lifecycle, it can be useful to use interviews to clarify or expand on data captured in the previous stage. However, also consider using other fact-finding techniques, including examining the sample online forms and report shown in Section 5.4.1. We should now analyze the data collected so far to define the boundary of the database system. One way to define the boundary of the *StayHome Online Rentals* database system is to show the aspects of the company operations that will be supported by the database and those that will not be supported, as shown in Figure 5.9. This figure shows that, although mentioned by the users, the supply of DVDs from suppliers and the selling of DVDs to members will not be included in the new database system, at this time.

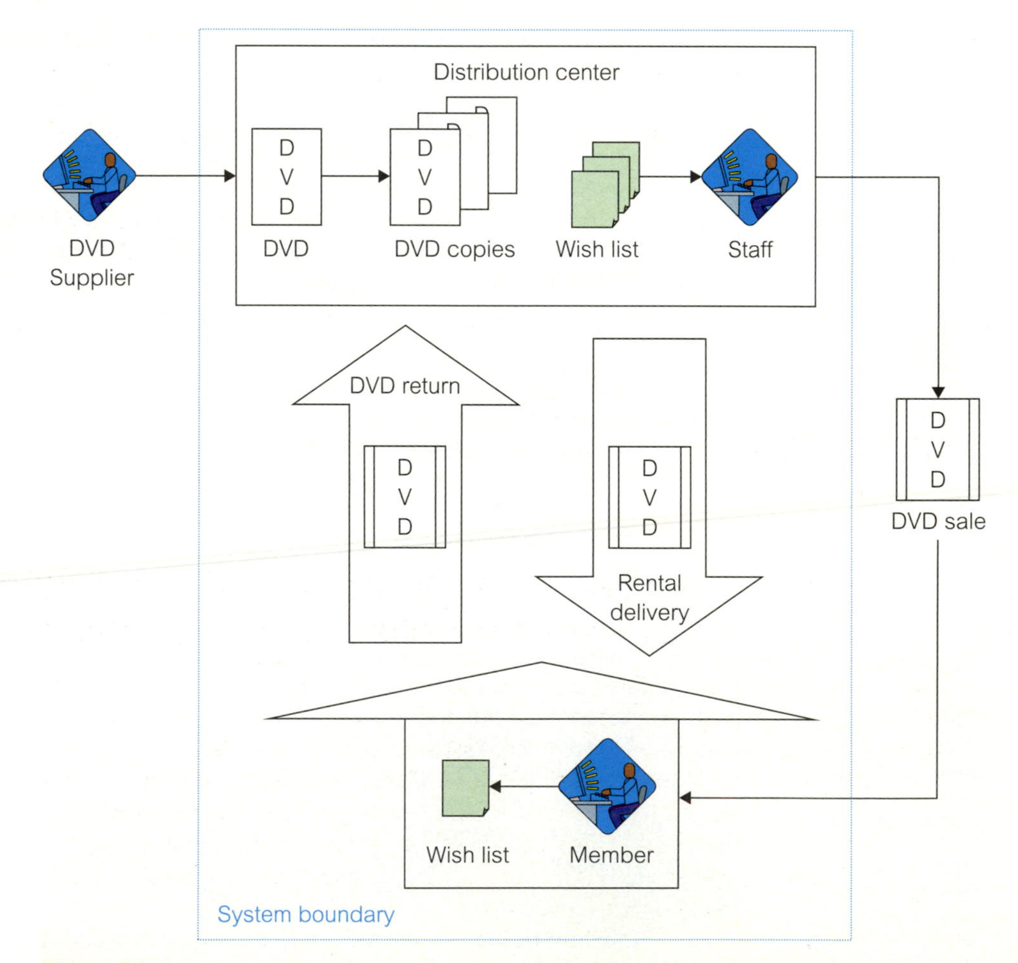

Figure 5.9 System boundary for the *StayHome Online Rentals* database system

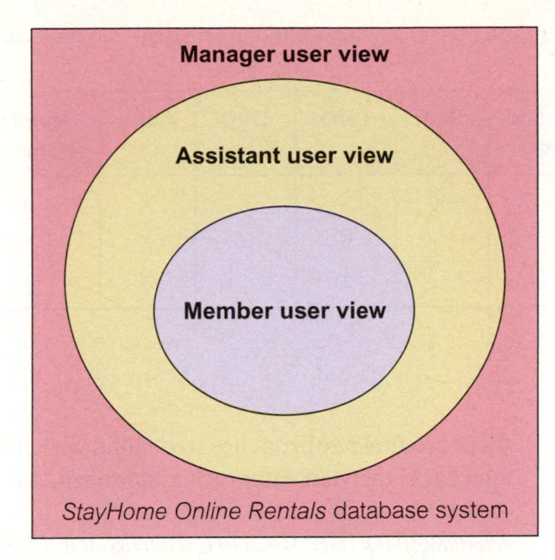

Figure 5.10 Main user views of the *StayHome Online Rentals* database system

An alternative way to represent a system boundary using an *extended* version of the *StayHome Online Rentals* case study was shown in Figure 4.2.

Identifying the major user views for the StayHome Online Rentals *database system*

User view

Defines what is required of a database system from the perspective of a particular job (such as manager or supervisor) or business application area (such as marketing, personnel, or stock control).

We now analyze the data collected so far to define the **user views** of the database system.

The majority of data about user views was collected during interviews with staff. Analysis of this data reveals that there are three major user views of the *StayHome Online Rentals* database system: namely the Manager, Assistant, and Member user views.

One way to represent the relationship between the user views in terms of data requirements is shown in Figure 5.10. This figure shows that the Member user view uses a subset of the data used by the Assistant user view, and that the Assistant user view uses a subset of the data used by the Manager user view.

5.4.4 The *StayHome Online Rentals* case study – requirements collection and analysis

Requirements collection and analysis

The process of collecting and analyzing information about the organization to be supported by the database system, and using this information to identify the requirements for the new database system.

During this stage, we continue to gather more details on the user views identified in the previous stage, to create a *users' requirements specification* that describes the data to be held in the database and how the data is to be used.

While collecting data on the requirements we learn about how the current system works. Of course, if we are building a new database system, we should try to retain the good things about the old system while introducing the benefits of using the new system. However, as *StayHome Online Rentals* is a new company there is no old system to investigate.

An important activity associated with this stage is deciding how to deal with the situation where we have more than one user view. As we discussed in Section 4.6,

Table 5.8 Cross-reference of user views with the main types of data to be stored in the *StayHome Online Rentals* database system

	Distribution Center	Staff	DVD	DVD Copy	Actor	Member Personal	Membership Type	Member Wish	Rental Delivery
Manager	X	X	X	X	X	X	X	X	X
Assistant			X	X	X	X	X	X	X
Member			X		X	X	X	X	X

Centralized approach

Requirements for each user view are merged into a single list of requirements for the new database system. A data model representing all user views is created during the database design stage.

View integration approach

Requirements for each user view remain as separate lists. Data models representing each user view are created and then merged later during the database design stage.

there are three approaches to dealing with multiple user views, namely the **centralized approach**, the **view integration approach**, and a combination of both approaches.

Managing the requirements for the major user views of the StayHome Online Rentals *database system*

How do we decide whether to use the centralized or view integration approach or a combination of both to manage multiple user views? One way to help make a decision is to examine in more detail the sharing of data between the user views identified during the system definition stage. Table 5.8 cross-references the Manager, Assistant, and Member user views with the main types of data to be stored in the *StayHome Online Rentals* database system (namely, Distribution Center, Staff, DVD, DVD Copy, Actor, Member Personal, Membership Type, Member Wish, and Rental Delivery).

We see from this table that there is a significant overlap in the data used by all user views and this confirms the findings shown previously in Figure 5.10. While Managers require access to all the main data types, Assistants require only a subset of this data (DVD, DVD copy, Actor, Member Personal, Membership Type, Member Wish, and Rental Delivery), and Members require an even smaller subset (DVD, Actor, Member Personal, Membership Type, Member Wish, and Rental Delivery).

We now decide how to best manage the data requirements of the main user views to help the process of designing a database capable of supporting all user groups. It is difficult to give precise rules as to when it is appropriate to use the centralized or view integration approaches. The decision should be based on an assessment of the complexity of the database system and the degree of overlap between the various user views. However, whether we use the centralized or view integration approach or a mixture of both to build the underlying database, ultimately we need to create the original user views for the working database system.

As shown in Figure 5.10 and Table 5.8, the different user views share a significant portion of the data and the database system is not overly complex, therefore the centralized approach is the better approach for managing the requirements of *StayHome Online Rentals*. We therefore merge the user requirements for the Manager, Assistant, and Member user views. We will discuss the re-establishment of the user views for the database in Chapter 11.

Note We demonstrate only the centralized approach to managing user views in this book. However, in Appendix A, we present an *extended* version of the *StayHome Online Rental* case study, which includes an additional user view called Buyer. This extended version can be used to work through the steps of the view integration approach. The additional steps necessary for the view integration approach are given in Appendix D, Step 2.6.

Gathering more information on the user views of the StayHome Online Rentals *database system*

It is important to note that the type of analysis of data usage conducted so far is high-level and does not take into account how the user views differ in the types of access required–such as the ability to create, update, or delete records and/or view one record at a time or as reports. We now continue the process of requirements collection and analysis by asking more specific questions about how each user uses or intends to use specific types of data.

To find out more about the requirements for each user view, we again use a selection of fact-finding techniques including interviews and, where possible, observing the organization in operation. Examples of the types of questions that we may ask about the data (represented as X) required by a user includes:

'What type of data do you need to hold on X?'

'What sorts of things do you do with the data on X?'

'How important is X to your ability to carry out your work?'

We need to ask similar questions about all the important data to be stored in the database. Responses to these questions should help identify the necessary details for the users' requirements specification.

Creating the users' requirements specification for the StayHome Online Rentals *database system*

The users' requirements specification for the merged user views is listed in two sections; the first describes how the data is to be used by the three main user views as use case diagrams and use case descriptions; the second describes the data used by all user views in the form of a data dictionary.

Use case diagrams and descriptions form part of the Unified Modeling Language (UML) object-oriented approach to software design and implementation. UML is an increasingly popular approach and is currently the standard notation for object methods as specified by the Object Management Group (OMG). Although in this book we use the traditional approach to database design, some of the concepts and notation of UML can be very helpful in analyzing, designing, and developing a relational database system.

The use cases shown in the figures that follow describe the required functionality of the *StayHome Online Rentals* database system from the perspective of the three main user views of the database system: namely Member, Assistant, and Manager. The use cases define the scope of the database system and represent the users'

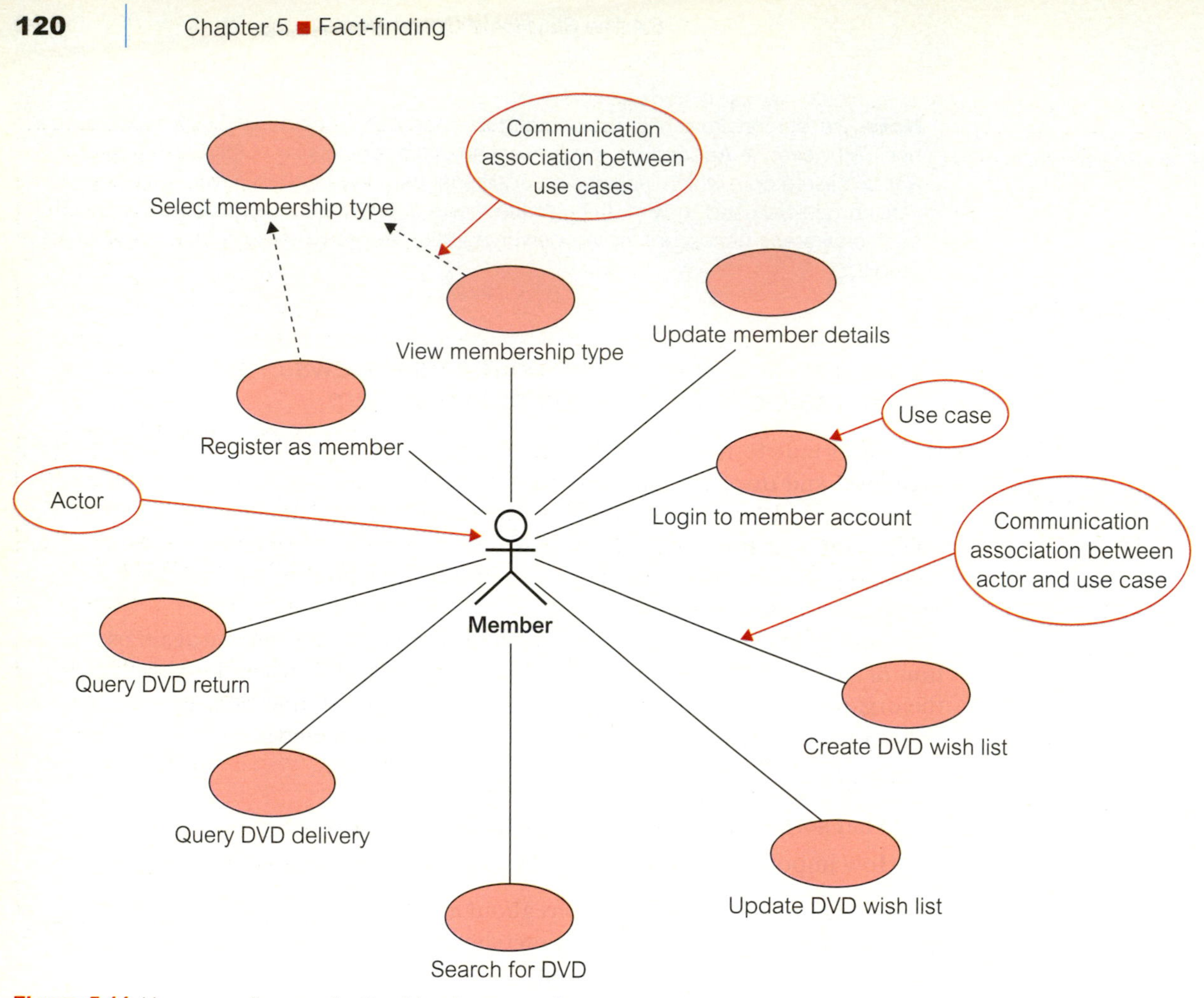

Figure 5.11 Use case diagram for the Member user view

understanding of their requirements for the database system. In a use case diagram such as Figure 5.11, each use case (shown as an ellipse) is connected through a communication association (shown as a line) to a particular user view (shown as an actor). Different kinds of associations can be represented in a use case diagram. For example, Figure 5.11 also shows communication between one use case and another (as a dashed line with arrow), which represents a use case (such as Register as member) requiring the functionality of another use case (such as Select membership type).

The descriptions that accompany the use case diagrams shown in the tables that follow provide a textual statement of the interaction between the main users (user views) of the system, termed *actors*, and the high-level functions within the system, namely the use cases. These textual statements can be in summary form as shown in Table 5.9 or in a more detailed form in which the interaction between the actors and use cases is described in a step-by-step fashion. Whatever approach is taken, it is important to note that the use cases describe the interactions between the users and the

Table 5.9 Use case descriptions for the Member user view

1. Register as member	Before renting a DVD, a customer is required to first join as a member of *StayHome Online Rentals*. When a customer joins, he or she is requested to complete the online member registration form. As well as providing personal details including an email address and postal address, the new member must provide a password.
2. View membership type	*StayHome Online Rentals* offers three types of membership, which are dependent on the number of DVDs a member wishes to rent out at any one time. The memberships available are 1-at-a-time, 3-at-a-time, and 5-at-a-time and each has a different monthly charge.
3. Select membership type	As part of the registration process, a member selects the type of DVD rental membership he/she wishes to hold with the company.
4. Update member details	A member can update his or her own personal and login details.
5. Login to member account	A member's email address and password are requested whenever a member wishes to access his or her account with *StayHome Online Rentals*.
6. Create DVD wish list	On completion of the online registration form, a new member is requested to identify the DVDs he or she wishes to view, up to a maximum of 25 DVDs. These DVDs will appear ranked in order of member preference as a wish list.
7. Update DVD wish list	A member can update the entries in his or her own DVD wish list.
8. Search for DVD	To assist in the compilation of a wish list, the *StayHome Online Rentals* web site provides a DVD search facility including the ability to find a DVD based on its title, main actors, and genre.
9. Query DVD delivery	A member can view his or her own current and past DVD deliveries.
10. Query DVD return	A member can view the date that a returned DVD was received at the distribution center.

system from the users' point of view and is not a description of the internal processes of the database system. For more information on using use cases and UML in general the interested reader is referred to Jacobson *et al.* (1992) and Bennet *et al.* (1999).

The use case diagram and descriptions for the Member user view is shown in Figure 5.11 and Table 5.9, respectively. The use case diagram and descriptions for the Assistant user view is shown in Figure 5.12 and Table 5.10, respectively. The use case diagram and descriptions for the Manager user view is shown in Figure 5.13 and Table 5.11, respectively. The use case diagrams and descriptions are presented in this order as the access requirements for the user views becomes progressively more complex as we consider the Member, Assistant, and finally the Manager user view. The use case diagrams were produced using a CASE tool called Rational Rose, which supports the development of software systems using UML.

A draft version of a data dictionary describing the merged data requirements for all the user views – namely Manager, Assistant, and Member – is shown in Table 5.12. Additional details will be added to this dictionary, as well as refinements, as we learn more about the data required by the main user views of the *StayHome Online Rentals* database system.

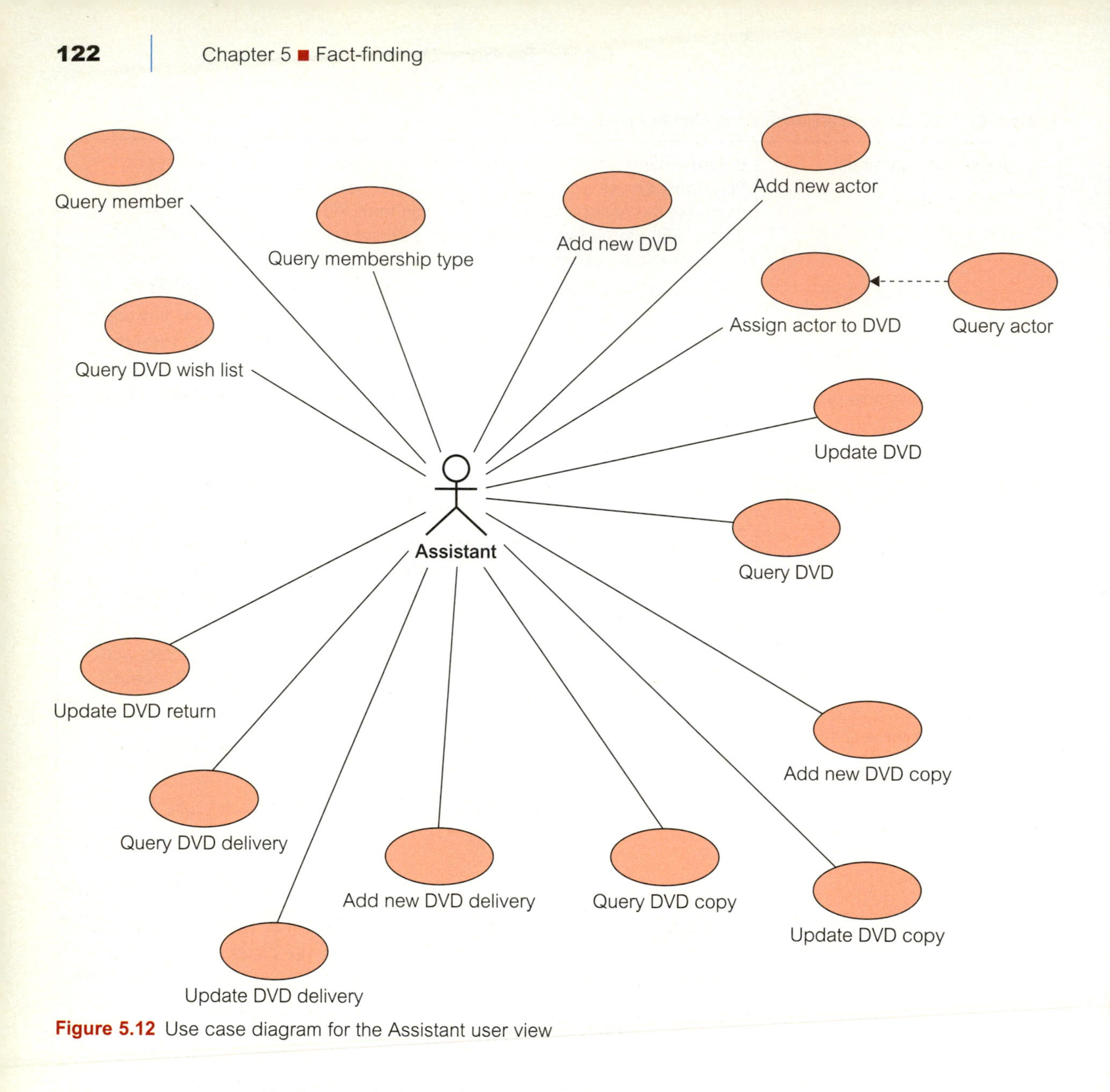

Figure 5.12 Use case diagram for the Assistant user view

In the remainder of this chapter, we present the general systems specification for the *StayHome Online Rentals* database system.

Creating the systems specification *for the* StayHome Online Rentals *database system*

There are requirements that are not associated with a particular user view but relate to the database system in general. The purpose of gathering this information is to create a *systems specification*, which describes any features to be included in the database system such as networking and shared access requirements, performance requirements, and the levels of security required.

Table 5.10 Use case descriptions for the Assistant user view

1. Query DVD wish list	To identify the DVD(s) that a member wants to rent out.
2. Query member	To view member address details to post requested DVD(s).
3. Query membership type	To view membership type to identify maximum number of DVD rentals allowed at any one time.
4. Add new DVD	To create a record for each new DVD. Each DVD is uniquely identified using a catalog number.
5. Add new actor	To create a record for each new actor. Each actor is identified using an actor number.
6. Assign actor to DVD	When a new DVD record is created, one or more actors are assigned to a DVD, where appropriate.
7. Query Actor	To view actor details.
8. Update DVD	To update DVD details.
9. Query DVD	To view DVD details.
10. Add new DVD copy	To create a DVD record for each new copy of a DVD. There are many copies of each DVD and the individual copies are identified using the DVD number.
11. Update DVD copy	To update details of a DVD copy. In particular to identify the status of a DVD copy.
12. Query DVD copy	To view DVD copy details.
13. Add new DVD delivery	To create a new DVD delivery record to identify the DVD(s) being sent to a member.
14. Update DVD delivery	To update DVD delivery details.
15. Query DVD delivery	To view details of DVD delivery. In particular, to allow staff to answer member queries about a DVD delivery.
16. Update DVD return	To record the date when the rented out DVD is returned to the distribution center.

While conducting interviews about user views, we should also collect more general information on the system requirements. Examples of the types of questions that we may ask about the system include:

'What transactions run frequently on the database?'

'What transactions are critical to the operation of the organization?'

'When do the critical transactions run?'

'When are the low, normal, and high workload periods for the critical transactions?'

'What type of security do you want for the database system?'

'Is there any highly sensitive data that should only be accessed by certain members of staff?'

'What historical data do you want to hold?'

'What are the networking and shared access requirements for the database system?'

'What type of protection from failures or data loss do you want for your database system?'

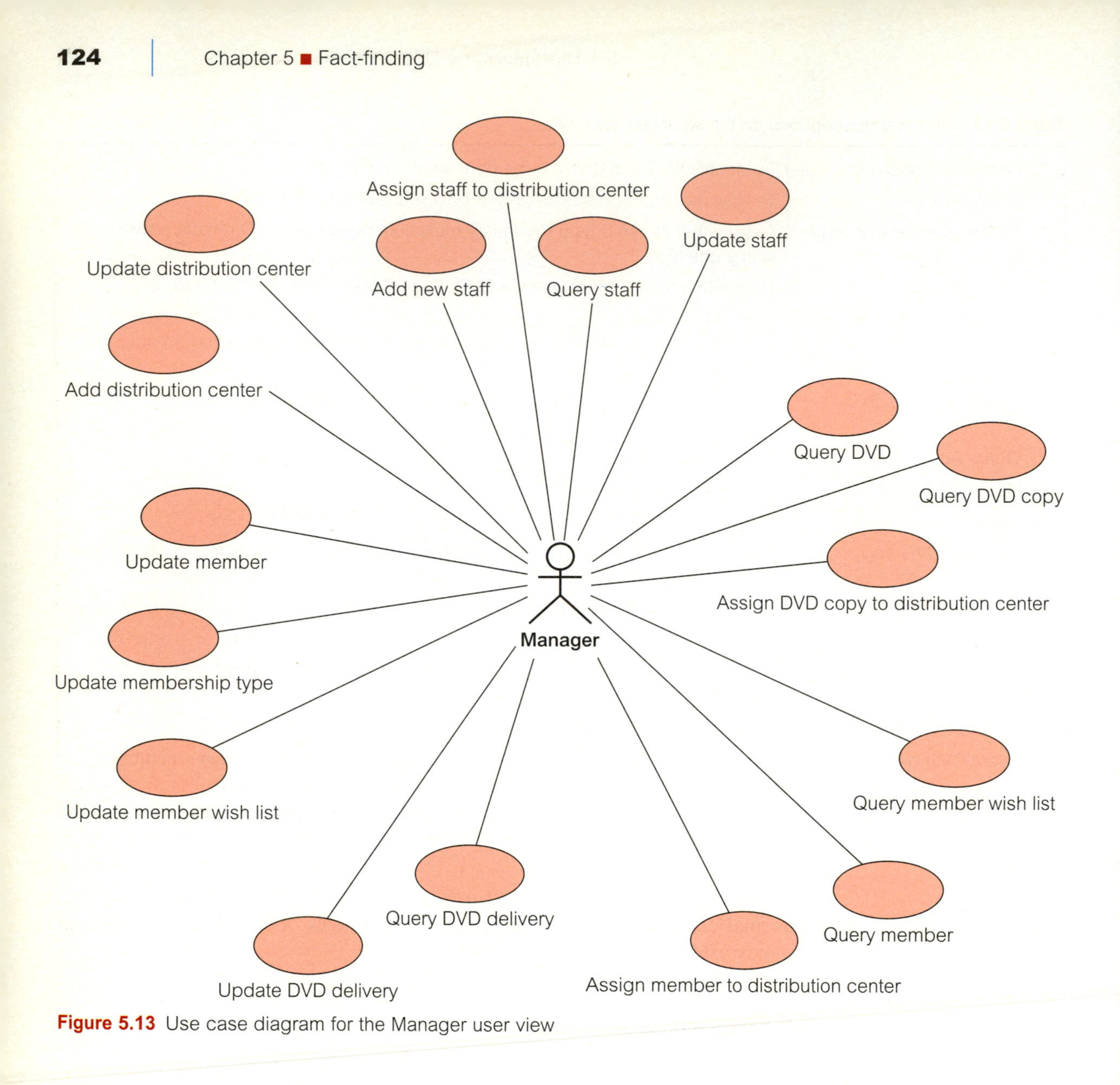

Figure 5.13 Use case diagram for the Manager user view

We need to ask similar questions about all the important aspects of the system. Responses to these questions should help identify the necessary details for the systems specification.

Creating the systems specification for the StayHome Online Rentals *database system*

The systems specification should list all the important features for the *StayHome Online Rentals* database system. Examples of the types of features that should be described in the systems specification include:

Table 5.11 Use case descriptions for the Manager user view

Use case	Description
1. Add new distribution center	To create a record for each new distribution center. Each center is uniquely identified using a distribution center number.
2. Update distribution center	To update distribution center details.
3. Add new staff	To create a record for each new member of staff. Each member of staff is identified using a staff number.
4. Assign staff to distribution center	When a new member of staff joins the company, he or she is assigned to work at a particular distribution center.
5. Query Staff	To view staff details.
6. Update staff	To update staff details.
7. Query DVD	To view DVD details.
8. Query DVD copy	To view DVD copy details.
9. Assign DVD copy to distribution center	A new copy of a DVD is assigned to a particular distribution center.
10. Query member wish list	To view DVD wish list entries.
11. Query member	To view member details.
12. Assign member to distribution center	When a new member joins the company, he or she is assigned to receive and return borrowed DVDs to their nearest distribution center.
13. Query DVD delivery	To view DVD delivery details.
14. Update DVD delivery	To update DVD delivery details.
15. Update member wish list	To update member wish list entries. It may be necessary to remove a DVD from a member's wish list due to the inability to re-stock a particular DVD.
16. Update membership type	To update membership type details.
17. Update member	To update member details.

- initial database size;
- database rate of growth;
- the types and average number of record searches;
- networking and shared access requirements;
- performance;
- security;
- backup and recovery;
- user interface;
- legal issues.

Table 5.12 A draft version of a data dictionary describing the data required for all user views of *StayHome Online Rentals*

Data	Description
Distribution Center	There are four distribution centers. The main work carried out at each center is monitoring the stock of DVDs and the posting out and receiving back of DVDs from members. Each center has members of staff including a Manager and Assistants. The Director is also the Manager of the Seattle center.
number	The distribution center number uniquely identifies each site.
address	This is made up of street, city, state, and zip code.
manager name	The name of the member of staff who manages the distribution center.
Staff	Staff are allocated to work at a distribution center.
number	This uniquely identifies each member of staff.
name	The full name of a member of staff.
position	The current position of a member of staff. There are two positions – namely, Manager and Assistant.
salary	The salary in US dollars of a member of staff.
staff email	The email address for a member of staff.
DVD	Each distribution center has a stock of DVDs.
catalog number	This uniquely identifies each DVD.
genre	Each DVD is described as belonging to a particular genre from one of the following: Action, Adult, Children, Fantasy, Horror, Sci-Fi, or Thriller.
title	The title of the DVD.
rating	Each DVD is described as having a particular rating from one of the following: U, G, PG, PG-13, and R.
DVD Copy	Each DVD has many copies.
DVD number	Each DVD copy is uniquely identified using the DVD number.
available	Indicates whether a particular copy of a DVD is available for renting. Y – indicates that the DVD copy is available. N – indicates that a DVD copy is not available. A DVD copy may not be available because it is already rented out or is unavailable due to damage, loss, or theft.
Actor	An actor is in one or more DVDs.
number	This uniquely identifies each actor.
name	The full name of an actor.
character	The name of the character an actor played in a given DVD. (An actor can play many characters in many DVDs.)
Member	A member holds a particular membership type, which enables them to receive DVDs from their nearest distribution center.
member number	This uniquely identifies each member.
member name	The first name and last name of the member.
member address	This is made up of street, city, state, and zip code.
member email	The email address for a member.

Table 5.12 (*Cont'd*)

Data	Description
member password	Each member has a password.
membership type	The membership type indicates the number of DVDs a member may rent out at any one time.
Membership Type	Each member selects one of three different type of membership, which are dependent on the number of DVDs a member wishes to rent out at any one time.
membership type number	Uniquely identifies the type of membership. There are three different memberships: 1-at-a-time, 3-at-a-time, and 5-at-a-time.
monthly charge	Each different membership is charged at a different monthly rate.
maximum rental	Indicates the maximum number of DVDs a member can rent out at any one time. This number is set by the membership type selected by the member.
Rental Delivery	Each rental delivery is a package of one or more DVDs, which is sent to a member's home address. The number of DVDs sent in a single delivery package is between one and five. The maximum number of DVDs in any single delivery is set by the membership type of a member.
delivery number	This uniquely identifies each delivery of one or more DVDs sent to a member.
DVD title	The title of the DVD sent to a member. A delivery can be of one or more DVDs.
DVD number	This uniquely identifies each DVD copy. A delivery can be of one or more DVD copies.
date out	The date that a particular delivery of one or more DVDs is posted out to a member.
date returned	The date that a particular DVD copy is received back at a distribution center from a member.
Wish	A member can specify one or more DVD that he or she wishes to rent out. The list of DVDs that a member wishes to rent out is called a 'wish list.'
title	Identifies the DVD title that a member wishes to rent. (A member can identify up to a maximum of 25 DVDs.)
ranking	Identifies the preference that a member has to rent out a particular DVD. (A member can rank up to a maximum of 25 DVDs.)

Initial database size

(a) There are approximately 10 000 DVD titles available on the *StayHome Online Rental* web site with a total number of 1 million DVDs copies of these titles distributed over four distribution centers.

(b) There are currently 20 members of staff. It is predicted that 20 additional members of staff will be employed in the first year of operating, giving an average of 10 staff at each distribution center.

(c) It is predicted that within one year of operating, there will be approximately 100 000 members registered across all four distribution centers.

(d) It is predicted that by the end of one year of operating, there will have been approximately 2 million DVD rentals across all four distribution centers.

(e) There are approximately 5000 main actors in 10 000 DVDs.

Database rate of growth

(a) Approximately 100 new DVD titles will be added to the database each month.

(b) It is predicted that after one year of operating, approximately two members of staff will join and leave the company every six months. The records of staff that leave the company will be deleted after six months.

(c) It is predicted that during the first year of operating, approximately 8000 new members will register with the company each month. Members can cancel their DVD rental contact after one year. It is predicted that after one year, approximately 1000 members will cancel their contact with *StayHome Online Rentals* and that the number of members joining the company will expand to roughly 200 000.

(d) It is predicted that after one year of operating, approximately 200 000 new DVD rentals will be processed each month across all four distribution centers.

The types and average number of record searches

(a) Searching for the details of a distribution center – approximately one per day.

(b) Searching for the details of a member of staff at a distribution center – approximately one per day.

(c) Searching for the details of a given DVD – approximately 10 000 per day.

(d) Searching for the details of a copy of a DVD – approximately 2000 per day.

(e) Searching for the details of a specified member – approximately 500 per day.

(f) Searching for the details of a DVD rental – approximately 2000 per day.

Networking and shared access requirements

(a) All distribution centers will be securely networked to a centralized database located at the company's HQ in Seattle.

(b) The system should allow for at least three people concurrently accessing the system from each distribution center. Consideration needs to be given to the licensing requirements for this number of concurrent accesses.

Performance

(a) Expect less than 1 second response for all single record searches.

(b) Expect less than 5 second response for all multiple record searches.

(c) Expect less than 1 second response for all updates/saves.

Security

(a) The database should be password protected.

(b) Members must user their email address and password to access their account.

(c) Users will be assigned database access privileges appropriate to a particular user view: namely the Member, Assistant, or Manager user view.

(d) Staff should see only the data necessary to do his or her job in a form that suits what they are doing.

Backup and recovery

The database should be backed up each day at 4.00am.

User interface

The user interface will be web-based and menu-driven. Online help should be easy to locate and access.

Legal issues

Each country has laws that govern the way that the computerized storage of personal data is handled. As the *StayHome Online Rentals* database holds data on staff and members, any legal issues that must be complied with should be investigated and implemented.

5.4.5 The *StayHome Online Rentals* case study – database design

In this chapter, we have demonstrated some of the useful documentation that can be created during the database planning, systems definition, and requirements collection and analysis stages of the database systems lifecycle. These documents are the source of information for the next stage of the lifecycle, called database design. In Chapters 9, 10, and 11 we will provide a step-by-step methodology for database design, and we will use some of the documents created in this chapter to demonstrate the methodology in practice.

Chapter summary

- **Fact-finding** is the formal process of using techniques such as interviews and questionnaires to collect facts about systems, requirements, and preferences.
- Fact-finding is particularly crucial to the early stages of the database system development lifecycle including the database planning, system definition, and requirements collection and analysis stages.
- The five most common fact-finding techniques are examining documentation, interviewing, observing the organization in operation, secondary research, and questionnaires.
- The first step in the **database planning stage** is to clearly define the mission statement and mission objectives for the database project. The **mission statement** defines the major aims of the database system. Each **mission objective** should identify a particular task that the database must support.

- The purpose of the **system definition stage** is to define the boundaries and user views of the database system.
- There are two main documents created during the **requirements collection and analysis stage**, namely the users' requirements specification and the systems specification.
- The **users' requirements specification** describes in detail the data to be held in the database and how the data is to be used.
- The **systems specification** describes any features to be included in the database system, such as the required performance and the levels of security.

Review questions

5.1 Describe the main purpose of using fact-finding techniques when developing a database system.

5.2 Describe how fact-finding is used throughout the stages of the database system development lifecycle.

5.3 For each stage of the database system development lifecycle, identify examples of the facts captured and the documentation produced.

5.4 The five most commonly used fact-finding techniques are examining documentation, interviewing, observing the organization in operation, conducting secondary research, and using questionnaires. Describe each fact-finding technique and identify the advantages and disadvantages of each.

5.5 Describe the purpose of defining a mission statement and mission objectives for a database system.

5.6 What is the purpose of identifying the systems boundary for a database system?

5.7 How do the contents of a user's requirements specification differ from a systems specification?

5.8 Describe one approach to deciding whether to use centralized, view integration, or a combination of both when developing a database system for multiple user views.

5.9 Discuss the purpose of use case diagrams and descriptions.

5.10 Discuss how the system specification differs from the users' specification.

Exercise

5.11 Read the the *PerfectPets* case study described in Appendix B and undertake the following tasks.

(a) Create a mission statement and mission objectives.
(b) Define the systems boundary.
(c) Identify user views.
(d) Create use case diagrams and descriptions for the user views.
(e) Create a data dictionary.

CHAPTER

6

Entity–relationship modeling

Preview

In Chapter 5, you learned about the techniques for gathering and capturing information about what the users require of a database system. Once the requirements collection and analysis stage of the database system development lifecycle (described in Chapter 4) is complete and the requirements for the database system are documented, we are now ready to begin database design.

One of the most difficult aspects of database design is the fact that designers, programmers, and end-users tend to view data and its use in different ways. Unfortunately, unless there is a common understanding that reflects how the organization operates, the design produced will fail to meet the users' requirements. To ensure that we get a precise understanding of the nature of the data and how the organization uses it, we need to have a model for communication that is non-technical and free of ambiguities. The entity–relationship (ER) model is one such example. Since the introduction of ER modeling in 1976, the model has been extended to include additional enhanced modeling concepts. We cover the basic ER concepts in this chapter and introduce some of the more useful enhanced ER concepts in Chapter 7.

Entity–relationship modeling is a top-down approach to database design. We begin ER modeling by identifying the important data (called entities) and relationships between the data that must be represented in the model. We then add more details such as the information we want to hold about the entities and relationships (called attributes) and any constraints on the entities, relationships, and attributes.

The basic concepts that make up an ER model are introduced throughout this chapter. Although there is general agreement about what each concept means, there are a number of different ways that we can represent each concept in a diagram. The diagrammatic notation used throughout this book is the increasingly popular object-oriented modeling language called **UML (Unified Modeling Language)**. However, examples of alternative popular notations for ER models are shown in Appendix C.

Key point UML is the successor to a number of object-oriented analysis and design methods introduced in the 1980s and 1990s and is the standard modeling language.

Key point As the ER model forms the basis of the methodology presented in this book, it is important that the concepts covered in this book are well understood. If you do not understand the concepts immediately, try reading the chapter again, then look at the examples we give in the methodology for additional help.

Throughout this chapter we use examples taken from the *StayHome Online Rentals* case study described in Section 5.4. However, on occasion it is necessary to use examples not included in the case study to allow discussion on a particular topic. We start by introducing the main concepts associated with ER modeling: entities, relationships, and attributes.

Learning objectives

In this chapter you will learn:

- How to use ER modeling in database design.
- The basic concepts of an ER model called entities, relationships, and attributes.
- A diagrammatic technique for displaying an ER model using UML.
- How to identify and solve problems in an ER model called connection traps.

6.1 Entities

Entity

A set of objects with the same properties, which is identified by a user or organization as having an independent existence.

The basic concept of the ER model is an **entity**, which represents a set of objects in the 'real world' that share the same properties. Each **object**, which should be uniquely identifiable within the set, is called an **entity occurrence**. An entity has an independent existence and can represent objects with a physical (or 'real') existence or objects with a conceptual (or 'abstract') existence, as shown in Figure 6.1.

Physical existence	Conceptual existence
Member	MembershipType
DistributionCenter	Wish

Figure 6.1 Examples of entities with physical and conceptual existence

We identify each entity by a unique name and a list of properties, called **attributes**. Although an entity has a distinct set of attributes, each entity has its own values for each attribute. A database normally contains many different entities. Attributes are discussed in Section 6.3.

Diagrammatic representation of entities

Each entity is shown as a rectangle labeled with the name of the entity, which is normally a singular noun. In UML, the first letter of each word in the entity name is uppercase (for example, `Member` and `DistributionCenter`). Figure 6.2 demonstrates the diagrammatic representation of the `Member`, `Wish`, and `DVD` entities.

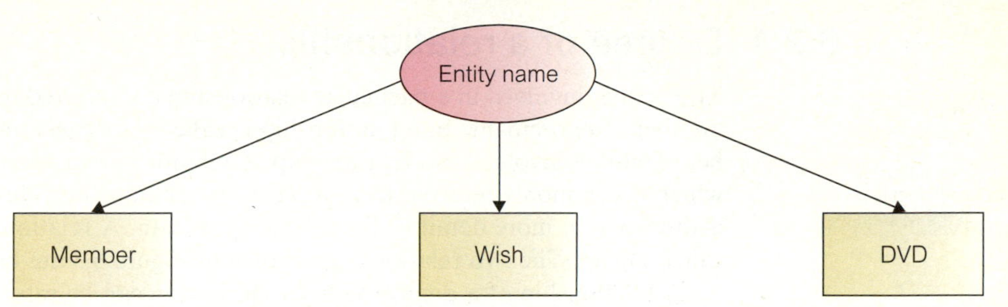

Figure 6.2 Diagrammatic representation of the `Member`, `Wish`, and `DVD` entities

6.2 Relationships

Relationship

A set of meaningful associations among entities.

A **relationship** is a set of associations between participating entities. As with entities, each association should be uniquely identifiable within the set. A uniquely identifiable association is called a **relationship occurrence**.

Each relationship is given a name that describes its function. For example, the `Member` entity is associated with the `Wish` entity through a relationship called *`Makes`*.

Diagrammatic representation of relationships

Each relationship is shown as a line connecting the associated entities, labeled with the name of the relationship. Normally, a relationship is named using a verb (for example, *`Selects`* or *`Makes`*) or a short phrase including a verb (for example, *`AppearsIn`*). Again, the first letter of each word in the relationship name is shown in uppercase. Whenever possible, a relationship name should be unique for a given ER model.

A relationship is only labeled in one direction, which usually means that the name of the relationship only makes sense in one direction (for example, `Member` *`Makes`* `Wish` makes sense but not `Wish` *`Makes`* `Member`). So once the relationship name is chosen, an arrow symbol is placed beside the name indicating the correct direction for a reader to interpret the relationship name (for example, `Member` *`Makes`* ▶ `Wish`). Figure 6.3 demonstrates the diagrammatic representation of the relationships `Member` *`Makes`* `Wish` and `DVD` *`AppearsIn`* `Wish`.

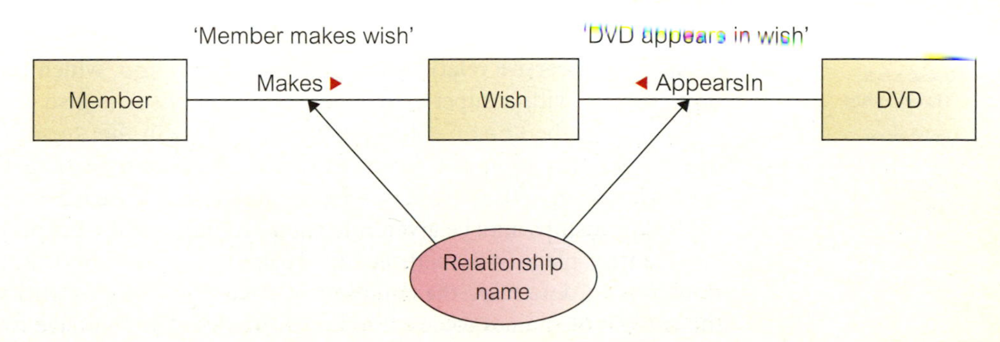

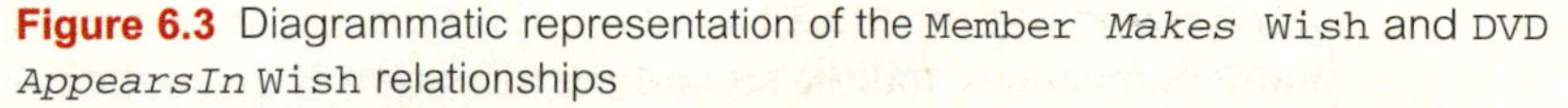
Figure 6.3 Diagrammatic representation of the `Member` *`Makes`* `Wish` and `DVD` *`AppearsIn`* `Wish` relationships

6.2.1 Degree of a relationship

Degree of a relationship

The number of participating entities in the relationship.

The entities involved in a particular relationship are referred to as participants. The number of participants in a relationship is called the **degree** and indicates the number of entities involved in a relationship. A relationship of degree one is called **unary**, which is commonly referred to as a *recursive* relationship. This type of relationship is discussed in more detail in the following section. A relationship of degree two is called **binary**. The two relationships shown in Figure 6.3 are binary relationships.

A relationship of a degree higher than binary can be referred to using the general term **complex relationship**. However, there are also specific names for complex relationships according to the number of entities involved. For example, a relationship of degree three is also called **ternary**. An example of a ternary relationship is *Complains* with three participating entities, namely DVDCopy, Staff, and Member, as shown in Figure 6.4. The purpose of this relationship is to represent the situation where a member complains about a copy of a DVD, which is dealt with by a member of staff.

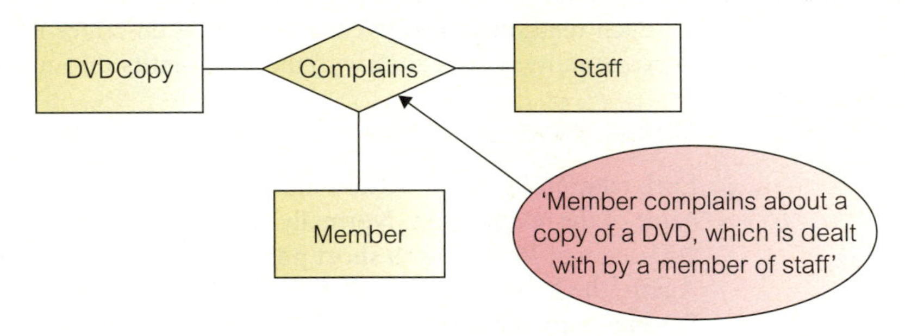

Figure 6.4 Example of a ternary relationship called *Complains*

A relationship of degree four is called quaternary, and a relationship of a higher degree is called *n*-ary. The most popular type of relationship is binary, but occasionally we will identify recursive or ternary, and less frequently quaternary.

6.2.2 Recursive relationships

Recursive relationship

A relationship where the *same* entity participates more than once in *different* roles.

Consider a **recursive relationship** called *Supervises*, which represents an association of staff with a supervisor where the supervisor is also a member of staff. In other words, the Staff entity participates twice in the *Supervises* relationship; the first participation as a supervisor, and the second participation as a member of staff who is supervised (supervisee), as shown in Figure 6.5.

Relationships may be given *role names* to indicate the purpose that each participating entity plays in a relationship. Role names are important for recursive relationships to determine the function of each participating entity. Figure 6.5 shows the use of role names to describe the *Supervises* recursive relationship. The first participation of the Staff entity in the *Supervises* relationship is given the role name Supervisor and the second participation is given the role name Supervisee.

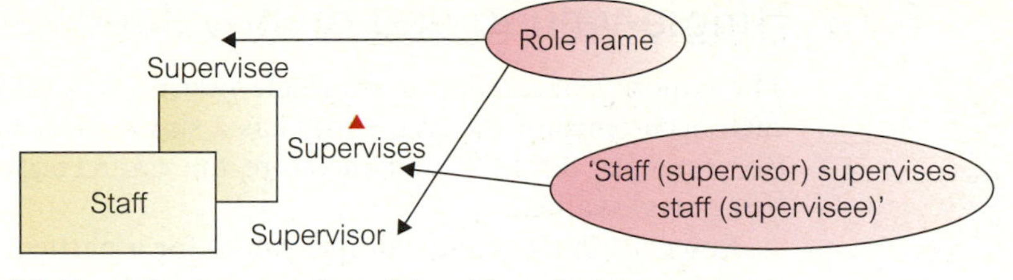

Figure 6.5 Example of a recursive relationship called *Supervises*

> **Note** The *StayHome Online Rental* case study described in Section 5.4 has no example of a recursive relationship.

6.3 Attributes

> **Attribute**
> A property of an entity or a relationship.

The particular properties of entities are called attributes. Attributes represent what we want to know about entities. For example, a DVD entity may be described by the catalogNo, title, genre, and rating attributes. These attributes hold values that describe each DVD occurrence, and represent the main source of data stored in the database.

> **Note** A relationship between entities can also have attributes similar to those of an entity, but we defer the discussion of such attributes until Section 6.6.

As we now discuss, we can classify attributes as being simple or composite, single-valued or multi-valued, or derived.

6.3.1 Simple and composite attributes

> **Simple attribute**
> An attribute composed of a single component.

> **Composite attribute**
> An attribute composed of multiple components.

Simple attributes cannot be further subdivided. Examples of simple attributes include the genre and rating attributes of the DVD entity. Simple attributes are sometimes called *atomic attributes.*

Composite attributes can be further divided to yield smaller components with an independent existence. For example, the name attribute of the Member entity with the value 'Don Nelson' can be subdivided into mFName ('Don') and mLName ('Nelson').

> **Key point** The decision to model the name attribute as a simple attribute or to subdivide the attribute into mFName and mLName is dependent on whether the users' transactions access the name attribute as a single component or as individual components.

6.3.2 Single-valued and multi-valued attributes

Single-valued attribute

An attribute that holds a single value for an entity occurrence.

Multi-valued attribute

An attribute that holds multiple values for an entity occurrence.

The majority of attributes are **single-valued** for a particular entity. For example, each occurrence of the DVD entity has a single value for the catalogNo attribute (for example, 207132), and therefore the catalogNo attribute is referred to as being single-valued.

Some attributes have multiple values for a particular entity. For example, each occurrence of the DVD entity may have multiple values for the genre attribute (for example, 'Children' and 'Comedy') and therefore the genre attribute in this case would be multi-valued. A **multi-valued attribute** may have a set of values with specified lower and upper limits. For example, the genre attribute may have between one and three values.

Key point The classification of simple and composite, and the classification of single-valued and multi-valued, are not mutually exclusive. In other words, we can have simple single-valued, composite single-valued, simple multi-valued, and composite multi-valued attributes.

6.3.3 Derived attributes

Derived attribute

An attribute that represents a value that is derivable from the value of a related attribute, or set of attributes, not necessarily in the same entity.

Some attributes may be related for a particular entity. For example, the age of a member (age) is derivable from the date of birth (DOB) attribute, and therefore the age and DOB attributes are related. We refer to the age attribute as a **derived attribute**, the value of which is derived from the DOB attribute.

Key point Age is not normally stored in a database because it would have to be updated regularly. On the other hand, as a date of birth never changes and age can be derived from date of birth, date of birth is stored instead, and age is derived from the DOB attribute when needed.

In some cases, the value of an attribute is derived from the values in a single entity, like age. But in other cases, the value of an attribute may be derived from the values in more than one entity.

6.3.4 Keys

Superkey

An attribute, or set of attributes, that uniquely identifies each entity occurrence.

In Section 2.3.3, we introduced the concept of keys associated with tables (relations). These concepts also apply to entities.

For example, dCenterNo (the distribution center number) and dZipCode (the distribution center's zip code) are **candidate keys** for the DistributionCenter entity, as each has a distinct value for every distribution center occurrence. If we

Candidate key

A superkey that contains only the minimum number of attributes necessary for unique identification of each entity occurrence.

Primary key

The candidate key that is selected to identify each entity occurrence.

Alternate keys

The candidate key(s) that are not selected as the primary key of the entity.

choose `dCenterNo` as the **primary key** for the `DistributionCenter` entity, then `dZipCode` becomes an **alternate key**.

Diagrammatic representation of attributes

If an entity is to be displayed with its attributes, we divide the rectangle representing the entity in two. The upper part of the rectangle displays the name of the entity and the lower part lists the names of the attributes. For example, Figure 6.6 shows the ER model for the `Member`, `Wish`, and `DVD` entities and their associated attributes.

The first attribute(s) to be listed is the primary key for the entity, if known. The name(s) of the primary key attribute(s) can be labeled with the tag {PK}. In UML, the name of an attribute is displayed with the first letter in lowercase and, if the name has more than one word, with the first letter of each subsequent word in uppercase (for example, `memberNo`, `catalogNo`, `rating`). Additional tags that can be used include partial primary key {PPK}, when an attribute only forms part of a composite primary key, and alternate key {AK}.

For simple, single-valued attributes, there is no need to use tags and so we simply display the attribute names in a list below the entity name.

For composite attributes, we list the name of the composite attribute followed below and indented to the right by the names of its simple component parts. For example, in Figure 6.6 the composite attribute `name` is shown followed below by the `names` of its component attributes, `mFName` and `mLName`.

For multi-valued attributes, we label the attribute name with an indication of the range of values available for the attribute. For example, if we label the `genre` attribute with the range [1..*]; this means that there are one or more values for the `genre` attribute. If we know the precise maximum number of values, we can label

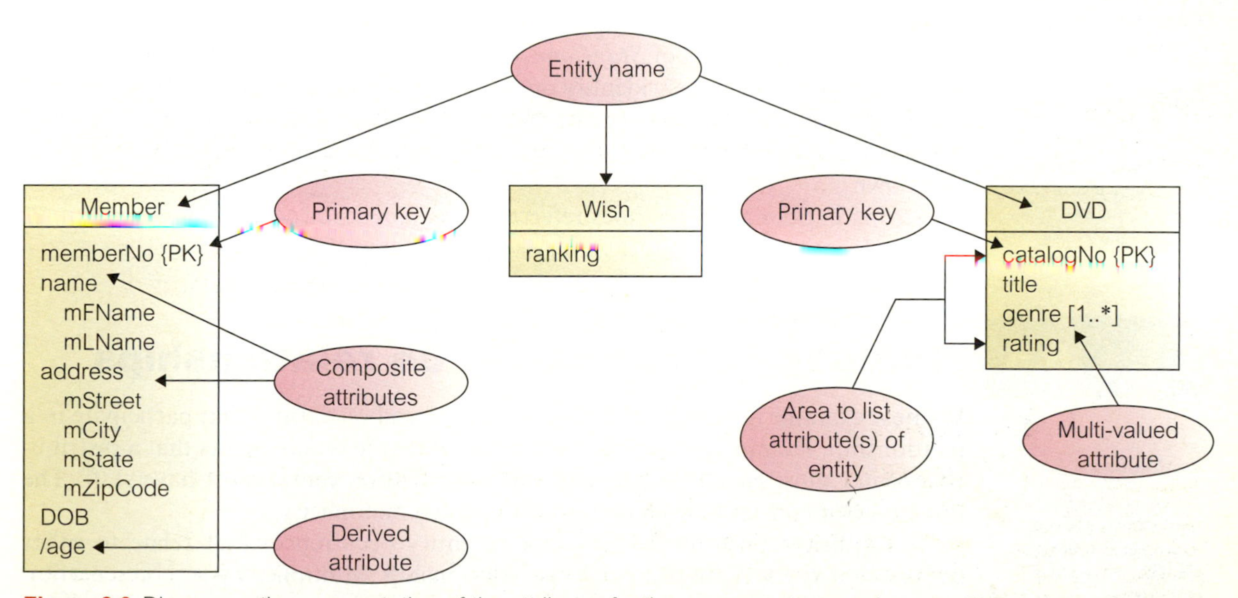

Figure 6.6 Diagrammatic representation of the attributes for the `Member`, `Wish`, and `DVD` entities

the attribute with an exact range. For example, if the `genre` attribute holds one to a maximum of three values, we could label the attribute with [1..3]. However, as the maximum value is not set, the `genre` attribute is labelled with [1..*]. For derived attributes, we prefix the attribute name with a '/'. For example, the derived attribute `age` is shown in Figure 6.6 as /`age`.

For a simple database, it is possible to show all the attributes for each entity on the data model. However, for a more complex database we normally display just the attribute, or attributes, that form the primary key of each entity. When only the primary key attributes are shown in the ER model, we can omit the {PK} tag.

Note In the *StayHome Online Rental* case study in Section 5.4, the `genre` attribute is described as being single-valued and the `Member` entity has no `DOB` or derived `age` attributes.

Figure 6.6 shows that no primary key has been identified for the `Wish` entity. The presence or absence of a primary key allows us to identify whether an entity is weak or strong. We discuss the concept of strong and weak entities in the following section.

6.4 Strong and weak entities

Strong entity

Entity that is *not* dependent on the existence of another entity for its primary key.

Weak entity

Entity that is partially or wholly dependent on the existence of another entity, or entities, for its primary key.

Entities can be classified as being either strong or weak. For example, as we can distinguish one member from all other members and one DVD from all other DVDs without the existence of any other entity, `Member` and `DVD` are referred to as being **strong entities**. In other words, the `Member` and `DVD` entities are strong because they have their own primary keys, as shown in Figure 6.6.

Figure 6.6 also has an example of a **weak entity** called `Wish`, which represents wishes made by members of *StayHome Online Rentals* to rent out particular DVDs. If we are unable to uniquely identify one `Wish` entity occurrence from another without the existence of the `Member` and `DVD` entities, then `Wish` is referred to as being a weak entity. In other words, the `Wish` entity is weak because it has no primary key of its own.

Strong entities are sometimes referred to as *parent, owner*, or *dominant entities* and weak entities as *child, dependent*, or *subordinate entities.*

6.5 Multiplicity constraints on relationships

Multiplicity

The number of occurrences of one entity that may relate to a single occurrence of an associated entity.

We now examine the constraints that may be placed on entities that participate in a relationship. Examples of such constraints include the requirements that a distribution center must have members and each distribution center must have staff. The main type of constraint on relationships is called **multiplicity**.

Multiplicity constrains the number of entity occurrences that relate to other entity occurrences through a particular relationship. Multiplicity is a representation of the policies established by the user or organization, and is referred to as an

integrity constraint. Ensuring that all appropriate integrity constraints are identified and represented is an important part of modeling an organization.

As we mentioned earlier, the most common degree for relationships is binary. The multiplicity for a binary relationship is generally referred to as one-to-one (1:1), one-to-many (1:*), or many-to-many (*:*). We examine these three types of relationships using the following integrity constraints:

- A member of staff manages a distribution center.
- A distribution center has members of staff.
- DVDs star actors.

For each integrity constraint, we demonstrate how to work out the multiplicity if, as is sometimes the case, it is not clearly specified in the constraint, and show how to represent it in an ER model. In Section 6.5.4, we examine multiplicity for relationships of degrees higher than binary.

Key point

Not all integrity constraints are easily and clearly represented in an ER model. For example, the requirement that a member of staff receives an additional day's holiday for every year of employment with the organization may be difficult to represent clearly in an ER model.

6.5.1 One-to-One (1:1) relationships

Consider the relationship called *Manages*, which relates the `Staff` and `DistributionCenter` entities. Figure 6.7(a) displays individual examples of the *Manages* relationship using values for the primary key attributes of the `Staff` and `DistributionCenter` entities.

Working out the multiplicity

Working out the multiplicity normally requires examining the precise relationships between the data given in an integrity constraint using sample data. The sample data may be obtained by examining filled-in forms or reports or, if possible, from further discussions with the users. However, to reach the right conclusions about an integrity constraint, it is essential that the sample data examined or discussed is a true representation of all the data.

In Figure 6.7(a), we see that `staffNo` S1500 manages `dCenterNo` D001 and `staffNo` S0010 manages `dCenterNo` D002, but `staffNo` S0003 does not manage any distribution center. In other words, a member of staff can manage zero or one distribution center and each distribution center is managed by a single member of staff. As there is a maximum of *one* distribution center for each member of staff and a maximum of *one* member of staff for each distribution center involved in the relationship, we refer to this relationship, as *one-to-one*, which we usually abbreviate as (1:1).

Diagrammatic representation of 1:1 relationships

An ER model of the `Staff` *Manages* `DistributionCenter` relationship is shown in Figure 6.7(b). To represent that a member of staff can manage zero or one

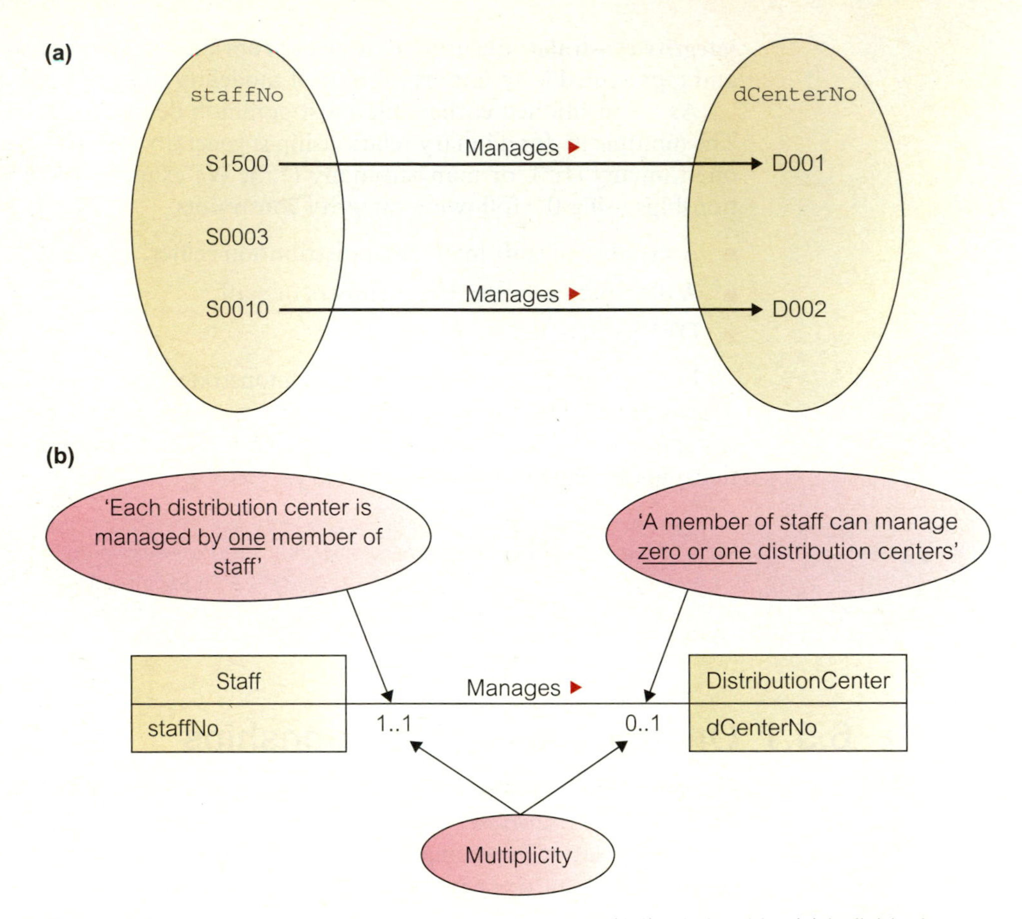

Figure 6.7 `Staff` *`Manages`* `DistributionCenter` (1:1) relationship: (a) individual examples; (b) multiplicity

distribution centers, we place a '0..1' beside the `DistributionCenter` entity. To represent that a distribution center always has one manager, we place a '1..1' beside the `Staff` entity.

6.5.2 One-to-many (1:*) relationships

Consider the relationship called *`Has`*, which also relates the `Distribution-Center` and `Staff` entities. Figure 6.8(a) displays individual examples of the `DistributionCenter` *`Has`* `Staff` relationship using values for the primary key attributes of the `DistributionCenter` and `Staff` entities.

Working out the multiplicity

In Figure 6.8(a), we see that `dCenterNo` D001 has `staffNo` S0003 and S1500, and `dCenterNo` D003 has `staffNo` S0415. Therefore, each distribution center has one or more members of staff and each member of staff works at a single distribution

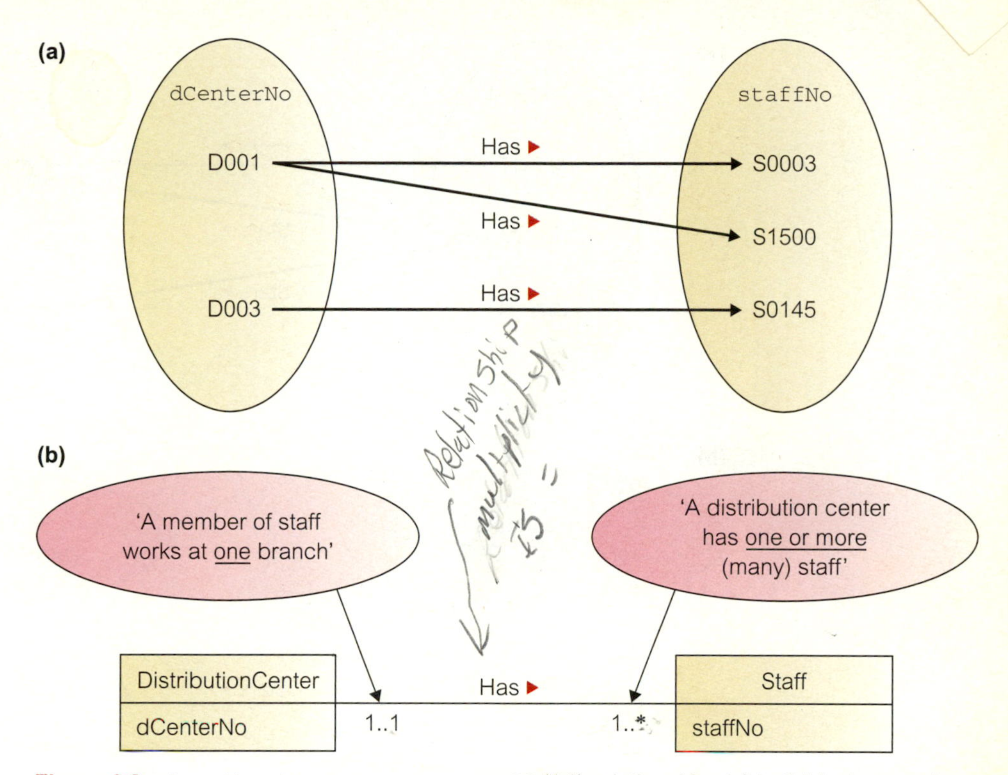

Figure 6.8 `DistributionCenter` *`Has`* `Staff` (1:*) relationship: (a) individual examples; (b) multiplicity

center. As *one* distribution center can have one or more staff, in other words *many* staff, we refer to this type of relationship as *one-to-many*, which we usually abbreviate as (1:*).

Diagramatic representation of 1: relationships*

An ER model of the `DistributionCenter` *`Has`* `Staff` relationship is shown in Figure 6.8(b). To represent that each distribution center can have one or more staff, we place a '1..*' beside the `Staff` entity. To represent that each member of staff works at a single distribution center, we place a '1..1' beside the `DistributionCenter` entity.

> **Key point**
>
> If we know the actual minimum and maximum values for the multiplicity, we can display these instead. For example, if a distribution center has between two and ten staff, we can replace the '1..*' with '2..10.'

6.5.3 Many-to-many (*:*) relationships

Consider the relationship called *`Stars`*, which relates the `DVD` and `Actor` entities. Figure 6.9(a) displays individual examples of the `DVD` *`Stars`* `Actor` relationship using values for the primary key attributes of the `DVD` and `Actor` entities.

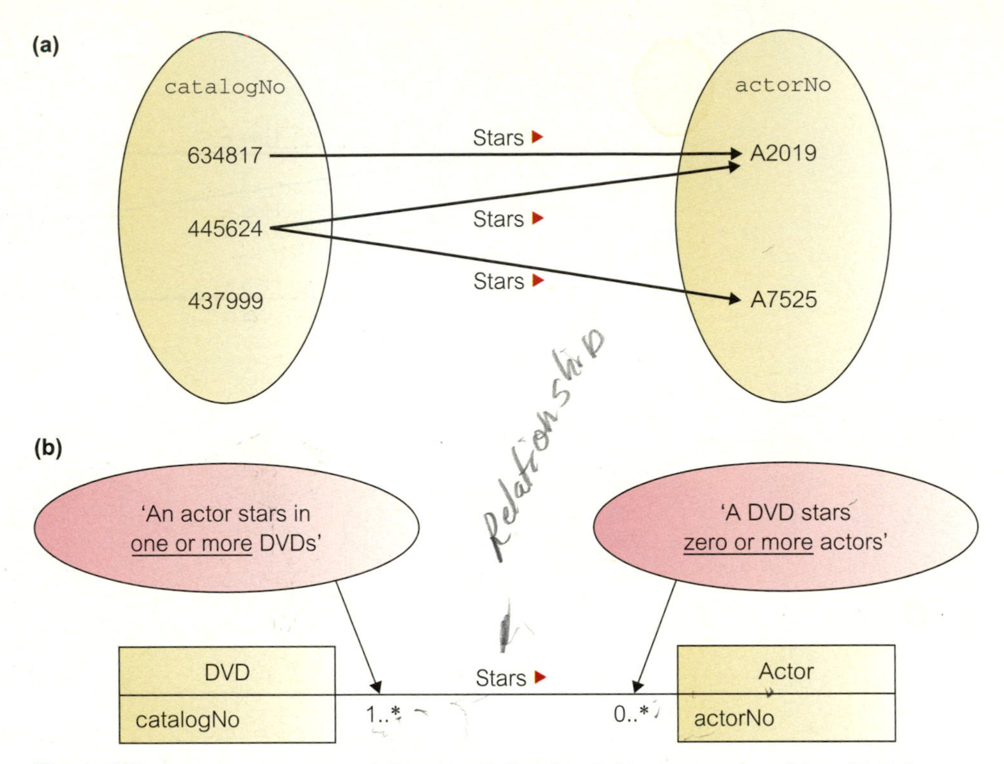

Figure 6.9 DVD *Stars* Actor relationship (*:*): (a) individual examples; (b) multiplicity

Working out the multiplicity

In Figure 6.9(a), we see that actorNo A2019 stars in DVD catalogNo 634817 and 445624, and actorNo A7525 stars in DVD catalogNo 445624. In other words, a single actor can star in one or more DVDs. We also see that DVD catalogNo 445624 has two starring actors but catalogNo 437999 does not have any actors in it, and so we conclude that a single DVD can star zero or more actors.

In summary, the *Stars* relationship is 1:* from the viewpoint of both the Actor and DVD entities. We represent this relationship as two 1:* relationships in both directions, which are collectively referred to as a *many-to-many* relationship, which we usually abbreviate as (*:*).

*Diagrammatic representation of *:* relationships*

An ER model of the DVD *Stars* Actor relationship is shown in Figure 6.9(b). To represent that each actor can star in one or more DVDs, we place a '1..*' beside the DVD entity. To represent that each DVD can star zero or more actors, we place a '0..*' beside the Actor entity.

6.5.4 Multiplicity for complex relationships

Multiplicity for relationships beyond degree two is slightly more complex. For example, the multiplicity for a ternary relationship represents the potential number

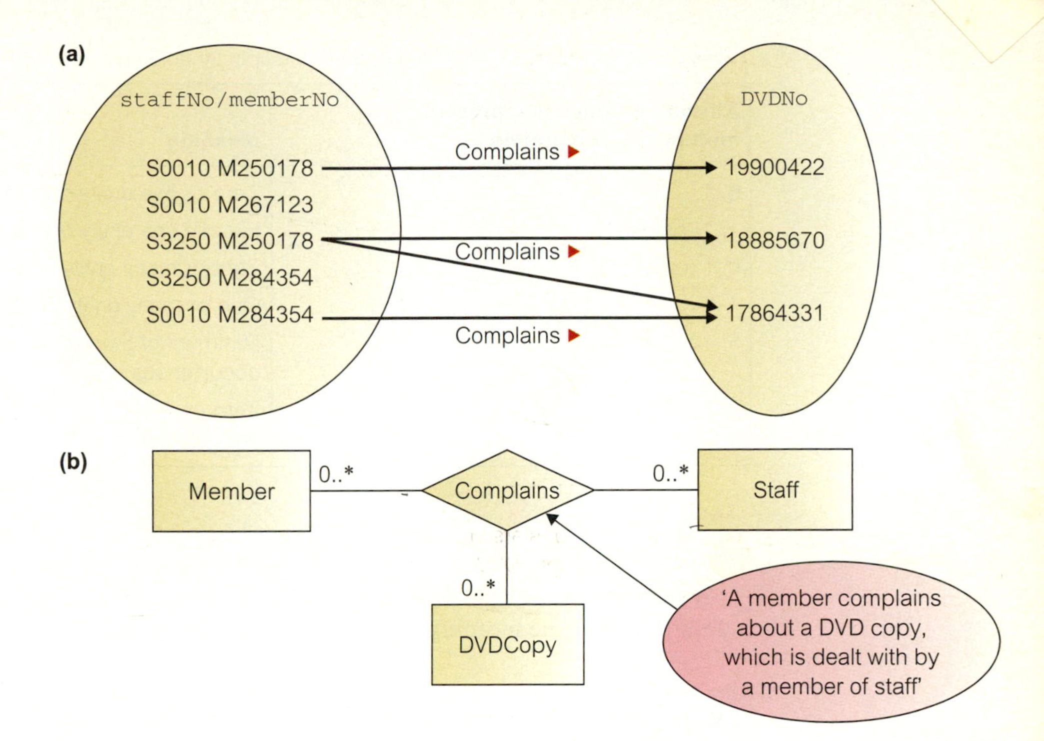

Figure 6.10 The ternary *Complains* relationship from the DVDCopy perspective with the values for Staff and Member fixed: (a) individual examples; (b) multiplicity of relationship

of entity occurrences in the relationship when the other two values are fixed. Consider the ternary *Complains* relationship between Member, DVDCopy, and Staff shown in Figure 6.4. Figure 6.10(a) displays individual examples of the *Complains* relationship when the values for the Staff and Member entities are fixed.

Working out the multiplicity

In Figure 6.10(a), we see that for the sample staffNo/memberNo values there are zero or more DVDNo values. In particular, member (M250178) complains about DVD copy (19900422) and this complaint is dealt with by staffNo S0010 and the same member complains about two other DVD copies (1885670 and 17864331), which are dealt with by another member of staff (S3250). A second member (M284354) complains about DVD copy (17864331) and this complaint was deal with by staff (S0010). The *Complains* relationship represents that a member can make zero or many complaints about one or more DVD copies and that each complaint is deal with by a member of staff, not necessarily the same one.

If we repeat this test from the Staff perspective, we find that the multiplicity for this relationship is 0..*, and if we examine it from the Member perspective, we find it is 0..*. An ER model of the ternary *Complains* relationship showing multiplicity is shown in Figure 6.10(b).

Key point In general, the multiplicity for *n*-ary relationships represents the potential number of entity occurrences in the relationship when the other $(n - 1)$ values are fixed.

Table 6.1 A summary of ways to represent multiplicity constraints

Alternative ways to represent multiplicity constraints	Meaning
0..1	Zero or one entity occurrence
1..1 (or just 1)	Exactly one entity occurrence
0..* (or just *)	Zero or many entity occurrences
1..*	One or many entity occurrences
5..10	Minimum of 5 up to a maximum of 10 entity occurrences
0, 3, 6–8	Zero or three or six, seven, or eight entity occurrences

A summary of the possible ways to represent multiplicity constraints along with a description of the meaning for each is shown in Table 6.1.

Note As an exercise, identify the multiplicity for the `Member` *`Makes`* `Wish` and the `DVD` *`AppearsIn`* `Wish` relationships shown in Figure 6.3. The answers to this exercise are shown in Figure 9.12.

6.5.5 Cardinality and participation constraints

Multiplicity actually consists of two separate constraints known as cardinality and participation.

Cardinality

Describes the number of possible relationships for each participating entity.

Participation constraint (ER)

Describes whether all or only some entity occurrences participate in a relationship.

The **cardinality** of a binary relationship is what we have been referring to as one-to-one, one-to-many, and many-to-many. A **participation constraint** represents whether all entity occurrences are involved in a particular relationship (*mandatory participation*) or only some (*optional participation*). In an ER model, cardinality is shown as the *maximum* values and participation is shown as the *minimum* values of the multiplicity ranges on either side of a relationship.

In Figure 6.11, we illustrate the cardinality and participation constraints for the `Staff` *`Manages`* `DistributionCenter` relationship shown in Figure 6.7(b). The maximum values of the multiplicity ranges show that the cardinality is a one-to-oneand the minimum values show that `DistributionCenter` has mandatory and `Staff` has optional participation in the `Manages` relationship.

Participation constraints are used in the logical database design methodology steps to determine:

(a) how to create tables for one-to-one relationships (covered in Step 2.1);

(b) whether a foreign key can have nulls (covered in Step 2.4).

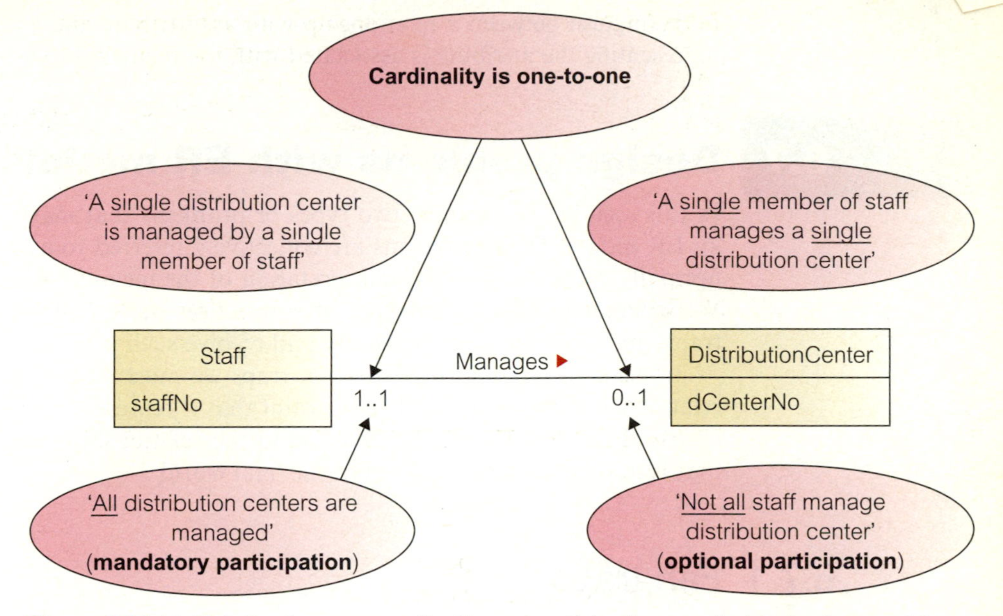

Figure 6.11 Multiplicity shown as cardinality and participation constraints for the `Staff` *`Manages`* `DistributionCenter` (1:1) relationship shown in Figure 6.7(b)

6.6 Attributes on relationships

As briefly mentioned in Section 6.3, attributes can also be assigned to relationships. For example, consider the relationship *`Stars`*, which associates the `DVD` and `Actor` entities. We may wish to record the character played by an actor in a given DVD. This information is associated with the *`Stars`* relationship rather than the `DVD` or `Actor` entities. We create an attribute called `character` to store this information and assign it to the *`Stars`* relationship, as illustrated in Figure 6.12. Note, in this figure the `character` attribute is shown using the symbol for an entity; however,

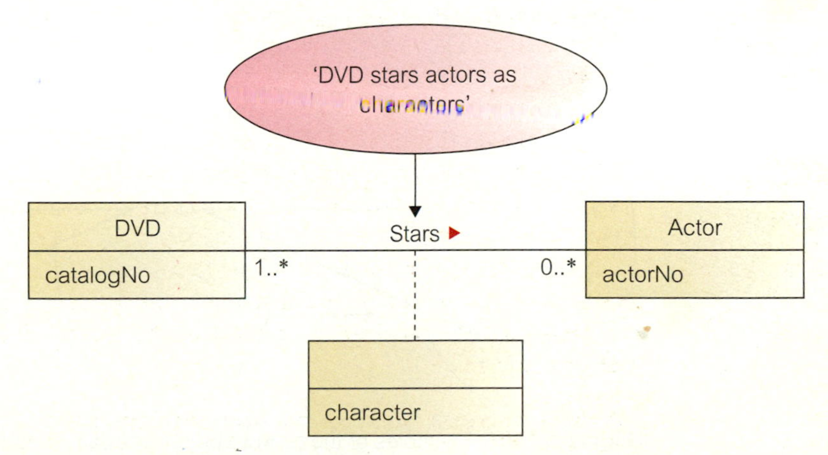

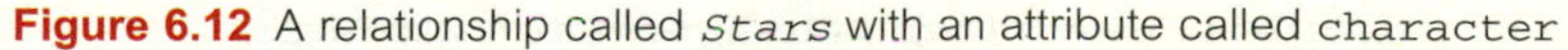

Figure 6.12 A relationship called *`Stars`* with an attribute called `character`

to distinguish between a relationship with an attribute and an entity, the rectangle representing the attribute is associated with the relationship using a dashed line.

6.7 Design problems with ER models

In this section, we examine two types of problems that may arise when designing an ER model. These problems are collectively referred to as *connection traps*, and normally occur due to a misinterpretation of the meaning of certain relationships. We examine the two main types of connection traps, called fan traps and chasm traps, and illustrate how to identify and resolve such problems in ER models.

In general, to identify connection traps we must ensure that the meaning of a relationship (and the integrity constraint that it represents) is fully understood and clearly defined. If we do not understand the relationships we may create a model that is not a true representation of the 'real world.'

6.7.1 Fan traps

Fan trap

Occurs between related entities that are not directly connected and the indirect pathway that connects them includes two 1:* relationships that fan out from a central entity. This means that certain entity occurrences that are related can only be connected using a pathway that can be ambiguous.

A potential **fan trap** is illustrated in Figure 6.13(a), which shows two 1:* relationships (*`Has`* and *`IsAssigned`*) emanating from the same entity called `Distribution-Center`. This model tells us that a single distribution center has many staff and is assigned many cars. However, a problem arises if we want to know which member of staff uses a particular car. To appreciate the problem, examine some examples of the *`Has`* and *`IsAssigned`* relationships, using values for the primary key attributes of the `Staff`, `DistributionCenter`, and `Car` entities, as shown in Figure 6.13(b).

(a)

Staff | ◀ Has | DistributionCenter | IsAssigned ▶ | Car
staffNo | 1..* 1..1 | dCenterNo | 1..1 1..* | vehLicenseNo

Figure 6.13(a) Example of a fan trap

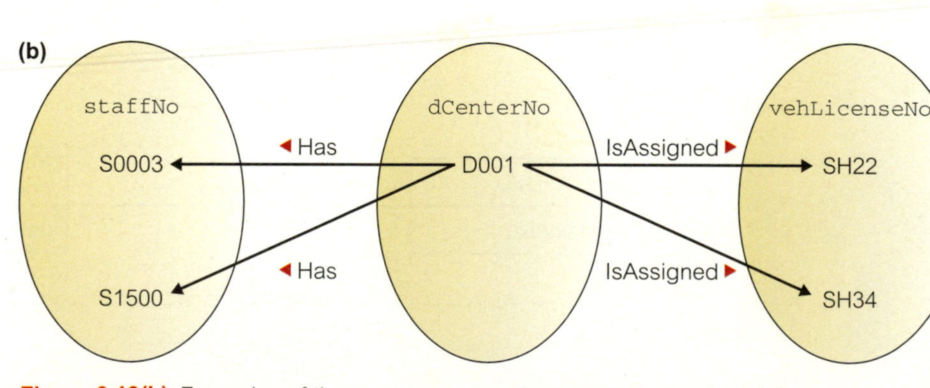

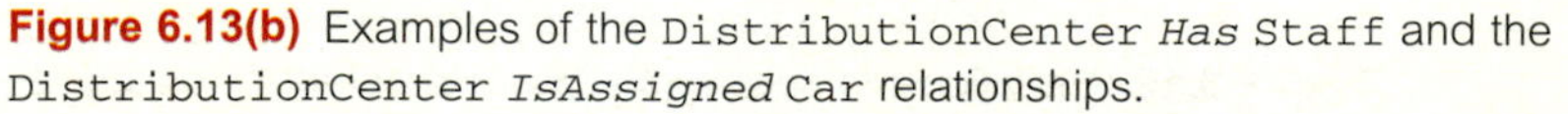
Figure 6.13(b) Examples of the `DistributionCenter` *`Has`* `Staff` and the `DistributionCenter` *`IsAssigned`* `Car` relationships.

If we attempt to answer the question 'Which member of staff uses car SH34?' it is impossible to give a specific answer with the current structure. We can determine only that car SH34 is assigned to distribution center D001 but we cannot tell whether staff S0003 or S1500 uses this car. The inability to answer this question specifically is the result of a fan trap.

We resolve this fan trap by adding a new relationship called `Staff` *`Uses`* `Car` to the original ER model, as shown in Figure 6.13(c). If we now examine the examples of the *`Has`*, *`IsAssigned`*, and *`Uses`* relationships shown in Figure 6.13(d), we can see that staff S1500 uses car SH34.

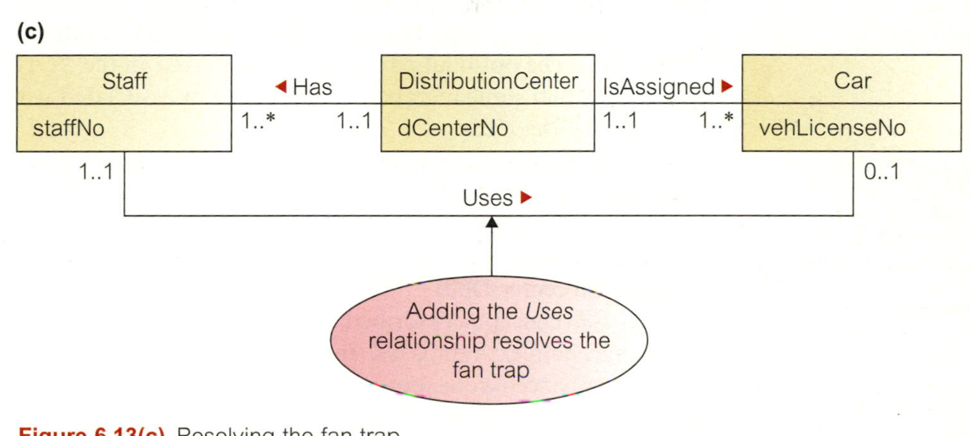

Figure 6.13(c) Resolving the fan trap

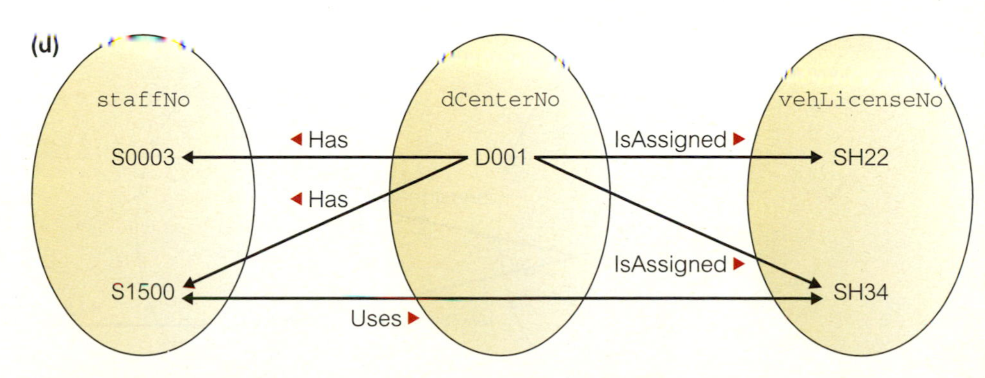

Figure 6.13(d) Examples of the `DistributionCenter` *`Has`* `Staff`, `DistributionCenter` *`IsAssigned`* `Car`, and `Staff` *`Uses`* `Car` relationships.

6.7.2 Chasm traps

Chasm trap

Occurs between related entities that are not directly connected and the indirect pathway that connects them includes partial participation. This means that certain entity occurrences that are related have no means of connection.

A **chasm trap** may occur where there is a relationship with optional participation that forms part of the pathway between entities that are related. A potential chasm trap is illustrated in Figure 6.14(a), which shows the relationships between the `DistributionCenter`, `Car`, and `Staff` entities. This model tells us that a single distribution center is assigned many cars and a member of staff may use one car. In particular, note that not all staff use a car. A problem arises when we want to know at which distribution center a member of staff works? To appreciate the problem, examine some examples of the *`IsAssigned`* and *`Uses`* relationships, using values for the primary key attributes of the `DistributionCenter`, `Car`, and `Staff` entities, as shown in Figure 6.14(b).

If we attempt to answer the question: 'At which distribution center does staff S0003 work?', we cannot tell with the current structure as not all staff use cars. The inability to answer this question is considered to be a loss of information (as we know a member of staff must work at a distribution center) and is the result of a chasm trap. The optional participation of `Staff` in the `Staff` *`Uses`* `Car` relationship means that some members of staff are not associated with a distribution center through the use of cars.

Therefore, to solve this problem and remove the chasm trap, we add a relationship called *`Has`* between the `DistributionCenter` and `Staff` entities, as shown in Figure 6.14(c). If we now examine the examples of the *`Has`*, *`IsAssigned`*, and *`Uses`* relationships shown in Figure 6.14(d), we can see that staff S0003 works at distribution center D001.

The ER concepts described in this chapter sometimes prove inadequate for modeling complex databases. In Chapter 7, we will introduce some of the more popular enhanced concepts associated with ER models that can be useful when modeling more complex data.

(a)

DistributionCenter
dCenterNo
IsAssigned ▶
1..1
1..*
Car
vehLicenseNo
◀ Uses
0..1
1..1
Staff
staffNo

Figure 6.14(a) Example of a chasm trap

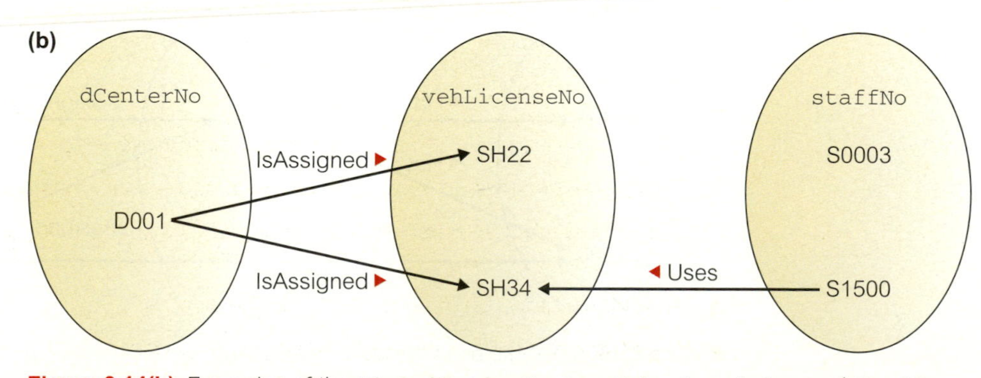

Figure 6.14(b) Examples of the `DistributionCenter` *`IsAssigned`* `Car` and `Staff` *`Uses`* `Car` relationships.

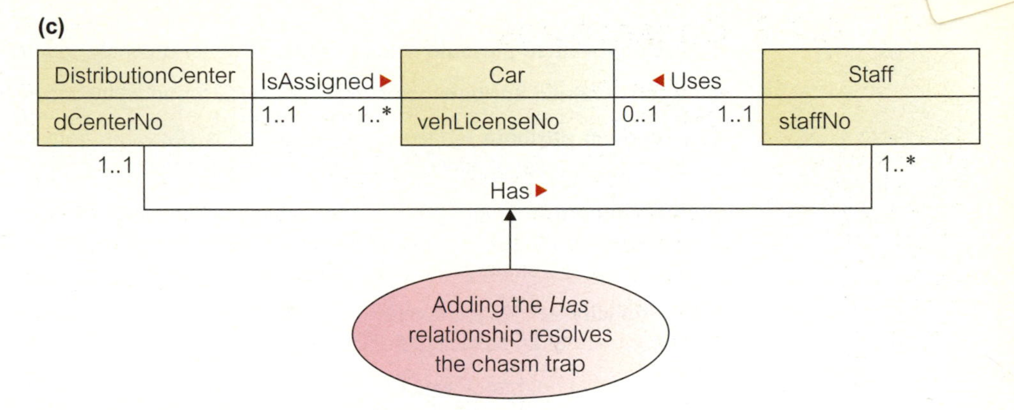

Figure 6.14(c) Resolving the chasm trap

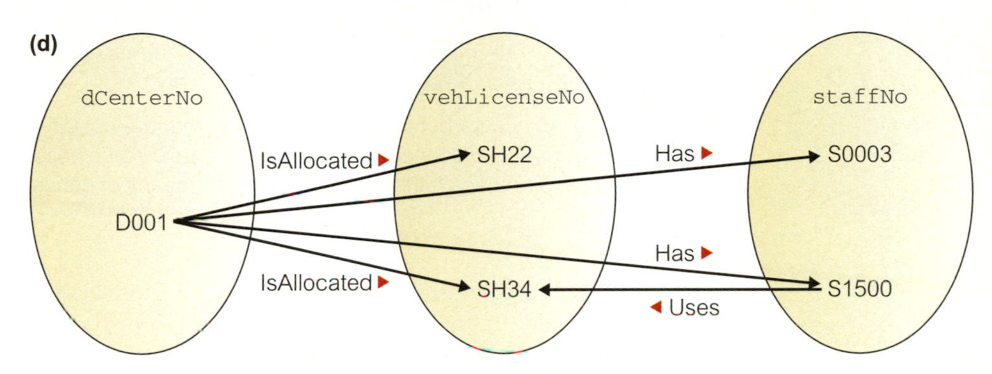

Figure 6.14(d) Examples of the `DistributionCenter` *`Has`* `Staff`, `DistributionCenter` *`IsAssigned`* `Car`, and `Staff` *`Uses`* `Car` relationships.

Chapter summary

- An **entity** is a set of objects with the same properties that are identified by a user or organization as having an independent existence. A uniquely identifiable object is called an **entity occurrence**.
- A **relationship** is a set of meaningful associations among entities. A uniquely identifiable association is called a **relationship occurrence**.
- The **degree** of a relationship is the number of participating entities in a relationship.
- A **recursive relationship** is a relationship where the *same* entity participates more than once in *different* roles.
- An **attribute** is a property of an entity or a relationship.
- A **simple attribute** is composed of a single component.
- A **composite attribute** is composed of multiple components.

- A **single-valued attribute** holds a single value for an entity occurrence.
- A **multi-valued attribute** holds multiple values for an entity occurrence.
- A **derived attribute** represents a value that is derivable from the value of a related attribute, or a set of attributes, not necessarily in the same entity.
- A **strong entity** is *not* dependent on the existence of another entity for its primary key. A **weak entity** is partially or wholly dependent on the existence of another entity, or entities, for its primary key.
- **Multiplicity** defines the number of occurrences of one entity that may relate to a single occurrence of an associated entity.
- Multiplicity consists of two separate constraints – namely **cardinality**, which describes the number of possible relationships for each participating entity, and **participation**, which describes whether all or only some entity occurrences participate in a relationship.
- A **fan trap** occurs between related entities that are not directly connected and the indirect pathway that connects them includes two 1:* relationships that fan out from a central entity. This means that certain entity occurrences that are related can only be connected using a pathway that can be ambiguous.
- A **chasm trap** occurs between related entities that are not directly connected and the indirect pathway that connects them includes partial participation. This means that certain entity occurrences that are related have no means of connection.

Review questions

6.1 Describe what entities represent in an ER model, and provide examples of entities with a physical or conceptual existence.

6.2 Describe what relationships represent in an ER model, and provide examples of unary, binary, ternary, and quaternary relationships.

6.3 Describe what attributes represent in an ER model, and provide examples of simple, composite, single-value, multi-value, and derived attributes.

6.4 Describe what multiplicity represents for a relationship.

6.5 What are integrity constraints and how does multiplicity model these constraints?

6.6 How does multiplicity represent both the cardinality and the participation constraints on a relationship?

6.7 Provide an example of a relationship with attributes.

6.8 Describe how strong and weak entities differ and provide an example of each.

6.9 Describe how fan and chasm traps can occur in an ER model and how they can be resolved. Give examples to illustrate your answers.

Exercises

6.10 Create an ER model for each of the following descriptions:

(a) Each company operates four departments, and each department belongs to one company. Each company has a unique name, and each department has a unique number and name.

(b) Each department in part (a) employs one or more employees, and each employee works for one department. Each employee has a number, name (including first and last name), date of birth, and age.

(c) Each of the employees in part (b) may or may not have one or more dependants, and each dependant belongs to one employee. Each dependant has a name, relationship to employee, and contact telephone numbers up to a maximum of three.

(d) Each employee in part (c) may or may not have an employment history. Each employment history has the name of the organization that the employee worked for and in what capacity, the start date and finish date for each employment.

(e) Represent all the ER models described in (a), (b), (c), and (d) as a single ER model. Provide any assumptions necessary to support your model.

The final answer to this exercise is shown as Figure 7.5 of Exercise 7.8.

6.11 Create an ER model for each of the following descriptions:

(a) A large organization has several car parks, which are used by staff.

(b) Each car park has a unique name, location, capacity, and number of floors (where appropriate).

(c) Each car park has car parking spaces, which are uniquely identified using a space number.

(d) Members of staff can request the use of a car parking space. Each member of staff has a unique number, name, telephone extension number, and vehicle license number.

(e) Represent all the ER models described in (a), (b), (c), and (d) as a single ER model. Provide any assumptions necessary to support your model.

The final answer to this exercise is shown as Figure 7.6 of Exercise 7.9.

6.12 Create an ER model for each of the following descriptions:

(a) A sailing club has members. Each member has a unique member number, name, date of birth, and gender.

(b) Most members own at least one dinghy. However, a dinghy can be owned by more than one member. Each dinghy has a boat name, sail number, and boat class (such as Topper, Mirror, Contender). (Hint: The sail number uniquely identifies each boat in the same class.)

(c) The sailing club offers a range of membership types including adult, child, and a non-sailing social membership. Each membership type has an annual subscription rate, which runs for a year from 1st March. The date that each member pays his or her annual membership is recorded.

(d) The sailing club also owns dinghies, which can be borrowed by members for a daily fee.

(e) Represent the ER models described in (a), (b), (c), and (d) as a single ER model. Provide any assumptions necessary to support your model.

CHAPTER

7 Enhanced ER modeling

Preview

We covered the basic concepts associated with entity–relationship (ER) modeling in Chapter 6. These basic concepts are often perfectly adequate for the representation of the data requirements for many different database systems. However, the basic ER concepts can be limiting for more complex database systems that require modeling with either a large amount of data and/or data with complex interrelationships. This stimulated the need to develop additional 'semantic' modeling concepts. The original ER model with additional semantic concepts is referred to as the **enhanced entity–relationship (EER)** model. In this chapter, we describe some of the more useful concepts associated with the EER model called specialization/generalization and show how these concepts can be applied.

The database design methodology presented in Appendix D provides an option to use the enhanced concepts of the EER model in Step 1.6. The choice of whether to include this step is largely dependent on whether the designer considers that using these enhanced modeling concepts facilitates or hinders the process of database design.

Throughout this chapter we use, adapt, and or extend examples taken from the *StayHome Online Rentals* case study described in Section 5.4. We also use examples not included in this case study to allow discussion on a particular topic.

Learning objectives

In this chapter you will learn:

- The limitations of the basic ER modeling concepts and the requirements to model more complex applications using enhanced data modeling concepts.
- The main concepts associated with the enhanced entity–relationship (EER) model called specialization/generalization.
- A notation for displaying specialization/generalization in an EER diagram using UML.

7.1 Specialization/generalization

The concept of specialization/generalization is associated with special types of entities known as superclasses and subclasses, and the process of **attribute inheritance**. We begin this section by defining what superclasses and subclasses are and by examining superclass/subclass relationships. We describe the process of attribute inheritance and contrast the process of specialization with generalization. We also show how to represent specialization/generalization in a diagram using the UML (Unified Modeling Language) notation.

7.1.1 Superclasses and subclasses

Superclass

An entity that includes one or more distinct groupings of its occurrences, which require to be represented in a data model.

A general entity called a **superclass** includes groupings of more specific kinds of entities called **subclasses**. For example, an entity that may have many distinct subclasses is `Staff`. The entities that are members of the `Staff` entity may be classified as `Manager` and `Assistant`. In other words, the `Staff` entity is the superclass of the `Manager` and `Assistant` subclasses.

7.1.2 Superclass/subclass relationships

Subclass

A distinct grouping of occurrences of an entity, which require to be represented in a data model.

The relationship between a superclass and any one of its subclasses is one-to-one (1:1) and is called a superclass/subclass relationship. For example, `Staff/Manager` forms a superclass/subclass relationship. Each member of a subclass is also a member of the superclass but has a distinct role.

Superclasses and subclasses can be used to avoid describing different types of entities with possibly different attributes within a single entity. For example, `Manager` may have special attributes such as `mgrStartDate` and `bonus`, and so on. If all staff attributes and those specific to particular jobs are represented by a single `Staff` entity, this may result in a lot of nulls for the job specific attributes. Clearly, managers have common attributes with other staff, such as `staffNo`, `name`, `position`, and `salary`, but it is the unshared attributes that cause problems when trying to represent all members of staff within a single entity. Defining superclasses/subclasses can also show relationships that are associated only with particular subclasses of staff and not with staff in general. For example, managers may have distinct relationships that are not appropriate for all staff, such as `Manager` *`Requires`* `Car`.

To illustrate some of the points being made above, consider the table called `AllStaff` in Figure 7.1. The table holds the details of all members of staff no matter what position they hold. A consequence of holding the details of all members of staff in one table is that while the columns appropriate to all staff are filled (namely, `staffNo`, `name`, `position`, `salary`, and `dCenterNo`), those that are only applicable to particular job roles will be only partially filled. (Note that a column called `eMail`, which is associated with all staff of the *StayHome Online Rental* case study is not included in this example.) For example, the columns associated with the `Manager` subclass (namely `mgrStartDate` and `bonus`) have no values for those members of staff holding the position of Assistant.

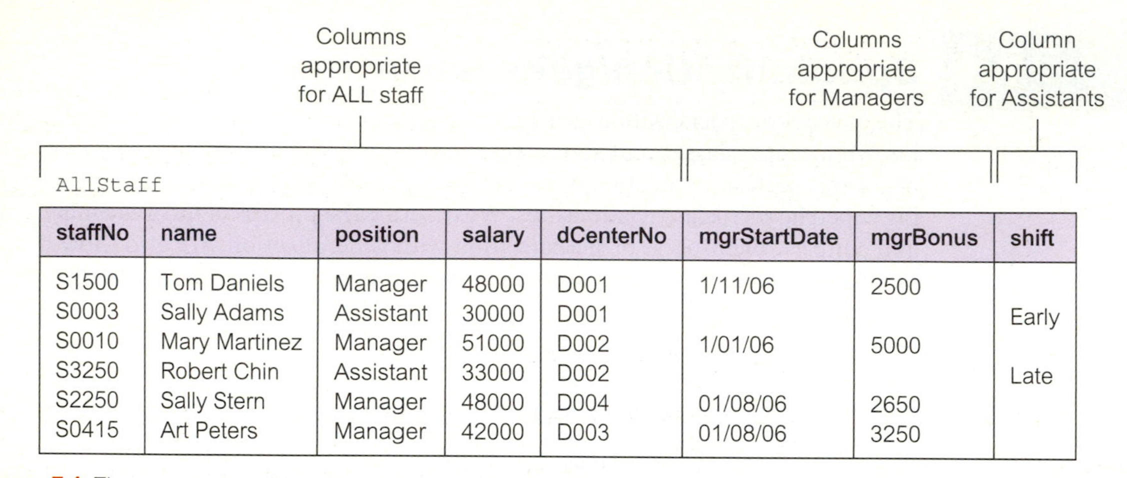

staffNo	name	position	salary	dCenterNo	mgrStartDate	mgrBonus	shift
S1500	Tom Daniels	Manager	48000	D001	1/11/06	2500	
S0003	Sally Adams	Assistant	30000	D001			Early
S0010	Mary Martinez	Manager	51000	D002	1/01/06	5000	
S3250	Robert Chin	Assistant	33000	D002			Late
S2250	Sally Stern	Manager	48000	D004	01/08/06	2650	
S0415	Art Peters	Manager	42000	D003	01/08/06	3250	

Figure 7.1 The `AllStaff` table holding details of all members of staff

> **Note** There are two important reasons for introducing the concepts of superclasses and subclasses into an ER model. The first reason is that it avoids describing similar concepts more than once, thereby saving time and making the ER model more readable. The second reason is that it adds more semantic information to the design in a form that is familiar to many people. For example, the assertions that 'Manager IS-A member of staff' and 'van IS-A type of vehicle' communicate significant semantic content in an easy-to-follow form.

7.1.3 Attribute inheritance

As mentioned above, an entity occurrence in a subclass represents the same 'real world' object as in the superclass. Hence, a member of a subclass inherits those attributes associated with the superclass, but may also have subclass-specific attributes. For example, a member of the `Manager` subclass has subclass-specific attributes, `mgrStartDate`, and `bonus`, and all the attributes of the `Staff` superclass, namely `staffNo`, `name`, `position`, `salary`, and `dCenterNo`.

A subclass is an entity in its own right and so it may also have one or more subclasses. A subclass with more than one superclass is called a *shared subclass*. In other words, a member of a shared subclass must be a member of the associated superclasses. As a consequence, the attributes of the superclasses are inherited by the shared subclass, which may also have its own additional attributes. This process is referred to as *multiple inheritance*.

> **Note** An entity and its subclasses and their subclasses, and so on, is called a **type hierarchy**. Type hierarchies are known by a variety of names including **specialization hierarchy** (for example, `Manager` is a specialization of `Staff`), **generalization hierarchy** (for example, `Staff` is a generalization of `Manager`), and **IS-A hierarchy** (for example, `Manager` IS-A [member of] `Staff`). We describe the process of specialization and generalization in the following sections.

7.1.4 Specialization process

Specialization

The process of maximizing the differences between members of an entity by identifying their distinguishing characteristics.

Specialization is a top-down approach to defining a set of superclasses and their related subclasses. The set of subclasses is defined on the basis of some distinguishing characteristics of the entities in the superclass. When we identify a subclass of an entity, we then associate attributes specific to the subclass (where necessary), and also identify any relationships between the subclass and other entities or subclasses (where necessary).

7.1.5 Generalization process

Generalization

The process of minimizing the differences between entities by identifying their common features.

The process of **generalization** is a bottom-up approach, which results in the identification of a generalized superclass from the original subclasses. The process of generalization can be viewed as the reverse of the specialization process. For example, consider a model where `Manager` and `Assistant` are represented as distinct entities. If we apply the process of generalization on these entities, we attempt to identify any similarities between them such as common attributes and relationships. As stated earlier, these entities share attributes common to all staff, and therefore we would identify `Manager` and `Assistant` as subclasses of a generalized `Staff` superclass.

Diagrammatic representation

UML has a special notation for representing subclasses and superclasses. For example, consider the specialization/generalization of the `Staff` entity into subclasses that represent job roles. The `Staff` superclass and the `Manager` and `Assistant` subclasses can be represented in the EER diagram illustrated in Figure 7.2. Note that the `Staff` superclass and the subclasses, being entities, are represented as rectangles. Specialization/generalization subclasses are attached by lines to a triangle that points towards the superclass. The label below the triangle, shown as {Optional, And}, describes the constraints on the specialization/generalization relationship. These constraints are discussed in more detail in the following section.

Attributes that are specific to a given subclass are listed in the lower section of the rectangle representing that subclass. For example, the `mgrStartDate` and `bonus` attributes are associated only with the `Manager` subclass, and are not applicable to the `Assistant` subclass. Similarly, we also show the attribute specific to the `Assistant` subclass, namely `shift`.

Figure 7.2 also shows relationships that are applicable to specific subclasses or to just the superclass. For example, the `Manager` subclass is related to the `DistributionCenter` entity through the *Manages* relationship, whereas the `Staff` entity is related to the `DistributionCenter` entity through the *Has* relationship.

Note The multiplicity of `Manager` in the *Manages* relationship is 1..1, whereas previously, in Figure 6.7, the multiplicity of `Staff` in the *p* relationship was 0..1 (in other words, `Manager` has mandatory participation whereas `Staff` had optional participation).

In Figure 7.3, the `Staff` specialization/generalization has been expanded to show a shared subclass called `AssistantManager` and the `Assistant` subclass

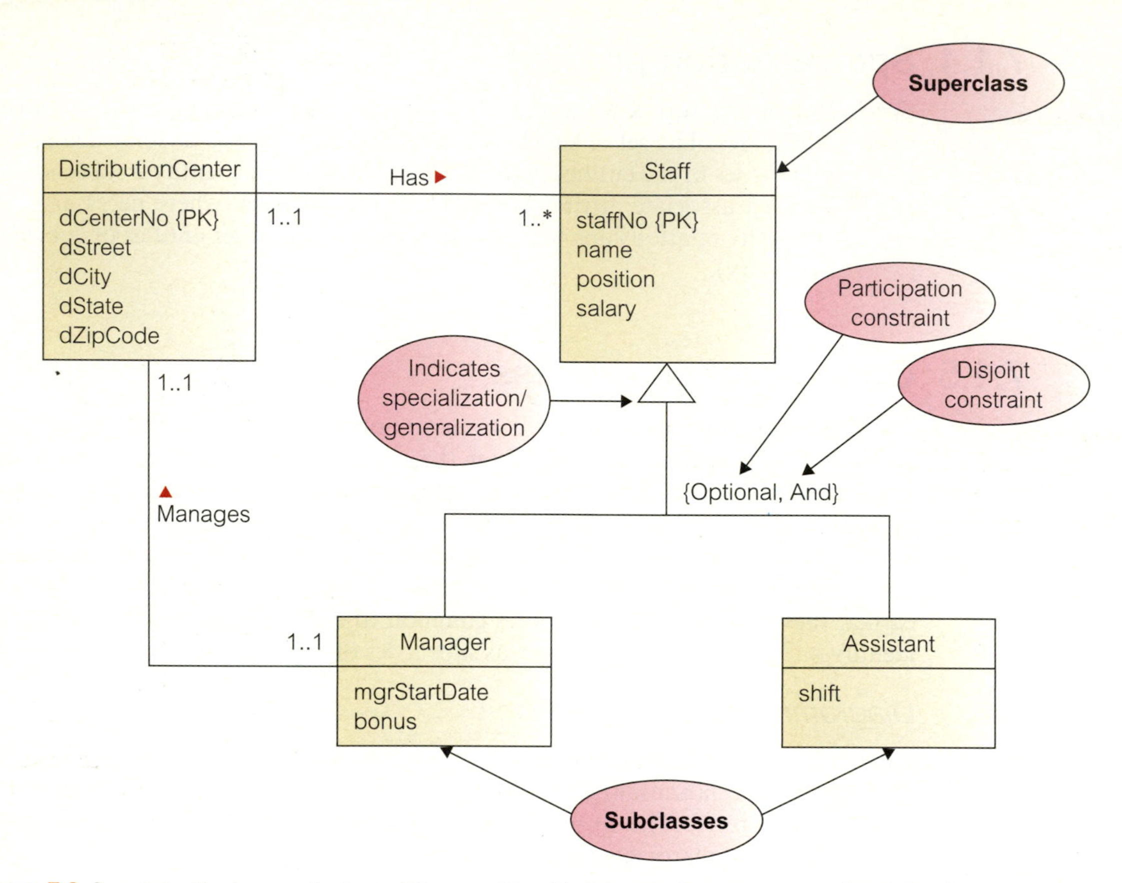

Figure 7.2 Specialization/generalization of the `Staff` entity into subclasses representing job roles

with its own subclass called `TraineeAssistant`. In other words, a member of the `AssistantManager` shared subclass must be a member of the `Manager` and `Assistant` subclasses and `Staff` superclass. As a consequence, the attributes of the `Staff` superclass (`staffNo`, `name`, `position`, `salary`), and the attributes of the subclasses `Manager` (`mgrStartDate` and `bonus`) and `Assistant` (`shift`) are inherited by the `AssistantManager` subclass.

`TraineeAssistant` is a subclass of `Assistant`, which is a subclass of `Staff`. This means that a member of the `TraineeAssistant` subclass must be a member of the `Assistant` subclass and the `Staff` superclass. As a consequence, the attributes of the `Staff` superclass (`staffNo`, `name`, `position`, `salary`) and the attribute of the `Assistant` subclass (`shift`) are inherited by the `TraineeAssistant` subclass, which also has its own additional attribute called `startDate`.

> **Note** The *StayHome Online Rental* case study in Section 5.4 described only Manager and Assistant staff roles in any detail. However, to allow discussions of a superclass/subclasses relationship with {Optional, And} constraints, we have allowed for other staff roles and for staff to exist that are not associated with any subclasses.

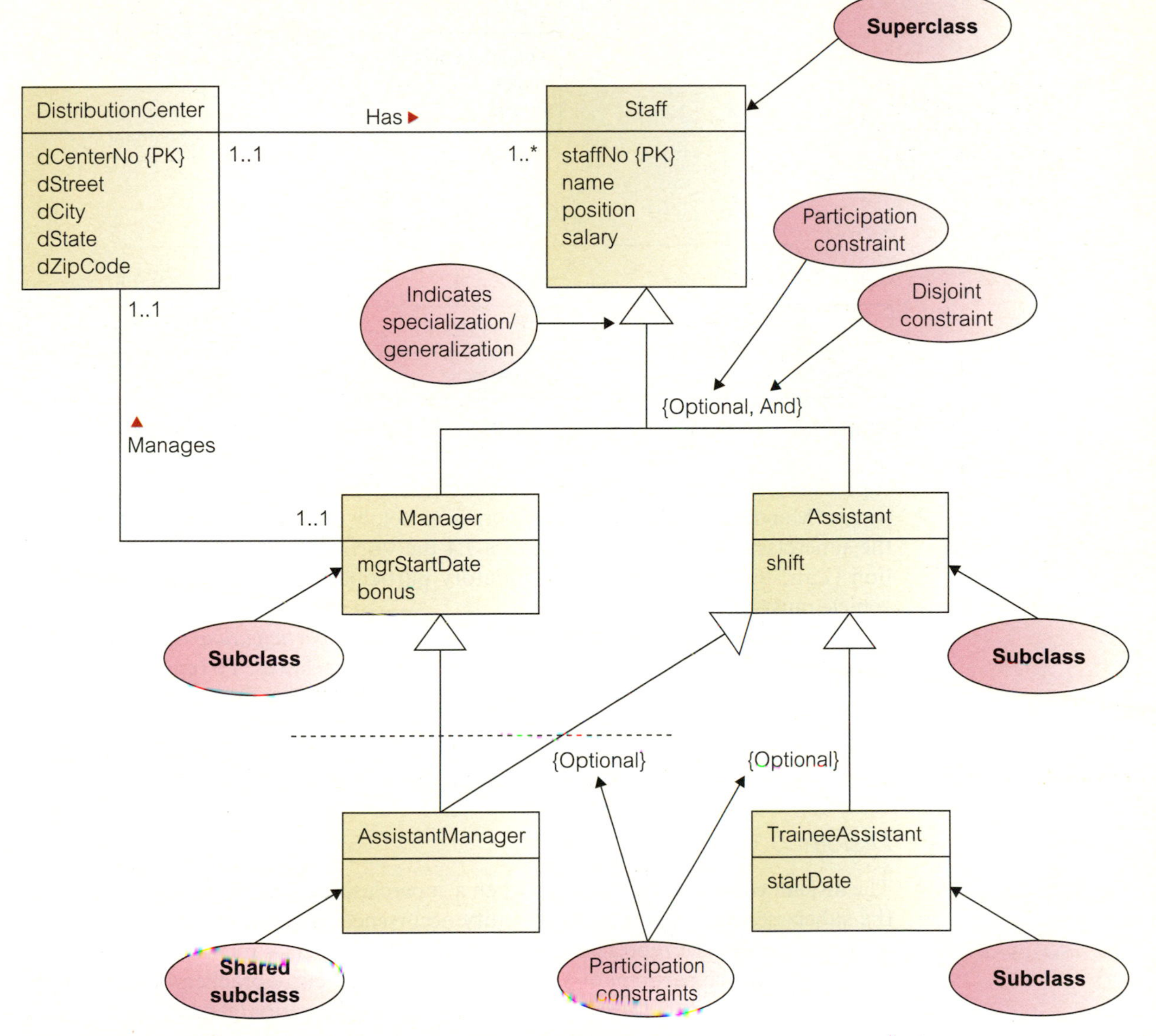

Figure 7.3 Specialization/generalization of the `Staff` entity including a shared subclass called `AssistantManager` and a subclass called `Assistant` with its own subclass called `TraineeAssistant`

7.1.6 Constraints on superclass/subclass relationships

> **Participation constraint (EER)**
>
> Determines whether every occurrence in the superclass must participate as a member of a subclass.

There are two constraints that may apply to a superclass/subclass relationship called participation constraints and disjoint constraints.

Participation constraints

A **participation constraint** may be mandatory or optional. A superclass/subclass relationship with a *mandatory participation* specifies that every entity occurrence in the

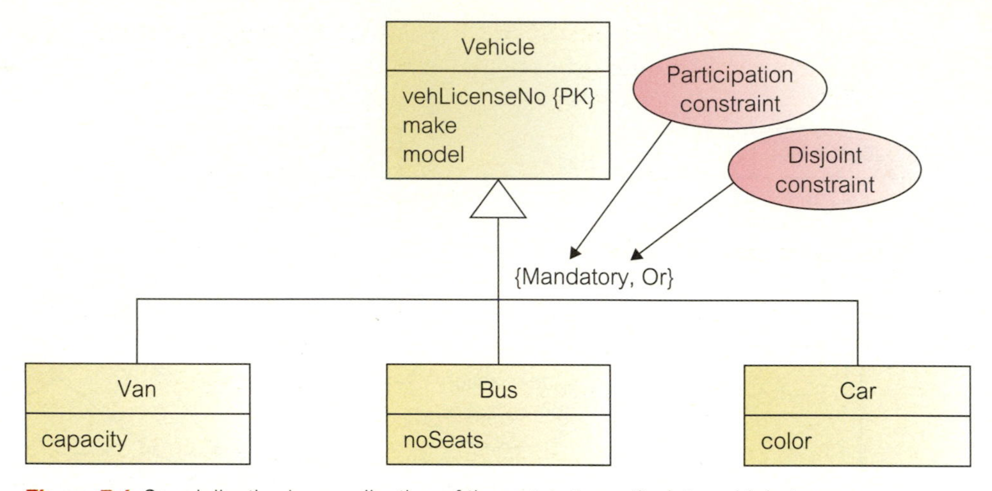

Figure 7.4 Specialization/generalization of the `Vehicle` entity into vehicle types

superclass must also be a member of a subclass. To represent mandatory participation, a 'Mandatory' is placed in curly brackets below the triangle that points towards the superclass. For example, in Figure 7.4 the `Vehicle` specialization/generalization (`Van`, `Bus`, and `Car`) has mandatory participation, which means that every vehicle must be a van, bus, or car.

A superclass/subclass relationship with *optional participation* specifies that a member of a superclass need not belong to any of its subclasses. To represent optional participation, an 'Optional' is placed in curly brackets below the triangle that points towards the superclass. For example, in Figure 7.2 the job role specialization/generalization has optional participation, which means that a member of staff need not have an additional job role such as a Manager or Assistant.

Disjoint constraints

> **Disjoint constraint**
>
> Describes the relationship between members of the subclasses and indicates whether it is possible for a member of a superclass to be a member of one, or more than one, subclass.

The **disjoint constraint** applies only when a superclass has more than one subclass. If the subclasses are *disjoint*, then an entity occurrence can be a member of only one of the subclasses. To represent a disjoint superclass/subclass relationship, an 'Or' is placed next to the participation constraint within the curly brackets. For example, in Figure 7.4 the subclasses of the `Vehicle` specialization/generalization (`Van`, `Bus`, and `Car`) are disjoint, which means that a vehicle is a van, bus, or car.

If subclasses of a specialization/generalization are not disjoint (called nondisjoint), then an entity occurrence may be a member of more than one subclass. To represent a *nondisjoint* superclass/subclass relationship, an 'And' is placed next to the participation constraint within the curly brackets. For example, in Figure 7.2 the subclasses of the job role specialization/generalization (`Manager` and `Assistant`) are nondisjoint, which means that an entity occurrence can be a member of both the `Manager` and `Assistant` subclasses. This is also confirmed by the presence of the shared subclass called `AssistantManager` shown in Figure 7.3.

The participation and disjoint constraints of specialization/generalization are distinct giving the following four categories: mandatory and nondisjoint, optional and nondisjoint, mandatory and disjoint, and optional and disjoint.

In Chapter 10, we describe how to create tables from a data model built using the basic and the enhanced concepts of the ER model. For the enhanced concepts we illustrate this process using Figures 7.2 and 7.4.

Chapter summary

- A **superclass** is an entity that includes one or more distinct groupings of its occurrences, which require to be represented in a model.
- A **subclass** is a distinct grouping of occurrences of an entity, which require to be represented in a data model.
- **Attribute inheritance** is the process by which a member of a subclass may possess subclass-specific attributes, and inherit those attributes associated with the superclass.
- **Specialization** is the process of maximizing the differences between members of an entity by identifying their distinguishing characteristics.
- **Generalization** is the process of minimizing the differences between entities by identifying their common features.
- The constraints that may apply on a superclass/subclass relationship are called **participation** and **disjoint constraints**.
- A **participation constraint** determines whether every occurrence in the superclass must participate as a member of a subclass.
- A **disjoint constraint** describes the relationship between members of the subclasses and indicates whether it is possible for a member of a superclass to be a member of one, or more than one, subclass.

Review questions

7.1 Describe what a superclass and a subclass represent.

7.2 Describe the relationship between a superclass and its subclass.

7.3 Describe and illustrate, using an example, the process of attribute inheritance.

7.4 What are the main reasons for introducing the concepts of superclasses and subclasses into an EER model?

7.5 Describe what a shared subclass represents.

7.6 Describe and contrast the process of specialization with the process of generalization.

7.7 Describe the two main constraints that apply to a specialization/generalization relationship.

Exercises

7.8 Introduce specialization/generalization concepts into the ER model shown in Figure 7.5 and described in Exercise 6.10. Use the enhanced concepts to show that there are two types of employees, namely permanent and temporary. The total number of days off due to sickness is recorded for all staff. The total annual holiday entitlement and the number of days taken are recorded for permanent staff only. Only permanent staff are required to provide an employment history, if previously employed.

The final answer to this exercise is shown as Figure 10.17 of Exercise 10.9.

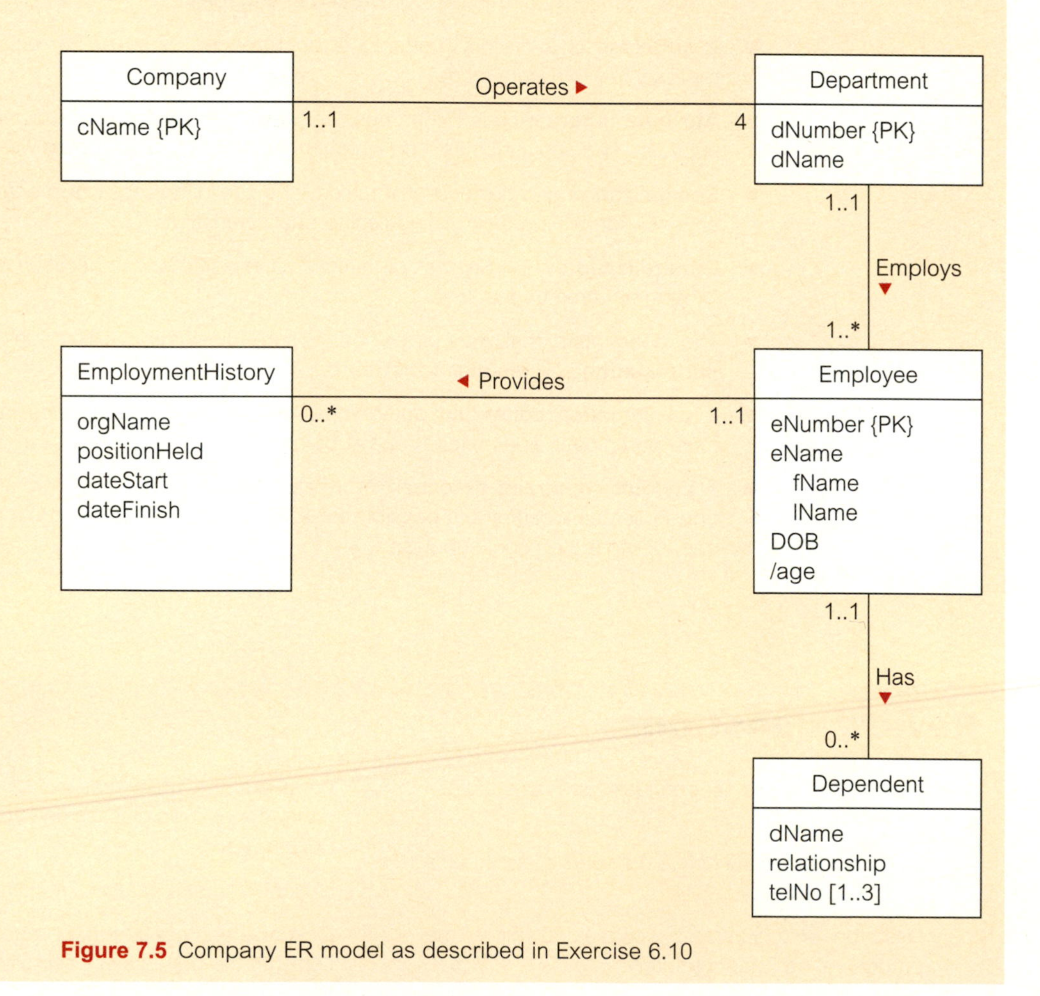

Figure 7.5 Company ER model as described in Exercise 6.10

7.9 Introduce specialization/generalization concepts into the ER model shown in Figure 7.6 and described in Exercise 6.11 to show the following:

(a) The majority of car parking spaces are under cover and each can be allocated for use by a member of staff for a monthly charge out rate.
(b) Car parking spaces that are not under cover are free to use when available.
(c) Up to 20 covered car parking spaces are available for use by visitors to the company. However, only members of staff are able to book out a car park space for the day of the visit. There is no charge for this type of booking but the member of staff must provide the visitor's vehicle license number.

The final answer to this exercise is shown as Figure 10.18 of Exercise 10.10.

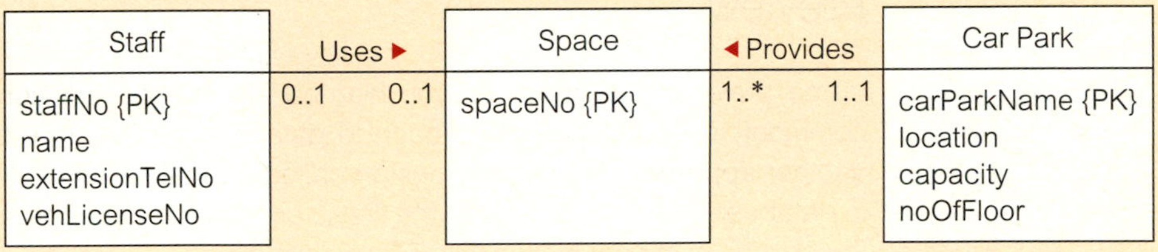

Staff
staffNo {PK}
name
extensionTelNo
vehLicenseNo

Uses ▶
0..1 0..1

Space
spaceNo {PK}

◀ Provides
1..* 1..1

Car Park
carParkName {PK}
location
capacity
noOfFloor

Figure 7.6 Car park ER model as described in Exercise 6.11

CHAPTER

8 Normalization

Preview

In the previous two chapters, you learned about entity–relationship (ER) modeling, a commonly used top-down approach to database design. In this chapter, we consider another approach to database design called normalization. Normalization can be used in database design in two ways: the first is as a bottom-up approach to database design; the second is in conjunction with ER modeling.

Using normalization as a **bottom-up approach** involves analyzing the associations between attributes and, based on this analysis, grouping the attributes together to form tables that represent entities and relationships. However, this approach becomes difficult with a large number of attributes, where it becomes progressively more complex to establish all the important associations between the attributes. For this reason, in this book we present a methodology that recommends that we first attempt to understand the data using a **top-down approach** to database design. In this approach, we use ER modeling to create a model that represents the main entities, relationships, and attributes of the data. The ER model is then translated into a set of tables. It is at this point that we use normalization (see Step 2.2 of Chapter 10) to check whether the tables are well designed.

The purpose of this chapter is to examine why normalization is a useful technique in database design and, in particular, how normalization can be used to check the structure of tables created from an ER model.

Learning objectives

In this chapter you will learn:

- How the technique of normalization is used in database design.
- How tables that contain redundant data can suffer from update anomalies, which can introduce inconsistencies into a database.
- The rules associated with the most commonly used normal forms, namely first (1NF), second (2NF), and third (3NF) normal forms.
- How tables that break the rules of 1NF, 2NF, or 3NF are likely to contain redundant data and suffer from update anomalies.
- How to correct errors in tables that break the rules of 1NF, 2NF, or 3NF to remove the presence of redundant data.

8.1 Introduction

Normalization

A technique for producing a set of tables with minimal redundancy that support the data requirements of an organization.

In 1972, Dr E. F. Codd developed the technique of **normalization** to support the design of databases based on the *relational model* described in Chapter 2. Normalization is often performed as a series of tests on a table to determine whether it satisfies or violates the rules for a given **normal form**. There are several normal forms, the most commonly used ones being first normal form (1NF), second normal form (2NF), and third normal form (3NF). All these normal forms are based on rules about relationships among the columns of a table.

In the following sections, we first demonstrate how a badly structured table, which contains **redundant data**, can potentially suffer from problems called **update anomalies**. Badly structured tables may occur due to errors in the original ER model or in the process of translating the ER model into tables. We then present definitions for first normal form (1NF), second normal form (2NF), and third normal form (3NF), and demonstrate how each normal form can be used to identify and correct problems in our tables.

Note that the examples of tables shown in this chapter use, alter, or extend the data requirements of the *StayHome Online Rentals* case study described in Section 5.4 to fully illustrate how normalization can be applied to identify and correct problems found in tables.

8.2 Data redundancy and update anomalies

A major aim of relational database design is to group columns into tables to minimize data redundancy and reduce the file storage space required by the implemented base tables. To illustrate the problems associated with data redundancy, compare the `Staff` and `DistributionCenter` tables shown in Figure 8.1 with the `StaffDistributionCenter` table shown in Figure 8.2.

> **Note** For simplicity, the column called `eMail`, which is associated with `Staff` of the *StayHome Online Rental* case study described in Section 5.4, is not included in these example tables.

The `StaffDistributionCenter` table is an alternative form of the `Staff` and `DistributionCenter` tables. The structure of these tables is described using a database definition language (DBDL), which is described in Chapter 10 Step 2.1:

`Staff (staffNo, name, position, salary, dCenterNo)`
Primary key `staffNo`
Foreign key `dCenterNo`

`DistributionCenter (dCenterNo, dAddress, dTelNo)`
Primary key `dCenterNo`

`StaffDistributionCenter (staffNo, name, position, salary, dCenterNo, dAddress, dTelNo)`
Primary key `staffNo`

Staff

staffNo	name	position	salary	dCenterNo
S1500	Tom Daniels	Manager	48000	D001
S0003	Sally Adams	Assistant	30000	D001
S0010	Mary Martinez	Manager	51000	D002
S3250	Robert Chin	Assistant	33000	D002
S2250	Sally Stern	Manager	48000	D004
S0415	Art Peters	Manager	42000	D003

DistributionCenter

dCenterNo	dAddress	dTelNo
D001	8 Jefferson Way, Portland, OR 97201	503-555-3618
D002	City Center Plaza, Seattle, WA 98122	206-555-6756
D003	14 – 8th Avenue, New York, NY 10012	212-371-3000
D004	2 W. El Camino, San Francisco, CA 94087	822-555-3131

Figure 8.1 `Staff` and `DistributionCenter` tables

StaffDistributionCenter

staffNo	name	position	salary	dCenterNo	dAddress	dTelNo
S1500	Tom Daniels	Manager	48000	D001	8 Jefferson Way, Portland, OR 97201	503-555-3618
S0003	Sally Adams	Assistant	30000	D001	8 Jefferson Way, Portland, OR 97201	503-555-3618
S0010	Mary Martinez	Manager	51000	D002	City Center Plaza, Seattle, WA 98122	206-555-6756
S3250	Robert Chin	Assistant	33000	D002	City Center Plaza, Seattle, WA 98122	206-555-6756
S2250	Sally Stern	Manager	48000	D004	2 W. El Camino, San Francisco, CA 94087	822-555-3131
S0415	Art Peters	Manager	42000	D003	14 – 8th Avenue, New York, NY 10012	212-371-3000

Figure 8.2 `StaffDistributionCenter` table

In the `StaffDistributionCenter` table there is **redundant data**; the details of a distribution center are repeated for every member of staff located at that distribution center. In contrast, the details of each distribution center appear only once in the `DistributionCenter` table and only the distribution center number (`dCenterNo`) is repeated in the `Staff` table, to represent where each member of staff is located. Tables that have redundant data may have problems called **update anomalies**, which are classified as insertion, deletion, or modification anomalies.

8.2.1 Insertion anomalies

There are two main types of insertion anomalies, which we illustrate using the `StaffDistributionCenter` table shown in Figure 8.2.

(1) To insert the details of a new member of staff located at a given distribution center into the `StaffDistributionCenter` table, we must also enter the

correct details for that distribution center. For example, to insert the details of a new member of staff at distribution center D002, we must enter the correct details of distribution center D002 so that the distribution center details are consistent with values for distribution center D002 in other records of the `StaffDistributionCenter` table. The tables shown in Figure 8.1 do not suffer from this potential inconsistency, because for each staff member we enter only the appropriate distribution center number into the `Staff` table. In addition, the details of distribution center D002 are recorded only once in the database as a single record in the `DistributionCenter` table.

(2) To insert details of a new distribution center that currently has no members of staff into the `StaffDistributionCenter` table, it is necessary to enter nulls into the staff-related columns, such as `staffNo`. However, as `staffNo` is the primary key for the `StaffDistributionCenter` table, attempting to enter nulls for `staffNo` violates entity integrity (described in Section 2.4.2) and is not allowed. The design of the tables shown in Figure 8.1 avoids this problem because new distribution center details are entered into the `DistributionCenter` table separately from the staff details. The details of staff ultimately located at a new distribution center can be entered into the `Staff` table at a later date.

8.2.2 Deletion anomalies

If we delete a record from the `StaffDistributionCenter` table that represents the last member of staff located at a distribution center, the details about that distribution center are also lost from the database. For example, if we delete the record for staff Art Peters (S0415) from the `StaffDistributionCenter` table, the details relating to distribution center D003 are lost from the database. The design of the tables in Figure 8.1 avoids this problem because distribution center records are stored separately from staff records and only the column `dCenterNo` relates the two tables. If we delete the record for staff Art Peters (S0415) from the `Staff` table, the details on distribution center D003 in the `DistributionCenter` table remain unaffected.

8.2.3 Modification anomalies

If we want to change the value of one of the columns of a particular distribution center in the `StaffDistributionCenter` table, for example the telephone number for distribution center D001, we must update the records of all staff located at that distribution center. If this modification is not carried out on all the appropriate records of the `StaffDistributionCenter` table, the database will become inconsistent. For example, to change the telephone number for distribution center D001 we have to update two records in the `StaffDistributionCenter` table. If only one record is updated, the database will be inconsistent.

The above examples illustrate that the `Staff` and `DistributionCenter` tables of Figure 8.1 have more desirable properties than the `StaffDistribution-Center` table of Figure 8.2. In the following sections, we examine how normal forms can be used to formalize the identification of tables that have desirable properties from those that may potentially suffer from update anomalies.

8.3 First normal form (1NF)

First normal form (1NF)

A table in which the intersection of every column and record contains only *one* value.

The only normal form that is critical in creating appropriate tables for relational databases is **first normal form (1NF)**. All the subsequent normal forms are optional. However, to avoid the update anomalies discussed in Section 8.2, it is normally recommended that we proceed to third normal form (3NF).

We examine the `DistributionCenter` table shown in Figure 8.3, with primary key `dCenterNo`. We see that all the columns of this version of the `DistributionCenter` table comply with our definition of 1NF with the exception of the column `dTelNos`. There are multiple values at the intersection of the `dTelNos` column for three of the four records shown. For example, `dCenterNo` D001 has three telephone numbers, 503-555-3618, 503-555-2727, and 503-555-6534. As a result, the `DistributionCenter` table is not in 1NF.

Although the `dAddress` column may appear to hold multiple values, this representation of address does not break 1NF. In this example, we have simply chosen the option to hold all the details of an address as a single value.

dCenterNo	dAddress	dTelNos
D001	8 Jefferson Way, Portland, OR 97201	503-555-3618, 503-555-2727, 503-555-6534
D002	City Center Plaza, Seattle, WA 98122	206-555-6756, 206-555-8836
D003	14 – 8th Avenue, New York, NY 10012	212-371-3000
D004	2 W. El Camino, San Francisco, CA 94087	822-555-3131, 822-555-4112

Figure 8.3 The `DistributionCenter` table is not in 1NF due to the presence of multiple telephone numbers in the `dTelNos` column

Normalizing the `DistributionCenter` table

To convert the `DistributionCenter` table to comply with the rules for 1NF, we must remove the `dTelNos` column along with a copy of the primary key, namely `dCenterNo` to a new table called `DistributionCenterTelephone`. The `dTelNos` column is renamed `dTelNo` and this column becomes the primary key for the new table. The structures for the altered `DistributionCenter` table and the `DistributionCenterTelephone` table are shown in Figure 8.4. The `DistributionCenter` and `DistributionCenterTelephone` tables are in at least 1NF as there is a single value at the intersection of every column with every record for each table.

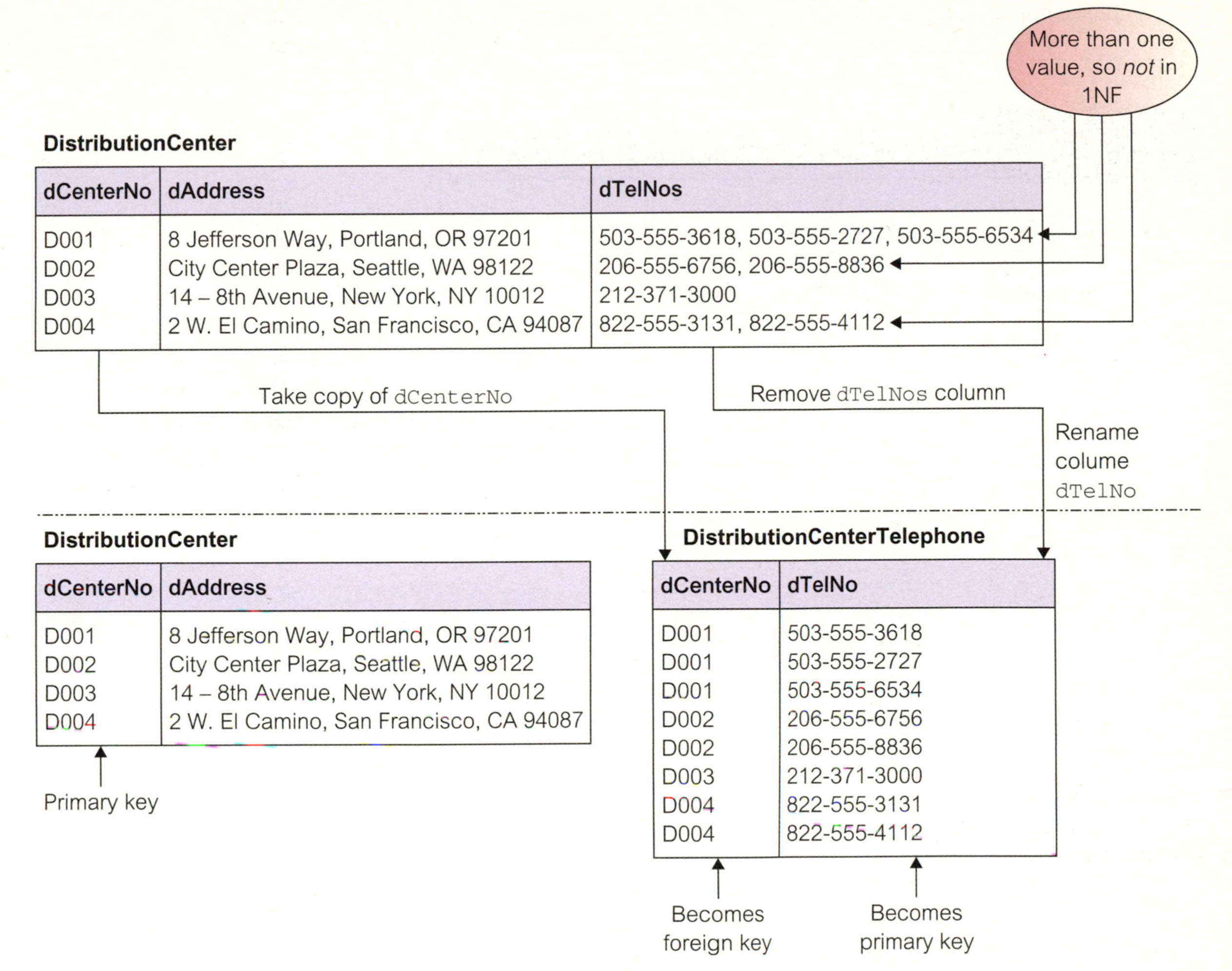

Figure 8.4 The altered `DistributionCenter` table complies with the rules for 1NF after removing the `dTelNos` column to a new table called `DistributionCenterTelephone`

8.4 Second normal form (2NF)

> **Second normal form (2NF)**
>
> A table that is in 1NF and in which the values in each non-primary-key column are determined by the values in *all* the columns that make up the primary key.

Second normal form (2NF) applies only to tables with composite primary keys, that is, tables with a primary key composed of two or more columns. A 1NF table with a single column primary key is automatically in at least 2NF. A table that is not in 2NF may suffer from the update anomalies discussed in Section 8.2.

To discuss 2NF, we examine the `TempStaffAllocation` table shown in Figure 8.5. This table represents the hours worked per week for temporary staff at each distribution center. The primary key for the `TempStaffAllocation` table is made up of both the `staffNo` and `dCenterNo` columns.

Composite primary key

TempStaffAllocation

staffNo	dCenterNo	name	position	hoursPerWeek
S4555	D002	Ellen Layman	Assistant	16
S4555	D004	Ellen Layman	Assistant	9
S4612	D002	Dave Sinclair	Assistant	14
S4612	D004	Dave Sinclair	Assistant	10

(fd1) ← Values in hoursPerWeek column are determined by (staffNo, dCenterNo)

(fd2) ← Values in name and position columns are only determined by staffNo, so table *not* in 2NF. This is an example of a partial dependency.

Figure 8.5 The TempStaffAllocation table is not in 2NF due to the presence of the partial dependency (fd2)

Key Point We use the term 'non-primary-key' columns to refer to those columns that are not part of the primary key. For example, the non-primary-key columns for the TempStaffAllocation table are name, position, and hoursPerWeek.

Functional dependency (fd)

Describes the relationship between columns in a table and indicates how columns relate to one another. For example, consider a table with columns a and b, where column a determines column b (denoted a → b). If we know the value of a, we find only *one* value of b in all the records that has this value for a, at any moment in time. However, for a given value of b there may be several different values of a.

The arrows shown below the TempStaffAllocation table of Figure 8.5 indicate particular relationships between the primary key columns and the non-primary-key columns. These relationships are more formally referred to as **functional dependencies (fd)**.

The formal definition of second normal form (2NF) is a table that is in 1NF and every non-primary-key column is *fully functionally dependent* on the primary key. The type of functional dependency that can cause problems for 2NF tables is called a **partial dependency**. An example of this type of dependency is in the TempStaffAllocation table and is shown as fd2 in Figure 8.5.

The presence of the partial dependency (fd2) in the TempStaffAllocation table is the reason why we see redundant data in the name and position columns, and this data may suffer from the update anomalies described in Section 8.2. For example, to change the name of 'Ellen Layman', we have to update two records in the TempStaffAllocation table. If only one record is updated, the database will be inconsistent. The existence of a partial dependency means that TempStaffAllocation table does not comply with our definition for 2NF.

Before we correct the problem with the TempStaffAllocation table, we discuss the partial dependency (fd2) in more detail. This dependency describes the association between the staffNo, name, and position columns. Note that the values in the name and position columns can be determined by the values in the staffNo column (part of the primary key). For example, every time S4555 appears in the staffNo column, the name 'Ellen Layman' and position 'Assistant' appears in the name and position columns. In summary, we say that staffNo determines name and position.

Full functional dependency

If a and b are columns of a table, b is fully determined by a, if b is not determined by any subset of a. If b is determined by a subset of a, this is referred to as a **partial dependency**.

The other functional dependency in the TempStaffAllocation table, namely fd1, describes the association between the staffNo, dCenterNo, and hoursPerWeek columns. The values in the hoursPerWeek column can only be determined from the values in both the staffNo and dCenterNo columns (the whole primary key). For example, when S4555 appears in the staffNo column at the same time that D002 appears in the dCenterNo column, then the value '16' appears in the hoursPerWeek column. In summary, we say that (staffNo, dCenterNo) determines hoursPerWeek. This is an example of a **full functional dependency** and as such will not cause redundant data in the TempStaffAllocation table.

Normalizing the TempStaffAllocation table

To convert the TempStaffAllocation table shown in Figure 8.5 to comply with the rules of 2NF, we need to remove the partial dependency (fd2). In other words, we need to remove the non-primary-key columns that can be determined by only part of the primary key, namely staffNo. This means that we must remove the name and position columns from the TempStaffAllocation table and place these columns in a new table called TempStaff, along with a copy of the part of the primary key that the columns are related to, which in this case is staffNo. The TempStaff table will now contain the dependency fd2; however in this new table the fd2 dependency is a *full* functional dependency indicating that the primary key for the table, staffNo, determines the other non-primary key columns, namely name, and position.

It is not necessary to remove the hoursPerWeek column as the presence of this column in the TempStaffAllocation table does not break the rules of 2NF. To ensure that we maintain the relationship between a temporary member of staff and the distribution centers at which he or she works for a set number of hours, we leave a copy of staffNo to act as a foreign key in the TempStaffAllocation table.

The structure for the altered TempStaffAllocation table and the new TempStaff table are shown in Figure 8.6. The primary key for the new TempStaff table is staffNo and this means that the table is automatically in at least 2NF as it is impossible to suffer from a partial dependency with a single column primary key. The altered TempStaffAllocation table is also in at least 2NF because the non-primary-key column hoursPerWeek is determined by the (staffNo, dCenterNo) columns.

When a table is normalized from a lower to a higher normal form (such as 1NF to 2NF/3NF), the functional dependencies in the original table must not be lost during the process. Furthermore, each of the original functional dependencies must appear in one of the resulting tables. For example, the two functional dependencies (denoted fd1 and fd2) in the original TempStaffAllocation table are now present in the resulting tables. While the altered TempStaffAllocation table has retained function dependency fd1, the new TempStaff table has acquired functional dependency fd2.

8.5 Third normal form (3NF)

Although 2NF tables have less redundancy than tables in 1NF, they may still suffer from update anomalies.

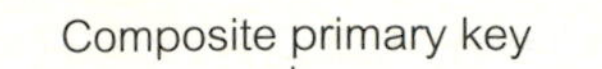

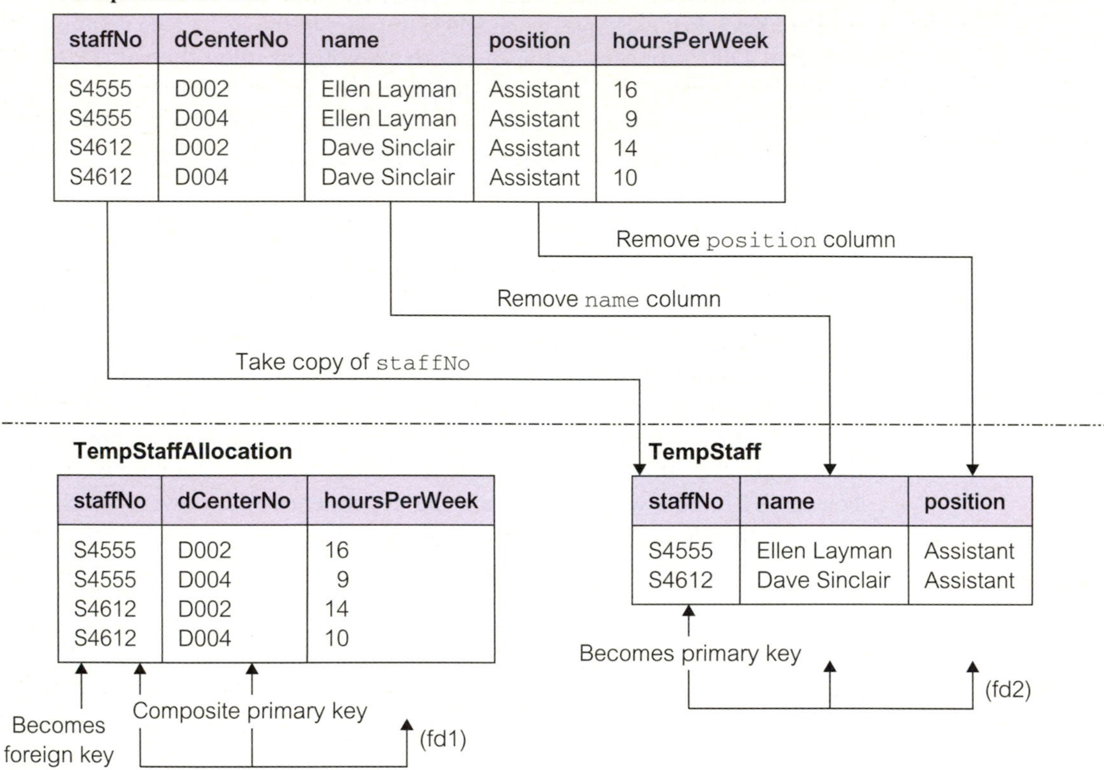

TempStaffAllocation

staffNo	dCenterNo	name	position	hoursPerWeek
S4555	D002	Ellen Layman	Assistant	16
S4555	D004	Ellen Layman	Assistant	9
S4612	D002	Dave Sinclair	Assistant	14
S4612	D004	Dave Sinclair	Assistant	10

TempStaffAllocation

staffNo	dCenterNo	hoursPerWeek
S4555	D002	16
S4555	D004	9
S4612	D002	14
S4612	D004	10

TempStaff

staffNo	name	position
S4555	Ellen Layman	Assistant
S4612	Dave Sinclair	Assistant

Figure 8.6 The altered `TempStaffAllocation` table complies with the rules for 2NF after removing the `name` and `position` columns into a new table called `TempStaff`

Third normal form (3NF)

A table that is already in 1NF and 2NF, and in which the values in all non-primary-key columns can be determined from *only* the primary key column(s) and no other columns.

To discuss **third normal form (3NF)**, examine the `StaffDistributionCenter` table with primary key `staffNo` shown in Figure 8.2. In Figure 8.7, we indicate the particular relationships (functional dependencies) between the columns in this table. The types of functional dependencies that cause problems for 3NF tables are called **transitive dependencies** and three examples exist in the `StaffDistributionCenter` table; denoted fd2, fd3, and fd4. The formal definition of third normal form (3NF) is a table that is in 1NF and 2NF and in which no non-primary-key column is transitively dependent on the primary key.

The presence of transitive dependencies (denoted fd2, fd3, and fd4) in the `StaffDistributionCenter` table has caused redundant data to appear in the `dCenterNo`, `dAddress`, and `dTelNo` columns and this data may suffer from the update anomalies described in Section 8.2. For example, to change the telephone number of distribution center D001, we have to update two records in the `StaffDistributionCenter` table. If only one record is updated, the database will be inconsistent. Therefore, the `StaffDistributionCenter` table does not comply with our definition of 3NF.

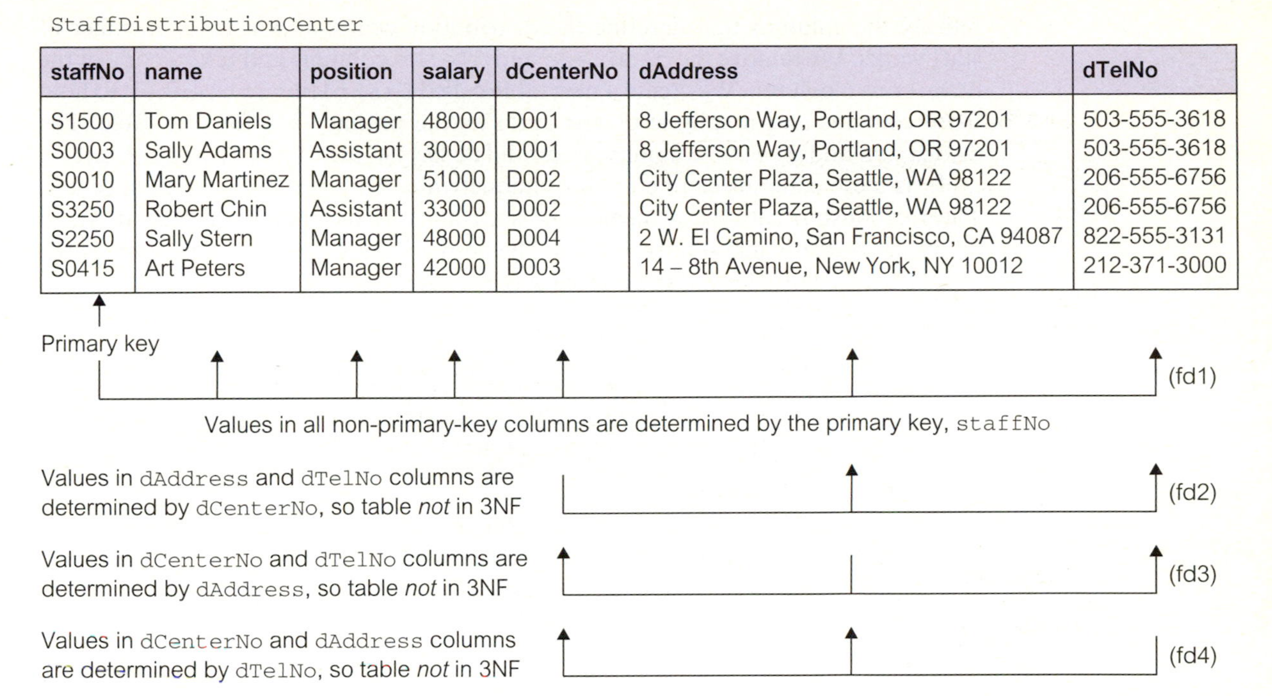
StaffDistributionCenter

staffNo	name	position	salary	dCenterNo	dAddress	dTelNo
S1500	Tom Daniels	Manager	48000	D001	8 Jefferson Way, Portland, OR 97201	503-555-3618
S0003	Sally Adams	Assistant	30000	D001	8 Jefferson Way, Portland, OR 97201	503-555-3618
S0010	Mary Martinez	Manager	51000	D002	City Center Plaza, Seattle, WA 98122	206-555-6756
S3250	Robert Chin	Assistant	33000	D002	City Center Plaza, Seattle, WA 98122	206-555-6756
S2250	Sally Stern	Manager	48000	D004	2 W. El Camino, San Francisco, CA 94087	822-555-3131
S0415	Art Peters	Manager	42000	D003	14 – 8th Avenue, New York, NY 10012	212-371-3000

Primary key
(fd1)
Values in all non-primary-key columns are determined by the primary key, staffNo
Values in dAddress and dTelNo columns are determined by dCenterNo, so table *not* in 3NF
(fd2)
Values in dCenterNo and dTelNo columns are determined by dAddress, so table *not* in 3NF
(fd3)
Values in dCenterNo and dAddress columns are determined by dTelNo, so table *not* in 3NF
(fd4)

Figure 8.7 The StaffDistributionCenter table is not in 3NF due to the presence of transitive dependencies (denoted fd2, fd3, and fd4)

Transitive dependency

Describes a relationship between columns a, b, and c. If a determines b ($a \rightarrow b$) and b determines c ($b \rightarrow c$), then c is transitively dependent on a via b (provided that b or c does not determine a).

Before correcting the problems associated with the StaffDistribution-Center table, we first discuss the *transitive* dependencies (fd2, fd3, and fd4), which describe the associations between the dCenterNo, dAddress, and dTelNo columns. The StaffDistributionCenter table is not in 3NF due to the presence of these dependencies. Although we can determine the distribution center number, distribution center address, and telephone number that a member of staff works at from the primary key, staffNo, we can also determine the details for a given distribution center if we know the distribution center number, distribution center address, or distribution center telephone number. In other words, we can determine information using values from non-primary-key columns, namely dCenterNo, dAddress, or dTelNo. For example, when S1500 appears in the staffNo column, '8 Jefferson Way, Portland, OR 97201' appears in the dAddress column. However, when D001 appears in dCenterNo, '8 Jefferson Way, Portland, OR 97201' also appears in the dAddress column. In other words, the address that a member of staff works at can be determined by the value in the dCenterNo column. This is not allowed in 3NF as thevalues in all non-primary-key columns must be determined from only the values in the primary key column(s).

Normalizing the StaffDistributionCenter table

To convert the StaffDistributionCenter table shown in Figure 8.7 to comply with the rules for 3NF, we need to remove the non-primary-key columns that can be determined by another non-primary-key column. In other words, we need to remove the columns that describe the distribution center at which the member of staff works. We remove the dAddress and dTelNo columns and take a copy of the dCenterNo column. We create a new table called DistributionCenter to hold these columns and nominate dCenterNo as the primary key for this table. The dAddress and dTelNo columns are candidate keys in the DistributionCenter table as these columns can be used to uniquely identify a given distribution center. The relationship between a member of staff and the distribution center at which he or she works is maintained because the copy of the dCenterNo column in the StaffDistributionCenter table acts because a foreign key.

Note We could have left a copy of any one of the other two columns to act as a foreign key as they share the same property as dCenterNo; in other words we can also determine where a member of staff works by leaving a copy of the dAddress or the dTelNo column in the StaffDistributionCenter table.

The structure for the altered StaffDistributionCenter table (renamed Staff table) and the new DistributionCenter tables are shown in Figure 8.8. The Staff table is in 3NF because each non-primary-key column can only be determined from the primary key, staffNo.

The new DistributionCenter table is also in 3NF because all of the non-primary-key columns can be determined from the primary key, dCenterNo. Although the other two non-primary-key columns in this table, dAddress and dTelNo, can also determine the details of a given distribution center, this does not violate 3NF because these columns are candidate keys for the DistributionCenter table.

Key point

The structure of the DistributionCenter table illustrates that the definition for 3NF can be generalized to include all candidate keys of a table, if any exist. Therefore, for tables with more than one candidate key we can use the generalized definition for 3NF, which is a table that is in 1NF and 2NF, and in which the values in all the non-primary-key columns can be determined from only *candidate key* column(s) and no other columns. Furthermore, this generalization is also true for the definition of 2NF, which is a table that is in 1NF and in which the values in each non-primary-key column can be determined from all the columns that makes up a *candidate key* and no other columns. This generalization does not alter the definition for 1NF as this normal form is independent of keys and particular relationships between columns of a table.

Note that the original functional dependencies (denoted fd1 to fd4) in the original StaffDistributionCenter table are now present in the resulting tables. While the altered StaffDistributionCenter table (renamed Staff table) has retained function dependency fd1, the new DistributionCenter table has acquired functional dependencies fd2, fd3, and fd4.

There are normal forms that go beyond 3NF such as Boyce-Codd normal form (BCNF), fourth normal form (4NF), and fifth normal form (5NF). However, these later normal forms are not commonly used as they attempt to identify and solve problems in tables that occur relatively infrequently. However, if you would like to find out more about BCNF, 4NF, and 5NF you should consult Connolly and Begg (2009).

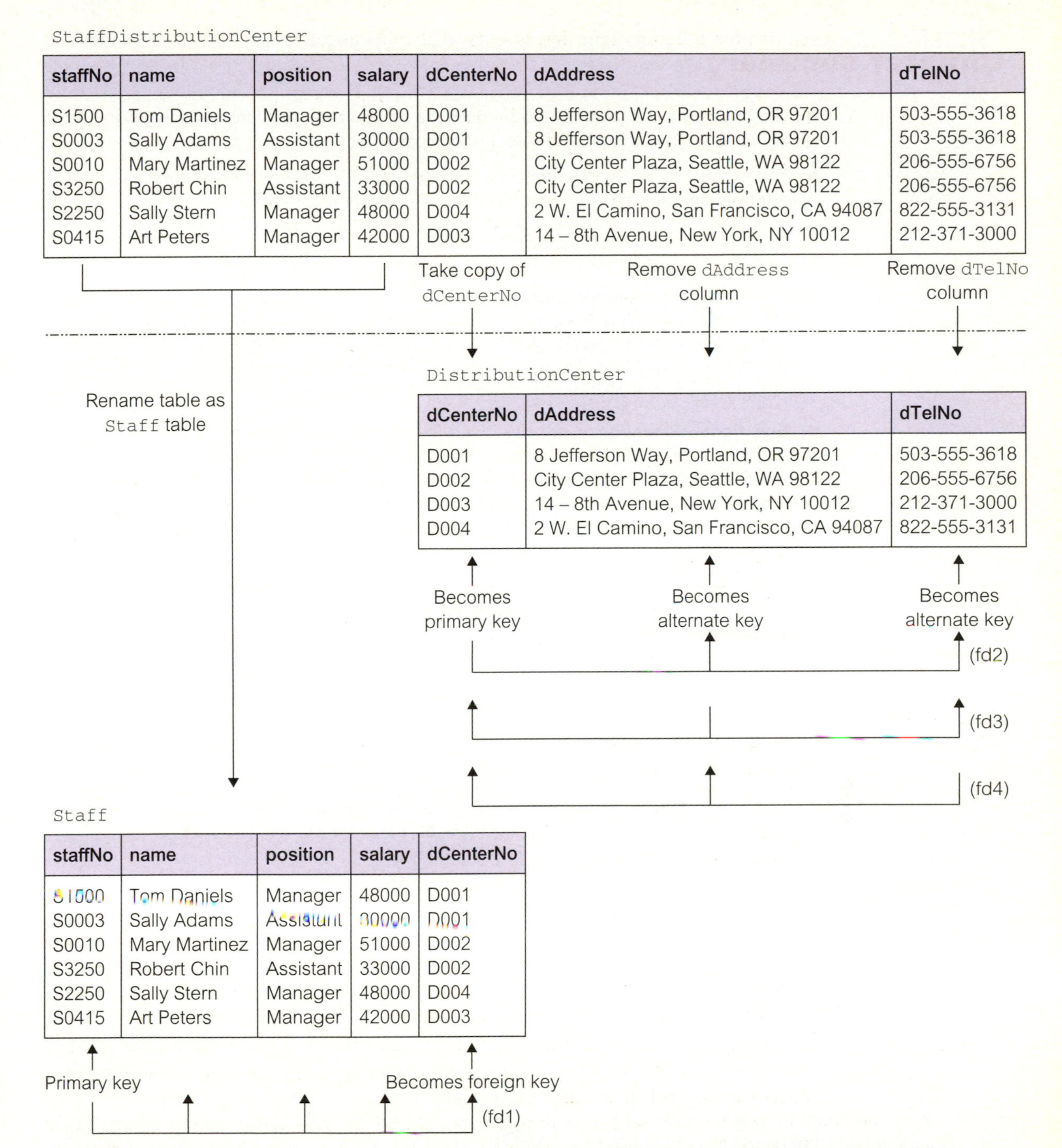

StaffDistributionCenter

staffNo	name	position	salary	dCenterNo	dAddress	dTelNo
S1500	Tom Daniels	Manager	48000	D001	8 Jefferson Way, Portland, OR 97201	503-555-3618
S0003	Sally Adams	Assistant	30000	D001	8 Jefferson Way, Portland, OR 97201	503-555-3618
S0010	Mary Martinez	Manager	51000	D002	City Center Plaza, Seattle, WA 98122	206-555-6756
S3250	Robert Chin	Assistant	33000	D002	City Center Plaza, Seattle, WA 98122	206-555-6756
S2250	Sally Stern	Manager	48000	D004	2 W. El Camino, San Francisco, CA 94087	822-555-3131
S0415	Art Peters	Manager	42000	D003	14 – 8th Avenue, New York, NY 10012	212-371-3000

DistributionCenter

dCenterNo	dAddress	dTelNo
D001	8 Jefferson Way, Portland, OR 97201	503-555-3618
D002	City Center Plaza, Seattle, WA 98122	206-555-6756
D003	14 – 8th Avenue, New York, NY 10012	212-371-3000
D004	2 W. El Camino, San Francisco, CA 94087	822-555-3131

Staff

staffNo	name	position	salary	dCenterNo
S1500	Tom Daniels	Manager	48000	D001
S0003	Sally Adams	Assistant	30000	D001
S0010	Mary Martinez	Manager	51000	D002
S3250	Robert Chin	Assistant	33000	D002
S2250	Sally Stern	Manager	48000	D004
S0415	Art Peters	Manager	42000	D003

Figure 8.8 The altered StaffDistributionCenter table (renamed Staff table) complies with the rules for 3NF after removing the dAddress and dTelNo columns and creating a new table called DistributionCenter

Chapter summary

- **Normalization** is a technique for producing a set of tables with minimal redundancy that supports the requirements of a user or company.
- Tables that have redundant data may have problems called **update anomalies**, which are classified as insertion, deletion, or modification anomalies.
- The definition for **first normal form (1NF)** is a table in which the intersection of every column and record contains only *one* value.
- The definition for **second normal form (2NF)** is a table that is already in 1NF and in which the values in each non-primary-key column can be determined from the values in *all* the column(s) that makes up the primary key. (The formal definition for 2NF is a table that is in 1NF and every non-primary-key column is fully functionally dependent on the primary).
- **Functional dependency (fd)** describes the relationship between columns in a table and indicates how columns relate to one another. For example, consider a table with columns **a** and **b**, where column **a** determines column **b** (denoted $\mathbf{a} \rightarrow \mathbf{b}$). If we know the value of **a**, we find only *one* value of **b** in all the records that has this value for **a**, at any moment in time. However, for a given value of **b** there may be several different values of **a**.
- **Full functional dependency** is described when **a** and **b** are columns of a table, **b** is fully determined by **a**, if **b** is not determined by any subset of **a**. If **b** is determined by a subset of **a**, this is referred to as a **partial dependency**.
- The definition for **third normal form (3NF)** is a table that is already in 1NF and 2NF, and in which the values in all non-primary-key columns can be determined from *only* the primary-key column(s) and no other columns. (The formal definition for 3NF is a table that is in 1NF and 2NF and in which no non-primary-key column is transitively dependent on the primary key).
- **Transitive dependency** describes a relationship between columns **a**, **b**, and **c**. If **a** determines **b** ($\mathbf{a} \rightarrow \mathbf{b}$) and **b** determines **c** ($\mathbf{b} \rightarrow \mathbf{c}$), then **c** is transitively dependent on **a** via **b** (provided that **b** or **c** does not determine **a**).

Review questions

8.1 Discuss how normalization may be used in database design.

8.2 Describe the types of update anomalies that may occur in a table that has redundant data.

8.3 Describe the characteristics of a table that violates first normal form (1NF) and then describe how such a table is converted to 1NF.

8.4 What is the minimal normal form that a relation must satisfy? Provide a definition for this normal form.

8.5 Describe an approach to converting a first normal form (1NF) table to second normal form (2NF) table(s).

8.6 Describe the characteristics of a table in second normal form (2NF).

8.7 Describe what a functional dependency represents.

8.8 How does a *full* functional dependency differ from a *partial* functional dependency?

8.9 Describe what is meant by partial functional dependency and describe how this type of dependency relates to 2NF. Provide an example to illustrate your answer.

8.10 Describe the characteristics of a table in third normal form (3NF).

8.11 Describe the characteristics of a transitive dependency.

8.12 Describe what is meant by transitive dependency, and describe how this type of dependency relates to 3NF. Provide an example to illustrate your answer.

Exercises

8.13 In Exercise 6.10 we described companies that have departments, which employ employees. Some employees have had one or more jobs before starting their current employment. The table in Figure 8.9 shows five sample records that represent the employment histories for three members of staff. Each employee is uniquely identified using employee number (`eNumber`). (Note in this example we do not include the details concerning companies, departments, and dependants.)

(a) The table shown in Figure 8.9 is susceptible to update anomalies. Provide examples of insertion, deletion, and modification anomalies.
(b) Identify the functional dependencies represented by the data shown in the table of Figure 8.9. State any assumptions you make about the data shown in this table.
(c) Describe and illustrate the process of normalizing the table shown in Figure 8.9 to 3NF. Identify the primary key and, where appropriate, alternate and foreign keys in each table.
(d) Demonstrate that the functional dependencies identified in part (b) are present in the 3NF tables described in part (c).

eNumber	eName	DOB	orgName	positionHeld	dateStart	dateFinish
0056	Kate Brown	12/12/76	Paterson & Co	IT Assistant	01/11/90	30/04/95
0057	Gillian Bradford	01/03/71	Willies and Sons	Technician	01/06/88	31/03/91
0057	Gillian Bradford	01/03/71	Willies and Sons	Assistant Researcher	01/04/91	31/03/94
0057	Gillian Bradford	01/03/71	Willies and Sons	Project Manager	01/04/94	31/01/96
0089	Stephen Widden	09/09/83	Paterson & Co	IT Assistant	01/03/91	31/08/95

Figure 8.9 Table displaying records of the employment histories for three employees

8.14 In Exercise 6.11 we described the data requirements of an organization that has several car parks, which are used by staff. The table in Figure 8.10 shows five sample records that represent members of staff who have been allocated a car parking space. Each car park space provided by the organization is uniquely identified using a space number (`spaceNo`). (Note in this example we do not include the extension number and vehicle license number data associated with staff.)

staffNo	name	carParkName	location	capacity	noOfFloors	spaceNo
S1156	Jane Jones	Yellow	Block E	120	3	123
S2311	Karen Gilmore	Yellow	Block E	120	3	145
S1167	Richard Blight	Yellow	Block E	120	3	156
S2345	Guy Ritchie	Green	Block D	45	2	26
S3434	Stephen Williams	Green	Block D	45	2	34

Figure 8.10 Table displaying records of members of staff who have been allocated car parking spaces

(a) The table shown in Figure 8.10 is susceptible to update anomalies. Provide examples of insertion, deletion, and modification anomalies.
(b) Identify the functional dependencies represented by the data shown in the table of Figure 8.10. State any assumptions you make about the data shown in this table.
(c) Describe and illustrate the process of normalizing the table shown in Figure 8.10 to 3NF. Identify the primary key and, where appropriate, alternate and foreign keys in each table.
(d) Demonstrate that the functional dependencies identified in part (b) are present in the 3NF tables described in part (c).

8.15 The table shown in Figure 8.11 lists dentist/patient appointment data. A patient is given an appointment at a specific time and date with a dentist located at a particular surgery. On each day of patient appointments, a dentist is allocated to a specific surgery for that day.

(a) The table shown in Figure 8.11 is susceptible to update anomalies. Provide examples of insertion, deletion, and modification anomalies.
(b) Identify the functional dependencies represented by the data shown in the table of Figure 8.11. State any assumptions you make about the data shown in this table.

staffNo	dentistName	patientNo	patientName	appointment		surgeryNo
				date	time	
S1011	Tony Smith	P100	Gillian White	12-Aug-09	10.00	S10
S1011	Tony Smith	P105	Jill Bell	13-Aug-09	12.00	S15
S1024	Helen Pearson	P108	Ian MacKay	12-Sept-09	10.00	S10
S1024	Helen Pearson	P108	Ian MacKay	14-Sept-09	10.00	S10
S1032	Robin Plevin	P105	Jill Bell	14-Oct-09	16.30	S15
S1032	Robin Plevin	P110	John Walker	15-Oct-09	18.00	S13

Figure 8.11 Table displaying records of patient dental appointments

(c) Describe and illustrate the process of normalizing the table shown in Figure 8.11 to 3NF. Identify the primary key and, where appropriate, alternate and foreign keys in each table.

(d) Demonstrate that the functional dependencies identified in part (b) are present in the 3NF tables described in part (c).

8.16 An agency called *InstantCover* supplies part-time/temporary staff to hotels throughout Scotland. The table shown in Figure 8.12 lists the time spent by agency staff working at two hotels. The National Insurance Number (NIN) is unique for every member of staff.

NIN	contractNo	hoursPerWeek	eName	hotelNo	hotelLocation
113567WD	C1024	16	John Smith	H25	Edinburgh
234111XA	C1024	24	Diane Hocine	H25	Edinburgh
712670YD	C1025	28	Sarah White	H4	Glasgow
113567WD	C1025	16	John Smith	H4	Glasgow

Figure 8.12 Table displaying employees records for agency called *InstantCover*

(a) The table shown in Figure 8.12 is susceptible to update anomalies. Provide examples of insertion, deletion, and modification anomalies.

(b) Identify the functional dependencies represented by the data shown in the table of Figure 8.12. State any assumptions you make about the data shown in this table.

(c) Describe and illustrate the process of normalizing the table shown in Figure 8.12 to 3NF. Identify the primary key and, where appropriate, alternate and foreign keys in each table.

(d) Demonstrate that the functional dependencies identified in part (b) are present in the 3NF tables described in part (c).

PART III

Database design methodology

In this part of the book, we present a methodology that will guide you through the three phases of database design, namely conceptual database design (Chapter 9), logical database design (Chapter 10), and physical database design (Chapter 11). Each phase is presented as a series of steps, and each step is illustrated using the *StayHome Online Rentals* case study described in Section 5.4.

As we progress through the methodology, we take the users' requirements for a database towards a physical design for a database that will meet all of their requirements. Ensuring that the physical database design is correct means that for quite complex systems we cannot get there directly, but must first carefully translate the users' requirements into a conceptual design (as an ER model) and then second translate this representation into a logical design (as a description of the relational tables also known as the relational schema). Finally, the logical design is translated into a physical design (as a description of the base tables for the target DBMS).

Ensuring that we build the correct design at each phase of the database design process is the main purpose of the methodology, and the phased format ensures that we do not attempt to build everything at the same time. Furthermore, the phases allow the design to be validated not at the end but throughout; in other words the design is continually checked against what the users want from their database.

After reading this part of the book you will know how to progress through the database design process and have a clear overview of what should be achieved at each phase. However, database design is a practical exercise and your ability to build the correct database will only improve with each repetition of the exercise.

CHAPTER
9 Conceptual database design

Preview

In Chapter 4, we described the stages of the database system development lifecycle, one of which is database design. Database design is made up of three main phases: *conceptual database design*, *logical database design,* and *physical database design*. In this chapter, we introduce a step-by-step methodology for database design and then describe in detail the steps for the first phase of database design, namely conceptual database design.

Learning objectives

In this chapter you will learn:

- What a design methodology is.
- That database design has three main phases: conceptual, logical, and physical design.
- About critical success factors in database design.
- About a step-by-step methodology for database design.
- The steps involved in conceptual database design.
- The documentation produced during conceptual database design.

9.1 Introduction to the database design methodology

If the database we require is reasonably complex, we will need a systematic approach to design and build a database that satisfies users' requirements and achieves stated performance requirements (such as response times). This systematic approach is called a *database design methodology*. Before presenting an overview of the methodology, we first discuss what a database design methodology is, and then identify the critical success factors in database design.

9.1.1 What is a design methodology?

Design methodology

A structured approach that uses procedures, techniques, tools, and documentation aids to support and facilitate the process of design.

A **design methodology** consists of phases made up of steps, which guide the designer in the techniques appropriate at each stage of the project. The phases also help the designer to plan, manage, control, and evaluate development projects. In addition, it is a structured approach for analyzing and modeling a set of requirements in a standardized and organized manner.

9.1.2 Phases of database design

Conceptual database design

Process of constructing a model of the data used in an organization independent of *all* physical considerations.

Logical database design

Process of constructing a model of the data used in an organization based on a specific data model, but independent of a particular DBMS and other physical considerations.

In this book we present a methodology that separates the database design into three main phases: conceptual, logical, and physical database design.

In the **conceptual database design** phase we build a conceptual data model of the data used by the organization, which is entirely independent of *all* implementation details such as the underlying data model (for example, the relational data model) or any other physical considerations. The conceptual data model identifies the important entities and relationships to be represented in the database (see later in this chapter). The conceptual database design is a source of information for the logical design phase.

In the **logical database design** phase we build the logical representation of the database. In this book we use the relational data model (see Chapter 2) as the basis of our logical design, and therefore we represent important entities and relationships as a set of relational tables (see Chapter 10). The logical database design is a source of information for the physical design phase, providing the physical database designer with a vehicle for making tradeoffs that are very important to the design of an efficient database.

In the **physical database design** phase we decide how the logical design is to be physically implemented in the target relational DBMS (see Chapter 11). This phase allows the designer to make decisions on how the database is to be implemented. Therefore, physical design is tailored to a specific DBMS such as Access, SQL Server, or Oracle.

9.1.3 Critical success factors in database design

Physical database design

Process of producing a description of the implementation of the database on secondary storage; it describes the base tables, file organizations, and indexes used to achieve efficient access to the data, and any associated integrity constraints and security restrictions.

The following guidelines are important to the success of database design:

- Work interactively with the users as much as possible.
- Follow a structured methodology throughout the data modeling process.
- Employ a data-driven approach.
- Incorporate structural and integrity considerations into the data models.
- Use normalization and transaction validation techniques in the methodology.
- Use diagrams to represent as much of the data models as possible.
- Use a database design language.
- Build a data dictionary to supplement the data model diagrams.
- Be willing to repeat steps.

All these guidelines are built into the methodology we are about to introduce.

9.2 Overview of the database design methodology

In this section, we present an overview of the database design methodology. The steps in the methodology are shown in Figure 9.1 and the chapter in which the step is discussed in detail is noted in the adjacent column.

- In *conceptual database design (Step 1)* we create an ER model (a high-level conceptual data model), which is a complete and accurate representation of the data requirements of the organization (or part of the organization) that is to be supported by the database. The model is checked to ensure that it has minimal redundancy and is capable of supporting the required transactions.

	Chapter
Conceptual database design	**9**
Step 1 Create ER model	
Step 1.1 Identify entities	
Step 1.2 Identify relationships	
Step 1.3 Identify and associate attributes with entities or relationships	
Step 1.4 Determine attribute domains	
Step 1.5 Determine candidate, primary, and alternate key attributes	
Step 1.6 Specialize/generalize entities (optional step)	
Step 1.7 Check the model for redundancy	
Step 1.8 Check that the model supports user transactions	
Step 1.9 Review the conceptual database design with users	
Logical database design	**10**
Step 2 Map ER model to tables	
Step 2.1 Create tables	
Step 2.2 Check table structures using normalization	
Step 2.3 Check that the tables support user transactions	
Step 2.4 Check integrity constraints	
Step 2.5 Review the logical database design with users	
Physical database design	**11**
Step 3 Translate the logical database design for target DBMS	
Step 3.1 Design base tables	
Step 3.2 Design representations of derived data	
Step 3.2 Design remaining integrity constraints	
Step 4 Choose file organisations and indexes	
Step 4.1 Analyze transactions	
Step 4.2 Choose file organizations	
Step 4.3 Choose indexes	
Step 5 Design user views	
Step 6 Design security mechanisms	
Step 7 Consider the introduction of controlled redundancy	
Step 8 Monitor and tune the operational system	

Figure 9.1 Steps in the methodology for conceptual, logical, and physical database design

- In *logical database design* (*Step 2*) we map (translate) the ER model to a set of relational tables. The structure of each table is checked to ensure that it has minimal redundancy using normalization. The tables are also checked to ensure that they are capable of supporting the required transactions. The required integrity constraints on the database are also defined.

Physical database design is divided into six main steps:

- In *Step 3* we translate the logical description of the relational tables into a physical description of base tables using the available functionality of the target DBMS. The implementations of the required integrity constraints on the physical database are also defined.
- In *Step 4* we choose file organizations and indexes for the base tables. Typically, DBMSs provide a number of alternative file organizations for data, with the exception of PC DBMSs, which tend to have a fixed storage structure.
- In *Step 5* we design the user views originally identified in the requirements collection and analysis stage of the database system development lifecycle.
- In *Step 6* we design the security measures to protect the data from unauthorized access.
- In *Step 7* we consider relaxing the normalization constraints imposed on the tables to improve the overall performance of the system. This step is considered only if the benefits outweigh the inherent problems involved in introducing redundancy while still maintaining consistency.
- In *Step 8* we monitor and tune the operational system to identify and resolve any performance problems resulting from the design and we implement new or changing requirements.

Appendix D presents a summary of the methodology for readers already familiar with database design and simply requiring an overview of the main steps.

Key point

Database design is an iterative process that has a starting point and an almost endless procession of refinements. Although we present the database design methodology as a procedural process, it must be emphasized that this does not imply that it should be performed in this manner. It is likely that the knowledge gained in one step may alter decisions made in a previous step. Similarly, we may find it useful to briefly look at a later step to help with an earlier step. The methodology should act as a framework to help guide us through the database design activity effectively.

9.3 Step 1: Conceptual database design methodology

In Chapter 5, we used the *StayHome Online Rentals* case study described in Section 5.4 to illustrate how fact-finding techniques can be used in the first three stages of the database system development lifecycle to capture and document the users' requirements for a database system. The documentation produced at each stage is a useful source of information for the database design stage. In particular, we discuss how the data dictionary is used and extended throughout Step 1 of database design.

Step 1 Create an ER model

Objective

To build an ER model of the data requirements of an organization (or part of an organization) to be supported by the database.

Each ER model comprises:

- entities;
- relationships;
- attributes and attribute domains;
- primary keys and alternate keys;
- integrity constraints.

The ER model is described in documentation and includes ER diagrams and a data dictionary. The tasks involved in Step 1 are:

- Step 1.1 Identify entities.
- Step 1.2 Identify relationships.
- Step 1.3 Identify and associate attributes with entities or relationships.
- Step 1.4 Determine attribute domains.
- Step 1.5 Determine candidate, primary, and alternate key attributes.
- Step 1.6 Specialize/generalize entities (optional step).
- Step 1.7 Check the model for redundancy.
- Step 1.8 Check that the model supports user transactions.
- Step 1.9 Review the conceptual database design with users.

Step 1.1 Identify entities

Objective

To identify the required entities.

The first step in building an ER model is to define the main objects that the users are interested in. These objects are the entities for the model. One method of identifying entities is to examine the users' requirements specification, and in particular the data dictionary.

The data shown in a data dictionary lists nouns or noun phrases that are mentioned (for example staff number, staff name, catalog number, and title). To facilitate analysis, the data can be shown in groups, for example we may group `staff number` and `staff name` with `Staff` and group `catalog number` and `title` with `DVD`.

Entities are identified from the data shown in the dictionary by looking for major objects such as people, places, or concepts of interest, and excluding those nouns that are merely qualities of other objects. Alternatively, entities can be identified by looking for objects that have an existence in their own right. For example, `Staff` is an entity because staff exists whether or not we know their names, addresses, and salaries. If possible, encourage the user to assist with this activity.

It is sometimes difficult to identify entities because of the way they are presented in the users' requirements specification. Users often talk in terms of examples or analogies. Instead of talking about staff in general, users may mention people's names. In some cases, users talk in terms of job roles, particularly where people or companies are involved. These roles may be job titles or responsibilities, such as Manager or Assistant. To further confuse matters, users frequently use synonyms and homonyms.

Key point

Two words are *synonyms* (or aliases) when they have the same meaning, for example 'Distribution Center' and 'Warehouse.' *Homonyms* occur when the same word can have different meanings depending on the context. For example, the word 'program' has several alternative meanings such as a series of events, a plan of work, a piece of software, and a course of study.

It is not always obvious whether a particular object is an entity, a relationship, or an attribute. For example, how should we model program? In fact, depending on the actual requirements we could model program as any or all of these. Analysis is subjective, and different designers may produce different, but equally valid, interpretations. The activity therefore relies, to a certain extent, on judgment and experience. Database designers must take a very selective view of the world and categorize the things that they observe within the context of the organization. Thus, there may be no unique set of entities deducible from a given users' requirements specification. However, successive iterations of the analysis process should lead to the choice of entities that are at least adequate for the system required.

StayHome Online Rentals entities

In Chapter 5, we produced the users' requirements specification for the *StayHome Online Rentals* database systems, which includes a first draft version of a data dictionary shown in Table 5.12. Analysis of the data listed in the data dictionary allows the identification of the main objects (entities) that the users are interested in. For the *StayHome Online Rentals* case study, we identify the following entities:

```
Actor               DistributionCenter
DVD                 DVDCopy
Member              MembershipType
RentalDelivery      Staff
Wish
```

Document entities

As we learn more about the entities, we extend the data dictionary to include additional information such as whether the entity is known by different names and the expected number of occurrences of each entity. Figure 9.2 shows this information on each entity for *StayHome Online Rentals*.

Step 1.2 Identify relationships

Objective

To identify the important relationships that exists between the entities.

Having identified the entities, the next step is to identify all the relationships (see Section 6.2) that exist between these entities. We examine the users' requirements specification to identify any relationships between entities. Typically, relationships are indicated by verbs or verbal expressions. For example:

```
DistributionCenter Has Staff
DistributionCenter Stocks DVDCopy
DVDCopy IsSentAs RentalDelivery
```

Entity	Description	Aliases	Occurrence
Actor	An actor stars in a DVD		5000 actors
DistributionCenter	A place of work	Warehouse	4 distribution centers
DVD	A film DVD		10 000 DVDs
DVDCopy	A copy of a film DVD		1 000 000 DVD copies
Member	A member is registered with *StayHome* to rent DVDs		100 000 members (predicted after 1 year)
MembershipType	A membership type describes the number of DVDs possible to borrow at any one time and the monthly charge		3 membership types
RentalDelivery	A delivery of one or more DVDs sent to a member's home address		700 000 DVD rental deliveries (predicted after 1 year)
Staff	A member of staff works at a distribution center	Employee	20 members of staff
Wish	A wish identifies the DVD that a member wishes to rent		2 500 000 member wishes (predicted after 1 year)

Figure 9.2 Extract from the data dictionary showing additional information on the entities for *StayHome Online Rentals*

Key point

We are interested only in required relationships between entities. In the previous example, we identified the `DistributionCenter` *`Stocks`* `DVDCopy` and `DVDCopy` *`IsSentAs`* `RentalDelivery` relationships. We may also include a relationship between `DistributionCenter` and `RentalDelivery` (for example, `DistributionCenter` *`Processes`* `RentalDelivery`). However, although this is a possible relationship, from the requirements it is not a relationship that we are interested in modeling. We discuss this further in Step 1.7.

Take great care to ensure that all the relationships that are either explicit or implicit in the users' requirements specification are noted. In principle, it should be possible to check each pair of entities for a potential relationship between them, but this would be a daunting task for a large system comprising hundreds of entities. However, it is unwise not to perform some such check, although missing relationships should become apparent when we check if the model supports the transactions that the users require in Step 1.8. Yet it is possible that an entity can have no relationship with other entities in the database but still play an important part in meeting the users' requirements.

In most instances, the relationships we find will be binary; in other words, the relationships exist between exactly two entities. However, look out for complex relationships that involve more than two entities, and recursive relationships that involve only one entity.

StayHome Online Rentals relationships

In Chapter 5, we produced the users' requirements specification for the *StayHome Online Rentals* database systems, which includes use case descriptions shown in Tables 5.9 to 5.11. Analysis of these descriptions reveals relationships between entities such as `Member` *`Selects`* `MembershipType` (see Table 5.9). Relationships are also identified by reviewing the answers given by the users during interviews or on questionnaires. The relationships for the *StayHome Online Rentals* case study are shown in Figure 9.3. Note that there are no complex relationships for this case study.

Use ER modeling

It is often easier to visualize a complex system rather than decipher long textual descriptions of such a system. The use of ER diagrams helps to more easily represent entities and how they relate to one another. We represent the above entities and relationships in the first-draft ER diagram shown in Figure 9.4.

Key point

Throughout the database design phase, it is recommended that ER diagrams are used whenever necessary, to help build up a picture of what we are attempting to model. Different people use different notations for ER diagrams. In this book, we have used the latest object-oriented notation called **UML (Unified Modeling Language)**, but other notations perform a similar function, as shown in Appendix C.

Determine the multiplicity constraints of relationships

Having identified the relationships we wish to model, we now want to determine the multiplicity (see Section 6.5) of each relationship. If specific values for the multiplicity are known, or even upper or lower limits, then document these values as well.

Entity	Relationship	Entity
DistributionCenter	Stocks	DVDCopy
DistributionCenter	Supplies	Member
DistributionCenter	Has	Staff
DVD	Stars	Actor
DVD	Is	DVDCopy
DVD	AppearsIn	Wish
DVDCopy	IsSentAs	RentalDelivery
Member	Selects	MembershipType
Member	Makes	Wish
Member	Receives	RentalDelivery
Staff	Manages	DistributionCenter

Figure 9.3 Main relationships for *StayHome Online Rentals*

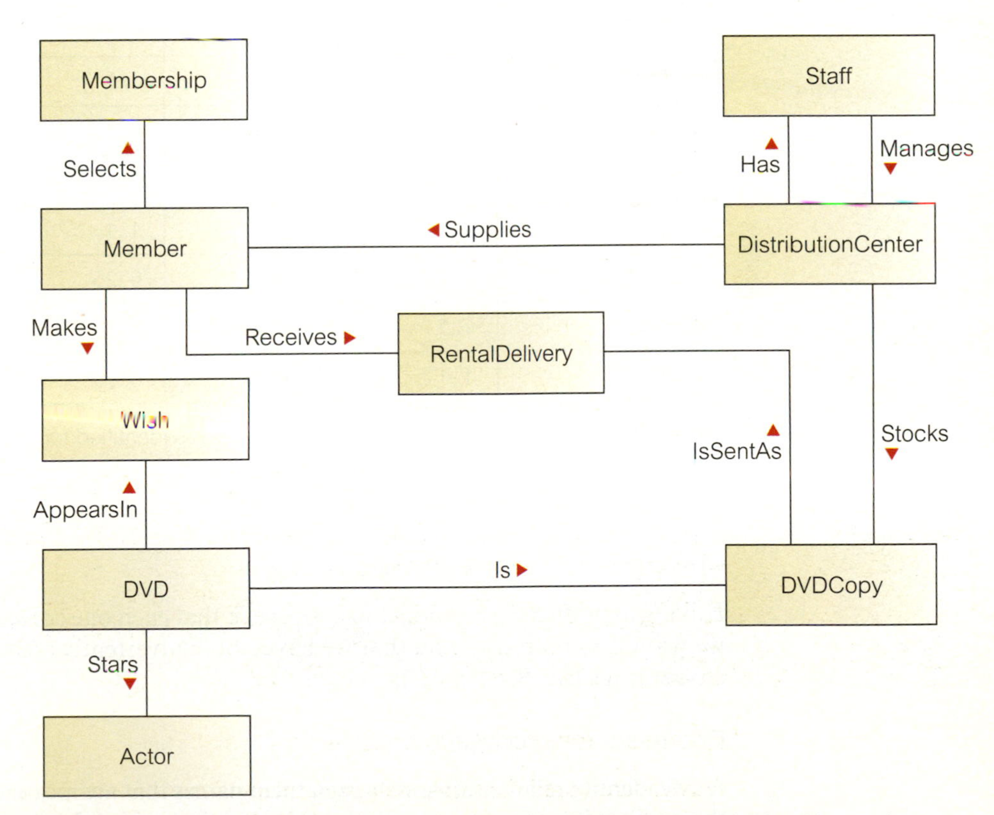

Figure 9.4 First draft ER diagram for *StayHome Online Rentals* showing entities and relationships

A model that includes multiplicity constraints represents the meaning of the relationship more explicitly and consequently results in a better representation of what we are trying to model. Multiplicity constraints are used to check and maintain the quality of the data. These constraints can be applied when the database is updated to determine whether or not the updates violate the stated integrity constraints.

StayHome Online Rentals multiplicity constraints

We continue the analysis of the users' requirements specification for the *StayHome Online Rentals* database systems to identify the multiplicity constraints for the relationships identified in Figure 9.4. For the *StayHome Online Rentals* case study, we identify the multiplicity constraints shown in Figure 9.5. Figure 9.6 shows the updated ER diagram with this information added.

Entity	Multiplicity	Relationship	Multiplicity	Entity
DistributionCenter	1..1	Stocks	1..*	DVDCopy
DistributionCenter	1..1	Supplies	1..*	Member
DistributionCenter	1..1	Has	1..*	Staff
DVD	1..*	Stars	0..*	Actor
DVD	1..1	Is	1..*	DVDCopy
DVD	1..1	AppearsIn	0..*	Wish
DVDCopy	1..5	IsSentAs	0..*	RentalDelivery
Member	1..*	Selects	1..1	MembershipType
Member	1..1	Makes	0..25	Wish
Member	1..1	Receives	1..*	RentalDelivery
Staff	1..1	Manages	0..1	DistributionCenter

Figure 9.5 Multiplicity constraints for the relationships identified for *StayHome Online Rentals*

Check for fan and chasm traps

Having identified the relationships, we check that each one correctly represents what we want it to represent, and that we have not inadvertently created any fan traps or chasm traps (see Section 6.7).

Document relationships

As we identify relationships, we assign them names that are meaningful and obvious to the user, and document each relationship description and the multiplicity constraints.

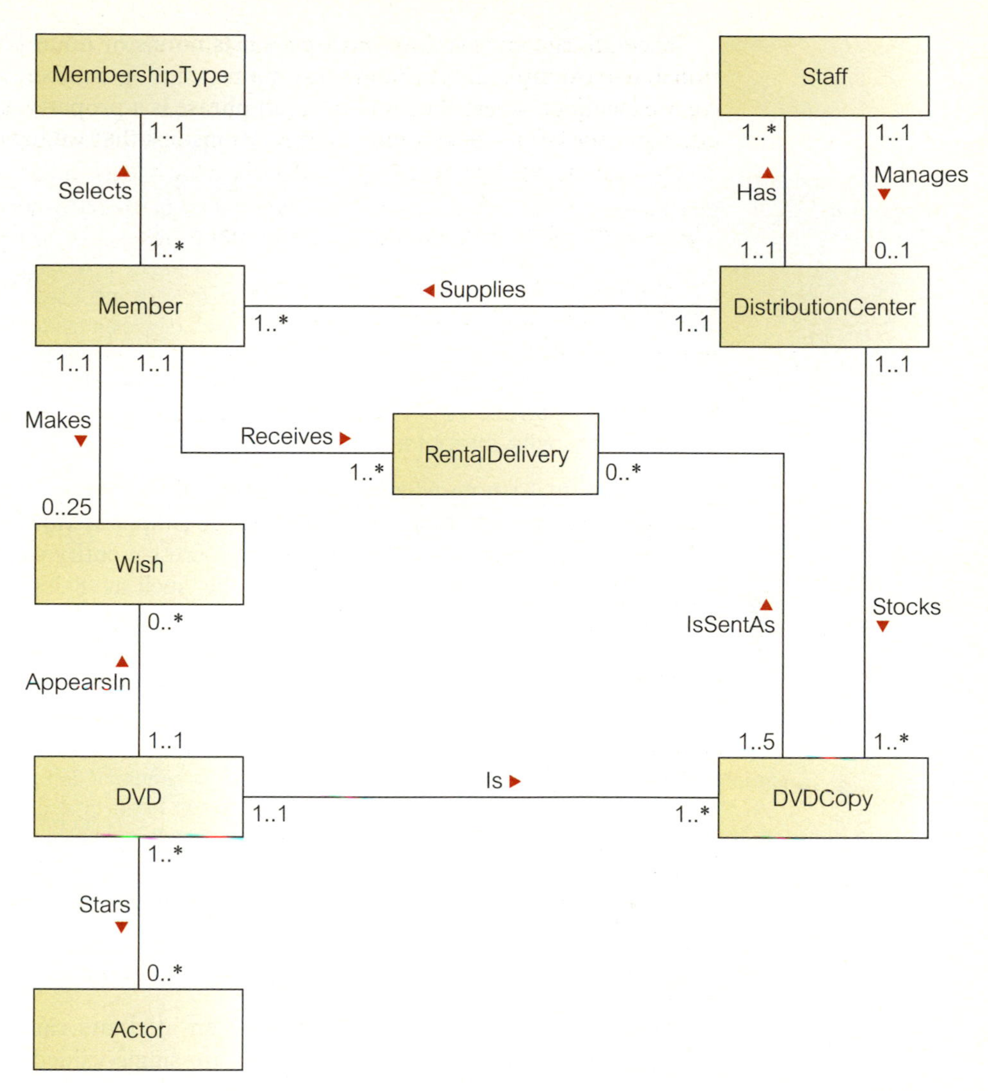

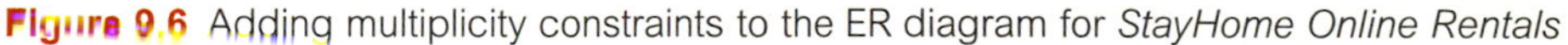
Figure 9.6 Adding multiplicity constraints to the ER diagram for *StayHome Online Rentals*

Step 1.3 Identify and associate attributes with entities or relationships

Objective

To associate attributes with the appropriate entities or relationships.

The next step in building an ER model is to identify the types of facts about the entities and relationships that we wish to be represented in the database. These facts are the attributes for the model. One method of identifying attributes is to examine the users' requirements specification, and in particular the data dictionary.

The data shown in a data dictionary lists nouns or noun phrases that are mentioned (for example staff number, staff name, catalog number, and title). Attributes can be identified where the noun or noun phrase is a property, quality, identifier, or characteristic of one of the entities or relationships that we have previously found.

Key point By far the easiest thing to do when identifying an entity or a relationship in the users' requirements specification is to consider '*What information are we required to hold on . . . ?*' The answer to this question should be described in the users' specification, and in particular the data dictionary. However, in some cases, it may be necessary to ask the users to clarify the requirements. Unfortunately, their answers may also contain other concepts, and so users' responses must be carefully considered.

Simple/composite attributes

It is important to note whether an attribute is simple or composite (see Section 6.3.1). Composite attributes are made up of simple attributes. For example, the `address` attribute of the `DistributionCenter` entity can be simple and hold all the details of an address as a single value, such as '8 Jefferson Way, Portland, OR, 97201.' However, the `address` attribute may also represent a composite attribute, made up of simple attributes that hold the address details as separate values in the attributes `dStreet` ('8 Jefferson Way'), `dCity` ('Portland'), `dState` ('OR'), and `dZipCode` ('97201').

Note The option to represent address details as a simple or composite attribute is determined by the users' requirements. If users do not need to access the separate components of an address then represent the `address` attribute as a simple attribute. If users do need to access the individual components of an address then represent the `address` attribute as being composite, made up of the required simple attributes.

Single/multi-valued attributes

In addition to being simple or composite, an attribute can also be single-valued or multi-valued. Although most attributes are single-valued, occasionally a multi-valued attribute (see Section 6.3.2) will be identified; that is, an attribute that holds multiple values for a single entity occurrence.

The *StayHome Online Rentals* case study has no multi-valued attributes but imagine that `Member` had a multi-valued attribute called `telNo`. There are two ways to model this situation. Either `telNo` is shown as a multi-valued attribute for the `Member` entity or identify `Telephone` as a separate entity, which is related to `Member` through a one-to-many (1:*) relationship. Both representations are equally valid ways to model this situation. As we will see shortly, in Step 2.1 of Chapter 10, multi-valued attributes are mapped to tables anyway, so both approaches produce the same end result.

Derived attributes

Attributes whose values can be found by examining the values of other attributes are known as derived attributes (see Section 6.3.3). All derived attributes must be shown in the data model to avoid a potential loss of information, which may occur if the attribute or attributes on which the derived attribute is based are deleted or modified.

We will consider the representation of derived attributes during physical database design. Depending on how the attribute is used, new values for a derived attribute may be calculated each time it is accessed or when the value(s) it is derived from changes. However, this issue is not the concern of conceptual database design, and we will discuss how best to physically represent derived attributes in Step 3.2 in Chapter 11.

Attributes for relationships

It is important to note that attributes can be associated with relationships. For example, the attribute called `character` was shown in the data dictionary of Table 5.12 as being associated with `Actor`. However, as `character` represents the name of the role played by an actor in a given DVD, it is associated with the *`Stars`* relationship and not the `DVD` or `Actor` entities. The reason for this placement is that the *`Stars`* relationship is a many-to-many relationship. However, attributes for relationships can also be found on relationships with different cardinalities, such as one-to-one. For example, if we recorded the date when a member of staff started to manage a distribution center, we would assign a `dateStart` attribute to the one-to-one *`Manages`* relationship. An additional example of an attribute associated with a relationship is discussed below in item (2).

Potential problems

When assigning attributes to entities and relationships, it is not uncommon for it to become apparent that one or more entities have been omitted from the original selection. In this case, return to the previous steps, document the new entities, and re-examine the associated relationships.

We must also be aware of cases where attributes appear to be associated with more than one entity as this can indicate the following:

(1) We have identified several entities that can be represented as a single entity. For example, we may have identified entities `Manager` and `Assistant`. Each have the attributes `staffNo` (staff number), `name`, `position`, `salary`, and `eMail`. Therefore these entities could be represented as a single entity called `Staff`.

> **Note** On the other hand, it may be that these entities share many attributes but there are also attributes that are unique to each entity. In Chapter 7, we looked at enhanced ER modeling concepts known as specialization/generalization, and provided guidelines for their use. These enhanced concepts allow us to represent this type of situation more accurately. We omit these concepts here and consider them as a separate optional step (Step 1.6) to keep the database design methodology as simple as possible.

(2) We have identified a relationship between entities. In this case, you must associate the attribute with only *one* entity, namely the parent entity, and ensure that the relationship was previously identified in Step 1.2. If this is not the case,

the documentation should be updated with details of the newly identified relationship. For example, we identified the entities `DistributionCenter` and `Staff` with the following attributes (as shown in the first draft version of the data dictionary in Table 5.12):

`DistributionCenter`	`dCenterNo`, `street`, `city`, `state`, `zipCode`, `managerName`
`Staff`	`staffNo`, `name`, `position`, `salary`, `eMail`

The presence of the `managerName` attribute in `DistributionCenter` is intended to represent the relationship `Staff` *Manages* `DistributionCenter`. In this case, however, the `managerName` attribute should be omitted from `DistributionCenter` and the relationship *Manages* should be part of the model.

StayHome Online Rentals attributes for entities and relationships

For *StayHome Online Rentals* case study, we identify and associate attributes with entities and relationships as follows:

Attributes associated with entities

`DistributionCenter`	`dCenterNo`, `address` (composite: `dStreet`, `dCity`, `dState`, `dZipCode`)
`Staff`	`staffNo`, `name`, `position`, `salary`, `eMail`
`DVD`	`catalogNo`, `title`, `genre`, `rating`
`Actor`	`actorName`
`Member`	`memberNo`, `name` (composite: `mFName`, `mLName`), `address` (composite: `mStreet`, `mCity`, `mState`, `mZipCode`), `mEMail`, `mPword`
`MembershipType`	`mTypeNo`, `mTypeDesc`, `maxRentals`, `monthlyCharge`
`RentalDelivery`	`deliveryNo`, `dateOut`
`DVDCopy`	`DVDNo`, `available`
`Wish`	`ranking`

Attributes associated with relationships

Stars	`character`
IsSentAs	`dateReturn`

Note The `address` attribute in the `DistributionCenter` and `Member` entities and the `name` attribute in `Member` are composite, whereas the `name` attribute in `Staff` and `Actor` is simple. This reflects the users' access requirements for these attributes.

Document attributes

As we identify attributes, assign them names that are meaningful and obvious to the user. Where appropriate, record the following information for each attribute:

Entity	Attribute Name	Description	Data type and length	Nulls	Multi-valued
Distribution Center	dCenterNo	Uniquely identifies each distribution center	4 fixed characters	No	No
	dStreet	Street location of distribution center	60 variable characters	No	No
	dCity	City location of distribution center	20 variable characters	No	No
	dState	State location of distribution center	20 variable characters	No	No
	dZipCode	ZipCode location of distribution center	5 variable characters	No	No
Staff	staffNo	Uniquely identifies each member of staff	5 fixed characters	No	No
	name	Full name of member of staff	30 variable characters	No	No
	position	Position of a member of staff	10 variable characters	No	No
	salary	Salary of member of staff	Currency US dollars	No	No
	eMail	email address of member of staff	50 variable characters	No	No

Figure 9.7 Extract from the data dictionary for *StayHome Online Rentals* showing descriptions of attributes

- attribute name and description;
- data type and length;
- any **aliases** that the attribute is known by;
- whether the attribute must always be specified (in other words, whether the attribute allows or disallows nulls);
- whether the attribute is multi-valued;
- whether the attribute is composite, and if so which simple attributes make up the composite attribute;
- whether the attribute is derived, and if so how it should be computed;
- default values for the attribute (if specified).

Figure 9.7 shows examples of additional information about attributes for *StayHome Online Rentals* documented in an extended version of a data dictionary.

Step 1.4 Determine attribute domains

Objective

To determine domains for the attributes in the ER model.

The objective of this step is to determine domains for the attributes in the ER model. A **domain** is a pool of values from which one or more attributes draw their values. Examples of the attribute domains for *StayHome Online Rentals* include:

- the attribute domain of valid `dCenterNo` numbers as being a four-character fixed-length string, with the first character as letter 'D' and the next three characters as digits in the range 000–999;
- the possible values for the `available` attribute of the `DVDCopy` entity as being either 'Y' or 'N'. In other words, the domain of the `available` attribute is a character string consisting of the values 'Y' or 'N'.

A fully developed data model specifies the domains for each of the model's attributes and includes:

- the allowable set of values for the attribute;
- the size and format of the attribute.

Document attribute domains

As we identify attribute domains we record their names and characteristics in the data dictionary. We also update the data dictionary entries for attributes to record their domain in place of the data type and length information.

Step 1.5 Determine candidate, primary, and alternate key attributes

Objective

To identify the candidate key(s) for each entity and, if there is more than one candidate key, to choose one to be the primary key, and to identify the others as alternate keys.

This step is concerned with identifying the candidate key(s) for an entity and then selecting one to be the primary key (see Sections 2.3.3 and 6.3.4). Be careful to choose a candidate key that can never be null (if the candidate key consists of more than one attribute, then this applies to each attribute). If we identify more than one candidate key, we must choose one to be the primary key; the remaining candidate keys are called alternate keys.

Key point People's names generally do not make good candidate keys, as we discussed in Section 2.3.3. For example, we may think that a suitable candidate key for the `Staff` entity would be `name`, the member of staff's name. However, it is possible for two people with the same name to work for *StayHome Online Rentals*, which would clearly invalidate the choice of `name` as a candidate key. We can make a similar argument for the names of members. In such cases, rather than coming up with combinations of attributes that may provide uniqueness, it may be better to define a new attribute that would always ensure uniqueness, such as a `staffNo` attribute for the `Staff` entity and a `memberNo` attribute for the `Member` entity.

When choosing a primary key from among the candidate keys, we should use the following guidelines to help make the selection:

- the candidate key with the minimal set of attributes;
- the candidate key that is less likely to have its values changed;
- the candidate key that is less likely to lose uniqueness in the future;
- the candidate key with fewest characters (for those with textual attribute(s));
- the candidate key with the smallest maximum value (for numerical attributes);
- the candidate key that is easiest to use from the users' point of view.

In the process of identifying primary keys, note whether an entity is strong or weak (see Section 6.4). If we can assign a primary key to an entity, the entity is referred to as being *strong*. If we cannot identify a primary key for an entity, the entity is referred to as being *weak*. However, it is possible that one or more of the attributes associated with a weak entity may form part of the final primary key, but they do not provide uniqueness by themselves.

Note The primary key of a weak entity can only be identified when we map the weak entity to a table, which we will describe in Step 2.1 in Chapter 10.

StayHome Online Rentals primary keys

Examination of the users' requirements for *StayHome Online Rentals*, and in particular the data dictionary (see Table 5.12), revealed that there are no primary keys for the `Actor` and `Wish` entities. However, for the `Actor` entity, a new primary key attribute called `actorNo` is created as the only other attribute associated with this entity, that is the actor's name is considered not suitable for distinguishing one actor from another.

The process of creating a new primary key attribute is not repeated for the `Wish` entity and therefore this entity remains as a weak entity. The only other attribute associated with this entity is the `ranking` attribute and as such is not suitable as a primary key. At this stage it appears that each `Wish` entity occurrence cannot be uniquely identified, however this problem is resolved when ER models are mapped to tables.

In summary, all of the entities for *StayHome Online Rentals* shown in Figure 9.8 are strong with the exception of the `Wish` entity, which is weak.

Document candidate, primary, and alternate keys

Record the identification of candidate, primary, and alternate keys (when available).

Step 1.6 Specialize/generalize entities (optional step)

Objective

To identify superclass and subclass entities, where appropriate.

In this step, we have the option to continue the development of the ER model using the process of specialization/generalization discussed in Chapter 7. The modeling of superclasses and subclasses adds more information to the data model, but also adds more complexity as well. As *StayHome Online Rentals* is a relatively simple case

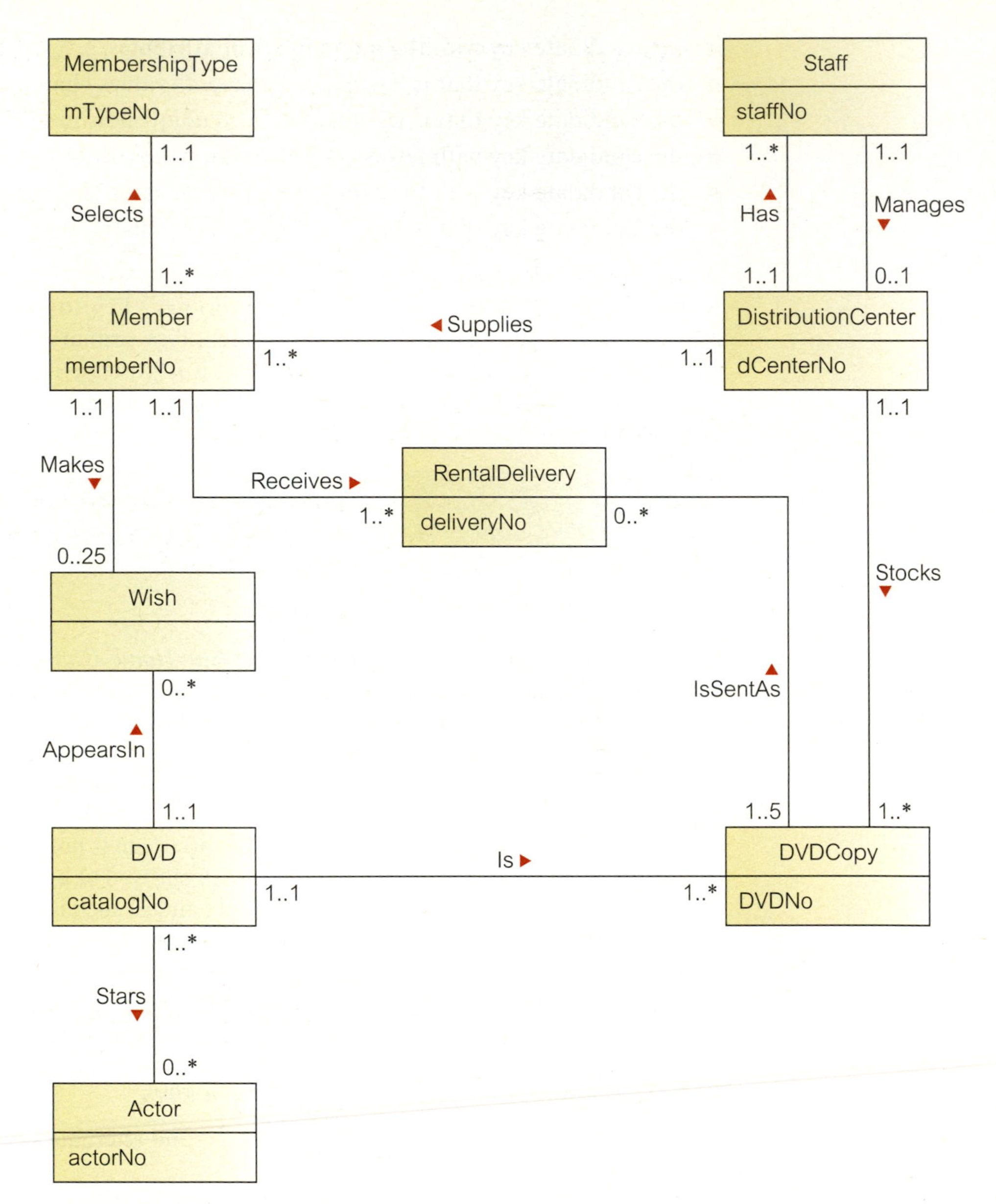

Figure 9.8 ER diagram for *StayHome Online Rentals* showing primary keys

study and has no obvious areas where the use of specialization/generalization would be beneficial, we therefore choose to omit this step.

> **Note** If *StayHome Online Rentals* decided to sell, as well as rent out DVDs, in the future, it may be necessary to introduce a `DVD` superclass with two subclasses called `DVDForRent` and `DVDForSale`. We leave this as an exercise for the reader to consider the attributes and relationships associated with the superclass and each subclass.

Step 1.7 Check the model for redundancy

Objective

To check for the presence of redundancy in the ER model.

In this step, we examine the ER model with the specific objectives of identifying whether there is any redundancy present and removing any that does exist. The two activities in this step are:

(1) re-examine one-to-one (1:1) relationships;

(2) remove redundant relationships.

(1) Re-examine one-to-one (1:1) relationships

In the identification of entities, we may have identified two entities that represent the same object in the organization and as such may be related through a 1:1 relationship (see Section 6.5.1). For example, imagine that we identified two entities named `DistributionCenter` and `Warehouse` that are actually the same; in other words, `DistributionCenter` is a synonym for `Warehouse`. In this case, the two entities should be merged. If the primary keys are different, choose one of them to be the primary key and leave the other as an alternate key, as shown in Figure 9.9. However, in this case `dCenterNo` and `warehouseNo` are the same, so `dCenterNo` is selected to be the primary key.

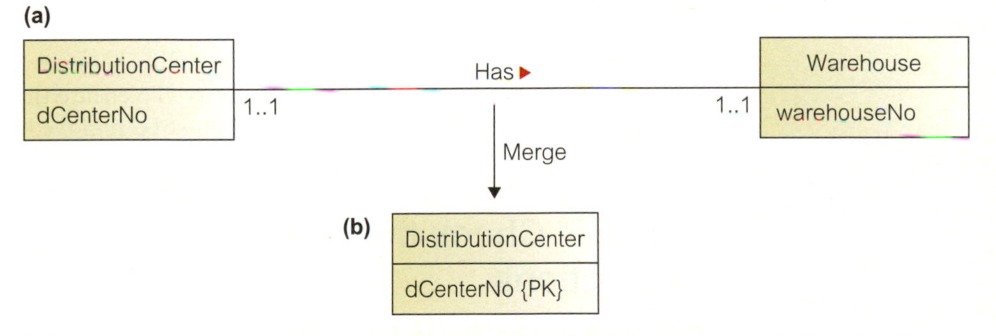

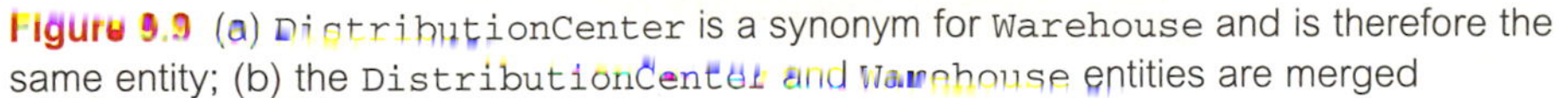
Figure 9.9 (a) `DistributionCenter` is a synonym for `Warehouse` and is therefore the same entity; (b) the `DistributionCenter` and `Warehouse` entities are merged

(2) Remove redundant relationships

A relationship is redundant if the same information can be obtained via other relationships. We are trying to develop a minimal data model and as redundant relationships are unnecessary then they should be removed. It is relatively easy to identify whether there is more than one path between two entities. However, this does not necessarily imply that one of the relationships is redundant, as they may represent different associations in the organization.

For example, consider the relationships between the `Staff`, `Rental`, and `Car` entities shown in Figure 9.10. There are two ways to find out which members of staff rent out which cars. There is the direct route using the *`Drives`* relationship between

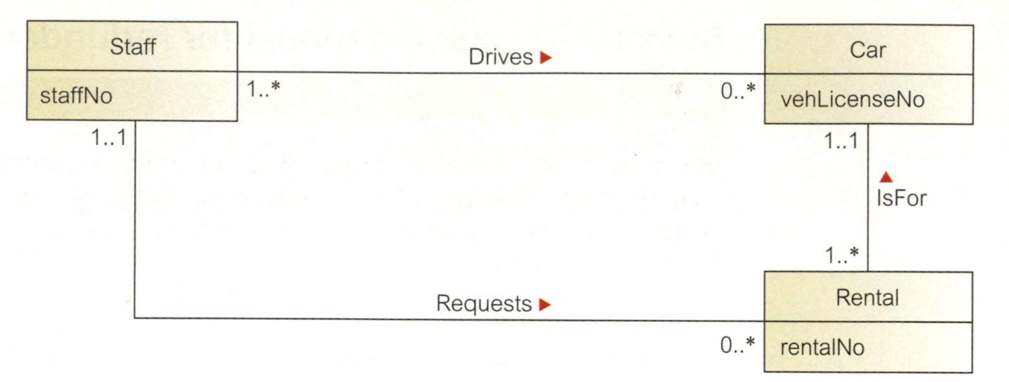

Figure 9.10 Remove the redundant *Drives* relationship as it does not convey any additional information about the relationship between *Staff* and *Car*

the Staff and Car entities and there is the indirect route using the *Requests* and *IsFor* relationships via the Rental entity. Before we can assess whether both routes are required, we need to establish the purpose of each relationship. The *Drives* relationship indicates which members of staff drive which cars. On the other hand, the *Requests* relationship indicates which members of staff request to rent (in order to drive) which car, while the *IsFor* relationship indicates which cars are associated with which rentals. Although it is true that there is a relationship between members of staff and the cars they drive, this is not a direct relationship in terms of the data model and the association is more accurately represented through a rental agreement. The *Drives* relationship is therefore redundant and does not convey any additional information about the relationship between Staff and Car that cannot be found out through the Rental entity. To ensure that we create a minimal model, the redundant *Drives* relationship must be removed.

Step 1.8 Check that the model supports user transactions

Objective

To ensure that the ER model supports the required transactions.

We now have an ER model that represents the database requirements of the organization (or part of the organization). The objective of this step is to check the ER model to ensure that the model supports the required transactions. The transaction requirements for *StayHome Online Rentals* are presented as use case diagrams and descriptions (see Section 5.4.4).

Using the ER model and the data dictionary, we attempt to perform the operations manually. If we resolve all transactions in this way, we have checked that the ER model supports the required transactions. However, if we are unable to perform a transaction manually then there must be a problem with the data model, which must be resolved. In this case, it is likely that we have omitted an entity, a relationship, or an attribute from the data model.

We examine two approaches to ensuring that the ER model supports the required transactions.

(1) Describing the transaction

In the first approach, we check that all the information (entities, relationships, and their attributes) required by transactions given in the use case descriptions is provided by the model, by documenting a description of the transaction's requirements. For example, consider the 'Search for DVD' transaction of the Member user view of *StayHome Online Rentals* shown in Figure 5.11 and described in Table 5.9. A specific example of this type of transaction could be when a member wishes to find an answer to the following question.

> **'What are the titles of all DVDs starring Kevin Spacey?'**
> DVD details, including DVD title, are stored in the `DVD` entity and actor details, including actor name, are stored in the `Actor` entity. In this case, we use the `DVD` *`Stars`* `Actor` relationship to find the title of each DVD which stars 'Kevin Spacey'.

(2) Using transaction pathways

The second approach to validating the data model against the required transactions involves representing the pathways taken by transactions directly on the ER diagram. We demonstrate this approach using the transactions use case descriptions (see Table 5.9) for the Member user view as shown in Figure 9.11. Clearly, the more transactions that exist, the more complex this diagram would become, so for readability we may need several such diagrams to cover all the transactions.

Step 1.9 Review the conceptual database design with users

Objective

To review the ER model with the users to ensure that the model is a 'true' representation of the data requirements of the organization (or the part of the organization) to be supported by the database.

Before completing conceptual database design (Step 1), we should review the ER model (high-level conceptual data model) with the users. The ER diagram for *StayHome Online Rentals* showing all entities, relationships, and attributes is shown in Figure 9.12.

This ER diagram forms only part of the ER model, which also includes all the documentation that describes what the ER diagram shows and also what cannot easily be represented by an ER diagram. For example, the details of attribute domains cannot be easily shown on an ER model.

If any anomalies are present in the data model, we must make the appropriate changes, which may require repeating the previous step(s). We should repeat this process until the users are prepared to 'sign off' the model as being a 'true' representation of the data requirements of the organization (or part of the organization) to be supported by the database.

In the following chapter we proceed to the next major step, namely logical database design, which maps the ER model to a set of tables and checks that the tables satisfy users' requirements.

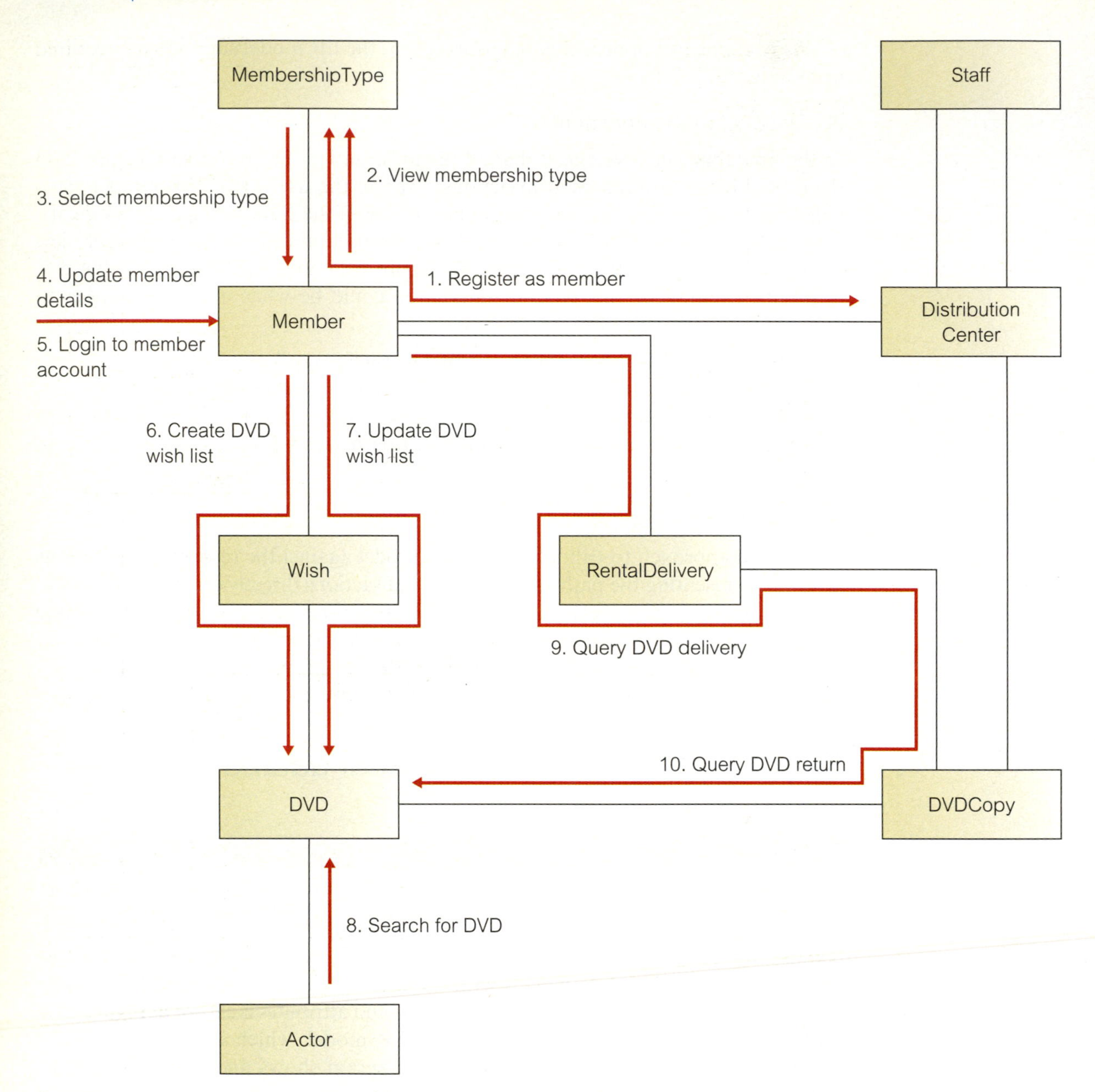

Figure 9.11 Using use case descriptions to check that the ER model supports the Member user view of *StayHome Online Rentals*

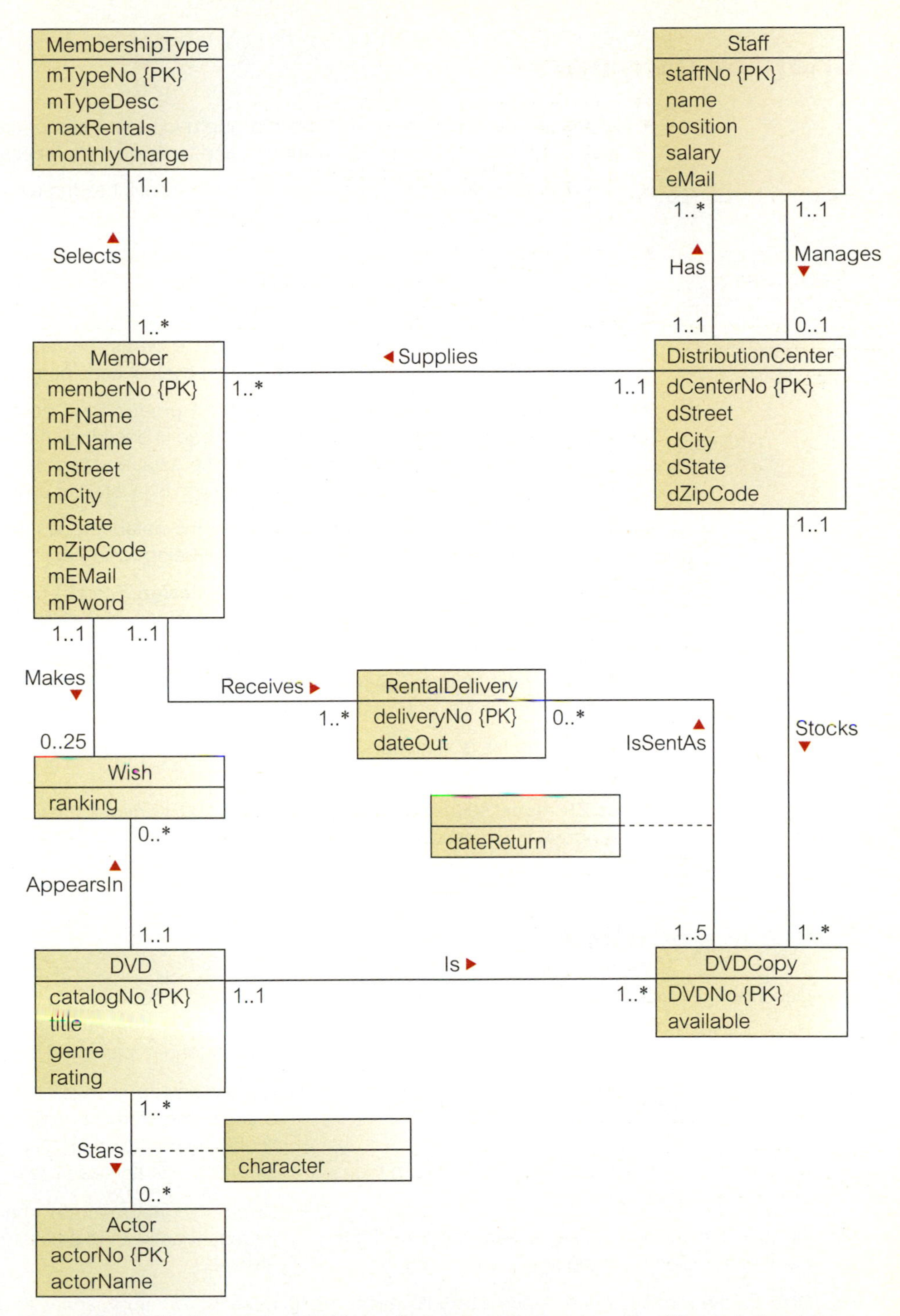

Figure 9.12 ER diagram for *StayHome Online Rentals* showing all entities, relationships, and attributes

Chapter summary

- A **design methodology** is a structured approach that uses procedures, techniques, tools, and documentation aids to support and facilitate the process of design.
- The **database design methodology** used in this book has three main phases: conceptual, logical, and physical database design.
- **Conceptual database design** is the process of constructing a model of the data used in an organization independent of *all* physical considerations.
- **Logical database design** is the process of constructing a model of the data used in an organization based on a specific data model such as the relational data model, but independent of a particular DBMS and other physical considerations.
- **Physical database design** is the process of producing a description of the implementation of the database on secondary storage; it describes the file organizations and indexes used to achieve efficient access of the data, and any associated integrity constraints and security restrictions. Physical design is tailored to a specific DBMS system.
- There are **critical factors** for the success of the database design stage including, for example, working interactively with users and being willing to repeat steps.
- The main objective of **conceptual database design** (Step 1) of the methodology is to build an ER model to represent the data requirements of the organization (or part of the organization) to be supported by the database.
- An **ER model** includes entities, relationships, attributes, attribute domains, candidate keys, primary keys, and alternate keys.
- An **ER model** is described by documentation including **ER diagrams** and a **data dictionary**.
- An **ER model** should be checked to ensure that it does not have any **redundancy** and supports the transactions required by the users.

Review questions

9.1 Describe the purpose of a design methodology.

9.2 Describe the main phases involved in database design.

9.3 Identify important factors in the success of database design.

9.4 Discuss the important role played by users in the process of database design.

9.5 Discuss the main purpose of each step of the database design methodology.

9.6 Discuss the main activities associated with each step of conceptual database design methodology.

9.7 Discuss an approach to identifying entities and relationships from a users' requirements specification (and in particular the data dictionary).

9.8 Discuss an approach to identifying attributes from a users' requirements specification (and in particular the data dictionary) and the association of attributes with entities or relationships.

9.9 Discuss an approach to checking an ER model for redundancy. Give an example to illustrate your answer.

9.10 Describe two approaches to checking that an ER model supports the transactions required by the user.

Exercises

9.11 The Director of *StayHome Online Rentals* has submitted the following additional requirements.

(a) A stronger connection between a member's wish to view a particular DVD and the sending out of that DVD to the member's home. This will mean that when a member is sent a particular DVD, the corresponding entry in the member's wish list can be removed from the wish list. (Hint: Create a new attribute called wish number (`wishNo`) to uniquely identify each wish.)

(b) To capture the date a member makes a wish to view a particular DVD. This will allow analysis of the time interval between requesting and receiving a particular DVD. (Hint: Create a new attribute called wish date (`wishDate`).)

(c) To allow DVDs to be described using one or more genres. (Hint: This means that the `genre` attribute will change from being single-valued to multi-valued.)

(d) To capture and store the number of DVDs sent in a single rental delivery package. (Hint: Create a new derived attribute called number of DVDs sent (`noDVDSent`).)

(e) To capture members' complaints about DVDs, and for each complaint to identify the member of staff who dealt with it and the action taken to resolve it. (Hint: Create a new entity called `Complaint` with attributes called complaint description (`complaintDesc`), date complaint received (`dateReceived`), and action taken to resolve the complain (`actionTaken`).)

Consider how accommodating these new requirements affect the current ER model for *StayHome Online Rental*. Alter the ER model shown in Figure 9.12 to include these new requirements. The answers to this exercise are shown in Figure 10.15 of Exercise 10.7.

9.12 Create an ER model for the Buyer user view of the *StayHome Online Rentals* case study described in Appendix A.

9.13 Create an ER model for the *PerfectPets* case study described in Appendix B. (If appropriate, use the enhanced ER concepts.)

9.14 Merge the ER model created for Exercise 9.13 to the ER model (representing the data merged requirements for the Member, Assistant, and Manager user views of the *StayHome Online Rentals* case study) shown in Figure 9.12 using the optional Step 2.6 of the database design methodology given in Appendix D.

9.15 Identify the entities, relationships, and the associated attributes for each case study given in Appendix I, and then create an ER model without first looking at the answer ER model that accompanies each case study. Compare your ER model with the answer ER model and justify any differences found.

9.16 Read the following case study that describes the data requirements for the *EasyDrive School of Motoring*.

The *EasyDrive School of Motoring* has many well-qualified instructors who have an unbeatable record of success in teaching people to drive. A new client must first attend an interview with an instructor to discuss an appropriate plan of learning. During this interview the client provides personal details, including his or her provisional driving license number. Each client is uniquely identified using a client number. A client may request individual lessons or book a block of five, ten, or twenty lessons.

The more lessons a client books in advance, the less they are charge per hour for a lesson. An individual driving lesson is for one hour, which begins and ends at the *EasyDrive School of Motoring* office. A lesson is with a particular instructor in a particular car at a given time. Lessons can start as early as 8am or as late as 8pm. After each lesson, the instructor records the progress made by the client and notes the mileage used during the lesson. The school has a pool of cars, which are adapted for the purposes of teaching. Each instructor has the sole use of a particular car. Once ready, a client applies to take a theoretical and then a practical driving test. If a client fails to pass, the instructor must record the reasons for the failure. Only the results of the latest attempt to pass the theoretical and practical test are recorded.

(a) Identify the main entities of the *EasyDrive School of Motoring*.
(b) Identify the main relationships between the entities.
(c) Determine the multiplicity constraints for each relationship.
(d) Identify attributes and associate them with an entity or relationship. (Hint: As few attributes are described in the case study, you will need to create your own.)
(e) Determine candidate and primary key attributes for each entity.
(f) Using your answers (a) to (e), represent the data requirements of the *EasyDrive School of Motoring* as an ER model. State any assumptions necessary to support your design. The final answer to this exercise is shown as Figure 10.16 of Exercise 10.8.

9.17 Read the following case study for a brief description of a taxi company called *FastCabs*.

Each office has a manager, several taxi owners, drivers and administrative staff. The manager is responsible for the day-to-day running of the office. An owner provides one or more taxis to *FastCabs* and each taxi is allocated for use to a number of drivers. The majority of owners are also drivers. *FastCabs* taxis are not available for hire by the public hailing a taxi in the street but must be requested by first phoning the company to attend a given address. There are two kinds of clients, namely private and business. The business provided by private clients is on an *ad hoc* basis. The details of private clients are collected on the first booking of a taxi. However, the business provided by business clients is more formal and involves agreeing a contract of work with the business. A contract stipulates the number of jobs that *FastCabs* will undertake for a fixed fee. When a job comes into *FastCabs* the name, phone number and contract number (when appropriate) of the client is taken and then the pick-up date/time and pick-up/drop-off addresses are noted. Each job is allocated a unique jobID. The nearest driver to the pick-up address is called by radio and is informed of the details of the job. When a job is completed, the driver should note the mileage used and the charge made (for private clients only). If a job is not complete, the reason for the failed job should be noted.

(a) Identify the main entities of *FastCabs*.
(b) Identify the main relationships between the entities.
(c) Determine the multiplicity constraints for each relationship.
(d) Identify attributes and associate them with an entity or relationship. (Hint: As few attributes are described in the case study, you will need to create your own.)
(e) Determine candidate and primary key attributes for each entity.

(f) Using your answers (a) to (e) represent the data requirements of the *FastCabs* as an enhanced ER (EER) model. (Hint: Use optional Step 1.6 of the methodology to identify private clients (subclass) and business clients (subclass) as being special types of clients (superclass).) State any assumptions necessary to support your design.

CHAPTER

10 Logical database design

Preview

This chapter describes the second step of our database design methodology, namely logical database design. The source of information for this step is the ER model created in Step 1 – conceptual database design, described in Chapter 9. We translate the conceptual database design into a logical database design, which for our methodology is based on the relational model. (The relational model was described in Chapter 2.)

Learning objectives

In this chapter you will learn:

- How to create a set of tables from an ER model.
- How to check that the tables are well – structured using normalization.
- How to check that the tables are capable of supporting the required transactions.
- How to define and document integrity constraints on the tables.

10.1 Step 2: Map the ER model to tables

Objective

To create tables based on the ER model and to check that these tables are well – structured and support the required transactions.

The main purpose of this step is to produce a description of tables based on the ER model created in conceptual database design (Step 1) of the methodology. The structure of each table is checked using normalization to ensure that no unnecessary duplication of columns exists. The tables are also checked to ensure that they are able to support the data requirements of the user transactions. Finally, integrity constraints associated with the tables are checked to ensure that each is represented in the final logical database design.

The tasks involved in Step 2 are:

- Step 2.1 Create tables.
- Step 2.2 Check table structures using normalization.
- Step 2.3 Check that the tables support user transactions.
- Step 2.4 Check integrity constraints.
- Step 2.5 Review the logical database design with users.

We demonstrate logical database design (Step 2) of the methodology using the ER model for the *StayHome Online Rentals* case study created in conceptual database design (Step 1).

Step 2.1 Create tables

Objective

To create a set of tables from the ER model.

In this step, we create tables from the ER model to represent the entities, relationships, attributes, and constraints. The structure of each table is created from the information that describes the ER model, including ER diagrams, data dictionary, and any other supporting documentation. To describe the composition of each table we use a database definition language for relational databases. Using the DBDL, we first specify the name of the table, followed by a list of the names of the table's simple attributes enclosed in brackets. We then identify the primary key, and where appropriate any alternate key(s) and/or foreign key(s) of the table. (Relational keys were described in Section 2.3.3.)

We illustrate this process using the ER model for *StayHome Online Rentals* shown as a diagram in Figure 9.12. However, in some cases it is necessary to add examples not shown in this model to illustrate particular points.

How to represent entities

For each entity in the ER model, create a table that includes all the entity's simple attributes. For composite attributes, include only the simple attributes that make up the composite attribute in the table. (Simple and composite attributes were described in Section 6.3.1.) For example, for the composite `address` attribute of the `DistributionCenter` entity, we include its simple attributes `dStreet`, `dCity`, `dState`, and `dZipCode`. Where possible, identify the column(s) that make up the primary key for each table. For the entities shown in Figure 9.12, we document the initial table structures in Figure 10.1.

For some tables, only an incomplete set of columns will be identified at this stage because we are yet to represent the relationships that exist between the entities shown in Figure 9.12. In particular, this means that we cannot identify the columns that make up the primary key for weak entities. For example, we are unable to identify

Actor (actorNo, actorName) **Primary key** actorNo	**DistributionCenter** (dCenterNo, dStreet, dCity, dState, dZipCode) **Primary key** dCenterNo **Alternate key** dZipCode
DVD (catalogNo, title, genre, rating) **Primary key** catalogNo	**DVDCopy** (DVDNo, available) **Primary key** DVDNo
DVDRental (deliveryNo, dateOut) **Primary key** deliveryNo	**Member** (memberNo, mFName, mLName, mStreet, mCity, mState, mZipCode, mEMail, mPword) **Primary key** memberNo **Alternate key** mEMail
MembershipType (mTypeNo, mTypeDesc, maxRentals, monthlyCharge) **Primary key** mTypeNo **Alternate key** mTypeDesc	**Staff** (staffNo, name, position, salary, eMail) **Primary key** staffNo **Alternate key** eMail
Wish (ranking) **Primary key** Not identified so far	

Figure 10.1 Initial table structures representing the entities in *StayHome Online Rentals* as shown in Figure 9.12

a primary key for the Wish table because this table represents a weak entity, which does not have all the necessary attributes so far to form a primary key. We discuss the identification of primary key columns for weak entities, and in particular for the Wish entity, at the end of this step. (Weak entities were described in Section 6.4.)

How to represent relationships

The relationship that an entity has with another entity is represented by the primary key/foreign key mechanism. In deciding where to *post* (or place) the foreign key attribute(s), we must first identify the 'parent' and 'child' entities involved in the relationship. The parent entity refers to the entity that posts a copy of its primary key into the table that represents the child entity, to act as the foreign key. (Relationships were described in Section 6.2.)

We consider the identification of parent/child entities for different types of relationships and for multi-valued attributes.

(a) one-to-many (1:*) binary relationships;
(b) one-to-many (1:*) recursive relationships;
(c) one-to-one (1:1) binary relationships;
(d) one-to-one (1:1) recursive relationships;
(e) many-to-many (*:*) binary relationships;
(f) complex relationships;
(g) multi-valued attributes.

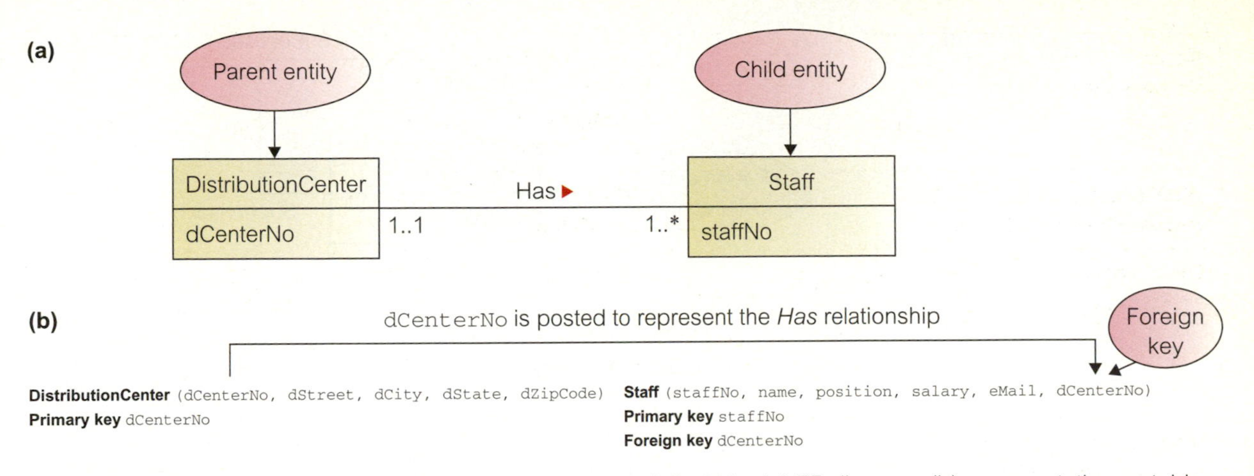

Figure 10.2 The 1:* `DistributionCenter` *`Has`* `Staff` relationship: (a) ER diagram; (b) representation as tables

One-to-many (1:*) binary relationships

For each 1:* binary relationship, the entity on the 'one side' of the relationship is designated as the *parent entity* and the entity on the 'many side' is designated as the *child entity*. To represent this relationship, a copy of the primary key of the parent entity is placed into the table representing the child entity, to act as a foreign key. (1:* relationships were described in Section 6.5.2.)

Consider the `DistributionCenter` *`Has`* `Staff` relationship shown in Figure 9.12 to illustrate how to represent a 1:* relationship as tables. In this example, `DistributionCenter` is on the 'one side' and represents the parent entity and `Staff` is on the 'many side' and represents the child entity. The relationship between these entities is established by placing a copy of the primary key of the `DistributionCenter` (parent) entity, namely `dCenterNo`, into the `Staff` (child) table. Figure 10.2(a) shows the `DistributionCenter` *`Has`* `Staff` ER diagram and Figure 10.2(b) shows the corresponding tables.

There are several other examples of 1:* relationships in Figure 9.12 such as `DistributionCenter` *`Stocks`* `DVDCopy` and `Member` *`Receives`* `RentalDelivery`. We should repeat the rule given above for every 1:* relationship in the ER model.

> **Note** In the case where a 1:* relationship has one or more attributes, these attributes should follow the posting of the primary key to the child table. For example, if the `DistributionCenter` *`Has`* `Staff` relationship had an attribute called `dateStart` representing when a member of staff started at a distribution center, this attribute should also be posted to the `Staff` table along with the copy of the primary key of the `DistributionCenter` table, namely `dCenterNo`.

One-to-many (1:*) recursive relationships

The representation of a 1:* recursive relationship is similar to that described above. (Recursive relationships were described in Section 6.2.2). As there are no recursive

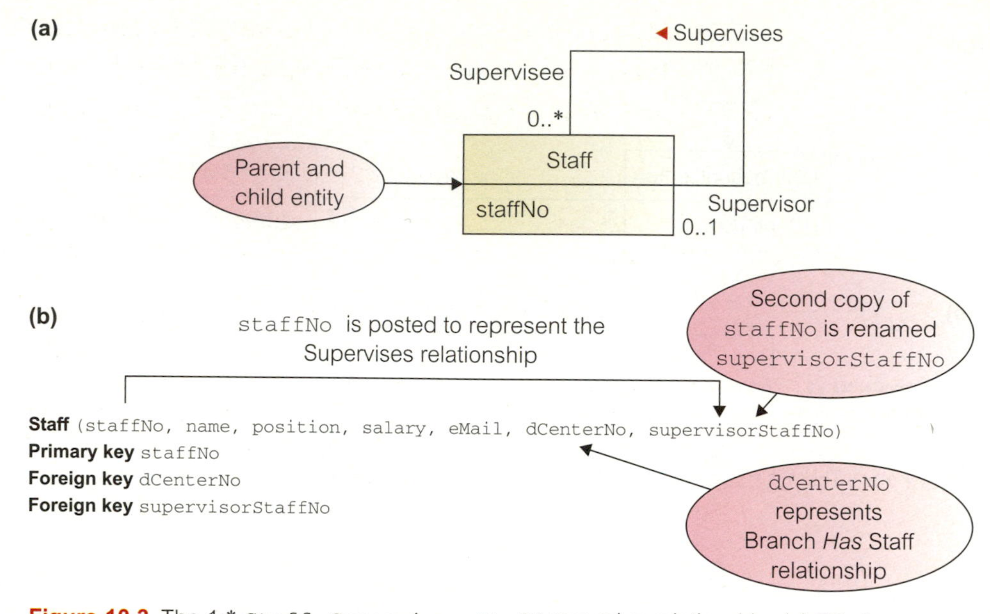

Figure 10.3 The 1:* `Staff` *`Supervises`* `Staff` recursive relationship: (a) ER diagram; (b) representation as a table

relationships in Figure 9.12, we invent a 1:* recursive relationship called `Staff` *`Supervises`* `Staff` as shown in Figure 10.3(a). In this case, both the parent and child entity is `Staff`. Following the rule given above, we represent the *`Supervises`* relationship by posting a copy of the primary key of the `Staff` (parent) entity, `staffNo`, to the `Staff` (child) table, creating a second copy of this column to act as the foreign key. This copy of the column is renamed `supervisorStaffNo` to indicate its purpose. Figure 10.3(a) shows the `Staff` *`Supervises`* `Staff` ER diagram and Figure 10.3(b) shows the corresponding table (with `dCenterNo` included to represent the `DistributionCenter` *`Has`* `Staff` relationship). Note that role names are included to help clarify the purpose that each entity plays in the relationship. For example, `Staff` (supervisor) *`Supervises`* `Staff` (supervisee).

Note that the foreign key `supervisorStaffNo` will not appear in the `Staff` table for the rest of this chapter as the *`Supervises`* relationship was invented to allow discussion of mapping of recursive relationships but is not part of the *StayHome Online Rentals* case study.

One-to-one (1:1) binary relationships

Creating tables to represent 1:1 relationships is slightly more complex as we cannot use the cardinality to help identify the parent and child entities in a relationship. Instead, we need to use participation to help decide whether it is best to represent the relationship by combining the entities involved into one table or by creating two tables and posting a copy of the primary key from one table to the other. (1:1 relationships were described in Section 6.5.1 and participation constraints were described in Section 6.5.5). We consider how to create tables to represent the following participation constraints:

(1) *Mandatory* participation on *both* sides of a 1:1 relationship.

(2) *Mandatory* participation on *one* side of a 1:1 relationship.

(3) *Optional* participation on *both* sides of a 1:1 relationship.

Mandatory participation on *both* sides of 1:1 relationship

In this case, we should combine the entities involved into one table and choose one of the primary keys of the original entities to be the primary key of the new table, while the other is used as an alternate key.

As we do not have an example of such a relationship in Figure 9.12 we invent a 1:1 relationship called `Staff` *`Uses`* `Car`. This relationship has mandatory participation for both entities, as shown in Figure 10.4(a). The primary key for the `Car` entity is the vehicle license number (`vehLicenseNo`), and the other attributes include `make` and `model`. In this example, we place all the attributes for the `Staff` and `Car` entities into one table. We choose one of the primary keys to be the primary key of the new table, namely `staffNo`, and the other becomes an alternate key, as shown in Figure 10.4(b).

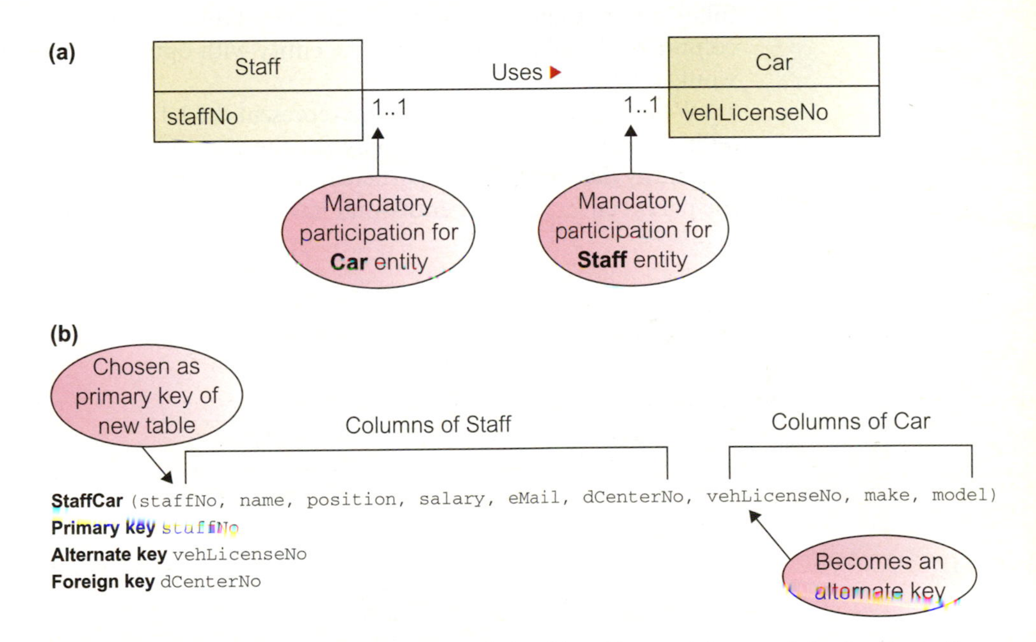

Figure 10.4 The 1:1 `Staff` *`Uses`* `Car` relationship with mandatory participation for both entities: (a) ER diagram; (b) representation as a table

Note In the case where a 1:1 relationship with mandatory participation on both sides has one or more attributes, these attributes should also be included in the table that represents the entities and relationship. For example, if the `Staff` *`Uses`* `Car` relationship had an attribute called `dateAssigned`, this attribute would also appear as a column in the `StaffCar` table.

Note that it is possible to merge two entities into one table only when there are no other relationships between these entities that would prevent this, such as a 1:* relationship. If this were the case, we would need to represent the `Staff` *`Uses`* `Car` relationship using the primary key/foreign key mechanism. We discuss how to designate the parent and child entities in this type of situation shortly.

Mandatory participation on *one* side of a 1:1 relationship

In this case, we are able to identify the parent and child entities for the 1:1 relationship using the participation constraints. The entity that has optional participation in the relationship is designated as the *parent entity*, and the entity that has mandatory participation in the relationship is designated as the *child entity*. As described above, a copy of the primary key of the parent entity is placed in the table representing the child entity.

The reason for posting a copy of the primary key of the entity that has optional participation (parent entity) to the entity that has mandatory participation (child entity) is that this copy of the primary key (foreign key) will always hold a value and hence avoid the presence of nulls in this column of the resulting table. If we did not follow this rule and chose to represent this relationship by positioning the foreign key column in the table representing the entity with optional participation, this column would contain nulls.

We now consider how we would represent the 1:1 `Staff` *`Uses`* *`Car`* relationship with mandatory participation only for the `Car` entity, as shown in Figure 10.5(a). The entity that has optional participation in the relationship (`Staff`) is designated as the parent entity, and the entity that has mandatory participation in the relationship

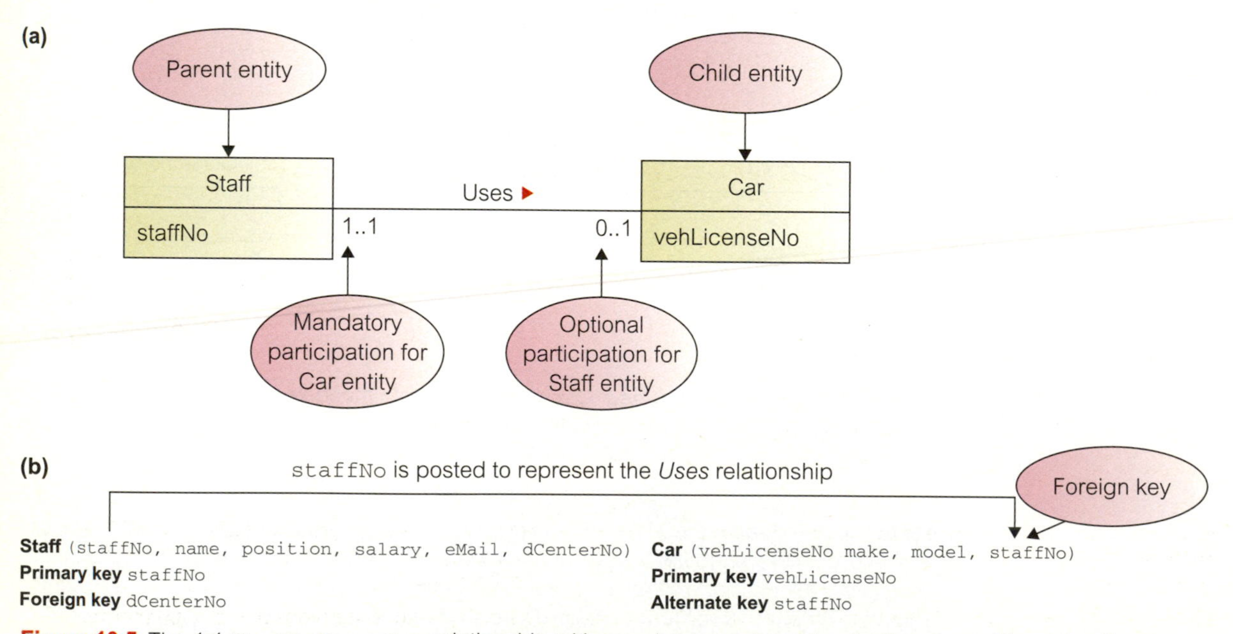

Figure 10.5 The 1:1 `Staff` *`Uses`* `Car` relationship with mandatory participation for the `Car` entity and optional participation for the `Staff` entity: (a) ER diagram; (b) representation as tables

(Car) is designated as the child entity. Therefore, a copy of the primary key of the Staff (parent) entity, staffNo, is placed in the Car (child) table, as shown in Figure 10.5(b). In this case, staffNo also becomes an alternate key for the Car table.

Figure 9.12 has a second example of a 1:1 relationship with mandatory participation on only one side, namely Staff *Manages* DistributionCenter with mandatory participation only for the DistributionCenter entity. Following the rule given above, the Staff entity is designated as the parent entity and the DistributionCenter entity is designated as the child entity. Therefore, a copy of the primary key of the Staff (parent) entity, staffNo, is placed in the DistributionCenter (child) table and renamed as mgrStaffNo, to indicate the purpose of the foreign key in the DistributionCenter table. Figure 10.6(a) shows the Staff *Manages* DistributionCenter ER diagram and Figure 10.6(b) shows the corresponding tables.

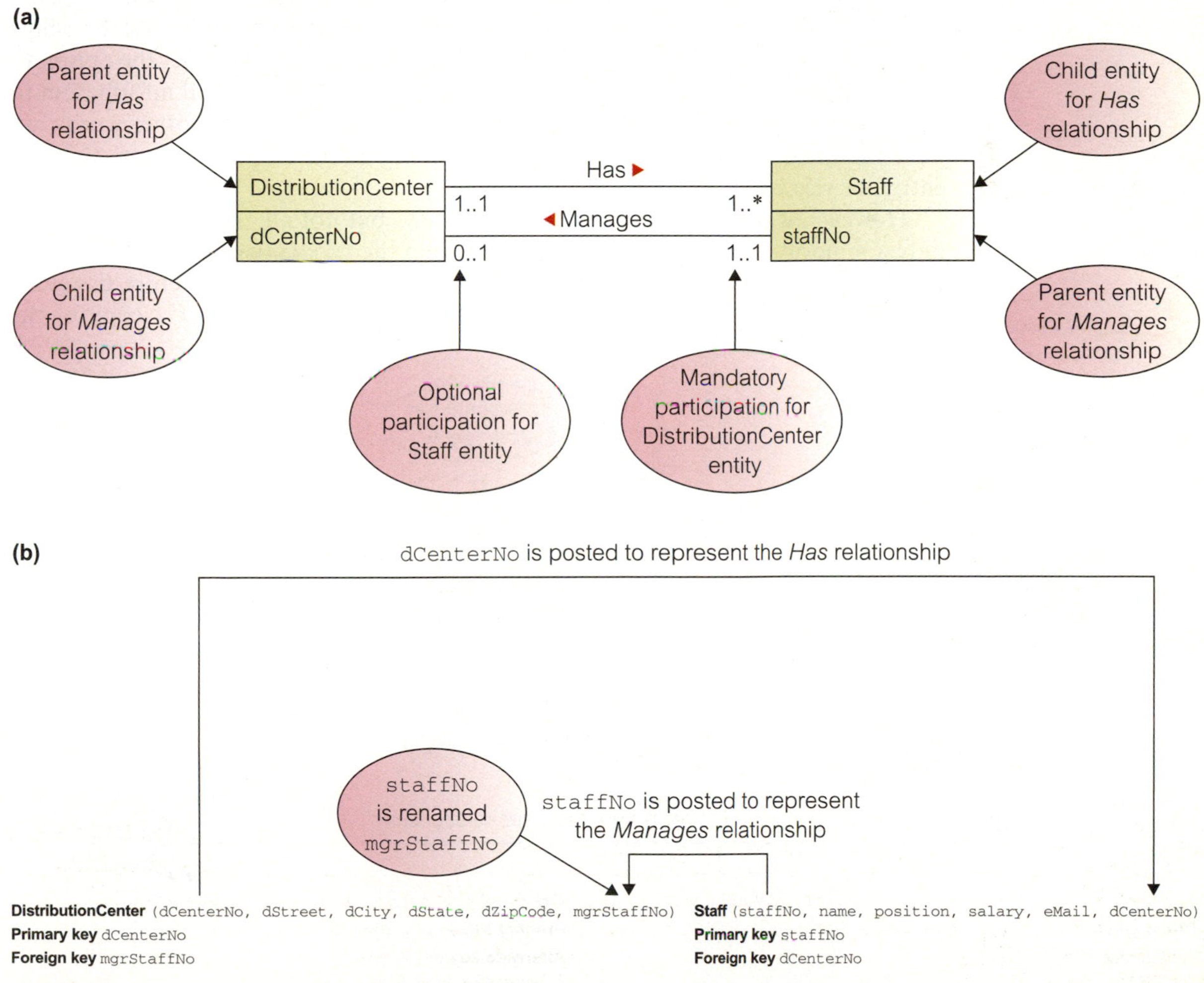

Figure 10.6 The 1:1 Staff *Manages* DistributionCenter relationship with mandatory participation for the DistributionCenter entity and optional participation for the Staff entity: (a) ER diagram; (b) representation as tables

> **Note** In the case where a 1:1 relationship with only mandatory participation for one entity in a relationship has one or more attributes, these attributes should follow the posting of the primary key to the child table. For example, if the `Staff` *`Manages`* `DistributionCenter` relationship had an attribute called `dateStart`, this attribute would appear as a column in the `DistributionCenter` table, along with a copy of `staffNo` (renamed `mgrStaffNo`).

Optional participation on *both* sides of a 1:1 relationship

In this case, the designation of the parent and child entities is arbitrary unless we can find out more about the relationship that can help us reach a decision one way or the other.

We consider how we would represent the 1:1 `Staff` *`Uses`* `Car` relationship, with optional participation on both sides of the relationship, as shown in Figure 10.7(a). (Note that the discussion that follows is also relevant for 1:1 relationships with mandatory participation for both entities where we cannot select the option to put everything into a single table.) If we do not have any additional information to help select the parent and child entities, the choice is arbitrary. In other words, we have the choice to post a copy of the primary key of the `Staff` entity to the `Car` entity, or vice versa.

However, if we find that the majority of cars, but not all, are used by staff and only a minority of staff use cars, we can say that the `Car` entity, although optional, is closer to being mandatory than the `Staff` entity. We can therefore designate `Staff` as the *parent entity* and `Car` as the *child entity*, and post a copy of the

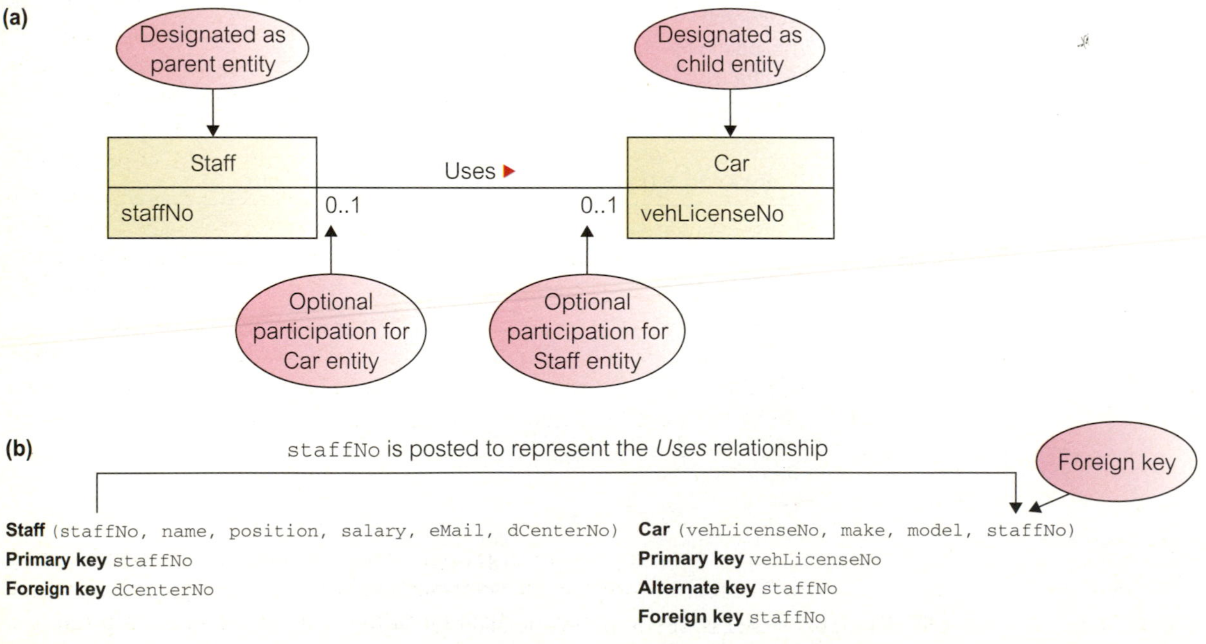

Figure 10.7 The 1:1 `Staff` *`Uses`* `Car` relationship with optional participation for both entities: (a) ER diagram; (b) representation as tables

primary key of the Staff entity (staffNo) into the Car table, as shown in Figure 10.7(b). (Note that the composition of the Staff and Car tables is the same as the example used in the discussion above on 1:1 relationships with mandatory participation on only one side.)

One-to-one (1:1) recursive relationships

For a 1:1 recursive relationship, we should follow the rules for participation as described above for a 1:1 relationship. However, in this special case of a 1:1 relationship, the entity on both sides of the relationship is the same. For a 1:1 recursive relationship with mandatory participation on both sides, we should represent the recursive relationship as a single table with two copies of the primary key. As before, one copy of the primary key represents a foreign key and should be renamed to indicate the relationship it represents.

For a 1:1 recursive relationship with mandatory participation on only one side, we have the option to create a single table with two copies of the primary key as described above, or to create a new table to represent the relationship. The new table would have only two columns, both copies of the primary key. As before, the copies of the primary keys act as foreign keys and have to be renamed to indicate the purpose of each in the table.

For a 1:1 recursive relationship with optional participation on both sides, we should create a new table as described above.

Many-to-many (*:*) binary relationships

For each *:* binary relationship, create a table to represent the relationship and include any attributes that are part of the relationship. We post a copy of the primary key attribute(s) of the entities that participate in the relationship into the new table, to act as foreign keys. One or both of the foreign keys will also form the primary key of the new table, possibly in combination with some of the attributes of the relationship. (*:* relationships were described in Section 6.5.3.)

For example, consider the *:* relationship DVD *Stars* Actor shown in Figure 9.12. The two participating entities, namely DVD and Actor, act as *parent entities* and post copies of their primary keys (catalogNo and actorNo) to a new table called DVDActor that represents the relationship. The character attribute associated with the *Stars* relationship is also included in the new table. Figure 10.8(a) shows the DVD *Stars* Actor ER diagram and Figure 10.8(b) shows the corresponding tables.

Note that the new table called DVDActor has a composite primary key made up of two foreign keys, catalogNo and actorNo. There is another example of a *:* relationships in Figure 9.12; namely DVDCopy *IsSentAs* RentalDelivery. We repeat the rule given above for this *:* relationship.

Complex relationship types

For each complex relationship, that is relationship with more than two participating entities, create a table to represent the relationship. We post a copy of the primary key attribute(s) of the entities that participate in the complex relationship into the new table, to act as foreign keys, and include any attributes that are associated with the relationship. One or more of the foreign keys will also form the primary key of

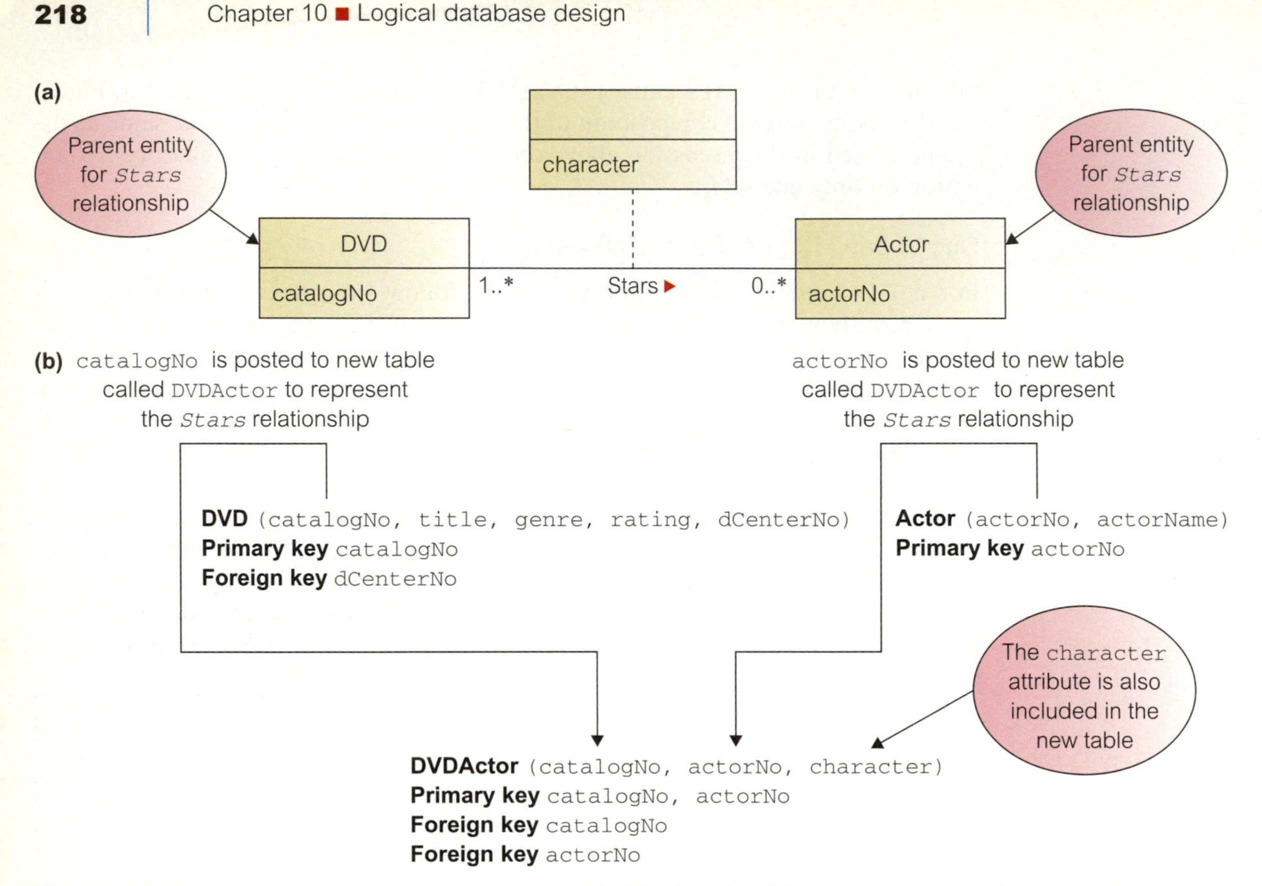

Figure 10.8 The *:* DVD *Stars* Actor relationship: (a) ER diagram; (b) representation as tables

the new table, possibly in combination with some of the attributes of the relationship. (Complex relationships were described in Section 6.5.4.)

As we do not have an example of a complex relationship in Figure 9.12, we use the complex (ternary) relationship called *Complains* shown in Figure 6.10. This relationship represents the association between a member of staff who deals with a complaint from a member about a particular DVD copy, as shown in Figure 10.9(a). The entities enclosing the complex relationship, namely Staff, Member and DVDCopy, act as parent entities and we post copies of their primary keys (staffNo, memberNo, and DVDNo) to a new table called Complaint that represents the relationship. Note that the *Complains* relationship has an attribute called dateReceived, complaintDesc, actionTaken, which is also included in the Complaint table. Figure 10.9(a) shows the *Complains* complex (ternary) relationship ER diagram and Figure 10.9(b) shows the corresponding tables. Note that the new table called Complaint has a composite primary key, namely (DVDNo, memberNo, dateReceived), which includes two foreign keys.

The Complaint table will not appear in the list of tables for the *StayHome Online Rentals* case study shown in Figure 10.11 on page 223 because the *Complains* relationship was invented to allow discussion of mapping of complex relationships, but is not part of the case study described in Section 5.4.

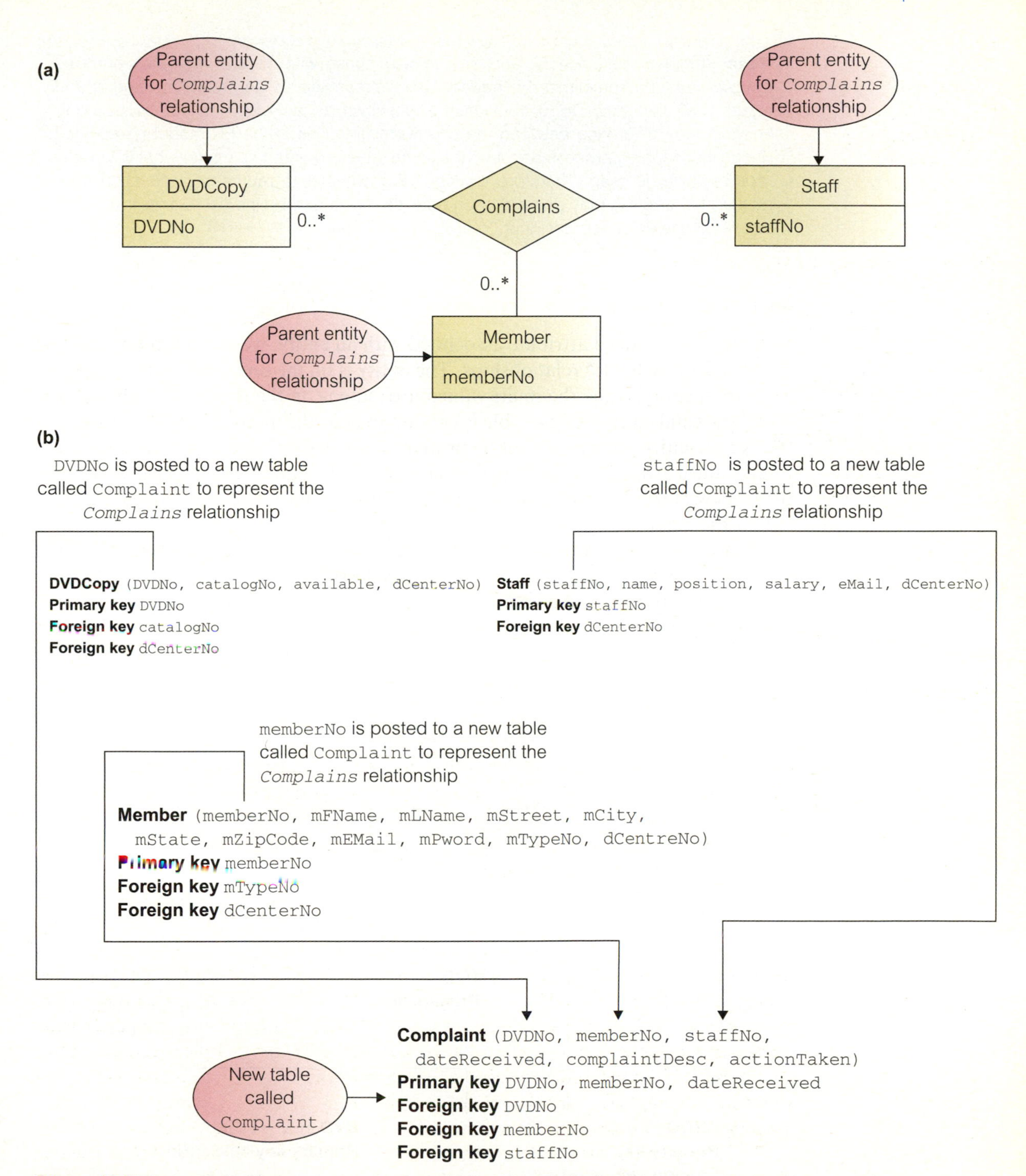

Figure 10.9 The complex (ternary) *Complains* relationship: (a) ER diagram; (b) representation as tables

Note Complex relationships, and in particular those with several attributes such as *Complains*, can sometimes be equally well represented as an entity. For example in Figure 10.9 the *Complains* relationship is shown as an entity called Complaint. However, the difference between the two representations in the ER model is resolved during the mapping process because the same table is created no matter what ER model representation is used. Therefore the choice of whether to represent a situation as a relationship or entity may depend upon how it is described by the users and/or the preference of the database designer.

Multi-valued attributes

For each multi-valued attribute associated with an entity, we should follow the rule described above for 1:* relationships. The entity is on the one side and is designated the parent entity, while the multi-valued attribute is on the many side and is designated the child entity. A new table is created to hold the multi-valued attribute, and the parent entity posts a copy of its primary key, to act as a foreign key. Unless the multi-valued attribute is itself an alternate key of the parent entity, the primary key of the new table is composed of the multi-valued attribute and the original primary key of the parent entity.

As we have no examples of multi-valued attributes in Figure 9.12, we invent the situation where a single DVD can be described using one or more genres, therefore the genre attribute of the DVD entity is defined as being a multi-valued attribute. To represent this, we create a new table called DVDGenre to represent the multi-valued attribute genre. Figure 10.10(a) shows the ER diagram of the DVD entity with the

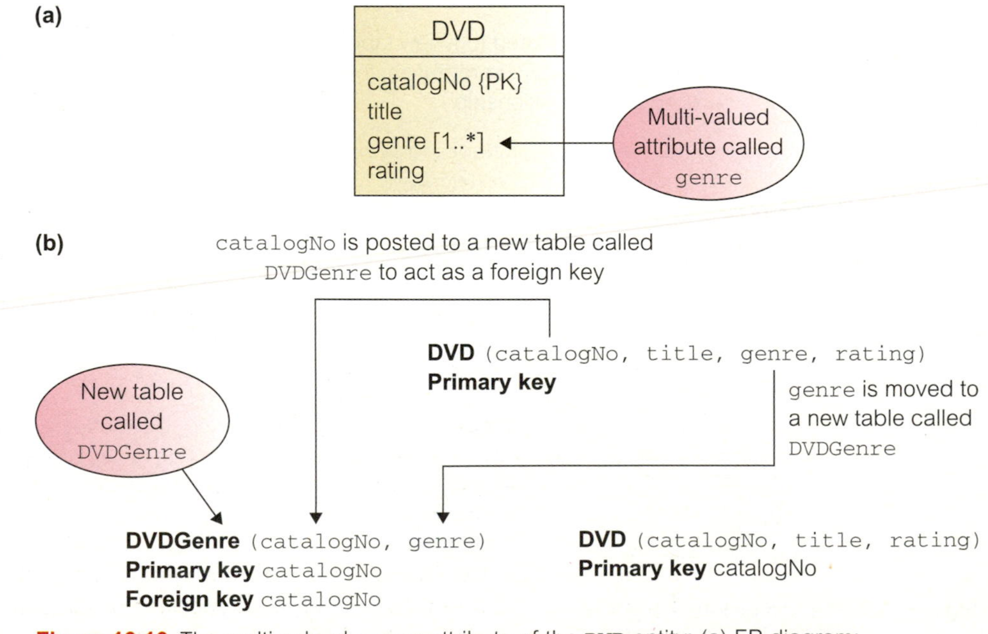

Figure 10.10 The multi-valued genre attribute of the DVD entity: (a) ER diagram; (b) representation as tables

multi-valued attribute `genre` and Figure 10.10(b) shows hows `DVD` and `genre` are represented as tables.

In Table 10.1 we summarize how to represent entities, relationships and multi-valued attributes as tables.

Table 10.1 Summary of how to represent entities, relationships and multi-valued attributes as tables

Entity/relationship	Mapping
Strong or weak entity	Create table that includes all simple attributes.
1:* binary relationship	Post a copy of primary key of entity on the 'one' side to table representing the entity on 'many' side. Any attributes of the relationship are also posted to the 'many' side.
1:* recursive relationship	As the entity on 'one' and 'many' sides is the same, the table representing the entity receives a second copy of the primary key, which is renamed, and also any attributes of the relationship.
1:1 binary relationship:	
Mandatory participation on *both* sides	Combine entities into one table.
Mandatory participation on *one* side	Post a copy of primary key of the entity with optional participation to the table representing the entity with mandatory participation. Any attributes of the relationship are also posted to the table representing the entity with mandatory participation.
Optional participation on *both* sides	Without further information, post a copy of the primary key of one entity to the other. However, if information is available, treat the entity that is closer to having mandatory participation as being the child entity.
: binary relationship Complex relationship	Create a table to represent the relationship and include any attributes associated with the relationship. Post a copy of the primary key from each parent entity into the new table to act as foreign keys.
Multi-valued attribute	Create a table to represent the multi-valued attribute and post a copy of the primary key of the parent entity into the new table to act as a foreign key.

Note Although the guidelines above propose the creation of a new table to represent a multi-valued attribute, if the maximum number of values is fixed and/or the majority of entity occurrences have few values for that attribute, then an alternative representation is to create a table with many columns to represent the multi-valued attribute. For example, if the maximum number of values for the `genre` attribute was between one and three, shown as [1..3}, then an alternative representation is to introduce new columns called `genre1`, `genre2`, and `genre3` into the `DVD` table.

In Step 1.6 of the database design methodology, we have the option to represent entities using the enhanced ER concepts of specialization/generalization, which we described in Chapter 7. We also discussed how to map those enhanced concepts to tables.

How to represent superclasses and subclasses

We illustrate how to represent a specialization/generalization hierarchy using the EER models shown in Figures 7.2 and 7.4. For each superclass/subclass relationship in the EER model, identify the superclass as the parent entity and the subclass as the child entity. There are various options on how to best represent such a relationship as one or more tables. The selection of the most appropriate option is dependent on the participation and disjoints constraints on the superclass/subclass relationship, as shown in Table 10.2.

Table 10.2 Options available for the representation of a superclass/subclass relationship based on the participation and disjoint constraints

Participation constraint	Disjoint constraint	Tables required
Mandatory	Nondisjoint {And}	Single table
Optional	Nondisjoint {And}	Two tables: one table for superclass and one table for all subclasses
Mandatory	Disjoint {Or}	Many tables: one table for each combined superclass/subclass
Optional	Disjoint {Or}	Many tables: one table for superclass and one for each subclass

We use the `Staff` specialization/generalization in Figure 7.2 as our first example. The relationship that the `Staff` superclass has with its subclasses (`Manager` or `Assistant`) is *optional*, as a member of staff may not belong to any of the subclasses, and *nondisjoint*, as a member of staff may belong to more than one subclass. Based on the options given in Table 10.2, the `Staff` superclass/subclass relationship should be represented by creating a table for the superclass and a table for all of the subclasses, as shown in Figure 10.11.

Note The *StayHome Online Rental* case study in Section 5.4 only described the Manager and Assistant staff roles in any detail. However, to allow discussions of a superclass/subclasses relationship with {Optional, And} constraints, we have allowed for other staff roles and for staff to exist that are not associated with any subclasses.

We use the `Vehicle` specialization/generalization in Figure 7.4 as our second example. The relationship that the `Vehicle` superclass has with its subclasses (`Van`, `Bus`, or `Car`) is *mandatory*, as all members of the `Vehicle` superclass must belong to one of the subclasses; and *disjoint*, as a member of the `Vehicle` superclass, can belong to only one subclass. Based on the options given in Table 10.2, the `Vehicle` superclass/subclass relationship should be represented by creating a table for each combined superclass/subclass, as shown in Figure 10.12.

Although the options described in Table 10.2 provide some guidelines for how best to represent a superclass/subclass relationship, there are other factors that may influence the final selection such as:

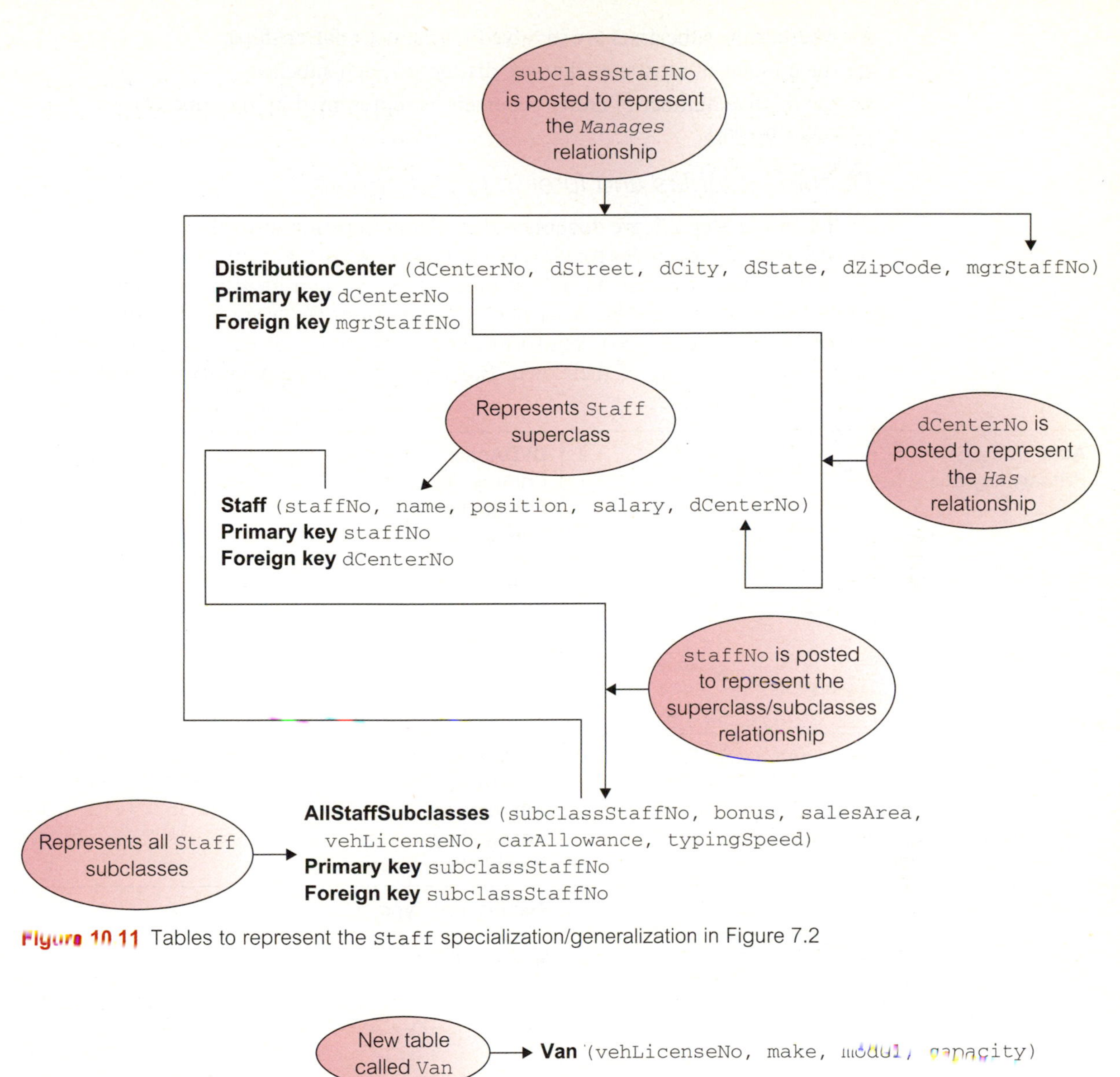

Figure 10.11 Tables to represent the Staff specialization/generalization in Figure 7.2

New table called Van → **Van** (vehLicenseNo, make, model, capacity)

Primary key vehLicenseNo

New table called Bus → **Bus** (vehLicenseNo, make, model, noSeats)

Primary key vehLicenseNo

New table called Car → **Car** (vehLicenseNo, make, model, color)

Primary key vehicleLicenseNo

Figure 10.12 Tables to represent the Vehicle specialization/generalization shown in Figure 7.4

- whether the subclasses are involved in distinct relationships;
- the number of attributes that are distinct to each subclass;
- the relative number of entity occurrences represented by the superclass and by each subclass.

Document tables and foreign key attributes

At the end of Step 2.1, we document the full composition of the tables created from the ER model. The tables for *StayHome Online Rentals* are shown in Figure 10.13. Now that each table has its full set of columns, we can identify any new primary and/or alternate keys. This is particularly important for weak entities that rely on the posting of the primary key from the parent entity (or entities) to form all or part of a primary key of their own. For example, the weak entity `Wish` shown in

Actor `(actorNo, actorName)` **Primary key** `actorNo`	**DVDActor** `(actorNo, catalogNo, character)` **Primary key** `actorNo, catalogNo` **Foreign key** `actorNo` **Foreign key** `catalogNo`
DistributionCenter `(dCenterNo, dStreet, dCity, dState, dZipCode, mgrStaffNo)` **Primary key** `dCenterNo` **Alternate key** `dZipCode` **Foreign key** `mgrStaffNo (original name is staffNo)`	**DVD** `(catalogNo, title, genre, rating)` **Primary key** `catalogNo`
DVDCopy `(DVDNo, catalogNo, available, dCenterNo)` **Primary key** `DVDNo` **Foreign key** `catalogNo` **Foreign key** `dCenterNo`	**DVDRental** `(deliveryNo, DVDNo, dateReturn)` **Primary key** `deliveryNo, DVDNo` **Alternate key** `DVDNo, dateReturn` **Foreign key** `DVDNo` **Foreign key** `deliveryNo`
Member `(memberNo, mFName, mLName, mStreet, mCity, mState, mZipCode, mEMail, mPword, mTypeNo, dCenterNo)` **Primary key** `memberNo` **Alternate key** `mEMail` **Foreign key** `mTypeNo` **Foreign key** `dCenterNo`	**MembershipType** `(mTypeNo, mTypeDesc, maxRentals, monthlyCharge)` **Primary key** `mTypeNo` **Alternate key** `mTypeDesc`
RentalDelivery `(deliveryNo, memberNo dateOut)` **Primary key** `deliveryNo` **Foreign key** `memberNo`	**Staff** `(staffNo, name, position, salary, eMail, dCenterNo)` **Primary key** `staffNo` **Alternate key** `eMail` **Foreign key** `dCenterNo`
Wish `(memberNo, catalogNo, ranking)` **Primary key** `memberNo, catalogNo` **Foreign key** `memberNo` **Foreign key** `catalogNo`	

Figure 10.13 Tables for *StayHome Online Rentals*

Figure 9.12 has a composite primary key made up of a copy of the primary key of the `Member` entity (`memberNo`) and a copy of the primary key of the `DVD` entity (`catalogNo`) as shown in Figure 10.13.

There are also two new tables called `DVDActor` and `DVDRental` in Figure 10.13 that did not appear in Figure 10.1. These tables represent the *:* relationships `DVD` *`Stars`* `Actor` and `DVDCopy` *`IsSentAs`* `RentalDelivery` relationships. Each table has a composite primary key made up using a copy of the primary key from each parent entity. For example, the primary key for the `DVDActor` table is made up from the primary key of the `DVD` entity (`catalogNo`) and a copy of the primary key of the `Actor` entity (`actorNo`) as shown in Figure 10.13.

The data dictionary should also be updated to indicate the presence of foreign keys and any new primary and alternate keys identified in this step.

Step 2.2 Check table structures using normalization

Objective

To check that each table has an appropriate structure, using normalization.

The purpose of this step is to examine the groupings of columns in each table created in Step 2.1. We check the composition of each table using the rules of normalization, to avoid unnecessary duplication of data. (Normalization was described in Chapter 8.)

We should ensure that each table created in Step 2.1 is in at least third normal form (3NF). If we identify tables that are not in 3NF, this may indicate that part of the ER model is incorrect, or that we have introduced an error while creating the tables from the model. If necessary, we may need to restructure the data model and/or tables.

Step 2.3 Check that the tables support user transactions

Objective

To ensure that the tables support the required transactions.

The objective of this step is to check that the tables created in Step 2.1 support the required transactions, as documented in the users' requirements specification. This type of check was carried out in Step 1.8 to ensure that the ER model supported the required transactions. In this step, we check that the tables created in the previous steps also support these transactions, and thereby ensure that no error has been introduced while creating tables.

One approach to checking that the tables support a transaction is to examine the transaction's data requirements to ensure that the data is present in one or more tables. Also, if a transaction requires data in more than one table we should check that these tables can be linked through the primary key/foreign key mechanism. We demonstrate this approach using the transactions given as use case descriptions for the Member user view of the *StayHome Online Rentals* case study in Section 5.4.4. Table 10.2(a) presents the tables/columns required to support use case descriptions (1, 2, and 3). For each description, we highlight the tables/columns required.

Table 10.2(a) The tables/columns required by the use case descriptions 1, 2, and 3 for the Member user view of *StayHome Online Rentals*

Transaction	Table(s) required	Column(s) required (in bold)
1. Register as member	Member	(memberNo, mFName, mLName, mStreet, mCity, mState, mZipCode, mEMail, mPword, mTypeNo, dCenterNo)
2. View membership type	MembershipType	(mTypeNo, mTypeDesc, maxRentals, monthlyCharge)
3. Select membership type	Member	(memberNo, mFName, mLName, mStreet, mCity, mState, mZipCode, mEMail, mPword, mTypeNo, dCenterNo) ↕
	MembershipType	(mTypeNo, mTypeDesc, maxRentals, monthlyCharge)

This analysis is repeated for the other use case descriptions of the Member user view and the Assistant and Manager user views of *StayHome Online Rentals*. On completion of the analysis, we conclude that the tables shown in Figure 10.13 support all the transactions for *StayHome Online Rentals*.

Note As with Step 1.8 covered in the last chapter, this may look like a lot of hard work and it certainly can be. As a result, we may be tempted to omit this step. However, it is very important that we do these checks now rather than later when it will be much more difficult and costly to resolve any errors in the data model.

Step 2.4 Check integrity constraints

Objective

To check that integrity constraints are represented in the logical database design.

Integrity constraints are the constraints that we wish to impose in order to protect the database from becoming incomplete, inaccurate, or inconsistent. Although we may not be able to implement some integrity constraints within the DBMS, this is not the question here. At this stage, we are concerned only with high-level design that is specifying *what* integrity constraints are required, irrespective of *how* this might be achieved. Having identified the integrity constraints, we will have a logical database design that is a complete and accurate representation of the data requirements of the organization (or part of the organization) to be supported by the database.

We consider the following types of integrity constraints:

- required data;
- column domain constraints;

- entity integrity;
- multiplicity;
- referential integrity;
- other integrity constraints.

Required data

Some columns must always contain a value; in other words, they are not allowed to hold nulls. For example, every member of staff must have a job position (such as Manager or Assistant). These constraints should have been identified when we documented the columns (attributes) in the data dictionary in Step 1.3. (Nulls were described in Section 2.4.1.)

Column domain constraints

Every column has a domain (a set of values that are legal for it). For example, the position of a member of staff is Manager or Assistant, so the domain of the `position` column consists of only these values. These constraints should have been identified when we chose the column (attribute) domains for the data in Step 1.4. (Domains were described in Section 2.3.1.)

Entity integrity

The primary key of an entity cannot hold nulls. For example, each record of the `Staff` table must have a value for the primary key column, `staffNo`. These constraints should have been considered when we identified the primary keys for each entity in Step 1.5. (Entity integrity was described in Section 2.4.2.)

Multiplicity

Multiplicity represents the constraints that are placed on relationships between data in the database. Examples of such constraints include the requirements that a distribution center has members and each distribution center has staff. Ensuring that all appropriate integrity constraints are identified and represented is an important part of modeling the data requirements of an organization. In Step 1.2 we defined the relationships between entities and all integrity constraints that can be represented in this way were defined and documented in this step. (Multiplicity was described in Section 6.5.)

Referential integrity

A foreign key links each record in the child table to the record in the parent table containing the matching primary key value. Referential integrity means that if the foreign key contains a value then that value must refer to an existing record in the parent table. For example, the `dCenterNo` column in the `Staff` table links the member of staff to the record in the `DistributionCenter` table where he or she works. If `dCenterNo` is not null, it must contain a value that exists in the `dCenterNo` column of the `DistributionCenter` table, or the member of staff will be assigned to a non-existent distribution center. (Referential integrity was described in Section 2.4.3.) There are two issues regarding foreign keys that must be addressed.

(1) Are nulls allowed for the foreign key?
For example, can we store the details of a member of staff without having a distribution center number for the employee? The issue is not whether the distribution center number exists, but whether a distribution center number must be specified. In general, if the participation of the child table in the relationship is mandatory, then nulls are not allowed. On the other hand, if the participation of the child table is optional, then nulls should be allowed. (Participation constraints were described in Section 6.5.5.)

(2) How do we ensure referential integrity?
To do this, we specify *existence constraints*, which define conditions under which a primary key or foreign key may be inserted, updated, or deleted. Consider the 1:* relationship `DistributionCenter` *`Has`* `Staff`. The primary key of the `DistributionCenter` table (`dCenterNo`) is a foreign key in the `Staff` table. We consider the following six cases.

Case 1: Insert record into child table (`Staff`)
To ensure referential integrity, check that the foreign key column (`dCenterNo`) of the new `Staff` record is set to null or to a value of an existing `DistributionCenter` record.

Case 2: Delete record from child table (`Staff`)
If a record in the child table is deleted, referential integrity is unaffected.

Case 3: Update foreign key of child record (`Staff`)
This is similar to Case 1. To ensure referential integrity, check that the foreign key column (`dCenterNo`) of the updated `Staff` record is set to null or to a value of an existing `DistributionCenter` record.

Case 4: Insert record into parent table (`DistributionCenter`)
Inserting a record into the parent table (`DistributionCenter`) does not affect referential integrity; it simply becomes a parent without any children – in other words, a distribution center without members of staff.

Case 5: Delete record from parent table (`DistributionCenter`)
If a record of the parent table is deleted, referential integrity is lost if there is a child record referencing the deleted parent record. In other words, referential integrity is lost if the deleted distribution center currently has one or more members of staff working in it. There are several strategies we can consider in this case:

- NO ACTION Prevent a deletion from the parent table if there are any referencing child records. In our example, 'We cannot delete a distribution center if there are currently members of staff working there.'
- CASCADE When the parent record is deleted; automatically delete any referencing child records. If any deleted child record also acts as a parent record in another relationship then the delete operation should be applied to the records in this child table, and so on in a cascading manner. In other words, deletions from the parent table cascade to the child table. In our example, 'Deleting a distribution center automatically deletes all members of staff working there.' Clearly, in this situation, this strategy would not be wise.
- SET NULL When a parent record is deleted, the foreign key values in all related child records are automatically set to null. In our example, 'If a distribution center is deleted, indicate that the current distribution center for those members of staff previously working there is unknown.' We can

consider this strategy only if the columns comprising the foreign key can accept nulls, as defined in Step 1.3.

- SET DEFAULT When a parent record is deleted, the foreign key values in all related child records are automatically set to their default values. In our example, 'If a distribution center is deleted, indicate that the current assignment of members of staff previously working there is being assigned to another (default) distribution center.' We can consider this strategy only if the columns comprising the foreign key have default values, as defined in Step 1.3.
- NO CHECK When a parent record is deleted, do nothing to ensure that referential integrity is maintained. This strategy should only be considered in extreme circumstances.

Case 6: Update primary key of parent record (`DistributionCenter`)
If the primary key value of a parent table record is updated, referential integrity is lost if there exists a child record referencing the old primary key value; that is, if the updated distribution center currently has staff working there. To ensure referential integrity, the strategies described above can be used. In the case of CASCADE, the updates to the primary key of the parent record are reflected in any referencing child records, and so on in a cascading manner.

The referential integrity constraints for the tables that have been created for *StayHome Online Rentals* are shown in Figure 10.14.

Other integrity constraints

Finally, we consider any remaining integrity constraints that have not been defined so far. Integrity constraints should be represented as constraints on the database to ensure that only permitted updates to tables governed by 'real world' transactions are allowed. For example, *StayHome Online Rentals* has an integrity constraint rule that prevents a member from renting more than five DVDs at any one time.

Document all integrity constraints

Document all integrity constraints for consideration during physical database design. The DBDL can be extended to show, for each foreign key, the parent table being referenced and the Update and Delete referential integrity constraints.

Step 2.5 Review logical database design with users

Objective

To ensure that the logical database design is a true representation of the data requirements of the organization (or part of the organization) to be supported by the database.

The logical database design should now be complete and fully documented. However, to finish this step we should review the design with the users.

If we are designing a database that has only a single user view, or we are using the centralized approach and have merged the user requirements for two or more user views, then we are ready to proceed to physical database design, which is described in Chapter 11. If, however, we are designing a more complex database

Actor (actorNo, actorName)
Primary key actorNo

DistributionCenter (dCenterNo, dStreet, dCity, dState, dZipCode, mgrStaffNo)
Primary key dCenterNo
Alternate key dZipCode
Foreign key mgrStaffNo references Staff (staffNo) on Update Cascade on Delete Set Null

DVD (catalogNo, title, genre, rating)
Primary key catalogNo

DVDActor (actorNo, catalogNo, character)
Primary key actorNo, catalogNo
Foreign key actorNo references Actor (actorNo) on Update Cascade on Delete Cascade
Foreign key catalogNo references DVD (catalogNo) on Update Cascade on Delete Cascade

DVDCopy (DVDNo, catalogNo, available, dCenterNo)
Primary key DVDNo
Foreign key catalogNo references DVD (catalogNo) on Update Cascade on Delete Cascade
Foreign key dCenterNo references DistributionCenter (dCenterNo) on Update Cascade on Delete No Action

DVDRental (deliveryNo, DVDNo, dateReturn)
Primary key deliveryNo, DVDNo
Alternate key DVDNo, dateReturn
Foreign key DVDNo references DVDCopy (DVDNo) on Update Cascade on Delete Cascade
Foreign key deliveryNo references RentalDelivery (deliveryNo) on Update Cascade on Delete Cascade

Member (memberNo, mFName, mLName, mStreet, mCity, mState, mZipCode, mEMail, mPword, mTypeNo, dCenterNo)
Primary key memberNo
Alternate key mEMail
Foreign key mTypeNo references MembershipType (mTypeNo) on Update Cascade on Delete Set Default
Foreign key dCenterNo references DistributionCenter (dCenterNo) on Update Cascade on Delete No Action

MembershipType (mTypeNo, mTypeDesc, maxRentals, monthlyCharge)
Primary key mTypeNo
Alternate key mTypeDesc

RentalDelivery (deliveryNo, memberNo dateOut)
Primary key deliveryNo
Foreign key memberNo references Member (memberNo) on Update Cascade on Delete No Action

Staff (staffNo, name, position, salary, eMail, dCenterNo)
Primary key staffNo
Alternate key eMail
Foreign key dCenterNo references DistributionCenter (dCenterNo) on Update Cascade on Delete No Action

Wish (memberNo, catalogNo, ranking)
Primary key memberNo, catalogNo
Foreign key memberNo references Member (memberNo) on Update Cascade on Delete Cascade
Foreign key catalogNo references DVD (catalogNo) on Update Cascade on Delete Set Default

Figure 10.14 Tables with referential integrity constraints defined for *StayHome Online Rentals*

that has numerous and varied user views and we are using the view integration approach to manage those user views, then you should read Appendix A before we proceed to physical database design. (Centralization and view integration approaches were described in Sections 4.6 and 5.4.4.)

Chapter summary

- The main purpose of logical database design (Step 2) is to describe a set of tables based on the ER model created in conceptual database design (Step 1) of the methodology.
- The structures of the tables are checked using normalization.
- The structures of the tables are checked to ensure that they support the transactions defined in the users' requirements.
- Integrity constraints protect the database from becoming incomplete, inaccurate, or inconsistent. These rules include integrity constraints, required data, column domain constraints, entity integrity, multiplicity, referential integrity, and any additional integrity constraints.
- Existence constraints ensure referential integrity by defining conditions under which a primary key or foreign key may be inserted, updated, or deleted.
- There are several strategies to consider when a child record references the parent record that we are attempting to delete/update: NO ACTION, CASCADE, SET NULL, SET DEFAULT, and NO CHECK.

Review questions

10.1 Describe the main purpose and tasks of logical database design (Step 2).

10.2 Describe the rules for creating tables that represent:
(a) strong and weak entities;
(b) one-to-many (1:*) binary relationships;
(c) one-to-many (1:*) recursive relationships;
(d) one-to-one (1:1) binary relationships;
(e) one-to-one (1:1) recursive relationships;
(f) many-to-many (*:*) binary relationships;
(g) complex relationships;
(h) multi-valued attributes.

Give examples to illustrate your answers.

10.3 Discuss how the technique of normalization can be used to check the structure of the tables created from an ER model.

10.4 Discuss an approach to check that the tables support the required transactions.

10.5 Discuss what integrity constraints represent. Give examples to illustrate your answers.

10.6 Describe the alternative strategies that can be applied if there is a child record referencing a parent record that we wish to delete.

Exercises

10.7 In Exercise 9.11 the Director of *StayHome Online Rentals* submitted additional requirements and these requirements are now shown in Figure 10.15 as (a) to (e). Discuss how these additional requirements will alter the tables shown in Figure 10.14.

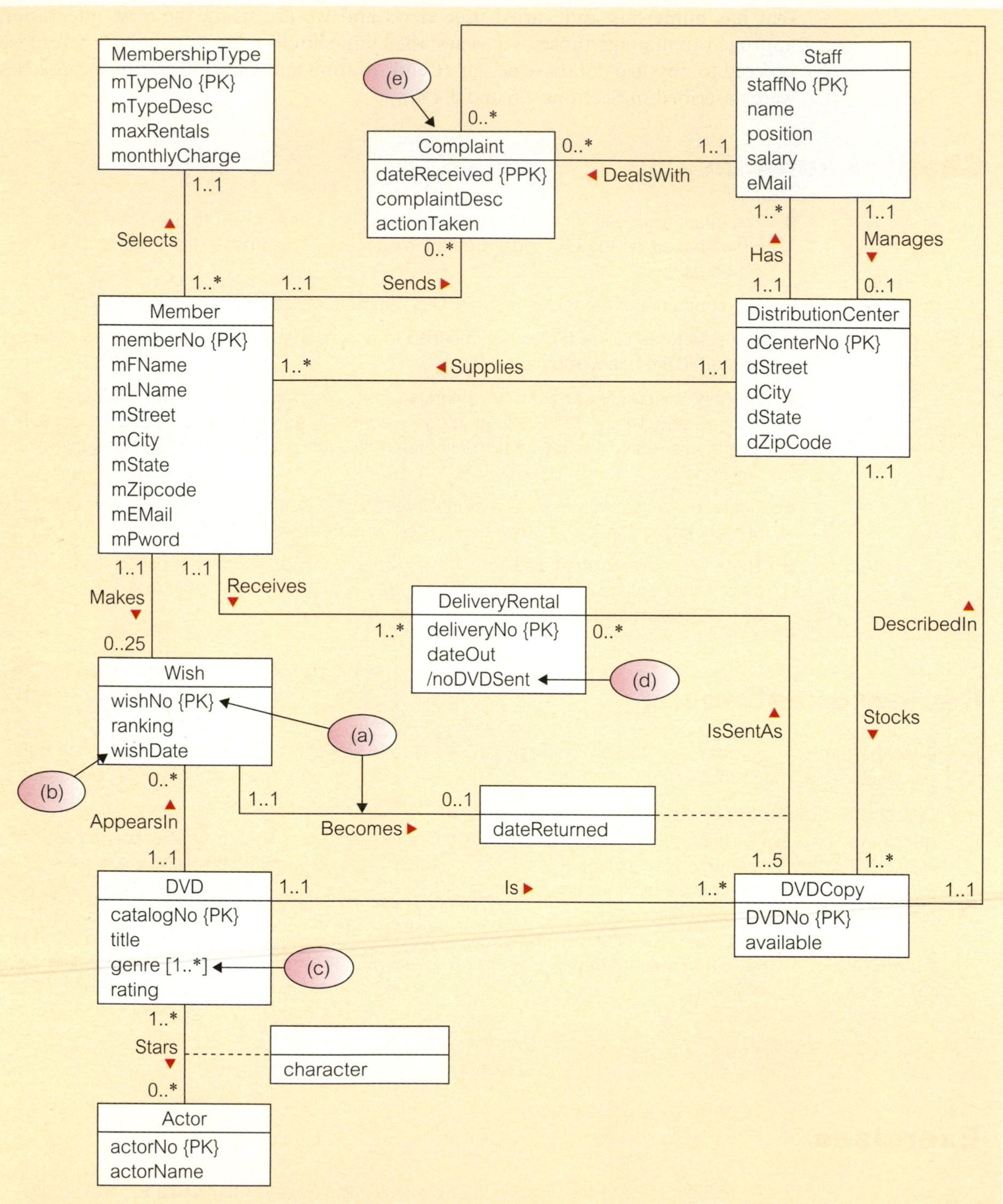

Figure 10.15 ER model for *StayHome Online Rentals* including the new requirements described in Exercise 9.11 (a) to (e)

10.8 Create a description of the tables mapped from the ER model for the *EasyDrive School of Motoring* case study described shown in Figure 10.16 and described in Exercise 9.16.

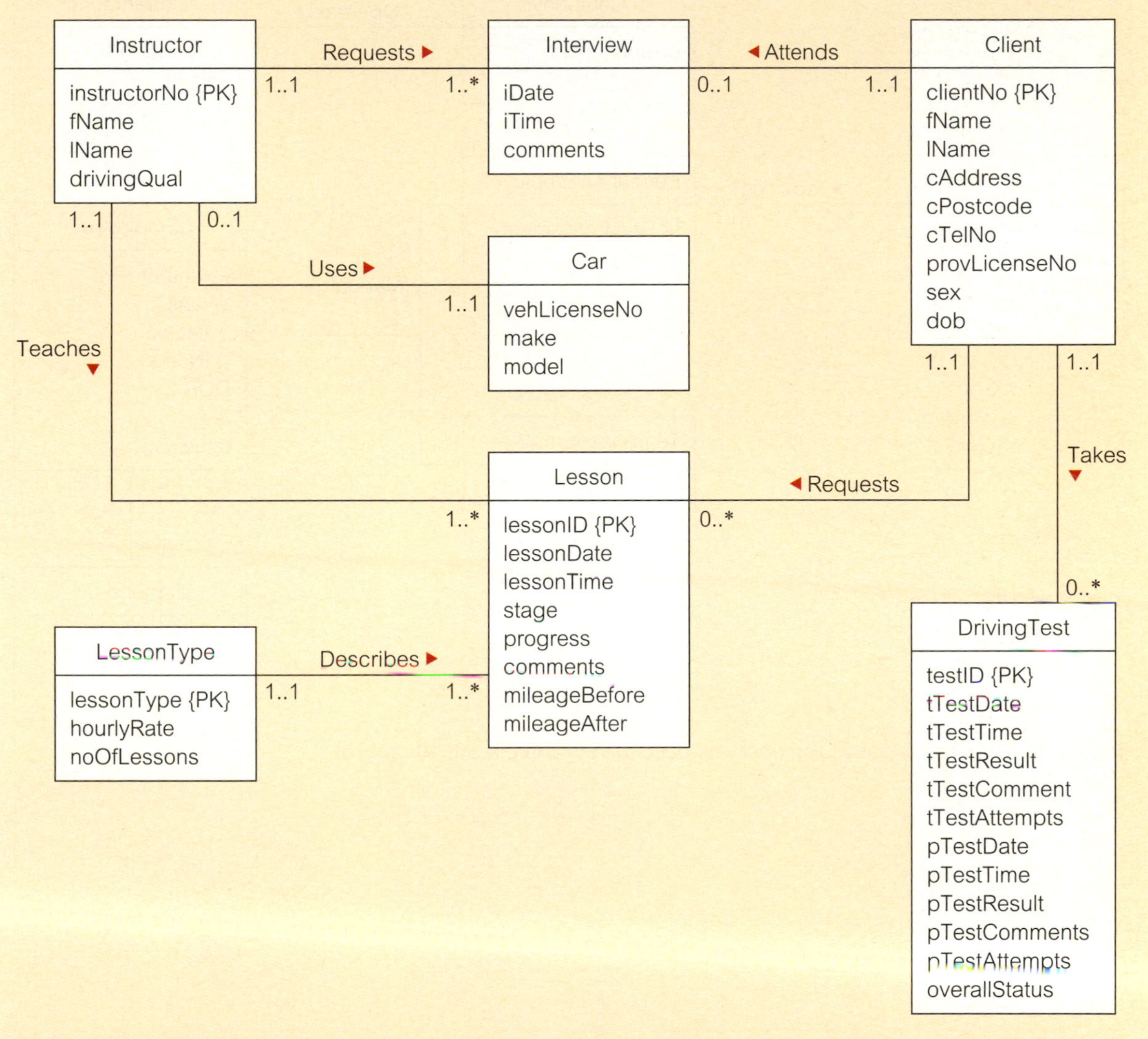

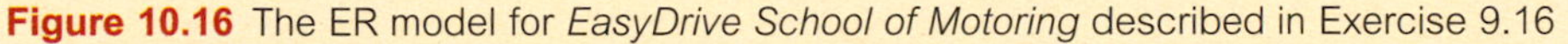
Figure 10.16 The ER model for *EasyDrive School of Motoring* described in Exercise 9.16

10.9 Create a description of the tables mapped from the company ER model shown in Figure 10.17 and described in Exercises 6.10 and 7.8.

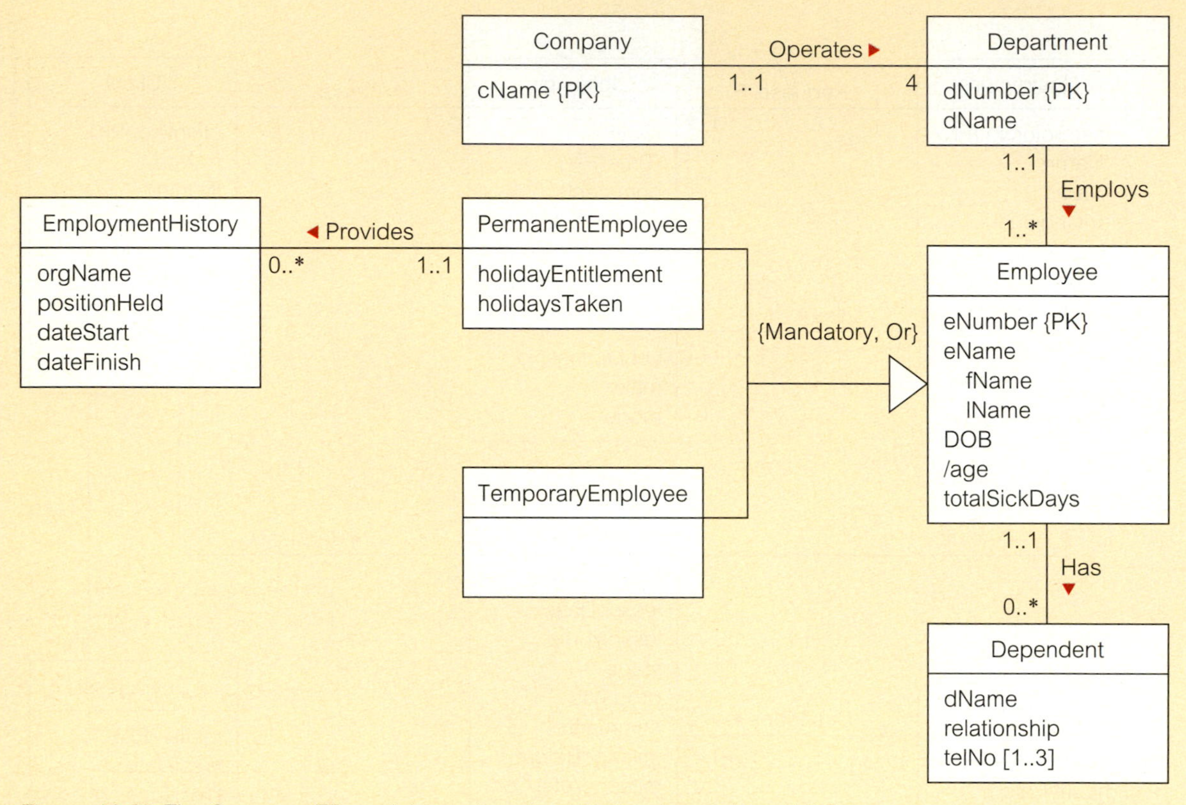

Figure 10.17 The Company ER model was described in Exercises 6.10 and 7.8

10.10 Create a description of the tables mapped from the *Car Park* model shown in Figure 10.18 and described in Exercises 6.11 and 7.9.

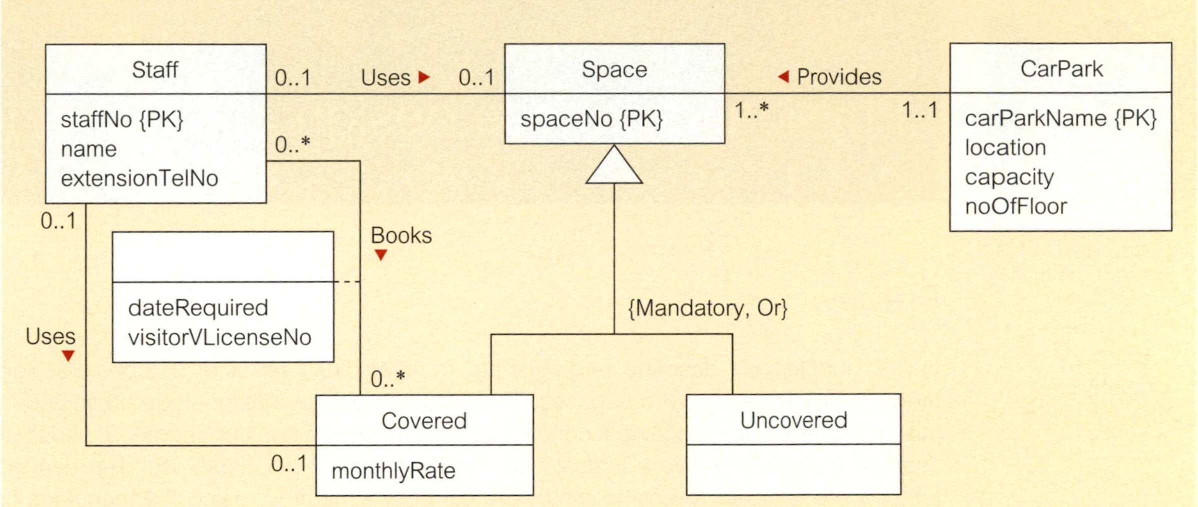

Figure 10.18 The Car park ER model was described in Exercises 6.11 and 7.9

10.11 Create a description of the tables mapped from the ER model created in Exercise 9.12 for the Buyer user view of *StayHome Online Rentals* case study described in Appendix A.

10.12 Create a description of the tables mapped from the ER model created in Exercise 9.13 for the *PerfectPets* case study described in Appendix B.

10.13 Merge the tables created for Exercise 10.11 to the tables (representing the merged data requirements for the Member, Assistant, and Manager user views of *StayHome Online Rentals*) shown in Figure 10.13 using the optional Step 2.6 of the database design methodology given in Appendix D.

10.14 Create each case study given in Appendix I without first looking at the answer tables that accompany each case study. Compare your tables with the answer tables and justify any differences found.

10.15 Create a description of the tables mapped from the ER model created for Exercise 9.18 to support part of the organization/university/college that you identified and described for Exercise 5.12.

CHAPTER 11

Physical database design

Preview

In this chapter, we describe and illustrate by example a physical database design methodology for relational databases. The database design methodology presented in this book started by producing a conceptual data model in Step 1 in Chapter 9, and then used this model to derive a logical data model in Step 2 in Chapter 10. The derived tables were checked to ensure they were correctly structured, using the technique of normalization, and to ensure they supported the transactions the users require. The starting point for this chapter is the logical data model and the documentation that describes the model produced in the previous two steps.

In the third phase of the database design methodology, namely physical database design, we decide how to translate the logical database design (that is the tables, columns, and integrity constraints) into a physical database design that can be implemented in the target DBMS. As many parts of physical database design are highly dependent on the target DBMS, there may be more than one way of implementing any given part of the database. Therefore, to carry out physical database design properly, we need to be fully aware of the functionality of the target DBMS and we need to understand the advantages and disadvantages of each alternative for a particular implementation. For some systems, we may also need to select a suitable storage strategy that takes account of intended database usage. Before we present the methodology for physical database design, we briefly review the design process.

Learning objectives

In this chapter you will learn:

- The purpose of physical database design.
- How to map the logical database design to a physical database design.
- How to design base tables for the target DBMS.
- How to design the representation of derived data.
- How to design integrity constraints for the target DBMS.
- How to analyze the users' transactions to identify characteristics that may impact on performance.

- That a database represents an essential corporate resource that must be made secure.
- The meaning of denormalization.
- About the importance of monitoring and tuning the operational system.
- How to measure efficiency.

11.1 Comparison of logical and physical database design

Logical database design is based on a specific data model (in this methodology we base it on the relational data model) but is independent of implementation details, such as the specific functionality of the target DBMS, application programs, programming languages, or any other physical considerations. The output of this process is a description of a set of relational tables together with supporting documentation, such as a data dictionary. These represent the sources of information for the physical design process, and they provide a vehicle for making trade-offs that are so important to an efficient database design.

Whereas logical database design is concerned with the *what*, physical database design is concerned with the *how*. In particular, the physical database designer must know how the computer system hosting the DBMS operates, and must also be fully aware of the functionality of the target DBMS. As the functionality provided by current systems varies widely, physical design must be tailored to a specific DBMS system. However, physical database design is not an isolated activity – there is often feedback between physical, logical, and application design. For example, decisions taken during physical design to improve performance, such as merging tables together, might affect the logical database design.

11.2 Overview of the physical database design methodology

Physical database design

The process of producing a description of the implementation of a database on secondary storage; it describes the base tables, file organizations, and indexes used to achieve efficient access to the data, and any associated integrity constraints and security restrictions.

The steps for **physical database design** are shown in Figure 11.1. We have divided the physical database design methodology into six main steps, numbered consecutively from Step 3 to follow the two steps of the conceptual and logical database design methodology.

We summarize each of the steps in Table 11.1. Appendix D presents a summary of the methodology for those readers who are already familiar with database design and who simply require an overview of the main steps. In this chapter we demonstrate the close association between physical database design and implementation by describing how alternative designs can be implemented for the *StayHome Online Rentals* case study (described in Section 5.4) using Microsoft Office Access 2007.

Step 3 Translate the logical database design for the target DBMS
  Step 3.1 Design base tables
  Step 3.2 Design representation of derived data
  Step 3.3 Design remaining integrity constraints
Step 4 Choose file organizations and indexes
  Step 4.1 Analyze transactions
  Step 4.2 Choose file organizations
  Step 4.3 Choose indexes
Step 5 Design user views
Step 6 Design security mechanisms
Step 7 Consider the introduction of controlled redundancy
Step 8 Monitor and tune the operational system

Figure 11.1 Steps in the physical database design methodology

Table 11.1 Summary of the main activities for the steps in the physical database design methodology

Step	Activities
3	Involves the design of the base tables and integrity constraints using the available functionality of the target DBMS. Also considers how to represent any derived data present in the model.
4	Involves analyzing the transactions that have to be supported and, based on this analysis, choosing appropriate file organizations and indexes for the base tables.
5	Involves deciding how each user view should be implemented.
6	Involves designing the security measures to protect data from unauthorized access, including the access controls that are required on the base tables.
7	Considers relaxing the normalization constraints imposed on the logical data model to improve the overall performance of the system. This is a step that should be undertaken only if necessary because of the inherent problems involved in introducing redundancy while maintaining data consistency.
8	The ongoing process of monitoring and tuning the operational system to identify and resolve any performance problems resulting from the design, and to design and then implement new or changing requirements.

11.3 Step 3: Translate the logical database design for the target DBMS

Objective

To produce a basic working relational database from the logical database design.

The first step of physical database design involves the translation of the tables in the logical data model into a form that can be implemented in the target relational

DBMS. The first part of this process entails collating the information gathered during logical database design and documented in the data dictionary, along with the information gathered during the requirements collection and analysis stage and documented in the systems specification. The second part of the process uses this information to produce the design of the base tables. This process requires intimate knowledge of the functionality offered by the target DBMS. For example, you will need to know:

- how to create base tables;
- whether the system supports the definition of primary keys, foreign keys, and alternate keys;
- whether the system supports the definition of required data, as defined in Section 2.3.1 (that is, whether the system allows columns to be defined as NOT NULL);
- whether the system supports the definition of domains;
- whether the system supports the relational integrity rules;
- whether the system supports the definition of other integrity constraints.

The three tasks in Step 3 are:

- Step 3.1 Design base tables.
- Step 3.2 Design representation of derived data.
- Step 3.3 Design remaining integrity constraints.

Step 3.1 Design the base tables

Objective

To decide how to represent the base tables identified in the logical database design in the target DBMS.

To start the physical design process, you first need to collate and assimilate the information about the tables that was produced during logical database design. The necessary information is obtained from the data dictionary and the definition of the tables that were defined using the Database Design Language (DBDL) (see Step 2.1 in Chapter 10). For each table identified in the logical data model, there should be a definition consisting of:

- the name of the table;
- a list of simple columns in brackets;
- the primary key and, where appropriate, alternate keys (AK) and foreign keys (FK);
- referential integrity constraints for any foreign keys identified.

For each column there should also be a specification of:

- its domain, consisting of a data type, length, and any constraints on the domain;

- an optional default value for the column;
- whether the column can hold nulls;
- whether the column is derived and, if so, how it should be computed.

To represent the design of the base tables, we use an extended form of the DBDL to define domains, default values, and null indicators. For example, for the `DistributionCenter` table of the *StayHome Online Rentals* database defined in Figure 10.13, you may produce the basic design shown in Figure 11.2. The next step is to decide how to implement the base tables. As we have already noted, this decision is dependent on the target DBMS; some systems provide more facilities than others for defining base tables and associated integrity constraints. If the target DBMS is compliant with the ISO SQL:2006 standard then we can use the CREATE TABLE statement discussed in Appendix E.1. If the target DBMS is not fully compliant with this standard, we will have to use the facilities offered by the DBMS. To illustrate this latter situation we demonstrate how to create base tables and associated integrity constraints in Microsoft Office Access 2007.

```
domain dCenter_Numbers      fixed length character string length 4
domain Street_Names         variable length character string maximum length 60
domain City_Names           variable length character string maximum length 20
domain State_Codes          fixed length character string length 2
domain Zip_Codes            fixed length character string length 5
domain Staff_Numbers        fixed length character string length 5

DistributionCenter(
    dCenterNo        dCenter_Numbers      NOT NULL,
    dStreet          Street_Names         NOT NULL,
    dCity            City_Names           NOT NULL,
    dState           State_Codes          NOT NULL,
    dZipCode         Zip_Codes            NOT NULL,
    mgrStaffNo       Staff_Numbers        NOT NULL)
    PRIMARY KEY dCenterNo
    ALTERNATE KEY dZipCode
    FOREIGN KEY mgrStaffNo REFERENCES Staff(staffNo)
                         ON UPDATE CASCADE ON DELETE SET NULL
)
```

Figure 11.2 The physical design of the `DistributionCenter` table using an extended DBDL

Implementing base tables in Microsoft Office Access 2007

Note When discussing Microsoft Office Access, we use the vendor's terminology and use the term 'field' in place of 'column.'

One way to create a blank (empty) table in Microsoft Office Access 2007 is to use Design View to specify all table details from scratch. This DBMS does not support domains so we need to decide how each field is to be represented. The data types that Access supports, which are slightly different from the SQL standard, are shown in

Table 11.2 Microsoft Office Access 2007 data types

Data Type	Use	Size
Text	Text or text/numbers. Also numbers that do not require calculations, such as telephone numbers.	Up to 255 characters
Memo	Lengthy text and numbers, such as notes or descriptions.	Up to 65 536 characters
Number	Numeric data to be used for mathematical calculations, except calculations involving money (use Currency type).	1, 2, 4, or 8 bytes
Date/Time	Dates and times.	8 bytes
Currency	Currency values. Use the Currency data type to prevent rounding off during calculations.	8 bytes
Autonumber	Unique sequential (incrementing by 1) or random numbers automatically inserted when a record is added.	4 bytes
Yes/No	Fields that will contain only one of two values, such as Yes/No, True/False, On/Off.	1 bit
OLE Object	Objects (such as Microsoft Word documents, Microsoft Excel spreadsheets, pictures, sounds, or other binary data) created in other programs using the OLE protocol, that can be linked to, or embedded in, a Microsoft Access table.	Up to 1 gigabyte
Hyperlink	Field that will store hyperlinks.	Up to 64 000 characters
Lookup Wizard	A field that allows you to choose a value from another table or from a list of values using a combo box. Choosing this option in the data type list starts a wizard to define this for you.	Typically 4 bytes

Table 11.2. In addition, when defining fields, Access allows us to specify among other things:

- whether the field (or combination of fields) represents the primary key;
- an input mask (which determines the type of character allowed for each position of the field);
- an optional default value;
- a validation rule (which we discuss shortly);
- whether the field is required (that is, whether it can accept nulls or not);
- whether the field is to be indexed – setting this property to 'Yes (No Duplicates)' supports the specification of alternate keys.

Figure 11.3 shows the Design View for the creation of the `DistributionCenter` table. Design View can also be used afterwards to customize the table further, such as adding new fields, changing default values or input masks.

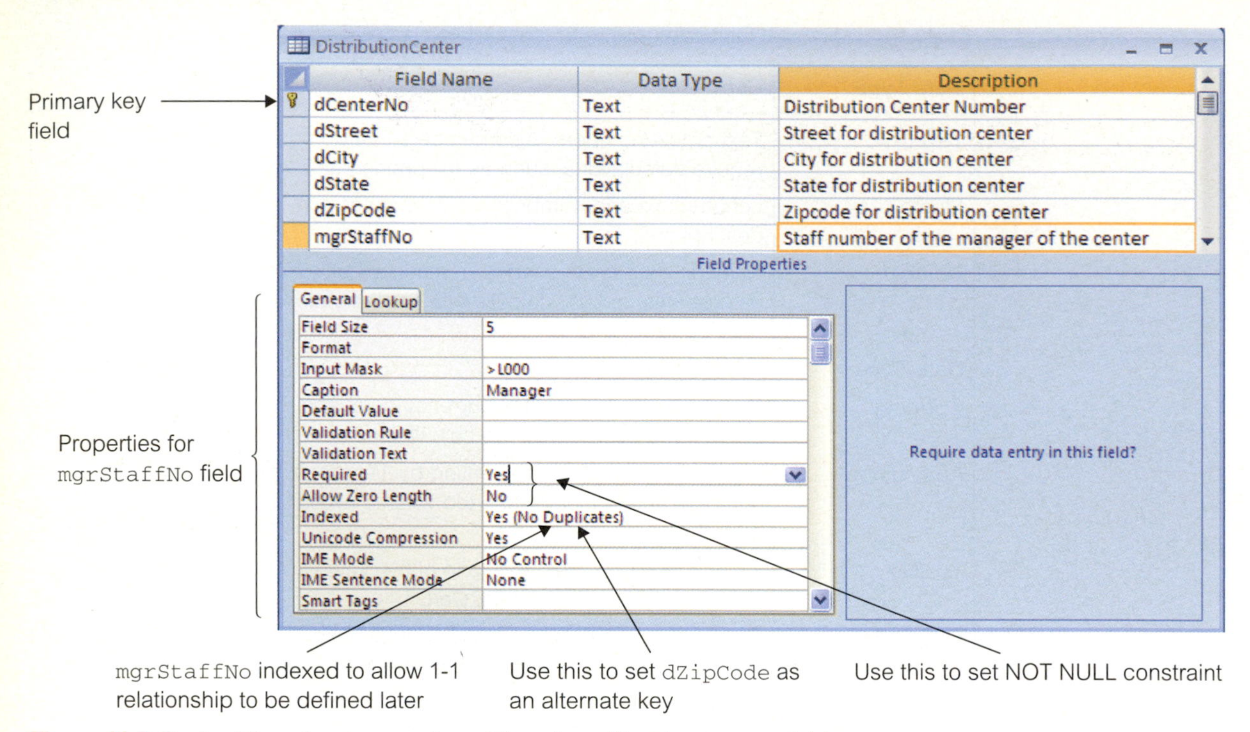

Figure 11.3 Design View showing creation of the `DistributionCenter` table

Creating a relationship between two tables in Access

Relationships are created in Access in the Relationships window. To create a relationship, we display the tables we want to create the relationships between and then drag the primary key attribute of the parent table to the foreign key attribute of the child table. At this point, Access displays a window allowing us to specify the referential integrity constraints. Figure 11.4(a) shows the Edit Relationships dialog box that is displayed when creating the one-to-one (1:1) relationship `Staff` *Manages* `DistributionCenter` and Figure 11.4(b) shows the Relationships window after the relationship has been created.

There are a couple of things to note about setting referential integrity constraints in Microsoft Office Access:

(1) A one-to-many (1:*) relationship (see Section 6.5.2) is created if only one of the related fields is a primary key or has a unique index; a 1:1 relationship (see Section 6.5.1) is created if both the related fields are primary keys or have unique indexes. Therefore, to ensure that the *Manages* relationship is 1:1, we must not only ensure that the `staffNo` field in the `Staff` table has been set as the primary key, but also that the `mgrStaffNo` field in the `DistributionCenter` table has the Indexed property set to 'Yes (No Duplicates)', as shown in Figure 11.3.

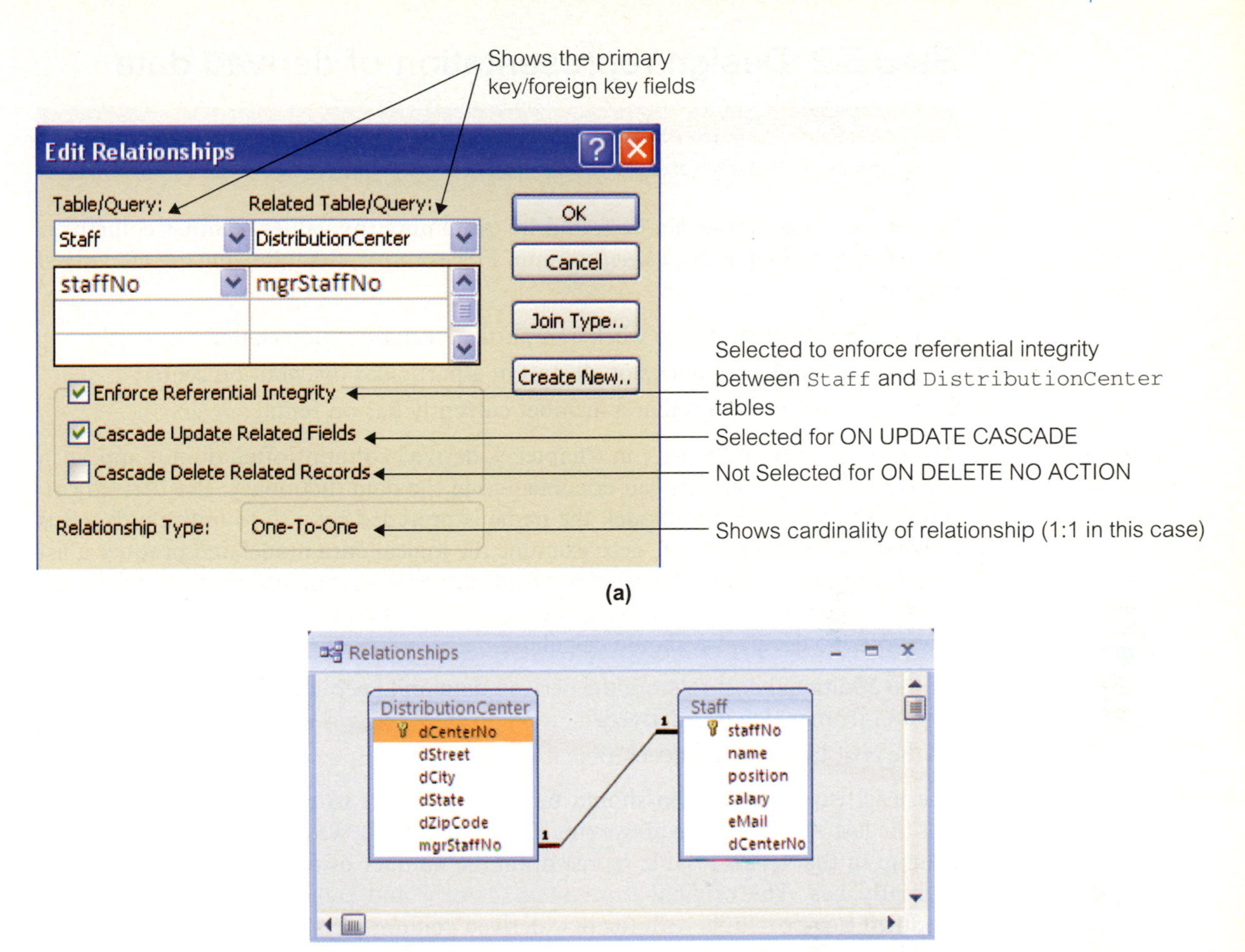

Figure 11.4 (a) Setting the referential integrity constraints for the 1:1 `Staff` *`Manages`* `DistributionCenter` relationship; (b) Relationship window showing the 1:1 `Staff` *`Manages`* `DistributionCenter` relationship

(2) There are only two referential integrity actions for update and delete that correspond to NO ACTION and CASCADE. Therefore, if we have identified other actions during Step 2.4 Check integrity constraints in Chapter 10, we must consider whether to modify these constraints to fit in with the constraints available in Access, or we must investigate how to implement these constraints in application code.

Document design of base tables

The design of the base tables should be fully documented along with the reasons for selecting the proposed design. In particular, document the reasons for selecting one approach where many alternatives exist.

Step 3.2 Design representation of derived data

Objective

To design the representation of derived data in the database.

A column whose value can be found by examining the values of other columns is known as a *derived* or *calculated* column. For example, the following are all derived columns:

- the number of staff who work at a particular distribution center;
- the total monthly salaries of all staff at a particular distribution center;
- the number of DVDs that a member currently has on rental.

As we mentioned in Step 1.3 in Chapter 9, derived columns often do not appear in the ER model, but are instead documented in the data dictionary. If a derived column is shown in the ER model, the name is preceded by a '/' to indicate that it is derived. The first step, then, is to examine the logical data model and produce a list of all derived columns. From a physical database design perspective, whether a derived column is stored in the database or calculated every time it is needed is a trade-off. To decide, we should calculate:

- the additional cost to store the derived data and keep it consistent with the data from which it is derived;
- the cost to calculate it each time it is required.

The least expensive option should be chosen subject to performance constraints. For the last example given above (the DVDs on rental), we could store an additional column in the `Member` table representing the number of rentals that each member currently has. The original `RentalDelivery` and `DVDRental` tables and the modified `Member` table with the new derived column are shown in Figure 11.5.

The additional storage overhead for this new derived column would not be particularly significant. However, the `noOfRentals` column would need to be updated every time a member rented or returned a DVD. We would need to ensure that this change was made consistently to maintain the correct count, and thereby ensure the integrity of the database. By storing the data in this way, when a query requires this information, the value is immediately available and does not have to be calculated.

If the `noOfRentals` column is not stored directly in the `Member` table, it must be calculated each time it is needed. This involves a join of the `Member`, `RentalDelivery`, and `DVDRental` tables. For example, to calculate the number of DVDs that member Don Nelson currently has on rental we could use the following SQL query:

```
SELECT COUNT(*) AS noOfRentals
FROM Member m, RentalDelivery r, DVDRental d
WHERE m.memberNo= r.memberNo AND
  m.mFName = 'Don' AND m.mLName = 'Nelson' AND
  r.deliveryNo = d.deliveryNo AND
  dateReturn IS NULL;
```

RentalDelivery

deliveryNo	memberNo	dateOut
R75346191	M284354	4-Feb-06
R75346282	M284354	4-Feb-06
R66825673	M115656	5-Feb-06
R66818964	M115656	2-Feb-06

DVDRental

deliveryNo	DVDNo	dateReturn
R75346191	24545663	6-Feb-06
R75346282	24343196	6-Feb-06
R66825673	19900422	7-Feb-06
R66818964	17864331	

Member

memberNo	mFName	mLName	. . .	noOfRentals
M250178	Bob	Adams	. . .	0
M166884	Art	Peters	. . .	0
M115656	Serena	Parker	. . .	1
M284354	Don	Nelson	. . .	0

Figure 11.5 The original `RentalDelivery` and `DVDRental` tables and the modified `Member` table with the additional derived column `noOfRentals`

If this type of query is frequent, or is considered to be critical for performance purposes, it may be more appropriate to store the derived column rather than calculate it each time. In our example, *StayHome Online Rentals* run this type of query every time a member attempts to rent a new DVD. Through discussion with *StayHome* staff, it is estimated that the size of the `DVDRental` table is about 2 million records (and the `RentalDelivery` table is about one-third this size). Therefore, as these tables are very large and the query frequent, we may decide that it is more efficient to add the derived column to the `Member` table. The same query could now be written as:

```
SELECT noOfRentals
FROM Member
WHERE mFName = 'Don' AND mLName = 'Nelson';
```

Document design of derived data

The design of how to represent derived data should be fully documented along with the reasons for selecting the proposed design. In particular, document the reasons for selecting one approach where many alternatives exist.

Step 3.3 Design remaining integrity constraints

Objective

To design the remaining integrity constraints for the target DBMS.

Updates to tables may be restricted by constraints that the organization imposes on the underlying data. At this point, we have already designed required the data constraints, domain constraints, and relational integrity constraints. The objective of this step is to design any other integrity constraints that have to be imposed on the data. The design of such constraints is again dependent on the choice of DBMS; some systems provide more facilities than others for defining integrity constraints. As in the previous step, if the system is compliant with the SQL standard, some constraints may be easy to implement. For example, *StayHome Online Rentals* has a rule that prevents a member from ever renting more than five DVDs at any one time (although the membership type may specify fewer than this). We could design this rule into the SQL CREATE TABLE statement (see Appendix E.1) for the `RentalDelivery` table, using the following clause:

```
CONSTRAINT member_not_renting_too_many
    CHECK (NOT EXISTS (SELECT memberNo
                       FROM RentalDelivery r, DVDRental d
                       WHERE r.deliveryNo = d.deliveryNo AND
                             dateReturn IS NULL
                       GROUP BY memberNo
                       HAVING COUNT(*) >= 5))
```

Alternatively, in some systems a **trigger** could be used to enforce some constraints. We provide an example of a trigger to enforce the above rule in Appendix E.6.

Creating integrity constraints in Microsoft Office Access 2007

There are several ways to create integrity constraints in Microsoft Office Access using, for example:

(a) validation rules for fields;

(b) validation rules for records;

(c) validation for forms using VBA (Visual Basic for Applications).

We illustrate some of these below with some simple examples.

Validation rules for fields

We can ensure that data is entered correctly into a field by defining a field validation rule, which is used to check the value entered into a field as the user leaves the field. A message we define is displayed if the value breaks the validation rule. For example, *StayHome Online Rentals* has a simple constraint that the date DVD rentals are returned cannot be later than the current date, although the date will be unspecified until the DVD is returned. We can implement this constraint at the field level in the `DVDRental` table using the function Date( ), which returns the current date, as shown in Figure 11.6.

Validation rules for records

A record validation rule controls when an entire record can be saved. Unlike field validation rules, record validation rules can refer to other fields. This makes them useful when we want to compare values from different fields in a table.

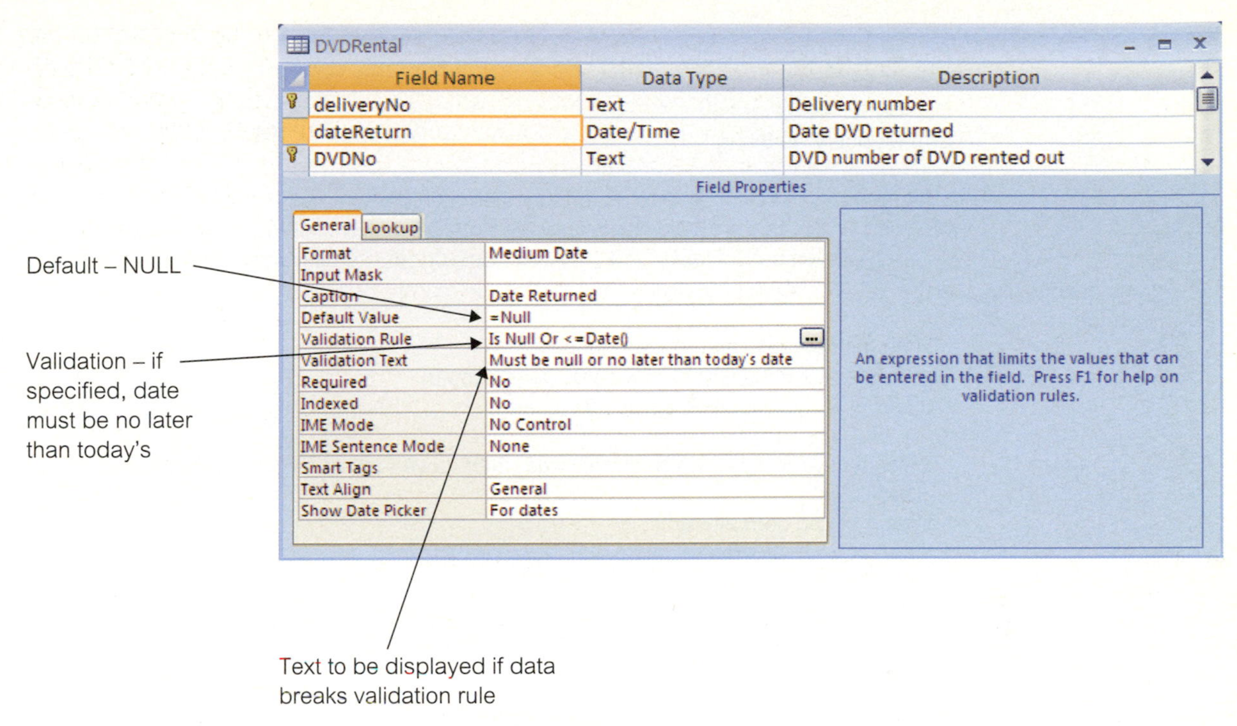

Figure 11.6 Example of field validation in Microsoft Office Access

Validation for forms using VBA (Visual Basic for Applications)

As we have just mentioned, *StayHome* has a constraint that members are not allowed to rent more than five DVDs at any one time. This is a more complex constraint, which requires that we check how many rentals the member currently has. One way to implement this constraint in Access is to use an event procedure (BeforeUpdate). The BeforeUpdate event is triggered before a record is updated and we can associate code with this event on a form, as shown in Figure 11.7.

In some systems, there will be no support for some types of integrity constraints and it will be necessary to design the constraints into the application, as we have shown with the last example that has built the constraint into the application's VBA code. Implementing an integrity constraint in application code is, of course, potentially dangerous and can lead to duplication of effort and, worse still, to inconsistencies if the constraint is not implemented everywhere it should be.

Document design of integrity constraints

The design of integrity constraints should be fully documented. In particular, document the reasons for selecting one approach where many alternatives exist.

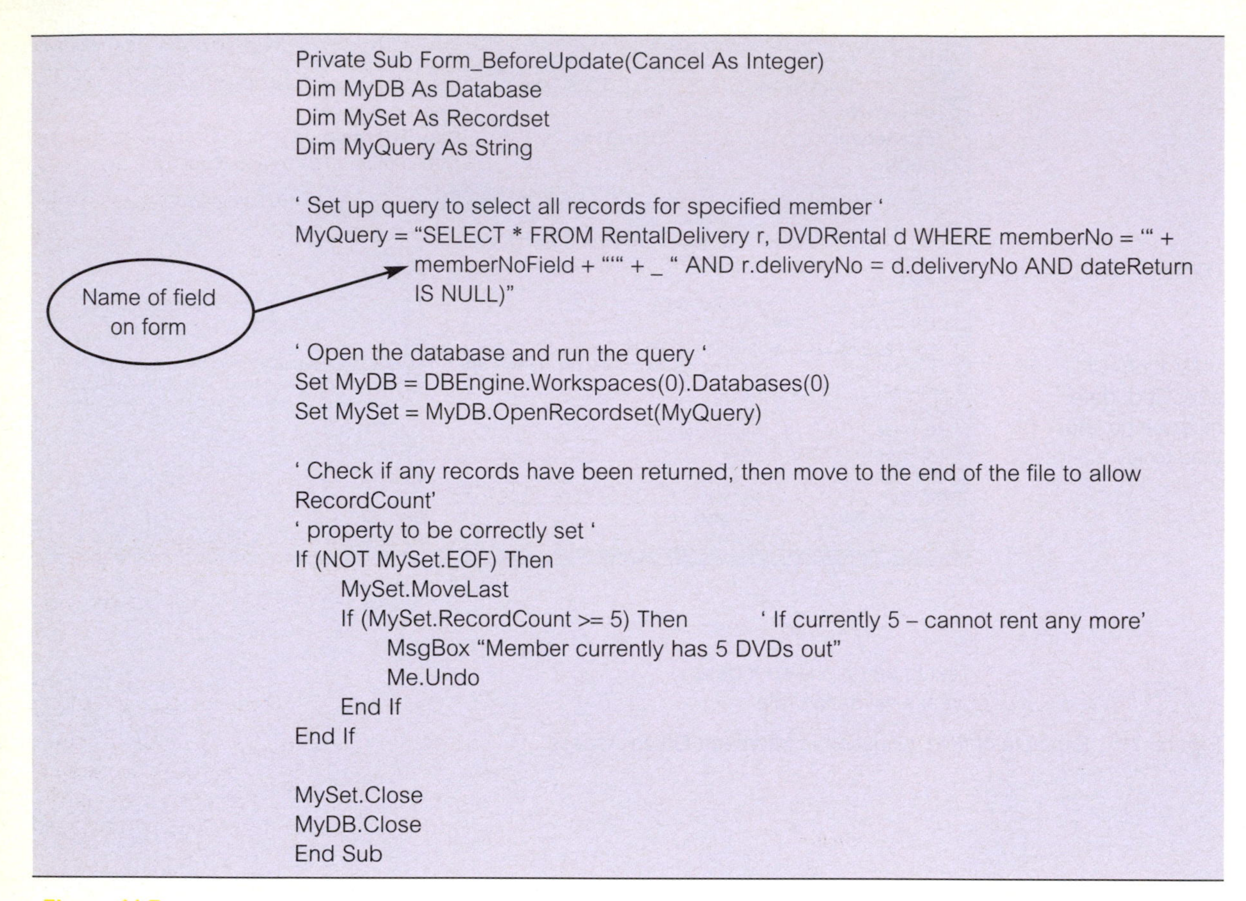


```
Private Sub Form_BeforeUpdate(Cancel As Integer)
Dim MyDB As Database
Dim MySet As Recordset
Dim MyQuery As String

' Set up query to select all records for specified member '
MyQuery = "SELECT * FROM RentalDelivery r, DVDRental d WHERE memberNo = '" +
          memberNoField + "'" + _ " AND r.deliveryNo = d.deliveryNo AND dateReturn
          IS NULL)"

' Open the database and run the query '
Set MyDB = DBEngine.Workspaces(0).Databases(0)
Set MySet = MyDB.OpenRecordset(MyQuery)

' Check if any records have been returned, then move to the end of the file to allow
RecordCount'
' property to be correctly set '
If (NOT MySet.EOF) Then
    MySet.MoveLast
    If (MySet.RecordCount >= 5) Then        ' If currently 5 – cannot rent any more'
        MsgBox "Member currently has 5 DVDs out"
        Me.Undo
    End If
End If

MySet.Close
MyDB.Close
End Sub
```

Figure 11.7 VBA code to check that a member cannot rent more than 5 DVDs

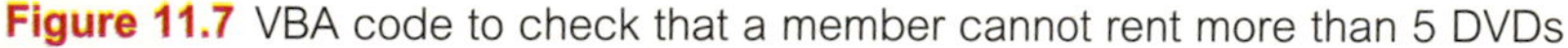

11.4 Step 4: Choose file organizations and indexes

Objective

To determine the optimal file organizations to store the base tables and the indexes that are required to achieve acceptable performance.

File organization

A way of arranging the records in a file when the file is stored on disk.

The physical database designer must provide the physical design details to both the DBMS and the operating system. For the DBMS, this includes specifying the **file organizations** that are to be used to represent each table; for the operating system, this includes specifying details such as the location and protection for each file. Typically, PC DBMSs have a fixed file organization, but other DBMSs tend to provide a small number of alternative file structures for data. The types of file organization available are dependent on the target DBMS; some systems provide more choice of file organizations than others. It is important that we fully understand the structures that are available and how the target system uses these structures. From the user's viewpoint, the internal storage representation for tables should be invisible – the user should be able to access tables and records without having to specify where or how the records are stored.

We cannot make meaningful physical design decisions about file organizations and **indexes** until we understand in detail the typical workload that the database must support. The workload consists of both read and write transactions supplemented with frequency information and performance goals for the transactions. As a result, we have decomposed the tasks in Step 4 into:

Index

A data structure that allows the DBMS to locate particular records in a file more quickly, and thereby improve the response to user queries. An index is similar to an index in a book where we look up a keyword to get a list of one or more pages the keyword appears on.

- Step 4.1 Analyze transactions.
- Step 4.2 Choose file organizations.
- Step 4.3 Choose indexes.

Step 4.1 Analyze transactions

Objective

To analyze the functionality of the transactions that will run on the database to identify those that may impact on performance.

Key point

In many situations it would be far too time-consuming to analyze all the expected transactions, so we should at least investigate the 'most important' ones; that is, the ones that run most frequently and/or the ones that are critical to the running of the company. It has been suggested that the most active 20% of user queries account for 80% of the total data access (Wiederhold, 1983). This 80/20 rule may be a useful guideline when carrying out the analysis.

In analyzing the transactions, we are attempting to identify performance criteria, such as:

- the transactions that run frequently and will have a significant impact on performance;
- the transactions that are critical to the operation of the business;
- the times of the day/week when there will be a high demand made on the database (called the *peak load*).

In considering each transaction, it is important that we know not only the average and maximum number of times it runs per hour, but also the day and time that the transaction is run, including when the peak load is likely. For example, some transactions may run at the average rate for most of the time, but have a peak loading between 14.00 and 16.00 on a Thursday prior to a meeting on Friday morning. Other transactions may run only at specific times, for example 18.00–21.00 on Friday/Saturday, which is also their peak loading.

We use this information to identify the parts of the database that may cause performance problems. At the same time, we need to identify the high-level functionality of the transactions, such as the columns that are updated in an update transaction or the columns that are retrieved in a query. We use this information to select

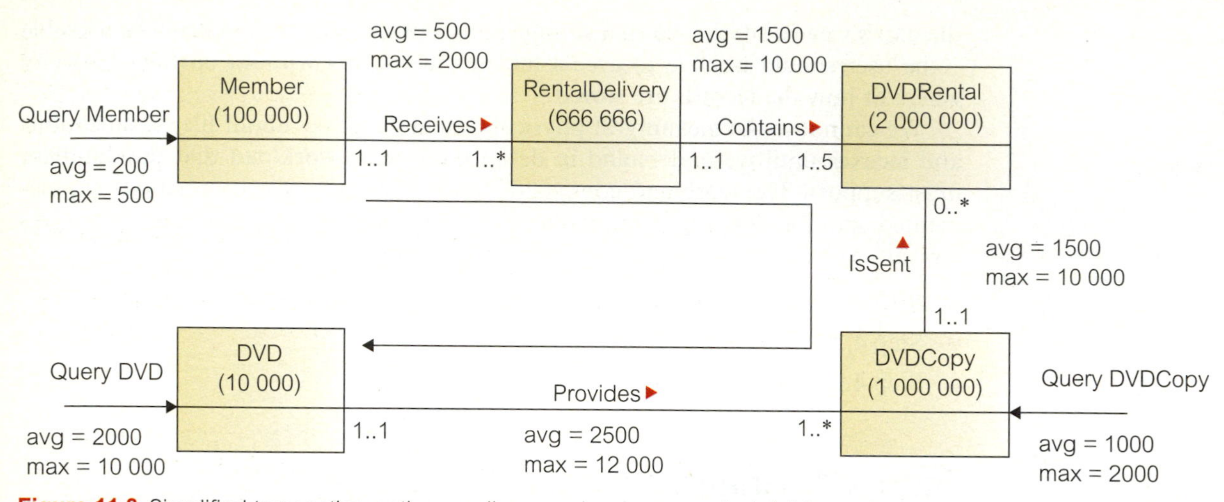

Figure 11.8 Simplified transaction pathways diagram showing expected daily occurrences

appropriate file organizations and indexes. For the most important transactions identified, determine which tables they access and indicate the average and maximum number of accesses over some time interval (for example hourly, daily, weekly.) One way to do this is to use the transaction pathways diagram that was created in Step 1.8 of the conceptual database design methodology (see Figure 9.11). This diagram summarizes, in a visual way, the access patterns of the transactions that will run on the database. Figure 11.8 shows a portion of this diagram with *daily* frequency information added focusing on the tables that appear to have the highest access rates. Due to the size of the `DVDCopy`, `RentalDelivery`, and `DVDRental` tables, it is important that access to these tables is as efficient as possible. We may now decide that a closer analysis of transactions involving these tables is useful. We provide more details on the analyzing transaction usage and discuss how this information is used to produce a 'wish-list' of possible indexes in Appendix F.

Step 4.2 Choose file organizations

Objective

To determine an efficient file organization for each base table.

One of the main objectives of physical database design is to store data in an efficient way. For example, if we want to retrieve staff records in alphabetical order of name then sorting the file by staff name is a good file organization. However, if we want to retrieve all staff whose salary is in a certain range, a file ordered by staff name would not be a good file organization. To complicate matters, some file organizations are efficient for bulk loading data into the database but inefficient after that. In other words, we may use an efficient storage structure to set up the database and then change it for normal operational use.

The objective of this step is to choose an optimal file organization for each table, if the target DBMS allows this. In many cases, we may find that the target DBMS gives little or no choice for choosing file organizations, although some may be established as we specify indexes. If the target DBMS does not support the choice of file organization, we can omit this step and move onto the next step, Step 4.3. For example, Microsoft Office Access 2007 has a fixed file organization and so for this DBMS we can omit this step. On the other hand, the Oracle DBMS supports *index-organized tables* and *clustered tables*:

- An **index-organized table** differs from an ordinary table in that the data for the table is held in its associated index. Changes to the table data, such as adding new records, updating records, or deleting records, result only in updating the index. Because data records are stored in the index, index-organized tables provide faster key-based access to table data for queries that involve exact match or range search or both.
- **Clusters** are groups of one or more tables physically stored together because they share common columns and are often used together. With related records being physically stored together, disk access time is improved. The related columns of the tables in a cluster are called the *cluster key*. The cluster key is stored only once, and so clusters store a set of tables more efficiently than if the tables were stored individually (not clustered). Clustering can be an efficient file organization if the clustered tables are frequently joined together. However, it can be an inefficient file organization if a full search of one of the tables is often required.

One approach to selecting an appropriate file organization for a table is to keep the records unordered and create as many **secondary indexes** as we need (we discuss how to choose secondary indexes shortly). Another approach is to order the records in the table by specifying a **primary** or **clustering index**. In this case, we should choose the column for ordering or clustering the records as:

- the column that is used most often for join operations, because this makes the join operation more efficient; or
- the column that is used most often to access the records in a table in order of that column.

A fuller discussion of choosing file organizations is beyond the scope of this book but the interested reader is referred to Connolly and Begg (2005).

Document choice of file organizations

The choice of file organizations should be fully documented, along with the reasons for the choice. In particular, document the reasons for selecting one file organization where many alternatives exist.

Step 4.3 Choose indexes

Objective

To determine whether adding indexes will improve the performance of the system.

Secondary indexes provide a mechanism for specifying an additional key for a base table that can be used to retrieve data more efficiently. (Appendix F.1 provides an overview of indexes for those readers unfamiliar with the concept.) For example, the `Member` table may be hashed on the member number, `memberNo`, the *primary index*. On the other hand, there may be frequent access to this table based on the `mLName` (last name) column. In this case, we may decide to add `mLName` as a *secondary index*. However, there is an overhead involved in the maintenance and use of secondary indexes that we have to balance against the performance improvement gained when retrieving data. This overhead includes:

- adding an index record to every secondary index whenever a record is inserted in the table;
- updating a secondary index when the corresponding record in the table is updated;
- the increase in disk space needed to store the secondary index;
- possible performance degradation during query optimization, as the query optimizer may consider all secondary indexes before selecting an optimal execution strategy;
- adding an index to a table may improve the performance of one application, but it may adversely affect another, perhaps more important, application.

We provide guidelines for choosing indexes in Appendix F and use the guidelines to create indexes for *StayHome Online Rentals*.

Document choice of secondary indexes

The choice of indexes should be fully documented, along with the reasons for the choice. In particular, if there are performance reasons why some columns should not be indexed these should also be documented.

11.5 Step 5: Design user views

Objective

To design the user views that were identified during the requirements collection and analysis stage of the database system development lifecycle.

The first step of the database design methodology involved the production of a conceptual data model for either the single user view or a number of combined user views identified during the requirements collection and analysis stage (see Section 4.5.1). In Section 5.4.4, we identified three user views for *StayHome* named Manager, Assistant, and Member. The objective of this step is to design all the user views identified previously. In a standalone DBMS on a PC, views are usually a convenience, defined to simplify queries. However, in a multi-user DBMS views play a central role in defining the structure of the database and enforcing security. To illustrate this process we show two particular ways to create views using:

(1) the ISO SQL:2006 standard;

(2) Microsoft Office Access 2007.

The ISO SQL:2006 standard

Normally, views are created using SQL or a QBE-like facility. For example, for Assistants at distribution center D001 we may create a view of the base table `Staff` that excludes salary information. The SQL statement to create this view would be:

```
CREATE VIEW Staff1View
AS  SELECT staffNo, name, position, eMail
    FROM Staff
    WHERE dCenterNo = 'D001';
```

This creates a view called `Staff1View` with the same columns as the `Staff` table, but excluding the `salary` and `dCenterNo` columns. If we query this view we get the data shown in Figure 11.9.

`Staff1View`

staffNo	name	position	eMail
S1500	Toma Daniels	Manager	tdaniels@stayhome.com
S0003	Sally Adams	Assistant	sadams@stayhome.com

Figure 11.9 List of the `Staff1View` view

To ensure that only the distribution center manager can see the `salary` column, Assistants are not given access to the base table `Staff`. Instead, they are given *access privilege* to the view `Staff1View`, thereby denying them access to sensitive salary data. We discuss access privileges further in Step 6.

Creating views in Microsoft Office Access 2007

Microsoft Office Access does not support the SQL CREATE VIEW statement. Instead, we can create a (stored) query using QBE or SQL. For example, we could create the view `Staff1View` using the QBE query shown in Figure 11.10(a) or using the SQL statement shown in Figure 11.10(b). This query can now be used to

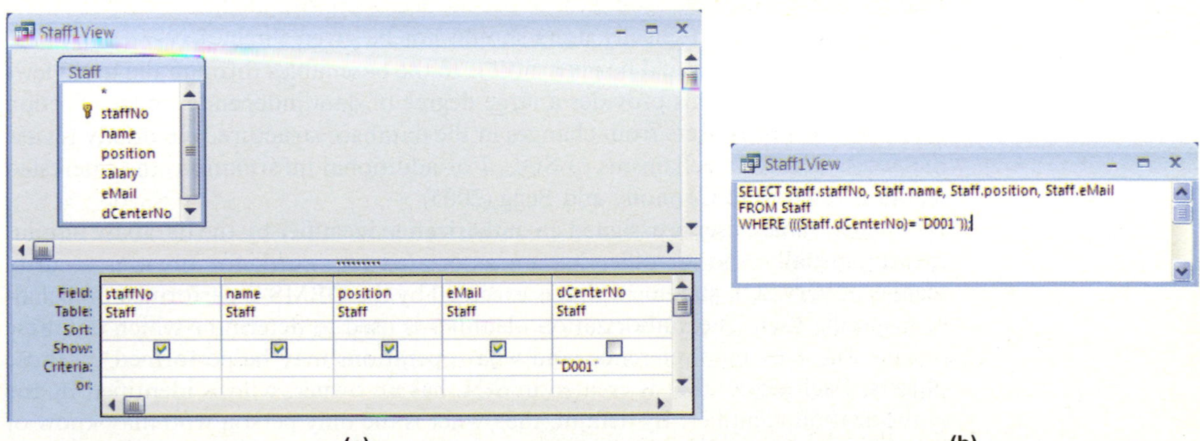

Figure 11.10 Creating a (stored) query in Microsoft Office Access: (a) using QBE; (b) using SQL

create other queries, update/delete records in the base table `Staff`, and can be used as the basis for creating forms and reports.

11.6 Step 6: Design security mechanisms

Objective

To design the security measures for the database as specified by the users during the requirements collection and analysis stage of the database system development lifecycle.

A database represents an essential corporate resource and so security of this resource is extremely important. There may have been specific security requirements documented during the requirements collection and analysis stage of the database system development lifecycle. The objective of this step is to decide how these security requirements are to be realized. Different DBMSs offer slightly different security facilities and therefore we must be aware of the facilities offered by the target DBMS. As we will discuss in Chapter 12, relational DBMSs generally provide two types of database security:

- system security;
- data security.

System security covers access and use of the database at the system level, such as a username and password. **Data security** covers access and use of database objects (such as tables and views) and the actions that users can have on the objects. To illustrate this process we show two particular ways to design security mechanisms using:

(1) the ISO SQL:2006 standard;
(2) Microsoft Office Access 2007.

The ISO SQL:2006 standard

One way to provide data security is to use the access control facilities of SQL. As we have just mentioned, typically users should not be given direct access to the base tables. Instead, they should be given access to the base tables through the user views designed in Step 5. This provides a large degree of data independence (see Section 1.2.2) and insulates users from changes in the database structure. We briefly review the access control mechanisms of SQL. For additional information, the interested reader is referred to Connolly and Begg (2005).

Each database user is assigned an **authorization identifier** by the database administrator; usually, the identifier has an associated password, for obvious security reasons. Every SQL statement that is executed by the DBMS is performed on behalf of a specific user. The authorization identifier is used to determine which database objects that user may reference, and what operations may be performed on those objects. Each object that is created in SQL has an owner, who is identified by the authorization identifier. By default, the owner is the only person who may know of the existence of the object and perform any operations on the object.

Privileges are the actions that a user is permitted to carry out on a given base table or view. For example, SELECT is the privilege to retrieve data from a table and UPDATE is the privilege to modify records of a table. When a user creates a table using the SQL CREATE TABLE statement, he or she automatically becomes the owner of the table and receives full privileges for the table. Other users initially have no privileges on the newly created table. To give them access to the table, the owner must explicitly grant them the necessary privileges using the SQL GRANT statement. A WITH GRANT OPTION clause can be specified with the GRANT statement to allow the receiving user(s) to pass the privilege(s) on to other users. Privileges can be revoked using the SQL REVOKE statement.

When a user creates a view with the CREATE VIEW statement, he or she automatically becomes the owner of the view, but does not necessarily receive full privileges on the view. To create the view, a user must have SELECT privilege to all the tables that make up the view. However, the owner will get other privileges only if he or she holds those privileges for every table in the view.

For example, to allow the user MANAGER to retrieve records from the `Staff` table and to insert, update, and delete data from the `Staff` table, we could use the following SQL statement:

```
GRANT ALL PRIVILEGES
ON Staff
TO Manager WITH GRANT OPTION;
```

In this case, MANAGER will also be able to reference the table and all the columns in any table he or she creates subsequently. The clause WITH GRANT OPTION is specified so that MANAGER can pass these privileges on to other users whom he or she sees fit. As another example, we could give the user with authorization identifier ADMIN the privilege SELECT on the `Staff` table using the following SQL statement:

```
GRANT SELECT
ON Staff
TO Admin;
```

The clause WITH GRANT OPTION is omitted this time so that ADMIN will not be able to pass this privilege on to other users.

Security in Microsoft Office Access 2007

Microsoft Office Access 2007 does not support the SQL GRANT and REVOKE statements. Instead, Access provides a number of security features including the following two methods:

(a) setting a password for opening a database (system security);

(b) user-level security, which can be used to limit the parts of the database that a user can read or update (data security).

Setting a password

The simpler method is to set a password for opening the database. Once a password has been set (from the *Tools*, *Security* menu), a dialog box requesting the password

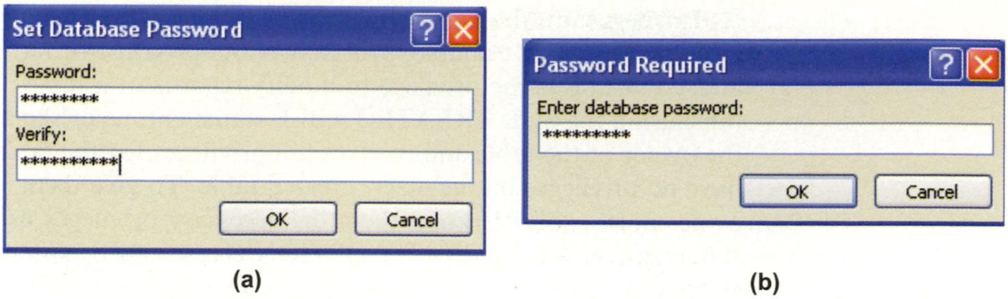

Set Database Password
Password:
Verify:
OK Cancel

Password Required
Enter database password:
OK Cancel

(a) (b)

Figure 11.11 Securing the *StayHome* database using a password: (a) the Set Database Password dialog box; (b) the Password Required dialog box shown at startup

will be displayed whenever the database is opened. The dialog box to set the password and the dialog box requesting the password whenever the database is opened are shown in Figure 11.11. Only users who type the correct password will be allowed to open the database. This method is secure because Microsoft Office Access encrypts the password so that it cannot be accessed by reading the database file directly. However, once a database is open all the objects contained within the database are available to the user.

User-level security

User-level security in Microsoft Office Access is similar to methods used in most network systems. Users are required to identify themselves and type a password when they start Microsoft Office Access. Within the workgroup information file, users are identified as members of a group. Access provides two default groups: administrators (*Admins* group) and users (*Users* group), but additional groups can be defined. Figure 11.12 displays the dialog box used to define the security level for user and group accounts. It shows a non-default group called Assistants, and a user called Assistant who is a member of the Users and Assistants groups.

Permissions are granted to groups and users to regulate how they are allowed to work with each object in the database using the User and Group Permissions dialog box. Figure 11.13 shows the dialog box for a user called Assistant in *StayHome* who has only read access to the `Staff1View` created previously. In a similar way, all access to the base table `Staff` would be removed so that the Assistant user can only view the data in the `Staff` table using this view.

Other security features of Microsoft Office Access

In addition to the above two methods of securing a Microsoft Office Access database, other security features include:

- *Encryption/decryption:* encrypting a database compacts the database file and makes it indecipherable by a utility program or word processor. This is useful if we wish to transmit a database electronically or when we store it on a pendrive or compact disk. Decrypting a database reverses the encryption.
- *Securing VBA code:* this can be achieved by setting a password that is entered once per session or by saving the database as an MDE file, which compiles the

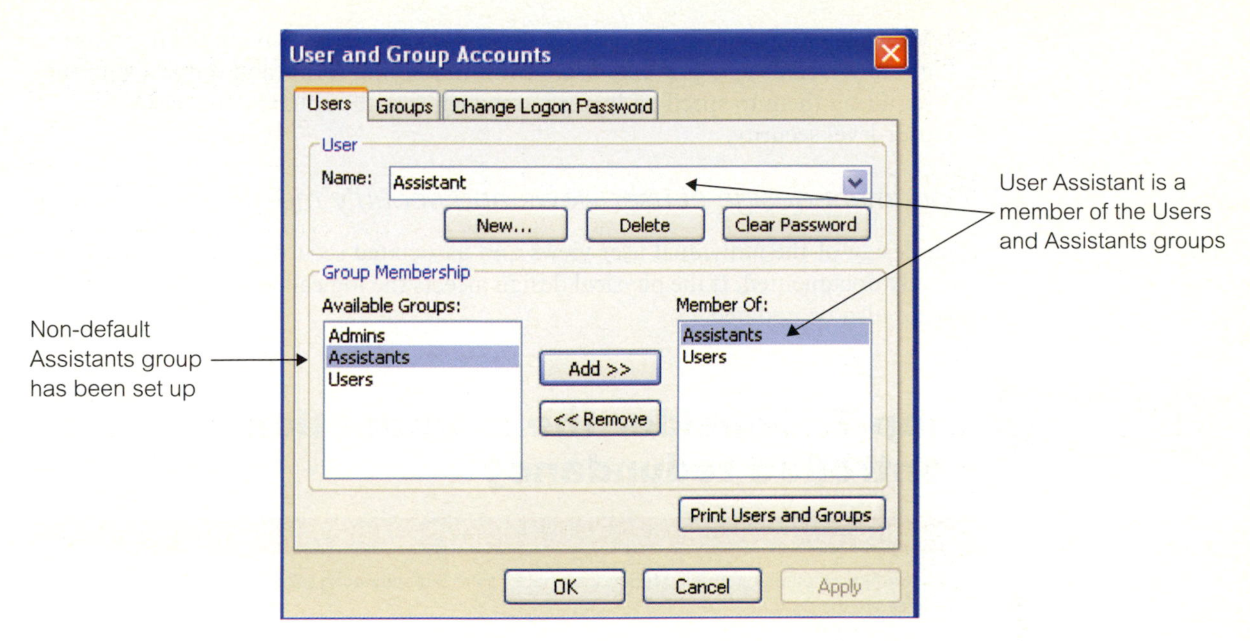

Figure 11.12 The User and Group Accounts dialog box for the *StayHome* database

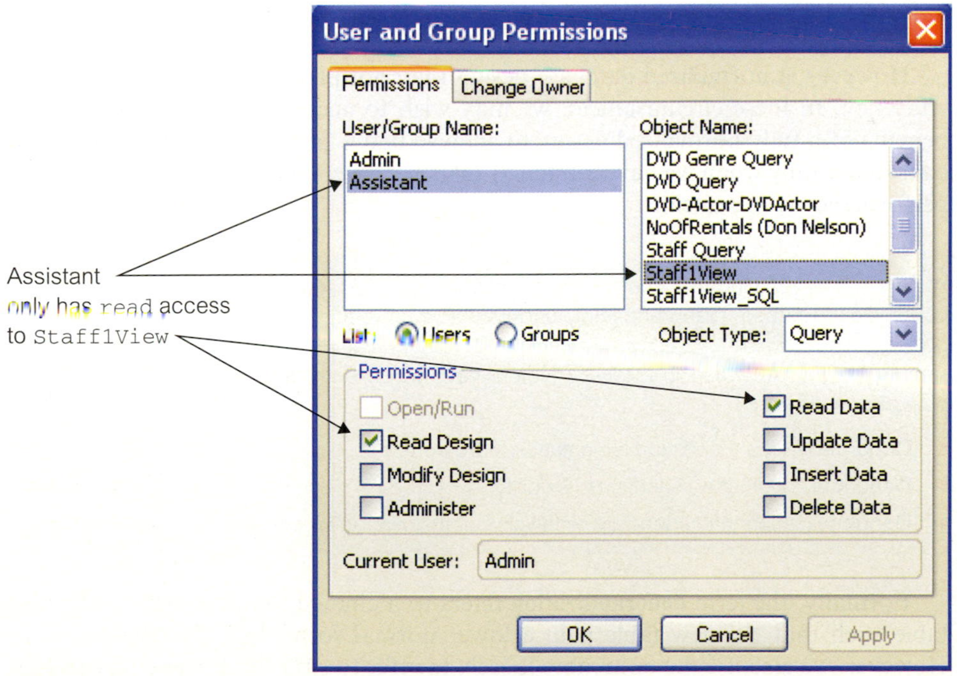

Figure 11.13 User and Group Permissions dialog box showing that the Assistant user has only read access to the `Staff1View` query

VBA source code before removing it from the database. Saving the database as an MDE file also prevents users from modifying forms and reports without requiring them to specify a logon password or without having to set up user-level security.

Document design of user views and security measures

The design of the individual user views and associated security mechanisms should be fully documented. If the physical design affects the logical data model, this model should also be updated.

11.7 Step 7: Consider the introduction of controlled redundancy

Objective

To determine whether introducing redundancy in a controlled manner by relaxing the normalization rules will improve the performance of the system.

As discussed in Chapter 8, normalization is a technique for deciding which columns belong together in a table. One of the basic aims of relational database design is to group columns together in a table because there is a direct relationship (called a *functional dependency*) between them. The result of performing normalization on data is a logical database design that is structurally consistent and has minimal redundancy.

However, a normalized database design may not provide maximum processing efficiency. In these circumstances, we may wish to accept the loss of some of the benefits of a fully normalized design to achieve better performance. This should be considered only when we have estimated that the system will not be able to meet its performance requirements.

Key point

We are not advocating that normalization should be omitted from logical database design: normalization forces us to completely understand each column in each table in the database. Undertaking this process may be the most important factor that contributes to the overall success of the system. The following factors have to be considered if denormalization is being considered:

- Denormalization makes implementation more complex.
- Denormalization often sacrifices flexibility.
- Denormalization may speed up retrievals but it slows down updates.

Formally, the term **denormalization** refers to a change to the structure of a base table such that the new table is in a lower normal form than the original table. However, we also use the term more loosely to refer to situations where we combine two tables into one new table, where the new table is in the same normal form but contains more nulls than the original tables.

Key point As a general rule of thumb, if performance is unsatisfactory and a table has a low update rate and a very high query rate, denormalization may be a viable option.

Indirectly, we have encountered an implicit example of denormalization when dealing with addresses. For example, consider the definition of the `Member` table:

Member (memberNo, mFName, mLName, mStreet, mCity, mState, mZipCode, mEMail, mPword, mTypeNo, dCenterNo)

Strictly speaking, this table is not in third normal form (3NF): `mStreet`, `mCity`, and `mState` are functionally dependent on `mZipCode`; in other words, if we know the zip code, we also know the street, city, and state. Therefore, to normalize the table it is necessary to split the table into two, as follows:

Member (memberNo, mFName, mLName, mZipCode, mEMail, mPword, mTypeNo, dCenterNo)

ZipCode (mZipCode, mStreet, mCity, mState)

However, we rarely wish to access a member's address without the `mStreet`, `mCity`, and `mState` columns. This means that we have to perform a join whenever we want a complete address for a member. As a result, we normally implement the original `Member` table and settle for second normal form (2NF).

Unfortunately, there are no fixed rules for determining when to denormalize tables. However, we discuss some of the more common situations for considering denormalization to speed up frequent or critical transactions in Appendix G.

Consider the implications of denormalization

We should consider the implications of denormalization on the previous steps in the methodology. For example, we may have to reconsider the choice of indexes on the tables that have been denormalized to check whether existing indexes should be removed or additional indexes added. In addition, we need to consider how data integrity will be maintained. Common solutions are:

- *Triggers*: These can be used to automate the updating of derived or duplicated data (see Appendix E.6).
- *Transactions*: By building transactions into each application that make the updates to denormalized data as a single (*atomic*) action.
- *Batch reconciliation*: Run batch programs at appropriate times to make the denormalized data consistent.

The advantages and disadvantages of denormalization are summarized in Table 11.3.

Document introduction of redundancy

The introduction of redundancy should be fully documented, along with the reasons for introducing it. In particular, document the reasons for selecting one approach where many alternatives exist. Update the logical data model to reflect any changes made as a result of denormalization.

Table 11.3 Advantages and disadvantages of denormalization

Advantages
Can improve performance by: – precomputing derived data; – minimizing the need for joins; – reducing the number of foreign keys in tables; – reducing the number of indexes (thereby saving storage space); – reducing the number of tables.
Disadvantages
May speed up retrievals but can slow down updates. Always application-specific and needs to be re-evaluated if the application changes. Can increase the size of tables. May simplify implementation in some cases but may make it more complex in others. Sacrifices flexibility.

11.8 Step 8: Monitor and tune the operational system

Objective

To monitor the operational system and improve the performance of the system to correct inappropriate design decisions or to reflect changing requirements.

One of the main objectives of physical database design is to store data in an efficient way. There are a number of factors that we may use to measure efficiency:

- *Transaction throughput:* this is the number of transactions processed in a given time interval. In some systems, such as airline reservations, high **transaction throughput** is critical to the overall success of the system.
- *Response time:* this is the elapsed time for the completion of a single transaction. From a user's point of view, we want to minimize response time as much as possible. However, there are some factors that influence response time that we may have no control over, such as system loading or communication times. We can shorten response time by:
  - reducing contention and wait times, particularly disk I/O wait times;
  - reducing the amount of time resources are required;
  - using faster components.
- *Disk storage:* this is the amount of disk space required to store the database files. We may wish to minimize the amount of disk storage used.

However, there is no one factor that is always correct. Typically, we have to trade off one factor against another to achieve a reasonable balance. For example, increasing the amount of data stored may decrease the response time or transaction throughput.

We should not regard the initial physical database design as static, but as an estimate of how the operational system might perform. Once the initial design has been implemented, we should monitor the system and tune it as a result of observed performance and changing requirements. Many DBMSs provide the database administrator with utilities to monitor the operation of the system and tune it.

There are many benefits to be gained from tuning the database:

- It may avoid the procurement of additional hardware.
- It may be possible to downsize the hardware configuration. This results in less, and cheaper, hardware and potentially less expensive maintenance.
- A well-tuned system produces faster response times and better throughput, which in turn makes the users, and hence the organization, more productive.
- Improved response times can improve staff morale.
- Improved response times can increase customer satisfaction.

These last two benefits are more intangible than the others. However, we can certainly state that slow response times demoralize staff and potentially lose customers. To tune a database system, we need to understand how the various system components interact and affect database performance.

11.8.1 Understanding system resources

To improve performance, we must be aware of how the four basic hardware components interact and affect system performance:

- main memory;
- CPU;
- disk I/O;
- network.

Each of these resources may affect other system resources. Equally well, an improvement in one resource may effect an improvement in other system resources. For example:

- Adding more main memory should result in less paging. This should help avoid CPU bottlenecks.
- More effective use of main memory may result in less disk I/O.

Main memory

Main memory accesses are significantly faster than secondary storage accesses, sometimes tens or even hundreds of thousands of times faster. In general, the more main memory available to the DBMS and the database applications, the faster the application programs will run. However, it is sensible to always have a minimum of 5% of main memory available. Equally well, it is advisable not to have any more than 10% available, otherwise main memory is not being used optimally. When there is insufficient memory to accommodate all processes, the operating system transfers pages of processes to disk to free up memory. When one of these pages is next required, the operating system has to transfer it back from disk. Sometimes, it is necessary to swap entire processes from main memory to disk and back again to free up memory. Problems occur with main memory when *paging* (also called *swapping*) becomes excessive.

To ensure efficient usage of main memory, we need to understand how the target DBMS uses main memory, what buffers it keeps in main memory, what parameters exist to allow us to adjust the size of these buffers, and so on. For example, Oracle keeps a data dictionary cache in main memory that ideally should be large enough to handle 90% of data dictionary accesses without having to retrieve the information from disk. We also need to understand the access patterns of users: an increase in the number of concurrent users accessing the database will result in an increase in the amount of memory being utilized.

CPU

The CPU controls the tasks of the other system resources and executes user processes – it is the most costly resource in the system and so needs to be correctly utilized. The main objective for this component is to prevent *CPU contention* in which processes are waiting for the CPU. CPU bottlenecks occur when either the operating system or application programs make too many demands on the CPU. This is often a result of excessive paging.

We need to understand the typical workload through a 24-hour period and ensure that sufficient resources are available for not only the normal workload but also the peak workload. (If we find that there is, for example, 90% CPU utilization and 10% idle during the normal workload, there may not be sufficient scope to handle the peak workload.) One option is to ensure that during peak load no unnecessary jobs are being run and that such jobs are instead run in off-hours. Another option may be to consider multiple CPUs, which allows the processing to be distributed and operations to be processed in parallel.

CPU MIPS (millions of instructions per second) can be used as a guide in comparing platforms and determining their ability to meet the organization's throughput requirements.

Disk I/O

With any large DBMS, there is a significant amount of disk I/O involved in storing and retrieving data. While CPU clock speeds have increased dramatically in recent years, I/O speeds have not increased proportionately. The way in which data is organized on disk can have a major impact on the overall disk performance. One problem that can arise is *disk contention*. This occurs when multiple processes try to access the same disk simultaneously. Most disks have limits on both the number of accesses and the amount of data they can transfer per second and when these limits are reached, processes may have to wait to access the disk. To avoid this, it is recommended that storage should be evenly distributed across available drives to reduce the likelihood of performance problems occurring. Figure 11.14 illustrates the basic principles of distributing the data across disks:

- The operating system files should be separated from the database files.
- The main database files should be separated from the index files.
- The recovery log file, if available and if used, should be separated from the rest of the database.

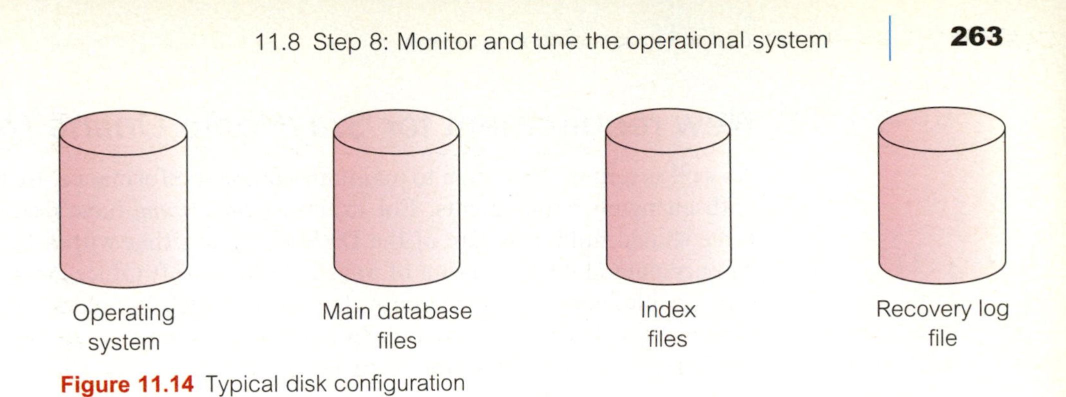

Figure 11.14 Typical disk configuration

If a disk still appears to be overloaded, we can move one or more of its heavily accessed files to a less active disk (this is known as *distributing I/O*). We can achieve **load balancing** by applying this principle to each of the disks until they all have roughly the same amount of I/O. Once again, we have to understand how the DBMS operates, the characteristics of the hardware, and the accesses patterns of the users.

Network

When the amount of data being transferred across the network is too great, network bottlenecks occur.

11.8.2 Summary

Tuning is an activity that is never complete. Throughout the life of the system, we will need to monitor performance, particularly to account for changes in the environment and user requirements. However, making a change to one area of an operational system to improve performance may have an adverse effect on another area. For example, adding an index to a table may improve the performance of one application, but it may adversely affect another, perhaps more important, application. Therefore, care must be taken when making changes to an operational system. If possible, test the changes either on a test database, or alternatively, when the system is not being fully used (for example, out of working hours).

Key point Most of the gains in performance come from good database design, through transaction analysis and use of appropriate indexes, as we discussed in Step 4 of the methodology. Although it is tempting to skip or rush through some of the steps, we strongly advocate against this and believe that spending sufficient time on database design will pay dividends subsequently.

Document tuning activity

The mechanisms we have used to tune the system should be fully documented, along with the reasons for tuning it the way we have. In particular, document the reasons for selecting one approach where many alternatives exist.

11.8.3 New requirement for *StayHome Online Rentals*

As well as tuning the system to maintain optimal performance, we may have to cope with changing requirements. For example, *StayHome* have decided that the DVD table should hold a picture of the DVD cover together with a brief story line. We can accommodate the storing of images in Microsoft Office Access using the OLE (Object Linking and Embedding) data type, which is used to store data such as Microsoft Word or Excel documents, pictures, sound, and other types of binary data created in other programs. OLE objects can be linked to, or embedded in, a field in a Microsoft Office Access table and then displayed in a form or report.

To satisfy this new requirement, we restructure the DVD table to add:

(1) a field called DVDCover specified as an OLE Object data type; this field holds graphical images of DVD covers, created by scanning photographs of the covers and saving the images in an appropriate format, for example as BMP (Bit Mapped) graphic files;

(2) a field called storyLine specified as a Memo data type, capable of storing lengthy text.

A form using these new fields is shown in Figure 11.15. The main problem with the addition of these two extra fields is the potentially large amount of disk space required to store the graphics files and the large amounts of text for the story line.

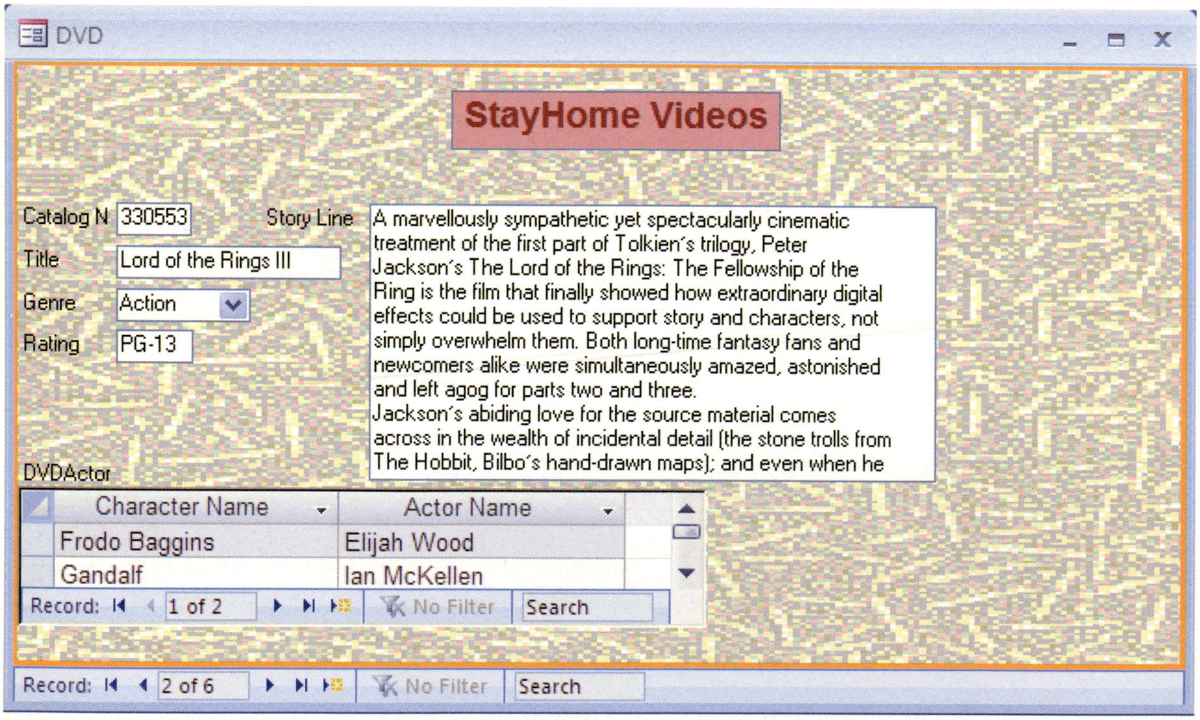

Figure 11.15 Form based on a revised DVD table with the new DVDCover and storyLine fields added

We will therefore need to continue to monitor the performance of the *StayHome* database to ensure that satisfying this new requirement does not compromise the system's performance.

Chapter summary

- **Physical database design** is the process of producing a description of the implementation of the database on secondary storage. It describes the base tables, file organizations and indexes used to access this data effectively, and any associated integrity constraints and security restrictions. The design of the base tables can be undertaken only once you are fully aware of the facilities offered by the target DBMS.
- In the initial step (**Step 3**) of physical database design, you translate the logical data model into a form that can be implemented in the target relational DBMS. This involves designing the base tables, the representation of derived data, and the integrity constraints.
- In the next step (**Step 4**), you analyze the transactions and, based on this analysis, design the file organizations and indexes that will be used to store the base tables.
- A database represents an essential corporate resource, and so security of this resource is extremely important. The objective of **Steps 5** and **6** is to design how the security measures identified during logical database design will be realized. This may include the creation of user views and the use of access control mechanisms.
- Relational DBMSs generally provide two types of database security: system security and data security. **System security** covers access and use of the database at the system level, such as a username and password. **Data security** covers access and use of database objects (such as tables and views) and the actions that users can have on the objects.
- In **Step 7**, you consider the introduction of controlled redundancy to improve performance. There may be circumstances where it may be necessary to accept the loss of some of the benefits of a fully normalized design in favor of performance. This should be considered only when it is estimated that the system will not be able to meet its performance requirements. As a rule of thumb, if performance is unsatisfactory and a table has a low update rate and a very high query rate, **denormalization** may be a viable option.
- **Step 8** involves the ongoing process of monitoring and tuning the operational system to achieve maximum performance.
- One of the main objectives of physical database design is to store data in an efficient way. There are a number of factors that we may use to measure efficiency, including throughput, response time, and disk storage. To improve performance, you must be aware of how the following four basic hardware components interact and affect system performance: main memory, CPU, disk I/O, and network.

Review questions

11.1 Explain the difference between logical and physical database design. Why might these tasks be carried out by different people?

11.2 Describe the inputs and outputs of physical database design.

11.3 Describe the purpose of the steps in the physical design methodology.

11.4 Describe the types of information required to design the base tables.

11.5 Describe how you would handle the representation of derived data in the database. Give an example to illustrate your answer.

11.6 Discuss the purpose of analyzing the transactions that have to be supported, and describe the types of information you would collect and analyze.

11.7 Discuss the difference between system security and data security.

11.8 Describe the access control facilities of SQL.

11.9 Explain the meaning of denormalization.

11.10 What factors can be used to measure the efficiency of a database system?

11.11 Discuss how the four basic hardware components interact and affect system performance.

11.12 How should you distribute data across disks?

Exercises

11.13 Create a complete physical database design for the Manager, Assistant, and Member users view of *StayHome Online Rentals*.

11.14 Create a complete physical database design for the Buyer user view (see Appendix A) of *StayHome Online Rentals*.

11.15 Using the guidelines provided in Appendix F, choose indexes for the transactions listed in Appendix A for the Buyer view of *StayHome Online Rentals*.

11.16 Using the guidelines provided in Appendix G, decide when you might consider denormalization for the Buyer view of *StayHome Online Rentals*.

PerfectPets case study

11.17 Create a physical database design for the *PerfectPets* case study specified in Appendix B.

11.18 Using the guidelines provided in Appendix F, choose indexes for the transactions listed in Appendix B for *PerfectPets*.

11.19 Using the guidelines provided in Appendix G, decide when you might consider denormalization for *PerfectPets*.

Additional exercises

11.20 *StayHome Online Rentals* have decided that they wish to extend the online information offered to their clients. They have identified the following new requirements:

(a) Store data on film directors.
(b) Store a short biography on each actor along with photograph.
(c) Stock video games for the Sony Playstation 3 and PSP, Microsoft Xbox 2, Nintendo Wii, and DS Lite.
(d) Provide an online facility for clients to write a comment and grade each DVD viewed or game played.
(e) Store data on client preferences so that when they revisit the web site, the system can provide recommendations on new DVDs/games stock they may be interested in.

Provide a revised conceptual, logical, and physical data model to reflect these new requirements. How do these new requirements impact on indexes chosen previously?

11.21 *PerfectPets* have identified the following new requirements:

(a) Store data on suppliers for surgical, non-surgical, and pharmaceutical supplies.
(b) Store data on invoicing for suppliers.
(c) Store data on staff holidays and staff absences.
(d) Store data relating to all salary payments and deductions made to staff.
(e) Store data relating to staff qualifications, staff reviews, and work history.

Provide a revised conceptual, logical, and physical data model to reflect these new requirements. How do these new requirements impact on indexes chosen previously?

PART IV

Current and emerging trends

In this final part of the book, we cover many of the key areas associated with current and emerging database systems. These include areas that are fundamental to any database system, such as the database administration and security (Chapter 12) and the management of transactions (Chapter 14). For databases that store personal data we discuss the additional professional, legal, and ethical issues associated with the management of such data (Chapter 13). We also include areas that, when combined with database systems, support the way business is commonly conducted, namely through eCommerce (Chapter 15) and distributed and mobile DBMSs (Chapter 16). We consider alternative ways to store and manage data using object DBMSs (Chapter 17). Finally we discuss how operational data can be exploited to support the corporate decision-maker using business intelligence technologies (Chapter 18).

CHAPTER

12 Database administration and security

Preview

In Chapter 4, you learned about the stages of the database system development lifecycle. In this chapter we discuss the roles played by the data administrator (DA) and database administrator (DBA), and the relationship between these roles and the stages of the database system development lifecycle. An important function of a DA and DBA is ensuring the security of the database. We discuss the potential threats to a database system and the types of computer-based countermeasures that can be applied to minimize such threats.

Learning objectives

In this chapter you will learn:

- The distinction between *data* administration and *database* administration.
- The purpose and tasks associated with data administration and database administration.
- The scope of database security.
- Why database security is a serious concern for an organization.
- The type of threats that can affect a database system.
- How to protect a database system using computer-based controls.

12.1 Data administration and database administration

The *data administrator* and *database administrator* are responsible for managing and controlling the activities associated with corporate data and corporate database, respectively. The DA is more concerned with the early stages of the lifecycle, from planning through to logical database design. In contrast, the DBA is more concerned with the later stages, from application/physical database design to operational maintenance. Depending on the size and complexity of the organization and/or database systems, the DA and DBA can be the responsibility of one or more people.

We begin by discussing the purpose and tasks associated with the DA and DBA roles within an organization.

12.1.1 Data administration

The data administrator is responsible for the corporate data, which includes non-computerized data, and in practice is often concerned with managing the shared data of users or business application areas of an organization. In addition, the DA must be concerned with how data 'enters' the organization and how data 'exits' the organization. The DA has the primary responsibility of consulting with and advising senior managers, and ensuring that the application of database technologies continues to support corporate objectives. In some organizations, **data administration** is a distinct business area, in others it may be combined with database administration. The typical tasks associated with data administration are listed in Table 12.1.

Data administration

The management and control of the corporate data, including database planning, development and maintenance of standards, policies and procedures, and logical database design.

Table 12.1 Typical data administration tasks

Typical data administration tasks
Selecting appropriate productivity tools
Assisting in the development of the corporate IT/IS and business strategies
Undertaking feasibility studies and planning for database development
Developing a corporate data model
Determining the organization's data requirements
Setting data collection standards and establishing data formats
Determining data access requirements and safeguards for both legal and ethical corporate requirements
Liaising with database administration staff and application developers to ensure that applications meet all stated requirements
Educating users on data standards, legal, and ethical responsibilities
Keeping up to date with IT/IS and business developments
Ensuring that documentation is complete, including the corporate data model, standards, policies, procedures, and controls on end-users
Managing the data dictionary
Liaising with end-users and database administration staff to determine new requirements and to resolve data access or performance problems
Developing a security policy

12.1.2 Database administration

The Database Administrator is more technically oriented than the DA, requiring knowledge of specific DBMSs and the operating system environments. The primary responsibilities of the DBA are centered on developing and maintaining systems using the DBMS software to its fullest extent. The typical tasks of **database administration** are listed in Table 12.2.

Database administration

The management and control of the physical realization of the corporate database system, including physical database design and implementation, setting security and integrity controls, monitoring system performance, and reorganizing the database as necessary.

Table 12.2 Typical database administration tasks

Evaluating and selecting DBMS products
Undertaking physical database design
Implementing a physical database design using a target DBMS
Estimating volumes of data and likely growth
Determining patterns and frequencies of data usage
Defining security and integrity constraints
Liaising with database system developers
Developing test strategies
Training users
Responsibility for 'signing off' on the implemented database system
Monitoring system performance and tuning the database
Performing routine backups
Ensuring that recovery mechanisms and procedures are in place
Ensuring that documentation is complete including in-house produced material
Keeping up to date with software and hardware developments and costs, and installing updates as necessary

12.1.3 Comparison of data and database administration

The preceding sections examined the purpose and tasks associated with data administration and database administration. In this section, we briefly contrast these roles. Table 12.3 summarizes the *main* task differences of the DA and DBA. Perhaps the most obvious difference lies in the nature of the work carried out. The work of DA staff tends to be much more managerial, whereas the work of DBA staff tends to be more technical.

Table 12.3 DA and DBA – main task differences

Data administration	Database administration
Involved in strategic IS planning	Evaluates new DBMSs
Determines long-term goals	Executes plans to achieve goals
Determines standards, policies, and procedures	Enforces standards, policies, and procedures
Determines data requirements	Implements data requirements
Develops logical database design	Develops physical database design
Develops and maintains corporate data model	Implements physical database design
Coordinates database development	Monitors and controls database use
Managerial orientation	Technical orientation
DBMS independent	DBMS dependent

12.2 Database security

Database security

The mechanisms that protect the database against intentional or accidental threats.

In the remainder of this chapter we concentrate on one of the key tasks of both data and database administration, namely **database security**. We describe the scope of database security and discuss why organizations must take potential threats to their database systems seriously. We also identify the range of threats and their consequences on database systems. We then examine mechanisms that can be used to keep the database secure.

Security considerations do not apply only to the data held in a database. Breaches of security may affect other parts of the system, which may in turn affect the database. Consequently, database security encompasses hardware, software, people, and data. To implement security effectively requires appropriate controls, which are defined in specific mission objectives for the system. This need for security, often neglected or overlooked in the past, is now increasingly recognized by organizations. The reason for this turn-around is due to the increasing amounts of crucial corporate data being stored on computers and the acceptance that any loss or unavailability of this data could be potentially disastrous.

A database represents an essential corporate resource that should be properly secured using appropriate controls. We consider database security in relation to the following outcomes:

- theft and fraud;
- loss of confidentiality (secrecy);
- loss of privacy;
- loss of integrity;
- loss of availability.

These outcomes represent the areas in which an organization should address to reduce risk; that is, the possibility of incurring loss or damage. In some situations, these outcomes are closely related such that an activity that leads to loss in one area may also lead to loss in another. In addition, outcomes such as fraud or loss of privacy may arise because of either intentional or unintentional acts, and do not necessarily result in any detectable changes to the database or the computer system.

Confidentiality

The mechanism for ensuring that data or information is accessible only to those authorized to have access.

Theft and fraud affect not only the database environment but also the entire organization. As it is people who perpetrate such activities, attention should focus on reducing the opportunities for this to occur. Theft and fraud do not necessarily alter data, which is also true for activities that result in either loss of confidentiality or loss of privacy.

Privacy

The ability of an individual or group to stop data or information about themselves from becoming known to people other than those whom they choose to give access.

Confidentiality refers to the need to maintain secrecy over data, usually only that which is critical to the organization, whereas **privacy** refers to the need to protect data about individuals. Breaches of security resulting in loss of confidentiality could, for instance, lead to loss of competitiveness, and loss of privacy could lead to legal action being taken against the organization.

Loss of data integrity results in invalid or corrupted data, which may seriously affect the operation of an organization. Many organizations are now seeking virtually continuous operation, the so-called 24/7 availability (that is, 24 hours a day, seven days a week). Loss of availability means that the data, the system or both, cannot be accessed, which can seriously impact an organization's financial performance. In some cases, events that cause a system to be unavailable may also cause data corruption.

In recent times, computer-based criminal activities have increased significantly and are forecast to continue to rise over the next few years. For example, according to the US National Fraud Information Center (www.fraud.com), personal losses from computer-based fraud increased from US$5 787 170 in 2004 to US$13 863 003 in 2005. The 2007 CSI/FBI Computer Crime and Security Survey (Richardson, 2007) revealed that over 46% of the companies that responded reported unauthorized use of computer systems in the previous 12 months. The average annual loss reported by the 494 companies responding to the survey increased from $168 000 in 2006 to $350 424 in 2007. The report further notes that the most critical computer security issue for the next two years will be data protection and application software vulnerability security.

Database security aims to minimize losses caused by anticipated events in a cost-effective manner without unduly constraining the users.

12.2.1 Threats

Threat

Any situation or event, whether intentional or unintentional, that may adversely affect a system and consequently the organization.

A **threat** may be caused by a situation or event involving a person, action, or circumstance that is likely to be detrimental to an organization. The loss to the organization may be tangible, such as loss of hardware, software, or data, or intangible, such as loss of credibility or client confidence. The problem facing any organization is to identify all possible threats. Therefore, as a minimum, an organization should invest time and effort identifying the most serious threats.

In the previous section we identified outcomes that may result from intentional or unintentional activities. While some types of threat can be either intentional or unintentional, the impact remains the same. Intentional threats involve people and may be carried out by both authorized users and unauthorized users, some of whom may be external to the organization.

Any threat must be viewed as a potential breach of security, which if successful will have a certain impact. Table 12.4 presents examples of various types of threats and the possible outcomes for an organization. For example, 'using another person's means of access' as a threat may result in theft and fraud, loss of confidentiality, and loss of privacy for an organization.

The extent to which an organization suffers as a result of a threat succeeding depends upon a number of factors, such as the existence of countermeasures and contingency plans. For example, if a hardware failure occurs corrupting secondary storage, all processing activity must cease until the problem is resolved. The recovery will depend upon a number of factors, which include when the last backups were taken and the time needed to restore the system.

An organization must identify the types of threats it may be subjected to and initiate appropriate plans and countermeasures, bearing in mind the costs of implementing them. Obviously, it may not be cost-effective to spend considerable time, effort, and money on potential threats that may result in only minor inconveniences.

Table 12.4 Examples of threats and the possible outcomes

Threat	Theft and fraud	Loss of confidentiality	Loss of privacy	Loss of integrity	Loss of availability
Using another person's means of access	√	√	√		
Unauthorized amendment or copying of data	√			√	
Program alteration	√			√	√
Inadequate policies and procedures that allow a mix of confidential and normal output	√	√	√		
Wire tapping	√	√	√		
Illegal entry by hacker	√	√	√		
Blackmail	√	√	√		
Creating 'trapdoor' into system	√	√	√		
Theft of data, programs, and equipment	√	√	√		√
Failure of security mechanisms, giving greater access than normal	√	√	√		
Staff shortage or strikes				√	√
Inadequate staff training		√	√	√	√
Viewing and disclosing unauthorized data	√	√	√		
Electronic interference and radiation				√	√
Data corruption due to power loss or surge				√	√
Fire (electrical fault, lightning strike, arson), flood, hurricane, bomb				√	√
Physical damage to equipment				√	√
Breaking cables or disconnection of cables				√	√
Software (DBMS) and operating system crashes				√	√
Exposure to viruses				√	√

The organization's business may also influence the types of threats that should be considered, some of which may be rare. However, rare events should be taken into account, particularly if their impact would be significant. A summary of the potential threats to computer systems is presented in Figure 12.1.

12.2.2 Countermeasures – computer-based controls

The types of countermeasures to threats on database systems range from physical controls to administrative procedures. Despite the range of computer-based controls that are available, it is worth noting that, generally, the security of a DBMS is only as good as that of the operating system, due to their close association. Representation of a typical multi-user computer environment is shown in Figure 12.2. In this section, we focus on the following computer-based security controls for a multi-user environment (some of which may not be available in the PC environment):

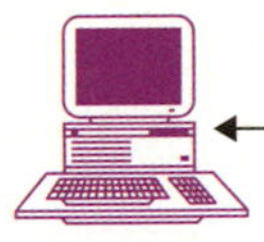

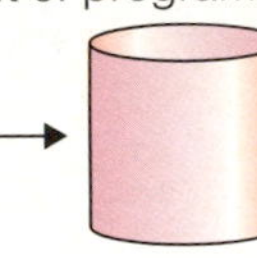

Figure 12.1 Summary of potential threats to computer systems

- authorization;
- views;
- backup and recovery;
- integrity;
- encryption;
- redundant array of independent disks (RAID).

> **Authorization**
>
> The granting of a right or privilege that enables a subject to have legitimate access to a database system or a database system's object.

Authorization

Authorization controls can be built into the software and govern not only what database system or object a specified user can access but also what the user may do

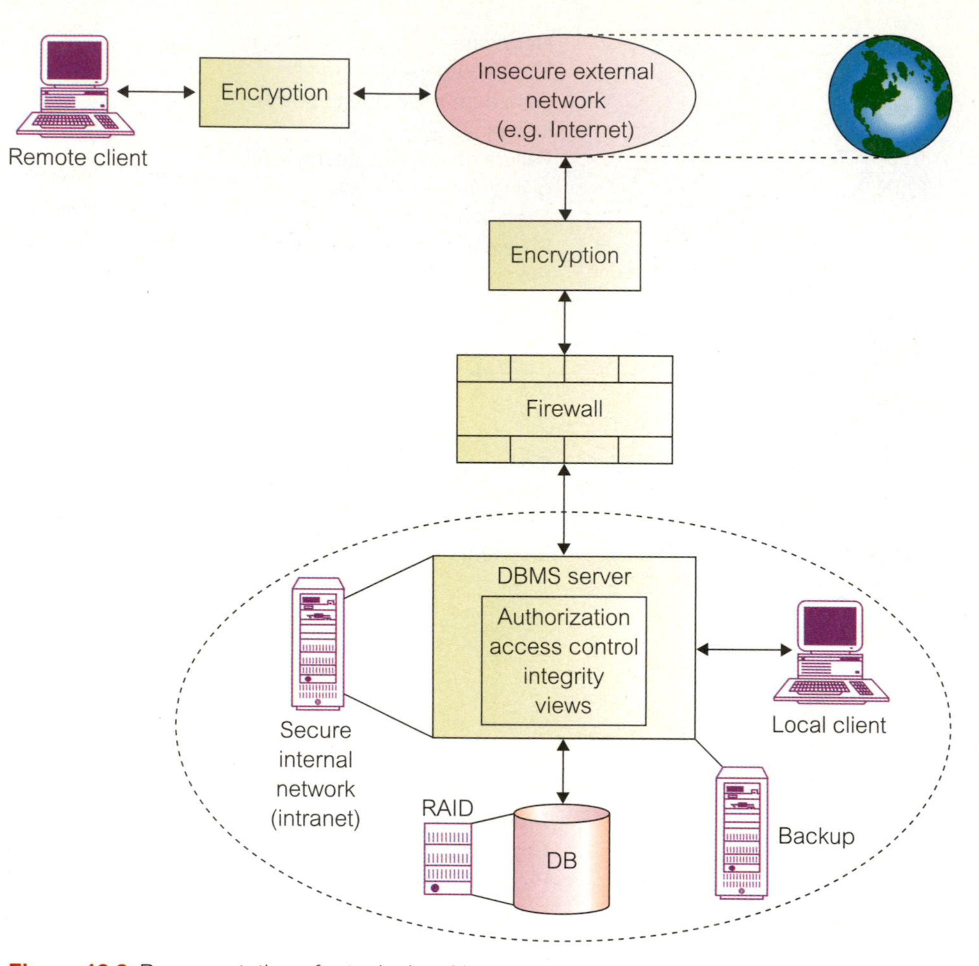

Figure 12.2 Representation of a typical multi-user computer environment

Authentication

A mechanism that determines whether a user is who he or she claims to be.

with it. For this reason, authorization controls are sometimes referred to as *access controls* (see Step 6 of Chapter 11). The process of authorization involves **authentication** of a subject requesting access to an object, where 'subject' represents a user or program and 'object' represents a database table, view, procedure, trigger, or any other object that can be created within the database system.

A system administrator is usually responsible for permitting users to have access to a computer system by creating individual user accounts. Each user is given a unique identifier, which is used by the operating system to determine who they are. Associated with each identifier is a password, chosen by the user and known to the operating system, which must be supplied to enable the operating system to authenticate (or verify) who the user claims to be.

This procedure allows authorized use of a computer system, but does not necessarily authorize access to the DBMS or any associated database applications. A separate, similar procedure may have to be undertaken to give a user the right to use the DBMS. The responsibility to authorize use of the DBMS usually rests with the DBA, who must also set up individual user accounts and passwords using the facilities provided by the DBMS.

Some DBMSs maintain a list of valid user identifiers and associated passwords, which can be distinct from the operating system's list. However, other DBMSs maintain a list whose entries are validated against the operating system's list based on the current user's login identifier. This prevents a user from logging onto the DBMS with one name, having already logged onto the operating system using a different name.

Privileges

Privilege

A right granted by one user to allow another user or group of users access to a database system or an object in the database system.

Once a user is given permission to use a DBMS, various other **privileges** may also be automatically associated with it. For example, privileges may include the right to access or create certain database objects such as tables, views, and indexes, or to run various DBMS utilities. Privileges are granted to users to accomplish the tasks required for their jobs. As excessive granting of unnecessary privileges can compromise security, a privilege should only be granted to a user who absolutely requires the privilege to accomplish his or her work.

Some DBMSs operate as *closed systems* so that while users may be authorized to access the DBMS, they require authorization to access specific objects. Either the DBA or owners of particular objects provide this authorization. An *open system* by default allows users to have complete access to all objects within the database and privileges have to be explicitly removed from users to control access.

Ownership and privileges

Some objects in the DBMS are owned by the DBMS itself, usually in the form of a specific superuser, such as the DBA. Ownership of objects gives the owner all appropriate privileges on the objects owned. The same situation applies to other authorized users if they own objects. The creator of an object owns the object and can assign appropriate privileges for the object. These privileges can be passed on to other authorized users. For example, an owner of several tables may authorize other users to query the tables, but not to carry out any updates.

Where a DBMS supports several different types of authorization identifier, there may be different priorities associated with each type. For example, a DBMS may permit both individual user identifiers and group identifiers to be created, with the user identifier having a higher priority than the group identifier. For such a DBMS, user and group identifiers may be defined as shown in Figure 12.3.

Figure 12.3(a) lists each user of the system together with the user type, which distinguishes individual users from groups. Figure 12.3(b) lists each group and the user members of that group. Certain privileges may be associated with specific identifiers that indicate what kind of privilege (such as Select, Update, Insert, Delete, or All) is allowed with certain database objects.

On some DBMSs, a user has to tell the system under which identifier he or she is operating, especially if the user is a member of more than one group. It is essential to become familiar with the available authorization and other control mechanisms provided by the DBMS, particularly where priorities may be applied to different authorization identifiers and where privileges can be passed on. This will enable the

(a) User identifiers

User identifier	Type
S0099	User
S2345	User
S1500	User
Sales	Group

(b) Group identifiers

Group	Member identifier
Sales	S0099
Sales	S2345

Figure 12.3 User identifiers and group identifiers

correct types of privileges to be granted to users based on their requirements and those of the database applications that many of them will use. Privileges were discussed in Step 6 of the physical database design methodology in Chapter 11.

Views

View

A virtual table that does not necessarily exist in the database but can be produced on request by a particular user, at the time of request.

We introduced the concept of **views** in Section 1.2.5. The view mechanism provides a powerful and flexible security mechanism by hiding parts of the database from certain users. The user is not aware of the existence of any columns or rows that are missing from the view. A view can be defined over several tables, with a user being granted the appropriate privilege to use it but not to use the base tables. In this way, using a view can be more secure than simply having certain privileges granted to a user on the base table(s).

Backup and recovery

Backup

The process of periodically taking a copy of the database and log file (and possibly programs) onto offline storage media.

A DBMS should provide **backup** facilities to assist with the recovery of a database following failure. To keep track of database transactions, the DBMS maintains a special file called a **log file** (or journal) that contains information about all updates to the database. It is always advisable to make backup copies of the database and log file at regular intervals and to ensure that the copies are in a secure location. In the event of a failure that renders the database unusable, the backup copy and the details captured in the log file are used to restore the database to the latest possible consistent state.

Journaling

The process of keeping and maintaining a log file (or journal) of all changes made to the database to enable recovery to be undertaken effectively in the event of a failure.

A DBMS should provide logging facilities, sometimes referred to as **journaling**, which keep track of the current state of transactions and database changes, to provide support for recovery procedures. The advantage of journaling is that, in the event of a failure, the database can be recovered to its last known consistent state using a backup copy of the database and the information contained in the log file. If no journaling is enabled on a failed system, the only means of recovery is to restore the database using the latest backup version of the database. However, without a log file, any changes made after the last backup to the database will be lost. We will discuss the use of the log file for database recovery in more detail in Section 14.3.

We can categorize backup facilities by examining the following two choices:

- whether the database is running and processing transactions ('hot' backup) or if the database is shut down ('cold' backup);
- whether the entire database (all of the data) is backed up (full backup) or if only a part of the database is backed up (incremental or differential backup).

Depending on these options, the backup task can take anywhere from a few minutes to several hours. State of the art backup devices such as SDLT 600 and LTO-4 tape drives can copy data from disk to tape at approximately 120 megabytes per second (MB/s). Backing up all of the data in a 400 GB database would thus take just under an hour. As the cost of hard disk storage has plummeted, backing up data from one disk to another can also be used as an alternative to backup to tape for many situations.

Backup window

The time period during which the database can be backed up.

The time during which the backup can occur is referred to as the **backup window**. The backup window can vary by the needs of the organization. For example, an organization that operates only from 9:00am to 5:00pm has a rather large window during which backup can occur. An eCommerce business that must be available all of the time may have only a small window during which backup can occur.

Backing up a database while it is running and processing transactions can cause problems with the integrity of the data. For example, suppose that during the two hours it takes to backup a database, a number of transactions are executed that add, change, or delete data after a table's data has been copied to tape. Upon restoring the backup, the data would be inconsistent with some data missing and other data present that should have been deleted. The obvious solution to these sorts of problems would be to shut the database down, backup the data, and then restart the database. Given a sufficient window, this is clearly the best solution. However, as mentioned, there are business situations that dictate that the database cannot be shut down.

The next set of options considers how much data should be backed up at a time. There are three popular choices:

1) Full backup – a backup all of the data in the database.
2) Incremental backup – a backup all of the data that has changed since the last backup.
3) Differential backup – a backup all of the data that has changed since the last full backup.

To illustrate these three choices, consider the following example using the *StayHome* database system:

- A full backup of all data is performed every Sunday night.
- On Monday, 10 new customers were added, 50 new rentals were processed, and 3 new DVDs were added.
- On Tuesday 5 new customers were added, 20 new rentals were processed, and 4 new DVDs were added.

A full backup performed each night would backup all of the data in the database. Each day, the full backup would grow in size according to how much data was added to the database each day. Restoring the data would simply be a matter of choosing the most recent full backup and copying the data from tape back to disk. For example, a disk failure on Wednesday morning would be remedied by restoring the full backup from Tuesday night.

An incremental backup would start with the full backup on Sunday, and then only the data that has been added or changed each day would be backed up at night. For Monday, this would mean only 10 customer records, 50 rental records, and 3 DVD records would be backed up. On Tuesday, only 5 customer records, 20 rental records, and 4 DVD records would be backed up. To recover from a disk failure on Wednesday morning, first the full backup from Sunday night would be restored, then the incremental backup from Monday night would be restored and finally the incremental backup from Tuesday night would be restored.

A differential backup would also start with a full backup on Sunday, and then only the data that has changed since Sunday will be backed up each night. For Monday, this would mean only 10 customer records, 50 rental records, and 3 DVD records would be backed up. On Tuesday, 15 customer records, 70 rental records, and 7 DVD records would be backed up. To recover from a disk failure on Wednesday morning, first the full backup from Sunday night would be restored, then the differential backup from Tuesday night would be restored.

In comparing the three approaches, trade-offs occur between the time required to perform the backups and the time and effort required to restore the data in the event of a disk failure. Full backups take the longest but provide the fastest restore time. Incremental backups take the shortest time but require the longest time to restore the data. This is especially true as the time between the last full backup and the failure increases. Differential backups fall in the middle in terms of backup time and restore times.

Commercial DBMSs such as Oracle and Microsoft SQL Server provide a variety of methods to back up data both when the databases are shut down and when they are running. Both offer support for 'hot' backups by keeping track of transactions that have executed while the data is being backed up. For example, Oracle calls this facility the Archived REDO logs.

Integrity

Integrity constraints also contribute to maintaining a secure database system by preventing data from becoming invalid, and hence giving misleading or incorrect results. Integrity constraints were introduced in Section 1.7 and were discussed in detail in the methodology we present for database design (see Step 2.4 in Chapter 10 and Step 3 in Chapter 11).

Encryption

Encryption

The encoding of the data by a special algorithm that renders the data unreadable by any program without the decryption key.

If a database system holds particularly sensitive data, it may be deemed necessary to encode it as a precaution against possible external threats or attempts to access it. For example, sensitive data such as social security numbers, drivers' license numbers, credit card numbers, bank account numbers, passwords, and so on are typically encrypted on storage to prevent attempts to directly read this data. Some DBMSs provide an **encryption** facility for this purpose. The DBMS can access the data (after decrypting it), although there is degradation in performance because of the time taken to decrypt it. Encryption also protects data transmitted over communication lines. There are a number of techniques for encrypting data to conceal the information; some are termed irreversible and others reversible. *Irreversible techniques*, as the name implies, do not permit the original data to be known. However, the data can be used to obtain valid statistical information. *Reversible techniques* are more commonly used. To transmit data securely over insecure networks requires the use of a **cryptosystem**, which includes:

- an encryption key to encrypt the data (plaintext);
- an encryption algorithm that, with the encryption key, transforms the plain text into ciphertext;
- a decryption key to decrypt the ciphertext;
- a decryption algorithm that, with the decryption key, transforms the ciphertext back into plain text.

One technique, called *symmetric encryption*, uses the same key for both encryption and decryption and relies on safe communication lines for exchanging the key. As most users do not have access to a secure communication line, to be really secure the keys need to be as long as the message. However, most working systems are based on using keys shorter than the message. One scheme used for encryption is the Data Encryption Standard (DES), which is a standard encryption algorithm developed by IBM. This scheme uses one key for both encryption and decryption, which must be kept secret, although the algorithm need not be. The algorithm transforms each 64-bit block of plaintext using a 56-bit key. The DES is not universally regarded as being very secure, and some maintain that a larger key is required. For example, Triple DES uses a sequence of three encryption stages, each with a different 56-bit key, and a scheme called PGP (Pretty Good Privacy) uses a 128-bit symmetric algorithm for encryption of the data it sends.

Keys with 64 bits are now breakable with modest hardware. While it is envisaged that keys with 80 bits will also become breakable in the future, it is probable that keys with 128 bits will remain unbreakable for the foreseeable future. The terms 'strong authentication' and 'weak authentication' are sometimes used to distinguish between algorithms that, to all intents and purposes, cannot be broken with existing technologies and knowledge from those that can be.

Another type of cryptosystem uses different keys for encryption and decryption, and is referred to as *asymmetric encryption*. One example is *public key cryptosystems*, which use two keys, one of which is public and the other private. The encryption algorithm may also be public, so that anyone wishing to send a user a message can use the user's publicly known key in conjunction with the algorithm to encrypt it. Only the owner of the private key can then decipher the message. Public key cryptosystems can also be used to send a 'digital signature' with a message and prove that the message came from the person who claimed to have sent it. The most well-known asymmetric encryption is RSA (the name is derived from the initials of the three designers of the algorithm: Rivest, Shamir, and Adelman).

Generally, symmetric algorithms are much faster to execute on a computer than those that are asymmetric. However, in practice they are often used together, so that a public key algorithm is used to encrypt a randomly generated encryption key, and the random key is used to encrypt the actual message using a symmetric algorithm. In eCommerce systems (covered in Chapter 15), the Secure Sockets Layer (SSL) protocol employs exactly this algorithm. Web sites maintain a public key/private key pair and 'publish' their public keys in 'Certificates.' When a browser makes a request for a secure connection, the Web server sends a copy of the certificate and the browser uses the public key contained in it to transmit a secret (symmetric) key that will be used to secure all subsequent transmissions.

RAID

RAID

A set, or array, of physical disk drives that appear to the database user (and programs) as if they form one large logical storage unit.

Disk Input/Output (I/O) has been revolutionized with the introduction of **RAID** technology. RAID originally stood for *Redundant Array of Inexpensive Disks*, but more recently the 'I' in RAID has come to stand for *Independent*. RAID works on having a large disk array comprising an arrangement of several independent disks that are organized to increase performance and at the same time improve reliability.

Performance is increased through *data striping*: the data is segmented into equal-size partitions (the *striping unit*), which are transparently distributed across multiple disks. This gives the appearance of a single large, very fast disk where in actual fact the data is distributed across several smaller disks. Striping improves overall I/O performance by allowing multiple I/Os to be serviced in parallel. At the same time, data striping also balances the load among disks. Reliability is improved through storing redundant information across the disks using a *parity* scheme or an *error-correcting* scheme. In the event of a disk failure, the redundant information can be used to reconstruct the contents of the failed disk.

There are a number of disk configurations, referred to as **RAID levels**, each providing a slightly different trade-off between performance and reliability. The RAID levels are:

- RAID 0 – Non-redundant: This level maintains no redundant data and so has the best write performance since updates do not have to be replicated. Data striping is performed at the level of blocks.
- RAID 1 – Mirrored: This level maintains (*mirrors*) two identical copies of the data across different disks. To maintain consistency in the presence of disk failure, writes may not be performed simultaneously. This is the most expensive storage solution.
- RAID 1+0 (Sometimes written as RAID 10) – Non-redundant and Mirrored: This level combines striping and mirroring.
- RAID 2 – Error-Correcting Codes: With this level, the striping unit is a single bit and error-correcting codes are used as the redundancy scheme.
- RAID 3 – Bit-Interleaved Parity: This level provides redundancy by storing parity information on a single disk in the array. This parity information can be used to recover the data on other disks should they fail. This level uses less storage space than RAID 1 but the parity disk can become a bottleneck.
- RAID 4 – Block-Interleaved Parity: With this level, the striping unit is a disk block – a parity block is maintained on a separate disk for corresponding disks from a number of other disks. If one of the disks fails, the parity block can be

used with the corresponding blocks from the other disks to restore the blocks of the failed disk.

- RAID 5 – Block-Interleaved Distributed Parity: This level uses parity data for redundancy in a similar way to RAID 3 but stripes the parity data across all the disks, similar to the way in which the source data is striped. This alleviates the bottleneck on the parity disk.
- RAID 6 – P + Q Redundancy: This level is similar to RAID 5 but additional redundant data is maintained to protect against multiple disk failures. Error-correcting codes are used instead of using parity.

For most database applications, RAID 1, RAID 1+0, or RAID 5 tends to be chosen. Oracle, for example, recommends use of RAID 1 for the redo log files. For the database files, Oracle recommends either RAID 5, provided the write overhead is acceptable, otherwise Oracle recommends either RAID 1 or RAID 1+0.

12.2.3 Countermeasures – network security

The previous set of countermeasures focused on internal controls within the DBMS and database. Modern database systems however are rarely implemented in isolation. Instead, two- and three-tier architectures, especially three-tier architectures implemented with Web servers (as detailed in Chapter 15), involve networks that connect various layers of the system. For example, in typical eCommerce architectures, the user works on a browser that is connected to the company's Web server over various networks that make up the Internet. This Web server in turn is connected to the company's internal database server (where the DBMS and database reside) using a private network that is internal to the company. Network security, therefore, becomes an important aspect of securing database resources.

Network security

The protection of servers from intruders.

A basic **network security** architecture for a three-tier database system is shown in Figure 12.4. Note that a detailed discussion of network security issues and alternate network architecture is beyond the scope of this book; however we will present some general definitions.

Firewall

A server or router with two or more network interfaces and special software that filters or selectively blocks messages traveling between networks.

A **firewall** can be configured to allow only certain kinds of messages to pass between one network and another. In Figure 12.4, for example, the external firewall might be configured to block all messages coming from the Internet with the exception of requests for web pages and incoming email messages. In this way, customers can view web pages on the company's Web server and send the company email messages. However all other messages, which could contain attempts to exploit weaknesses in other services, are blocked 'at the border' of the organization. The internal firewall in Figure 12.4 is even more restrictive in that it would be configured to only allow connections between the Web server and database for the purposes of running transactions. This interaction is explained in further detail in Section 15.2.

De-Militarized Zone (DMZ)

A special, restricted network that is established between two firewalls.

In Figure 12.4, the **De-Militarized Zone (DMZ)** is indicated by the dashed outline area between the two firewalls. The intent is that servers in the DMZ are partially 'exposed' to the Internet and are very restricted in their functions.

In larger organizations, the DBA interacts with the network security staff to ensure the database is not vulnerable to direct network attacks from the Internet. In

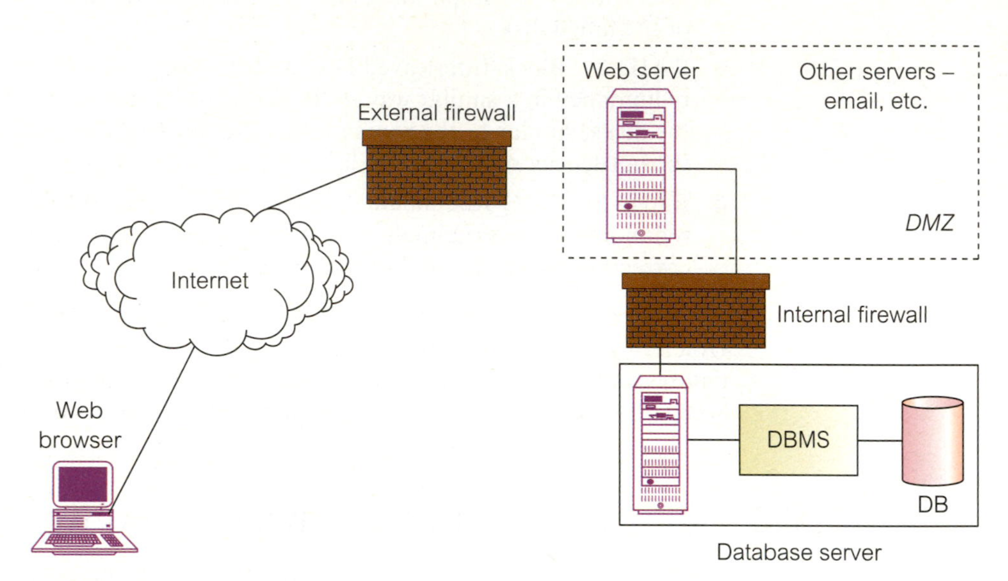

Figure 12.4 Basic network security architecture for three-tier database system architecture

smaller organizations, the DBA may well be asked to assume this responsibility. We emphasize again that the architecture shown in this figure is but one of many different possible network security architectures.

Chapter summary

- **Data administration** is the management and control of corporate data, including database planning, development and maintenance of standards, policies and procedures, and logical database design.
- **Database administration** is the management and control of the physical realization of the corporate database system, including physical database design and implementation, setting security and integrity controls, monitoring system performance, and reorganizing the corporate database as necessary.
- **Database security** is concerned with avoiding the following outcomes: theft and fraud, loss of confidentiality (secrecy), loss of privacy, loss of integrity, and loss of availability.
- **Confidentiality** refers to the need to maintain secrecy over data, usually only that which is critical to the organization, whereas **privacy** refers to the need to protect data about individuals.
- A **threat** is any situation or event, whether intentional or unintentional, that will adversely affect a system and consequently an organization.
- **Computer-based security controls** for the multi-user environment include authorization, views, backup and recovery, journaling, integrity, encryption, and RAID.

- **Authorization** is the granting of a right or privilege that enables a subject to have legitimate access to a system or a system's object.
- **Authentication** is a mechanism that determines whether a user is who he or she claims to be.
- A **view** is a virtual table that does not necessarily exist in the database but can be produced on request by a particular user, at the time of request.
- **Backup** is the process of periodically taking a copy of the database and log file (and possibly programs) onto offline storage media.
- **Backup window** is the time period during which the database can be backed up.
- **Journaling** is the process of keeping and maintaining a log file (or journal) of all the changes made to the database to enable recovery to be undertaken effectively in the event of a failure.
- **Integrity constraints** also contribute to maintaining a secure database system by preventing data from becoming invalid, and hence giving misleading or incorrect results.
- **Encryption** is the encoding of the data by a special algorithm that renders the data unreadable by any program without the decryption key.
- **RAID** is a set, or array, of physical disk drives that appear to the database user (and programs) as if they form one large logical storage unit. The disk drives are organized to improve reliability and at the same time increase performance.
- **Network security** is concerned with the protection of servers from intruders by implementing a network security architecture.

Review questions

12.1 Define the purpose and tasks associated with data administration and database administration.

12.2 Compare and contrast the main tasks carried out by the data administrator and database administrator.

12.3 Explain the purpose and scope of database security.

12.4 What is the difference between confidentiality and privacy?

12.5 List the main types of threats that could affect a database system, and for each describe the controls that you would use to counteract each of them.

12.6 Explain the following in terms of providing security for a database:

(a) authorization and authentication;
(b) views;
(c) backup and recovery;
(d) integrity;
(e) encryption;
(f) RAID.

12.7 What are the differences between full backup, incremental backup, and differential backup?

12.8 What is the difference between symmetric and asymmetric encryption?

12.9 What is a firewall, and how can it be used to protect a database system?

Exercises

12.10 Visit the Computer Security Institute's web site (http://www.gocsi.com/) and download the latest CSI/FBI Computer Crime and Security Survey. Discuss the current trends in types of attacks or misuse that are most critical to the security and integrity of data.

12.11 For any DBMS that you have access to, investigate how it supports the following functionality:

(a) authentication;
(b) ownership and privileges;
(c) backup and recovery;
(d) encryption.

12.12 Consider the *StayHome Online Rentals* case study discussed in Chapter 5. Produce a report for the Director of the company outlining the threats that may exist for its database system, and provide a set of recommendations on how to minimize these threats.

12.13 Consider the *PerfectPets* case study discussed in Appendix B. Produce a report for the Director of the company outlining the threats that may exist for its database system, and provide a set of recommendations on how to minimize these threats.

12.14 Assume that a database contains approximately 500 gigabytes (GB) of data that is required to be backed up daily.

(a) Given a tape backup device based on LTO-2 technology (200 GB per tape and 24 megabytes per second (MB/s) transfer rate), how long will it take to perform a full backup of the data?
(b) Research the latest LTO-4 tape format (Hewlett-Packard and Tandberg Data are two possible vendors) and describe the difference in backup times that could be achieved using this new technology.
(c) Current Serial Attached SCSI (SAS) and Serial ATA (SATA) disk drives transfer data at up to 300 MB/s. Describe the difference in backup times that could be achieved using one of the technologies for 'disk-to-disk' backup.

12.15 Produce a technical report that compares and contrasts asymmetric encryption algorithms and symmetric encryption algorithms.

12.16 Research two different approaches to securing Web access to databases by using firewalls. Prepare a report that presents what you believe to be the most secure alternative.

CHAPTER

13 Professional, legal, and ethical issues in data management

Preview

As discussed in Chapter 12, data and database administrators should be well versed in issues related to the day-to-day internal control over growing volumes of organizational data. Such managers, however, will increasingly find themselves delving deeply into the relatively unfamiliar territory of legal and ethical compliance. With the increased scrutiny of corporations brought on by the massive scandals emerging in the past several years (for example, Enron and WorldCom in the US, and Parmalat in Europe) have come new laws and regulations that will bring about significant changes in the way organizations operate. The rise in cases of identity theft has likewise brought increased scrutiny over data management practices. In the context of this book, the impact of legal and ethical issues on the IT function quite often revolves around the management of data. The aim of this chapter is therefore to define the underlying issues, to illustrate the data management context in which these issues present themselves, and to provide best practices for data and database administrators with respect to these issues.

Learning objectives

In this chapter you will learn:

- How to define ethical and legal issues in information technology.
- How to distinguish between legal and ethical issues and situations that data/database administrators face.
- How new regulations are placing additional requirements and responsibilities on data/database administrators.
- How legislation, such as the Sarbanes-Oxley Act and the Basel II accords, impact on data/database administration functions.
- Best practices for preparing for and supporting auditing and compliance functions.
- Intellectual property (IP) issues related to IT and data/database administration.

13.1 Defining legal and ethical issues in information technology

You may be wondering why we are including a chapter on legal and ethical issues in a book about database systems. The answer is simple: organizations around the world increasingly find themselves having to answer tough questions about the conduct and character of their employees and the manner in which their activities are carried out. At the same time, we need to develop knowledge of what constitutes professional and non-professional behavior.

13.1.1 Defining ethics in the context of information technology

In the past, information technology workers, in their roles supporting the organization, may have felt largely shielded from the actions and deeds (or misdeeds as the case may be) of their managers and executives. After all, it is the executives and managers who define how the organization operates, and IT staff simply implement what the managers dictate. Today, however, this is no longer the case. The confluence of massive increases in storage and processing power, and the increase in scrutiny by shareholders, watchdogs, the media, and, quite possibly, insiders, have placed IT staff in the limelight. It is not unusual, for example, for even a small eCommerce vendor to amass many terabytes (10^{12} bytes) of **click stream** data from users. Financial services firms deal with petabytes (10^{15} bytes) of financial transactions involving hundreds of millions of individuals and business entities. Within such a technology climate, IT departments are being asked to leverage these mountains of data to achieve business advantages. As discussed in Chapter 12, individuals intent on identity theft and fraud (who could come from inside or outside the organization), find these volumes of data extremely tempting. At the same time, overzealous managers may become tempted by the possibilities of business intelligence technologies whose usage can push against ethical boundaries (we discuss business intelligence in Chapter 18). Needless to say, legislators and government regulations are having a hard time keeping up with the rapidly shifting technological landscape. Further, as we will see, a number of new and emerging regulations require accurate data and analyses to demonstrate compliance and conformity.

> **Click stream**
>
> A web or application log that traces where and when a user clicks the links on a website or application.

For the purposes of this chapter, we start with some basic definitions and discuss some example scenarios to illustrate best practices.

There are many definitions of **ethics** and most seem quite distant from what the business or technology person faces on a daily basis. It might be helpful therefore to think of ethical behavior as 'doing what is right' according to the standards of society. This, of course, begs the question of 'whose society' as what might be

> **Ethics**
>
> A set of principles of right conduct or a theory or a system of moral values.

considered ethical behavior in one culture (country, religion, and ethnicity) might not be considered so in another. Tackling this particular debate is well beyond the scope of this book.

13.1.2 The difference between ethical and legal behavior

Another point of confusion may be the contrast between what is *ethical* and what is *legal*. We may think of laws as simply enforcing certain ethical behaviors. For example, most would agree that it is unethical to steal from another. Enough individuals seem capable of dismissing this aspect of 'doing what is right' that, in most societies, laws must be enacted to enforce this particular ethical behavior. This line of thinking leads to two familiar ideas: what is ethical is legal, and what is unethical is illegal. Many examples can be provided to support these claims.

This however brings up the question: Is all unethical behavior illegal? Consider a lonely database administrator for *StayHome Online Rentals* who, using their administrative access privileges, queries the *StayHome* database for customers of the opposite gender and whose rental patterns suggest that they are unmarried and close to the DBA's age. It may very well be the case that no laws are broken, while at the same time the company would consider this unethical behavior.

Another question that can be asked is: Is all ethical behavior legal? Consider, for example, the US Securities and Exchange Commission (SEC) Regulation NMS (National Market System). This sweeping set of regulations aims to alter the way in which equities (stocks) are traded in US markets. One aspect of Regulation NMS is called the 'order protection rule,' which states that a trade cannot execute at one price if a better price can be found in a different 'fast' exchange or market (fast being a market capable of subsecond executions). Institutional investors such as mutual funds and retirement funds trading very large blocks of shares need to trade on the market that has the most shares available to buy or sell, and may not necessarily be concerned about obtaining the best price. As a result, Regulation NMS, which was intended to ensure best price execution for all customers, changes what appears to be ethical for an institutional investor, to be illegal if carried out by a broker or the exchange receiving the order.

In essence, ethics precedes the law. Ethical codes of practice help determine whether specific laws should be introduced. Ethics fills the gap between the time when technology creates problems and the time when laws are introduced.

13.1.3 Ethical behavior in information technology

A survey conducted by TechRepublic, an IT-oriented Web portal maintained by CNET Networks (techrepublic.com), reported that 57% of the IT workers polled indicated they had been asked to do something 'unethical' by their supervisors (Thornberry, 2002). While the survey did not delve into specific actions, clearly this is a troubling figure. Actions that most consider to be unethical (and also illegal) include installing unlicensed software (see Section 13.4.4), accessing personal information, and divulging trade secrets.

Another aspect of database technology concerns the use of data mining and data warehousing to aggregate and find associations and patterns among disparate data. Such business intelligence tools have evolved significantly over the past decade and, coupled with the tremendous increases in processing power and storage, afford even small and medium sized businesses the ability to examine customer behavior on an extremely fine-grained level.

There are many clearly ethical uses for such technology. For example, consider the case of a suspect who is placed near the scene of a crime by linking the suspect's car (identified by a video scan of the license plate) to the suspect's bank cash machine transaction. However, just as easily, we can think of many examples of situations that would violate ethical and privacy standards. For example, as a database administrator, imagine you are asked to implement a schema for a loan application process that includes the applicant's race or national origin.

A growing number of daily events trigger data collection on a grand scale; for example, making a cell phone call, making a purchase with a credit or debit card, applying for a loan, passing through an automated toll booth or subway turnstyle, driving around London, visiting a doctor or a pharmacy, or simply clicking on a link on a web site – all these generate transaction logs that can potentially be correlated, joined, and otherwise mined for patterns that many business and government entities would take great interest in. The temptation to collect and mine data is made even greater as businesses are pressured to gain competitive advantage.

These examples illustrate legal behavior that many would consider unethical. The issue comes down to recognizing the fact that while advances in IT make these kinds of analyses possible, governments and legal communities have been slow to recognize the potential threats to privacy, and thus the decision of whether or not these activities *should* be carried out is left up to the individual organization. Such decisions, in turn, necessarily depend upon the organization's culture and awareness of what constitutes ethical behavior. In Section 13.3, we discuss best practices for developing a culture of ethical behavior among information technology workers.

13.2 Legislation and its impact on the IT function

As mentioned in the previous section, the distinction between what is legal and what is ethical often becomes blurred by the introduction of, or amendments to, laws and regulations that affect how data may be collected, processed, and distributed. In this section we discuss several recent regulations and discuss the impact such regulations have on data and database administration functions.

13.2.1 Securities and Exchange Commission (SEC) Regulation National Market System (NMS)

In the context of activities that appear to be ethical but are in fact illegal, we considered the US Securities and Exchange Commission's Regulation NMS and the 'order protection rule' under which an activity that is acceptable to one facet of the investment community (purchasing a large block of shares at an inferior price) was deemed illegal under the new regulation. As a result of this regulation, financial services firms are now required to collect market data so that they can demonstrate that a better price was indeed not available at the time the trade was executed. The data administrator for a financial services firm would thus need to be aware of this regulation and how it impacts the operations of trading within the firm. Additional databases would need to be developed that link the trading activity to the market data, and reporting tools would be required to generate confirmation reports and *ad hoc* reports to satisfy SEC inquiries.

13.2.2 The Sarbanes–Oxley Act, COBIT, and COSO

In the aftermath of major financial frauds allegedly carried out within companies such as Enron, WorldCom, Parmalat, and others, both the US and European governments have put forth legislation to tighten requirements on how companies form their board of directors, interact with auditors, and report their financial statements. In the US, this legislation has taken the form of the Sarbanes–Oxley Act of 2002 (SOX), which also affects European companies listed on US exchanges. While the focus of SOX is on accounting and finance related issues, data management and auditing of databases and applications have been thrust to the forefront as companies must now certify the accuracy of their financial data. From a data administrator's perspective, SOX places increased requirements on the security and auditing of financial data and this has implications for how data is collected, processed, secured, and (possibly) reported both internally and externally to the organization.

Internal controls

A set of rules an organization adopts to ensure policies and procedures are not violated, data is properly secured and reliable, and operations can be carried out efficiently.

In order to comply with SOX, companies must adopt a formal **internal control** framework for information management risks. Two leading frameworks are the 'Control Objectives for Information and related Technology' (COBIT) and the 'Committee of Sponsoring Organizations of the Treadway Commission' (COSO), as we now discuss.

COBIT was created in 1996 by the IT Governance Institute (ITGI) and has since gone though three revisions to its current form, COBIT 4.0, released in 2005 by the Information Systems Audit and Control Association (ISACA) and ITGI. The ISACA web site for COBIT (http://www.isaca.org/cobit) explains:

> '*COBIT is an IT governance framework and supporting toolset that allows managers to bridge the gap between control requirements, technical issues and business risks. COBIT enables clear policy development and good practice for IT control throughout organizations.*'

The COBIT framework covers the four domains of *Plan and Organize* (PO), *Acquire and Implement* (AI), *Deliver and Support* (DS), and *Monitor and Evaluate* (ME).

Within these domains are a total of 38 high-level objectives. Data administrators should be most concerned with objectives such as:

- *Defining an information architecture (PO)* – to optimize the organization of information systems taking into consideration, among other things, an automated data depository and dictionary, data syntax rules and **data ownership**.
- *Managing performance and capacity (DS)* – to ensure that adequate capacity is available and that best and optimal use is made of it to meet required performance requirements.
- *Ensuring system security (DS)* – the use of logical access controls to safeguard information against unauthorized use, disclosure or modification, damage or loss.
- *Managing data (DS)* – the use of controls over the IT operations to ensure that data remains complete, accurate and valid during its input, update, and storage.
- *Monitoring and evaluating internal controls on data (ME)* – accessing internal control adequacy to ensure the achievement of the internal control objectives set for the IT processes.

On the other hand, the COSO framework focuses more narrowly on internal controls and consists of five major components including:

- *control environment* – establishes a culture of control, accountability, and ethical behavior;
- *risk assessment* – evaluates the risks faced in carrying out the organization's objectives;
- *control activities* – implements controls necessary to mitigate risks;
- *information and communications* – specifies the paths of reporting and communication within an organization and between the organization and its trading partners;
- *monitoring* – assessing the effectiveness of controls put in place.

Clearly data administrators should be directly involved in each of these components. In large organizations, this would mean working closely with senior management to make them aware of the impact of implementing these controls from the IT perspective. Significant resources (new software, hardware, databases, training, and new personnel) will need to be lobbied for.

13.2.3 The Health Insurance Portability and Accountability Act

The Health Insurance Portability and Accountability Act (HIPAA) of 1996 is administered by the Department of Health and Human Services in the United States and affects all providers of healthcare and health insurance. Provisions of the Act are being rolled out in stages with deadlines for implementation that depend upon the size and nature of the health care provider. The Act has several main provisions, of which the following five are of direct importance to database management.

1. *Privacy of patient information* (mandated by April 2003 for most organizations). Patients are now required to sign consent forms to allow their healthcare providers to share medical information with other providers and insurers. Data administrators must ensure that databases and systems track patient consent and allow or deny data transfers (either electronically or on paper) accordingly.
2. *Standardizing electronic health/medical records and transactions between health care organizations* (mandated by October, 2003). A series of standards have been developed that cover typical healthcare transactions such as claims, enrollment, patient eligibility, payments, and others. For data administrators, this has meant changing enterprise data models to include additional attributes and to work with **electronic data interchange (EDI)** software vendors to ensure that healthcare data can be exchanged in a standard format between organizations.

Electronic data interchange (EDI)

The computer-to-computer exchange of business data over a network. Typical transactions include purchase orders, invoices, payments, etc.

3. *Establishing a nationally recognized identifier for employees to be used by all employee health plans* (July 2004 for most organizations). Such an identifier (which may not be the social security number) will then be used in all subsequent transactions between healthcare organizations. Again, data administrators need to introduce changes to enterprise data models to include these alternate identifiers.
4. *Standards for the security of patient data and transactions involving this data* (April 2005 for most organizations). Patient data must be secured both within database systems as well as when transmitted between organizations. Failure to secure patient data can result in large fines. Database vendors such as Oracle and IBM now offer tools to encrypt data within columns of database tables and provide facilities to enable fine-grained auditing of database transactions.
5. *Need for a nationally recognized identifier for healthcare organizations and individual providers*. The implications for this provision are similar to those for the standardized employee identifier discussed above.

13.2.4 The European Union (EU) Directive on Data Protection of 1995

The official title of the EU's data protection directive is 'Directive 95/46/EC of the European Parliament and of the Council of 24 October 1995 on the protection of individuals with regard to the processing of personal data and on the free movement of such data' (OJEC, 1995). This Directive, adopted by all EU members in 1995, spans 34 Articles and is perhaps the most comprehensive of all similar Directives or Acts in the world today. An in-depth treatment of all aspects of the Directive is beyond the scope of this book, however, some Articles of the Directive merit particular attention.

- Articles 6 and 7 consist of 11 requirements, of which eight were used as a basis for the UK's data protection principles described in the next section.

- Article 8 focuses on the processing of 'personal data revealing racial or ethnic origin, political opinions, religious or philosophical beliefs, trade-union membership, and the processing of data concerning health or sex life.' This activity is generally prohibited, however ten exceptions are noted including, if the subject gives consent, the processor is ordered by law or does the work in accordance with its normal business functions, etc.
- Articles 10, 11, and 12 address how data is collected and the rights of individuals to see their data and appeal for corrections.
- Articles 16 and 17 address the confidentiality and security measures taken while data is collected and processed.
- Articles 18 through 21 deal with how a processor notifies an EU member of its intention to process data, and situations under which the EU member will publicize the processing operations.

13.2.5 The United Kingdom's Data Protection Act of 1998

The intent of the United Kingdom's Data Protection Act of 1998 (OPSI, 1998) is to uphold eight data protection principles that are outlined below. These eight principles, shown in Table 13.1, were borrowed from the 1995 EU Directive on Data Protection. Under this Act, citizens have the right to request to inspect copies of data any organization keeps about them and to request inaccuracies to be corrected.

Table 13.1 UK Data Protection Act 1998 (OPSI, 1998)

1. Personal data shall be processed fairly and lawfully and, in particular, shall not be processed unless it is consented to or is 'necessary.' The conditions under which processing is considered necessary are explicitly listed in Schedule 2 and Schedule 3 of the Act.
2. Personal data shall be obtained only for one or more specified and lawful purposes, and shall not be further processed in any manner incompatible with that purpose or those purposes.
3. Personal data shall be adequate, relevant, and not excessive in relation to the purpose or purposes for which they are processed.
4. Personal data shall be accurate and, where necessary, kept up to date.
5. Personal data processed for any purpose or purposes shall not be kept for longer than is necessary for that purpose or those purposes.
6. Personal data shall be processed in accordance with the rights of data subjects under this Act.
7. Appropriate technical and organizational measures shall be taken against unauthorized or unlawful processing of personal data and against accidental loss or destruction of, or damage to, personal data.
8. Personal data shall not be transferred to a country or territory outside the European Economic Area unless that country or territory ensures an adequate level of protection for the rights and freedoms of data subjects in relation to the processing of personal data.

Organizations that collect and maintain such data must have clear policies regarding how to respond to requests to inspect data as well as requests to share data with other organizations. Such policies clearly need to be consistent with the law as well as the ethical standards of the organization.

13.2.6 International banking – Basel II Accords

The *International Convergence of Capital Measurement and Capital Standards*, otherwise known as 'Basel II,' is a 2004 revision to the 1998 Basel Capital Accord (Basel I). These are recommended policies that must be enacted into law in each individual country and monitored by the appropriate national regulators. In the US that would be the Federal Reserve Bank, for the 10 largest internationally active US banks, and the Securities and Exchange Commission for securities firms. These two regulators were created to level the playing field among globally competitive institutions and set standards to minimize systemic risk in the world financial system. Institutions in the international banking system are interconnected in a number of ways through agreements, loans, and other credit and debt obligations. The fear has been that the failure of one large firm could cause defaults in countries and organizations far removed from the failing institution.

The Basel II framework consists of three main 'pillars':

1. *Minimum capital requirements* – institutions must maintain sufficient capital (funds) given the level of risk inherent in their portfolio of assets (loans, securities, etc.). The measurement of risk has been revised and expanded to include:
   (a) Credit risk – the risk that creditors will not be able to repay their debts (principle and interest.)
   (b) Market risk – the risk that all investments will decline in value as the entire market (or economy) declines, or due to industry or firm-specific causes, including interest rate and currency risks.
   (c) Interest rate risk – the risk that investment will lose value as a result of interest rate increases.
   (d) Operational risk – the risk of loss as a result of poor internal controls, operations, systems or human resources, or the risk of loss as a result of some external event (such as a natural disaster.)
2. *Supervisory review process* – management must understand and actively control the risks, have sufficient internal risk controls and timely reporting, including compensation plans that reward appropriate risk management behavior.
3. *Market discipline* – institutions must publicly disclose information about their capital adequacy, risk exposures, and the processes by which they measure and mitigate risks.

Value at Risk (VaR)

The minimum expected financial loss under normal circumstances calculated at a specific (e.g. 95%) confidence level.

In order to calculate market risks, firms must aggregate positions from all trading, loans (credit card, cars, homes, business, etc.), and financial operations at least daily and for trading in real time. **Value at risk (VaR)** calculations need historical data over one or two years or more for each asset to be able to calculate the variance–covariance matrices required by risk models, including Monte Carlo simulations. Credit risk models use external sources such as Standard & Poors credit rating for public companies and large liquid instruments, but banks must still maintain significant data to execute their internal risk models. This includes credit histories, business financial data, loan officer reports, etc. Assessing operational risk is even more data intensive as Basel II requires at least five years of data. Operational risk assessment requires analysis of both high frequency but low value events and, more critically, high value infrequent events, for which there is little statistical evidence upon which to base capital requirements. In the US and Europe, consortiums are being established, where banks are sharing operational risk events so that each member has a base upon which to develop their internal models of operational risk. As with the Sarbanes–Oxley legislation, having effective internal controls in place plays a large role in mitigating operation risk.

13.3 Establishing a culture of legal and ethical data stewardship

The complexity and IT implications of the recent legislation discussed in the previous section raise issues that are vital to employees throughout an organization. Senior managers such as board members, presidents, chief information officers (CIOs), and data administrators are increasingly finding themselves liable for any violations of these laws. It is therefore mandatory that official policies be created and articulated to employees at all organizational levels. An obvious question arises: 'Where do we start?' Some basic steps are outlined below.

13.3.1 Developing an organization-wide policy for legal and ethical behavior

First, it is important that the senior management team is aware of new legislation and changes in industry practice. An assessment of how these changes impact the organization is also a critical first step. Often issues will arise as a result of the growing interconnected nature of global business. For example, a firm may find it is subject to the stricter laws of a foreign country in which it does business, and as a result may have to adjust its entire operations according to the most stringent standard.

Next, data administrators and CIOs will need to assess how legislation affects the flow of data through the organization. Special attention must be paid to how data is collected, stored, secured, and accessed by users who may be internal or external to the organization. Many of the security techniques discussed in Chapter 12 can be applied in this case. Following this, new or revised operating procedures must be documented and communicated to all affected parties. Again an assessment may reveal additional employees or trading partners involved in working with sensitive data or processes that were previously overlooked.

Once explicit rules for conducting business within legal parameters have been developed, a similar set of ethical principles for the business should be developed.

Many organizations already have a corporate-wide statement of ethics that can be used as a starting point. As already noted, any resulting policies must be documented and articulated to all employees in such a way that they come to understand the seriousness with which senior management takes these issues.

Finally, lapses in legal and ethical behavior must be dealt with swiftly and fairly, and within the guidelines made known to all employees. These cases can also serve to help refine policies and procedures going forward such that legal and ethical policy statements evolve over time to adapt to new business situations.

Another potential source of general guidelines can be existing codes of ethics, codes of conduct, and/or codes of practice that have been adopted by a professional IT-related society or organization. The next section discusses two such codes.

13.3.2 Professional organizations and codes of ethics

Many professional organizations have a code of ethics that all members pledge to uphold. Perhaps the most comprehensive code of ethics for IT comes from the Association for Computing Machinery (ACM), an organization in existence since 1947 with over 80 000 members worldwide (www.acm.org). The ACM Code of Ethics and Professional Conduct (ACM, 1992) consists of 24 statements of personal responsibility in four main categories:

- *Fundamental ethical considerations* – this category addresses eight areas, including:
  - Contribute to society and human well-being.
  - Avoid harm to others.
  - Be honest and trustworthy.
  - Be fair and take action not to discriminate.
  - Honor property rights including copyrights and patent.
  - Give proper credit for intellectual property.
  - Respect the privacy of others.
  - Honor confidentiality.
- *Specific considerations of professional conduct* – this category addresses eight areas:
  - Strive to achieve the highest quality, effectiveness and dignity in both the process and products of professional work.
  - Acquire and maintain professional competence.
  - Know and respect existing laws pertaining to professional work.
  - Accept and provide appropriate professional review.
  - Give comprehensive and thorough evaluations of computer systems and their impacts, including analysis of possible risks.
  - Honor contracts, agreements, and assigned responsibilities.
  - Improve public understanding of computing and its consequences.

  - Access computing and communication resources only when authorized to do so.
- *Considerations for individuals in leadership roles* – this category covers six areas:
  - Articulate the social responsibilities of members of an organizational unit and encourage full acceptance of those responsibilities.
  - Manage personnel and resources to design and build information systems that enhance the quality of working life.
  - Acknowledge and support proper and authorized uses of an organization's computing and communication resources.
  - Ensure that users and those who will be affected by a system have their needs clearly articulated during the assessment and design of requirements; later the system must be validated to meet requirements.
  - Articulate and support policies that protect the dignity of users and others affected by a computing system.
  - Create opportunities for members of the organization to learn the principles and limitations of computer systems.
- *Compliance with the code* – this last category addresses two main points:
  - Uphold and promote the principles of this code.
  - Treat violations of this code as inconsistent with membership in the ACM.

The British Computer Society (www.bcs.org) was founded in 1957 and currently has over 50 000 members in 100 countries. The BCS Code of Conduct (BCS, 2001), which all BCS members agree to uphold, specifies conduct in four main areas:

- *The public interest*
  - You shall carry out work or study with due care and diligence in accordance with the relevant authority's requirements, and the interests of system users. If your professional judgment is overruled, you shall indicate the likely risks and consequences.
  - In your professional role you shall have regard for the public health, safety and environment.
  - You shall have regard to the legitimate rights of third parties.
  - You shall ensure that within your professional field/s you have knowledge and understanding of relevant legislation, regulations and standards, and that you comply with such requirements.
  - You shall conduct your professional activities without discrimination against clients or colleagues.
  - You shall reject any offer of bribery or inducement.
- *Duty to relevant authority (e.g. a member's superiors)*
  - You shall avoid any situation that may give rise to a conflict of interest between you and your relevant authority. You shall make full and immediate disclosure to them if any conflict is likely to occur or be seen by a third party as likely to occur.

  - You shall not disclose or authorise to be disclosed, or use for personal gain or to benefit a third party, confidential information, except with the permission of your relevant authority, or at the direction of a court of law.
  - You shall not misrepresent or withhold information on the performance of products, systems or services, or take advantage of the lack of relevant knowledge or inexperience of others.
- *Duty to the profession*
  - You shall uphold the reputation and good standing of the BCS in particular, and the profession in general, and shall seek to improve professional standards through participation in their development, use and enforcement.
  - You shall act with integrity in your relationships with all members of the BCS and with members of other professions with whom you work in a professional capacity.
  - You shall have due regard for the possible consequences of your statements on others. You shall not make any public statement in your professional capacity unless you are properly qualified and, where appropriate, authorised to do so. You shall not purport to represent the BCS unless authorised to do so.
  - You shall notify the Society if convicted of a criminal offence or upon becoming bankrupt or disqualified as company director.
- *Professional competence and integrity*
  - You shall seek to upgrade your professional knowledge and skill, and shall maintain awareness of technological developments, procedures and standards which are relevant to your field, and encourage your subordinates to do likewise.
  - You shall not claim any level of competence that you do not possess. You shall only offer to do work or provide a service that is within your professional competence.
  - You shall observe the relevant BCS Codes of Practice and all other standards which, in your judgment, are relevant, and you shall encourage your colleagues to do likewise.
  - You shall accept professional responsibility for your work and for the work of colleagues who are defined in a given context as working under your supervision.

The ACM Code and BCS Code are similar in that both begin by establishing grounding in providing an overall benefit to society. From that point, performing one's professional duties to the highest possible standard and carrying out duties in a legal and ethical manner are paramount. Recognition of intellectual property rights (discussed next) and acknowledgement of sources, respecting privacy and confidentiality, and overall concern for public health, safety, and the environment are also common themes. Both codes explicitly mention a member's duty to understand and comply with all relevant laws, regulations, and standards – something that is highly relevant as discussed in this chapter. Both codes also mention duties to one's superiors as well as to the public at large.

It should not be surprising that the two major computer societies in the US and the UK share much common ground due to their common language, and general common ground regarding law and ethics. However, not all countries share the same societal values as the US and Britain. Therefore, we can find situations in several countries where concepts such as an individual's right to privacy and anti-discrimination are not consistent with US and UK norms.

These existing codes, and others as cited by Lee (2006), can be used as a resource for organizations wishing to establish their own similar codes.

13.3.3 Developing an organization-wide policy for legal and ethical behavior for *StayHome*

In this section, we outline the steps the *StayHome Online Rentals* company might take to develop an organization-wide policy that addresses legal and ethical behavior. As a business, *StayHome* interacts with customers, wholesalers, and a variety of other organizations on a daily basis. Some of the data that *StayHome* maintains, such as the price they pay a DVD wholesaler for a particular title, would be considered sensitive information. In a similar fashion, a customer's rental history and payment information are also considered to be very sensitive. *StayHome's* policy should therefore explicitly address:

- *Interactions between StayHome staff and customers and business partners.* Some critical points would include:
  - Treating customers with respect (e.g. in email and over the phone).
  - Treating business partners with respect.
  - Taking special care to limit information disclosure to business partners, including the proper procedures for handling information requests.
- *The security of customer and other business data.* Some critical points would include:
  - Raising awareness of the sensitivity of a customer's personal data, payment history, credit card numbers, and rental history.
  - Ensuring that appropriate security measures are maintained to protect this sensitive data.
  - Proper procedures for handling data requests from:
    - internal employees (e.g. proposals for data mining or accessing sensitive customer data)
    - customers (e.g. request to reset a password)
    - business partners (if such data sharing is allowed)
    - and possibly law enforcement (e.g. a request for a customer's payment information or rental history.)

- The use of company resources (hardware, software, Internet, etc.). Some critical points would include:
  - Computer hardware may not be removed from the premises without departmental manager's approval.
  - Licensed computer software may not be copied, distributed or otherwise used improperly.
  - Additional software may not be installed without IT department approval.
  - Internet resources may not be used for non-company business.
- *Ramifications for violating the security and/or trust of customer and business partner data*. Some critical points would include:
  - All violations will be documented and presented before an oversight board consisting of representatives from different business areas as well as management levels. Serious violations will also be reported to the appropriate authorities.
  - Willful or malicious violations will be met with dismissal and prosecution.
  - Other violations will result in sanctions commensurate with the seriousness of the violation as determined by the oversight board.

Finally, *StayHome* should further establish a procedure by which the policy is reviewed annually and/or in the wake of any major violations of the policy or other incidents to ensure that the policy does not become outdated as the technology and business environment changes.

13.4 Intellectual property

Intellectual property (IP)

The product of human creativity in the industrial, scientific, literary, and artistic fields.

In this final section, we introduce some of the main concepts underlying **intellectual property** (sometimes referred to by the simple acronym **IP**). It is important that data and database administrators as well as business analysts and software developers recognize and understand the issues surrounding IP both to ensure that their ideas can be protected and to ensure that other people's rights are not infringed.

Intellectual property covers inventions, inventive ideas, designs, patents and patent applications, discoveries, improvements, trademarks, designs and design rights (registered and unregistered), written work (including computer software) and know-how devised, developed, or written by an individual or set of individuals. IP generated through the course of employment legally belongs to the employer unless specifically agreed otherwise. In the same way that ownership of tangible products gives the owner rights, the ownership of intangible property attempts to provide similar rights to allow owners the rights of exclusivity to give away, license, or sell their intellectual property. While the exclusive nature of IP rights can seem strong, the strength of IP laws are tempered by limitations placed on their duration and/or scope, as well as the owner's freedom not to enforce their rights.

We can distinguish two types of IP:

- **background IP** – IP that exists before an activity takes place.
- **foreground IP** – IP that is generated during an activity.

A project may make use of background IP owned by someone other than the organization but in this case relevant contractual arrangements should be put in place with the owner of the IP. There are three main ways to protect IP rights: patents, copyright, and trademarks, as we now discuss.

13.4.1 Patents

Patent

Provides an exclusive (legal) right for a set period of time to make, use, sell or import an invention.

Patents are granted by a government when an individual or organization can demonstrate:

- the invention is *new*;
- the invention is in some way *useful*;
- the invention involves an *inventive step*.

In addition, one of the key considerations of the patent system is that the patent application must disclose how the invention works. This information is then disseminated to the public once a patent is issued, thereby increasing the wealth of public knowledge. Patents give effective protection for new technology that will lead to a product, composition, or process with significant long-term commercial gain. Note, however, that artistic creations, mathematical models, plans, schemes, or other purely mental processes cannot be patented.

13.4.2 Copyright

Copyright

Provides an exclusive (legal) right for a set period of time to reproduce and distribute a literary, musical, audiovisual, or other 'work' of authorship.

Unlike a patent where rights are granted through a formal application process, **copyright** comes into effect as soon as what is 'created' takes a fixed form (for example, in writing or in sound). Copyright covers not just works like books, articles, song lyrics, music CDs, videos, DVDs, TV programs, but also computer software, databases, technical drawings and designs, and multimedia. Copyright holders can sell the rights to their works to individuals or organizations in return for payment, which are often referred to as *royalties*. There are some exceptions to copyright so that some minor uses may not infringe copyright (for example, limited use for non-commercial research, private study, and teaching purposes).

Copyright also gives *moral rights* to be identified as the creator of certain kinds of material and to object to distortion or mutilation of it. Although copyright does not require registration, many countries allow for registration of works, for example to identify titles of works or to serve as *prima facie* evidence in a court of law when copyright is infringed or disputed.

13.4.3 Trademarks

Trademark

Provides an exclusive (legal) right to use a word, symbol, image, sound, or some other distinctive element that identifies the source of origin in connection with certain goods or services.

A third form of protection is the **trademark**. Generally, trademarks are intended to be associated with specific goods and services and as a result they assist consumers in identifying the nature and quality of the products they purchase. Like patents and copyright, trademarks give the owner exclusive legal rights to use, license, or sell it for the goods and services for which it is registered. Like copyright, a trademark does not have to be registered although registration may be advisable as it can be expensive and time-consuming to take action under common law. For the *StayHome Online Rentals* case study, the company may decide to trademark their business name.

13.4.4 IPR issues for software

As noted earlier, it is important to understand intellectual property rights (IPR) for a number of reasons:

- to understand your own right or your organization's right as a producer of original ideas and works;
- to recognize the value of original works;
- to understand the procedures for protecting and exploiting such work;
- to know the legal measures that can be used to defend against the illegal use of such work;
- to be fair and sensible about legitimate use of your work for non-profit purposes.

In this section, we briefly discuss some of the issues related specifically to IPR and software.

Software and patentability

In the 1970s and 1980s, there were extensive discussions on whether patents or copyright should provide protection for computer software. These discussions resulted in a generally accepted principle that software should be protected by copyright, whereas apparatus using software should be protected by patent. However, this is less clear nowadays. While the UK specifically excludes software from patent protection, there has been some latitude in the interpretation where software forms part of the overall machinery or industrial process. Therefore, an application to just patent a piece of software will be refused but an application to patent some technical effect that is produced by a piece of software will be considered, subject to constraints discussed in Section 13.4.1. In the US, patentability has been extended to cover what are termed 'business methods' and many software patents have been granted and more have been applied for, particularly with the growth of the Internet and eCommerce.

Software and copyright

All software has one or more authors who assert the right to their intellectual property in what they have written. Copyright applies, therefore, to all software whether or not you have paid money for it, and the distribution and use of software is subject to a 'license' that specifies the terms of use. The conditions that apply to a particular piece of software depend on a number of things, but in general there are four types of license as we now discuss.

- *Commercial software (perpetual use)*: In this case a fee is paid for the software and the license allows the software to be used for as long as you like on one machine, and to make copies only for the purpose of backup if something goes wrong with the machine. If software can be transferred to a different machine, it *must* be deleted from the old one first. In some cases a license may permit use on more than one machine, but this would be explicit in the license terms.
- *Commercial software (annual fee)*: This is similar to the perpetual use license, but a fee may be required for each year of continued use, and in most cases the software stops working unless the fee is paid and a new 'license key' is issued by the supplier. Annual rental often applies to site licenses (where once the fee is paid, the organization may use the software on as many machines as it likes) and to software on mainframe or server computers. Again the license terms will be explicit as to what use is allowed.
- *Shareware*: Software made available initially for a free 'trial' period. If after the initial period (for example, 30 days) you wish to continue using the software, you are asked to send a (usually small) fee to the author(s) of the software. In some cases the software enforces this by refusing to work after the trial period, but irrespective of this in using the software you are accepting the license terms and are infringing the author's copyright if you continue to use the software after the trial period. In return for the fee, a more up-to-date version of the software may be provided that does not constantly remind the user to register and pay for the software.
- *Freeware*: Software made available free for certain categories of use (such as education or personal use). There are two main types of freeware: software that is distributed without the source code, preventing modification by users, and open source software (OSS). The latter is usually issued under a license such as the GNU Public License (GPL) that specifies the terms and conditions of free use. The main restrictions are that the software cannot be used for commercial purposes, although you are usually allowed to modify the software but are duty bound to submit any improvements that you make to the author(s) so that they can incorporate them in future releases. A second restriction is that the text of the copyrighted GPL license itself be included with any redistribution.

Note In neither of the first two cases concerning commercial software are you permitted to attempt to modify or reverse engineer the software or remove any copyright messages, etc. All software has license conditions, even software downloaded free from the Internet, and failure to comply with the license conditions is an infringement of copyright.

13.4.5 IPR issues for data

Consideration must also be paid to data that an organization collects, processes, and possibly shares with its trading partners. In conjunction with senior management and legal counsel, data administrators must define and enforce policies that govern when data can be shared and in what ways it can be used within the organization. For example, consider the data that *StayHome Online Rentals* maintains on its customers' rental habits. It is entirely possible that other retailers, target marketing firms, or even law enforcement, would be interested in gaining access to detailed transaction histories of customers. For some businesses, sharing limited data (such as purchase patterns without revealing individual identities) or aggregated data may make sense from a revenue standpoint. In the event that a business case is made for sharing data, appropriate licensing of the data must be put into effect so that it is not 'reshared' with other parties.

Chapter summary

- Recent failures of well-known organizations have lead to increased scrutiny of organizations. This scrutiny has been formalized in a number of acts of legislation in the US and elsewhere.
- **Ethics** as defined as 'doing what is right' within a given society or culture.
- What constitutes legal behavior is most often aligned with ethical behavior, although this is not always the case.
- Most of the legislation discussed in this chapter was put into place to help diminish the possibility of unintended information disclosure.
- Most of the legislative acts discussed have at their core a mandate to protect the data of customers, clients, etc. while at the same time increasing the reporting requirements of companies to official agencies. Both of these general items have at their core data management issues.
- Establishing a corporate-wide (and certainly IT-wide) awareness of security, privacy and reporting, as it relates to the data an organization collects and processes, is a critical task, especially given the current regulatory environment.
- **Intellectual property** (**IP**) covers inventions, inventive ideas, designs, patents and patent applications, discoveries, improvements, trademarks, designs and design rights, written work and know-how devised, developed, or written by an individual or set of individuals.

Review questions

13.1 Define ethics in terms of how organizations conduct business.

13.2 Describe business situations in which an individual's or business's behavior would be considered:

(a) illegal and unethical;
(b) legal but unethical;
(c) illegal but ethical.

13.3 Explain how a company that is adhering to the 'industry norms' can find itself in violation of a law.

Exercises

13.4 Suppose you are a data administrator for a large European pharmaceutical manufacturer that has significant sales and marketing efforts in Europe, Japan, and the United States. What data management issues would you have to be most concerned with?

13.5 Suppose you have just joined a large financial services company as the head of IT and are asked to create a formal code of ethics for IT. What steps would you take to research this, and what resources would you consider?

13.6 Access Peter Neumann's 'Inside Risks' article archives for the Communications of the ACM (visit http://www.csl.sri.com/users/neumann/insiderisks.html). Summarize, in a few paragraphs, a recent article from these archives dealing with legal and/or ethical issues related to information technology.

13.7 Access the ACM Code of Ethics and Professional Conduct and the BCS Code of Conduct and Code of Good Practice. When comparing the two, discuss elements that are emphasized more (or less) in one code than the other.

13.8 Access the Singapore Computer Society's Code of Conduct (http://www.scs.org.sg/code_of_conduct.php). Compare this code with either the ACM or the BCS code and note any differences.

13.9 Consider the *StayHome Online Rentals* case study discussed in Chapter 5. Produce a report for the Director of the company outlining the legal and ethical issues that need to be considered, and make any recommendations you think appropriate.

13.10 Consider the *PerfectPets* case study discussed in Appendix B. Produce a report for the Director of the company outlining the legal and ethical issues that need to be considered, and make any recommendations you think appropriate.

CHAPTER

14 Transaction management

Preview

In Chapter 1, we discussed the functions that a DBMS should provide. Among these are three closely related functions that are intended to ensure that the database is reliable and remains in a consistent state. These three functions are transaction support, concurrency control, and recovery. The reliability and consistency of the database must be maintained in the presence of failures of both hardware and software components, and when multiple users are accessing the database. In this chapter we concentrate on these three functions.

Although each function can be discussed separately, they are mutually dependent. Both concurrency control and recovery are required to protect the database from data inconsistencies and data loss. Many DBMSs allow users to undertake simultaneous operations on the database. If these operations are not controlled, the accesses may interfere with each other and the database can become inconsistent. To overcome this, the DBMS implements a concurrency control protocol that prevents database accesses from interfering with each other.

Database recovery is the process of restoring the database to a correct state following a failure. The failure may be the result of a system crash due to hardware or software errors, a media failure, such as a head crash, or a software error in the application, such as a logical error in the program that is accessing the database. It may also be the result of unintentional or intentional corruption or destruction of data or facilities by system administrators or users. Whatever the underlying cause of the failure, the DBMS must be able to recover from the failure and restore the database to a consistent state.

Central to an understanding of both concurrency control and recovery is the notion of a transaction, which we describe in Section 14.1. In Section 14.2, we discuss concurrency control and examine the protocols that can be used to prevent conflict. In Section 14.3, we discuss database recovery and examine the techniques that can be used to ensure the database remains in a consistent state in the presence of failures.

Learning objectives

In this chapter you will learn:

- The purpose of concurrency control.
- The purpose of database recovery.

- The function and importance of transactions.
- The properties of a transaction.
- How locks can be used to ensure transactions do not interfere with one another.
- The meaning of deadlock and how it can be resolved.
- How timestamps can be used to ensure transactions do not interfere with one another.
- How optimistic concurrency control techniques work.
- Some causes of database failure.
- The purpose of the transaction log file.
- The purpose of checkpoints during transaction logging.
- How to recover following database failure.

14.1 Transaction support

Transaction

An action, or series of actions, carried out by a single user or database application, which reads or updates the contents of the database.

A **transaction** is a *logical unit of work* on the database. It may be an entire program, a part of a program, or a single statement (for example, the SQL statement INSERT or UPDATE), and it may involve any number of operations on the database. In the database context, the execution of a database application can be thought of as a series of transactions with non-database processing taking place in between. To illustrate the concepts of a transaction, we use a simple account table that maintains the status of each member's payments in the *StayHome Online Rentals* database. A simple transaction against this table is to update the balance for a particular member, bal_x, say. At a high level, we could write this transaction as shown in Figure 14.1(a). In this chapter, we denote a database read or write operation on a data item x as read(x) or write(x). In this example, we have a transaction consisting of two database operations (read and write) and a non-database operation ($bal_x = bal_x + 10$). A more complicated transaction is to transfer \$10 from one account (bal_x) to another (bal_y), as shown in Figure 14.1(b). If both these updates are not made, the database will be in an *inconsistent state* (\$10 will have been 'lost').

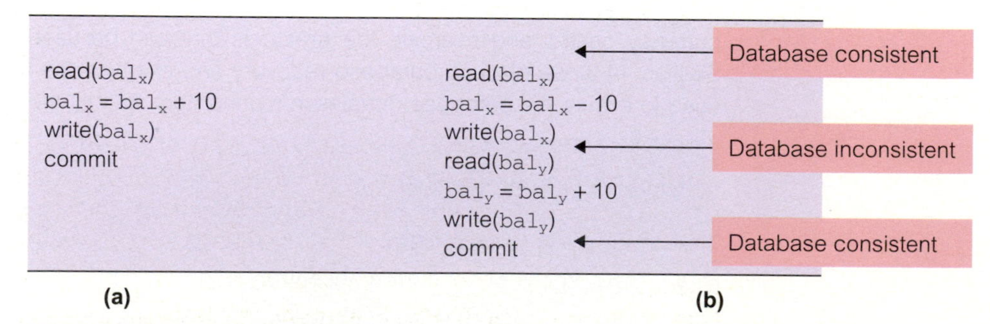

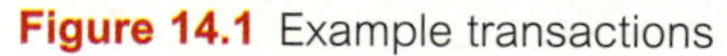
Figure 14.1 Example transactions

A transaction should always transform the database from one consistent state to another, although we accept that consistency may be violated while the transaction is in progress. For example, at the start of the transaction in Figure 14.1(b), we assume that the database is in a consistent state. Following the first update, $10 has been removed from one account but has not yet been added to the second account, so at this point the database is not in a consistent state. However, at the end of the transaction, the transfer has been successfully completed and the database is once again in a consistent state.

A transaction can have one of two outcomes. If it completes successfully, the transaction is said to have *committed* and the database reaches a new consistent state. If the transaction does not execute successfully, the transaction is *aborted*. If a transaction is aborted, the database must be restored to the consistent state it was in before the transaction started. Such a transaction is *rolled back* or *undone*. A committed transaction cannot be aborted. If we decide that the committed transaction was a mistake, we must perform another *compensating transaction* to reverse its effects. However, an aborted transaction that is rolled back can be restarted later and, depending on the cause of the failure, may successfully execute and commit at that time.

The DBMS has no inherent way of knowing which updates are grouped together to form a single logical transaction. It must therefore provide a method to allow the user to indicate the boundaries of a transaction. The keywords BEGIN TRANSACTION, COMMIT, and ROLLBACK (or their equivalent[1]) are available in many data manipulation languages to delimit transactions. If these delimiters are not used, the entire program is usually regarded as a single transaction, with the DBMS automatically performing a COMMIT when the program terminates correctly and a ROLLBACK if it does not.

14.1.1 Properties of a transaction

There are four basic, or so-called **ACID**, properties that all transactions should possess:

- **Atomicity**. The 'all or nothing' property. A transaction is an indivisible unit that is either performed in its entirety or it is not performed at all. It is the responsibility of the recovery subsystem of the DBMS to ensure atomicity.
- **Consistency**. A transaction must transform the database from one consistent state to another consistent state. It is the responsibility of both the DBMS and the application developers to ensure consistency. The DBMS can ensure consistency by enforcing all the integrity constraints that have been specified on the database schema. However, in itself this is insufficient to ensure consistency. For example, suppose we have a transaction that is intended to transfer money from one bank account to another and the programmer makes an error in the transaction logic and debits one account but credits the wrong

[1] With the ISO SQL standard, BEGIN TRANSACTION is implied by the first *transaction-initiating* SQL statement.

account, then the database is in an inconsistent state. However, the DBMS would not have been responsible for introducing this inconsistency and would have had no ability to detect the error.

- **Isolation**. Transactions execute independently of one another. In other words, the partial effects of incomplete transactions should not be visible to other transactions. It is the responsibility of the concurrency control subsystem to ensure isolation.
- **Durability**. The effects of a successfully completed (committed) transaction are permanently recorded in the database and must not be lost because of a subsequent failure. It is the responsibility of the recovery subsystem to ensure durability.

14.2 Concurrency control

In this section, we examine the problems that can arise with concurrent access and the techniques that can be employed to avoid these problems. We start with the working definition of **concurrency control**, as shown in the margin below.

14.2.1 The need for concurrency control

Concurrency control

The process of managing simultaneous operations on the database without having them interfere with one another.

A major objective in developing a database is to enable many users to access shared data concurrently. Concurrent access is straightforward if all transactions are only reading data, as there is no way that they can interfere with one another. However, when two or more transactions are accessing the database simultaneously and at least one is updating data, there may be interference that can result in inconsistencies. We examine three examples of potential problems caused by concurrency: the *lost update problem*, the *uncommitted dependency problem*, and the *inconsistent analysis problem*. To illustrate the concepts, we continue with the simple account table that maintains the status of each member's payments. In this context, we are using the transaction as the *unit of concurrency control*.

Example 14.1 The lost update problem

An apparently successfully completed update operation by one user can be overridden by another user. This is known as the *lost update problem* and is illustrated in Figure 14.2, in which transaction T_1 is executing concurrently with transaction T_2. T_1 is withdrawing \$10 from an account with balance bal_x, initially \$100, and T_2 is depositing \$100 into the same account. If these transactions are executed *serially*, one after the other with no interleaving of operations, the final balance would be \$190 no matter which transaction is performed first.

Transactions T_1 and T_2 start at nearly the same time and both read the balance as \$100. T_2 increases bal_x by \$100 to \$200 and stores the update in the database. Meanwhile, transaction T_1 decrements its copy of bal_x by \$10 to \$90 and stores this value in the database, overwriting the previous update and thereby 'losing' the $100 previously added to the balance.

The loss of T_2's update is avoided by preventing T_1 from reading the value of bal_x until after T_2's update has been completed. We discuss how this can be achieved shortly.

Time	T_1	T_2	bal_x
t_1		begin_transaction	100
t_2	begin transaction	read(bal_x)	100
t_3	read(bal_x)	$bal_x = bal_x + 100$	100
t_4	$bal_x = bal_x - 10$	write(bal_x)	200
t_5	write(bal_x)	commit	90
t_6	commit		90

Figure 14.2 The lost update problem

Example 14.2 The uncommitted dependency (or dirty read) problem

The uncommitted dependency problem occurs when one transaction is allowed to see the intermediate results of another transaction before it has committed. Figure 14.3 shows an example of an uncommitted dependency that causes an error, using the same initial value for balance bal_x as in the previous example. Here, transaction T_4 updates bal_x to $200, but it aborts the transaction so that bal_x should be restored to its original value of $100. However, by this time, transaction T_3 has read the new value of bal_x ($200) and is using this value as the basis of the $10 reduction, giving a new (incorrect) balance of $190, instead of $90. The value of bal_x read by T_3 is called *dirty data*, giving rise to the alternative name, *the dirty read problem*.

The reason for the rollback is unimportant; it may be that the transaction was in error, perhaps crediting the wrong account. The effect is the assumption by T_3 that T_4's update completed successfully, although the update was subsequently rolled back. This problem is avoided by preventing T_3 from reading bal_x until after the decision has been made to either commit or abort T_4's effects. Again, we discuss how this can be achieved shortly.

Time	T_3	T_4	bal_x
t_1		begin_transaction	100
t_2		read(bal_x)	100
t_3		$bal_x = bal_x + 100$	100
t_4	begin_transaction	write(bal_x)	200
t_5	read(bal_x)	⋮	200
t_6	$bal_x = bal_x - 10$	rollback	100
t_7	write(bal_x)		190
t_8	commit		190

Figure 14.3 The uncommitted dependency problem

The two problems above concentrate on transactions where both are updating the database and their interference may corrupt the database. However, as illustrated in the next example, transactions that only read the database can also produce inaccurate results if they are allowed to read partial results of incomplete transactions that are simultaneously updating the database.

Example 14.3 The inconsistent analysis problem

The problem of inconsistent analysis occurs when a transaction reads several values from the database, but a second transaction updates some of them during the execution of the first. For example, a transaction that is summarizing data in a database (for example, totaling balances) will obtain inaccurate results if, while it is executing, other transactions are updating the database. One example is illustrated in Figure 14.4, in which a summary transaction T_6 is executing concurrently with transaction T_5. Transaction T_6 is totaling the balances of account x ($100), account y ($50), and account z ($25). However, in the meantime transaction T_5 has transferred $10 from bal_x to bal_z, so that T_6 now has the wrong result ($10 too high). This problem is avoided by preventing transaction T_6 from reading bal_x and bal_z until after T_5 has completed its updates.

Time	T_5	T_6	bal_x	bal_y	bal_z	sum
t_1		begin_transaction	100	50	25	
t_2	begin_transaction	sum = 0	100	50	25	0
t_3	read(bal_x)	read(bal_x)	100	50	25	0
t_4	$bal_x = bal_x - 10$	sum = sum + bal_x	100	50	25	100
t_5	write(bal_x)	read(bal_y)	90	50	25	100
t_6	read(bal_z)	sum = sum + bal_y	90	50	25	150
t_7	$bal_z = bal_z + 10$		90	50	25	150
t_8	write(bal_z)		90	50	35	150
t_9	commit	read(bal_z)	90	50	35	150
t_{10}		sum = sum + bal_z	90	50	35	185
t_{11}		commit	90	50	35	185

Figure 14.4 The inconsistent analysis problem

Another problem can occur when a transaction T re-reads a data item it has previously read, but in between another transaction has modified it. Thus, T receives two different values for the same data item. This is sometimes referred to as a **nonrepeatable** (or **fuzzy**) **read**. A similar problem can occur if transaction T executes a query that retrieves a set of records from a table satisfying a certain predicate, re-executes the query at a later time, but finds that the retrieved set contains an additional (*phantom*) record that has been inserted by another transaction in the meantime. This is sometimes referred to as a **phantom read**.

14.2.2 Serializability and concurrency control techniques

The objective of a concurrency control protocol is to schedule transactions in such a way as to avoid any interference between them, and hence prevent the types of problems described above. One obvious solution is to allow only one transaction to execute at a time: one transaction is *committed* before the next transaction is allowed to *begin*. This is referred to as a *serial schedule* (a **schedule** is simply a particular sequencing of the operations from a set of concurrent transactions). The three problems described above resulted from the mismanagement of concurrency, which left the database in an inconsistent state in the first two examples, and presented the user with the wrong result in the inconsistent analysis example. Serial execution prevents such problems occurring. No matter which serial schedule is chosen, serial execution never leaves the database in an inconsistent state so every serial schedule is considered correct, although different results may be produced. However, the aim of a multi-user DBMS is also to maximize the degree of concurrency or parallelism in the system, so that transactions that can execute without interfering with one another can run in parallel. For example, transactions that access different parts of the database can be scheduled together without interference. The objective of **serializability** is to find a *nonserial* ordering of the operations in a set of concurrently executing transactions that allow the transactions to execute without interfering with one another, and thereby produce a database state that could be produced by a serial execution.

Serializability can be achieved in several ways but the two main concurrency control techniques that allow transactions to execute safely in parallel, subject to certain constraints, are **locking** and **timestamp** based. These are essentially *conservative* (or *pessimistic*) approaches in that they cause transactions to be delayed in case they conflict with other transactions at some time in the future. *Optimistic* methods, as we see later, are based on the premise that conflict is rare so they allow transactions to proceed unsynchronized and only check for conflicts when a transaction is about to commit. We discuss locking, timestamping, and optimistic concurrency control techniques in the following sections.

14.2.3 Locking methods

Locking

A procedure used to control concurrent access to data. When one transaction is accessing the database, a lock may deny access to other transactions to prevent incorrect results.

Locking methods are the most widely used approach to ensure serializability of concurrent transactions. There are several variations but all share the same fundamental characteristic, namely that a transaction must claim a **shared** (*read*) or **exclusive** (*write*) **lock** on a data item before the corresponding database read or write operation. The lock prevents another transaction from modifying the item or, in the case of an exclusive lock, even reading it. Data items of various sizes, ranging from the entire database down to a field, may be locked. The size of the item determines the fineness, or **lock granularity**. The basic rules for locking are as follows:

- *Shared lock* – if a transaction has a shared lock on a data item, it can read the item but not update it.
- *Exclusive lock* – if a transaction has an exclusive lock on a data item, it can both read and update the item.

Since read operations cannot conflict, it is permissible for more than one transaction to hold shared locks simultaneously on the same item. However, an exclusive lock gives a transaction exclusive access to that item. Thus, as long as a transaction holds the exclusive lock on the item, no other transactions can read or update that data item. Locks are used in the following way:

- Any transaction that needs to access a data item must first lock the item, requesting a shared lock for read only access or an exclusive lock for both read and write access.
- If the item is not already locked by another transaction, the lock will be granted.
- If the item is currently locked, the DBMS determines whether the request is compatible with the existing lock. If a shared lock is requested on an item that already has a shared lock on it, the request will be granted; otherwise, the transaction must *wait* until the existing lock is released.
- A transaction continues to hold a lock until it explicitly releases it, either during execution or when it terminates (aborts or commits). It is only when the exclusive lock has been released that the effects of the write operation will be made visible to other transactions.

Using locks in transactions, as described above, does not guarantee serializability of schedules by themselves, as the following example shows.

Example 14.4 Incorrect locking schedule

Consider the (valid) schedule shown in Figure 14.5 that uses the above locking rules. If prior to execution, $\texttt{bal}_x$ = 100 and $\texttt{bal}_y$ = 400, the result should be $\texttt{bal}_x$ = 220, $\texttt{bal}_y$ = 330 if T_7 executes before T_8, or $\texttt{bal}_x$ = 210 and $\texttt{bal}_y$ = 340 if T_8 executes before T_7. However, the result of executing the schedule gives $\texttt{bal}_x$ = 220 and $\texttt{bal}_y$ = 340 (Schedule is *not* a serializable schedule.)

Two-phase locking (2PL)

A transaction follows the two-phase locking protocol if all locking operations precede the first unlock operation in the transaction.

The problem in this example is that the transactions release the locks they hold as soon as the associated read/write is executed and that lock item (say $\texttt{bal}_x$) no longer needs to be accessed. However, the transaction itself is locking other items ($\texttt{bal}_y$), after it releases its lock on $\texttt{bal}_x$. Although this may seem to allow greater concurrency, it permits transactions to interfere with one another, resulting in the loss of total isolation and atomicity. To guarantee serializability, we must follow an additional protocol concerning the positioning of the lock and unlock operations in every transaction. The best known protocol is **two-phase locking (2PL)**.

Two-phase locking (2PL)

According to the rules of this protocol, every transaction can be divided into two phases: first a *growing phase* in which it acquires all the locks needed but cannot release any locks, and then a *shrinking phase* in which it releases its locks but cannot acquire any new locks. There is no requirement that all locks be obtained simultaneously. Normally, the transaction acquires some locks, does some processing, and goes on to acquire additional locks as needed. However, it never releases any lock until it has reached a stage where no new locks are needed. The rules are:

Time	T_7	T_8	bal_x	bal_y
t_1	write_lock(bal_x)		100	400
t_2	read(bal_x)		"	"
t_3	$bal_x = bal_x + 100$		"	"
t_4	write(bal_x)		200	"
t_5	unlock(bal_x)		"	"
t_6		write_lock(bal_x)	"	"
t_7		read(bal_x)	"	"
t_8		$bal_x = bal_x * 1.1$	"	"
t_9		write(bal_x)	220	"
t_{10}		unlock(bal_x)	"	"
t_{11}		write_lock(bal_y)	"	"
t_{12}		read(bal_y)	"	"
t_{13}		$bal_y = bal_y * 1.1$	"	"
t_{14}		write(bal_y)	"	440
t_{15}		unlock(bal_y)	"	"
t_{16}		commit	"	"
t_{17}	write_lock(bal_y)		"	"
t_{18}	read(bal_y)		"	"
t_{19}	$bal_y = bal_y - 100$		"	"
t_{20}	write(bal_y)		"	340
t_{21}	unlock(bal_y)		"	"
t_{22}	commit		220	340

Figure 14.5 Incorrect locking schedule

- A transaction must acquire a lock on an item before operating on the item. The lock may be shared or exclusive, depending on the type of access needed.
- Once the transaction releases a lock, it can never acquire any new locks.

A further condition that may be imposed with two-phase locking is to leave the release of *all* locks until the end of the transaction. This is called **rigorous 2PL**. It can be shown that with rigorous 2PL, transactions can be serialized in the order in which they commit. Another variant of 2PL, called **strict 2PL**, holds *exclusive locks* only until the end of the transaction. Most database systems implement one of these two variants of 2PL. It can be proved that if *every* transaction in a schedule follows the 2PL protocol, then the schedule is guaranteed to be serializable (Eswaran *et al.*, 1976). We now look at how (rigorous) two-phase locking is used to resolve the three problems identified in Section 14.2.1.

Example 14.5 Preventing the lost update problem using 2PL

A solution to the lost update problem is shown in Figure 14.6. To prevent the lost update problem occurring, T_2 first requests an exclusive lock on bal_x. It can then proceed to read the value of bal_x from the database, increment it by $100, and write the new value back to the database. When T_1 starts, it also requests an exclusive lock on bal_x. However, because the data item bal_x is currently exclusively locked by T_2, the request is not immediately granted and T_1 has to *wait* until the lock is released by T_2. This only occurs once the commit of T_2 has been completed.

Time	T_1	T_2	bal_x
t_1		begin_transaction	100
t_2	begin_transaction	write_lock(bal_x)	100
t_3	write_lock(bal_x)	read(bal_x)	100
t_4	WAIT	$bal_x = bal_x + 100$	100
t_5	WAIT	write(bal_x)	200
t_6	WAIT	commit/unlock(bal_x)	200
t_7	read(bal_x)		200
t_8	$bal_x = bal_x - 10$		200
t_9	write(bal_x)		190
t_{10}	commit/unlock(bal_x)		190

Figure 14.6 Preventing the lost update problem

Example 14.6 Preventing the uncommitted dependency problem using 2PL

A solution to the uncommitted dependency problem is shown in Figure 14.7. To prevent this problem occurring, T_4 first requests an exclusive lock on bal_x. It can then proceed to read the value of bal_x from the database, increment it by $100, and write the new value back to the database. When the rollback is executed, the updates of transaction T_4 are undone and the value of bal_x in the database is returned to its original value of $100. When T_3 starts, it also requests an exclusive lock on bal_x. However, because the data item bal_x is currently exclusively locked by T_4, the request is not immediately granted and T_3 has to wait until the lock is released by T_4. This only occurs once the rollback of T_4 has been completed.

Time	T_3	T_4	bal_x
t_1		begin_transaction	100
t_2		write_lock(bal_x)	100
t_3		read(bal_x)	100
t_4	begin_transaction	$bal_x = bal_x + 100$	100
t_5	write_lock(bal_x)	write(bal_x)	200
t_6	WAIT	rollback/unlock(bal_x)	100
t_7	read(bal_x)		100
t_8	$bal_x = bal_x - 10$		100
t_9	write(bal_x)		90
t_{10}	commit/unlock(bal_x)		90

Figure 14.7 Preventing the uncommitted dependency problem

Example 14.7 Preventing the inconsistent analysis problem using 2PL

A solution to the inconsistent analysis problem is shown in Figure 14.8. To prevent this problem occurring, T_5 must precede its reads by exclusive locks, and T_6 must precede its reads with shared locks. Therefore, when T_5 starts it requests and obtains an exclusive lock on bal_x. Now, when T_6 tries to share lock bal_x the request is not immediately granted and T_6 has to wait until the lock is released, which is when T_5 commits.

Time	T_5	T_6	bal_x	bal_y	bal_z	sum
t_1		begin_transaction	100	50	25	
t_2	begin_transaction	sum = 0	100	50	25	0
t_3	write_lock(bal_x)		100	50	25	0
t_4	read(bal_x)	read_lock(bal_x)	100	50	25	0
t_5	$bal_x = bal_x - 10$	WAIT	100	50	25	0
t_6	write(bal_x)	WAIT	90	50	25	0
t_7	write_lock(bal_z)	WAIT	90	50	25	0
t_8	read(bal_z)	WAIT	90	50	25	0
t_9	$bal_z = bal_z + 10$	WAIT	90	50	25	0
t_{10}	write(bal_z)	WAIT	90	50	35	0
t_{11}	commit/unlock(bal_x, bal_z)	WAIT	90	50	35	0
t_{12}		read(bal_x)	90	50	35	0
t_{13}		sum = sum + bal_x	90	50	35	90
t_{14}		read_lock(bal_y)	90	50	35	90
t_{15}		read(bal_y)	90	50	35	90
t_{16}		sum = sum + bal_y	90	50	35	140
t_{17}		read_lock(bal_z)	90	50	35	140
t_{18}		read(bal_z)	90	50	35	140
t_{19}		sum = sum + bal_z	90	50	35	175
t_{20}		commit/unlock(bal_x, bal_y, bal_z)	90	50	35	175

Figure 14.8 Preventing the inconsistent analysis problem

Deadlock
An impasse that may result when two (or more) transactions are each waiting for locks to be released that are held by the other.

A problem with two-phase locking, which applies to all locking-based schemes, is that it can cause **deadlock**, since transactions can wait for locks on data items. If two transactions wait for locks on items held by the other, deadlock will occur and the deadlock detection and recovery scheme described next is needed.

14.2.4 Deadlock

Figure 14.9 shows two transactions, T_9 and T_{10}, that are deadlocked because each is waiting for the other to release a lock on an item it holds. At time t_2, transaction T_9 requests and obtains an exclusive lock on item bal_x, and at time t_3 transaction T_{10}

Time	T_9	T_{10}
t_1	begin_transaction	
t_2	write_lock(bal_x)	begin_transaction
t_3	read(bal_x)	write_lock(bal_y)
t_4	$bal_x = bal_x - 10$	read(bal_y)
t_5	write(bal_x)	$bal_y = bal_y + 100$
t_6	write_lock(bal_y)	write(bal_y)
t_7	WAIT	write_lock(bal_x)
t_8	WAIT	WAIT
t_9	WAIT	WAIT
t_{10}	⋮	WAIT
t_{11}	⋮	⋮

Figure 14.9 Deadlock between two transactions

obtains an exclusive lock on item bal_y. Then at t_6, T_9 requests an exclusive lock on item bal_y. Since T_{10} holds a lock on bal_y, transaction T_9 waits. Meanwhile, at time t_7, T_{10} requests a lock on item bal_x, which is held by transaction T_9. Neither transaction can continue because each is waiting for a lock it cannot obtain until the other completes. Once deadlock occurs, the applications involved cannot resolve the problem. Instead, the DBMS has to recognize that deadlock exists and break it in some way.

Unfortunately, there is only one way to break deadlock: abort one or more of the transactions. This usually involves undoing all the changes made by the aborted transaction(s). In Figure 14.9, the DBMS may decide to abort transaction T_{10}. Once this is complete, the locks held by transaction T_{10} are released and T_9 is able to continue again. Deadlock should be transparent to the user, so the DBMS should automatically restart the aborted transaction(s).

There are three general techniques for handling deadlock: timeouts, deadlock prevention, and deadlock detection and recovery. With *timeouts*, the transaction that has requested a lock waits for, at most, a specified period of time. Using deadlock prevention, the DBMS looks ahead to determine if a transaction would cause deadlock, and never allows deadlock to occur. Using deadlock detection and recovery, the DBMS allows deadlock to occur but recognizes occurrences of deadlock and breaks it. Since it is more difficult to prevent deadlock than using timeouts or testing for deadlock and breaking it when it occurs, systems generally avoid the deadlock prevention method.

14.2.5 Timestamp methods

Timestamp

A unique identifier created by the DBMS that indicates the relative starting time of a transaction.

The use of locks, combined with the two-phase locking protocol, guarantees serializability of transactions. The order of transactions in the equivalent serial schedule is based on the order in which the transactions lock the items they require. If a transaction needs an item that is already locked, it may be forced to wait until the item is released. A different approach that also guarantees serializability uses transaction **timestamps** to order transaction execution for an equivalent serial schedule.

Timestamp methods for concurrency control are quite different from locking methods. No locks are involved, and therefore there can be no deadlock. Locking methods generally prevent conflicts by making transactions wait. With timestamp methods, there is no waiting; transactions involved in conflict are simply rolled back and restarted.

Timestamps can be generated by simply using the system clock at the time the transaction started, or, more normally, by incrementing a logical counter every time a new transaction starts.

Timestamping

A concurrency control protocol that orders transactions in such a way that older transactions, transactions with *smaller* timestamps, get priority in the event of conflict.

With **timestamping**, if a transaction attempts to read or write a data item, then the read or write is only allowed to proceed if the *last update on that data item* was carried out by an older transaction. Otherwise, the transaction requesting the read/write is restarted and given a new timestamp. New timestamps must be assigned to restarted transactions to prevent them from being continually aborted and restarted. Without new timestamps, a transaction with an old timestamp might not be able to commit due to younger transactions having already committed.

14.2.6 Optimistic methods

In some environments, conflicts between transactions are rare, and the additional processing required by locking or timestamping protocols is unnecessary for many of the transactions. Optimistic techniques are based on the assumption that conflict is rare and that it is more efficient to allow transactions to proceed without imposing delays to ensure serializability (Kung and Robinson, 1981). When a transaction wishes to commit, a check is performed to determine whether conflict has occurred. If there has been a conflict, the transaction must be rolled back and restarted. Since the premise is that conflict occurs very infrequently, rollback will be rare. The overhead involved in restarting a transaction may be considerable, since it effectively means redoing the entire transaction. This could be tolerated only if it happened very infrequently, in which case the majority of transactions will be processed without being subjected to any delays. These techniques potentially allow greater concurrency than traditional protocols since no locking is required.

There are two or three phases to an optimistic concurrency control protocol, depending on whether it is a read-only or an update transaction:

- *Read phase*. This extends from the start of the transaction until immediately before the commit. The transaction reads the values of all data items it needs from the database and stores them in local variables. Updates are applied to a local copy of the data, not to the database itself.
- *Validation phase*. This follows the read phase. Checks are performed to ensure that serializability is not violated if the transaction updates are applied to the database. For a read-only transaction, this consists of checking that the data values read are still the current values for the corresponding data items. If no interference occurred, the transaction is committed. If interference occurred, the transaction is aborted and restarted. For a transaction that has updates, validation consists of determining whether the current transaction leaves the database in a consistent state, with serializability maintained. If not, the transaction is aborted and restarted.

- *Write phase.* This follows the successful validation phase for update transactions. During this phase, the updates made to the local copy are applied to the database.

14.3 Database recovery

Database recovery

The process of restoring the database to a correct state in the event of a failure.

At the start of this chapter, we introduced the concept of **database recovery** as a service that should be provided by the DBMS to ensure that the database is reliable and remains in a consistent state in the presence of failures. In this context, reliability refers to both the resilience of the DBMS to various types of failure and its capability to recover from them. In this section, we consider how this service can be provided. To gain a better understanding of the potential problems we may encounter in providing a reliable system, we start by examining the need for recovery and the types of failure that can occur in a database environment.

14.3.1 The need for recovery

The storage of data generally includes four different types of media with an increasing degree of reliability: main memory, magnetic disk, magnetic tape, and optical disk. Main memory is *volatile* storage that usually does not survive system crashes. Magnetic disks provide *online non-volatile* storage. Compared with main memory, disks are more reliable and much cheaper, but slower by three to four orders of magnitude. Magnetic tape is an *offline non-volatile* storage medium, which is far more reliable than disk and fairly inexpensive, but slower, providing only sequential access. Optical disk is more reliable than tape, generally cheaper, faster, and providing random access. Main memory is also referred to as *primary storage* and disks and tape as *secondary storage*. *Stable storage* represents data that has been replicated in several non-volatile storage media (usually disk) with independent failure modes. For example, it may be possible to simulate stable storage using RAID technology, which guarantees that the failure of a single disk, even during data transfer, does not result in loss of data (see Section 12.2.2).

There are many different types of failure that can affect database processing, each of which has to be dealt with in a different manner. Some failures affect main memory only, while others involve non-volatile (secondary) storage. Among the causes of failure are:

- **system crashes** – due to hardware or software errors, resulting in loss of main memory;
- **media failures** – such as head crashes or unreadable media, resulting in the loss of parts of secondary storage;
- **application software errors** – such as logical errors in the program that is accessing the database, which cause one or more transactions to fail;
- **natural physical disasters** – such as fires, floods, earthquakes, or power failures;
- **carelessness** – or unintentional destruction of data or facilities by operators or users;

- **sabotage** – or intentional corruption or destruction of data, hardware, or software facilities.

Whatever the cause of the failure, there are two principal effects that we need to consider: the loss of main memory, including the **database buffers** (an area of memory that the DBMS uses to read in data from disk and write data to disk), and the loss of the disk copy of the database. In the remainder of this chapter we discuss the concepts and techniques that can minimize these effects and allow recovery from failure.

14.3.2 Transactions and recovery

Transactions represent the basic *unit of recovery* in a database system. It is the role of the *recovery manager* to guarantee two of the four *ACID* properties of transactions, namely **atomicity** and **durability**, in the presence of failures. The recovery manager has to ensure that, on recovery from failure, either all the effects of a given transaction are permanently recorded in the database or none of them are. The situation is complicated by the fact that database writing is not an atomic (single step) action, and it is therefore possible for a transaction to have committed but for its effects not to have been permanently recorded in the database, simply because they have not yet reached the database.

Consider again the first example of this chapter, in which the balance of a member's account is being increased by $10, as shown at a high level in Figure 14.1(a). To implement the read operation, the DBMS carries out the following steps:

- find the address of the disk block that contains the appropriate record;
- transfer the disk block into a database buffer in main memory;
- copy the bal_x data from the database buffer into a local variable.

For the write operation, the DBMS carries out the following steps:

- find the address of the disk block that contains the appropriate record;
- transfer the disk block into a database buffer in main memory;
- copy the bal_x data from the local variable into the database buffer;
- write the database buffer back to disk.

The database buffers occupy an area in main memory where data is transferred to and from secondary storage. It is only once the buffers have been *flushed* to secondary storage that any update operations can be regarded as permanent. This flushing of the buffers to the database can be triggered by a specific command (for example, transaction commit) or automatically when the buffers become full. The explicit writing of the buffers to secondary storage is known as *force-writing*.

If a failure occurs between writing to the buffers and flushing the buffers to secondary storage, the recovery manager must determine the status of the transaction that performed the write at the time of failure. If the transaction had issued its commit, then to ensure durability the recovery manager would have to *redo* that transaction's updates to the database (also known as *rollforward*).

On the other hand, if the transaction had not committed at the time of failure, then the recovery manager would have to *undo* (*rollback*) any effects of that transaction on the database to guarantee transaction atomicity. If only one transaction has to be undone, this is referred to as *partial undo*. A partial undo can be triggered when a transaction is rolled back and restarted as a result of the concurrency control protocol, as described in the previous section. A transaction can also be aborted unilaterally, for example, by the user or by an exception condition in the application program. When all active transactions have to be undone, this is referred to as *global undo*.

Example 14.8 Use of UNDO/REDO

Figure 14.10 illustrates a number of concurrently executing transactions $T_1, \ldots, T_6$. The DBMS starts at time t_0, but fails at time t_f. We assume that the data for transactions T_2 and T_3 have been written to secondary storage before the failure.

Clearly, T_1 and T_6 had not committed at the point of the crash; therefore, at restart, the recovery manager must *undo* transactions T_1 and T_6. However, it is not clear to what extent the changes made by the other (committed) transactions T_4 and T_5 have been propagated to the database on non-volatile storage. The reason for this uncertainty is the fact that the volatile database buffers may or may not have been written to disk. In the absence of any other information, the recovery manager would be forced to *redo* transactions T_2, T_3, T_4, and T_5.

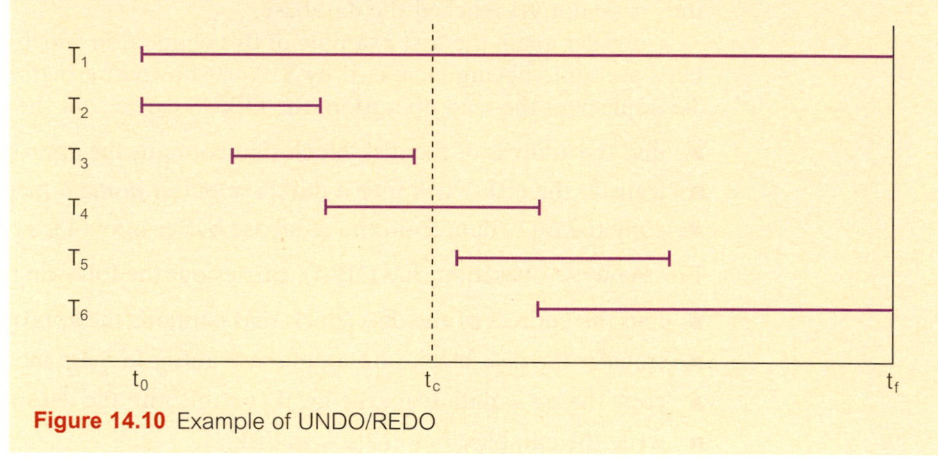

Figure 14.10 Example of UNDO/REDO

14.3.3 Recovery facilities

A DBMS should provide the following facilities to assist with recovery:

- a **backup mechanism** – makes periodic backup copies of the database;
- **logging facilities** – keep track of the current state of transactions and database changes;
- a **checkpoint facility** – enables updates to the database that are in progress to be made permanent;
- a **recovery manager** – allows the system to restore the database to a consistent state following a failure.

Backup mechanism

The DBMS should provide a mechanism to allow backup copies of the database and the *log file* (discussed next) to be made at regular intervals without necessarily having to first stop the system. The backup copy of the database can be used in the event that the database has been damaged or destroyed. A backup can be a complete copy of the entire database or an incremental backup, consisting only of modifications made since the last complete or incremental backup. Typically, the backup is stored on offline storage, such as optical disk.

Log file

To keep track of database transactions, the DBMS maintains a special file called a **log** (or **journal**) that contains information about all updates to the database. The log may contain the following data:

- **Transaction records** containing:
  - transaction identifier;
  - type of log record (transaction start, insert, update, delete, abort, commit);
  - identifier of data item affected by the database action (insert, delete, and update operations);
  - *before-image* of the data item: that is, its value before change (update and delete operations only);
  - *after-image* of the data item: that is, its value after change (insert and update operations only);
  - log management information, such as a pointer to previous and next log records for that transaction (all operations).
- **Checkpoint records**, which we describe shortly.

The log is often used for purposes other than recovery (for example, for performance monitoring and auditing). In this case, additional information may be recorded in the log file (for example database reads, user logons, logoffs, and so on), but these are not relevant to recovery and therefore are omitted from this discussion. Table 14.1 illustrates a segment of a log file, which shows three concurrently executing transactions T1, T2, and T3. The columns pPtr and nPtr represent pointers to the previous and next log records for each transaction.

Due to the importance of the transaction log file in the recovery process, the log may be duplexed or triplexed (that is, two or three separate copies are maintained) so that if one copy is damaged, another can be used. In the past, log files were stored on magnetic tape because tape was more reliable and cheaper than magnetic disk. However, nowadays DBMSs are expected to be able to recover quickly from minor failures. This requires that the log file be stored online on a fast direct-access storage device.

In some environments where a vast amount of logging information is generated every day (a daily logging rate of 10^4 megabytes is not uncommon), it is not possible to hold *all* this data online all the time. The log file is needed online for quick recovery following minor failures (for example, rollback of a transaction following deadlock).

Table 14.1 A segment of a log file

Tid	Time	Operation	Object	Before image	After image	pPtr	nPtr
T1	10.22	START				0	2
T1	10.23	UPDATE	STAFF S1500	(old value)	(new value)	1	8
T2	10.24	START				0	4
T2	10.26	INSERT	STAFF S0003		(new value)	3	5
T2	10.27	DELETE	STAFF S3250	(old value)		4	6
T2	10.27	UPDATE	MEMBER M250178	(old value)	(new value)	5	9
T3	10.28	START				0	11
T1	10.28	COMMIT				2	0
	10.29	CHECKPOINT	T2, T3				
T2	10.29	COMMIT				6	0
T3	10.30	INSERT	MEMBER M166884		(new value)	7	12
T3	10.31	COMMIT				11	0

Major failures, such as disk head crashes, obviously take longer to recover from and may require access to a large part of the log. In these cases, it would be acceptable to wait for parts of the log file to be brought back online from offline storage. It should be noted that the log file is a potential bottleneck, and the speed of the writes to the log file can be critical in determining the overall performance of the database system.

Checkpointing

The information in the log file is used to recover from a database failure. One difficulty with this scheme is that when a failure occurs, the DBMS does not know how far back in the log to search and may end up redoing transactions that have been safely written to the database. To limit the amount of searching and subsequent processing that needs to be carried out on the log file, the DBMS can use a technique called *checkpointing*.

Checkpoint

The point of synchronization between the database and the transaction log file. All buffers are force-written to secondary storage.

Checkpoints are scheduled at predetermined intervals and involve the following operations:

- writing all log records in main memory to secondary storage;
- writing the modified blocks in the database buffers to secondary storage;
- writing a checkpoint record to the log file. This record contains the identifiers of all transactions that are active at the time of the checkpoint.

If transactions are performed serially, when a failure occurs the DBMS checks the log file to find the last transaction that started before the last checkpoint. Any earlier transactions would have committed previously and would have been written to the database at the checkpoint. Therefore, the DBMS need only redo the ones that were active at the checkpoint and any subsequent transactions for which both start and commit records appear in the log. If a transaction is active at the time of failure then the transaction must be undone. If transactions are performed concurrently then the DBMS should redo all transactions that have committed since the checkpoint and undo all transactions that were active at the time of the crash.

Example 14.9 Use of UNDO/REDO with checkpointing

Returning to Example 14.8, if we now assume that a checkpoint occurred at point t_c, then the DBMS would know that the changes made by transactions T_2 and T_3 had been written to secondary storage. In this case, the recovery manager would be able to omit the redo for these two transactions. However, the recovery manager would have to redo transactions T_4 and T_5, which have committed since the checkpoint, and undo transactions T_1 and T_6, which were active at the time of the crash.

Generally, checkpointing is a relatively inexpensive operation, and it is often possible to take three or four checkpoints an hour. In this way, no more than 15–20 minutes of work will need to be recovered.

14.3.4 Recovery techniques

The particular recovery procedure to be used is dependent on the extent of the damage that has occurred to the database. We consider two cases:

- If the database has been extensively damaged, for example a disk head crash has occurred and destroyed the database, then it is necessary to restore the last backup copy of the database and reapply the update operations of committed transactions using the log file. This assumes, of course, that the log file has not been damaged as well. In Step 8 of the physical database design methodology presented in Chapter 11, it was recommended that, where possible, the log file is stored on a disk separate from the main database files. This reduces the risk of both the database files and the log file being damaged at the same time.
- If the database has not been physically damaged but has become inconsistent, for example the system crashed while transactions were executing, then it is necessary to undo the changes that caused the inconsistency. It may also be necessary to redo some transactions to ensure that the updates they performed have reached secondary storage. Here, we do not need to use the backup copy of the database, but can restore the database to a consistent state using the *before-* and *after-images* held in the log file.

We now look at one technique, called *immediate update*, for recovery from the latter situation: that is, the case where the database has not been destroyed but is in an inconsistent state.

Recovery techniques using immediate update

Using the *immediate update* recovery protocol, updates are applied to the database as they occur. The DBMS uses the log file to protect against system failures in the following way:

- When a transaction starts, write a *transaction start* record to the log.
- When a write operation is performed, write a record containing the necessary data to the log file.
- Once the log record is written, write the update to the database buffers.
- The updates to the database itself are written when the buffers are next flushed to secondary storage.
- When the transaction commits, write a *transaction commit* record to the log.

It is essential that log records (or at least certain parts of them) are written *before* the corresponding write to the database. This is known as the **write-ahead log protocol**. If updates were made to the database first, and failure occurred before the log record was written, then the recovery manager would have no way of undoing (or redoing) the operation. Under the write-ahead log protocol, the recovery manager can safely assume that if there is no *transaction commit* record in the log file for a particular transaction, then that transaction was still active at the time of failure, and must therefore be undone.

If a transaction aborts, the log can be used to undo it since it contains all the old values for the updated fields. As a transaction may have performed several changes to an item, the writes are undone *in reverse order*. Regardless of whether the transaction's writes have been applied to the database itself, writing the before-images guarantees that the database is restored to its state prior to the start of the transaction.

If the system fails, recovery involves using the log to undo or redo transactions:

- For any transaction for which both a *transaction start* and *transaction commit* record appear in the log, we redo using the log records to write the after-image of updated fields, as described above. Note that if the new values have already been written to the database, these writes, though unnecessary, will have no effect. However, any write that did not actually reach the database will now be performed.
- For any transaction for which the log contains a *transaction start* record but not a *transaction commit* record, we need to undo that transaction. This time the log records are used to write the before-image of the affected fields, and thus restore the database to its state prior to the transaction's start. The undo operations are performed *in the reverse order in which they were written to the log*.

For an extended discussion of concurrency and recovery, the interested reader is referred to Connolly and Begg (2005).

Chapter summary

- **Concurrency control** is the process of managing simultaneous operations on the database without having them interfere with one another. **Database recovery** is the process of restoring the database to a correct state after a failure. Both protect the database from inconsistencies and data loss.
- A **transaction** is an action, or series of actions, carried out by a single user or database application, which accesses or changes the contents of the database. A transaction is a logical *unit of work* that takes the database from one consistent state to another. Transactions can terminate successfully (**commit**) or unsuccessfully (**abort**). Aborted transactions must be **undone** or rolled back. The transaction is also the *unit of concurrency* and the *unit of recovery*.
- A transaction should possess the four basic, or so-called **ACID**, properties: atomicity, consistency, isolation, and durability. Atomicity and durability are the responsibility of the recovery subsystem; isolation and, to some extent, consistency are the responsibility of the concurrency control subsystem.
- Concurrency control is needed when multiple users are allowed to access the database simultaneously. Without it, problems of *lost update*, *uncommitted dependency*, and *inconsistent analysis* can arise. Serial execution means executing one transaction at a time, with no interleaving of operations. A set of transactions are **serializable** if it produces the same results as some serial sequence of these transactions.
- Two methods that guarantee serializability are **two phase-locking (2PL)** and **timestamping**. Locks may be shared (read) or exclusive (write). In **two-phase locking**, a transaction acquires all its locks before releasing any. With **timestamping**, transactions are ordered in such a way that older transactions get priority in the event of conflict.
- **Deadlock** occurs when two or more transactions are waiting to access data that the other transaction has locked. The only way to break deadlock once it has occurred is to abort one or more of the transactions.
- Some causes of failure are system crashes, media failures, application software errors, carelessness, natural physical disasters, and sabotage. These failures can result in the loss of main memory and/or the disk copy of the database. Recovery techniques minimize these effects.
- To facilitate recovery, one method is for the system to maintain a **log file** containing transaction records that identify the start/end of transactions and the before- and after-images of the write operations. Using **immediate updates**, an update may be made to the database itself any time after a log record is written. The log can be used to undo and redo transactions in the event of failure.
- **Checkpoints** are used to improve database recovery. At a checkpoint, all modified buffer blocks, all log records, and a checkpoint record identifying all active transactions are written to disk. If a failure occurs, the checkpoint record identifies which transactions need to be redone.

Review questions

14.1 Explain what is meant by a transaction.

14.2 Why are transactions important units of operation in a DBMS?

14.3 Give examples of simple transactions (that consist of a single database operation) and complex transactions (that consist of two or more database operations).

14.4 The consistency and reliability aspects of transactions are due to the 'ACIDity' properties of transactions. Discuss each of these properties and how they relate to the concurrency control and recovery mechanisms. Give examples to illustrate your answer.

14.5 Describe, with examples, the types of problem that can occur in a multi-user environment when concurrent access to the database is allowed.

14.6 Give full details of a mechanism for concurrency control that can be used to ensure the types of problem discussed in Question 14.5 cannot occur. Show how the mechanism prevents the problems illustrated from occurring.

14.7 Discuss how the concurrency control mechanism interacts with the transaction mechanism.

14.8 Discuss the types of problem that can occur with locking-based mechanisms for concurrency control and the actions that can be taken by a DBMS to prevent them.

14.9 What is a timestamp?

14.10 How do timestamp-based protocols for concurrency control differ from lock-based protocols?

14.11 Discuss the difference between pessimistic and optimistic concurrency control.

14.12 Discuss the types of failure that may occur in a database environment.

14.13 Explain why it is important for a multi-user DBMS to provide a recovery mechanism.

14.14 Discuss how the log file is a fundamental feature in any recovery mechanism.

14.15 Explain what is meant by undo and redo and describe how the log file is used in recovery.

14.16 What is the significance of the write-ahead log protocol?

14.17 How do checkpoints affect the recovery protocol?

14.18 Describe the immediate update recovery protocol.

Exercises

14.19 Analyze the DBMSs that you are currently using. What concurrency control protocol does each DBMS use? What type of recovery mechanism is used?

14.20 State whether the following schedules are serial or nonserial:

(a) read(T_1, bal_x), read(T_2, bal_x), write(T_1, bal_x), write(T_2, bal_x), commit(T_1), commit(T_2)
(b) read(T_1, bal_x), read(T_1, bal_y), write(T_1, bal_x), read(T_2, bal_y), read(T_2, bal_x), commit(T_1), commit(T_2)
(c) read(T_1, bal_x), write(T_2, bal_x), write(T_2, bal_x), abort(T_2), commit(T_1)
(d) write(T_1, bal_x), read(T_2, bal_x), write(T_1, bal_x), commit(T_2), abort(T_1)
(e) read(T_1, bal_x), write(T_2, bal_x), write(T_1, bal_x), read(T_3, bal_x), commit(T_1), commit(T_2), commit(T_3)

14.21 Determine if the following schedule is serializable:

S = [read(T_1, Z), read(T_2, Y), write(T_2, Y), read(T_3, Y), read(T_1, X), write(T_1, X), write(T_1, Z), write(T_3, Y), read(T_2, X), read(T_1, Y), write(T_1, Y), write(T_2, X), read(T_3, W), write(T_3, W)]

where read(T_i, w)/write(T_i, w) indicates a read/write by transaction T_i on data item w.

14.22 Would it be sensible to produce a concurrency control algorithm based on serializability? Give justification for your answer. How is serializability used in standard concurrency control algorithms?

14.23 Show how the problems of *lost update*, *uncommitted dependency*, and *inconsistent analysis* can be overcome using timestamping.

Additional exercises

14.24 Draw a Venn diagram showing the relationships between strict 2PL, rigorous 2PL, and timestamping. Extend the diagram to include optimistic concurrency control.

14.25 Discuss how you would test for deadlock. What issues need to be considered when you are deciding how to break deadlock?

14.26 Using your method, decide whether the following transactions are in deadlock:

Transaction	Data items locked by transaction	Data items transaction is waiting for
T_1	x_2	x_1, x_3
T_2	x_3, x_{10}	x_7, x_8
T_3	x_8	x_4, x_5
T_4	x_7	x_1
T_5	x_1, x_5	x_3
T_6	x_4, x_9	x_6
T_7	x_6	x_5

14.27 Consider Figure 14.12, which shows a set of concurrently executing transactions. If t_c is the time of a checkpoint and t_f is the time of failure, explain which transactions have to be redone and/or undone.

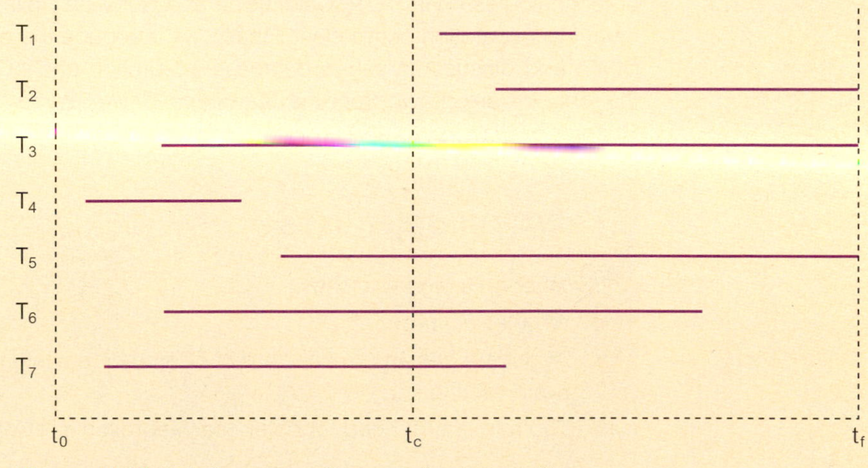

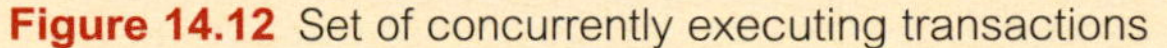

Figure 14.12 Set of concurrently executing transactions

CHAPTER

15 eCommerce and database systems

Preview

It's been 20 years since the conception of the Internet yet, in this relatively short time, it has had a profound effect on many aspects of society, including business, government, broadcasting, shopping, leisure, communication, and education and training. Its growth in the past few years has been near exponential and it has started an information revolution that will continue for many years to come. According to Internet World Stats (internetworldstats.com), as of December 2007 over 1.3 billion people were using the Internet representing approximately one-fifth of the world's population. Buying goods and services over the Internet is becoming commonplace and most organizations have recognized the potential of the Internet to market and sell to a global market. This has given rise to the term 'electronic commerce' or eCommerce for short.

Database systems play a crucial role in eCommerce systems by supporting functions such as catalog search and browsing, order management, payment systems, inventory management systems, online marketing, and customer relationship management (CRM). In this chapter we present a general architecture for an eCommerce system focusing specifically on the data management aspects. A common component of virtually all eCommerce systems is the integration layer that is situated between the DBMS and the Web server that delivers content to the end user's browser. We briefly explore a number of technologies (PHP, ASP, ColdFusion and Ruby on Rails) that can be used to implement this integration component. Finally, we introduce the eXtensible Markup Language (XML) and discuss its use in database integration and eCommerce. The examples in this chapter are drawn from the *StayHome Online Rentals* case study documented in Chapter 5.

Learning objectives

In this chapter you will learn:

- What eCommerce is.
- About the general architecture of eCommerce systems and where database systems fit in.
- The role of and need for database integration in eCommerce systems.

- About data management issues encountered in interorganizational systems.
- About a general architecture for Web–database integration.
- About some technologies for integrating the Web and databases.
- What the eXtensible Markup Language (XML) is and how it can be used in eCommerce systems integration.

15.1 eCommerce

Electronic commerce (eCommerce)

The distribution, buying, selling, and marketing of physical and information goods and services accomplished using computer networks such as the Internet.

Business activities within the scope of **eCommerce** are typically categorized according to the individuals or organizations participating in the transaction. For example, for most people the term 'electronic commerce' is most often associated with online shopping carried out by a consumer. This type of interaction would be considered '**business to consumer**' or '**B2C**' for short. Transactions between businesses are considered 'B2B' and transactions directly between consumers (individuals), such as participating in an online auction, is considered **consumer to consumer** or **(C2C)** or more recently **peer to peer (P2P)**. Governments have also entered this chain lending a 'G' component to the various combinations mentioned: **government to business (G2B)** and **government to consumer (G2C)**. In marketing terminology, eCommerce provides alternative *channels* by which individuals and organizations can advertise their goods and services, locate prospective counterparties, and complete a business transaction. The various styles of eCommerce are depicted in Figure 15.1.

A number of statistics are available to gauge the size of eCommerce markets. For example, according to (Burns 2006), online consumer spending (B2C travel and all other B2C online retail) grew from US$117.2 billion in 2004 to US$143.2 billion in 2005 worldwide. Projections from Forrester Research and eMarketer indicate this market segment will grow to US$316 billion by 2010. Forrester also reports the B2B market segment, which includes **Electronic Data Interchange (EDI)** grew from US$2.8 trillion in 2004 to US$4.1 trillion in 2005 and are projecting growth to US$6.8 trillion by 2007.

Electronic Data Interchange

The computer-to-computer transfer of business documents over a network using a standard format.

eCommerce systems are also considered to be a type of interorganizational information system as they link IT resources between organizations, typically by using network services on the Internet. For example, a student looking to purchase a textbook online is using the IT resources of the online book retailer by connecting to the retailer's web site from their desktop PC (B2C) as shown in Figure 15.2. An automobile manufacturer may send orders for parts from their purchase order management database system to a supplier's customer order database system by way of EDI over the Internet (B2B). Supply chain management systems, that link raw materials and parts suppliers to manufacturing and distribution organizations, rely heavily on B2B eCommerce technologies to link raw materials suppliers to processors and others in the value-added 'chain' of organizations leading up to the complete product's manufacturer. An example of an industry leading B2B infrastructure provider is shown in Figure 15.3.

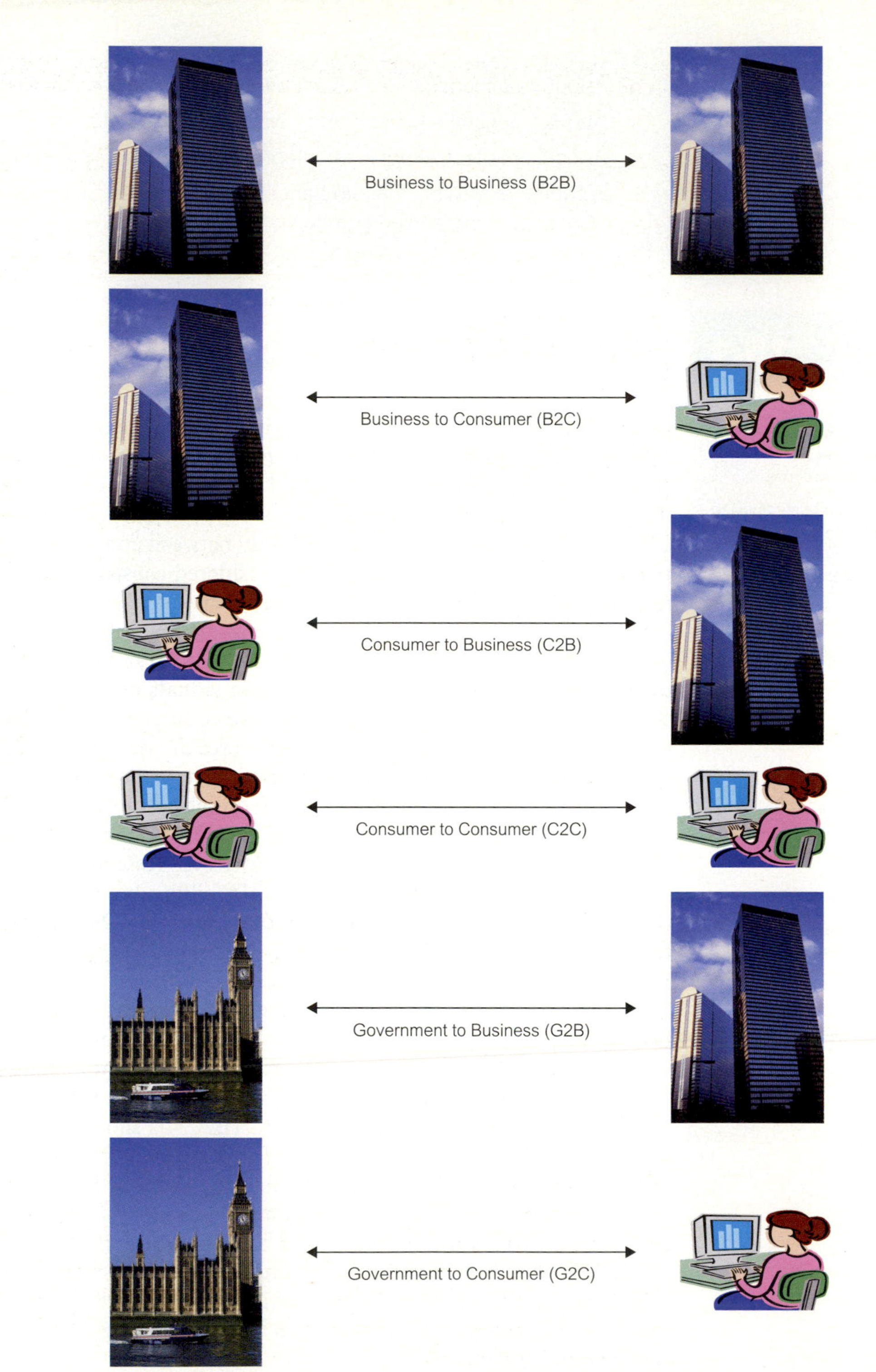

Figure 15.1 eCommerce styles

Figure 15.2 A B2C eCommerce site
Source: Bames & Noble, Inc.

15.1.1 A general architecture for eCommerce systems

A general architecture for an eCommerce system is presented in Figure 15.6. In this example, a large organization (indicated by the colored box) maintains systems for accounting (e.g. accounts payable and accounts receivable), inventory management, order management, and others such as human resources, payroll, and so on. Each system contains applications and a DBMS/database, and potentially each system may be provided by a different vendor. Such systems may be tightly integrated where a suite of applications shares the same database schema. Examples of tightly integrated systems include SAP and the Oracle Application Suite. Alternatively, systems may be loosely coupled, perhaps installed at different points in time. In this case data may be copied from one system to another. These systems are used directly by users internal to the organization. For example, a customer may telephone to

Figure 15.3 B2B Example
Source: Covisint Compuwave Corporation.

inquire about pricing and availability of various products or services, and then place an order. In this case an employee will use the various information systems to satisfy the customer's requests and to place the order in the order management system.

The next logical step is to allow customers to browse products and services and to place orders via a web site as demonstrated in the *StayHome Online Rentals* example introduced in Chapter 1 and demonstrated in Chapter 5. This requires the business to establish a Web server system, an eCommerce system, and an online payment system, such that:

- The Web server interacts with the web browsers of the external users.
- The eCommerce system includes features to support customer user registration, catalog searching and browsing, product comparison, shopping cart, e-mail list sign-up, and other typical eCommerce functionality.

Figure 15.4 Firstgov.gov is a portal for US government agencies – a G2C example
Source: Firstgov.gov.

- The online payment system acts as a gateway that sends out credit verification requests (for example, for a credit or debit card transaction). The payment system could be hosted with the company or outsourced to a third party.

> **Micropayment systems**
>
> Systems that support the transfer of small payment amounts (generally less than US$1.00) with low per transaction costs between parties.

In B2C situations, the products or services being sold may have a small unit value (such as songs, images, articles, or cell phone ringtones). Given that processing a credit card transaction costs about $0.25, purchasing a $0.50 article would not be commercially sensible. In P2P cases, a participant's low volume of transactions would preclude setting up a credit card processing system altogether (for example, consider a seller who wants to auction off an antique on eBay). **Micropayment systems** such as PayPal (www.paypal.com) and Chockstone (www.chockstone.com) have been developed to address these situations.

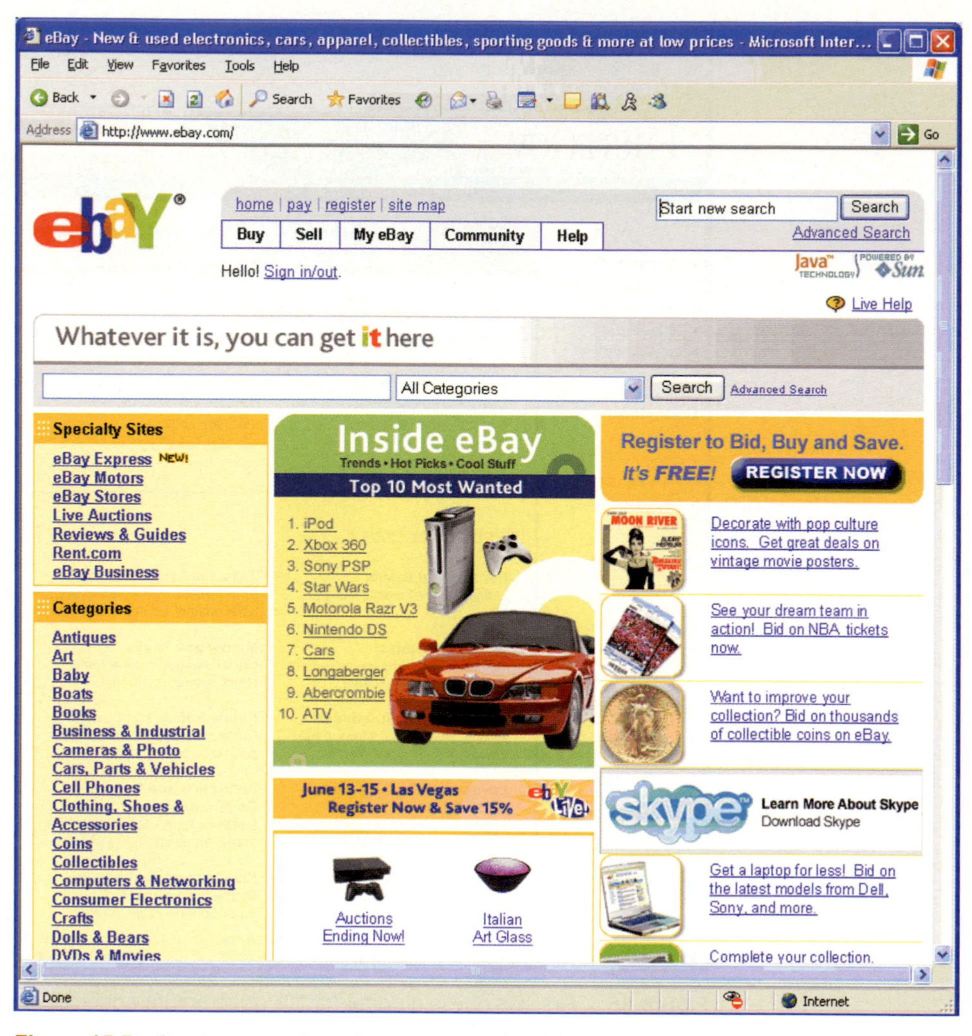

Figure 15.5 eBay is an auction site – an example of C2C marketplace.
Source: eBay, Inc.

Recommender systems

Software that attempts to predict what a user would like based on prior knowledge of the user's profile, or browsing or purchasing activity.

Supply chain

The flow of raw materials and components from and between suppliers that terminates at a manufacturer.

Software that supports user customization of the site can also be added. Business intelligence (BI) techniques, such as **Recommender systems**, might be employed to keep track of DVDs browsed and purchased by each customer, and then to recommend additional purchases based on associations with genre or actor. For example, *StayHome* could use BI software to track whether a user does frequent searches for their favorite movie actor and/or has rented a series of movies starring that actor. Then *StayHome* could recommend other movies starring that actor or movies in genres similar to those the favorite actor has starred in.

A further step the business could take would be to partially integrate their internal systems with those of other businesses such as key suppliers to form a **supply chain.** A B2B gateway would be employed to link a supplier's order management system, accounts receivables, and shipping systems with the businesses' purchasing,

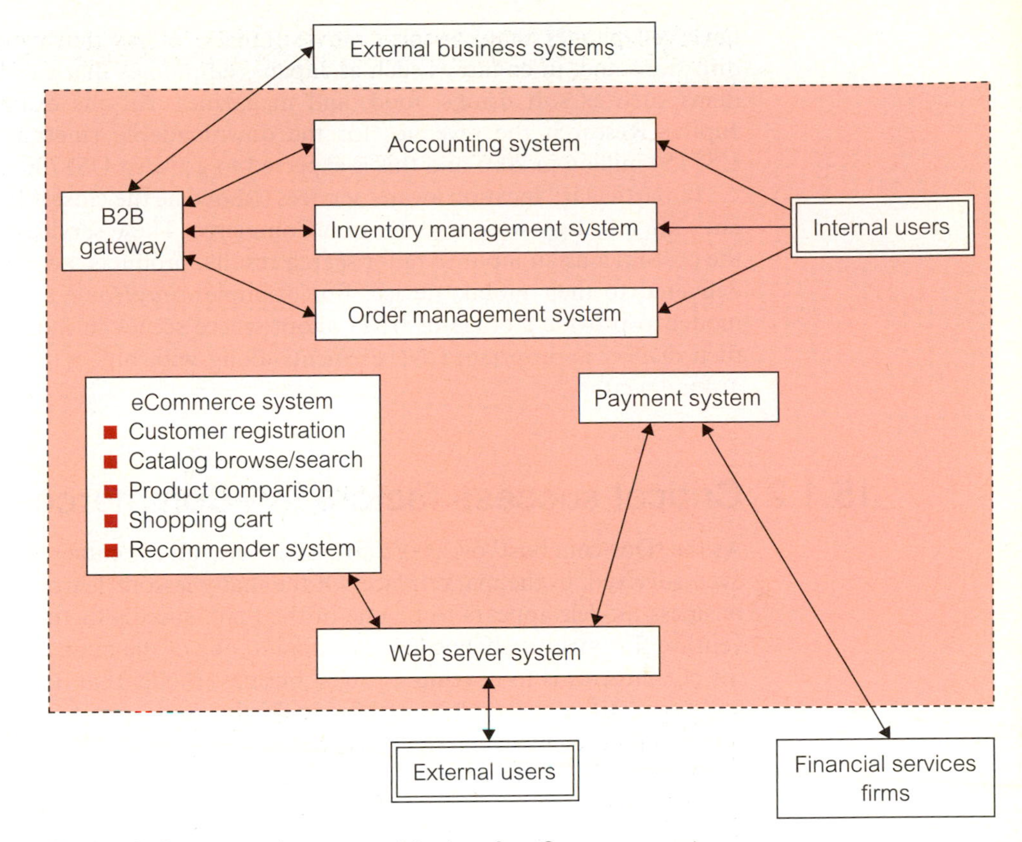

Figure 15.6 A general system architecture for eCommerce systems

accounts payable, and receiving systems. Supply chain management systems can then be used to more accurately schedule orders and deliveries of raw materials and components required for production of the final product. For example, if the order processing system at *StayHome* reports a surge in orders for a particular DVD, an order for more copies can automatically be sent to the supplier for delivery to the appropriate distribution centers.

Another variation of the eCommerce business would be to allow customers to interact directly in a P2P fashion. For example, *StayHome* might offer a service on its web site that allows their customers to auction off copies of DVDs they own but wish to sell. In this example, *StayHome* would provide database and Web server support for customers to post their DVD titles and asking prices. An auction system would then need to be provided to allow bidders to post prices, and finally a payment system that can operate between individuals would need to be provided.

mCommerce

Accessing eCommerce products and services using mobile devices.

A final variation of the eCommerce business would be to include services enabled and/or delivered to the customer's mobile device such as a cell phone, personal digital assistant (PDA), smartphone, or digital music player. Such **mobile commerce (mCommerce)** systems take advantage of faster and more robust wireless data networks to deliver services directly to the mobile device. For example, today we have cell phones that can play movie trailers, PDAs that can access maps and directions and, in countries such as Japan, cell phones that can be used to pay for items such as soft drinks, food, and magazines. As one example, according to Jupiter Research the revenues for the downloadable ringtones market reached US$450 million in 2005 and this is expected to grow to US$700 million by 2009.

In particular, 'location aware' services ('show me the closest Indian food restaurant') are a fast-growing segment of mCommerce. These services use the location of the customer as an input to tailor search results, products, advertising, and services delivered to their mobile device. For example, *StayHome* could expand its data model to provide storage of trivia about where scenes in movies were filmed and then display appropriate advertisements along with bits of trivia as a user roams around a city.

15.1.2 Critical success factors in eCommerce

As the 'Dot-com bust' of 2000/2001 proved, not all eCommerce ventures thrived, or even survived, in the marketplace. Of the many lessons learned, developing robust business models appears to be one of the main success factors in any eCommerce venture. From a purely business standpoint, one of the main critical success factors for eCommerce is to develop a robust business model that addresses market needs and competitive risks, while remaining flexible and open to change as technology and competition evolve in the marketplace.

As shown in the general architecture described above, eCommerce systems can be quite complex and need to support the interconnection of many different systems. As discussed in Chapters 12 and 13, the reliability and security of these systems is critical in order for the business to operate effectively and efficiently, and to engender the trust of customers. With competitors 'just a click away', having robust and secure systems is a critical success factor.

In the early days of eCommerce, a large number of payment systems were introduced and eventually most failed for various reasons, such as a failure to gain the trust of users and merchants leading to a lack of adoption. To date, no universally accepted micropayment system has survived, with the possible exception of PayPal. With credit card payments making up the majority of online purchases today, it is expected that this stage of the customer purchasing experience must also be supported by secure and reliable systems.

Business intelligence systems (discussed in Chapter 18) can provide the business with robust information about customers. Customer Relationship Management (CRM) systems, for example, specialize in documenting and aligning all of the customer's experiences with the business in a way that can support effective customer service. A CRM system might document when a customer made their purchases, when they checked shipping to see when the items would be delivered, when they sent requests for technical support, when they returned items to the store, and so on. Given such a history, it then becomes possible to identify patterns in customer behavior and to align service offerings in an appropriate fashion. eCommerce businesses that can harness these technologies and use them to their advantage stand a much better chance of attracting and retaining customers.

While CRM systems support the customer side of B2C, supply chain management systems support the business side of B2B. Again, leveraging information technology to effectively manage and streamline the flow of materials can give businesses a competitive advantage.

15.2 Web–database integration

A major task common to all eCommerce systems centers on the integration of the organization's web site with its internal database system(s). This requirement can be illustrated by examining the different languages 'spoken' by the respective components of such an integrated system. Web access to databases follows the three-tier architecture introduced in Chapter 1 and shown in Figure 1.8. As can be seen in Figure 15.7, a browser such as Microsoft Internet Explorer or Mozilla Firefox, makes its requests to a Web server, such as Apache or Microsoft Internet Information Server (IIS) using a protocol (language) called **HyperText Transfer Protocol (HTTP)**. For example, if a user clicks on a link to display an item from a catalog, the HTTP request might look something like:

```
GET /home/listings/catalog/Lord_of_the_Rings_III.html
```

When the Web server receives this request, it will look in the folder `/home/listings/catalog` for a file named `Lord_of_the_Rings_III.html` and send this file back to the browser. The file would contain text marked up by the **HyperText Markup Language (HTML)**. HTML uses a collection of tags that instruct the browser to display text, graphics, and other multimedia objects in a particular fashion. Small online stores may provide pre-written individual HTML pages for each of their products or services (such pages are called **static Web pages**). However, for more than a few dozen items, managing the HTML pages will become difficult. Integrating the web site with a database system that stores the products, descriptions, pricing, and inventory status information offers an opportunity to manage a much larger collection of products and services by turning requests for Web pages into database queries. Such pages are called **dynamic Web pages**, because the content of the page is dynamically created on request.

As discussed in Chapter 3, Structured Query Language (SQL) is the standard language implemented in relational DBMSs such as Microsoft Access, Microsoft SQL Server, Oracle, and MySQL. If the underlying DBMS is relational, the Web server must therefore express a query or transaction using SQL. In response, the DBMS will either return a set of records, an acknowledgement that the transaction was successful, or an error message. Based on this response, the Web server will generate an appropriate Web page and send it back to the browser. For example, suppose a user clicks on a link to display a list of all DVDs in a particular genre. The HTTP request might appear as:

```
GET /home/dvd_list.asp?genre=Action
```

In this case, the Web server will invoke a small program, called a **script**, written in Active Server Pages (ASP) and pass along the parameter `genre=Action`. Once at the Web server, this request will need to be unpacked, formed into a SQL query, and

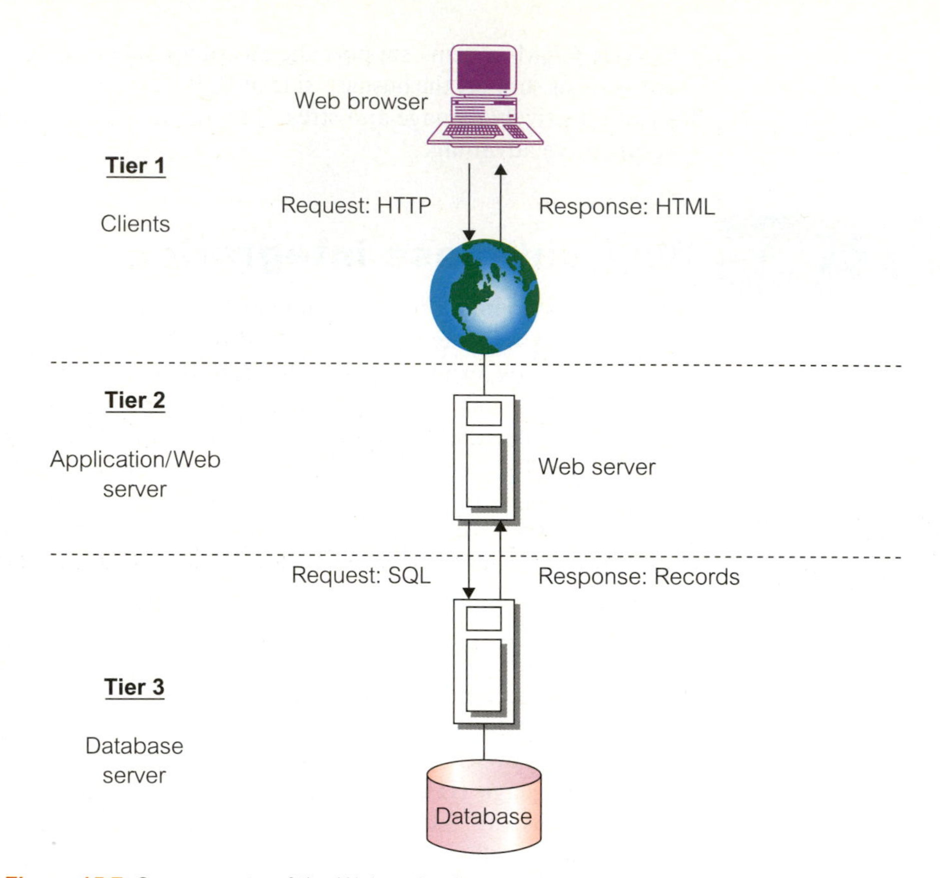

Figure 15.7 Components of the Web – database environment

submitted to the DBMS on the database server. In response, the DBMS will return a set of records to the Web server which then must apply the appropriate HTML markup tags to the records so that they display properly once sent back to the browser.

From the browser's point of view, an HTTP request was made and an HTML response was returned. From the DBMS's perspective, an SQL query was received and a set of records was returned. In between these two sits the Web server and some additional software that must carry out the 'translation' between web browser and DBMS. A more detailed set of steps follows:

Common Gateway Interface (CGI)

A standard for packaging parameters sent as part of an HTTP request between a browser and a Web server.

1. The browser packages up a request and sends it via the HTTP protocol to the Web server.
2. The Web server receives the HTTP request and invokes the appropriate script (such as `dvd_list.asp`) on the Web server passing along the contents of the HTTP request using the **Common Gateway Interface (CGI)** standard.
3. The script on the Web server unpacks the HTTP request, parses out the various parameters and values (such as `genre=Action`), and builds an appropriate SQL DML statement.

4. The script on the Web server then connects to the DBMS on the database server and submits the SQL statement.
5. The DBMS executes the SQL statement, packages up the resulting records or acknowledgement codes, and returns this to the Web server.
6. The script on the Web server receives the results from the database server and formats the results using HTML markup tags.
7. Finally, the Web server sends the newly created HTML back to the browser for interpretation and display.

The script on the Web server can be written in a number of different programming languages using a wide range of technologies. Regardless of the language or technology used, the same seven steps outlined above must still be followed. In the following section, a number of different languages and technologies are presented.

15.3 Web–database integration technologies

As the Web has developed and matured over the past decade, technologies for integrating Web servers and databases have gone through considerable evolution to the point where today there are literally dozens of technologies available. A high-level way of categorizing such technologies is by grouping them according to their development efforts (commercial or open source) and according to the integration approach taken, as shown in Table 15.1.

Early approaches to Web–database integration relied on existing compiled programming languages such as C and C++, as well as scripting languages such as Perl. For these languages, the programmer must write code to support each of the seven main steps shown above. While this approach affords the most freedom to customize the interaction, it also requires the most programming effort. Over time, developers recognized the common requirements of Web–database communications and specialized scripting languages such as Active Server Pages, Java Server Pages, ColdFusion, and PHP emerged as more productive tools for developing the server side

Table 15.1 Categorization of Web–database integration technologies

	Commercial	Open Source
Compiled languages	C, C++, C#	C, C++, Java
Scripting languages	MIcrosoft Active Server Pages (ASP) Oracle PSP (PL/SQL Server Pages) Adobe (formerly Macromedia) ColdFusion	Java Server Pages Perl PHP Python
Database connectivity	Open Database Connectivity (ODBC) ActiveX Data Objects (ADO)	JDBC Java Data Objects (JDO)
Components	IBM Websphere BEA Systems WebLogic Microsoft .NET	Ruby on Rails

code for Web-based applications. Deploying such applications on an enterprise scale requires yet another layer of refinement as legacy systems integration, transaction processing, session management, security, and the ability to serve applications to a variety of mobile devices became common requirements for Internet applications. Development platforms such as IBM WebSphere (www.ibm.com/software/websphere/), WebLogic from BEA Systems (www.bea.com/weblogic) (to be acquired by Oracle in 2008), and Microsoft .NET Framework (msdn.microsoft.com/netframework/) provide pre-built components that can be assembled into larger Internet applications.

15.3.1 Examples of Web–database integration technologies

HTML (HyperText Markup Language)

A standard markup language used to format text and multimedia on web pages.

PHP (PHP Hypertext processor)

An open source server-side scripting language.

In this section we present some brief examples of Web-database integration technologies. For each example, we assume that the Web page has a form that allows querying of a specific movie genre. The **HTML** code for this page is shown in Figure 15.8 and the resulting page displayed in a browser is shown in Figure 15.9. This is a simplified example of the *StayHome Online Rentals* Browse Selection page shown in Figure 5.5. In the sample HTML code, the `<FORM ACTION>` tag begins the HTML form and indicates the script that will be executed once the submit button is clicked. As shown in the code example, the ACTION for an ASP page will have the extension '.asp' (in our case, `dvd_list.asp`). For **PHP**, the extension would be '.php' (for example, `dvd_list.php`). For ColdFusion the extension would be '.cfm' (for example, `dvd_list.cfm`).

PHP Hypertext Processor

The PHP Hypertext Processor (www.php.net) is an open source scripting language that was developed in the mid 1990s by Rasmus Lerdorf, Zeev Suraski, and Andi Gutmans as well as a host of programmers from around the world. PHP is intended

```
<HTML>
<BODY>
<H1>DVD Genre Query Form</H1>
Select the DVD Genre from the list below and click the Submit button.
<P>
<FORM ACTION="dvd_list.asp">
   <SELECT NAME="q_genre">
      <OPTION VALUE=Action>Action
      <OPTION VALUE=Sci-Fi>Sci-Fi
      <OPTION VALUE=Children>Children
   </SELECT>
   <INPUT TYPE="submit" VALUE="Submit">
</FORM>
</BODY>
</HTML>
```

Figure 15.8 HTML source page for the DVD genre query form

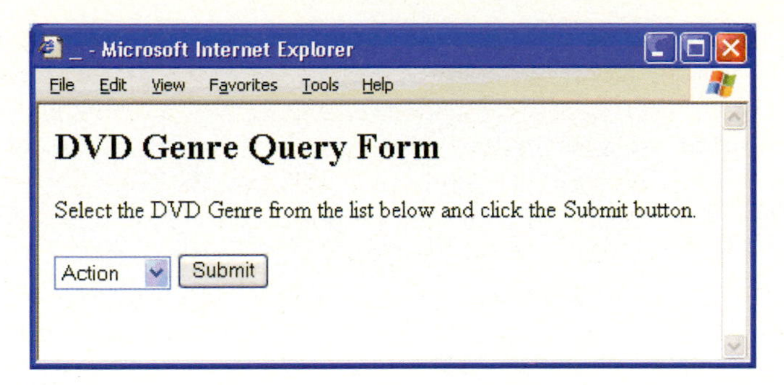

Figure 15.9 The DVD genre query form as displayed in a browser

to be embedded within HTML pages. When a PHP page is served, the HTML portions are sent directly back to the browser, however any code contained within the special PHP tags `<?php` and `?>` are executed by the PHP parser and the results of the execution are returned to the browser.

The sample code listed in Figure 15.10 carries out the steps 3 through 6 listed in the prior section by querying an Oracle database and returning the results of all DVDs within a specific genre. In PHP, two slashes indicate a comment and, as in the Perl programming language, variable names are preceded by the dollar sign. Note also that error checking, which would typically be included after each statement, has been omitted from this example.

Active Server Pages

Active server pages (ASP)

A server-side scripting language developed my Microsoft.

Active Server Pages (ASP) is a scripting language developed by Microsoft that works within Microsoft's Internet Information Server (IIS) Web server (msdn.microsoft.com/asp). The latest version, ASP.NET, is incorporated into Microsoft's .NET Framework. As with other server-side scripting languages such as JSP and PHP, an ASP page consists of HTML tags with scripting code placed inside the special HTML tags `<%` and `%>`. When a request arrives for an ASP page, the HTML portions are returned to the browser directly while the ASP code is executed on the server and the results of the execution are returned to the browser. ASP code can be written in a number of different languages including Microsoft's VBScript and JScript. The example shown in Figure 15.11 uses VBScript to carry out the Web–database integration steps 3 through 6. Fields from the requesting form are referenced using the `Request.Form` statement and HTML code is written back to the browser using the `Response.Write` statement. Comments in VBScript begin with a single quote.

ColdFusion

ColdFusion

A server-side scripting engine that operates on special tags that extend HTML.

ColdFusion is an extension to HTML offered by Adobe (http://www.adobe.com/products/coldfusion/). The ColdFusion Markup Language (CFML) consists of a collection of special HTML tags (all start with `<CF`) that are mixed within standard HTML to interact with the ColdFusion server to access databases and other server resources. When the Web server receives a request for a CFML page with a '.cfm' extension, the ColdFusion server handles the request, interprets the CFML tags

```
<!-- dvd_list.php -->
<HTML>
<BODY>
<H3>The results of your query are</H3>

<TABLE BORDER>
<TR><TH>CatalogNo <TH>Title <TH>Genre <TH>Rating </TR>


<?php
// PHP automatically unpacks the CGI request and sets up variables for each
// field on the HTML form that submitted the request.
// The following line creates a SQL query using the q_genre field from the form
$query = "SELECT catalogNo, title, genre, rating FROM dvd WHERE genre = $q_genre";

// Connect to an Oracle database
$connection = Ora_Logon ("username", "password");

// Declare a database cursor using the current open connection
$cursor = Ora_Open ($connection);

// Have the DBMS parse the query to ensure correct syntax
$result = Ora_Parse ($cursor, $query);

// Execute the query in the DBMS
$result = Ora_Exec ($cursor);

// Loop through the resulting records and print out an HTML table row for each record
while (Ora_Fetch_Into ($cursor, &$values)){
  echo
  "<tr><td>$values[0]<td>$values[1]<td>$values[2]<td>$values[3]</tr>\n";
}

// Close the cursor and the database connection
Ora_Close ($cursor);
Ora_Logoff ($connection);
?>

</TABLE>
</BODY>
</HTML>
```

Figure 15.10 PHP example code for querying the DVD table in the *StayHome* database

within the document and returns the resulting HTML to the Web server for delivery to the browser client. The example shown in Figure 15.12 uses ColdFusion to carry out the Web–database integration steps 3 through 6. Queries are defined using the CFQUERY tag. Fields from the requesting form are referenced using the `#Form.field#` statement and HTML code from the database is written back to the browser using the `CFOUTPUT` tag.

```
<!-- dvd_list.asp -->
<HTML>
<BODY>
<H3>The results of your query are</H3>

<TABLE BORDER>
<TR><TH>CatalogNo <TH> Title <TH> Genre <TH> Rating </TR>
<%
  ' Create a SQL Query using the q_genre field from the query form
  strSQL = "SELECT catalogNo, title, genre, rating FROM dvd WHERE genre = '" &
Request.Form("q_genre") & "'"

  ' Create a connection object and open the connection to a Microsoft Access
database
  Set cnn = Server.CreateObject("ADODB.Connection")
  cnn.Open "Provider=Microsoft.Jet.OLEDB.4.0;Data Source=C:\mydatabase\stayhome.mdb"

  ' Create a query result set object to hold the query results
  Set rstQuery = Server.CreateObject("ADODB.Recordset")

  ' Execute the query in the database and store the results
  rstQuery.Open strSQL, cnn

  ' Loop through the query results and for each record print out the record data
  Do Until rstQuery.EOF
     Response.Write "<TR><TD>" & rstQuery("catalogNo")
     Response.Write "<TD>" & rstQuery("title")
     Response.Write "<TD>" & rstQuery("genre")
     Response.Write "<TD>" & rstQuery("rating")
     rstQuery.MoveNext
  Loop
%>

</TABLE>
</BODY>
</HTML>
```

Figure 15.11 ASP example code for querying the DVD table in the *StayHome* database

Ruby on Rails

Ruby on Rails

A framework for creating database-driven web sites using Ruby programming language.

Ruby is an object-oriented programming language developed in Japan in the early 1990s (www.ruby-lang.org/en/). Rails (often referred to as '**Ruby on Rails**') is a framework for creating database-driven Web and interactive Web applications using the Ruby language (www.rubyonrails.org). It was developed and released in 2004 by David Heinemeier Hansson. In the Rails framework, objects are created automatically for each database table, along with a collection of default methods for retrieving, displaying, editing, and deleting database records. These existing methods can be extended relatively easily to perform custom operations on the data. When establishing a new Rail application, the database connection is specified once in a

```
<!-- dvd_list.cfm -->
<HTML>
<HEAD><TITLE>Query Results</TITLE></HEAD>
<BODY>
<B>Your query results are:</B>
<P>
<TABLE BORDER>
<TR><TH>CatalogNo <TH> Title <TH> Genre <TH> Rating </TR>

<!-- Create a query named findDVDGenre
     DATASOURCE is defined in a ColdFusion configuration file
     Fields in the calling form as passed into the #Form object.
-->
<CFQUERY NAME="findDVDGenre" DATASOURCE="StayHomeDatabase">
     SELECT catalogNo, title, genre, rating
     FROM dvd
     WHERE genre = '#Form.q_genre#'
</CFQUERY>

<!-- CFOUTPUT accesses the query results and loops through the records
     Values in the record's fields are displayed using #field name#
-->
<CFOUTPUT QUERY="findDVDGenre">
    <TR><TD>#catalogNo# <TD>#title# <TD>#genre# <TD>#rating#<BR>
</CFOUTPUT>

</TABLE>
</BODY>
</HTML>
```

Figure 15.12 ColdFusion example code for querying the DVD table in the *StayHome* database

configuration file named 'database.yml' so that all parts of the application can work using the same connection. An example configuration file is shown in Figure 15.13. Note there are three databases defined: one for development, one for testing, and one for production (deployment). As of June 2007, the following DBMSs were supported:

- Oracle 8i, 9i, and 10g;
- Microsoft SQL Server;
- IBM DB2;
- Informix;
- MySQL;
- PostgreSQL;
- SQLite;
- Firebird/Interbase.

While the example shown in Figure 15.14 hides much of the complexity of the complete application, it does show the code that would need to be written to respond to

```
# orcl on the localhost is our development database
development:
  adapter: oci
  host: localhost/orcl
  username: myuser
  password: mypassword

# orcl_test on the localhost is our test database
test
  adapter: oci
  host: localhost/orcl_test
  username: myuser
  password: mypassword

# oraprod on proddb.stayhome.com is our production Oracle database
production:
  adapter: oci
  host: proddb.stayhome.com/oraprod
  username: produser
  password: prodpass
```

Figure 15.13 Ruby on Rails database.yml configuration file for the *StayHome* database

```
<!-- dvd_list.rhtml -->
<HTML>
<BODY>
<H3>The results of your query are</H3>

<TABLE BORDER>
<TR><TH>CatalogNo <TH> Title <TH> Genre <TH> Rating </TR>

<!-- Loop through each record in the DVD table -->
<% @dvd.each do |dvd| %>
  <!-- If the current record matches the genre -->
  <% if (@q_genre == dvd.genre) %>
    <TR>
    <!-- Display the contents of each field -->
    <TD> <%= dvd.catalogno %>
    <TD> <%= dvd.title %>
    <TD> <%= dvd.genre %>
    <TD> <%= dvd.rating %>
    </TR>
  <% end %>
<% end %>

</TABLE>
</BODY>
</HTML>
```

Figure 15.14 Ruby on Rails example code for querying the DVD table in the *StayHome* database

a query on a specific movie genre. The code between the special tags <% and %> represent statements that the Ruby interpreter will execute.

As can be seen from these examples, there are many ways to achieve the same kinds of Web–database interaction. A more detailed treatment of these approaches can be found in any number of programming guides and tutorials in books as well as posted for free on the Web. In the following section we introduce the eXtensible Markup Language (XML), which has become an industry standard for data exchange and communications.

15.4 eXtensible Markup Language (XML)

Most documents on the Web are currently stored and transmitted in HTML. We have already commented that one of the strengths of HTML is its simplicity, allowing it to be used by a wide variety of users. However, its simplicity is arguably also one of its weaknesses, with the growing need from users who want tags to simplify some tasks and make HTML documents more attractive and dynamic. In an attempt to satisfy this demand, vendors have introduced some browser-specific HTML tags. However, this makes it difficult to develop sophisticated, widely viewable Web documents. In addition, HTML tags do not carry with them the *semantics*, or meaning of the data or text they contain.

In comparison, data stored in relational databases is highly structured and, as we introduced in Chapter 1, a major purpose of a database schema is to provide structure and meaning to the database contents. There is a great demand to bring this kind of formal structure and meaning to the huge amount of relatively unstructured data held in books, publications, Web pages, etc.

To address these issues, the World Wide Web Consortium (W3C) (www.w3.org) has produced a standard called the **eXtensible Markup Language (XML)**, which preserves the general application independence that makes HTML portable and powerful while providing meaning to the data that documents contain. The current XML standard, version 1.1, was released on 4 February 2004 (WC3 2004).

eXtensible Markup Language (XML)

A meta-language (a language for describing other languages) that enables designers to create their own customized tags to provide functionality not available with HTML

XML is not intended as a replacement for HTML. Instead, XML is designed to complement HTML by enabling different kinds of data to be exchanged over the Web. In fact, the use of XML is not limited to only text markup, but extensibility means that XML could also be applied to other types of data, such as sound markup or image markup. Four popular languages created with XML are XBRL (eXtensible Business Reporting Language), MathML (Mathematics Markup Language), SMIL (Synchronized Multimedia Integration Language), and CML (Chemistry Markup Language), among many others.

XML 1.0 was formally ratified by the W3C, and it has revolutionized computing. As a technology, it has impacted every aspect of programming, including graphical user interfaces, embedded systems, distributed systems, and, from our perspective, database management. It has become the *de facto* standard for data communication within the software industry and it is quickly replacing EDI systems as the primary medium for data interchange among businesses. Some analysts believe it will become the language in which most documents are created and stored, both on and off the Internet.

Semi-structured data

Data that may be irregular or incomplete and have a structure that may change rapidly or unpredictably.

Due to the nature of information on the Web and the inherent flexibility of XML, it is expected that much of the data encoded in XML will be **semi-structured**; that is, the data may be irregular or incomplete, and its structure may change rapidly or unpredictably. Unfortunately, relational, object-oriented, and object-relational DBMSs do not handle data of this nature particularly well. Some DBMS vendors such as Oracle have introduced native XML data storage engines that run alongside, and are integrated with, the relational and object-relational DBMSs.

15.4.1 Advantages of XML

Some of the advantages of using XML on the Web are listed in Table 15.2.

Table 15.2 Advantages of XML

Advantages of XML
Simplicity
Open standard and platform/vendor-independent
Extensibility
Reuse
Separation of content and presentation
Improved load balancing
Support for the integration of data from multiple sources
Ability to describe data from a wide variety of applications
More advanced search engines
New opportunities

- *Simplicity*. XML is a relatively simple standard, fewer than 50 pages long. It was designed as a text-based language that is human-legible and reasonably clear.
- *Open standard and platform/vendor-independent*. XML is both platform-independent and vendor-independent. It is also based on ISO 10646, the Unicode character set, and so has built-in support for texts in all the world's alphabets, including a method to indicate which language and encoding is being used.
- *Extensibility*. Unlike HTML, XML is extensible allowing users to define their own tags to meet their own particular application requirements.
- *Reuse*. Extensibility also allows libraries of XML tags to be built once and then reused by many applications.
- *Separation of content and presentation*. XML separates the content of a document from how the document will be presented (such as within a browser). This facilitates a customized view of the data – data can be delivered to the user through the browser where it can be presented in a customized way, perhaps based on factors such as user preference or configuration. In much the same way that Java is sometimes referred to as a 'write once, run anywhere' language, XML is referred to as a 'write once, publish anywhere' language,

with facilities such as stylesheets that allow the same XML document to be published in different ways using a variety of formats and media.

- *Improved load balancing*. Data can be delivered to the browser on the desktop for local computation, offloading computation from the server and thereby achieving better load balancing.
- *Support for the integration of data from multiple sources*. The ability to integrate data from multiple heterogeneous sources is extremely difficult and time-consuming. However, XML enables data from different sources to be combined more easily. Software agents can be used to integrate data from backend databases and other applications, which can then be delivered to other clients or servers for further processing or presentation.
- *Ability to describe data from a wide variety of applications*. As XML is extensible, it can be used to describe data contained in a wide variety of applications. Also, because XML makes the data *self-describing*, the data can be received and processed without the need for a built-in description of the data.
- *More advanced search engines*. At present, search engines work on information contained in the HTML meta-tags or on proximity of one keyword to another. With XML, search engines will be able to simply parse the description-bearing tags.
- *New opportunities*. Perhaps one of the great advantages of XML is the wealth of opportunities that are now presented by this new technology.

Some potential weaknesses of XML include:

- *Requires new software tools and training*. Working with XML requires new software tools and new skills to use them.
- *Size and complexity of syntax*. The XML syntax can be rather large as compared to the data. In some cases, syntax may be redundant.
- *Limited data types in native XML*. The original XML specification did not distinguish between numeric and character data types. However, XML Schema (defined in Section 15.4.3) does include this level of specification.
- *Storing XML documents in relational and object-oriented databases can be difficult*. This is often the case when XML documents are complex and contain many optional elements.

Virtually all commercial databases such as Oracle, Microsoft SQL Server and IBM DB2 support XML in a number of ways. For example, all three DBMSs provide both import and export functionality to bring XML data into the database and export existing data as XML files. Oracle10g supports a 'native' XML database in which XML documents are stored in their native format.

15.4.2 XML declaration

An example XML document is shown in Figure 15.15. XML documents begin with an optional XML declaration, which in our example indicates the version of XML

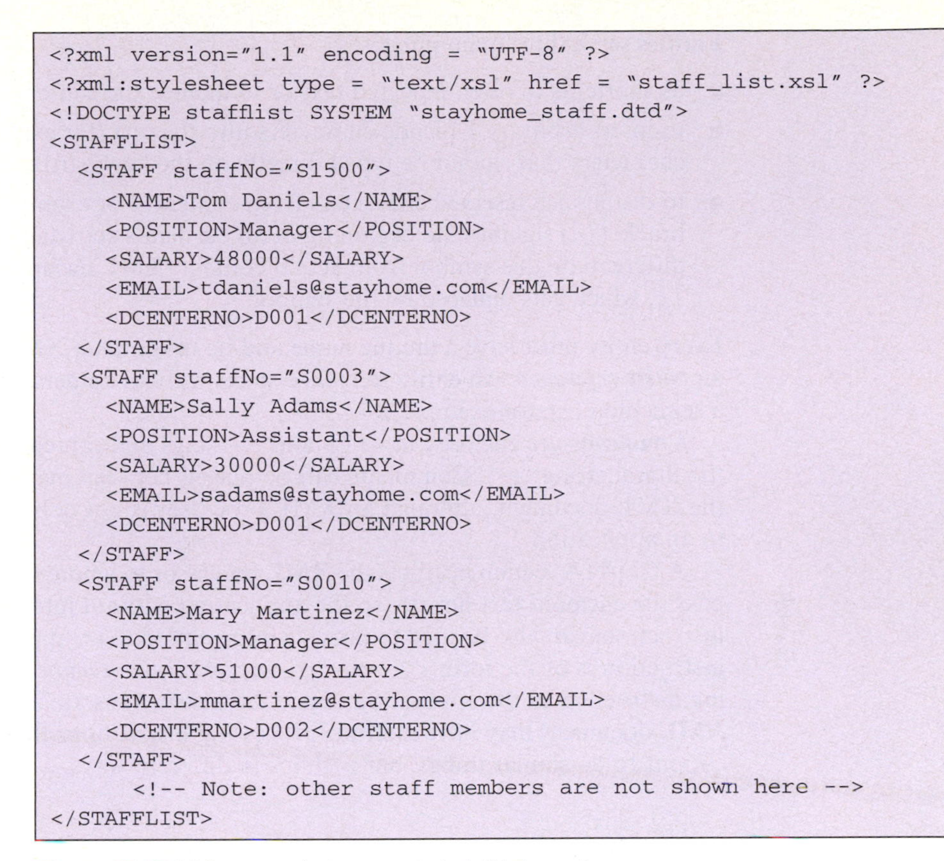

```
<?xml version="1.1" encoding = "UTF-8" ?>
<?xml:stylesheet type = "text/xsl" href = "staff_list.xsl" ?>
<!DOCTYPE stafflist SYSTEM "stayhome_staff.dtd">
<STAFFLIST>
  <STAFF staffNo="S1500">
    <NAME>Tom Daniels</NAME>
    <POSITION>Manager</POSITION>
    <SALARY>48000</SALARY>
    <EMAIL>tdaniels@stayhome.com</EMAIL>
    <DCENTERNO>D001</DCENTERNO>
  </STAFF>
  <STAFF staffNo="S0003">
    <NAME>Sally Adams</NAME>
    <POSITION>Assistant</POSITION>
    <SALARY>30000</SALARY>
    <EMAIL>sadams@stayhome.com</EMAIL>
    <DCENTERNO>D001</DCENTERNO>
  </STAFF>
  <STAFF staffNo="S0010">
    <NAME>Mary Martinez</NAME>
    <POSITION>Manager</POSITION>
    <SALARY>51000</SALARY>
    <EMAIL>mmartinez@stayhome.com</EMAIL>
    <DCENTERNO>D002</DCENTERNO>
  </STAFF>
      <!-- Note: other staff members are not shown here -->
</STAFFLIST>
```

Figure 15.15 XML example to represent staff information

used to author the document (1.1), the encoding system used (UTF-8 for Unicode), and whether or not there are external markup declarations referenced. The second and third lines of the XML document in Figure 15.15 relate to stylesheets and DTDs, which we discuss shortly.

Elements, or **tags**, are the most common form of markup. The first element must be a root element, which can contain other (sub)elements. An XML document must have one root element, in our example `<STAFFLIST>`. An element begins with a start-tag (for example, `<STAFF>`) and ends with an end-tag (for example, `</STAFF>`). An element can be empty, in which case it can be abbreviated to `<EMPTYELEMENT/>`. **Attributes** are name–value pairs that contain descriptive information about an element. The attribute is placed inside the start-tag after the corresponding element name with the attribute value enclosed in quotes. A given attribute may occur only once within a tag, while subelements with the same tag may be repeated. For example, we have chosen to represent the staffNo for the staff member in the element STAFF:

```
<STAFF staffNo="S1500">
```

Entities serve three main purposes:

- as shortcuts to often repeated text or to include the content of external files;
- to insert arbitrary Unicode characters into the text (for example, to represent characters that cannot be typed directly on the keyboard);
- to distinguish reserved characters from content. For example, the left angle bracket (<) signifies the beginning of an element's start-tag or end-tag. To differentiate this symbol from actual content, XML has introduced the entity `lt`, which gets replaced by the symbol '<'.

Every entity must have a unique name and its usage in an XML document is called an *entity reference*. An entity reference starts with an ampersand (`&`) and ends with a semicolon (`;`), for example, `<`.

Comments are enclosed in `<!--` and `-->` tags and can contain any data except the literal string '`--`'. Comments can be placed between markup anywhere within the XML document, although an XML processor is not obliged to pass comments to an application.

A CDATA section instructs the XML processor to ignore markup characters and pass the enclosed text directly to the application without interpretation. Processing instructions can also be used to provide information to an application. A processing instruction is of the form `<?name pidata?>`, where *name* identifies the processing instruction to the application. Since the instructions are application specific, an XML document may have multiple processing instructions that tell different applications to do similar things, but perhaps in different ways.

15.4.3 Document Type Definitions (DTDs) and XML Schema

Document Type Definitions and the XML Schema are similar ways of expressing the structure and syntax of an XML document. While DTDs were introduced with the original XML specification, they have, for the most part, been superseded by the newer XML Schema specification. We describe both standards in the next two subsections.

Document Type Definition

Document Type Definition (DTD)

Defines the valid syntax (rules of the language) of an XML document.

The **Document Type Definition (DTD)** defines the valid syntax of an XML document by listing the element names that can occur in the document, which elements can appear in combination with which other ones, how elements can be nested, what attributes are available for each element type, and so on. The term *vocabulary* is sometimes used to refer to the elements used in a particular application. Although a DTD is optional, it is recommended for document conformity, as we discuss shortly.

To continue the staff example, in Figure 15.16 we show a possible DTD for the XML document of Figure 15.15. We have specified the DTD as a separate external file, although the DTD can also be embedded within the XML document itself. There

```
<!DOCTYPE STAFFLIST [
  <!ELEMENT STAFFLIST (STAFF)*>
  <ELEMENT STAFF (NAME, POSITION, SALARY, EMAIL, DOB?, DCENTERNO)>
  <ELEMENT NAME (#PCDATA)>
  <ELEMENT POSITION (#PCDATA)>
  <ELEMENT SALARY (#PCDATA)>
  <ELEMENT EMAIL (#PCDATA)>
  <ELEMENT DOB (#PCDATA)>
  <ELEMENT DCENTERNO (#PCDATA)>
  <!ATTLIST STAFF staffNo CDATA #IMPLIED>
]>
```

Figure 15.16 Document Type Definition for XML staff document

are four types of DTD declarations: element type declarations, attribute list declarations, entity declarations, and notation declarations. We introduce the first two types here.

Element type declarations identify the rules for elements that can occur in the XML document. For example, in Figure 15.16 we have specified the following rule (or *content model*) for the element STAFFLIST:

```
<!ELEMENT STAFFLIST (STAFF)*>
```

which states that the element STAFFLIST consists of zero or more STAFF elements.

Commas between element names indicate that they must occur in succession; if commas are omitted, the elements can occur in any order. For example, we have specified the following rule for the element STAFF:

```
<ELEMENT STAFF (NAME, POSITION, SALARY, EMAIL, DOB?,
DCENTERNO)>
```

which states that the element STAFF consists of a NAME element, a POSITION element, a SALARY element, an EMAIL element, an optional DOB element, and a DCENTERNO element, in this order. Declarations for NAME, POSITION, EMAIL, DOB, and SALARY and all other elements used in a content model must also be present for an XML processor to check the validity of the document. These base elements have all been declared using the special symbol #PCDATA to indicate parseable character data. Note that an element may contain only other elements but it is possible for an element to contain both other elements and #PCDATA (which is referred to as *mixed content*).

Attribute list declarations identify which elements may have attributes, what attributes they may have, what values the attributes may hold, and what the optional default values are. Each attribute declaration has three parts: a name, a type, and an optional default value. The most common types are:

- CDATA – character data, containing any text. The string will not be parsed by the XML processor and is simply passed directly to the application.
- ID – used to identify individual elements in a document. IDs must correspond to an element name, and all ID values used in a document must be different.

For example, the following attribute declaration is used to define an attribute called staffNo for the element STAFF:

```
<!ATTLIST STAFF staffNo CDATA #IMPLIED>
```

This declaration states that the staffNo value is a string (CDATA – character data) and is optional (#IMPLIED) with no default provided. Apart from #IMPLIED, #REQUIRED can be specified to indicate that the attribute must always be provided. If neither of these qualifiers is specified, then the value contains the declared default value. The #FIXED keyword can be used to indicate that the attribute must always have the default value.

The XML specification provides for two levels of document processing: well-formed and valid. A non-validating processor ensures that an XML document is well-formed before passing the information in the document on to the application. An XML document that conforms to the structural and notational rules of XML is considered *well-formed*. Among others, well-formed XML documents must conform to the following rules:

- the document must start with the XML declaration `<?xml version "1.1"?>`;
- all elements must be contained within one root element;
- elements must be nested in a tree structure without any overlap;
- all non-empty elements must have a start-tag and an end-tag.

A validating processor will not only check that an XML document is well-formed but that it also conforms to a DTD, in which case the XML document is considered *valid*. As we mentioned earlier, the DTD can be contained within the XML document or referenced from it.

XML Schema

While XML 1.1 supplies the DTD mechanism for defining the content model (the valid order and nesting of elements) and, to a limited extent, the data types of attributes of an XML document, it has a number of limitations:

- it is written in a different (non-XML) syntax;
- it has no support for namespaces;
- it offers extremely limited data typing.

Therefore, a more comprehensive and rigorous method of defining the content model of an XML document is needed. W3C XML Schema overcomes these limitations and is much more expressive than DTDs (http://www.w3.org/XML/Schema). The additional expressiveness allows Web applications to exchange XML data much more robustly without relying on *ad hoc* validation tools. An **XML Schema** is the definition (both in terms of its organization and its data types) of a specific XML structure. The W3C XML Schema language specifies how each type of element in the schema is defined and what data type that element has associated with it. The schema is itself an XML document, using elements and attributes to express the semantics of the schema. As it is an XML document, it can be edited and processed

XML Schema

Defines the specific structure of an XML document including its organization and data types.

by the same tools that read the XML it describes. A sample XML Schema for stafflist is shown in Figure 15.17.

The major features of an XML Schema are:

- complexType: a named element that can contain other elements or other complexTypes.
- sequence: a named element that contains an ordered set of subelements.
- simpleType: a named element with a simple data type (such as boolean, string, date, or decimal).
- Cardinality: an element can be specified with minOccurs and maxOccurs indicating the minimum and maximum occurrences allowed.
- References: references (such as <xs:element ref = "STAFFNO"/>) can be used to refer to other elements defined elsewhere in the same XML document.
- Defining new data types.
- Defining groups of elements and attributes.
- Constraints on elements and attributes including uniqueness of values among a set of elements or attributes, as well as key constraints that require a non-null, as well as unique value.

Note that not all of these features are demonstrated in Figure 15.17.

```
<?xml version="1.0" encoding="UTF-8"?>
<xs:schema xmlns:xs="http://www.w3.org/2001/XMLSchema" name="stafflist">
  <xs:complexType>
    <xs:sequence maxOccurs="unbounded" minOccurs="0">
    <xs:element ref="staff"/>
    </xs:sequence>
  </xs:complexType>
  <xs:complexType>
    <xs:sequence>
      <xs:element ref="name" type="xs:string" />
      <xs:element ref="position" type="xs:string"/>
      <xs:element ref="salary" type="xs:decimal"/>
      <xs:element ref="email" type="xs:string"/>
      <xs:element minOccurs="0" ref="dob" type="xs:date"/>
      <xs:element ref="dcenterno" type="xs:string"/>
    </xs:sequence>
    <xs:attribute name="staffno" type="xs:string" use="required"/>
  </xs:complexType>
  <xs:key name="staffkey">
      <xs:selector xpath = "staff"/>
      <xs:field xpath = "staffno"/>
  </xs:key
</xs:schema>
```

Figure 15.17 XML Schema definition for the XML staff document

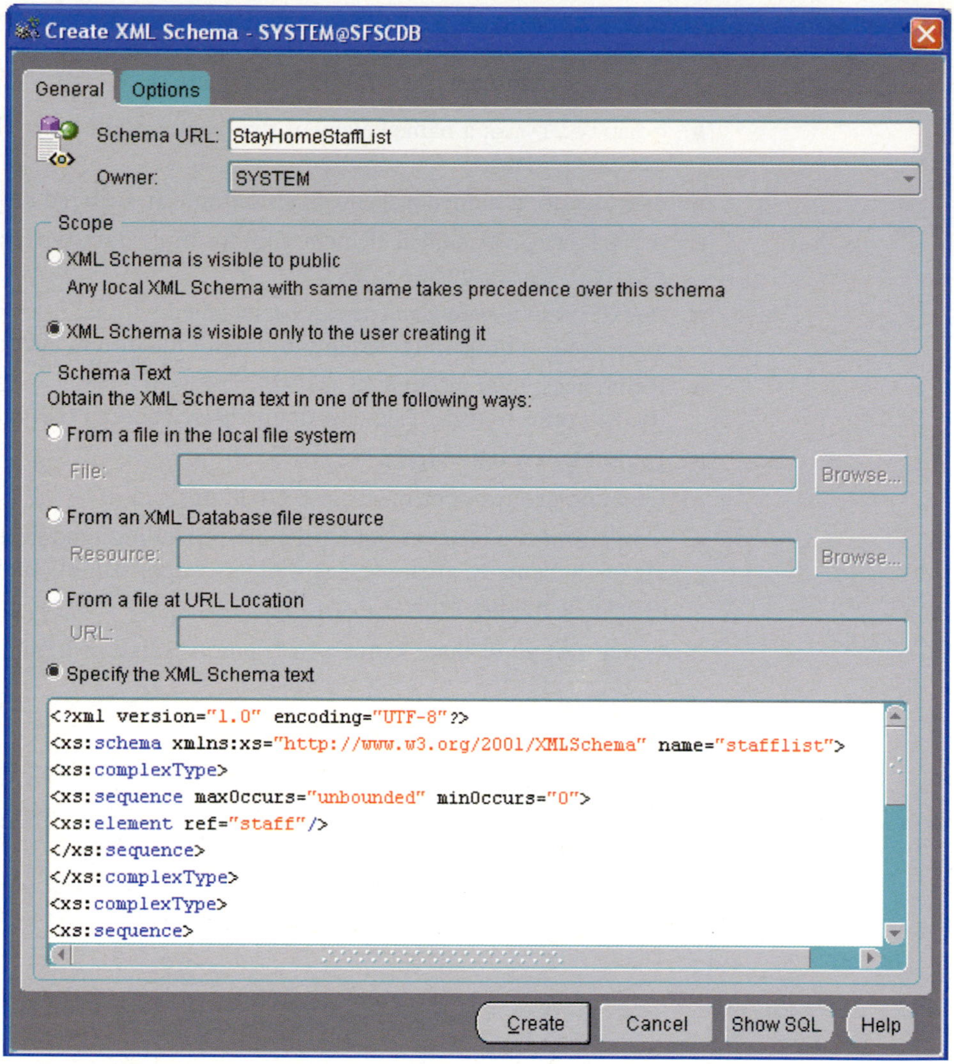

Figure 15.18 Creating an XML Schema for the *StayHome* staff XML document in Oracle10g

Because an XML Schema is an XML document, it can be processed by existing XML tools. In particular, an XML Schema can be used as the equivalent of an SQL Data Definition Language script to create either a schema in a relational DBMS or a schema in a native XML data store. Figure 15.18 shows the Oracle 10g XML Database interface for creating the XML Schema directly in Oracle's native XML Database (called XDB). The XML Schema text used was taken directly from Figure 15.17.

15.5 XML-related technologies

In this section we briefly discuss a number of additional technologies related to XML that are important to the understanding and development of XML applications, namely the eXtensible Stylesheet Language (XSL) and the eXtensible Stylesheet Language for Transformations (XSLT), and XHTML.

15.5.1 XSL and XSLT

In HTML, default styling is built into browsers because the tag set for HTML is predefined and fixed. The Cascading Stylesheet Specification (CSS) allows the developer to provide an alternative rendering for the tags. CSS can also be used to render an XML document in a browser but it has no ability to make structural alterations to a document. XSL is a formal W3C recommendation (http://www.w3.org/Style/XSL/) that has been created specifically to define how an XML document's data is rendered, and to define how one XML document can be transformed into another document. It is similar to CSS although more powerful.

XSLT forms a subset of XSL. It is a language in both the markup and the programming sense in that it provides a mechanism to transform XML structure into either another XML structure, HTML, or any number of other text-based formats (such as SQL). While it can be used to create the display output of a Web page, XSLT's main ability is to change the underlying structures rather than simply the media representations of those structures, as is the case with CSS.

XSLT is important because it provides a mechanism for dynamically changing the view of a document and for filtering data. It is also robust enough to encode business rules and it can generate graphics (not just documents) from data. It can even handle communicating with servers – especially in conjunction with scripting modules that can be integrated into XSLT – and it can generate the appropriate messages within the body of XSLT itself.

15.5.2 XHTML

XHTML 1.0 is a reformulation of HTML 4.01 written in XML and it is the next generation of HTML. The W3C released XHTML 1.0 in January of 2000 (http://www.w3.org/TR/xhtml1/). It is basically a stricter and cleaner version of HTML. For example:

- tags and attributes must be in lower case;
- all XHTML elements must have an end-tag;
- attribute values must be quoted and minimization is not allowed;
- the ID attribute replaces the name attribute;

- documents must conform to XML rules.
- All XHTML document must begin with the following DOCTYPE tag:

```
<!DOCTYPE html PUBLIC "-//W3C//DTD XHTML 1.0 Strict//EN"
"http://www.w3.org/TR/xhtml1/DTD/xhtml1-strict.dtd">
```

At this time, all major web browsers support XHTML.

15.6 XML query languages

Data extraction, transformation, and integration are well-understood database issues that rely on a query language. The Structured Query Language introduced in Chapter 3 does not apply directly to XML because of the irregularity of XML data. XML data is considered to be a form of semi-structured data. There are many semi-structured query languages that can be used to query XML documents, including XQuery, XML-QL (Deutsch *et al.*, 1998), UnQL (Buneman *et al.*, 1996), XQL from Microsoft (Robie *et al.*, 1998) and SQL/XML that is part of the ANSI/ISO SQL 2003 standard. Of these different approaches, the **XQuery** language has moved to the forefront. For example, Microsoft SQL Server 2005 edition includes support for XQuery, as does Oracle 10g in its native XML database. The XQuery language is described in more detail below. We also discuss the SQL/XML extensions to the SQL 2003 standard.

15.6.1 XQuery – a query language for XML

The W3C Query Working Group has proposed a query language for XML called **XQuery** (http://www.w3.org/XML/Query/). XQuery is derived from an XML query language called Quilt (Chamberlin *et al.*, 2000). XQuery is a functional language in which a query is represented as an expression. XQuery supports several kinds of expression, which can be nested (supporting the notion of a subquery.) We present two aspects of the language: XPath expressions and FLWR expressions. A fuller treatment of XQuery is beyond scope of this book and the interested reader is referred to the W3C document for additional information (W3C, 2005).

XQuery path expressions

XQuery path expressions use the abbreviated syntax of XPath, extended with a 'dereference' operator and a 'range predicate'. In XQuery, the result of a path expression is an ordered list of nodes representing data. The result of a path expression may contain duplicate values. A path expression can begin with the function `document(string)`, which refers to a named XML document. Two examples of XQuery path expressions are given in Example 15.1.

Example 15.1 Examples of XQuery path expressions

(a) *Find the staff number of the first member of staff in the XML document of Figure 15.15.*

```
document("staff_list.xml")/STAFF[1]//STAFFNO
```

This example uses a path expression consisting of three steps: the first step locates the root node of the document; the second step locates the first STAFF element that is a child of the root element; the third step finds STAFFNO elements occurring anywhere within this STAFF element.

(b) *Find the staff numbers of the first two members of staff.*

```
document("staff_list.xml")/STAFF[RANGE 1 TO 2]//STAFFNO
```

(c) *Find the names of the staff at distribution center D001.*

```
document("staff_list.xml")//STAFF[DCENTERNO = D001]/NAME
```

This example uses a path expression consisting of three steps: the first step finds STAFF elements; the second step determines whether the DCENTERNO element equals D001 and, if it does, the third step provides the name of the member of staff.

FLWR expressions

A FLWR (pronounced 'flower') expression is constructed from FOR, LET, WHERE, and RETURN clauses. As in an SQL query, these clauses must appear in order. The FOR clause is used to loop over a collection of elements so that each element can be inspected. The LET clause is used to reference a collection of elements for purposes of summarizing the set of data. The WHERE clause filters elements in the XML document according to some condition. It is similar to the WHERE clause in SQL. The RETURN clause is similar to the SELECT portion of an SQL statement in that it determines what elements should be returned by the FLWR expression. A FLWR expression may contain several FOR and LET clauses, and each of these causes may contain references to variables bound in previous clauses. The result of the sequence of FOR and LET clauses is a list of tuples. Examples of FLWR expressions are shown in Example 15.2.

Example 15.2 XQuery FLWR expressions

(a) *List the staff at distribution center D001 with a salary greater than $15 000.*

```
FOR $S IN document("staff_list.xml")//STAFF
WHERE $S/SALARY > 15 000 AND $S[DCENTERNO = D001]
RETURN $S/STAFFNO
```

(b) *List each distribution center and the average salary at the center.*

```
FOR $D IN DISTINCT(document("staff_list.xml")//DCENTERNO)
LET $avgSalary :=
avg(document("staff_list.xml")/STAFF[DCENTERNO= $D]/SALARY
RETURN
  <DCENTER>
    <DCENTERNO>$D/text()</DCENTERNO>,
    <AVGSALARY>$avgSalary</AVGSALARY>
  </DCENTER>
```

(c) *List the distribution centers that have more than 20 staff.*

```
<LARGECENTERS>
FOR $D IN DISTINCT(document("staff_list.xml")//DCENTERNO)
LET $S := document("staff_list.xml")/STAFF[DCENTERNO= $D]
WHERE count ($S) > 20
RETURN $D
</ LARGECENTERS>
```

15.6.2 SQL/XML – XML extensions for SQL

As discussed in the previous section, XQuery is an XML-centric query language that is based on the XML document data model and XML Schema-type systems. By contrast, SQL/XML adds the ability to create and manipulate XML structures using a small set of additional extensions to standard SQL. Oracle Corporation has supported, for the most part, the SQL 2003 standard, including the SQL/XML extensions since it released the Oracle9i product. IBM also supports the SQL/XML extensions in its DB2 Universal Database products.

The SQL/XML extensions add nine new functions to the language and a new data type called XML. From a querying standpoint, SQL/XML is most useful for generating XML output from existing relational tables. The SQL/XML functions to accomplish this are described below:

- `xmlelement()` creates an XML element from a column value. The function allows the name of the element to be specified. This functions works on one column at a time.
- `xmlattributes()` creates an XML attribute from a column value using the column name as the name of the attribute. This functions works on one column at a time.

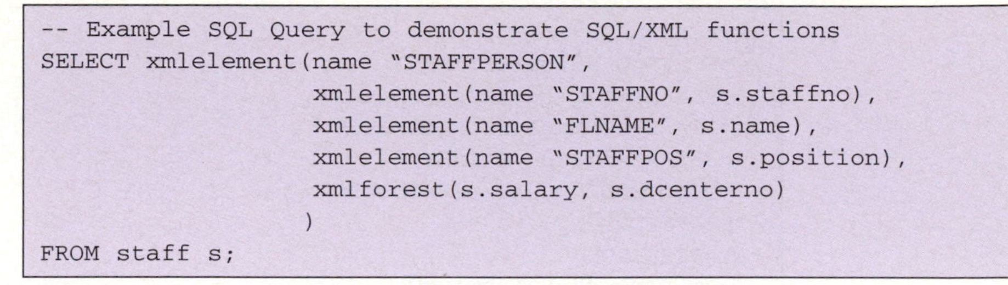

```
-- Example SQL Query to demonstrate SQL/XML functions
SELECT xmlelement(name "STAFFPERSON",
                  xmlelement(name "STAFFNO", s.staffno),
                  xmlelement(name "FLNAME", s.name),
                  xmlelement(name "STAFFPOS", s.position),
                  xmlforest(s.salary, s.dcenterno)
                 )
FROM staff s;
```

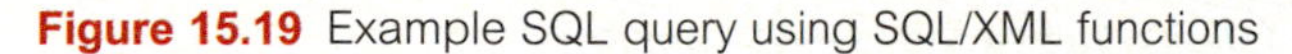

Figure 15.19 Example SQL query using SQL/XML functions

- `xmlforest()` creates a list of XML elements from a set of column names.
- `xmlconcat()` concatenates two or more XML values into one XML element.
- `xmlagg()` aggregates a collection of values into one XML element.

An example demonstrating some of these functions is shown in Figure 15.19 with the resulting output (from Oracle10g) shown in Figure 15.20.

15.7 Database integration in eCommerce systems

The combination of XML technologies and development tools and languages that support Web–database integration have resulted in a powerful set of tools that support database systems integration in eCommerce and in business in general. In this section, we introduce Web services and discuss some existing and potential applications of this technology in eCommerce.

15.7.1 Web services

Web service

A software system designed to support interoperable machine-to-machine interaction over a network.

In recent years **Web services** have emerged as a flexible way to build distributed applications. Web services are based on open standards and focus on communication and collaboration among people and applications. Unlike other Web-based applications, Web services have no user interface and are not targeted for browsers. Instead, they consist of reusable software components designed to be consumed by other applications, such as traditional client applications, Web-based applications, or other Web services.

A common example of a Web service is a stock quote facility, which receives a request for the current price of a specified stock and responds with the requested price. As a second example, Microsoft has produced a MapPoint Web service that allows high-quality maps, driving directions, and other location information to be integrated into a user application, business process, or web site.

```
<STAFFPERSON>
  <STAFFNO>S1500</STAFFNO>
  <FLNAME>Tom Daniels</FLNAME>
  <STAFFPOS>Manager</STAFFPOS>
  <SALARY>48000</SALARY>
  <DCENTERNO>D001</DCENTERNO>
</STAFFPERSON>
<STAFFPERSON>
  <STAFFNO>S0003</STAFFNO>
  <FLNAME>Sally Adams</FLNAME>
  <STAFFPOS>Assistant</STAFFPOS>
  <SALARY>30000</SALARY>
  <DCENTERNO>D001</DCENTERNO>
</STAFFPERSON>
<STAFFPERSON>
  <STAFFNO>S0010</STAFFNO>
  <FLNAME>Mary Martinez</FLNAME>
  <STAFFPOS>Manager</STAFFPOS>
  <SALARY>51000</SALARY>
  <DCENTERNO>D002</DCENTERNO>
</STAFFPERSON>
<STAFFPERSON>
  <STAFFNO>S3250</STAFFNO>
  <FLNAME>Robert Chin</FLNAME>
  <STAFFPOS>Assistant</STAFFPOS>
  <SALARY>33000</SALARY>
  <DCENTERNO>D002</DCENTERNO>
</STAFFPERSON>
<STAFFPERSON>
  <STAFFNO>S2250</STAFFNO>
  <FLNAME>Sally Stern</FLNAME>
  <STAFFPOS>Manager</STAFFPOS>
  <SALARY>48000</SALARY>
  <DCENTERNO>D004</DCENTERNO>
</STAFFPERSON>
<STAFFPERSON>
  <STAFFNO>S0415</STAFFNO>
  <FLNAME>Art Peters</FLNAME>
  <STAFFPOS>Manager</STAFFPOS>
  <SALARY>42000</SALARY>
  <DCENTERNO>D003</DCENTERNO>
</STAFFPERSON>
```

Figure 15.20 Query output using SQL/XML functions

Central to the Web services approach is the use of widely accepted technologies and commonly used standards, such as:

- The eXtensible Markup Language (XML).
- The SOAP (Simple Object Access Protocol) protocol, based on XML, is used for communication over the Internet.
- The WSDL (Web Services Description Language) protocol, again based on XML, is used to describe the Web service. WSDL adds a layer of abstraction between the interface and the implementation, providing a loosely-coupled service for future flexibility.
- The **UDDI (Universal Discovery, Description, and Integration)** protocol is used to register the Web service for prospective users.

These main components are shown in Figure 15.21 and will be described in more detail in the sections below. The specifications and protocols for Web services are still at an early stage of development and cannot cover all possible requirements. However, the Web Services Interoperability Group (WS-I), consisting of members from many of the major vendors involved in Web services development, has taken on the task of developing case studies, sample applications, implementation scenarios, and test tools to ensure that these specifications and protocols will work with each other irrespective of vendor product implementations.

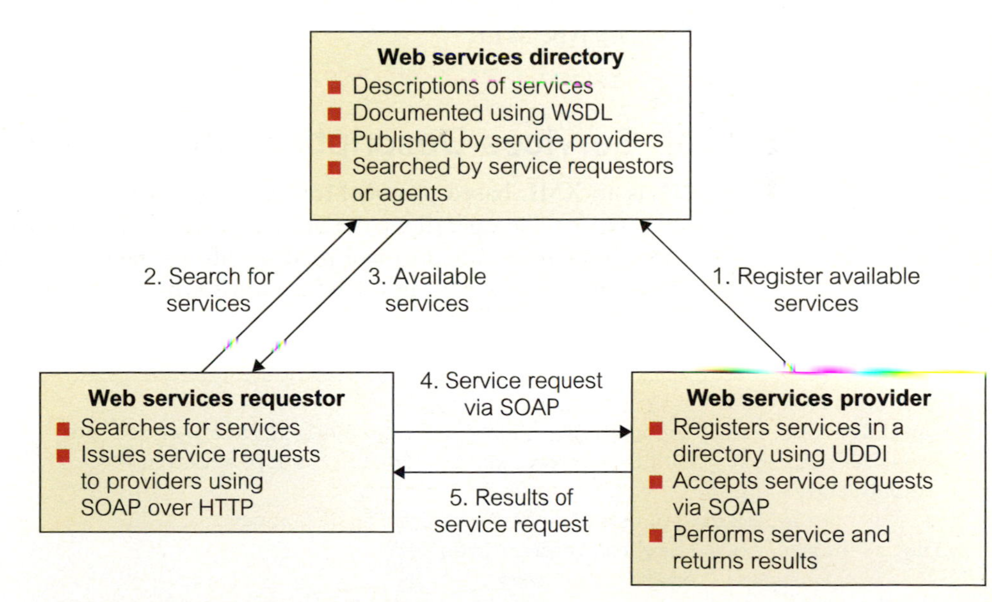

Figure 15.21 Web services interactions

15.7.2 Simple Object Access Protocol (SOAP)

SOAP (Simple Object Access Protocol)

An XML-based messaging protocol that defines a set of rules for structuring messages.

SOAP is an XML-based messaging protocol that defines a set of rules for structuring messages (http://www.w3.org/2000/xp/Group/). The protocol can be used for simple one-way messaging but is also useful for performing Remote Procedure Call (RPC)-style request–response dialogues. SOAP is not tied to any particular operating system or programming language, nor is it tied to any particular transport protocol, although HTTP is popular. This independence makes SOAP an important building block for developing Web services. In addition, an important advantage of SOAP is that most firewalls allow HTTP to pass right through, facilitating point-to-point SOAP data exchanges (although a system administrator could selectively block SOAP requests).

A SOAP message is an ordinary XML document containing the following elements:

- A required envelope element that identifies the XML document as a SOAP message.
- An optional header element that contains application specific information such as authentication or payment information. It also has three attributes that specify who should process the message, whether processing is optional or mandatory, and encoding rules that describe the data types for the application.
- A required body header element that contains call and response information.
- An optional fault element that provides information about errors that occurred while processing the message.

Figure 15.22 illustrates a simple SOAP message that obtains the monthly price membership type MT1.

15.7.3 Web Services Description Language (WSDL)

WSDL is an XML-based protocol for defining a Web service. It specifies the location of a service, the operations the service exposes, the (SOAP) messages involved, and the communications protocol used to talk to the service. The notation that a WSDL file uses to describe message formats is typically based on the XML Schema

```
<?xml version="1.1"?>
<soap:Envelope xmlns:soap="http://www.w3.org/2001/12/soap-envelope"
   soap:encodingStyle="http://www.w3.org/2001/12/soap-encoding">
   <soap:Body>
         <m:GetPriceRequest
xmlns:m="http://www.stayhome.com/prices">
               <m:Item>MT1</m:Item>
         </m:GetPriceRequest>
   </soap:Body>
</soap:Envelope>
```

Figure 15.22 Example SOAP message

standard, making it both language and platform neutral. Programmers or, more generally, automated development tools can create WSDL files to describe a service and can make the description available over the Web. Client-side programmers and development tools can use published WSDL descriptions to obtain information about available Web services, and thereafter build and create proxies or program templates that access these services.

WSDL 2.0 describes a Web service in two parts: an *abstract* part and a *concrete* part (http://www.w3.org/TR/wsd120-primer). At the abstract level, WSDL describes a Web service in terms of the messages it sends and receives; messages are described using a type system such as XML Schema.

15.7.4 Examples of web services

Mashup

An application that brings together data from multiple, often public, data sources.

Web services are being adopted by increasing numbers of companies. This is one aspect of eCommerce that is evolving very rapidly and is one of the underlying technologies that has enabled the 'Web 2.0' era of the internet. The term **mashups** is often used to describe the merging and filtering of data often accomplished through Web services. A number of companies now offer access to their internal services by way of Web services. Some more well- known examples include:

- The Google Applications Programming interface which allows other programmers to access Google search results by submitting Web services requests (http://www.google.com/apis/). For example, any developer can incorporate Google's advertising and search results into their own applications or web sites.
- Amazon Web Service (AWS) provides access to Amazon.com's products catalog as well as a variety of other services (http://www.amazon.com/gp/aws/landing.html). For example, any retailer can publish their products and make them available within Amazon's catalog for search, product comparison, and so on.
- OpenSearch, supported by a9.com an aggregate search engine developed by Amazon.com, provides a set of formats and Web services used for sharing search results. (http://opensearch.a9.com/)

Services such as these are growing in popularity as new business models emerge to take advantage of them.

Chapter summary

- **eCommerce** systems can be characterized by the participants in the business model. Some common business models include: B2C – business to consumer; B2B – business to business; C2C (or P2P) – consumer to consumer or peer to peer; G2C – government to citizen.
- The B2B market is considerably larger than all of the other business models combined.
- A general architecture of eCommerce systems includes: (possibly multiple) database management systems; Web servers; applications such as eCommerce shopping carts, payment systems, etc.; gateways to other businesses in the supply chain.
- eCommerce deployments can evolve over time to include: catalogs with browsing and searching capabilities; shopping cart/order placement; user customization; and integration with other businesses on the supply chain.
- **Electronic Data Interchange** (**EDI**) is the computer-to-computer transfer of business documents over a network using a standard format.
- Micropayment systems support the transfer of small payment amounts (generally less than US$1.00) with low per transaction costs between parties.
- mCommerce systems support accessing eCommerce products and services using mobile devices.
- Typical Web–database integration languages include: PHP Hypertext Processor; Active Server Pages (ASP); Ruby on Rails; ColdFusion; interpreted languages such as Perl and Python; compiled languages such as Java, C and C++.
- **eXtensible Markup Language** (**XML**) is a meta-language (a language for describing other languages) that enables designers to create their own customized tags to provide functionality not available with HTML.
- XML consists of the declaration and possibly an accompanying Document Type Definition (DTD) or XML Schema.
- XML technologies are varied and are in a constant state of growth. Some current XML based technologies include: XSL – the eXtensible Stylesheet Language; XSLT – eXtensible Stylesheet Language for Transformations; XHTML – eXtensible HTML; XML schema – the definition (both in terms of its organization and its data types) of a specific XML structure.
- A number of XML-based query languages have been developed. The **XQuery language** provides path expressions and FLWR (FOR, LET, WHERE, and RETURN) expressions.
- Web services are a way of integrating eCommerce systems over networks. Web services rely on technologies such as XML, SOAP, WSDL, and UDDI.

Review questions

15.1 Define eCommerce and give an example of an eCommerce service or organization characterized as
(a) B2C;
(b) B2B;
(c) G2C;
(d) C2C (or P2P).

15.2 Describe the purpose of micropayment systems.

15.3 Explain how business intelligence can be used to support customers.

15.4 Describe three potential or existing services for mCommerce systems.

15.5 Discuss the critical success factors in establishing eCommerce businesses.

15.6 Explain the difference between static and dynamic Web pages.

15.7 List the seven steps required to produce a dynamic Web page using a database query.

15.8 Explain the purpose of the common gateway interface.

15.9 Describe three approaches for carrying out Web–database integration.

15.10 Define XML and discuss its advantages and disadvantages.

15.11 Explain the purpose and uses of a Document Type Definition and XML Schema.

15.12 Describe four XML-related technologies.

15.13 Describe the two main methods for querying XML schemas using XQuery.

15.14 Define Web services and describe how SOAP and WSDL support Web services.

Exercises

15.15 Research a successful eCommerce business and discuss how it meets the critical success factors discussed in Section 15.1.2.

15.16 Research a successful G2C or G2B government entity and discuss how it meets the critical success factors discussed in Section 15.1.2.

15.17 Research a successful or emerging mCommerce business and discuss how it meets the critical success factors discussed in Section 15.1.2.

15.18 Sketch out the entities you believe a CRM system would need to contain in order to capture a wide range of customer interactions.

15.19 Research some examples of Java Server Pages (JSP) such as http://java.sun.com/products/jsp/. Write an example JSP page that would respond to a query for movie genre in a fashion similar to the Active Server Pages example given in Section 15.3.1

15.20 Research a commercial database vendor and discuss how their DBMSs support XML.

15.21 Research a commercial database vendor and discuss how their DBMSs and/or related software systems support Web services.

15.22 Locate a company that is offering access to its products or services using Web services and provide a description of the types of clients and services that will interact.

CHAPTER

16 Distributed and mobile DBMSs

Preview

Database technology has taken us from a paradigm of data processing in which each application program defined and maintained its own data to one in which data is defined and administered centrally. During recent times we have seen rapid developments in network and data communication technology, epitomized by Internet, mobile and wireless computing, and intelligent devices. Now, with the combination of these two technologies, distributed database technology may change the mode of working from centralized to decentralized. This combined technology is one of the major developments in the database systems area.

A major motivation behind the development of database systems is the desire to integrate the operational data of an organization and to provide controlled access to the data. Although we may think that integration and controlled access implies centralization, this is not the intention. In fact, the development of computer networks promotes a decentralized mode of work. This decentralized approach mirrors the organizational structure of many companies, which are logically distributed into divisions, departments, projects, and so on, and physically distributed into offices, plants, and factories, where each unit maintains its own operational data. The development of a distributed DBMS that reflects this organizational structure, makes the data in all units accessible, and stores data close to the location where it is most frequently used, should improve our ability to share the data and should improve the efficiency with which we can access the data.

In this chapter, we discuss the concepts associated with three decentralized DBMS technologies:

- distributed DBMSs (Sections 16.1–16.4);
- replication servers (Section 16.5);
- mobile DBMSs (Section 16.6).

The examples in this chapter are drawn from the *StayHome Online Rentals* case study documented in Section 5.4.

Learning objectives

In this chapter you will learn:

- The main concepts of distributed DBMSs (DDBMSs).
- The differences between DDBMSs and distributed processing.
- The advantages and disadvantages of DDBMSs.
- The main issues associated with distributed database design, namely fragmentation, replication, and allocation.
- How fragmentation should be carried out.
- The importance of allocation and replication in distributed databases.
- The levels of transparency that should be provided by a DDBMS.
- About comparison criteria for DDBMSs.
- The main concepts associated with database replication.
- The main concepts associated with mobile DBMSs.

16.1 DDBMS concepts

Distributed database management system (DDBMS)

The software system that permits the management of the distributed database and makes the distribution transparent to users.

Distributed database

A logically interrelated collection of shared data (and a description of this data), physically distributed over a computer network.

A **distributed database management system (DDBMS)** consists of a single logical database that is split into a number of **fragments**. Each fragment is stored on one or more computers (replicas) under the control of a separate DBMS, with the computers connected by a communications network. Each site is capable of independently processing user requests that require access to local data (that is, each site has some degree of **local autonomy**) and is also capable of processing data stored on other computers in the network.

Users access the **distributed database** using applications. Applications are classified as those that do not require data from other sites (*local applications*) and those that do require data from other sites (*global applications*). We require a DDBMS to have at least one global application. A DDBMS therefore has the following characteristics:

- a collection of logically related shared data;
- the data is split into a number of fragments (fragments can be horizontal or vertical, similar to the horizontal and vertical partitions that we discuss in Appendix G);
- fragments may be replicated;
- fragments/replicas are allocated to sites;
- the sites are linked by a communications network;
- the data at each site is under the control of a DBMS;
- the DBMS at each site can handle local applications, autonomously;
- each DBMS participates in at least one global application.

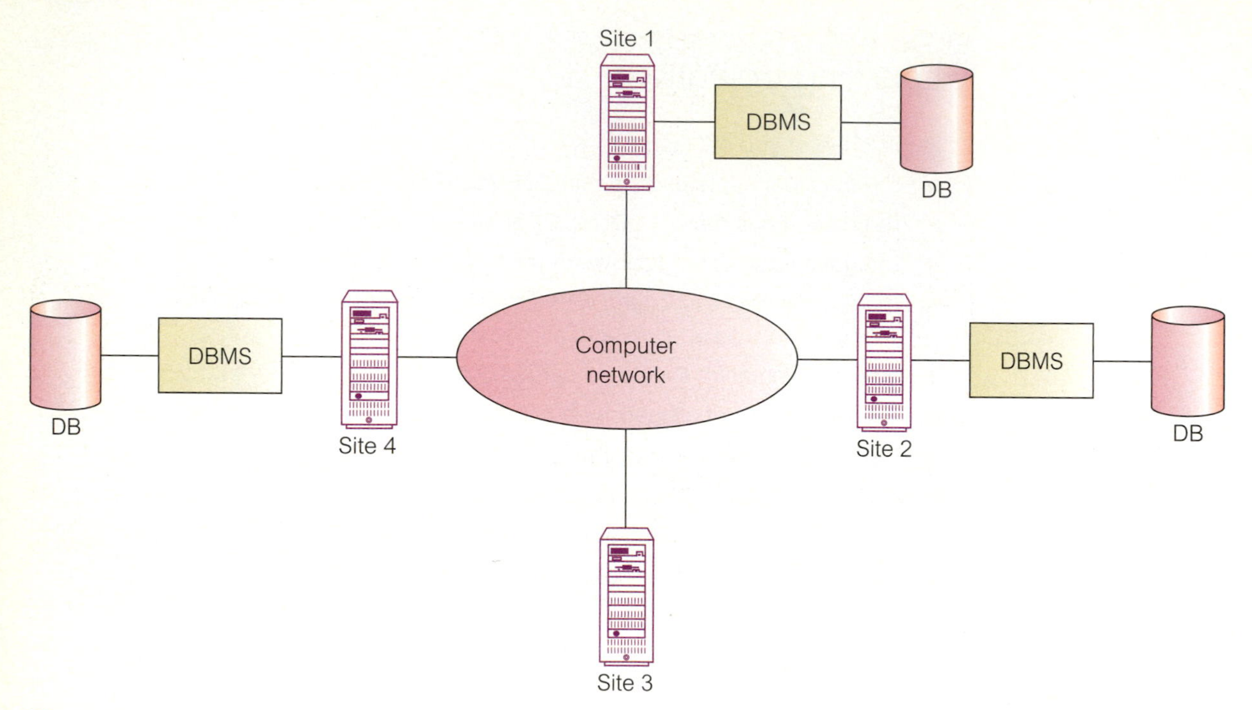

Figure 16.1 Distributed DBMS

It is not necessary for every site in the system to have its own local database, as illustrated by the topology of the DDBMS shown in Figure 16.1. From the definition of the DDBMS, the system is expected to make the distribution **transparent** (invisible) to the user. Thus, the fact that a distributed database is split into fragments that can be stored on different computers and perhaps replicated should be hidden from the user. The objective of transparency is to make the distributed system appear like a centralized system. This is sometimes referred to as the *fundamental principle* of distributed DBMSs. This requirement provides significant functionality for the end-user but, unfortunately, creates many additional problems that have to be handled by the DDBMS. We discuss transparency in more detail in Section 16.3.

Distributed processing

Distributed processing

A centralized database that can be accessed over a computer network.

It is important to make a distinction between a distributed DBMS and **distributed processing**.

The key point with the definition of a DDBMS is that the system consists of data that is physically distributed across a number of sites in the network. If the data is centralized, even though other users may be accessing the data over the network, we do not consider this to be a distributed DBMS, simply distributed processing. We illustrate the topology of distributed processing in Figure 16.2. Compare this figure, which has a central database at site 2, with Figure 16.1, which shows four sites, three of which have their own database.

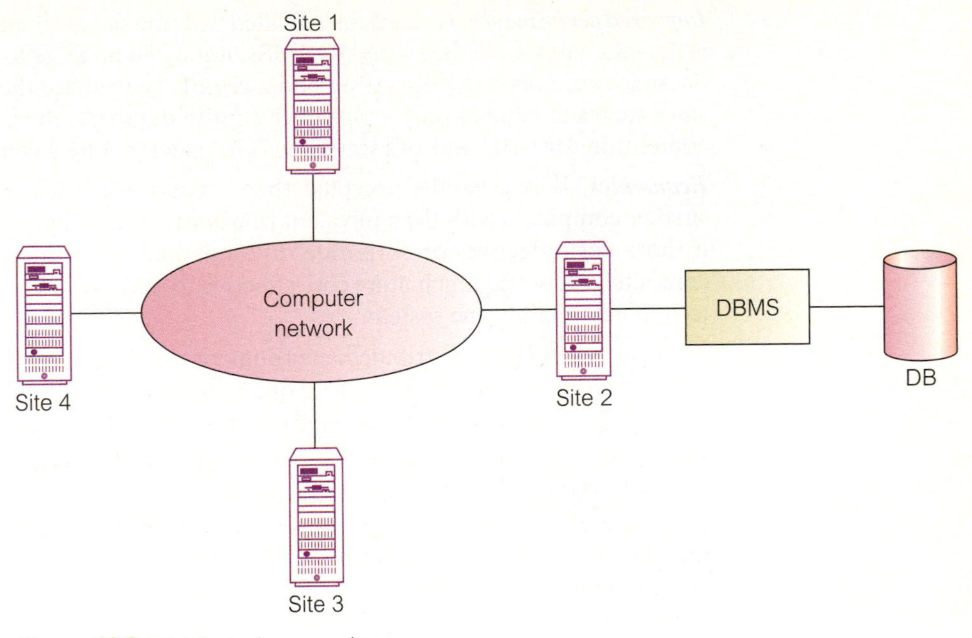

Figure 16.2 Distributed processing

16.1.1 Advantages and disadvantages of DDBMSs

The distribution of data and applications has potential advantages over traditional centralized database systems. Unfortunately, there are also disadvantages. In this section, we briefly review the advantages and disadvantages of DDBMSs.

Advantages

Reflects organizational structure. Many organizations are naturally distributed over several locations. It is natural for databases used in such a situation to be distributed over these locations.

Improved shareability and local autonomy. The geographical distribution of an organization can be reflected in the distribution of the data; users at one site can access data stored at other sites. Data can be placed at the site close to the users who normally work with that data. In this way, users have local control of the data, and they can consequently establish and enforce local policies regarding the use of this data.

Improved availability and reliability. Broadly speaking, **availability** is concerned with whether a system is continuously available during a given time period, whereas **reliability** is concerned with whether a system is running at a certain point in time. In a centralized DBMS, a computer failure terminates the operations of the DBMS. However, a failure at one site of a DDBMS, or a failure of a communication link making some sites inaccessible, does not make the entire system inoperable. Further, as data may be replicated so that it exists at more than one site, the failure of a node or a communication link does not necessarily make the data inaccessible.

Improved performance. As the data is located near the site of 'greatest demand' and there is the inherent parallelism with DDBMSs, it may be possible to improve the speed of database accesses more than if we had a remote centralized database. Furthermore, since each site handles only a part of the entire database, there may not be the same contention for CPU and I/O services as characterized by a centralized DBMS.

Economics. It is generally accepted that it costs much less to create a system of smaller computers with the equivalent power of a single large computer. This makes it more cost-effective for corporate divisions and departments to obtain separate computers. It is also much more cost-effective to add workstations to a network than to update a mainframe system.

Modular growth. In a distributed environment it is much easier to handle expansion. New sites can be added to the network without affecting the operations of other sites. This flexibility allows an organization to expand relatively easily.

Integration. At the start of this section, we noted that 'integration' was a key advantage of the DBMS approach, not 'centralization.' The integration of legacy systems is one particular example that demonstrates how some organizations are forced to rely on distributed data processing to allow their legacy systems to coexist with their more modern systems. At the same time, no one package can provide all the functionality that an organization requires nowadays. Thus, it is important for organizations to be able to integrate software components from different vendors to meet their specific requirements.

Remaining competitive. There are a number of relatively recent developments that rely heavily on distributed database technology such as eCommerce, computer-supported collaborative work, and workflow management. Many enterprises have had to reorganize their businesses and use distributed database technology to remain competitive.

Disadvantages

Complexity. A DDBMS that hides the distributed nature from the user and provides an acceptable level of performance, reliability, and availability is inherently more complex than a centralized DBMS. Replication also adds an extra level of complexity, which, if not handled adequately, will lead to degradation in availability, reliability, and performance compared with the centralized system, and the advantages we cited above will become disadvantages.

Cost. Increased complexity means that we can expect the procurement and maintenance costs for a DDBMS to be higher than those for a centralized DBMS. Furthermore, a DDBMS requires additional hardware to establish a network between sites. There are ongoing communication costs incurred with the use of this network. There are also additional manpower costs to manage and maintain the local DBMSs and the underlying network.

Security. In a centralized system, access to the data can be easily controlled. However, in a DDBMS not only does access to replicated data have to be controlled in multiple locations, but the network itself has to be made secure. In the past, networks were regarded as an insecure communication medium. Although this is still partially true, significant developments have been made recently to make networks more secure.

Integrity control more difficult. Enforcing integrity constraints generally requires access to a large amount of data that defines the constraint, but is not involved in the actual update operation itself. In a DDBMS, the communication and processing costs that are required to enforce integrity constraints may be prohibitive.

Lack of standards. Although DDBMSs depend on effective communication, we are only now starting to see the appearance of standard communication and data access protocols. This lack of standards has significantly limited the potential of DDBMSs. There are also no tools or methodologies to help users convert a centralized DBMS into a distributed DBMS.

Lack of experience. General-purpose DDBMSs have not been widely accepted, although many of the protocols and problems are well understood. Consequently, we do not yet have the same level of experience in industry as we have with centralized DBMSs. For a prospective adopter of this technology, this may be a significant deterrent.

Database design more complex. Besides the normal difficulties of designing a centralized database, the design of a distributed database has to take account of fragmentation of data, allocation of fragments to specific sites, and **data replication**. We discuss distributed database design in Section 16.2.

The advantages and disadvantages are summarized in Table 16.1. As we have just mentioned, to date general-purpose DDBMSs have not been widely accepted. Instead, *data replication*, the copying and maintenance of data on multiple servers, appears

Table 16.1 Advantages and disadvantages of DDBMSs

Advantages
Reflects organizational structure
Improved shareability and local autonomy
Improved availability and reliability
Improved performance
Economics
Modular growth
Integration
Remaining competitive
Disadvantages
Complexity
Cost
Security
Integrity control more difficult
Lack of standards
Lack of experience
Database design more complex

to be a more preferred solution. Every major database vendor has some form of replication solution and many non-database vendors also offer alternative methods for replicating data. The **replication server** is an alternative and potentially a more simplified approach to data distribution, as we discuss in Section 16.5.

16.1.2 Types of DDBMSs

Homogeneous versus heterogeneous

A DDBMS may be classified as homogeneous or heterogeneous. In a **homogeneous DDBMS**, all sites use the identical DBMS product. In a **heterogeneous DDBMS**, sites may run different DBMS products, which need not be based on the same underlying data model, and so the system may be composed of relational, network, hierarchical, and object-oriented DBMSs. Homogeneous systems are much easier to design and manage. This approach provides incremental growth, making the addition of a new site to the DDBMS easy, and it allows increased performance by exploiting the parallel processing capability of multiple sites.

Heterogeneous systems usually result when individual sites have implemented their own databases and integration is considered at a later stage. In a heterogeneous system, translations are required to allow communication between different DBMSs. To provide **DBMS transparency**, users must be able to make requests in the language of the DBMS at their local site and the system then has the task of locating the data and performing any necessary translation. Data may be required from another site that may have:

- different hardware;
- different DBMS products;
- different hardware and different DBMS products.

If the hardware is different but the DBMS products are the same, the translation is straightforward, involving the change of codes and word lengths. If the DBMS products are different, the translation is complicated, involving the mapping of data structures in one data model to the equivalent data structures in another data model. For example, relations in the relational data model are mapped to records and sets in the network model. It is also necessary to translate the query language used (for example, SQL SELECT statements are mapped to the network FIND and GET statements). If both the hardware and software are different, then these two types of translations are required. This makes the processing extremely complex.

The typical solution used by some relational systems that are part of a heterogeneous DDBMS is to use **gateways**, a type of **middleware** that convert the language and model of each different DBMS into the language and model of the relational system. However, the gateway approach has some serious limitations. First, it may not support transaction management, even for a pair of systems; in other words, the gateway between two systems may be only a query translator. For example, a system may not coordinate concurrency control and recovery of transactions that involve updates to the pair of databases. Second, the gateway approach is concerned

Middleware

Computer software that connects software components or applications. It is used most often in complex distributed applications.

only with the problem of translating a query expressed in one language into an equivalent expression in another language. As such, it does not generally address the issues of homogenizing the structural and representational differences between different schemas.

Degree of autonomy

A DDBMS may also be classified based on the degree of autonomy of the local DBMSs, which examines the distribution of control as opposed to distribution of data. There are four types of autonomy:

- *design*: each DBMS is free to use its own data model and transaction management technique;
- *participation*: each DBMS can decide how to participate in the distributed system – that is, it can decide what data to contribute and when it participates;
- *communication*: each DBMS can decide how and under what terms to communicate with other sites;
- *execution*: each DBMS can execute the transactions that are submitted to it in its own way.

At one extreme, there is no local autonomy and so there is full global control. A single conceptual schema exists and all access to the system is obtained through one site (the DDBMS looks like a centralized DBMS to the user). An example of such a system is a homogeneous DDBMS that was designed top-down. Effectively, the local DBMSs do not operate independently and there are no local users.

On the other hand, with *semi-autonomy* the local DBMSs do operate independently but have decided to participate in a federation to make their local data sharable. Each DBMS determines which parts of its database will be made available to other DBMSs. The local DBMSs are not fully autonomous because they need to be modified to allow the exchange of data with each other. Such systems are commonly referred to as **federated DBMSs**.

Finally, we have the case where the local DBMSs have *full autonomy*. Such systems are commonly referred to as **multi-database systems (MDBSs)**. One consequence of complete autonomy is that there can be no software modifications to the local DBMSs. Thus, an MDBS requires an additional software layer on top of the local systems to provide the necessary functionality. An MDBS allows users to access and share data without requiring full database schema integration. However, it still allows users to administer their own databases without centralized control, as with true DDBMSs. The DBA of a local DBMS can authorize access to particular portions of his or her database by specifying an *export schema*, which defines the parts of the database that may be accessed by non-local users.

In simple terms, an MDBS is a DBMS that resides transparently on top of existing database and file systems, and presents a single database to its users. An MDBS maintains a global schema against which users issue queries and updates; an MDBS maintains only the global schema and the local DBMSs themselves maintain all user data. The global schema is constructed by integrating the schemas of the local databases. The MDBS first translates the global queries and updates into queries and updates on the appropriate local DBMSs. It then merges the local results and generates the final global result for the user. Furthermore, the MDBS coordinates the commit and abort operations for global transactions by the local DBMSs that processed them, to maintain consistency of data within the local databases. It also controls multiple gateways and manages local databases through these gateways.

An additional complexity is the provision of a common conceptual schema, which is formed from the integration of individual local conceptual schemas. The integration of data models can be very difficult due to the semantic heterogeneity. For example, columns with the same name in two schemas may represent different things. Equally well, columns with different names may model the same thing. A complete discussion of detecting and resolving semantic heterogeneity is beyond the scope of this book, however, the interested reader is referred to the paper by Garcia-Solaco *et al.* (1996).

Figure 16.3 illustrates a partial taxonomy of DBMSs. The interested reader is referred to Sheth and Larson (1990) and Bukhres and Elmagarmid (1996) for a complete taxonomy of distributed DBMSs.

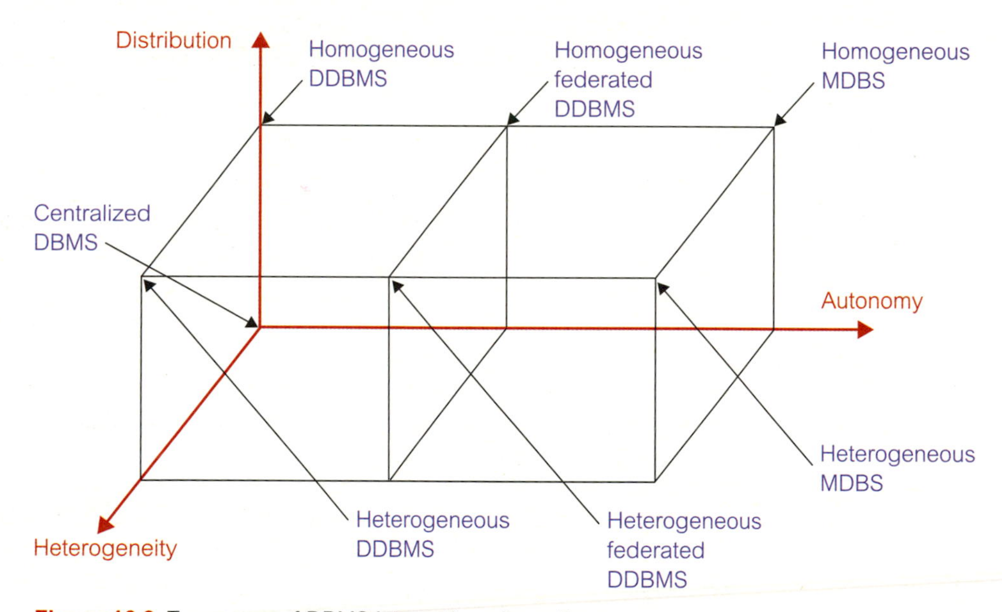

Figure 16.3 Taxonomy of DBMS integration alternatives

16.2 Distributed relational database design

In Chapters 9 and 10, we presented a methodology for the conceptual and logical design of a centralized relational database. In this section, we examine the additional factors that have to be considered for the design of a distributed relational database, namely:

- **Fragmentation**. A table may be divided into a number of subtables, called *fragments*, which are then distributed about the various local databases.

- **Allocation**. Each fragment is stored at the site with 'optimal' distribution.
- **Replication**. The DDBMS may maintain a copy of a fragment at several different sites.

As we noted in Section 1.5, in a centralized DBMS the conceptual schema describes the data that is stored in the database and the relationships between the data. In a DDBMS, as well as the (global) conceptual schema, we have a **fragmentation schema** (a description of how tables have been fragmented), an **allocation schema** (a description of how the fragments have been allocated to sites), and possibly a **replication schema** (a description of how fragments have been replicated) as we discuss in this section. The definition and allocation of fragments must be based on how the database is to be used. This involves analyzing transactions. Generally, it is not possible to analyze all transactions, so we concentrate on the most important ones. As noted in Section 11.4, it has been suggested that the most active 20% of user queries account for 80% of the total data access, and this 80/20 rule may be used as a guideline in carrying out this analysis (Wiederhold, 1983). The design should be based on both qualitative and quantitative information. Qualitative information is used in fragmentation; quantitative information is used in allocation. The qualitative information may include information about the transactions that are executed, such as:

- the tables, columns, and records accessed;
- the type of access (read or write);
- the search conditions specified in the WHERE clause of an SQL statement.

The quantitative information may include:

- the frequency with which a transaction is run (for example, transaction runs 50 times daily);
- the site from which a transaction is run;
- the performance criteria for transactions (for example, transaction must complete within 1 second).

The definition and allocation of fragments are carried out strategically to achieve the following objectives:

- *Locality of reference*. Where possible, data should be stored close to where it is used. If a fragment is used at several sites, it may be advantageous to store copies of the fragment at these sites.
- *Improved reliability and availability*. Reliability and availability are improved by replication: there is another copy of the fragment available at another site in the event of one site failing.
- *Acceptable performance*. Bad allocation may result in bottlenecks occurring: that is, a site may become overloaded with requests from other sites, perhaps causing a significant degradation in performance. Alternatively, bad allocation may result in under-utilization of resources.
- *Balanced storage capacities and costs*. Consideration should be given to the availability and cost of storage at each site so that cheap mass storage can be used, where possible. This must be balanced against *locality of reference*.

- *Minimal communication costs*. Consideration should be given to the cost of remote requests. Retrieval costs are minimized when *locality of reference* is maximized or when each site has its own copy of the data. However, when replicated data is updated, the update has to be performed at all sites holding a duplicate copy, thereby increasing communication costs.

16.2.1 Fragmentation

In this section, we discuss the following issues related to fragmentation:

- Why fragment a table?
- How to test the correctness of the fragmentation schema.
- The different types of fragmentation.

Why fragment?

Before we discuss fragmentation in detail, we list four reasons for fragmenting a table:

- *Usage*. In general, applications work with views rather than entire tables (see Section 1.2.5). Therefore, for data distribution it seems appropriate to work with subsets of tables as the *unit of distribution*.
- *Efficiency*. Data is stored close to where it is most frequently used. In addition, data that is not needed by local applications is not stored.
- *Parallelism*. With fragments as the unit of distribution, a transaction can be divided into several subqueries that operate on fragments. This should increase the degree of concurrency, or parallelism, in the system thereby allowing transactions, that can do so safely, to execute in parallel.
- *Security*. Data not required by local applications is not stored and consequently not available to unauthorized users.

Fragmentation has two primary disadvantages, which we have mentioned previously:

- *Performance*. The performance of global applications that require data from several fragments located at different sites may be slower.
- *Integrity*. Integrity control may be more difficult if data and functional dependencies (see Section 8.4) are fragmented and located at different sites.

Correctness of fragmentation

Fragmentation cannot be carried out haphazardly. There are three rules that must be followed during fragmentation:

(1) *Completeness*. If a table instance R is decomposed into fragments R_1, R_2, . . . R_n, each data item that can be found in R must appear in at least one fragment. This rule is necessary to ensure that there is no loss of data during fragmentation.

(2) *Reconstruction*. It must be possible to reconstruct the table R from the fragments. This rule ensures that functional dependencies are preserved.

(3) *Disjointness*. If a data item appears in fragment R_i, then it should not appear in any other fragment. Vertical fragmentation is the exception to this rule, where primary key columns must be repeated to allow reconstruction. This rule ensures minimal data redundancy.

In the case of horizontal fragmentation, a data item is a record; for vertical fragmentation, a data item is a column.

Types of fragmentation

There are two main types of fragmentation: *horizontal* and *vertical*. Horizontal fragments are subsets of records, and vertical fragments are subsets of columns, as illustrated in Figure 16.4. There are also two other types of fragmentation: *mixed*, illustrated in Figure 16.5, and *derived*, a type of horizontal fragmentation. We now

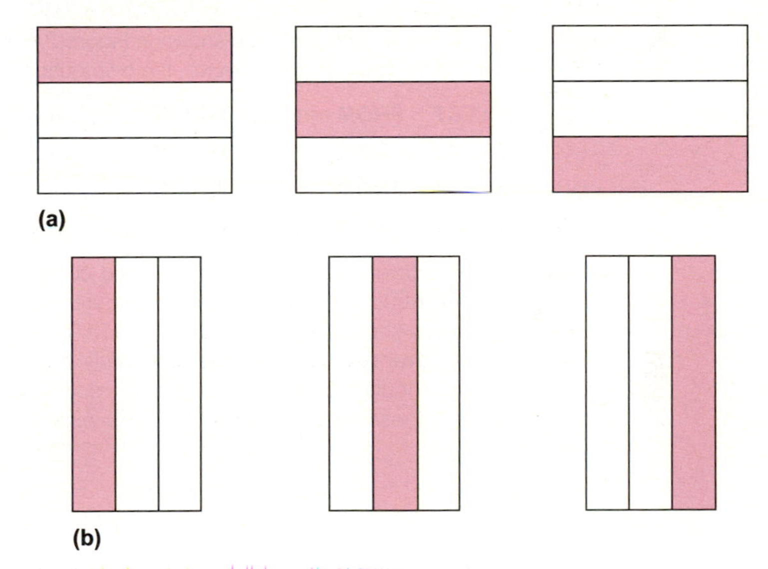

Figure 16.4 (a) Horizontal and (b) vertical fragmentation

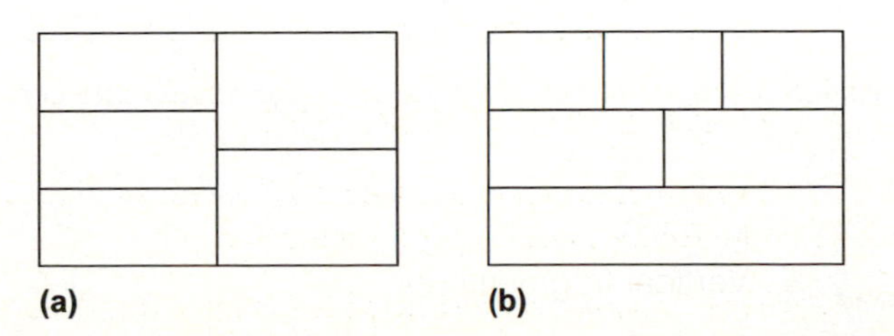

Figure 16.5 Mixed fragmentation: (a) vertical fragments, horizontally fragmented; (b) horizontal fragments, vertically fragmented

provide examples of the different types of fragmentation using the instance of the *StayHome Online Rentals* database shown in Figure 2.4.

Horizontal fragmentation

Horizontal fragment

Consists of a subset of the records of a table.

Horizontal fragmentation groups together the records in a table that are collectively used by the important transactions. A **horizontal fragment** is produced by specifying a predicate that performs a restriction on the records in the table (for example, by specifying a WHERE clause in an SQL SELECT statement, as the next example shows). Sometimes, the choice of horizontal fragmentation strategy is obvious. However, in other cases it is necessary to analyze the applications in detail. As noted above, this analysis involves an examination of the predicates (or search conditions) used by transactions or queries in the applications. The predicates may be *simple*, involving single columns, or *complex*, involving multiple columns.

Example 16.1 Horizontal fragmentation

Consider the DVDCopy table instance shown in Figure 2.4. We can define a horizontal fragmentation of DVDCopy by dCenterNo, the distribution center number, as follows:

DC_1: **SELECT** * **FROM** DVDCopy **WHERE** dCenterNo = 'D001';

DC_2: **SELECT** * **FROM** DVDCopy **WHERE** dCenterNo = 'D002;

DC_3: **SELECT** * **FROM** DVDCopy **WHERE** dCenterNo = 'D003

DC_4: **SELECT** * **FROM** DVDCopy **WHERE** dCenterNo = 'D004;

This produces four fragments (DC1, DC2, DC3, and DC4) each consisting of the records for a particular distribution center, as shown in Figure 16.6 (note, in Figure 2.4 there are currently no records shown for centers D003 and D004). This particular fragmentation strategy may be advantageous as we have separate applications dealing with DVD copies at each distribution center. We can easily verify that this fragmentation schema satisfies the correctness rules and leave this as an exercise for the reader (see Exercise 16.13).

DC_1

DVDNo	available	catalogNo	dCenterNo
19900422	Y	207132	D001
17864331	N	634817	D001

DC_2

DVDNo	available	catalogNo	dCenterNo
24545663	Y	207132	D002
24343196	Y	634817	D002

Figure 16.6 Horizontal fragmentation of DVDCopy by the dCenterNo column

Vertical fragmentation

Vertical fragment

Consists of a subset of the columns of a table.

Vertical fragmentation groups together the columns in a table that are used jointly by the important transactions.

Example 16.2 Vertical fragmentation

The *StayHome* payroll department requires the `staffNo`, `position`, and `salary` columns of each member of staff; the human resources department requires the `staffNo`, `name`, `eMail`, and `dCenterNo` columns. The vertical fragmentation of `Staff` for this example canbe obtained as follows:

S_1: **SELECT** `staffNo, position, salary` **FROM** `Staff;`

S_2: **SELECT** `staffNo, name, eMail, dCenterNo` **FROM** `Staff;`

This produces two fragments (S_1 and S_2), as shown in Figure 16.7. Note that both fragments contain the primary key, `staffNo`, to enable the original table to be reconstructed. The advantage of vertical fragmentation is that the fragments can be stored at the sites that need them. In addition, performance is improved, as the fragment is smaller than the original base table. We can easily verify that this fragmentation schema satisfies the correctness rules and leave this as an exercise for the reader (see Exercise 16.13).

S_1

staffNo	position	salary
S1500	Manager	48000
S0003	Assistant	30000
S0010	Manager	51000
S3250	Assistant	33000
S2250	Manager	48000
S0415	Manager	42000

S_2

staffNo	name	eMail	dCenterNo
S1500	Tom Daniels	tdaniels@stayhome.com	D001
S0003	Sally Adams	sadams@stayhome.com	D001
S0010	Mary Martinez	mmartinez@stayhome.com	D002
S3250	Robert Chin	rchin@stayhome.com	D002
S2250	Sally Stern	sstern@stayhome.com	D004
S0415	Art Peters	apeters@stayhome.com	D003

Figure 16.7 Vertical fragmentation of `Staff`

Mixed (or hybrid) fragment

Consists of a horizontal fragment that is subsequently vertically fragmented, or a vertical fragment that is then horizontally fragmented.

Mixed fragmentation

Sometimes, horizontal or vertical fragmentation of a database schema by itself is insufficient to adequately distribute the data for some applications. Instead, **mixed** or **hybrid fragmentation** is required.

Example 16.3 Mixed fragmentation

In Example 16.2, we vertically fragmented `Staff` for the payroll and human resources departments. We could now horizontally fragment S_2 according to the distribution center number (we assume that there are only four centers):

S_{21}: **SELECT** * **FROM** S_2 **WHERE** `dCenterNo` = 'D001';

S_{22}: **SELECT** * **FROM** S_2 **WHERE** `dCenterNo` = 'D002';

S_{23}: **SELECT** * **FROM** S_2 **WHERE** `dCenterNo` = 'D003';

S_{24}: **SELECT** * **FROM** S_2 **WHERE** `dCenterNo` = 'D004';

This produces four fragments (S_{21}, S_{22}, S_{23}, and S_{24}) each consisting of the records for a particular distribution center, as shown in Figure 16.8. We can easily verify that this fragmentation schema satisfies the correctness rules and leave this as an exercise for the reader (see Exercise 16.13).

S_1

staffNo	position	salary
S1500	Manager	48000
S0003	Assistant	30000
S0010	Manager	51000
S3250	Assistant	33000
S2250	Manager	48000
S0415	Manager	42000

S_{21}

staffNo	name	eMail	dCenterNo
S1500	Tom Daniels	tdaniels@stayhome.com	D001
S0003	Sally Adams	sadams@stayhome.com	D001

S_{22}

staffNo	name	eMail	dCenterNo
S0010	Mary Martinez	mmartinez@stayhome.com	D002
S3250	Robert Chin	rchin@stayhome.com	D002

S_{23}

staffNo	name	eMail	dCenterNo
S0415	Art Peters	apeters@stayhome.com	D003

S_{24}

staffNo	name	eMail	dCenterNo
S2250	Sally Stern	sstern@stayhome.com	D004

Figure 16.8 Mixed fragmentation of `Staff`

Derived horizontal fragmentation

Some applications may involve a join of two or more tables. If the tables are stored at different locations, there may be a significant overhead in processing the join. In such cases, it may be more appropriate to ensure that the tables, or fragments of tables, are at the same location. We can achieve this using **derived horizontal fragmentation**.

Derived fragment

A horizontal fragment that is based on the horizontal fragmentation of a parent table.

We use the term *child* to refer to the table that contains the foreign key and *parent* to the table containing the targeted primary key.

Example 16.4 Derived horizontal fragmentation

StayHome has an application that joins the `DVDCopy` and `DVDRental` tables. For this example, we assume that `DVDCopy` is horizontally fragmented as in Example 16.1 so that data relating to each center is stored locally:

```
DC1: SELECT * FROM DVDCopy WHERE dCenterNo = 'D001';
DC2: SELECT * FROM DVDCopy WHERE dCenterNo = 'D002';
DC3: SELECT * FROM DVDCopy WHERE dCenterNo = 'D003';
DC4: SELECT * FROM DVDCopy WHERE dCenterNo = 'D004';
```

It would be useful to store rental data using the same fragmentation strategy; that is, according to the distribution center. However, the `DVDRental` table does not have a column for the distribution center number (there is no direct relationship between `DVDRental` and `DistributionCenter`). However, we can still achieve this by fragmenting the table based on how the `DVDCopy` table has been fragmented (in other words, *deriving* the fragmentation of `DVDRental` from the `DVDCopy` table):

```
DR1: SELECT dr.* FROM DVDRental dr, DC1 WHERE dr.DVDNo = DC1.DVDNo;
DR2: SELECT dr.* FROM DVDRental dr, DC2 WHERE dr.DVDNo = DC2.DVDNo;
DR3: SELECT dr.* FROM DVDRental dr, DC3 WHERE dr.DVDNo = DC3.DVDNo;
DR4: SELECT dr.* FROM DVDRental dr, DC4 WHERE dr.DVDNo = DC4.DVDNo;
```

This produces four fragments (DR_1, DR_2, DR_3, and DR_4) each consisting of those rentals associated with DVD copies at a particular distribution center, as shown in Figure 16.9 (note, with the sample data in Figure 2.4 there are no rentals shown for centers D003 or D004). We can easily show that this fragmentation schema satisfies the correctness rules and we leave this as an exercise for the reader (see Exercise 16.13).

Now when we join the `DVDCopy` and `DVDRental` tables, we can perform the join locally and merge the local joins together; that is, we merge DC_1 and DR_1 fragments at site D001, DC_2 and DR_2 fragments at site D002, DC_3 and DR_3 fragments at site D003, and DC_4 and DR_4 fragments at site D004, then union these four results tables together.

If a table contains more than one foreign key, it will be necessary to select one of the referenced tables as the parent. For example, assuming that the `Member` table was also horizontally fragmented based on the distribution center, `dCenterNo`, then we could also have derived `DVDRental` from `Member`. The choice can be based on the fragmentation used most frequently or the fragmentation with better join characteristics; that is, the join involving smaller fragments or the join that can be performed in parallel to a greater degree.

DR_1

deliveryNo	DVDNo	dateReturn
R66825673	19900422	7-Feb-06
R66818964	17864331	

DR_2

deliveryNo	DVDNo	dateReturn
R75346191	24545663	6-Feb-06
R75346282	24343196	6-Feb-06

Figure 16.9 Derived fragmentation of `DVDRental` based on `DVDCopy`

No fragmentation

A final strategy is not to fragment a table. For example, the `DistributionCenter` table contains only a small number of records and is not updated very frequently. Rather than trying to horizontally fragment the table on, for example, distribution center number, it would be more sensible to leave the table whole and simply replicate the `DistributionCenter` table at each site.

16.2.2 Allocation

There are four alternative strategies regarding the placement of data (**allocation**): centralized, fragmented, complete replication, and selective replication. We now compare these strategies using the strategic objectives identified at the start of Section 16.2.

Centralized

This strategy consists of a single database and DBMS stored at one site with users distributed across the network (we referred to this previously as distributed processing). Locality of reference is at its lowest as all sites, except the central site, have to use the network for all data accesses; this also means that communication costs are high. Reliability and availability are low because a failure of the central site results in the loss of the entire database system.

Fragmented (or partitioned)

This strategy partitions the database into disjoint fragments, with each fragment assigned to one site. If data items are located at the site where they are used most frequently, locality of reference is high. As there is no replication, storage costs are low; similarly, reliability and availability are low, although they are higher than in the centralized case because the failure of a site results in the loss of only that site's data. Performance should be good and communications costs low if the distribution is designed properly.

Complete replication

This strategy consists of maintaining a complete copy of the database at each site. Therefore, locality of reference, reliability and availability, and performance are maximized. However, storage costs and communication costs for updates are the most expensive. To overcome some of these problems, **snapshots** are sometimes used. A snapshot is a copy of the data at a given time. The copies are updated on a periodic basis, for example hourly or weekly, so they may not be always up to date. Snapshots are also sometimes used to implement views in a distributed database to improve the time it takes to perform a database operation on a view. We discuss asynchronous replication in Section 16.5.

Selective replication

This strategy is a combination of fragmentation, replication, and centralization. Some data items are fragmented to achieve high locality of reference and others, which are used at many sites and are not frequently updated, are replicated; otherwise, the data items are centralized. The objective of this strategy is to have all the advantages of the other approaches but none of the disadvantages. This is the most commonly used strategy because of its flexibility.

The alternative strategies are summarized in Table 16.2. For further details on allocation, the interested reader is referred to Ozsu and Valduriez (1999).

Table 16.2 Comparison of strategies for **data allocation**

	Locality of reference	Reliability and availability	Performance	Storage costs	Communication costs
Centralized	**LOWEST** All sites, except central site, have to use the network for all data accesses	**LOWEST** Failure of central site results in loss of entire system	**UNSATISFACTORY**	**LOWEST** No replication	**HIGHEST** All sites, except central site, have to use the network for all data accesses
Fragmented	**HIGH**† Data items located at site where they are used most frequently	**LOW FOR ITEM; HIGH FOR SYSTEM** Failure of a site results in loss of only that site's data	**SATISFACTORY**†	**LOWEST** No replication	**LOW**† Due to high locality of reference
Complete replication	**HIGHEST** Database fully replicated at each site	**HIGHEST** Database fully replicated at each site	**BEST FOR READ** Poor for update as operation has to be performed at each site	**HIGHEST** Database fully replicated at each site	**HIGH FOR UPDATE; LOW FOR READ** Data can be read from any site but update operation has to be performed at each site
Selective replication	**HIGH**† Based on appropriate fragmentation and allocation design	**LOW FOR ITEM; HIGH FOR SYSTEM** Failure of a site results in loss of only the data at that site that has not been replicated	**SATISFACTORY**†	**AVERAGE** Some replication present	**LOW**† Based on appropriate fragmentation and allocation design

† Indicates subject to good design.

16.2.3 Overview of a distributed database design methodology

We are now in a position to summarize a methodology for distributed database design.

(1) Use the methodology described in Chapters 9 and 10 to produce a design for the global tables.

(2) Examine the topology of the system. For example, consider whether *StayHome* will have a database at each distribution center, or in each state, or possibly at some other level. In the first case, fragmenting tables on a distribution center number basis may be appropriate. However, in the second case it may be more appropriate to try to fragment tables on a state basis.

(3) Analyze the most important transactions in the system and identify where horizontal or vertical fragmentation may be appropriate.

(4) Decide which tables are not to be fragmented – these tables will be replicated everywhere. From the global ER diagram, remove the tables that are not going to be fragmented and any relationships these transactions are involved in. For example, for *StayHome* we would not fragment the `DistributionCenter` nor `MembershipType` tables but would replicate these at all sites.

(5) After that, typically examine the tables that are on the one-side of a relationship and decide a suitable fragmentation schema for these tables, taking into consideration the topology of the system. Tables on the many-side of a relationship may be candidates for derived fragmentation.

(6) During the previous step, check for situations where vertical/mixed fragmentation would be appropriate (that is, where transactions require access to a subset of the columns of a table).

16.3 Transparencies in a DDBMS

The definition of a DDBMS given in Section 16.1 states that the system should make the distribution *transparent* to the user. Transparency hides implementation details from the user. In a centralized DBMS, data independence is a form of transparency – it hides changes in the definition and organization of the data from the user. A DDBMS may provide various levels of transparency. However, they all participate in the same overall objective: to make the use of the distributed database equivalent to that of a centralized database. We can identify four main types of transparency in a DDBMS:

- distribution transparency;
- transaction transparency;
- performance transparency;
- DBMS transparency.

Note that all the transparencies we discuss below are rarely met by a single system.

16.3.1 Distribution transparency

Distribution transparency allows the user to perceive the database as a single, logical entity. If a DDBMS exhibits distribution transparency, then the user does not need to know that the data is fragmented (**fragmentation transparency**) or the location of data items (**location transparency**). If the user needs to know that the data is fragmented and the location of fragments then we call this **local mapping transparency**. These transparencies are ordered, as we now discuss. To illustrate these concepts, we consider the distribution of the `Staff` table given in Example 16.3, namely:

S_1:	**SELECT** staffNo, position, salary **FROM** Staff;	located at site 1
S_2:	**SELECT** staffNo, name, eMail, dCenterNo **FROM** Staff;	
S_{21}:	**SELECT** * **FROM** S_2 **WHERE** dCenterNo = 'D001';	located at site 1
S_{22}:	**SELECT** * **FROM** S_2 **WHERE** dCenterNo = 'D002';	located at site 2
S_{23}:	**SELECT** * **FROM** S_2 **WHERE** dCenterNo = 'D003';	located at site 3
S_{24}:	**SELECT** * **FROM** S_2 **WHERE** dCenterNo = 'D004';	located at site 4

Fragmentation transparency

This is the highest level of distribution transparency. If fragmentation transparency is provided by the DDBMS, then the user does not need to know that the data is fragmented. As a result, database accesses are based on the global schema, so the user does not need to specify fragment names or data locations. For example, to retrieve the names of all Managers, with fragmentation transparency we could write:

```
SELECT name
FROM Staff
WHERE position = 'Manager';
```

This is the same SQL statement as we would write in a centralized system.

Location transparency

This is the middle level of distribution transparency. With location transparency, the user must know how the data has been fragmented but still does not have to know the location of the data. The above query under location transparency now becomes:

```
SELECT name
FROM S21
WHERE staffNo IN (SELECT staffNo FROM S1 WHERE position = 'Manager')
  UNION
SELECT name
FROM S22
WHERE staffNo IN (SELECT staffNo FROM S1 WHERE position = 'Manager')
  UNION
SELECT name
FROM S23
```

```
WHERE staffNo IN (SELECT staffNo FROM S1 WHERE position = 'Manager')
  UNION
SELECT name
FROM S24
WHERE staffNo IN (SELECT staffNo FROM S1 WHERE position = 'Manager');
```

We now have to specify the names of the fragments in the query. We also have to use a join (or subquery) because the columns `position` and `name` appear in different vertical fragments. The main advantage of location transparency is that the database may be physically reorganized without impact on the application programs that access them.

Replication transparency

Closely related to location transparency is **replication transparency**, which means that the user is unaware of the replication of fragments. Replication transparency is implied by location transparency. However, it is possible for a system not to have location transparency but to have replication transparency.

Local mapping transparency

This is the lowest level of distribution transparency. With local mapping transparency, the user needs to specify both fragment names and the location of fragments, taking into consideration any replication that may exist. The example query under local mapping transparency becomes:

```
SELECT name
FROM S21 AT SITE 1
WHERE staffNo IN (SELECT staffNo FROM S1 AT SITE 1 WHERE position =
  'Manager') UNION
SELECT name
FROM S22 AT SITE 2
WHERE staffNo IN (SELECT staffNo FROM S1 AT SITE 1 WHERE position =
  'Manager') UNION
SELECT name
FROM S23 AT SITE 3
WHERE staffNo IN (SELECT staffNo FROM S1 AT SITE 1 WHERE position =
  'Manager') UNION
SELECT name
FROM S24 AT SITE 4
WHERE staffNo IN (SELECT staffNo FROM S1 AT SITE 1 WHERE position =
  'Manager');
```

For the purposes of illustration, we have extended SQL with the keyword **AT SITE** to express where a particular fragment is located. Clearly, this is a more complex and time-consuming query for the user to enter than the first two. It is unlikely that a system that provided only this level of transparency would be acceptable to end-users.

16.3.2 Transaction transparency

Transaction transparency in a DDBMS environment ensures that all transactions maintain the distributed database's integrity and consistency. In IBM's Distributed Relational Database Architecture (DRDA), there are four types of transaction, each with a progressive level of complexity in the interaction between the DBMSs, as illustrated in Figure 16.10:

(1) *Remote request*. An application at one site can send a request (SQL statement) to some remote site for execution. The request is executed entirely at the remote site and can only reference data at the remote site.

(2) *Remote unit of work*. An application at one (local) site can send all the SQL statements in a unit of work (transaction) to some remote site for execution. All SQL statements are executed entirely at the remote site and can only reference data at the remote site. However, the local site decides whether the transaction is to be committed or rolled back.

(3) *Distributed unit of work*. An application at one (local) site can send some or all of the SQL statements in a transaction to one or more remote sites for execution. Each SQL statement is executed entirely at the remote site and can only reference data at the remote site. However, different SQL statements can be executed at different sites. Again, the local site decides whether the transaction is to be committed or rolled back.

(4) *Distributed request*. An application at one (local) site can send some or all of the SQL statements in a transaction to one or more remote sites for execution. However, an SQL statement may require access to data from more than one site (for example, the SQL statement may need to join or union tables/fragments located at different sites).

In the latter two cases, the transaction is divided into a number of *subtransactions*, one for each site that has to be accessed. Atomicity is still fundamental to the transaction concept but, in addition, the DDBMS must also ensure the atomicity of each subtransaction (see Section 14.1.1). Therefore, not only must the DDBMS ensure synchronization of subtransactions with other local transactions that are executing concurrently at a site, it must also ensure synchronization of subtransactions with global transactions running simultaneously at the same or different sites. Transaction transparency in a DDBMS is complicated by the fragmentation, allocation, and replication schemas. We consider two further aspects of transaction transparency: **concurrency transparency** and **failure transparency**.

Concurrency transparency

Concurrency transparency is provided by the DDBMS if the results of all concurrent transactions (distributed and non-distributed) execute *independently* and are logically *consistent* with the results that are obtained if the transactions are executed one at a time, in some arbitrary serial order. These are the same fundamental principles as we discussed for a centralized DBMS in Section 14.2.2. However, there is the added complexity that the DDBMS must ensure that both global and local transactions do not interfere with each other. Similarly, the DDBMS must ensure the consistency of all subtransactions of the global transaction.

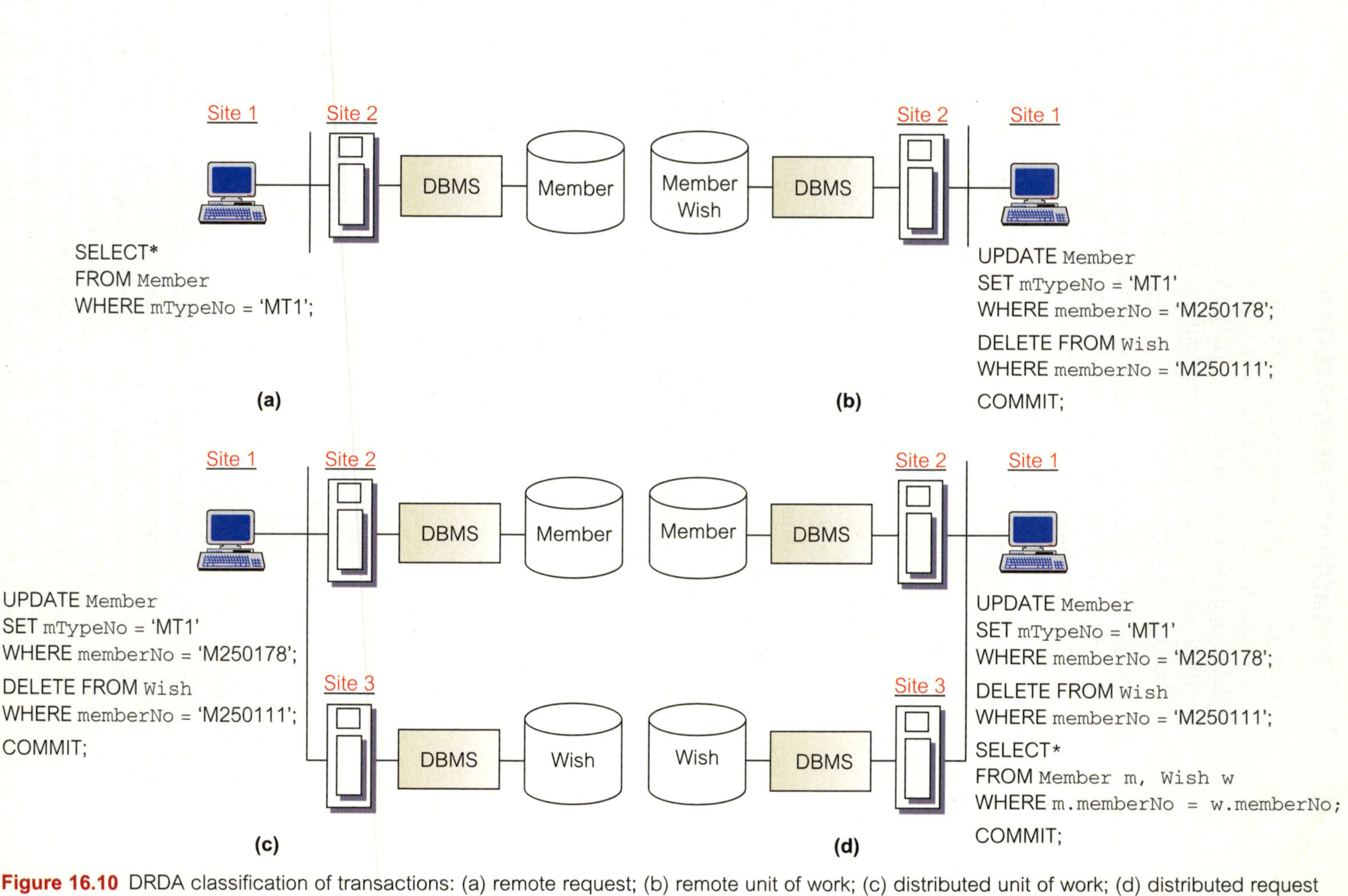

Figure 16.10 DRDA classification of transactions: (a) remote request; (b) remote unit of work; (c) distributed unit of work; (d) distributed request

Replication makes the issue of concurrency more complex. If a copy of a replicated data item is updated, the update must eventually be propagated to all copies. An obvious strategy is to propagate the changes as part of the original transaction, making it an atomic operation. However, if one of the sites holding a copy is not reachable when the update is being processed, either because the site or the communication link has failed, then the transaction is delayed until the site is reachable. If there are many copies of the data item, the probability of the transaction succeeding decreases exponentially. An alternative strategy is to limit the update propagation to only those sites that are currently available. The remaining sites must be updated when they become available again. A further strategy would be to allow the updates to the copies to happen *asynchronously*, sometime after the original update. The delay in regaining consistency may range from a few seconds to several hours. We discuss asynchronous replication in Section 16.5.

Failure transparency

In Section 14.3.2, we stated that a centralized DBMS must provide a recovery mechanism that ensures that, in the presence of failures, transactions are *atomic* – either all the operations of the transaction are carried out or none at all. Furthermore, once a transaction has committed, the changes are *durable*. We also examined the types of failure that could occur in a centralized system such as system crashes, media failures, software errors, carelessness, natural physical disasters, and sabotage. In the distributed environment, the DDBMS must also cater for:

- the loss of a message (generally this is handled by the underlying network protocol);
- the failure of a communication link;
- the failure of a site;
- network partitioning.

The DDBMS must ensure the atomicity of the global transaction, which means ensuring that subtransactions of the global transaction either all commit or all abort. Thus, the DDBMS must synchronize the global transaction to ensure that all subtransactions have completed successfully before recording a final COMMIT for the global transaction. For example, consider a global transaction that has to update data at two sites, S_1 and S_2, say. The subtransaction at site S_1 completes successfully and commits, but the subtransaction at site S_2 is unable to commit and rolls back the changes to ensure local consistency. The distributed database is now in an inconsistent state: we are unable to *uncommit* the data at site S_1 due to the durability property of the subtransaction at S_1.

The main recovery protocol for distributed systems is known as **two-phase commit (2PC)**. As the name implies, 2PC operates in two phases: a *voting phase* and a *decision phase*. The basic idea is that the coordinator of the distributed transaction (that is, the site where the transaction is initiated) asks all participant sites if they are prepared to commit the transaction. If one participant votes to abort, or fails to respond within a timeout period, then the coordinator instructs all participants to abort the transaction. If all vote to commit, then the coordinator instructs all participants to commit the transaction. The global decision must be adopted by all participants. If a participant votes to abort, then it is free to abort the transaction immediately; in fact, any site is free to abort a transaction at any time up until it votes to commit. This type of abort is known as a *unilateral abort*. If a participant votes to commit, then it must wait for the coordinator to broadcast either the *global commit* or *global abort* message. This protocol assumes that each site has its own local log, and can therefore rollback or commit the transaction reliably (see Section 14.3). The processing for the case when participants vote COMMIT and ABORT are shown in Figure 16.11.

Coordinator		**Participant**
Commit:		
write *begin_commit* to log		
send PREPARE to all participants	→	Prepare:
wait for responses		write *ready_commit* to log
	←	send READY_COMMIT to coordinator
Ready_commit:		wait for GLOBAL_COMMIT or GLOBAL_ABORT
if all participants have voted READY:		
write *commit* to log		
send GLOBAL_COMMIT to all participants	→	Global_commit:
wait for acknowledgements		write *commit* record to log
		commit transaction
Ack:		
if all participants have acknowledged:	←	send acknowledgements
write *end_of_transaction* to log		

(a)

Coordinator		**Participant**
Commit:		
write *begin_commit* to log		
send PREPARE to all participants	→	Prepare:
wait for responses		write *abort* to log
	←	send ABORT to coordinator
Abort:		abort transaction
if a participant has voted ABORT:		
write *abort* to log		
send GLOBAL_ABORT to all participants	→	
wait for acknowledgements		

(b)

Figure 16.11 Summary of 2PC: (a) 2PC protocol for participant voting COMMIT; (b) 2PC protocol for participant voting ABORT

Under 2PC it is possible for sites to become blocked in certain circumstances. For example, a participant that times out after voting COMMIT but before receiving the global instruction from the coordinator, is blocked if it can communicate only with sites that are similarly unaware of the global decision. The probability of blocking occurring in practice is sufficiently rare that most existing systems use 2PC.

16.3.3 Performance transparency

Performance transparency requires a DDBMS to perform as if it were a centralized DBMS. In a distributed environment, the system should not suffer any performance degradation due to the distributed architecture, for example the presence of the underlying network. Performance transparency also requires the DDBMS to determine the most cost-effective strategy to execute a request. In a centralized DBMS, the Query Processor (QP) must evaluate every database request (for example, an SQL SELECT statement) and find an optimal execution strategy. In a distributed environment, the Distributed Query Processor (DQP) maps a data request into an ordered sequence of operations on the local databases. It has the added complexity of taking into account:

- which fragment to access;
- which copy of a fragment to use, if the fragment is replicated;
- which location to use.

The DQP produces an execution strategy that is optimized with respect to some cost function. Typically, the costs associated with a distributed request include:

- the access time (I/O) cost involved in accessing the physical data on disk;
- the CPU time cost incurred when performing operations on data in main memory;
- the communication cost associated with the transmission of data across the network.

The first two factors are the only ones considered in a centralized system. In a distributed environment, the DDBMS must take account of the communication cost, which may be the most dominant factor in Wide Area Networks (WANs) with a bandwidth of a few kilobytes per second. In such cases, optimization may ignore I/O and CPU costs. However, Local Area Networks (LANs) have a bandwidth comparable with that of disks, so in such cases optimization should not ignore I/O and CPU costs entirely.

One approach to query optimization minimizes the total cost of time that will be incurred in executing the query (Sacco and Yao, 1982). An alternative approach minimizes the response time of the query, in which case the DQP attempts to maximize the parallel execution of operations (Epstein *et al.*, 1978). Sometimes, the response time will be significantly less than the total cost time. The following example, adapted from Rothnie and Goodman (1977), illustrates the wide variation in response times that can arise from different, but plausible, execution strategies.

Example 16.5 Distributed query processing

Consider a simplified *StayHome Online Rentals* relational schema consisting of the following three tables:

Member(memberNo, mCity)	100 000 records stored in Seattle
DVDCopy(DVDNo, catalogNo)	1 000 000 records stored in New York
Rental(memberNo, DVDNo)	2 000 000 records stored in Seattle

where Rental records each DVD each member has rented. To list the DVD copies of 'War of the Worlds' (catalogNo = '634817') that have been rented by members who live in Chicago, we can use the SQL query:

```
SELECT dc.DVDNo
FROM DVDCopy dc, Rental r, Member m
WHERE dc.DVDNo = r.DVDNo AND r.memberNo = m.memberNo AND
  dc.catalogNo = '634817' AND m.mCity = 'Chicago';
```

For simplicity, assume that each record in each table is 20 characters long, there are 1000 members in Chicago, there are 20 000 rentals of 'War of the Worlds', and computation time is negligible compared with communication time. We further assume that the communication system has a data transmission rate of 10 000 characters per second and a 1 second access delay to send a message from one site to another. We use the following formula to calculate response time:

```
Response time = C0 + (no_of_bits_in_message/transmission_rate)
```

where C_0 is a fixed cost of initiating a message (the access delay).

We consider six possible strategies for this query, as summarized in Table 16.3. Using the above formula, we calculate the response times for these strategies as follows:

Strategy 1: Move the DVDCopy table to Seattle and process query there:

Time = 1 + (1000 000 * 20/10000) ≅ 33.3 minutes

Strategy 2: Move the Member and Rental tables to New York and process query there:

Time = 2 + [(100000 + 2000000) * 20/10000] ≅ 1.17 hours

Strategy 3: Join the Member and Rental tables at Seattle, select records for Chicago members, and then for each of these records in turn check at New York to determine if the associated DVDCopy has a catalogNo = '634817'. The check for each record involves two messages: a query and a response.

Time = 1000 * (1 + 20/10000) + 1000 * 1 ≅ 33.3 minutes

Strategy 4: Select DVD copies with catalogNo = '634817' at New York and for each one found check at Seattle to see if there is a rental involving a member living in Chicago. Again, two messages are needed:

Time = 20000 * (1 + 20/10000) + 20000 * 1 ≅ 11.12 hours

Strategy 5: Join Member and Rental tables at Seattle, select records for Chicago members, project result over DVDNo, and move this result to New York for matching with catalogNo = '634817'. For simplicity, we assume that the projected result is 10 characters long:

Time = 1 + (1000 * 10/10000) ≅ 2 seconds

Strategy 6: Select DVD copies with catalogNo = '634817' at New York, and move the result to Seattle for matching with rentals associated with Chicago members:

Time = 1 + (20000 * 20/10000) ≅ 41 seconds

Table 16.3 Comparison of distributed query processing strategies

Strategy	Time
(1) Move `DVDCopy` table to Seattle and process query there.	33.3 minutes
(2) Move `Member` and `Rental` tables to New York and process query there.	1.17 hours
(3) Join `Member` and `Rental` tables at Seattle, select records for Chicago members, and for each of these in turn check at New York to determine if there is an associated `catalogNo` = '634817'.	33.3 minutes
(4) Select DVD copies with `catalogNo` = '634817' at New York and for each one found check at Seattle for a rental involving a member living in Chicago.	11.12 hours
(5) Join `Member` and `Rental` tables at Seattle, select Chicago members, project result over `DVDNo`, and move this result to New York for matching with `catalogNo` = '634817'.	2 seconds
(6) Select DVD copies with `catalogNo` = '634817' at New York and move the result to Seattle for matching with rentals associated with Chicago members.	41 seconds

The response times vary from 2 seconds to 11.12 hours, yet each strategy is a legitimate way to execute the query! Clearly, if the wrong strategy is chosen, then the effect on system performance can be devastating.

16.3.4 DBMS transparency

DBMS transparency hides the knowledge that the local DBMSs may be different and is therefore only applicable to heterogeneous DDBMSs. It is one of the most difficult transparencies to provide as a generalization. We discussed the problems associated with the provision of heterogeneous systems in Section 16.1.3.

16.4 Date's 12 rules for a DDBMS

In this section, we list Date's 12 rules (or objectives) for DDBMSs (Date, 1987). The basis for these rules is that a distributed DBMS should feel like a centralized DBMS to the user.

(0) Fundamental principle

> To the user, a distributed system should look exactly like a non-distributed system.

(1) Local autonomy

The sites in a distributed system should be autonomous. In this context, autonomy means that:

- local data is locally owned and managed;
- local operations remain purely local;
- all operations at a given site are controlled by that site.

(2) No reliance on a central site

There should be no one site without which the system cannot operate. This implies that there should be no central servers for services such as transaction management, deadlock detection, query optimization, and management of the global system catalog.

(3) Continuous operation

Ideally, there should never be a need for a planned system shutdown for operations such as adding or removing a site from the system, or the dynamic creation and deletion of fragments at one or more sites.

(4) Location independence

Location independence is equivalent to location transparency. The user should be able to access the database from any site. Furthermore, the user should be able to access all data as if it were stored at the user's site, no matter where it is physically stored.

(5) Fragmentation independence

The user should be able to access the data, no matter how it is fragmented.

(6) Replication independence

The user should be unaware that data has been replicated. Thus, the user should not be able to access a particular copy of a data item directly, nor should the user have to specifically update all copies of a data item.

(7) Distributed query processing

The system should be capable of processing queries that reference data at more than one site.

(8) Distributed transaction processing

The system should support the transaction as the unit of recovery. As discussed in Section 14.1.1, the system should ensure that both global and local transactions conform to the ACID rules for transactions, namely: atomicity, consistency, isolation, and durability.

(9) Hardware independence

It should be possible to run the DDBMS on a variety of hardware platforms.

(10) Operating system independence

As a corollary to the previous rule, it should be possible to run the DDBMS on a variety of operating systems.

(11) Network independence

Again, it should be possible to run the DDBMS on a variety of disparate communication networks.

(12) Database independence

It should be possible to run a DDBMS made up of different local DBMSs, perhaps supporting different underlying data models. In other words, the system should support heterogeneity.

The last four rules are ideals. As the rules are so general and as there is a lack of standards in computer and network architectures, we can expect only partial compliance from vendors in the foreseeable future.

16.5 Replication servers

From the users' perspective, the functionality offered by a DDBMS is highly attractive. However, from an implementation perspective, the protocols and algorithms required to provide this functionality are complex and give rise to several problems that may outweigh the advantages offered by this technology. An alternative, and potentially a more simplified, approach to data distribution is provided by a **replication server**, which handles the replication of data to remote sites. Every major database vendor has a replication solution of one kind or another, and many non-database vendors also offer alternative methods for replicating data. In this section, we consider the replication server as an alternative to a DDBMS. In particular, we examine synchronous versus asynchronous replication, the functionality of replication servers, and data ownership models. For further details the interested reader is referred to Buretta (1997).

Replication

The process of generating and reproducing multiple copies of data at one or more sites.

Replication is an important mechanism because it enables organizations to provide users with access to current data where and when they need it. Replication provides a number of benefits, including improved performance when centralized resources get overloaded, increased reliability and data availability, and support for mobile computing and data warehousing.

16.5.1 Synchronous versus asynchronous replication

Typically, protocols for updating replicated data in a DDBMS work on the basis that the replicated data is updated immediately when the source data is updated (that is, as part of the enclosing transaction.) This type of replication is called **synchronous replication**. While this mechanism may be appropriate for environments that, by necessity, must keep all replicas fully synchronized (such as financial transactions), it does have several disadvantages. For example, the transaction will be unable to fully complete if one or more of the sites that hold replicas are unavailable. Further, the number of messages required to coordinate the synchronization of data places a significant burden on corporate networks.

Many commercial DBMSs provide an alternative mechanism to synchronous replication, called **asynchronous replication**. With this mechanism, the target database is updated after the source database has been modified. The delay in regaining consistency may range from a few seconds to several hours or even days. However, the data eventually synchronizes to the same value at all replicated sites. Although this violates the principle of distributed data independence, it appears to be a practical compromise between data integrity and availability that may be more appropriate for organizations that are able to work with replicas that do not necessarily have to be synchronized and current.

16.5.2 Functionality of replication servers

At its basic level, we expect a distributed data replication service to be capable of copying data from one database to another, synchronously or asynchronously. However, there are many other functions that need to be provided, such as:

- *Specification of replication schema*. The system should provide a mechanism to allow a privileged user to specify the data and objects to be replicated.
- *Subscription mechanism*. The system should provide a mechanism to allow a privileged user to subscribe to the data and objects available for replication.
- *Initialization mechanism*. The system should provide a mechanism to allow for the initialization of a target replica.
- *Scalability*. The service should be able to handle the replication of both small and large volumes of data.
- *Mapping and transformation*. The service should be able to handle replication across different DBMSs and platforms. This may involve mapping and transforming the data from one data model into a different data model, or the data in one data type to a corresponding data type in another DBMS.
- *Object replication*. It should be possible to replicate objects other than data. For example, some systems allow indexes and stored procedures (or triggers) to be replicated.
- *Easy administration*. It should be easy for the DBA to administer the system and to check the status and monitor the performance of the replication system components.

16.5.3 Data ownership

Ownership relates to which site has the privilege to update the data. The main types of ownership are *master/slave*, *workflow*, and *update-anywhere* (sometimes referred to as *peer-to-peer* or *symmetric replication*).

Master/slave ownership

With master/slave ownership, asynchronously replicated data is owned by one site, the *master* or *primary* site, and can be updated by only that site. Using a '*publish-and-subscribe*' metaphor, the master site (the publisher) makes data available. Other sites 'subscribe' to the data owned by the master site, which means that they receive read-only copies on their local systems. Potentially, each site can be the master site for non-overlapping data sets. However, there can only ever be one site that can update the master copy of a particular data set, so update conflicts cannot occur between sites.

A master site may own the data in an entire table, in which case other sites subscribe to read-only copies of that table. Alternatively, multiple sites may own distinct fragments of the table, and other sites then subscribe to read-only copies of the fragments. This type of replication is also known as *asymmetric replication*.

The following are some examples showing the potential usage of this type of replication:

- *Decision support system (DSS) analysis*. Data from one or more distributed databases can be offloaded to a separate, local DSS for read-only analysis. For *StayHome Online Rentals*, we may collect all rentals information together with member details, and perform analysis to determine trends, such as which type of person is most likely to rent particular genres of DVDs in particular areas.
- *Distribution and dissemination of centralized information*. Data dissemination describes an environment where data is updated in a central location and then replicated to read-only sites. For example, product information such as price lists could be maintained at the corporate headquarters site and replicated to read-only copies held at remote distribution centers. This type of replication is shown in Figure 16.12(a).
- *Consolidation of remote information*. Data consolidation describes an environment where data can be updated locally and then brought together in a read-only repository in one location. This method gives data ownership and autonomy to each site. For example, member details maintained at each distribution center could be replicated to a consolidated read-only copy of the data at the corporate headquarters site. This type of replication is shown in Figure 16.12(b).
- *Mobile computing*. Mobile computing has become much more accessible in recent years, and in most organizations some people work away from the office. There are now a number of methods for providing data to a mobile workforce, one of which is replication. In this case, the data is downloaded on demand from a local workgroup server. Updates to the workgroup or central data from the mobile client, such as new customer or order information, are handled in a similar manner.

Workflow ownership

Like master/slave ownership, this model avoids update conflicts while at the same time providing a more dynamic ownership model. Workflow ownership allows the right to update replicated data to move from site to site. However, at any one

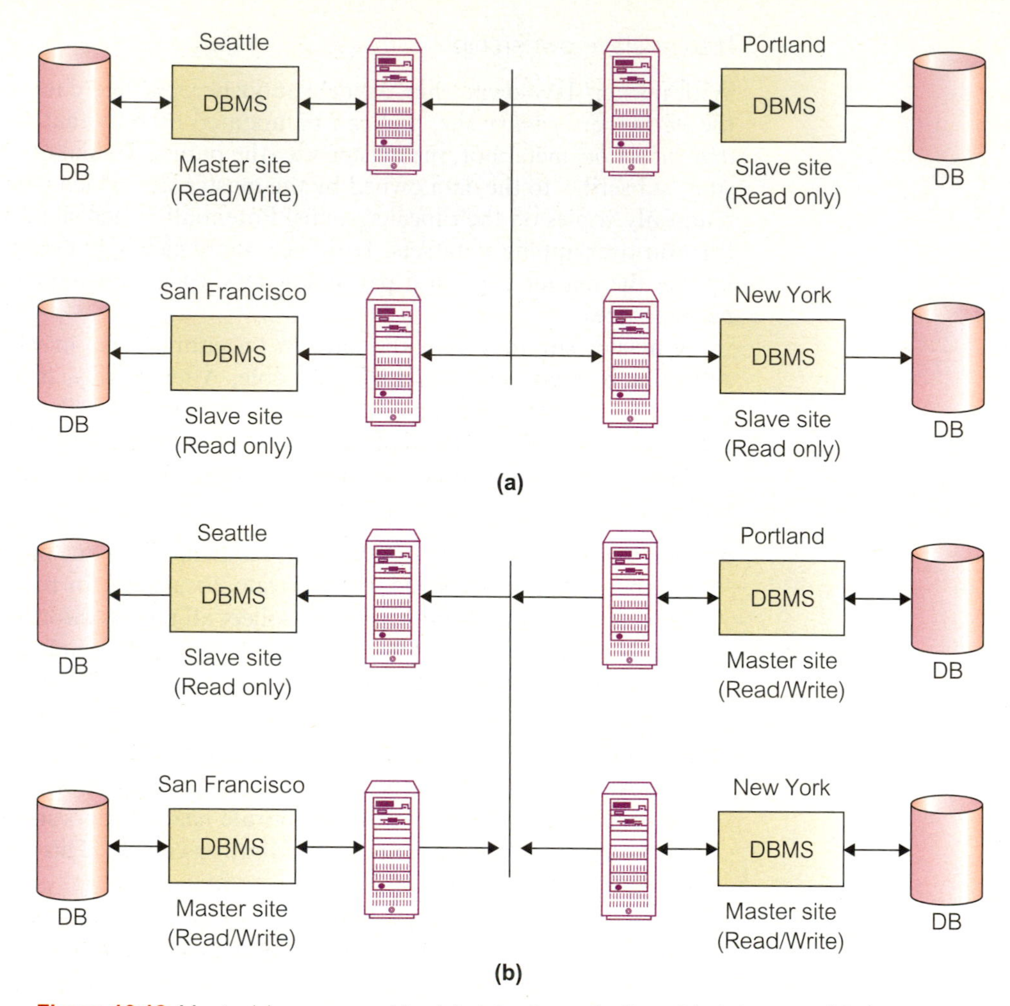

Figure 16.12 Master/slave ownership: (a) data dissemination; (b) data consolidation

moment, there is only ever one site that may update that particular data set. A typical example of workflow ownership is an order processing system, where the processing of orders follows a series of steps, such as order entry, credit approval, invoicing, shipping, and so on. In a centralized DBMS, applications of this nature access and update the data in one integrated database: each application updates the order data in sequence when, and only when, the state of the order indicates that the previous step has been completed.

Update-anywhere (symmetric replication) ownership

The two previous models share a common property: at any given moment only one site may update the data; all other sites have read-only access to the replicas. In some environments, this is too restrictive. The update-anywhere model creates an environment where multiple sites have equal rights to update replicated data. This allows local sites to function autonomously, even when other sites are not available.

For example, *StayHome* may decide to operate a hotline that allows potential members to telephone a freephone number to get a DVD sent out. Call centers have been established in each distribution center. Calls are routed to the nearest center. The telecommunications system attempts load-balancing, and so if one center is particularly busy, calls may be re-routed to another center. Each call center needs to be able to access and update data at any of the other distribution centers and have the updated records replicated to the other sites, as illustrated in Figure 16.13.

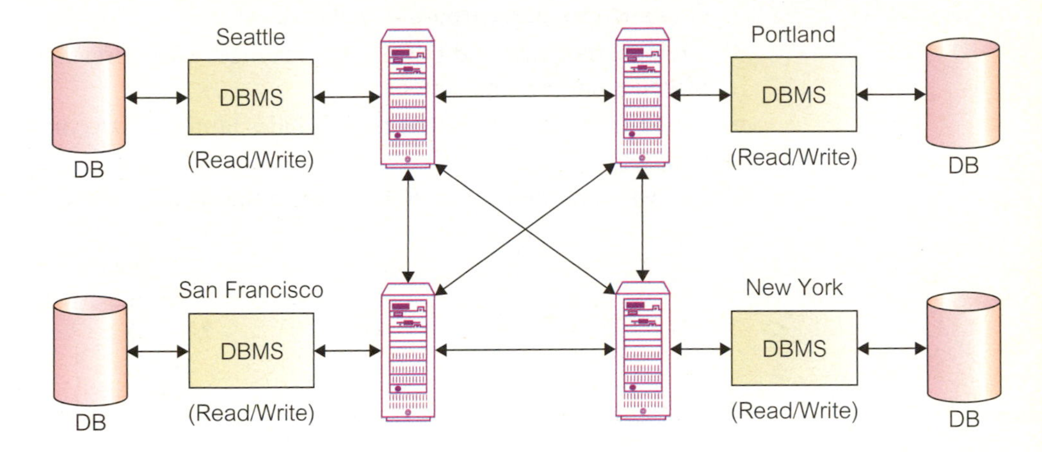

Figure 16.13 Update-anywhere (symmetric) ownership

Shared ownership can lead to conflict scenarios and the replication server has to be able to employ a methodology for conflict detection and resolution. A simple mechanism to detect conflict within a single table is for the source site to send both the old and new values (*before-* and *after-images*) for any records that have been updated since the last refresh. At the target site, the replication server can check each record in the target database that has also been updated against these values. However, consideration has to be given to detecting other types of conflict, such as violation of referential integrity between two tables. There have been many mechanisms proposed for conflict resolution, but some of the most common are earliest/latest timestamps, site priority, and holding for manual resolution.

16.6 Mobile databases

Currently, we are witnessing increasing demands on mobile computing to provide the types of support required by a growing number of mobile workers. Such a workforce may be required to work as if in the office but in reality they are working from remote locations including homes, clients' premises, or simply while en route to remote locations. The 'office' may accompany a remote worker in the form of a laptop, PDA (Personal Digital Assistant), or other Internet access device. With the rapid expansion of cellular, wireless, and satellite communications, it will soon be possible for mobile users to access any data, anywhere, at any time. However, business etiquette, practicalities, security, and costs may still limit communication such that

Mobile database

A database that is portable and physically separate from a centralized database server but is capable of communicating with that server from remote sites allowing the sharing of corporate data.

it is not possible to establish online connections for as long as users want, whenever they want. **Mobile databases** offer a solution for some of these restrictions.

With mobile databases, users have access to corporate data on their laptop, PDA, or other Internet access device at remote sites. The typical architecture for a mobile database environment is shown in Figure 16.14. The components of a mobile database environment include:

- a corporate database server and DBMS that manages and stores the corporate data and provides corporate applications;
- a remote database and DBMS that manages and stores the mobile data and provides mobile applications;
- a mobile database platform that includes laptop, PDA, or other Internet access devices;
- two-way communication links between the corporate and mobile DBMS.

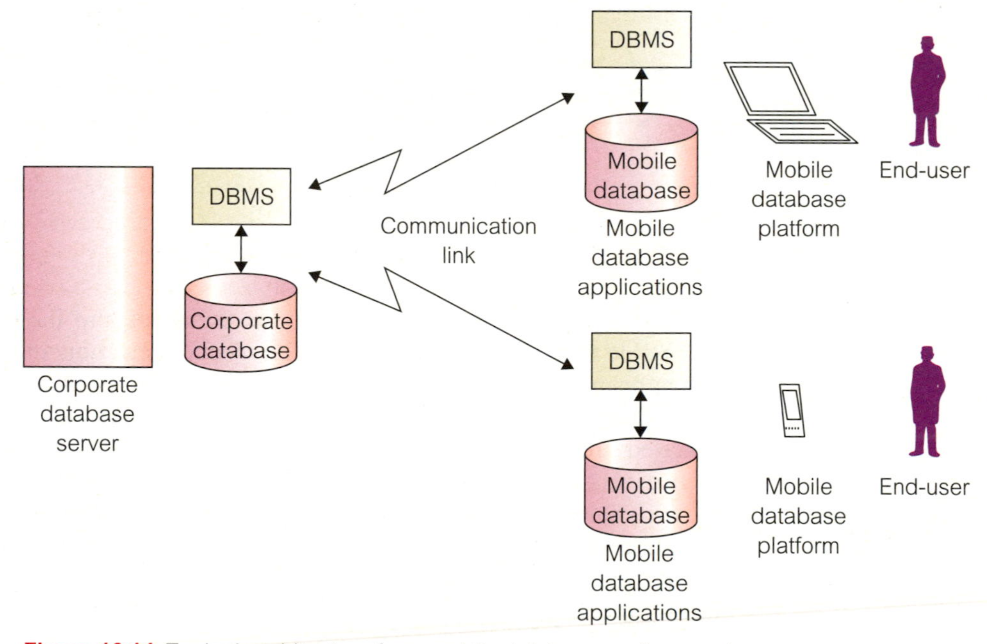

Figure 16.14 Typical architecture for a mobile database environment

Depending on the particular requirements of mobile applications, in some cases the user of a mobile device may log on to a corporate database server and work with data there, while in others the user may download data and work with it on a mobile device or upload data captured at the remote site to the corporate database.

The communication between the corporate and mobile databases is usually intermittent and is typically established for short periods of time at irregular intervals. Although unusual, there are some applications that require direct communication between the mobile databases. The two main issues associated with the mobile databases is the management of the mobile database and the communication between the mobile and corporate databases. In the following section, we identify the requirements of mobile DBMSs.

16.6.1 Mobile DBMSs

All the major DBMS vendors now offer a mobile DBMS. In fact, this development is partly responsible for driving the current dramatic growth in sales for the major DBMS vendors. Most vendors promote their mobile DBMS as being capable of communicating with a range of major relational DBMSs and in providing database services that require limited-computing resources to match those currently provided by mobile devices. The additional functionality required of mobile DBMSs includes the ability to:

- communicate with the centralized database server through modes such as wireless or Internet access;
- replicate data on the centralized database server and mobile device;
- synchronize data on the centralized database server and mobile device;
- capture data from various sources, such as the Internet;
- manage data on the mobile device;
- analyze data on a mobile device;
- create customized mobile applications.

DBMS vendors are driving the prices per user to such a level that it is now cost-effective for organizations to extend applications to mobile devices, which were previously available only in-house. Currently, most mobile DBMSs only provide pre-packaged SQL functions for the mobile application, rather than supporting any extensive database querying or data analysis. However, the prediction is that in the near future mobile devices will offer functionality which at least matches that available at the corporate site.

Chapter summary

- A **distributed database** is a collection of multiple, logically interrelated collection of shared data (and a description of this data), physically distributed over a computer network. The **DDBMS** is the software that transparently manages the distributed database. A DDBMS is distinct from **distributed processing**, where a centralized DBMS is accessed over a network.
- The advantages of a DDBMS are that it reflects the organizational structure, it makes remote data more shareable, it improves reliability and availability, and performance, it may be more economical, and provides for modular growth. The major disadvantages are cost, complexity, lack of standards, and experience.
- A DDBMS may be classified as homogeneous or heterogeneous. In a **homogeneous** system, all sites use the same DBMS product. In a **heterogeneous** system, sites may run different DBMS products, which need not be based on the same underlying data model, and so the system may be composed of relational, network, hierarchical, and object-oriented DBMSs.

- A **multi-database system** (MDBS) is a distributed DBMS in which each site maintains complete autonomy. An MDBS resides transparently on top of existing database and file systems, and presents a single database to its users. It maintains a global schema against which users issue queries and updates; an MDBS maintains only the global schema and the local DBMSs themselves maintain all user data.
- A table may be divided into a number of subtables called **fragments**, which are **allocated** to one or more sites. Fragments may be **replicated** to provide improved availability and performance.
- The definition and allocation of fragments are carried out strategically to achieve locality of reference, improved reliability and availability, acceptable performance, balanced storage capacities and costs, and minimal communication costs.
- There are four allocation strategies regarding the placement of data: **centralized** (a single centralized database), **fragmented** (fragments assigned to one site), **complete replication** (complete copy of the database maintained at each site), and **selective replication** (combination of the first three).
- There are two main types of fragmentation: **horizontal** and **vertical**. Horizontal fragments are subsets of records and vertical fragments are subsets of columns. There are also two other types of fragmentation: **mixed** and **derived**, a type of horizontal fragmentation where the fragmentation of one table is based on the fragmentation of another table.
- The DDBMS should appear like a centralized DBMS by providing a series of transparencies. With **distribution transparency**, users should not know that the data has been fragmented/replicated. With **transaction transparency**, the consistency of the global database should be maintained when multiple users are accessing the database concurrently and when failures occur. With **performance transparency**, the system should be able to efficiently handle queries that reference data at more than one site. With **DBMS transparency**, it should be possible to have different DBMSs in the system.
- **Replication** is the process of generating and reproducing multiple copies of data at one or more sites. It is an important mechanism because it enables organizations to provide users with access to current data where and when they need it. Replication provides a number of benefits, including improved performance when centralized resources get overloaded, increased reliability and availability, and support for mobile computing and data warehousing facilitating decision support.
- Although asynchronous updates violate the principle of distributed data independence, it appears to be a practical compromise between data integrity and availability that may be more appropriate for organizations that are able to work with replicas that do not necessarily have to be synchronized and current.
- A **mobile database** is a database that is portable and physically separate from the corporate database server but is capable of communicating with the server from remote sites allowing the sharing of corporate data. With mobile databases, users have access to corporate data on their laptop, PDA, or other Internet access device that is required for applications at remote sites.

Review questions

16.1 Explain what is meant by a DDBMS and discuss the motivation in providing such a system.

16.2 Compare and contrast a DDBMS with distributed processing. Under what circumstances would you choose a DDBMS over distributed processing?

16.3 Discuss the advantages and disadvantages of a DDBMS.

16.4 What is the difference between a homogeneous and a heterogeneous DDBMS? Under what circumstances would such systems generally arise?

16.5 What is a multi-database system (MDBS)?

16.6 What are the strategic objectives for the definition and allocation of fragments?

16.7 Define and contrast alternative schemes for fragmenting a global table. State how you would check for correctness to ensure that the database does not undergo change during fragmentation.

16.8 What layers of transparency should be provided with a DDBMS? Give examples to illustrate your answer. Give justification for your answer.

16.9 What are the four levels of transactions defined in IBM's DRDA? Compare and contrast these four levels. Give examples to illustrate your answer.

16.10 Compare and contrast the different ownership models for replication. Give examples to illustrate your answer.

16.11 Compare and contrast the database mechanisms for replication.

16.12 Describe the terms 'mobile database' and 'mobile DBMS.'

Exercises

16.13 Show that the fragmentation schemas defined in Examples 16.1, 16.2, 16.3, and 16.4 satisfy the correctness rules for fragmentation.

16.14 Consider the following table:

staffNo	Name	position	salary	eMail	dCenterNo
S1500	Tom Daniels	Manager	48000	tdaniels@stayhome.com	D001
S0003	Sally Adams	Assistant	30000	sadams@stayhome.com	D001
S0010	Mary Martinez	Manager	51000	mmartinez@stayhome.com	D002
S3250	Robert Chin	Assistant	33000	rchin@stayhome.com	
S2250	Sally Stern	Manager	48000	sstern@stayhome.com	D004
S0415	Art Peters	Manager	42000	apeters@stayhome.com	D003

(a) Give the SQL to horizontally fragment staff by `position`. Give the SQL to reconstruct the original table from the fragments. Under what conditions is the fragmentation complete?

(b) Give the SQL to horizontally fragment staff by `dCenterNo`. Give the SQL to reconstruct the original table from the fragments. Is the fragmentation complete and if not, why not?

16.15 Draw an ER diagram to represent this system.

Case study 1

A large real estate agency has decided to distribute its project management information at the regional level. A part of the current centralized relational schema is as follows:

`Staff`	(`NINo`, `fName, lName, address, DOB, sex, salary, taxCode, agencyNo`)
`Agency`	(`agencyNo`, `agencyAddress, managerNINo, propertyTypeNo, regionNo`)
`Property`	(`propertyNo`, `propertyTypeNo, propertyAddress, ownerNo, askingPrice, agencyNo, contactNINo`)
`Owner`	(`ownerNo`, `fName, lName, ownerAddress, ownerTelNo`)
`PropertyType`	(`propertyTypeNo`, `propertyTypeName`)
`Region`	(`regionNo`, `regionName`)

where:

`Staff`	contains staff details and the national insurance number `NINo` is the key.
`Agency`	contains agency details and `agencyNo` is the key. `managerNINo` identifies the employee who is the manager of the agency. There is only one manager for each agency; an agency only handles one type of property.
`Property`	contains details of the properties the company is dealing with and the key is `propertyNo`. The agency that deals with the property is given by `agencyNo`, and the contact in the estate agents by `contactNINo`; the owner is given by `ownerNo`.
`Owner`	contains details of the owners of the properties and the key is `ownerNo`.
`PropertyType`	contains the names of the property types and the key is `propertyTypeNo`.

and

`Region`	contains the names of the regions and the key is `regionNo`.

Agencies are grouped regionally as follows:

Region 1: North; Region 2: South; Region 3: East; Region 4: West

Properties are handled by the local estate agents office. As well as distributing the data on a regional basis, there is an additional requirement to access the employee data either by personal information (by Human Resources) or by salary-related information (by Payroll).

16.16 Using the ER diagram from the previous question, produce a distributed database design for this system, and include:

(a) a suitable fragmentation schema for the system;

(b) the reconstruction of global tables from fragments.

State any assumptions necessary to support your design.

StayHome Online Rentals

16.17 Repeat Exercise 16.16 for the *StayHome Online Rentals* case study documented in Section 5.4. State any assumptions necessary to support your design.

PerfectPets

16.18 Repeat Exercise 16.16 for the *PerfectPets* case study documented in Appendix B. State any assumptions necessary to support your design.

Additional exercises

16.19 Compare a distributed DBMS that you have access to against Date's 12 rules for a DDBMS. For each rule for which the system is not compliant, give your reasons why you think there is no conformance to this rule.

16.20 You have been asked by the Managing Director of *StayHome Online Rentals* to investigate the data distribution requirements of the organization and to prepare a report on the potential use of a distributed DBMS. The report should compare the technology of the centralized DBMS with that of the distributed DBMS, and should address the advantages and disadvantages of implementing a DDBMS within the organization, and any perceived problem areas. The report should also address the possibility of using a replication server to address the distribution requirements. Finally, the report should contain a fully justified set of recommendations proposing an appropriate solution.

16.21 Produce a conceptual data model for the system catalog for a DDBMS. The data model should represent, relations, attributes and their data types, key attributes (both primary key and foreign key), sites, horizontal fragmentation, vertical fragmentation, and replication. Hint: note that a fragment is itself a relation.

16.22 Draw an entity–relationship (ER) diagram to represent this system.

Case Study 2

Reliable Printing is a large printing company that does work for book publishers throughout Europe. The company currently has over 50 offices, most of which operate autonomously, apart from salaries which are paid by the head office in each country. To improve the sharing and communication of data, the company has decided to implement a distributed DBMS. *Reliable Printing* jobs consist of printing books or part of books. A printing job requires the use of materials, such as paper and ink, which are assigned to a job via purchase orders. Each printing job may have several purchase orders assigned to it. Likewise, each purchase order may contain several purchase order items. The centralized schema is as follows:

Office	(officeNo, oAddress, oTelNo, oFaxNo, mgrNIN, countryNo)
Staff	(NIN, fName, lName, sAddress, sTelNo, sex, DOB, position, taxCode, salary, officeNo)
Publisher	(pubNo, pName, pCity, pTelNo, pFaxNo, creditCode, officeNo)
Bookjob	(jobNo, pubNo, jobDate, jobDescription, jobType, supervisorNIN)
PurchaseOrder	(jobNo, poNo, poDate)
Item	(itemNo, itemDescription, amountInStock, price)
POItem	(jobNo, poNo, itemNo, quantity)
Country	(countryNo, countryName)

where:

Office	contains details of each office and the office number (officeNo) is the key. Each office has a Manager represented by the manager's national insurance number (mgrNIN).

`Staff`	contains details of staff and the national insurance number (`NIN`) is the key. The office that the member of staff works from is given by `officeNo`.
`Publisher`	contains details of publisher and the publisher number (`pubNo`) is the key. Publishers are registered with the nearest office in their country, given by `officeNo`.
`Bookjob`	contains details of publishing jobs and the job number (`jobNo`) is the key. The publisher is given by the publisher number (`pubNo`) and the supervisor for the job by `supervisorNIN`.
`PurchaseOrder`	contains details of the purchase orders for each job and the combination of job number and a purchase order number (`jobNo, poNo`) form the key.
`Item`	contains details of all materials that can be used in printing jobs and the item number (`itemNo`) is the key.
`POItem`	contains details of the items on the purchase order and (`jobNo, poNo, itemNo`) forms the key.
`Country`	contains the names of each country that *Reliable Printing* operates in and the country number (`countryNo`) is the key.

As well as accessing printing jobs based on the publisher, jobs can also be accessed on the job type (`jobType`), which can be: 1 – Normal; 2 – Rush.

The offices of *Reliable Printing* are grouped into countries as follows:

Country 1:	UK	Country 2:	France	Country 3:	Germany
Country 4:	Italy	Country 5:	Spain		

16.23 Using the ER diagram from the previous question, produce a distributed database design for this system, and include:

(a) a suitable fragmentation schema for the system;

(b) the reconstruction of global tables from fragments.

State any assumptions necessary to support your design.

CHAPTER 17 Object DBMSs

Preview

Object-orientation is an approach to software construction that shows considerable promise for solving some of the classic problems of software development. The underlying concept behind object technology is that all software should be constructed of standard, reusable components wherever possible. Traditionally, software engineering and database management have existed as separate disciplines. Database technology has concentrated on the static aspects of data storage, while software engineering has modeled the dynamic aspects of software. With the arrival of the next (third) generation of database management systems, namely Object-Oriented Database Management Systems (OODBMSs) and Object-Relational Database Management Systems (ORDBMSs), the two disciplines have been combined to allow the concurrent modeling of both data and the processes acting upon the data.

However, there is currently significant dispute regarding this next generation of DBMSs. The success of relational systems in the past two decades is evident, and the traditionalists believe that it is sufficient to extend the relational model with additional (object-oriented) capabilities. Others believe that an underlying relational model is inadequate to handle the type of complex applications we discuss shortly.

Putting the discussions into context, relational DBMSs[1] are currently the dominant database technology with estimated sales of between approximately $6–10 billion per year ($25 billion with application development tools sales included), and growing at a rate of possibly 25% per year. The OODBMS started initially in the engineering and design domains, and has also become the favored system for financial and telecommunications applications. Although the OODBMS market is still small, the OODBMS continues to find new application areas, such as the Web (which we discussed in Chapter 15). A few years ago, some industry analysts predicted the market for the OODBMS to grow at over 50% per year, a rate faster than the total database market, however, this growth has not been sustained. It is unlikely that OODBMS sales will overtake those of relational systems because of the wealth of businesses that find relational DBMSs acceptable, and because businesses have invested so much money and resources in their development that change is prohibitive (of course, this is the typical situation that creates legacy systems).

---

[1] All the main relational products now include object features and so are really ORDBMSs.

To help understand these new types of DBMSs, and the arguments on both sides, we discuss the technologies and issues behind them in this chapter. In Section 17.1, we examine the requirements for the advanced types of database applications that are becoming commonplace nowadays, and in Section 17.2 we discuss why traditional relational DBMSs are not well suited to supporting these new applications. In Section 17.3 we examine the problems associated with storing objects in a relational database. In Section 17.4, we consider OODBMSs and in Section 17.5 we consider ORDBMSs. The examples in this chapter are drawn from the *StayHome Online Rentals* case study documented in Section 5.4. Readers who are unfamiliar with object-oriented concepts should first read Appendix H.

Learning objectives

In this chapter you will learn:

- The requirements for advanced database applications.
- Why relational DBMSs are not well suited to supporting advanced database applications currently.
- The problems associated with storing objects in a relational database.
- A definition for an object-oriented DBMS (OODBMS).
- The main features of the ODMG Object Data Standard: the Object Model, Object Definition Language (ODL), and Object Query Language (OQL).
- The advantages and disadvantages of OODBMSs.
- How the relational DBMS has been extended into an object-relational DBMS (ORDBMS) to support advanced database applications.
- The advantages and disadvantages of ORDBMSs.
- The main object management features in the SQL:2006 standard.

17.1 Advanced database applications

The past decade has seen significant changes in the computer industry. In database systems, we have seen the widespread acceptance of relational DBMSs (RDBMSs) for traditional business applications, such as order processing, inventory control, banking, and airline reservations. However, existing RDBMSs have proven inadequate for applications with needs that are quite different from those of traditional business database applications. These applications include:

- interactive and dynamic web sites;
- office information systems and multimedia systems;
- geographic information systems;
- computer-aided software engineering.

Interactive and dynamic web sites

Consider a web site that has an online catalog for selling clothes. The web site maintains a set of preferences for previous visitors to the site and allows a visitor to:

- browse through thumbnails of the items in the catalog and select one to obtain a full-size image with supporting details;
- search for items that match a user-defined set of criteria;
- obtain a 3D rendering of any item of clothing based on a customized specification (for example color, size, fabric);
- select a voiceover commentary giving additional details of the item;
- view a running total of the bill, with appropriate discounts;
- conclude the purchase through a secure online transaction.

As well as handling complex data, the site has the added complexity of interactively modifying the display based on user preferences and user selections and providing 3D rendering.

As we discussed in Chapter 15, the Web now provides a relatively new paradigm for data management, and languages such as XML (eXtended Markup Language) hold significant promise, particularly for the eCommerce market. As the use of the Internet increases and the technology becomes more sophisticated, we will see web sites and business-to-business (B2B) transactions handle much more complex and interrelated data.

Office information systems (OIS) and multimedia systems

An OIS database stores data relating to the computer control of information in a business, including email, documents, invoices, and so on. To provide better support for this area, the applications need to handle a wider range of data types other than names, addresses, dates, and currency. Modern systems now handle free-form text, photographs, diagrams, and audio and video sequences. For example, a multimedia document may handle text, photographs, animation, spreadsheets, and voice commentary. The documents may have a specific structure imposed on them, perhaps described using a mark-up language such as SGML (Standardized Generalized Markup Language), HTML (HyperText Markup Language), or XML, as discussed in Chapter 15.

Documents may be shared among many users using systems such as email and bulletin boards based on Internet technology[2]. Again, such applications need to store data that has a much richer structure than records consisting of numbers and text strings. There is also an increasing need to capture handwritten notes using electronic devices. Although many notes can be transcribed into ASCII text using

[2] A criticism of database systems, as noted by a number of observers, is that the largest 'database' in the world – the World Wide Web – has developed with little or no use of database technology. We discussed the integration of the Web and DBMSs in Chapter 15.

handwriting analysis techniques, most such data cannot. In addition to words, handwritten data can include sketches, diagrams, and so on.

Geographic information systems (GIS)

A GIS database stores various types of spatial and temporal information, such as that used in land management and underwater exploration. Much of the data in these systems is derived from survey and satellite photographs, and tends to be very large. Searches may involve identifying features based, for example, on shape, color, or texture using advanced pattern-recognition techniques.

For example, EOS (Earth Observing System) is a collection of satellites launched by NASA over the last decade to gather information to support scientists concerned with long-term trends regarding the earth's atmosphere, oceans, and land. It is anticipated that these satellites will return over one-third of a petabyte (10^{15} bytes) of data per year. This data is integrated with other data sources and stored in EOSDIS (EOS Data and Information System). EOSDIS will supply the information needs of both scientists and non-scientists. For example, school children are able to access EOSDIS to see a simulation of world weather patterns. The immense size of this database and the need to support thousands of users with very heavy volumes of information requests will provide many challenges for DBMSs.

Computer-aided software engineering (CASE)

A CASE database stores data relating to the stages of the software development lifecycle: planning, requirements collection and analysis, design, implementation, testing, maintenance, and documentation. For example, software configuration management tools allow concurrent sharing of project design, code, and documentation. They also track the dependencies between these components and assist with change management. Project management tools facilitate the coordination of various project management activities, such as the scheduling of potentially highly complex interdependent tasks, cost estimation, and progress monitoring. Designs of this type have some common characteristics:

- Designs may be very large, perhaps consisting of millions of parts, often with many interdependent subsystem designs.
- The design is not static but evolves through time. When a design change occurs, the changes must be propagated through all design representations.
- Updates are far-reaching; one change is likely to affect a large number of design objects.
- Often, many design alternatives are being considered for each component, and the correct version for each part must be maintained. This involves some form of version control and configuration management.
- There may be hundreds of staff involved with the design, and they may work in parallel on multiple versions of a large design. Even so, the end product must be consistent and coordinated. This is sometimes referred to as *cooperative engineering*.

17.2 Weaknesses of relational DBMSs (RDBMSs)

In Chapter 2, we mentioned that the relational model has a strong theoretical foundation, based on first-order predicate logic. This theory supported the development of SQL, a declarative language that has now become the standard language for defining and manipulating relational databases. Other strengths of the relational model are its simplicity, its suitability for Online Transaction Processing (OLTP), and its support for data independence. However, the relational data model, and relational RDBMSs in particular, are not without their disadvantages. Table 17.1 lists some of the more significant disadvantages often cited by proponents of the object-oriented approach. We discuss these weaknesses in this section and leave readers to judge for themselves the applicability of these weaknesses.

Table 17.1 Summary of weaknesses of relational DBMSs

Weaknesses
Poor representation of 'real world' entities
Semantic overloading
Poor support for integrity constraints
Limited operations
Difficulty handling recursive queries
Impedance mismatch
Other problems with RDBMSs associated with concurrency, schema changes, and poor navigational access

Poor representation of 'real world' entities. Normalization generally leads to the creation of tables that do not correspond to entities in the 'real world'. The fragmentation of a 'real world' entity into many tables, with a physical representation that reflects this structure, is inefficient leading to many joins during query processing.

Semantic overloading. The relational model has only one construct for representing data and relationships between data, namely the table. For example, to represent a many-to-many (*:*) relationship between two entities A and B, we create three tables, one to represent each of the entities A and B, and one to represent the relationship. There is no mechanism to distinguish between entities and relationships, or to distinguish between different kinds of relationship that exist between entities. For example, a 1:* relationship might be *Has*, *Supervises*, or *Manages*. If such distinctions could be made, then it might be possible to build the semantics into the operations. It is said that the relational model is *semantically overloaded*.

Poor support for integrity constraints. In Section 2.4, we introduced the concepts of entity and referential integrity, and in Section 2.2.1 we introduced domains, which are also types of integrity constraints. Unfortunately, many commercial systems do not fully support these rules, and it is necessary to build them into the applications. This, of course, is dangerous and can lead to duplication of effort and, worse still, inconsistencies. Furthermore, there is no support for other types of integrity constraints in the relational model, which again means they have to be built into the DBMS or the application.

Limited operations. The relational model has only a fixed set of operations, such as set and record-oriented operations, operations that are provided in SQL. However, until recently SQL did not allow new operations to be specified. Again, this is too restrictive to model the behavior of many 'real world' objects. For example, a GIS application typically uses points, lines, line groups, and polygons and needs operations for distance, intersection, and containment.

Difficulty handling recursive queries. Atomicity of data means that repeating groups are not allowed in the relational model. As a result, it is extremely difficult to handle recursive queries: that is, queries about relationships that a table has with itself (directly or indirectly). To overcome this problem, SQL can be embedded in a high-level programming language, which provides constructs to facilitate iteration. Additionally, many RDBMSs provide a report writer with similar constructs. In either case, it is the application rather than the inherent capabilities of the system that provides the required functionality.

Impedance mismatch. In Section 3.1.1, we noted that until recently, SQL lacked computational completeness. To overcome this problem and to provide additional flexibility to help develop more complex database applications, the SQL standard provides a mechanism (called *embedded SQL*) to embed SQL statements in a high-level programming language. However, this approach produces an *impedance mismatch* because we are mixing different programming paradigms:

(1) SQL is a declarative language that handles rows of data, whereas a high-level language such as C++ is a procedural language that can handle only one row of data at a time.

(2) SQL and high-level programming languages like C++ use different models to represent data. For example, SQL provides the built-in data types Date and Interval, which are not available in traditional programming languages. Thus, it is necessary for the application program to convert between the two representations, which is inefficient both in programming effort and in the use of runtime resources. Furthermore, since we are using two different type systems, it is not possible to automatically type-check the application as a whole.

Other problems with relational DBMSs include the following:

- Transactions in business processing are generally short-lived and the concurrency control primitives and protocols such as two-phase locking (see Section 14.2) are not particularly suited for long-duration transactions, which are more common for complex design objects.
- Schema changes are difficult. Database administrators must intervene to change database structures and, typically, programs that access these structures must be modified to adjust to the new structures. These are slow and cumbersome processes even with current technologies. As a result, most organizations are locked into their existing database structures. Even if they are

willing and able to change the way they do business to meet new requirements, they are unable to make these changes because they cannot afford the time and expense required to modify their information systems (Taylor, 1992). To meet the requirement for increased flexibility, we need a system that caters for natural schema evolution.

- Relational DBMSs were designed to use content-based *associative access* and are poor at *navigational access* (that is, access based on movement between individual records.) Navigational access is important for many of the complex applications we discussed in the previous section.

Of these three problems, the first two are applicable to many DBMSs, not just relational systems. In fact, there is no underlying problem with the relational model that would prevent such mechanisms being implemented. The latest release of the SQL standard, SQL:2006, addresses some of the above deficiencies with the introduction of many new features, such as the ability to define new data types and operations as part of the data definition language (as we discuss in Section 17.5), and the addition of new constructs to make the language computationally complete (as we discuss in Appendix E).

17.3 Storing objects in a relational database

One approach to achieving persistence with an object-oriented programming language, such as C++ or Java, is to use a relational DBMS as the underlying storage engine. This requires mapping class instances (that is, objects) to one or more records distributed over one or more tables. This can be problematic as we discuss in this section. For the purposes of discussion, consider the inheritance hierarchy shown in Figure 17.1, which has a `Staff` superclass and three subclasses: `Manager`, `SalesPersonnel`, and `Secretary`.

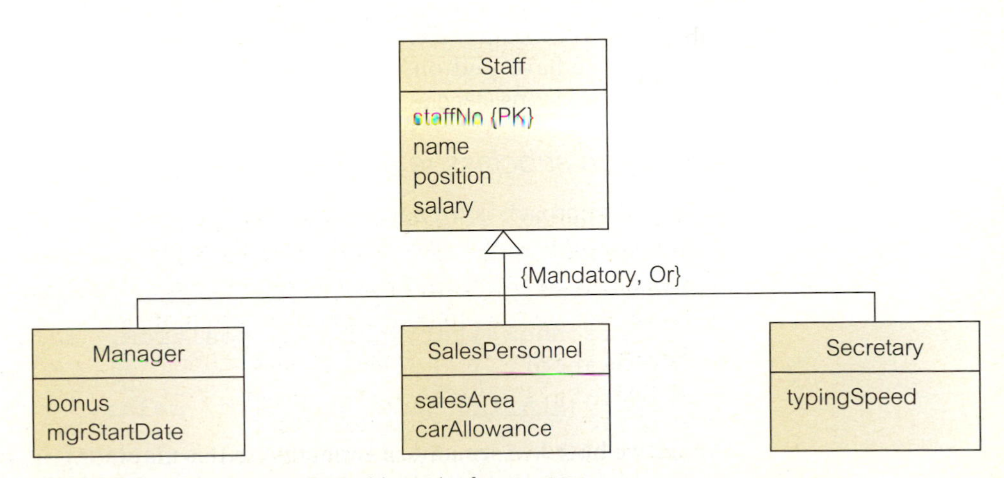

Figure 17.1 Sample inheritance hierarchy for `Staff`

To handle this type of class hierarchy, we have two basics tasks to perform:

(1) design the tables to represent the class hierarchy;
(2) design how objects will be accessed, which means:
   - writing code to decompose the objects into records and store the decomposed objects in tables;
   - writing code to read records from the tables and reconstruct the objects.

We describe the first task in some detail and leave the second task as an exercise for the reader (see Exercise 17.25).

17.3.1 Mapping classes to tables

There are a number of alternative strategies for mapping classes to tables, although each results in a loss of semantic information. The code to make objects persistent and to read the objects back from the database is dependent on the strategy chosen. We consider three alternatives below.

Map each class or subclass to a table

One approach is to map each class or subclass to a table. For the hierarchy given in Figure 17.1, this would give the following four tables (with the primary key underlined):

`Staff` (<u>`staffNo`</u>, `name, position, salary`)

`Manager` (<u>`staffNo`</u>, `bonus, mgrStartDate`)

`SalesPersonnel` (<u>`staffNo`</u>, `salesArea, carAllowance`)

`Secretary` (<u>`staffNo`</u>, `typingSpeed`)

We assume that the underlying data type of each attribute is supported by the relational DBMS, although this may not be the case – in which case we would need to write additional code to handle the transformation of one data type to another. Unfortunately, with this relational schema we have lost semantic information – it is no longer clear which table represents the superclass and which tables represent the subclasses. We would therefore have to build this knowledge into each application, which, as we have said on other occasions, can lead to duplication of code and potential for inconsistencies arising.

Map each subclass to a table

A second approach is to map each subclass to a table. For the hierarchy given in Figure 17.1, this would give the following three tables:

`Manager` (<u>`staffNo`</u>, `name, position, salary, bonus, mgrStartDate`)

`SalesPersonnel` (<u>`staffNo`</u>, `name, position, salary, salesArea, carAllowance`)

`Secretary` (<u>`staffNo`</u>, `name, position, salary, typingSpeed`)

Again, we have lost semantic information in this mapping – it is no longer clear that these tables are subclasses of a single generic class. In this case, to produce a list of all staff we would have to select the records from each table and then union the results together.

Map the hierarchy to a single table

A third approach is to map the entire inheritance hierarchy to a single table, giving in this case:

`Staff (staffNo, name, position, salary, bonus, mgrStartDate, salesArea, carAllowance, typingSpeed, typeFlag)`

The attribute `typeFlag` is a discriminator to distinguish which type each record is (for example, it may contain the value 1 for a `Manager` record, 2 for a `SalesPersonnel` record, and 3 for a `Secretary` record). Again, we have lost semantic information in this mapping. Further, this mapping will produce an unwanted number of nulls for columns that do not apply to that record. For example, for a `Manager` record, the columns `salesArea`, `carAllowance`, and `typingSpeed` will be null.

17.4 Object-oriented DBMSs (OODBMSs)

In Section 17.2, we reviewed the weaknesses of the relational model against the requirements for the types of advanced database applications that are emerging. In this section, we introduce one approach that attempts to overcome these perceived weaknesses, based on the concepts of object-orientation, namely the **Object-Oriented Database Management System (OODBMS)**. The OODBMS started initially in the engineering and design domains, and has also become the favored system for financial and telecommunications applications. There are many different definitions that have been proposed for an object-oriented data model. For example, Kim (1991) defines an **Object-Oriented Data Model (OODM)**, **Object-Oriented Database (OODB)**, and an **Object-Oriented DBMS (OODBMS)** as shown in the margin.

> **OODM**
> A (logical) data model that captures the semantics of objects supported in object-oriented programming.

> **OODB**
> A persistent and sharable collection of objects defined by an OODM.

> **OODBMS**
> The manager of an OODB.

These definitions are very non-descriptive and tend to reflect the fact that there is no one object-oriented data model equivalent to the underlying data model of relational systems. Each system provides its own interpretation of base functionality. Based on some of the current commercial OODBMSs, such as Gemstone from Gemstone Systems Inc., Objectivity/DB from Objectivity Inc., and ObjectStore from Progress Software Corporation, we can see that the concepts of object-oriented data models are drawn from different areas, as shown in Figure 17.2.

One of the early criticisms often cited about OODBMSs was that they lacked a formal data model. However, towards the end of the last decade, several important vendors (including Sun Microsystems, eXcelon Corporation, Objectivity Inc., POET Software, Computer Associates, and Versant Corporation) formed the Object Data Management Group (ODMG) to define standards for OODBMSs. The ODMG produced an object model that specifies a standard model for the semantics of database objects. The model is important because it determines the built-in semantics that the OODBMS understands and can enforce. As we discuss shortly, the ODMG also provide an Object Definition Language and an Object Query Language, which forms

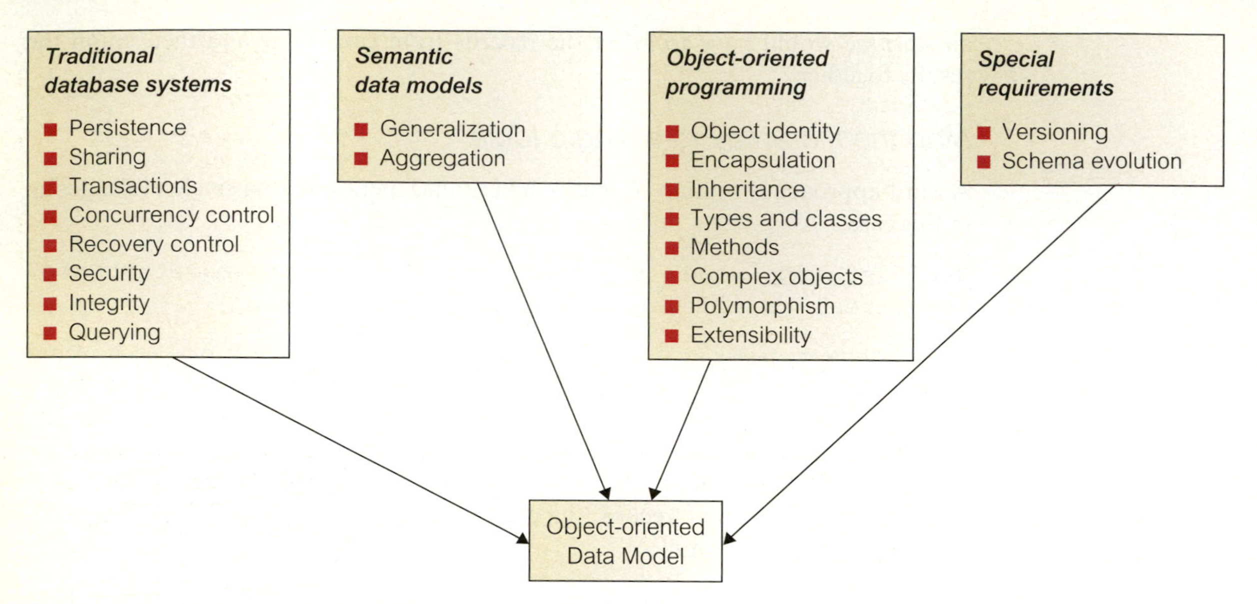

Figure 17.2 Origins of the object-oriented data model

a superset of SQL. Before we discuss the ODMG standard, we first examine how relationships can be modeled in an OODBMS.

17.4.1 Relationships and referential integrity

Relationships are represented in an object-oriented data model using **reference attributes**, typically implemented using object identifiers (OIDs). In this section, we discuss how to represent binary relationships based on their multiplicity: one-to-one (1:1), one-to-many (1:*), and many-to-many (*:*).

1:1 relationships

A 1:1 relationship between objects `A` and `B` is represented by adding a reference attribute to object `A` and, to maintain referential integrity, a reference attribute to object `B`. For example, the 1:1 relationship `Manager` *`Manages`* `DistributionCenter` is represented in Figure 17.3.

1: relationships*

A 1:* relationship between objects `A` and `B` is represented by adding a reference attribute to object `B` and an attribute containing a set of references to object `A`. For example, the 1:* relationship `DistributionCenter` *`Stocks`* `DVDCopy` is represented in Figure 17.4.

**:* relationships*

A *:* relationship between objects `A` and `B` is represented by adding an attribute containing a set of references to each object. For example, there is a *:* relationship

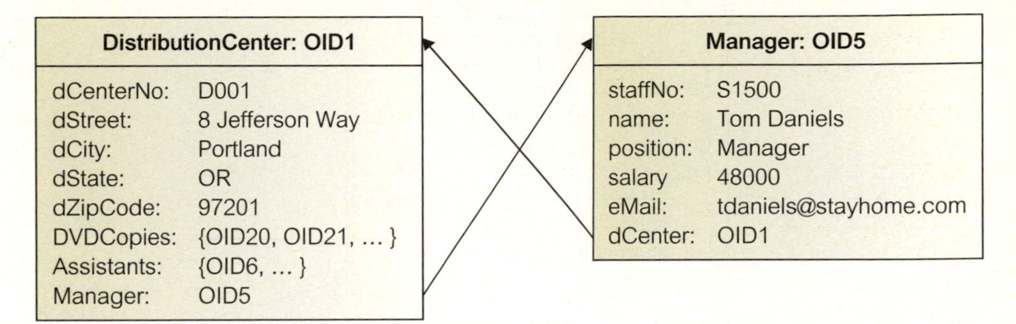

Figure 17.3 The 1:1 relationship `Manager` *`Manages`* `DistributionCenter` (and `Manager` *`WorksAt`* `DistributionCenter`)

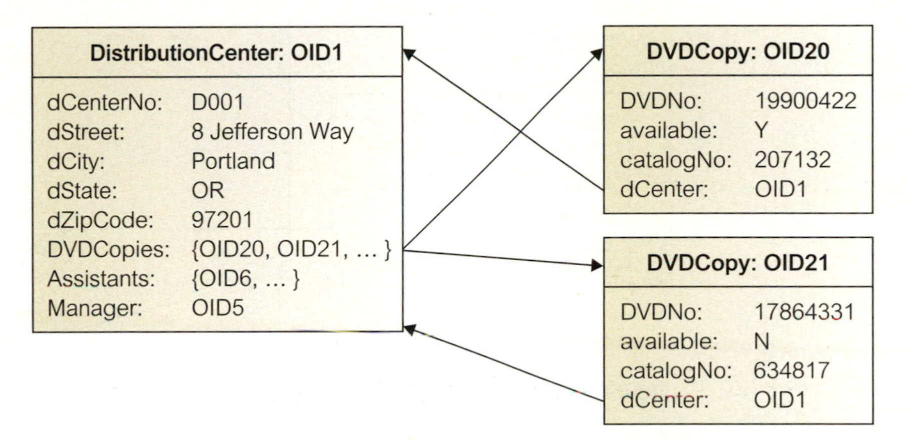

Figure 17.4 The 1:* relationship `DistributionCenter` *`Stocks`* `DVDCopy`

between `DVD` and `Actor`, as represented in Figure 17.5. For relational database design, we would decompose the *:* relationship into two 1:* relationships linked by an intermediate entity. It is also possible to represent this model in an OODBMS, as shown in Figure 17.6.

Referential integrity

In Section 2.4.3, we discussed referential integrity in terms of primary and foreign keys. Referential integrity requires that any referenced object must exist. For example, consider the 1:1 relationship between `Manager` and `DistributionCenter` in Figure 17.3. The `DistributionCenter` instance, OID1, references a `Manager` instance, OID5. If the user deletes this `Manager` instance without updating the `DistributionCenter` instance accordingly, referential integrity is lost. One approach to handling referential integrity is to get the system to automatically maintain the integrity of objects, possibly using inverse attributes. For example, in Figure 17.3 we have an inverse relationship from `Manager` to `DistributionCenter`. When a `Manager` object is deleted, it is easy for the system to use this inverse relationship to adjust the reference in the `DistributionCenter` object accordingly (e.g. set it to NULL – the null pointer).

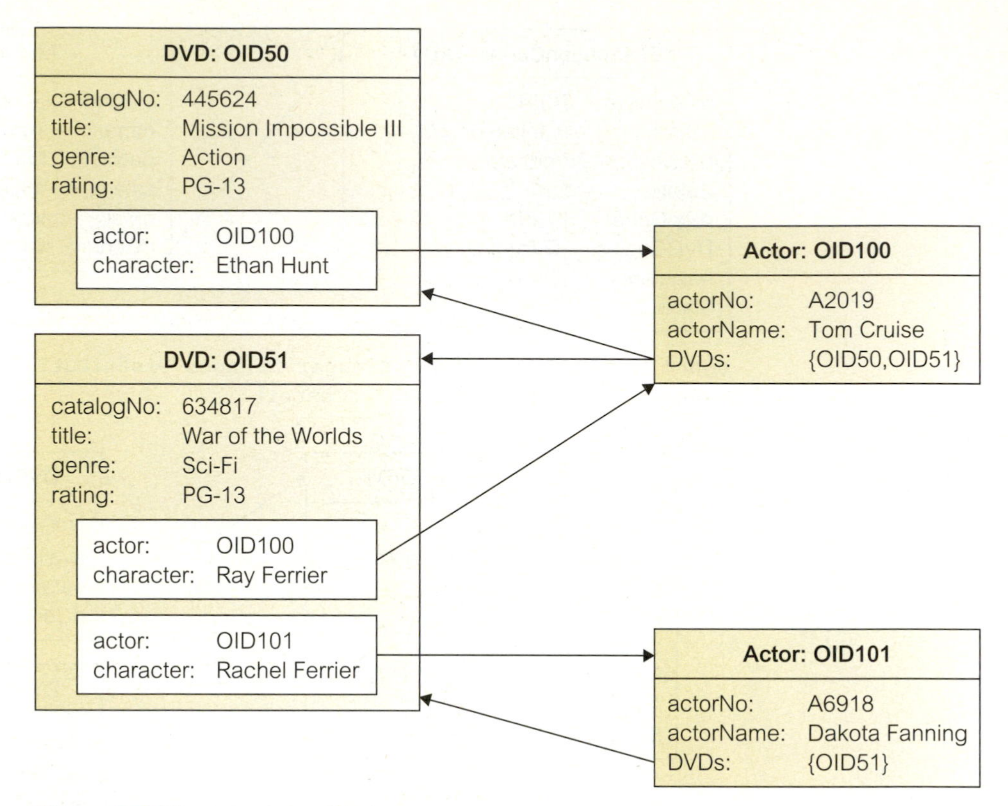

Figure 17.5 The *:* relationship between `DVD` and `Actor`

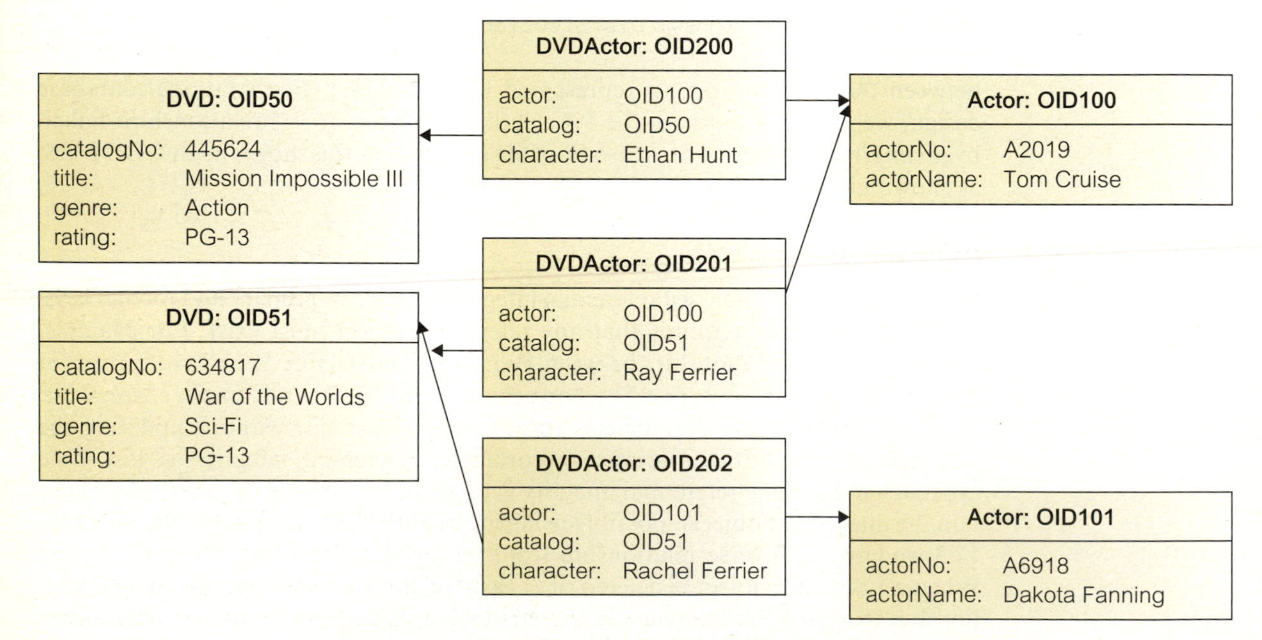

Figure 17.6 Alternative design of a *:* relationship with an intermediate class

17.4.2 ODMG Object Data Standard

The Object Data Management Group (ODMG) specification covers both Object-Oriented Database Management Systems (OODBMSs) that store objects directly and Object-to-Database Mappings (ODMs) that convert and store the objects in a relational or other database system representation. Both types of products are referred to generically as Object Data Management Systems (ODMSs). ODMSs make database objects appear as programming language objects in one or more existing (object-oriented) programming languages, and ODMSs extend the programming language with transparently persistent data, concurrency control, recovery, **associative queries**, and other database capabilities (Cattell, 2000). Before completing their work and disbanding in 2001, the ODMG submitted the Java binding to the Java Community Process as the basis of Java Data Objects (JDO), a persistence mechanism for the Java programming language. A full discussion of the standard is beyond the scope of this book but in this section we provide a brief introduction to the standard. For more details, the interested reader is referred to Cattell (2000) and Connolly and Begg (2005).

The Object Model

The ODMG Object Model specifies the following modeling primitives:

- The basic modeling primitives are the *object* and the *literal*. Only an object has a unique identifier, which does not change and is not reused when the object is deleted. An object may also be given one or more *names* that are meaningful to the user, provided each name identifies a single object within a database. Object names are intended to act as 'root' objects that provide entry points into the database.
- The lifetime of an object is specified when the object is created and may be either *persistent* (the object's storage is managed by the ODMS) or *transient* (object's memory is allocated and deallocated by the programming language's runtime system.)
- Objects and literals can be categorized into *types*. All objects and literals of a given type exhibit common behavior and state. A type is itself an object. An object is sometimes referred to as an *instance* of its type.
- There are two ways to specify object types: interfaces and classes. An *interface* is a specification that defines only the abstract behavior of an object type, using operation signatures. An interface is noninstantiable – in other words, we cannot create objects from an interface. Normally interfaces are used to specify abstract operations that can be inherited by classes or by other interfaces. On the other hand, a *class* defines both the abstract state and behavior of an object type, and is instantiable (thus, type is an abstract concept and class is an implementation concept). Inheritance can be defined through interfaces and classes, although only single inheritance is supported for classes.
- Behavior is defined by a set of *operations* that can be performed on or by the object. Operations may have a list of typed input/output parameters and may return a typed result.

- State is defined by the values an object carries for a set of *properties*. A property may be either an *attribute* of the object or a *relationship* between the object and one or more other objects. Typically, the values of an object's properties can change over time.
- Only binary relationships with cardinality 1:1, 1:*, and *:* are supported. A relationship does not have a name; instead *traversal paths* are defined for each direction of traversal.
- An ODMS stores objects, enabling them to be shared by multiple users and applications. An ODMS is based on a *schema* that is defined in the **Object Definition Language (ODL)**, and contains instances of the types defined by its schema.

The Object Definition Language (ODL)

The ODMG Object Definition Language (ODL) is a language for defining the specifications of object types for ODMG-compliant systems, equivalent to the Data Definition Language (DDL) of traditional DBMSs. Its main objective is to facilitate portability of schemas between compliant systems while helping to provide interoperability between ODMSs. The ODL defines the attributes and relationships of types and specifies the signature of the operations, but it does not address the implementation of signatures (this is done in the program code). A complete specification of the syntax of ODL is beyond the scope of this book, however, the following example illustrates some of the elements of the language. The general structure of a class definition is shown in Figure 17.7.

```
class className {
(extent extentName,
key attributeName)

//define attributes
attribute dataType attributeName
...
//define relationships
relationship [set]<className> traversalPathName
    inverse className::inverseTraversalPathName
...
//define methods
method signature
...
}
```

extent optional
keys optional; separate multiple keys by commas

repeat for each attribute

repeat for each relationship;
set specified for 1..* relationship

repeat for each method

Figure 17.7 Structure of a class definition in the ODMG ODL

Example 17.1 The Object Definition Language

Consider the simplified DVD rentals schema for *StayHome Online Rentals* shown in Figure 17.8. An example ODL definition for part of this schema is shown in Figure 17.9.

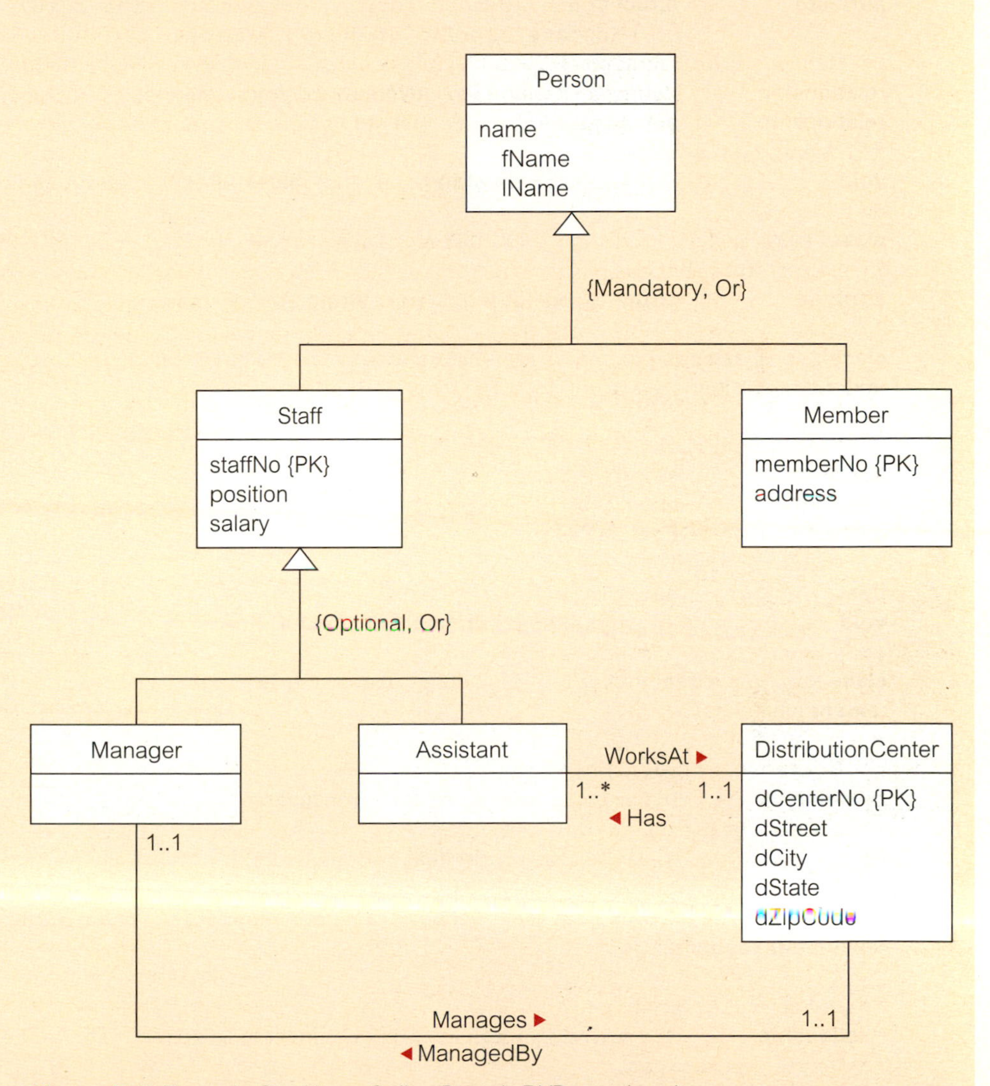

Figure 17.8 Example *StayHome Online Rentals* DVD rentals schema

```
module StayHome {
    class DistributionCenter     // Define class for DistributionCenter
    (extent distributionCenters key dCenterNo)
    {
    /* Define attributes */
    attribute          string dCenterNo;
    attribute          struct CenterAddress {string dStreet, string dCity, string,
                              dState, string dZipCode} address;
    /* Define relationships */
    relationship       Manager ManagedBy  inverse Manager::Manages;
    relationship       set<Assistant> Has inverse Assistant::WorksAt;
    /* Define operations */
    void               takeOnStaff (in string staffNo) raises(staffAlreadyPresent);
    };
    class  Person {                // Define class for Person
    /* Define attributes */
    attribute          struct PName {string fName, string lName}  name;
    };
    class Staff extends Person     // Define class for Staff that inherits from Person
    (extent staff key staffNo)
    {
    /* Define attributes */
    attribute          string staffNo;
    attribute          enum PositionType {Manager, Deputy, Assistant} position;
    attribute          float salary;
    /* Define operations */
    float              getSalary();
    void               increaseSalary(in float increment);
    };
    class Manager extends Staff   // Define class for Manager that inherits from Staff
    (extent managers)
    {
    /* Define relationships */
    relationship       DistributionCenter Manages inverse DistributionCenter::ManagedBy;
    /* Define operations */
    void               giveCommission(in float centerProfit);
    };
    class Assistant extends Staff // Define class for Assistant that inherits from Staff
    (extent assistants)
    {
    /* Define relationships */
    relationship       DistributionCenter WorksAt inverse DistributionCenter::Has;
    /* Define operations */
    void               transferStaff(in string fromdCenterNo, in string todCenterNo)
                       raises(doesNotWorkInCenter);
    };
};
```

Figure 17.9 ODL definition for part of the *StayHome Online Rentals* DVD rentals schema

The Object Query Language (OQL)

The ODMG Object Query Language (OQL) provides declarative access to the object database using an SQL-like syntax. It does not provide explicit update operators, but leaves this to the operations defined on object types. As with SQL, OQL can be used as a standalone language and as a language embedded in another language for which an ODMG binding is defined. The supported languages are Smalltalk, C++, and Java. OQL can also invoke operations methods written in these languages.

OQL can be used for both associative and navigational access:

- An *associative query* (that is, a declarative statement with selection based on one or more predicates) returns a collection of objects. How these objects are located is the responsibility of the ODMS, rather than the application program.
- A *navigational query* accesses individual objects, and object, relationships are used to navigate from one object to another. It is the responsibility of the application program to specify the procedure for accessing the required objects.

An OQL query is a function that delivers an object whose type may be inferred from the operator contributing to the query expression. OQL is essentially a superset of the SQL SELECT. For some queries, the query can be expressed quite succinctly simply by specifying an entry point to the database. When the SELECT statement is used, it has a similar structure to the standard SQL SELECT statement (see Section 3.2.1), as the next few examples illustrate.

Example 17.2 Object Query Language – Use of extents and traversal paths

(1) Get the set of all staff (with identity).

In general, for each query an entry point to the database is required, which can be any named persistent object (that is, an *extent* or a *named object*). In this case, we can use the extent of class `Staff` to produce the required set using the following simple expression:

```
staff
```

(2) Get the set of all distribution center managers (with identity).

In this case, we can use the name of the extent of the class `DistributionCenter` (`distributionCenters`) as an entry point to the database and then use the traversal path `ManagedBy` to find the set of center managers, to produce:

```
distributionCenters.ManagedBy
```

(3) Find all distribution centers in Seattle.

```
SELECT d.dCenterNo
FROM d IN distributionCenters
WHERE d.address.city = 'Seattle';
```

Again, we can use the extent `distributionCenters` as an entry point to the database and use the iterator variable `d` to range over the objects in this collection.

Note There is a slight difference in the format of the OQL FROM clause compared to the SQL FROM clause, which would have been written without the IN keyword and the alias d after the name of the corresponding table.

(4) Assume that `seattleCenters` *is a named object (corresponding to the object from the previous query.) Use this named object to find all staff who work at that center.*

We can express this query as:

```
seattleCenters.Has
```

which returns a set of `Assistant` objects. To access the salaries of assistants, intuitively we may think this can be expressed as:

```
seattleCenters.Has.salary
```

However, this is not allowed in OQL because there is ambiguity over the return result, which may or may not contain duplicates. Instead, we have to express this as:

```
SELECT [DISTINCT] s.salary
FROM s IN seattleCenters.Has;
```

Example 17.3 Object Query Language – Use of aggregates

How many staff work in New York?

The OQL aggregate functions can be applied within the SELECT clause or to the result of the SELECT operation. For example, the following two expressions are equivalent in OQL:

```
SELECT COUNT(a) FROM a IN assistants WHERE
a.WorksAt.address.city = 'New York';
COUNT(SELECT a FROM a IN assistants WHERE
a.WorksAt.address.city = 'New York');
```

Note OQL allows aggregate operations to be applied to any collection of the appropriate type and, unlike SQL, can be used in any part of the query. For example, the following is allowed in OQL (but not SQL):

```
SELECT a
FROM a IN assistants
WHERE COUNT(a.WorksAt) > 10;
```

17.4.3 Advantages and disadvantages of OODBMSs

OODBMSs can provide appropriate solutions for many types of advanced applications. However, there are also disadvantages. In this section, we briefly discuss the advantages and disadvantages.

Advantages of OODBMSs

Many of the advantages of OODBMSs are a result of the incorporation of object-orientation within the system. For example:

- enriched modeling capabilities;
- extensibility (that is, we can create new data types);
- removal of impedance mismatch;
- applicability to advanced database applications.

Others are the result of employing more appropriate protocols. For example:

- support for schema evolution;
- support for long-duration transactions.

Two other advantages often cited are:

- *More expressive query language*: OODBMSs generally use *navigational access* to move from one object to the next. This is in contrast to the *associative access* of SQL. Navigational access is more suitable for handling parts explosion, recursive queries, and so on.
- *Improved performance*: there have been a number of benchmarks that have suggested that OODBMSs provide significant performance improvements over RDBMSs. For example, in 1989 and 1990, the OO1 benchmark was run on the OODBMSs GemStone, Ontos, ObjectStore, Objectivity/DB, and Versant, and the RDBMSs INGRES and Sybase. The results showed an average 30-fold performance improvement for the OODBMS over the RDBMS.

Disadvantages of OODBMSs

Some of disadvantages often cited about the OODBMS are:

- lack of a universal data model;
- lack of standards;
- lack of experience;
- competition from RDBMSs/ORDBMSs;
- complexity;
- lack of support for views;
- lack of support for security.

17.5 Object-relational DBMSs (ORDBMSs)

ORDBMS

A set of extensions to the relational DBMS to incorporate some concept of 'object'.

Moving away from the traditional relational data model is sometimes referred to as a *revolutionary approach* to integrating object-oriented concepts with database systems. In contrast, the **Object-Relational DBMS (ORDBMS)** is a more *evolutionary approach* to integrating object-oriented concepts with database systems that extends the relational model.

Towards the end of the last decade, the choice of DBMS seemed to be between the RDBMS and the OODBMS. However, many vendors of RDBMS products were conscious of the threat and promise of the OODBMS. They agreed that traditional RDBMSs were not suited to the advanced applications discussed in Section 17.1, and that added functionality was required. However, they rejected the claim that extended RDBMSs would not provide sufficient functionality or would be too slow to cope adequately with the new complexity.

If we examine the advanced database applications that are emerging, we find they make extensive use of many object-oriented features such as a user-extensible type system, encapsulation, inheritance, polymorphism, complex objects, and object identity (see Figure 17.2). The most obvious way to remedy the shortcomings of the relational model is to extend the model with these types of features. This is the approach that has been taken by many extended RDBMSs, although each has implemented different combinations of features. Thus, there is no single extended relational model; rather, there is a variety of these models, whose characteristics depend upon the way and the degree to which extensions were made. However, all the models do share the same basic relational tables and query language, all incorporate some concept of 'object,' and some have the ability to store methods (or procedures or triggers) as well as data in the database.

Three of the leading RDBMS vendors – Oracle, Microsoft, and IBM – have all extended their systems into ORDBMSs, although the functionality provided by each is slightly different. The concept of the ORDBMS, as a hybrid of the RDBMS and the OODBMS, is very appealing, preserving the wealth of knowledge and experience that has been acquired with the RDBMS. So much so, that some analysts predict the ORDBMS will have a 50% larger share of the market than the RDBMS.

As might be expected, the standards activity in this area is based on extensions to the SQL standard. The national standards bodies have been working on object extensions to SQL since 1991. These extensions have become part of the SQL standard, with releases in 1999, referred to as SQL:1999, 2003, referred to as SQL:2003, and 2006 (SQL:2006). These releases are an on-going attempt to standardize extensions to the relational model and query language. After discussing the advantages and disadvantages of ORDBMSs, we briefly review some of the main object management features of SQL:2006.

17.5.1 Advantages and disadvantages of ORDBMSs

ORDBMSs can provide appropriate solutions for many types of advanced applications. However, there are also disadvantages. In this section, we briefly discuss the advantages and disadvantages.

Advantages of ORDBMSs

Apart from the advantages of resolving many of the weaknesses cited in Section 17.2, the main advantages of extending the relational data model come from *reuse* and *sharing*. Reuse comes from the ability to extend the DBMS server to perform standard functionality centrally, rather than have it coded in each application. For example, applications may require spatial data types that represent points, lines, and polygons, with associated functions that calculate the distance between two points, the distance between a point and a line, whether a point is contained within a polygon, and whether two polygonal regions overlap, among others. If we can embed this functionality in the server, it saves having to define it in each application that needs it, and consequently allows the functionality to be shared by all applications. These advantages also give rise to increased productivity both for the developer and for the end-user.

Another obvious advantage is that the extended relational approach preserves the significant body of knowledge and experience that has gone into developing relational applications. This is a significant advantage, as many organizations would find it prohibitively expensive to change. If the new functionality is designed appropriately, this approach should allow organizations to take advantage of the new extensions in an evolutionary way without losing the benefits of current database features and functions. Thus, an ORDBMS could be introduced in an integrative fashion, as proof-of-concept projects. The recent SQL:2003 and SQL:2006 standards are designed to be upwardly compatible with the SQL2 standard, and so any ORDBMS that complies with SQL:2006 should provide this capability.

Disadvantages of ORDBMSs

The ORDBMS approach has the obvious disadvantages of complexity and associated increased costs. Further, there are the proponents of the relational approach who believe the essential simplicity and purity of the relational model are lost with these types of extensions. There are also those who believe that the RDBMS is being extended for what will be a minority of applications that do not achieve optimal performance with current relational technology.

In addition, object-oriented purists are not attracted by these extensions either. They argue that the terminology of ORDBMSs is revealing. Instead of discussing object models, terms like 'user-defined data types' are used. The terminology of object-orientation abounds with terms like 'abstract types', 'class hierarchies', and 'object models'. However, ORDBMS vendors are attempting to portray object models as extensions to the relational model with some additional complexities. This potentially misses the point of object-orientation, highlighting the large semantic gap between these two technologies. Object applications are simply not as data-centric as relational-based ones. Object-oriented models and programs deeply combine relationships and encapsulated objects to more closely mirror the 'real world'. In fact, objects are fundamentally not extensions of data but a completely different concept with far greater power to express 'real world' relationships and behaviors.

17.5.2 SQL:2006

In this section, we examine the following object management features of the SQL:2006 standard:

- type constructors for row types and reference types;
- user-defined types (distinct types and structured types) that can participate in supertype/subtype relationships;

- user-defined procedures, functions, and operators;
- reference types and object identity;
- creating tables and subtables.

Row types

A **row type** is a sequence of field name/data type pairs that provides a data type to represent the types of rows in tables, so that complete rows can be stored in variables, passed as arguments to routines, and returned as return values from function calls. A row type can also be used to allow a column of a table to contain row values. In essence, the row is a table nested within a table.

Example 17.4 Use of row type

To illustrate the use of row types, we create a simplified `DistributionCenter` table consisting of the distribution center number and address, and insert a record into the new table:

```
CREATE TABLE DistributionCenter (
    dCenterNo  CHAR(4),
    dAddress  ROW(dStreet      VARCHAR(60),
                  dCity        VARCHAR(20),
                  dState       CHAR(2),
                  dZipCode     CHAR(5)));
INSERT INTO DistributionCenter
VALUES ('D001', ROW('8 Jefferson Way', 'Portland', 'OR', '97201'));
```

User-defined types (UDTs)

SQL:2006 allows the definition of *user-defined types (UDTs)*, which may be used in the same way as the predefined types such as CHAR, INT, FLOAT. UDTs are subdivided into two categories: distinct types and structured types. The simpler type of UDT is the *distinct type*, which allows differentiation between the same underlying base types. For example, we could create the following two distinct types:

```
CREATE TYPE ActorNumberType AS VARCHAR(5) FINAL;
CREATE TYPE StaffNumberType AS VARCHAR(5) FINAL;
```

If we now attempt to treat an instance of one type as an instance of the other type, an error would be generated.

Key point

Although SQL also allows the creation of domains to distinguish between different data types, the purpose of an SQL domain is solely to constrain the set of valid values that can be stored in a column with that domain, not to perform any form of type checking.

In its more general case, a UDT definition consists of one or more *attribute definitions* and zero or more *routine declarations* (methods). The value of an attribute can be accessed using the common dot notation (.). For example, assuming p is an instance of the UDT PersonType, which has an attribute name of type VARCHAR, we can access the name attribute as:

```
p.name
p.name = 'A. Smith'
```

Key point When referring to UDTs, SQL uses the term 'attribute' rather than the usual 'column', which is reserved for tables.

Encapsulation and observer and mutator functions

SQL encapsulates each attribute of structured types by providing a pair of built-in routines that are invoked whenever a user attempts to reference the attribute: an *observer* (get) and a *mutator* (set) function. The observer function returns the current value of the attribute; the mutator function sets the value of the attribute to a value specified as a parameter. These functions can be redefined in the definition of the UDT. In this way, attribute values are encapsulated and are accessible only by invoking these functions. For example, the observer function for the name attribute of PersonType would be:

```
FUNCTION name(p PersonType) RETURNS VARCHAR(15)
    RETURN p.name;
```

and the corresponding mutator function to set the value to *newValue* would be:

```
FUNCTION name(p PersonType RESULT, newValue VARCHAR(15))
RETURNS PersonType
BEGIN
    p.name = newValue
    RETURN p;
END;
```

Constructor functions and the NEW expression

A (public) *constructor* function is automatically defined to create new instances of the type. The constructor function has the same name and type as the UDT, takes zero arguments, and returns a new instance of the type with the attributes set to their default value. User-defined constructor methods can be provided by the user to initialize a newly created instance of the structured type, but the constructor must have the same name as the type and the parameters must be different from the system-supplied constructor. For example, we could initialize a constructor for type PersonType as follows:

```
CREATE CONSTRUCTOR METHOD PersonType (nm VARCHAR(15), DOB
DATE)
      RETURNS PersonType
  BEGIN
    SET SELF.name = nm;
    SET SELF.DOB = DOB;
    RETURN SELF;
  END;
```

The NEW expression can be used to invoke the system-supplied function, for example:

```
SET p = NEW PersonType();
```

User-defined constructor methods must be invoked in the context of the NEW expression. For example, we can create a new instance of `PersonType` and invoke the above user-defined constructor method as follows:

```
SET p = NEW PersonType('John White', '27-May-1950');
```

Example 17.5 Definition of a new user-defined type

To illustrate the creation of a new UDT, we create a UDT for a `PersonType`.

```
CREATE TYPE PersonType AS (
    name          VARCHAR(15),
    dateOfBirth   DATE)
INSTANTIABLE
NOT FINAL
INSTANCE METHOD age () RETURNS INTEGER,
INSTANCE METHOD age (DOB DATE) RETURNS PersonType;
CREATE INSTANCE METHOD age () RETURNS INTEGER
    FOR PersonType
  BEGIN
      RETURN /* age calculated from SELF.dateOfBirth */;
    END;
CREATE INSTANCE METHOD age (DOB DATE) RETURNS PersonType
    FOR PersonType
    BEGIN
    SELF.dateOfBirth = /* code to set dateOfBirth from DOB*/;
    RETURN SELF;
  END;
```

This example also illustrates the use of **stored** and **virtual attributes**. A *stored attribute* is the default type with an attribute name and data type. The data type can be any known data type, including other UDTs. In contrast, *virtual attributes* do not correspond to stored data, but to derived data. There is an implied virtual attribute age, which is derived using the (observer) age function and assigned using the (mutator) age function[3]. From the user's perspective, there is no distinguishable difference between a stored attribute and a virtual attribute – both are accessed using the corresponding observer and mutator functions. Only the designer of the UDT will know the difference.

The keyword INSTANTIABLE indicates that instances can be created for this type. If NOT INSTANTIABLE had been specified, we would not be able to create instances of this type, only from one of its subtypes. The keyword NOT FINAL indicates that we can create subtypes of this user-defined type.

[3] Note that the function name age has been **overloaded** here.

Subtypes and supertypes

SQL allows UDTs to participate in a subtype/supertype hierarchy using the UNDER clause. A type can have more than one subtype but currently only one supertype (that is, multiple inheritance is not supported). A subtype inherits all the attributes and behavior of its supertype and it can define additional attributes and functions like any other UDT and it can override inherited functions. An instance of a subtype is considered an instance of all its supertypes. SQL supports the concept of **substitutability**: that is, whenever an instance of a supertype is expected an instance of the subtype can be used in its place.

Example 17.6 Creation of a subtype using the UNDER clause

To create a subtype StaffType of the supertype PersonType we write:

```
CREATE TYPE StaffType UNDER PersonType AS (
    staffNo      VARCHAR(5),
    position     VARCHAR(10)     DEFAULT 'Assistant',
    salary       DECIMAL(7, 2),
    eMail        VARCHAR(20),
    dCenterNo    CHAR(4))
    INSTANTIABLE
    NOT FINAL
    REF IS SYSTEM GENERATED
    INSTANCE METHOD isManager () RETURNS BOOLEAN;
    CREATE INSTANCE METHOD isManager () RETURNS BOOLEAN
    BEGIN
        IF s.position = 'Manager' THEN
            RETURN TRUE;
        ELSE
            RETURN FALSE;
        END IF
    END;
```

`StaffType`, as well as having the attributes defined within the above CREATE TYPE statement, also has the inherited attributes of `PersonType`, along with the associated observer and mutator functions. In addition, we have defined a function `isManager` that checks whether the specified member of staff is a Manager. We discuss the clause REF IS SYSTEM GENERATED shortly.

User-defined routines (UDRs)

User-defined routines (UDRs) define methods for manipulating data and are an important adjunct to UDTs, providing the required behavior for the UDTs. In SQL, UDRs may be defined as part of a UDT or separately as part of a schema. An *SQL-invoked routine* may be a procedure or function. It may be externally provided in a standard programming language such as C/C++, or defined completely in SQL using extensions that make the language computationally complete (see Appendix E). There are three types of **methods**:

- *constructor methods*, which initialize a newly created instance of a UDT;
- *instance methods*, which operate on specific instances of a UDT;
- *static methods*, which are analogous to class methods in the some object-oriented programming languages and operate at the UDT level rather than at the instance level.

In the first two cases, the methods include an additional implicit first parameter called SELF whose data type is that of the associated UDT. We saw an example of the SELF parameter in the user-defined constructor method for `PersonType`. A method can be invoked in one of three ways:

- a constructor method is invoked using the NEW expression, as discussed previously;
- an instance method is invoked using the standard dot notation, for example, `p.name`, or using the generalized invocation format, for example, (`p AS StaffType`).name();
- a static method is invoked using ::, for example, if `totalStaff` is a static method of `StaffType`, we could invoke it as `StaffType::totalStaff`().

Reference types and object identity

Until SQL:2003, the only way to define relationships between tables was using the primary key/foreign key mechanism, which in SQL2 could be expressed using the referential table constraint clause REFERENCES, as discussed in Appendix E.1. In SQL:2003, **reference types** can be used to define relationships between row types and uniquely identify a row within a table. A reference type value can be stored in one table and used as a direct reference to a specific row in some base table that has been defined to be of this type (similar to the notion of a pointer type in C/C++). In this respect, a reference type provides a similar functionality as the **object identifier** (OID) of OODBMSs, which we discussed in Section 17.4.1. Thus, references allow a row to be shared among multiple tables, and enable users to replace complex join definitions in queries with much simpler path expressions.

REF IS SYSTEM GENERATED in a CREATE TYPE statement indicates that the actual values of the associated REF type are provided by the system, as in `StaffType` created above. Other options are available but we omit the details here; the default is REF IS SYSTEM GENERATED. As we see in the next example, a base table can be created to be of some structured type. Other columns can be specified for the table but at least one column must be specified, namely a column of the associated REF type, using a clause REF IS <columnName> SYSTEM GENERATED. This column is used to contain unique identifiers for the rows of the associated base table. The identifier for a given row is assigned when the row is inserted into the table and remains associated with that row until it is deleted.

Creating tables and subtables

To maintain upwards compatibility with the SQL2 standard, it is still necessary to use the CREATE TABLE statement to create a table, even if the table consists of a single UDT. In other words, a UDT instance can only persist if it is stored as the column value in a table. There are several variations of the CREATE TABLE statement, as we now illustrate.

Example 17.7 Creation of a table based on a UDT

To create a table using the `PersonType` UDT, we could write:

```
CREATE TABLE Person (
                info                PersonType);
```

or

```
CREATE TABLE Person OF PersonType;
```

In the first instance, we would access the columns of the `Person` table using a path expression such as '`Person.info.name`'; in the second version, we would access the columns using a path expression such as '`Person.name`'.

Example 17.8 Creation of a subtable using the UNDER clause

We can create a table for `Staff` using table inheritance:

```
CREATE TABLE Staff OF StaffType UNDER Person (
    REF IS staffID SYSTEM GENERATED);
```

When we insert rows into the `Staff` table, the values of the inherited columns are inserted into the `Person` table. Similarly, when we delete rows from the `Staff` table, the rows disappear from both the `Staff` and `Person` tables. As a result, when we access all rows of `Person`, this will include all the rows directly inserted into the `Person` table and all the rows indirectly inserted through the `Staff` table.

Example 17.9 Using a reference type to define a relationship

In this example, we model the relationship between `DistributionCenter` and `Staff` using a reference type.

```
CREATE TABLE DistributionCenter(
    dCenterNo    CHAR(4)          NOT NULL,
    dStreet      VARCHAR(60)      NOT NULL,
    dCity        VARCHAR(20)      NOT NULL,
    dState       CHAR(2)          NOT NULL,
    dZipCode     CHAR(5)          NOT NULL,
    mgrStaffID   REF(StaffType)   SCOPE Staff
                 REFERENCES ARE CHECKED ON DELETE CASCADE,
    PRIMARY KEY (dCenterNo));
```

We are using a reference type, REF(`StaffType`), to model the relationship between `DistributionCenter` and `Staff`. The SCOPE clause specifies the associated referenced table. REFERENCES ARE CHECKED indicates that referential integrity is to be maintained (alternative is REFERENCES ARE NOT CHECKED). ON DELETE CASCADE corresponds to the normal referential action that existed in SQL2. Note that an ON UPDATE clause is not required, because the column `staffID` in the `Staff` table cannot be updated.

Querying data

SQL:2006 provides the same syntax as SQL2 for querying and updating tables, with various extensions to handle objects. We briefly illustrate some of these extensions.

Example 17.10 Retrieve a specific column, specific rows

Find the names of all Managers.

```
SELECT s.name
FROM Staff s
WHERE s.position = 'Manager';
```

This query invokes the implicitly-defined observer function `position` in the WHERE clause to access the `position` column.

Example 17.11 Invoking a user-defined function

Find the names and ages of all Managers.

```
SELECT s.name, s.age
FROM Staff s
WHERE s.isManager;
```

This alternative method of finding Managers uses the user-defined function `isManager` as a predicate of the WHERE clause. This UDF returns the boolean value TRUE if the member of staff is a manager (see Example 17.6). In addition, this query also invokes the inherited virtual (observer) function `age` as an element of the SELECT list.

Example 17.12 Use of the dereference operator

Find the name of the member of staff who manages distribution center D001.

```
SELECT d.mgrStaffID->name AS name
FROM DistributionCenter d
WHERE d.dCenterNo = 'D001';
```

References can be used in path expressions that permit traversal of object references to navigate from one row to another. To traverse a reference, the dereference operator (`->`) is used. In the SELECT statement, `d.mgrStaffID` is the normal way to access a column of a table. In this particular case though, the column is a reference to a row of the `Staff` table, and so we must use the dereference operator to access the columns of the dereferenced table. In SQL2, this query would have required a join or nested subquery.

To retrieve the manager for distribution center D001, rather than the person's name, we would use the following query instead:

```
SELECT DEREF (d.mgrStaffID) AS Staff
FROM DistributionCenter d
WHERE d.dCenterNo = 'D001';
```

Although reference types are similar to foreign keys, there are significant differences. In SQL:2006, referential integrity is only maintained using a referential constraint definition specified as part of the table definition. By themselves, reference types do not provide referential integrity. Thus, the SQL reference type should not be confused with that provided in the ODMG object model. In the ODMG model, OIDs are used to model relationships between types and referential integrity is automatically defined.

A fuller discussion of the object management features of SQL:2006 is beyond the scope of this book but the interested reader is referred to Connolly and Begg (2005).

Chapter summary

- Advanced database applications include interactive and dynamic web sites, geographic information systems (GIS), office information systems (OIS) and multimedia systems, and computer-aided software engineering (CASE).
- The relational model, and relational systems in particular, have weaknesses such as poor representation of 'real world' entities, semantic overloading, poor support for

integrity constraints, difficulty handling recursive queries, limited operations, and impedance mismatch. The limited modeling capabilities of relational DBMSs have made them unsuitable for advanced database applications.

- An **OODBMS** is a manager of an OODB. An **OODB** is a persistent and sharable repository of objects defined in an OODM. An **OODM** is a data model that captures the semantics of objects supported in object-oriented programming. There is no universally agreed OODM.
- Several important vendors have formed the **Object Data Management Group** (ODMG) to define standards for OODBMSs. The ODMG has produced an Object Model that specifies a standard model for the semantics of database objects. The model is important because it determines the built-in semantics that the OODBMS understands and can enforce. The design of class libraries and applications that use these semantics should be portable across the various OODBMSs that support the Object Model.
- The ODMG OM enables both designs and implementations to be ported between compliant systems. The basic modeling primitives in the model are the **object** and the **literal**. Only an object has a unique identifier. Objects and literals can be categorized into **types**. All objects and literals of a given type exhibit common behavior and state. Behavior is defined by a set of **operations** that can be performed on or by the object. State is defined by the values an object carries for a set of **properties**. A property may be either an **attribute** of the object or a **relationship** between the object and one or more other objects.
- The **Object Query Language** (OQL) provides declarative access to the object database using an SQL-like syntax. It does not provide explicit update operators, but leaves this to the operations defined on object types. An OQL query is a function that delivers an object whose type may be inferred from the operator contributing to the query expression. OQL can be used both for both associative and navigational access.
- Advantages of OODBMSs include enriched modeling capabilities, extensibility, removal of impedance mismatch, more expressive query language, support for schema evolution and long duration transactions, applicability to advanced database applications, and performance. Disadvantages include lack of universal data model, lack of standards, lack of experience, competition from RDBMSs/ORDBMSs, complexity, and lack of support for views and security.
- There is no single extended relational data model; rather, there is a variety of these models, whose characteristics depend upon the way and the degree to which extensions were made. However, all the models do share the same basic relational tables and query language, all incorporate some concept of 'object', and some have the ability to store methods or procedures/triggers as well as data in the database.
- The relational model has been extended with the concept of an 'object' to create the **Object-Relational DBMS** (**ORDBMS**). Advantages of ORDBMSs come from reuse and sharing. There is also the obvious advantage that it preserves the significant body of knowledge and experience with relational DBMSs. Disadvantages include complexity and increased costs.
- SQL:2006 extensions include row types, user-defined types (UDTs) and user-defined routines (UDRs), inheritance, reference types, and object identity.

Review questions

17.1 Discuss the general characteristics of advanced database applications.

17.2 Discuss why the weaknesses of the relational data model and relational DBMSs may make them unsuitable for advanced database applications.

17.3 Define each of the following concepts in the context of an object-oriented data model (you may need to read Appendix H first):
(a) abstraction, encapsulation, and information hiding;
(b) objects and attributes;
(c) object identity;
(d) methods and messages;
(e) classes, subclasses, superclasses, and inheritance;
(f) overriding and overloading;

Give examples using the *StayHome Online Rentals* sample data shown in Figure 2.4.

17.4 Discuss the difficulties involved in mapping objects created in an object-oriented programming language to a relational database.

17.5 Describe the three generations of DBMSs.

17.6 Define an object-oriented DBMS (OODBMS).

17.7 List the advantages and disadvantages of an OODBMS.

17.8 Discuss the main concepts of the ODMG Object Model. Give an example to illustrate each of the concepts.

17.9 What is the function of the ODMG Object Definition Language (ODL)?

17.10 What is the function of the ODMG Object Query Language (OQL)?

17.11 What typical functionality would be provided by an ORDBMS?

17.12 What are the advantages and disadvantages of extending the relational data model?

17.13 What are the main object management features in SQL:2006?

Exercises

17.14 Investigate one of the advanced database applications discussed in Section 17.1, or a similar one that handles complex, interrelated data. In particular, examine its functionality and the data types and operations it uses.

17.15 Analyze one of the relational DBMSs that you currently use. Discuss the object-oriented features provided by the system. What additional functionality do these features provide?

17.16 You have been asked by the Managing Director of *StayHome Online Rentals* to investigate and prepare a report on the applicability of an object-oriented DBMS for the organization. The report should compare the technology of the relational DBMS with that of the object-oriented DBMS, and should address the advantages and disadvantages of implementing an OODBMS within the organization, and any perceived problem areas. Finally, the report should contain a fully justified set of conclusions on the applicability of the OODBMS for *StayHome*.

17.17 For the *StayHome Online Rentals* case study documented in Section 5.4, suggest attributes and methods that would be appropriate for the `DistributionCenter`, `Staff`, and `Member` classes.

17.18 Represent the classes from Question 17.17 using the ODMG Object Definition Language (ODL).

17.19 Produce an object-oriented design for the *PerfectPets* case study documented in Appendix B.

17.20 Represent the design from Question 17.19 using the ODMG Object Definition Language (ODL).

Additional exercises

17.21 Produce an object-oriented database design for the *Hotel case study* specified at the start of the exercises in Chapter 3 and then show how the following queries would be written in OQL:

(a) List all hotels.

(b) List all single rooms with a price below $20 per night.

(c) List the names and cities of all guests.

(d) List the price and type of all rooms at the Grosvenor Hotel.

(e) List all guests currently staying at the Grosvenor Hotel.

(f) List the details of all rooms at the Grosvenor Hotel, including the name of the guest staying in the room, if the room is occupied.

(g) List the guest details (`guestNo`, `guestName`, and `guestAddress`) of all guests staying at the Grosvenor Hotel.

17.22 Consider the relational schema for the *Hotel case study* given in the exercises of Chapter 3. Redesign this schema to take advantage of the new features of SQL:2006. Add user-defined functions that you consider appropriate.

17.23 Create SQL:2006 statements for the queries given in Chapter 3, Exercises 3.11–3.33.

17.24 Using a browser, look at some of the following web sites and discover the wealth of information held there:

(a) Gemstone	http://www.gemstone.com
(b) Objectivity/DB	http://www.objectivity.com
(c) ObjectStore	http://www.objectstore.net
(d) FastObjects for Poet	http://www.poet.com
(e) Oracle	http://www.oracle.com
(f) SQL Server	http://www.microsoft.com/sqlserver
(g) DB2	http://www.ibm.com/db2

17.25 For each of the different approaches to storing objects in a relation database discussed in Section 17.3, write some code (or pseudocode) to illustrate how objects would be inserted and retrieved from the database. What can you conclude from this?

CHAPTER

18 Business intelligence

Preview

In this final chapter of the book we examine the current and emerging trend of business intelligence (BI). We begin by defining what business intelligence represents and then focus on three associated technologies, namely data warehousing, online analytical processing (OLAP), and data mining. To illustrate some of the concepts associated with BI, we have extended the *StayHome Online Rentals* case study given in Section 5.4.

Learning objectives

In this chapter you will learn:

- What business intelligence (BI) represents.
- The technologies associated with business intelligence including data warehousing, online analytical processing (OLAP), and data mining.
- The main concepts associated with a data warehouse.
- The relationship between online transaction processing (OLTP) systems and a data warehouse.
- The main concepts associated with a data mart.
- About designing a database for decision-support using a technique called dimensionality modeling.
- The important concepts associated with online analytical processing (OLAP) systems.
- The main categories of OLAP tools.
- The main concepts associated with data mining.
- How a business intelligence (BI) tool such as Microsoft Analytical Services provides decision-support.

18.1 Business intelligence (BI)

Businesses have always sought ways to gain greater insight about their environment. This was true even before the emergence of computing where businesses commonly collected data about their environment from non-automated sources. However, the lack of computing resources to support the collection, storage, and analysis of data, meant that businesses often made decisions based primarily on intuition. As businesses began to automate more systems, more electronic data became available. However, even at this stage the collection and integration of data created by different systems remained a challenge due to lack of an infrastructure for data exchange or to incompatibilities between systems. Reports based on the gathered data sometimes took months to generate. Such reports allowed informed long-term strategic decision-making. However, short-term tactical decision-making continued to rely on intuition.

Business intelligence (BI)

The processes for collecting and analyzing data, the technologies used in these processes, and the information obtained from these processes with the purpose of facilitating corporate decision making.

In modern businesses, the emergence of standards in computing, automation, and technology have led to vast amounts of electronic data becoming available. Business intelligence involves sieving through large amounts of data, extracting information and turning that information into actionable knowledge. In 1989 Howard Dresner, a Research Fellow at Gartner Group popularized '**business intelligence**' or (**BI**) as a umbrella term to describe a set of concepts and methods to improve business decision-making by using fact-based support systems.

In the following sections we focus on three key technologies that can form part of a BI implementation, namely data warehousing, online analytical processing (OLAP), and data mining.

18.2 Data warehousing

Since the 1970s, organizations have largely focused their investment in new computer systems that automate business processes. In this way, organizations gained competitive advantage through systems that offered more efficient and cost-effective services to the customer. Throughout this period, organizations accumulated growing amounts of data stored in their operational databases. However, in recent times, where such systems are commonplace, organizations are focusing on ways to use operational data to support decision-making as a means of regaining competitive advantage.

Operational systems were never primarily designed to support business decision-making and so using such systems may never be an easy solution. The legacy is that a typical organization may have numerous operational systems with overlapping and sometimes contradictory definitions, such as data types. The challenge for an organization is to turn its archives of data into a source of information, so that a single integrated/consolidated view of the organization's data is presented to the user. The concept of a **data warehouse** was deemed the solution to meet the requirements of a system capable of supporting decision-making, receiving data from multiple data sources.

Data warehouse

A database system that is designed to support decision-making by presenting an integrated view of corporate data that is copied from disparate data sources.

The data held in a data warehouse is described as being subject-oriented, integrated, time-variant, and non-volatile (Inmon, 1993).

- *Subject-oriented* because the warehouse is organized around the major subjects of the organization (such as customers, products, and sales) rather than the major application areas (such as customer invoicing, stock control, and product sales.) This is reflected in the need to store decision-support data rather than application-oriented data.
- *Integrated* because of the coming together of source data from different organization-wide applications systems. The source data is often inconsistent, using for example different data types and/or formats. The integrated data source must be made consistent to present a unified view of the data to the users.
- *Time-variant* because data in the warehouse is accurate and valid only at some point in time or over some time interval. The time-variance of the data warehouse is also shown in the extended time that the data is held, the implicit or explicit association of time with all data, and the fact that the data represents a series of snapshots.
- *Non-volatile* because the data is not updated in real-time but is refreshed from operational systems on a regular basis. New data is always added as a supplement to the database, rather than a replacement. The database continually absorbs this new data, incrementally integrating it with the previous data.

18.2.1 Comparison of OLTP with data warehousing

An organization will normally have a number of different online transaction processing (OLTP) systems for business processes such as inventory control, customer invoicing, and point-of-sale. These systems generate operational data that is detailed, current, and subject to change. The OLTP systems are optimized for a high number of transactions that are predictable, repetitive, and update intensive. The OLTP data is organized according to the requirements of the transactions associated with the business applications and supports the day-to-day decisions of a large number of concurrent operational users. In contrast, an organization will normally have a single data warehouse which holds data that is historic, detailed, summarized to various levels and rarely subject to change (other than being supplemented with new data.) The data warehouse is designed to support relatively lower numbers of transactions that can be unpredictable in nature and require answers to queries that are *ad hoc*, unstructured, and heuristic. As a result the data warehouse data is structured in such a way (that is subject-oriented) to ensure that such transactions are supported and that the main users of the warehouse, namely the corporate decision-makers, are given access to the data they need in a form that suits their analysis. Compared with OLTP systems, the data warehouse serves a relatively lower number of users, who tend to be tactical and strategic decision-makers.

Although OLTP systems and data warehouses have different characteristics and are built with different purposes in mind, these systems are closely related in that the OLTP systems normally provide the majority of source data for the warehouse. A major problem with this relationship is that the data held by the OLTP systems

Table 18.1 Comparison of OLTP and data warehousing systems

OLTP system	Data warehousing
Holds current data	Holds historic data
Stores detailed data	Stores detailed, lightly, and highly summarized data
Data is dynamic	Data is largely static
Repetitive processing	*Ad hoc*, unstructured, and heuristic processing
High level of transaction throughput	Medium to low level of transaction throughput
Predictable pattern of usage	Unpredictable pattern of usage
Transaction driven	Analysis driven
Application oriented	Subject oriented
Supports day-to-day operational decisions	Supports tactical and strategic decisions
Serves large number of users	Serves lower number of users

can be inconsistent, fragmented, and subject to change, containing duplicate or missing entries. As such, the operational data must be 'cleaned up' before it can be used in the data warehouse.

OLTP systems are not built to quickly answer ***ad hoc* queries** that involve complex analysis of data. They also tend not to store historical data, which is necessary to analyze trends, because the focus is on data that is current. Basically, OLTP creates large amounts of raw data that is not easily analyzed. A summary of the main characteristics of OLTP systems compared with a data warehouse is shown in Table 18.1.

18.2.2 Data warehouse architecture

The typical architecture of a data warehouse is shown in Figure 18.1. In this section we briefly describe the important components that form this architecture.

- The source of *operational data* for the data warehouse is largely supplied from relational DBMS and also where applicable from proprietary file systems, private workstations and external systems such as the Internet.
- An **operational data store (ODS)** is a repository of current and integrated operational data used for analysis. It is often structured and supplied with data in the same way as the data warehouse, but may in fact act simply as a staging area for data to be moved into the warehouse.
- The ETL *manager* performs all the operations associated with the extraction, transformation and loading (ETL) of data into the warehouse.
- The *warehouse manager* performs all the operations associated with the management of the data, such as the transformation and merging of source data, creation of indexes and views on base tables, generation of aggregations, and backing-up and archiving data.

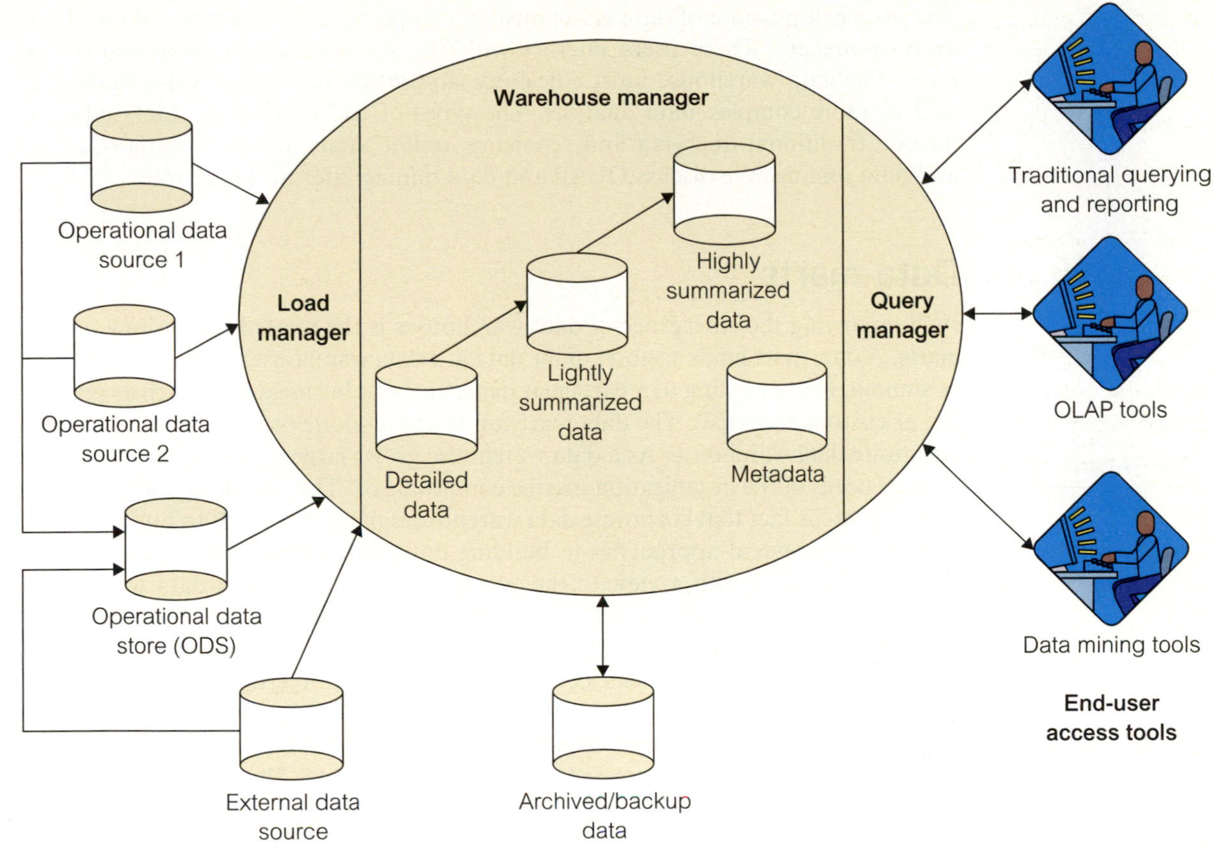

Figure 18.1 The typical architecture of a data warehouse

- The *query manager* performs all the operations associated with the management of user queries.
- *Detailed data* is not stored online but is made available by summarizing the data to the next level of detail. However, on a regular basis, detailed data is added to the warehouse to supplement the summarized data. The warehouse stores all the predefined *lightly and highly summarized data* generated by the warehouse manager. The purpose of summary information is to speed up the performance of queries. Although there are increased operational costs associated with initially summarizing the data, this is offset by removing the requirement to continually perform summary operations (such as sorting or grouping) when answering user queries. The summary data is updated continuously as new data is loaded into the warehouse. Detailed and summarized data is stored offline for the purposes of archiving and backup.
- *Metadata* (data about data) definitions are used by all the processes in the warehouse, including the extraction, transformation and loading processes, the warehouse management process, and the query management process.

The principal purpose of data warehousing is to provide information for corporate decision-makers. These users interact with the warehouse using *end-user access tools*. The data warehouse must efficiently support *ad hoc* and routine analysis as well as more complex data analysis. The types of end-user access tools typically include traditional querying and reporting, online analytical processing (OLAP), and data mining. We discuss OLAP and data mining later in this chapter.

18.2.3 Data marts

Data mart

A subset of a data warehouse, which supports the decision-making requirements of a particular department or business area.

Accompanying the emergence of data warehouses is the related technology of **data marts**. A data mart holds a subset of the data in a data warehouse normally in the form of summary data relating to a particular department or business area, such as marketing or customer services. The data mart can be stand-alone or linked centrally to the corporate data warehouse. As a data warehouse grows larger, the ability to serve the various needs of the organization may be compromised. The popularity of data marts stems from the fact that corporate data warehouses proved difficult to build and use.

There are several approaches to building data marts. One approach is to build several data marts with a view to the eventual integration into a data warehouse. Another approach is to build the infrastructure for a corporate data warehouse while at the same time building one or more data marts to satisfy immediate business needs.

Data mart architectures can be built as two-tier or three-tier database applications. The data warehouse is the optional first tier (if the data warehouse provides the data for the data mart), the data mart is the second tier, and the end-user workstation is the third tier. Data is distributed among the tiers. There are many reasons for creating a data mart:

- To give users access to the data they need to analyze most often.
- To provide data in a form that matches the collective view of the data by a group of users in a department or business area.
- To improve end-user response time due to the reduction in the volume of data to be accessed.
- To provide appropriately structured data as dictated by the requirements of end-user access tools such as OLAP and data mining tools, which may require their own internal database structures.
- Data marts normally use less data than data warehouses so tasks such as data cleansing, loading, transformation and integration are far easier, and hence implementing and setting up a data mart is simpler compared with establishing a corporate data warehouse.
- The cost of implementing data marts is normally less than that required to establish a data warehouse.
- The potential users of a data mart are more clearly defined and can be more easily targeted to obtain support for a data mart project rather than a corporate data warehouse project.

Databases designed to support data warehousing or data mart applications are necessarily different from those that support traditional OLTP applications. In the following section, we discuss how to design databases for decision-support.

18.2.4 Designing databases for decision-support

Dimensionality modeling

A technique that aims to build a data model that has a consistent and intuitive structure to facilitate efficient multi-dimensional analysis of data.

Star schema

A structure that has a fact table containing factual data in the center, surrounded by dimension tables containing reference data (which can be denormalized.)

Designing a database to support decision-making uses a technique called **dimensionality modeling**.

Dimensionality modeling uses the same diagrammatic notation as ER modeling with some important restrictions. Every dimensional model (DM) is composed of one table with a composite primary key, called the **fact table**, and a set of smaller tables called **dimension tables**. Each dimension table has a simple (non-composite) primary key that corresponds exactly to one of the components of the composite key in the fact table. In other words, the primary key of the fact table is made up of two or more foreign keys. This characteristic 'star-like' structure is called a **star schema** or **star join**.

In this section and the next, we use an extended version of the *StayHome Online Rentals* case study (described in Section 5.4) to include DVD sales. An example star schema for the DVD sales of *StayHome* is shown in Figure 18.2. Note that foreign keys (labeled {FK}) are included in a dimensional model.

Another important feature of a DM is that all natural keys are replaced with surrogate keys that use integer values. This means that every join between fact and dimension tables is based on surrogate keys, not natural keys. Each surrogate key should have a generalized structure based on simple integers. The use of surrogate keys allows the data in the decision-support database to have some independence from the data used and produced by the OLTP systems. For example, each DVD has a natural key, namely `catalogNo`, and also a surrogate key, namely `catalogID`.

The star schema exploits the characteristics of factual data such that facts are generated by events that occurred in the past, and are unlikely to change, regardless of how they are analyzed. As the bulk of data in a database for decision-support is represented as facts, the fact tables can be extremely large relative to the dimension tables. As such, it is important to treat fact data as read-only data that will not change over time. The most useful fact tables contain one or more numerical measures, or 'facts', that occur for each record. In Figure 18.2, the facts are `unitCost`, `retailPrice`, `actualSellingPrice` and `postage`. The most useful facts in a fact table are numeric and additive because database for decision-support applications almost never access a single record; rather, they access hundreds, thousands, or even millions of records at a time and the most useful thing to do with so many records is to aggregate them.

Dimension tables, by contrast, generally contain descriptive textual information. Dimension attributes are used as the constraints (search conditions) in queries. For example, the star schema shown in Figure 18.2 can support queries that require access to sales figures for children's DVDs in 2009 using the `genre` attribute in the `DVD` table and the `year` attribute in the `Time` table. In fact, the usefulness of a data warehouse corresponds to the appropriateness of the data held in the dimension tables.

Star schemas can be used to speed up query performance by denormalizing reference data into a single dimension table. For example, in Figure 18.2 note that several dimension tables (namely `Member` and `DistributionCenter`) contain location data (city and state), which is repeated in each. A particular city is located in a particular state, no matter whether it refers to a member's or distribution center's location. Denormalization is appropriate when there are a number of entities related to the dimension table that are often accessed, avoiding the overhead of having to join additional tables to access those attributes. Denormalization is not appropriate where

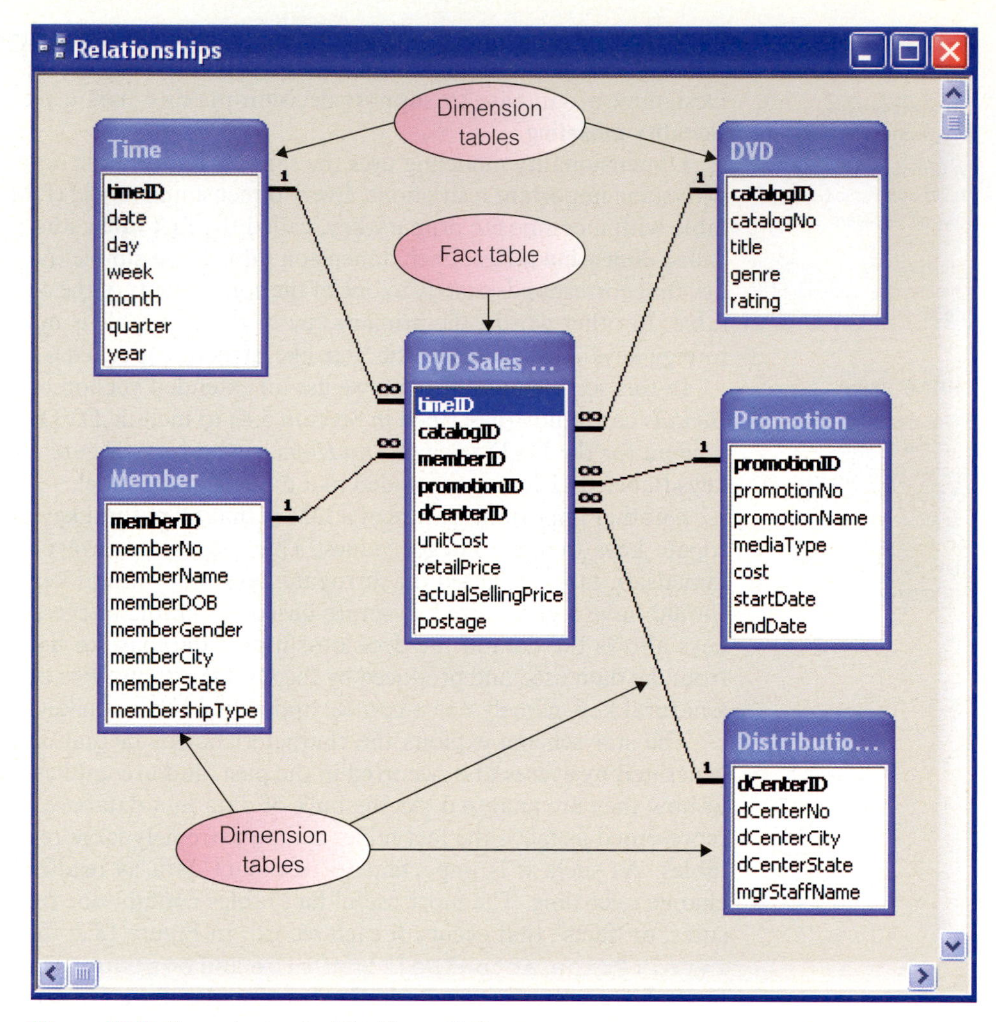

Figure 18.2 Star schema for *StayHome* DVD sales

the additional data is not accessed very often, because the overhead of scanning the expanded dimension table may not be offset by any gain in the query performance.

Databases designed for decision-support are structured to facilitate access to data required by business intelligence (BI) tools such as OLAP and data mining. We discuss OLAP in the following section.

18.3 Online analytical processing (OLAP)

Over the past few decades, we have witnessed the increasing popularity and prevalence of relational DBMSs such that we now find that a significant proportion of corporate data is held in such systems. Relational databases have been used primarily to support traditional **online transaction processing (OLTP) systems**, which create and maintain operational data as necessary to support the day-to-day running of an organization.

The databases that support OLTP systems have been developed to enable the highly efficient execution of a large number of relatively simple transactions involving insertion, updates and deletions, as well as read operations. However, these databases are not designed to primarily support decision-making and achieving appropriate support will always be difficult. When the operational data created by OLTP systems is no longer current, it is normally archived. It is at this point that a copy of the data can be shipped to a database designed for decision-support.

Online analytical processing (OLAP)

Supports advanced analysis of large volumes of multi-dimensional data that is aggregated (summarized) to various levels of detail.

Multi-dimensional data

Data that can be characterized through many different views. For example, multi-dimensional data such as DVD sales can be viewed in terms of properties associated with DVDs such as genre and/or properties associated with buyers such as home address and so on.

Online analytical processing is a term describing a technology that provides views of **multi-dimensional** aggregated (summarized) **data** to provide quick access to corporate data for the purposes of advanced analysis. OLAP enables users to gain a deeper understanding and knowledge about various aspects of their corporate data through fast, consistent, interactive access to a wide variety of possible views of the data. OLAP allows the user to view corporate data in such a way that it is a better model of the true dimensionality of the organization. The types of analysis available from OLAP ranges from basic navigation and browsing (referred to as 'slicing and dicing') to calculations, and to more complex analyses such as time series and complex modeling. There are many examples of OLAP applications in various business areas, as listed in Table 18.2.

Table 18.2 Examples of OLAP applications in various business areas

Business area	Examples of OLAP Applications
Finance	Budgeting, activity-based costing, financial performance analysis, and financial modeling.
Sales	Sales analysis and sales forecasting.
Marketing	Market research analysis, sales forecasting, promotions analysis, customer analysis, and market/customer segmentation.
Manufacturing	Production planning and defect analysis.

Although OLAP applications are found in widely divergent business areas, they all require multi-dimensional views of corporate data, support for complex calculations (such as forecasting), and time intelligence. Time intelligence is a key feature of almost any analytical application as performance is almost always judged over time, for example this month versus last month or this month versus the same month last year.

18.3.1 OLAP tools

OLAP tools are categorized according to the architecture of the underlying database (providing the data for the purposes of online analytical processing). There are three main categories of OLAP tools:

- multi-dimensional OLAP (MOLAP or MD-OLAP);
- relational OLAP (ROLAP);
- hybrid OLAP (HOLAP).

Multi-dimensional OLAP (MOLAP)

MOLAP does not store data in relational tables but as multi-dimensional cubes using array technology. To improve query performance the data is typically pre-calculated, aggregated, and stored according to predicted usage. MOLAP cubes provide fast data retrieval and are optimized for 'slicing and dicing' operations that allow the data to be viewed in various ways. A disadvantage of MOLAP is that only a limited amount of data can be stored because all data processing, in preparation for analysis, is performed before the cube is built. Another disadvantage is the additional investment required as MOLAP technology is often propriety and as such requires specific investments in new technology and training of staff. The typical architecture for MOLAP is shown in Figure 18.3.

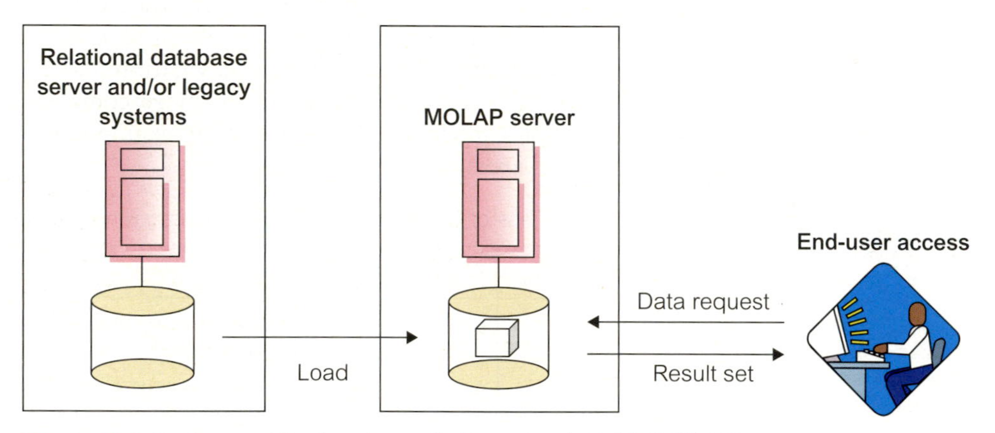

Figure 18.3 Typical architecture for multi-dimensional OLAP (MOLAP)

Relational OLAP (ROLAP)

ROLAP does store data in relational tables but manipulates the data to give the appearance of the 'slicing and dicing' functionality provided by MOLAP. Each 'slicing and dicing' operation is equivalent to adding a WHERE clause to the SQL statement. The main advantage of ROLAP tools is their ability to access large amounts of data; however, query performance can be poor because each ROLAP report is essentially an SQL query (or multiple SQL queries) on the relational database, and for large databases in particular the query time can be long. To improve performance, some ROLAP tools have enhanced SQL engines to support the complexity of multi-dimensional analysis, while others recommend, or require, the use of highly denormalized database designs such as the star schema, which was discussed in Section 18.2.4.

Therefore the main limitation of ROLAP tools is the requirement to use SQL statements that do not perform complex calculations easily. However, ROLAP vendors are extending the functionality of SQL by providing pre-built SQL OLAP functions as well as allowing users to define their own OLAP functions. The typical architecture for relational OLAP (ROLAP) tools is shown in Figure 18.4.

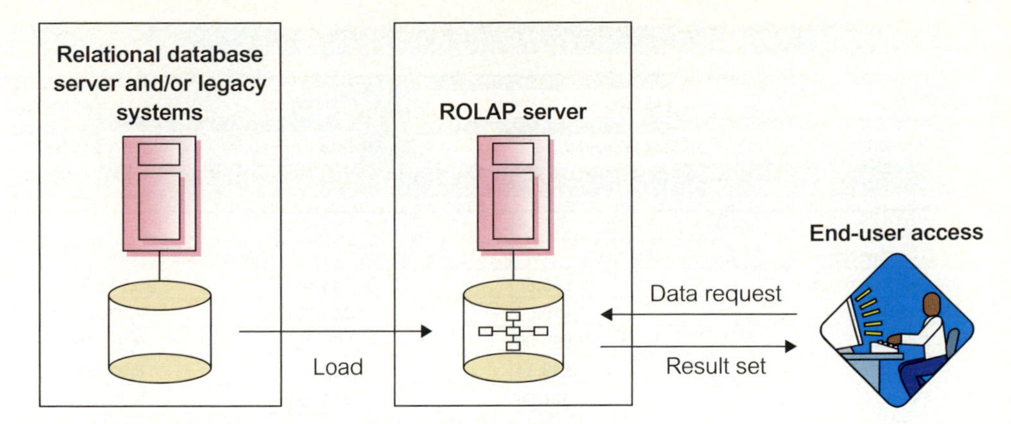

Figure 18.4 Typical architecture for relational OLAP (ROLAP)

Hybrid OLAP (HOLAP)

HOLAP technologies attempt to combine the advantages of MOLAP and ROLAP. HOLAP uses cube technology for fast performance when the query is predictable and the required pre-calculated and/or aggregated data required by the query is stored in the cube. When detailed information is needed, HOLAP provides the ability to 'drill down' from the cube into the underlying relational data. The typical architecture for HOLAP tools is shown in Figure 18.5.

Microsoft SQL Analytical Services is an example of a hybrid OLAP (HOLAP) tool offering both ROLAP and MOLAP services. Figure 18.6 shows the MOLAP Cube Browser of Microsoft SQL Analytical Services displaying *StayHome* DVD sales data. Various aspects of the data can be viewed by making selections using the drop-down boxes. Furthermore, the sales data can be viewed at various levels of detail.

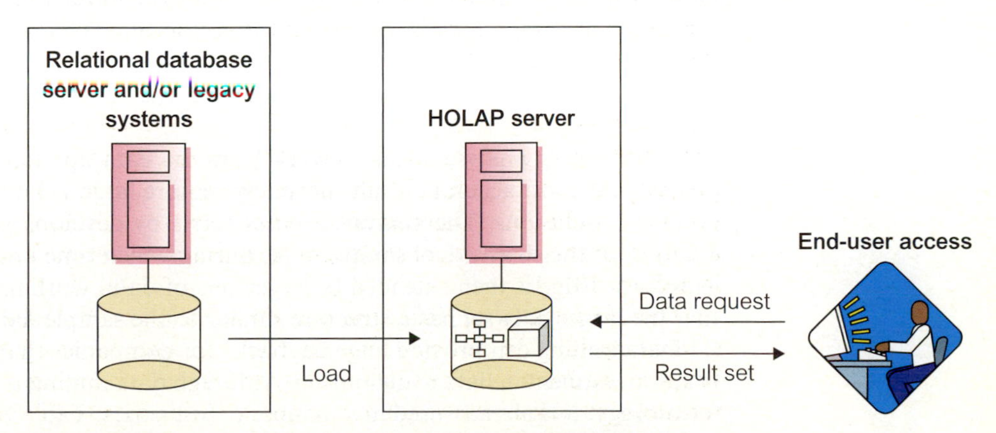

Figure 18.5 Typical architecture for hybrid OLAP (HOLAP)

	MeasuresLevel			
+ D Center No	Unit Cost	Retail Price	Actual Selling Price	Postage
All Distribution Center	10,560.68	32,746.48	28,291.38	2,499.64
+ D001	2,990.00	7,768.02	7,170.02	598.00
+ D002	2,990.00	10,758.02	8,360.04	651.82
+ D003	2,649.14	9,502.22	8,970.00	586.04
+ D004	1,931.54	4,718.22	3,791.32	663.78

Figure 18.6 Cube Browser of Microsoft SQL analytical services displaying *StayHome* DVD sales data

18.4 Data mining

Simply storing data in a data warehouse does not provide the benefits an organization is seeking. To realize the value of a data warehouse, it is necessary to extract the knowledge hidden within the warehouse. However, as the amount and complexity of the data in a data warehouse grows, it becomes increasingly difficult, if not impossible, for business analysts to identify trends and relationships in the data using simple query and reporting tools. **Data mining** is one of the best ways to extract meaningful trends and patterns from huge amounts of data. Data mining discovers knowledge within data warehouses that traditional queries and reports cannot effectively reveal.

> **Data mining**
> The process of extracting valid, previously unknown, comprehensible, and actionable knowledge from large databases and using it to provide decision-support.

Data mining is concerned with the analysis of data and the use of software techniques for finding hidden and unexpected patterns and relationships in sets of data. The focus of data mining is to reveal information that is hidden and unexpected, as there is less value in finding patterns and relationships that are already intuitive. Examining the underlying rules and features in the data identifies the patterns and relationships.

Data mining analysis tends to work from the data up, and the techniques that produce the most accurate results normally require large volumes of data to deliver reliable conclusions. The analysis process starts by developing an optimal representation of the structure of sample data, during which time knowledge is acquired. This knowledge is then extended to larger sets of data, working on the assumption that the larger data set has a structure similar to the sample data.

Data mining can provide huge paybacks for companies that have made a significant investment in data warehousing. Although data mining is still a relatively new technology, it is already used in a number of industries. Table 18.3 lists examples of applications of data mining in retail/marketing, banking, insurance, and medicine.

Table 18.3 Examples of data mining applications in various business areas

Business area	Examples of OLAP applications
Retail/Marketing	Identifying buying patterns of customers Finding associations among customer demographic characteristics Predicting response to mailing campaigns Market basket analysis
Banking	Detecting patterns of fraudulent credit card use Identifying loyal customers Predicting customers likely to change their credit card affiliation Determining credit card spending by customer groups
Insurance	Claims analysis Predicting which customers will buy new policies
Medicine	Characterizing patient behavior to predict surgery visits Identifying successful medical therapies for different illnesses

There are four main operations associated with data mining techniques: *predictive modeling*, *database segmentation*, *link analysis*, and *deviation detection*. Although any of the four major operations can be used for implementing any of the business applications listed in Table 18.3, there are certain recognized associations between the applications and the corresponding operations. For example, direct marketing strategies are normally implemented using the database segmentation operation, while fraud detection could be implemented by any of the four operations. Further, many applications work particularly well when several operations are used. For example, a common approach to customer profiling is to segment the database first and then apply predictive modeling to the resultant data segments.

Techniques are specific implementations of the data mining operations. However, each operation has its own strengths and weaknesses. With this in mind, data mining tools sometimes offer a choice of operations to implement a technique.

18.4.1 Data mining tools

There are a growing number of commercial data mining tools on the marketplace. The important features of data mining tools include data preparation, selection of data mining operations (algorithms), product scalability and performance, and facilities for understanding results.

Data preparation

Data preparation is the most time-consuming aspect of data mining. Whatever a tool can provide to facilitate this process will greatly speed up model development. Some of the functions that a tool may provide to support data preparation include:

data cleansing, such as handling missing data; data describing, such as the distribution of values; data transforming, such as performing calculations on existing columns; and data sampling for the creation of training and validation data sets.

Selection of data mining operations (algorithms)

It is important to understand the characteristics of the operations (algorithms) used by a data mining tool to ensure that they meet the user's requirements. In particular, it is important to establish how the algorithms treat the data types of the response and predictor variables, how fast they train, and how fast they work on new data. A predictor variable is the column in a database that can be used to build a predictor model to predict values in another column.

Another important feature of an algorithm is its sensitivity to noise. (Noise is the difference between a model and its predictions. Sometimes data is referred to as being noisy when it contains errors such as many missing or incorrect values or when there are extraneous columns.) It is important to establish how sensitive a given algorithm is to missing data, and how robust are the patterns it discovers in the face of extraneous and incorrect data.

Product scalability and performance

Scalability and performance are important considerations when seeking a tool that is capable of dealing with increasing amounts of data in terms of numbers of rows and columns, possibly with sophisticated validation controls. The need to provide scalability while maintaining satisfactory performance may require investigations into whether a tool is capable of supporting parallel processing using technologies such as symmetric multi-processing (SMP) or massively parallel processing (MPP).

Facilities for understanding results

A good data mining tool should help the user to understand the results by providing measures such as those describing accuracy and significance in useful formats such as confusion matrices, by allowing the user to perform sensitivity analysis on the result, and by presenting the result in alternative ways using, for example, visualization techniques. A confusion matrix shows the counts of the actual versus predicted class values. It shows not only how well the model predicts, but also presents the details needed to see exactly where things may have gone wrong. Sensitivity analysis determines the sensitivity of a predictive model to small fluctuations in the predictor value. Through this technique end-users can gauge the effects of noise and environmental change on the accuracy of the model. Visualization graphically displays data to facilitate better understanding of its meaning. Graphical capabilities range from simple scatter plots to complex multi-dimensional representations.

18.4.2 Examples of data mining operations

In this section we provide examples of two data mining operations, namely database segmentation and link analysis.

Database segmentation

The aim of database segmentation is to partition a database into an unknown number of *segments*, or *clusters*, of similar records; that is, records that share a number of properties and so are considered to be homogeneous. (Segments have high internal homogeneity and high external heterogeneity.) This approach uses *unsupervised learning* to discover homogeneous subpopulations in a database to improve the accuracy of the profiles.

The Data Mining Module Browser of Microsoft SQL Analytical Services is shown in Figure 18.7. This figure shows that when the data segmentation operation

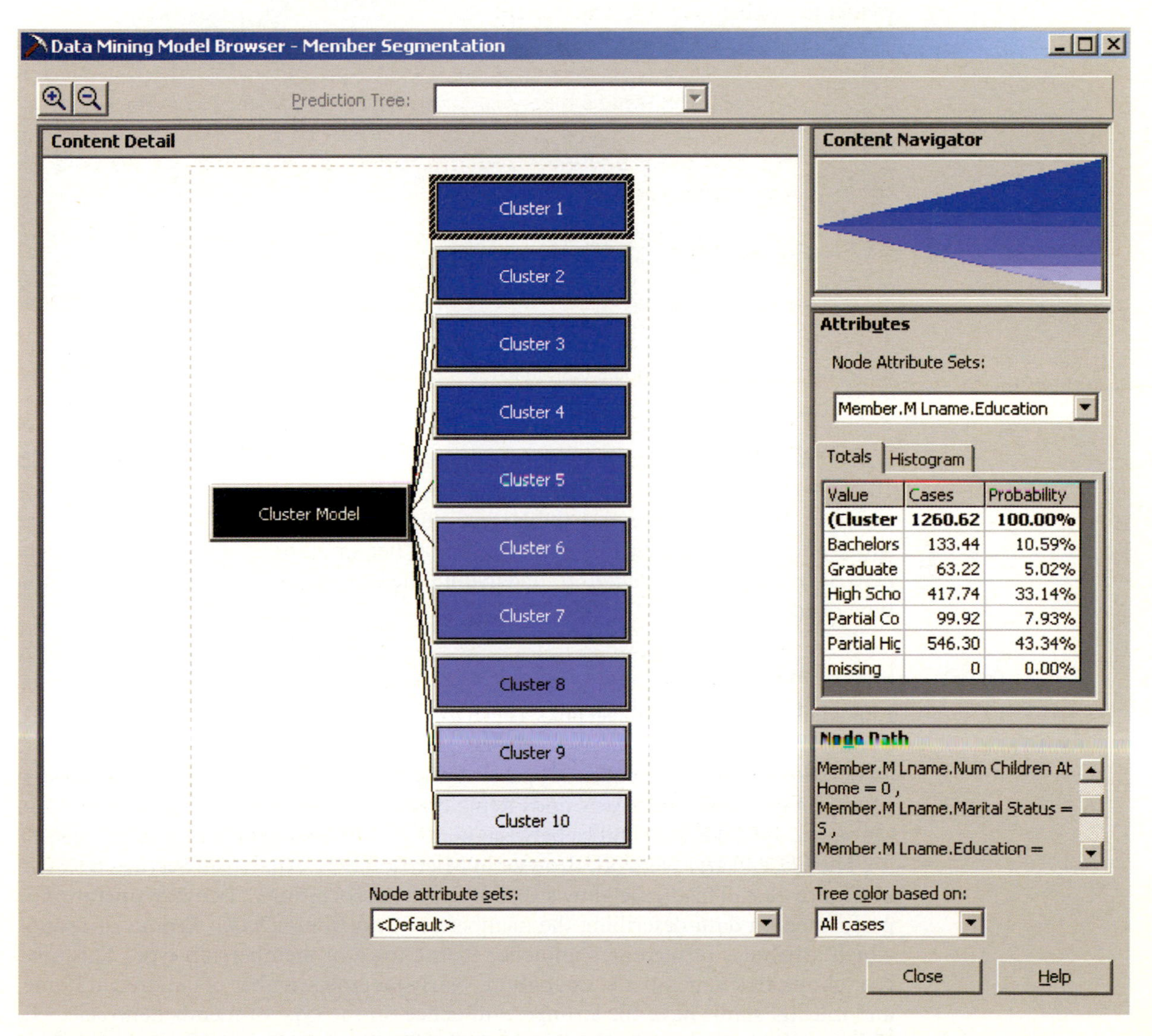

Figure 18.7 Data Mining Model Browser of Microsoft SQL Analytical Services displaying clusters of members of *StayHome Online Rentals*

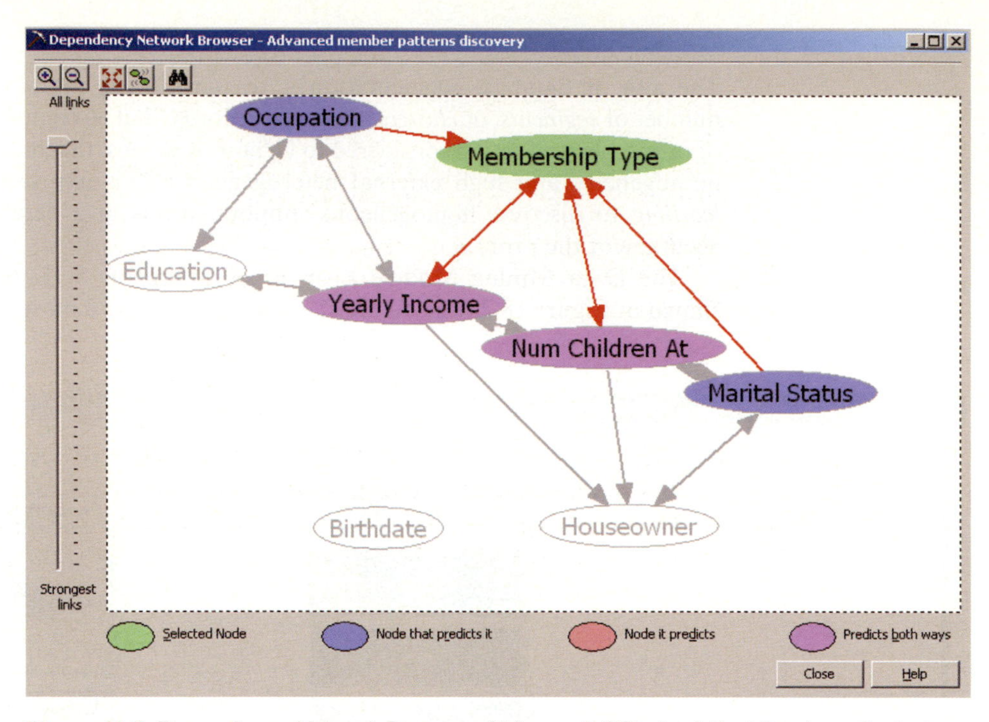

Figure 18.8 Dependency Network Browser of Microsoft SQL Analytical Services displaying associations between attributes that describe members of *StayHome Online Rentals*

is performed on data describing the members of *StayHome Online Rentals*, it reveals 10 clusters. Each cluster represents members who have properties in common. For example, Cluster 1 represents the largest cluster and represents members who are single and have no children at home, among other similarities. This knowledge may help *StayHome Online Rentals* to understand the characteristics of the most common type of member.

Link analysis

Link analysis aims to establish links, called *associations*, between the individual records, or sets of records, in a database. There are three specializations of link analysis: associations discovery, sequential pattern discovery, and similar time sequence discovery. **Associations discovery** finds items that imply the presence of other items in the same event. These affinities between items are represented by association rules.

The Dependency Network Browser of Microsoft SQL Analytical Services is shown in Figure 18.8. This figure shows that when the associations discovery operation is performed on data describing the members of *StayHome Online Rentals*, it reveals which attributes of members influence their choice of membership type. This analysis shows that a member's occupation, yearly income, number of children at home, and marital status have the strongest influence on the type of membership selected. This knowledge may help *StayHome Online Rentals* target potential new members with the type of membership that is most likely to attract them to join the company.

18.4.3 Data warehousing and data mining

One of the major challenges for organizations seeking to exploit data mining is identifying suitable data to mine. Data mining requires a single, separate, clean, integrated, and self-consistent source of data. A data warehouse is well-equipped for providing data for mining for the following reasons:

- Data quality and consistency is a prerequisite for mining to ensure the accuracy of the predictive models. Data warehouses are populated with clean, consistent data.
- It is advantageous to mine data from multiple sources to discover as many interrelationships as possible. Data warehouses contain data from a number of sources.
- Selecting the relevant subsets of records and fields for data mining requires the query capabilities of the data warehouse.
- The results of a data mining study are useful if there is some way to further investigate the uncovered patterns. Data warehouses provide the capability to go back to the data source.

Chapter summary

- **Business intelligence** concerns the processes for collecting and analyzing data, the technology used in these processes, and the information obtained from these processes with the purpose of facilitating corporate decision making.
- A **data warehouse** is a database system that is designed to support decision-making by presenting an integrated view of corporate data that is copied from disparate operational data sources. The data held in a data warehouse is described as being subject-oriented, integrated, time-variant, and non-volatile.
- A **data mart** is a subset of a data warehouse that supports the requirements of a particular department or business area.
- **Dimensionality modeling** is technique that aims to build a data model that has a consistent and intuitive structure to facilitate efficient multi-dimensional analysis of data.
- A **star schema** is a structure that has a fact table containing factual data in the center, surrounded by dimension tables containing reference data (which can be denormalized).
- **Online analytical processing (OLAP)** supports advanced analysis of large volumes of multi-dimensional data that is aggregated (summarized) to various levels of detail.
- **Multi-dimensional data** can be characterized through many different views. For example, multi-dimensional data such as DVD sales can be viewed in terms of properties associated with DVDs such as genre and/or properties associated with buyers such as location and so on).
- **Data mining** is the process of extracting valid, previously unknown, comprehensible, and actionable information from large databases and using it to provide decision-support.

Review questions

18.1 Describe what business intelligence represents.

18.2 Discuss the key technologies that can form part of business intelligence implementation.

18.3 Give a definition of a data warehouse, and discuss the benefits of implementing a data warehouse.

18.4 Describe the characteristics of the data held in a data warehouse.

18.5 Discuss what the relationship is between OLTP systems and a data warehouse.

18.6 Compare and contrast the main characteristics of OLTP systems with a data warehouse.

18.7 Describe the important components of a typical data warehouse.

18.8 Discuss how data marts differ from data warehouses, and identify the main reasons for implementing a data mart.

18.9 Discuss how designing a database for decision-support differs from designing a database for an operational system.

18.10 Describe how a dimensional model differs from an ER model.

18.11 Discuss what OLAP offers the business analyst.

18.12 Describe OLAP applications and identify the characteristics of such applications.

18.13 Discuss the important features of data mining tools.

18.14 Discuss how data mining can realize the value of a data warehouse.

Exercises

18.15 Discuss the types of business intelligence that would bring competitive advantage to your organization, college, or university.

18.16 Identify the OLTP systems used by your organization, college, or university. Investigate whether the OLTP systems provide decision-support.

18.17 Investigate whether your organization, college, or university has a data warehouse and/or data mart(s). If found, describe how the data warehouse and/or data marts provides decision-support.

18.18 Create a dimensional model for a database capable of analyzing data that describes members joining *StayHome Online Rentals* (given in Section 5.4). For the purposes of this exercise, it will be necessary to extend the case study to include additional attributes that would support such analysis including the date a member joins the company, and more details on the members such as date of birth and gender.

18.19 Investigate whether your organization, college, or university uses online analytical processing (OLAP) technologies. If found, describe the type of OLAP tool used and discuss how these tools support decision-making by providing examples.

18.20 Investigate whether your organization, college, or university uses data mining technologies. If found, describe the type of data mining tools used and discuss how these tools support decision-making by providing examples.

APPENDIX

A The Buyer user view for *StayHome Online Rentals*

Learning objectives

In this appendix you will learn:

- The requirements for the Buyer user view of *StayHome Online Rentals*.

The requirements for the Manager, Member, and Assistant user views of the *StayHome Online Rentals* case study are documented in Section 5.4. In this appendix, we document the Buyer user view.

A.1 Data requirements

The details held on a distribution center of *StayHome* are the center address and the telephone number. Each distribution center is given a distribution center number, which is unique throughout the company.

Each distribution center has staff, which includes a Manager. The details held on a member of staff are his or her name, position, and salary. Each member of staff is given a staff number, which is unique throughout the company.

Each distribution center is allocated a stock of DVDs. The details held on a DVD are the catalog number, DVD number, title, genre, and purchase price. The catalog number uniquely identifies each DVD. However, in most cases there are several copies of each DVD at a distribution center, and the individual copies are identified using the DVD number.

Each distribution center receives DVDs from DVD suppliers. The details held on DVD suppliers are the supplier number, name, address, telephone number, and status. Orders for DVDs are placed with these suppliers and the details held on a DVD order are the order number, supplier number, supplier address, DVD catalog number, DVD title, DVD purchase price, quantity, date order placed, date order received, and the address of the center receiving the order.

A customer of *StayHome Online Rentals* must first register as a member of a local distribution center of *StayHome*. The details held on a member are name, address, and the date that the member registered at a center. Each member is given a member number, which is unique throughout all centers of the company and is used even when a member chooses to register at more than one center.

The details held on each DVD rented are the rental number, full name and member number, the DVD number, title, and the dates the DVD is rented out and returned. The rental number is unique throughout the company.

A.2 Transaction requirements

Data entry

(a) Enter the details for a newly released DVD (such as details of a DVD called *Spiderman 3*).

(b) Enter the details of a DVD supplier (such as a supplier called *WorldView DVDs*).

(c) Enter the details of a DVD order (such as ordering 10 copies of *Spiderman 3* for distribution center D002).

Data update/deletion

(d) Update/delete the details of a given DVD.

(e) Update/delete the details of a given DVD supplier.

(f) Update/delete the details of a given DVD order.

Data Queries

(g) List the name, position, and salary of staff at all distribution centers, ordered by center number.

(h) List the name and telephone number of the Manager at a given distribution center.

(i) List the catalog number and title of all DVDs at a given distribution center, ordered by title.

(j) List the number of copies of a given DVD at a given distribution center.

(k) List the number of members at each distribution center, ordered by distribution center number.

(l) List the number of members who joined this year at each distribution center, ordered by distribution center number.

(m) List the number of DVD rentals at each distribution center between certain dates, ordered by distribution center number.

(n) List the number of DVDs in each genre at a given distribution center, ordered by genre.

(o) List the name, address, and telephone number of all DVD suppliers, ordered by supplier number.

(p) List the name and telephone number of a DVD supplier.

(q) List the details of all DVD orders placed with a given supplier, sorted by the date ordered.

(r) List the details of all DVD orders placed on a certain date.

(s) List the total daily rentals for DVDs at each distribution center between certain dates, ordered by distribution center number.

APPENDIX

B Second case study – *PerfectPets*

Learning objectives

In this appendix you will learn:

- The requirements for *PerfectPets*, a private health practice for domestic pets.

A practice called *PerfectPets* provides private healthcare for domestic pets throughout America. This service is provided through various clinics located in the main cities of America. The Director of *PerfectPets* is concerned that there is a lack of communication within the practice, and particularly in the sharing of information and resources across the various clinics. To resolve this problem the Director has requested the creation of a centralized database system to assist in the more effective and efficient running of the practice. The Director has provided the following description of the current system.

B.1 Data requirements

Veterinary clinics

PerfectPets has many veterinary clinics located in the main cities of America. The details of each clinic include the clinic number, clinic address (consisting of the street, city, state, and zipcode), and the telephone and fax numbers. Each clinic has a Manager and a number of staff (for example vets, nurses, secretaries, cleaners). The clinic number is unique throughout the practice.

Staff

The details stored on each member of staff include the staff number, name (first and last), address (street, city, state, and zipcode), telephone number, date of birth, sex, social security number (SSN), position, and current annual salary. The staff number is unique throughout the practice.

Pet owners

When a pet owner first contacts a clinic of *PerfectPets*, the details of the pet owner are recorded, which include an owner number, owner name (first name and last name), address (street, city, state, and zipcode), and home telephone number. The owner number is unique to a particular clinic.

Pets

The details of the pet requiring treatment are noted, which include a pet number, pet name, type of pet, description, date of birth (if unknown, an approximate date is recorded), date registered at clinic, current status (alive/deceased), and the details of the pet owner. The pet number is unique to a particular clinic.

Examinations

When a sick pet is brought to a clinic, it is examined by the vet on duty. The details of each examination are recorded and include an examination number, the date and time of the examination, the name of the vet, the pet number, pet name, type of pet, and a full description of the examination results. The examination number is unique to a particular clinic. As a result of the examination, the vet may propose treatment(s) for the pet.

Treatments

PerfectPets provides various treatments for all types of pets. These treatments are provided at a standard rate across all clinics. The details of each treatment include a treatment number, a full description of the treatment, and the cost to the pet owner. For example, treatments include:

T123	Penicillin antibiotic course	\$50.00
T155	Feline hysterectomy	\$200.00
T112	Vaccination course against feline flu	\$70.00
T56	Small dog – stay in pen per day (includes feeding)	\$20.00

A standard rate of \$20.00 is charged for each examination, which is recorded as a type of treatment. The treatment number uniquely identifies each type of treatment and is used by all *PerfectPets* clinics.

Pet treatments

Based on the results of the examination of a sick pet, the vet may propose one or more types of treatment. For each type of treatment, the information recorded includes the examination number and date, the pet number, name and type, treatment number, description, quantity of each type of treatment, and the dates the treatment is to begin and end. Any additional comments on the provision of each type of treatment are also recorded.

Pens

In some cases, it is necessary for a sick pet to be admitted to the clinic. Each clinic has 20–30 animal pens, each capable of holding between one and four pets. Each pen has a unique pen number, capacity, and status (an indication of availability). The sick pet is allocated to a pen and the details of the pet, any treatment(s) required by the pet, and any additional comments about the care of the pet are recorded. The details of the pet's stay in the pen are also noted, which include a pen number, and the dates the pet was put into and taken out of the pen. Depending on the pet's illness, there may be more than one pet in a pen at the same time. The pen number is unique to a particular clinic.

Invoices

The pet owner is responsible for the cost of the treatment given to a pet. The owner is invoiced for the treatment arising from each examination, and the details recorded on the invoice include the invoice number, invoice date, owner number, owner name and full address, pet number, pet name, and the details of the treatment given. The invoice provides the cost for each type of treatment and the total cost of all treatments given to the pet.

Additional data is also recorded on the payment of the invoice, including the date the invoice was paid and the method of payment (for example cash, Visa). The invoice number is unique throughout the practice.

Surgical, non-surgical, and pharmaceutical supplies

Each clinic maintains a stock of surgical supplies (for example syringes, sterile dressings, bandages) and non-surgical supplies (for example plastic bags, aprons, litter trays, pet name tags, pet food). The details of surgical and non-surgical supplies include the item number and name, item description, quantity in stock (this is ascertained on the last day of each month), reorder level, reorder quantity, and cost. The item number uniquely identifies each type of surgical or non-surgical supply. The item number is unique for each surgical or non-surgical item and is used throughout the practice.

Each clinic also maintains a stock of pharmaceutical supplies (for example, antibiotics, painkillers). The details of pharmaceutical supplies include a drug number and name, description, dosage, method of administration, quantity in stock (this is ascertained on the last day of each month), reorder level, reorder quantity, and cost. The drug number uniquely identifies each type of pharmaceutical supply. The drug number is unique for each pharmaceutical supply and is used throughout the practice.

Appointments

If the pet has to be seen by the vet at a later date, the owner and pet are given an appointment. The details of an appointment are recorded and include an appointment number, owner number, owner name (first name and last name), home telephone number, the pet number, pet name, type of pet, and the appointment date and time. The appointment number is unique to a particular clinic.

B.2 Transaction requirements

Listed below are the transactions that should be supported by the *PerfectPets* database.

1. The database should be capable of supporting the following maintenance transactions:
   - (a) Create and maintain records recording the details of *PerfectPets* clinics and the members of staff at each clinic.
   - (b) Create and maintain records recording the details of pet owners.
   - (c) Create and maintain the details of pets.
   - (d) Create and maintain records recording the details of the types of treatments available for pets.
   - (e) Create and maintain records recording the details of examinations and treatments given to pets.
   - (f) Create and maintain records recording the details of invoices to pet owners for treatment to their pets.
   - (g) Create and maintain records recording the details of surgical, non-surgical, and pharmaceutical supplies at each clinic.
   - (h) Create and maintain records recording the details of pens available at each clinic and the allocation of pets to pens.
   - (i) Create and maintain pet owner/pet appointments at each clinic.
2. The database should be capable of supporting the following example query transactions:
   - (a) Present a report listing the Manager's name, clinic address, and telephone number for each clinic, ordered by clinic number.
   - (b) Present a report listing the names and owner numbers of pet owners with the details of their pets.
   - (c) List the historic details of examinations for a given pet.
   - (d) List the details of the treatments provided to a pet based on the results of a given examination.
   - (e) List the details of an unpaid invoice for a given pet owner.
   - (f) Present a report on invoices that have not been paid by a given date, ordered by invoice number.
   - (g) List the details of pens available on a given date for clinics in New York, ordered by clinic number.
   - (h) Present a report that provides the total monthly salary for staff at each clinic, ordered by clinic number.
   - (i) List the maximum, minimum and average cost of treatments.
   - (j) List the total number of pets in each pet type, ordered by pet type.
   - (k) Present a report of the names and staff numbers for all vets and nurses over 50 years old, ordered by staff name.

(l) List the appointments for a given date and for a particular clinic.
(m) List the total number of pens in each clinic, ordered by clinic number.
(n) Present a report of the details of invoices for pet owners between 2004 and 2006, ordered by invoice number.
(o) List the pet number, name, and description of pets owned by a particular owner.
(p) Present a report listing the pharmaceutical supplies that need to be reordered at each clinic, ordered by clinic number.
(q) List the total cost of the non-surgical and surgical supplies currently in stock at each clinic, ordered by clinic number.

APPENDIX

C Alternative data modeling notations

Learning objectives

In this appendix you will learn:

- About alternative data modeling notations.

In Chapters 6 and 7, we discussed how to create an ER model using an increasingly popular notation called UML. In this appendix we show two additional notations that are often used to create ER models. The first ER notation is called the Chen notation and the second is called the Crow's Feet notation. We demonstrate each by presenting a table that shows the notation used for each of the main concepts of the ER model, and then we present the notation using as an example the ER model shown in Figure 9.12.

C.1 ER modeling using the Chen notation

Table C.1 shows the Chen notation for the main concepts of the ER model and Figure C.1 shows the ER model in Figure 9.12 redrawn using the Chen notation.

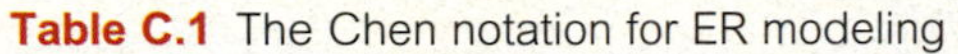

Table C.1 The Chen notation for ER modeling

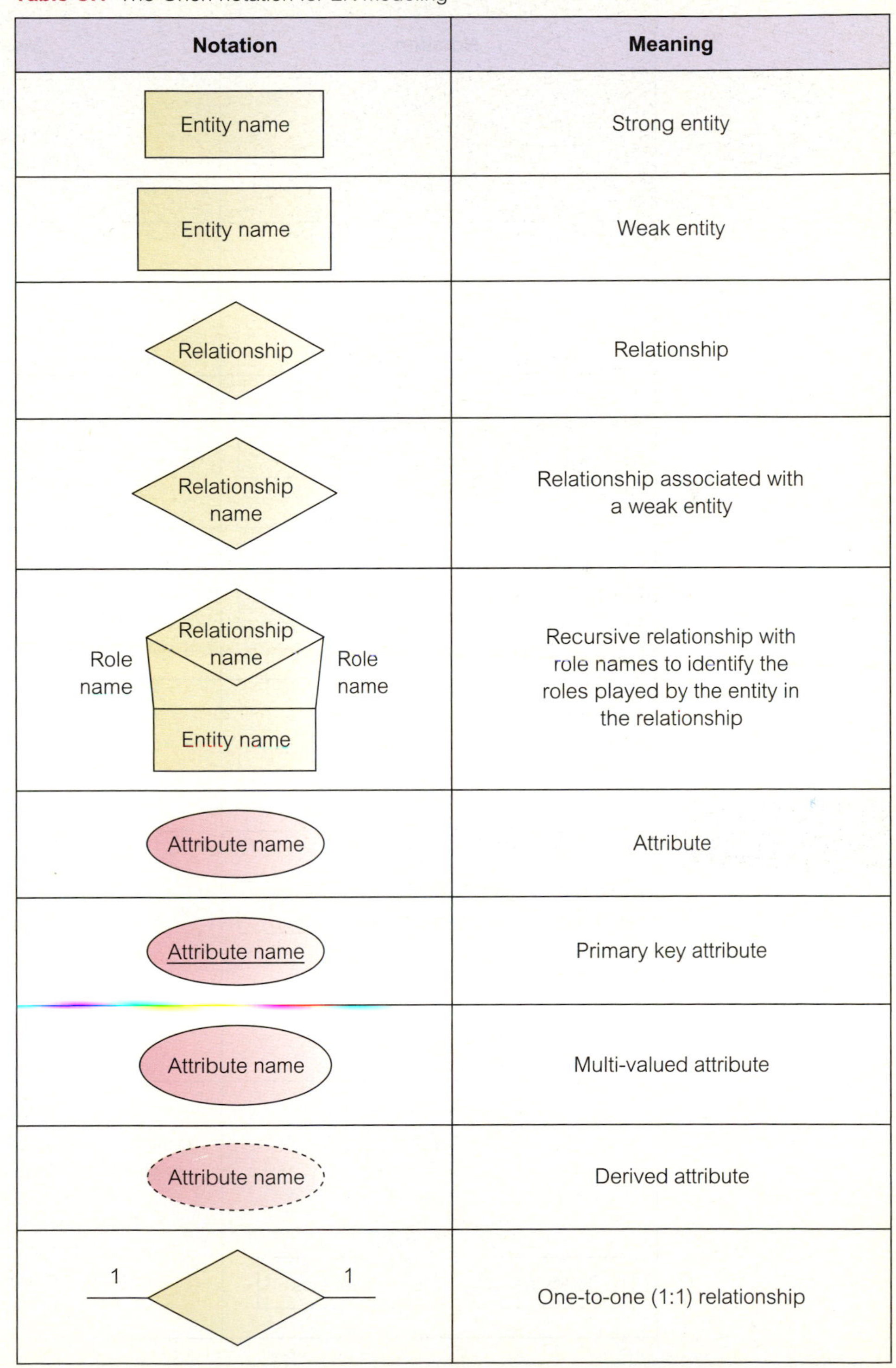

Notation	Meaning
Entity name	Strong entity
Entity name	Weak entity
Relationship	Relationship
Relationship name	Relationship associated with a weak entity
Role name / Relationship name / Role name / Entity name	Recursive relationship with role names to identify the roles played by the entity in the relationship
Attribute name	Attribute
Attribute name	Primary key attribute
Attribute name	Multi-valued attribute
Attribute name	Derived attribute
1 ◇ 1	One-to-one (1:1) relationship

Table C.1 *(continued)*

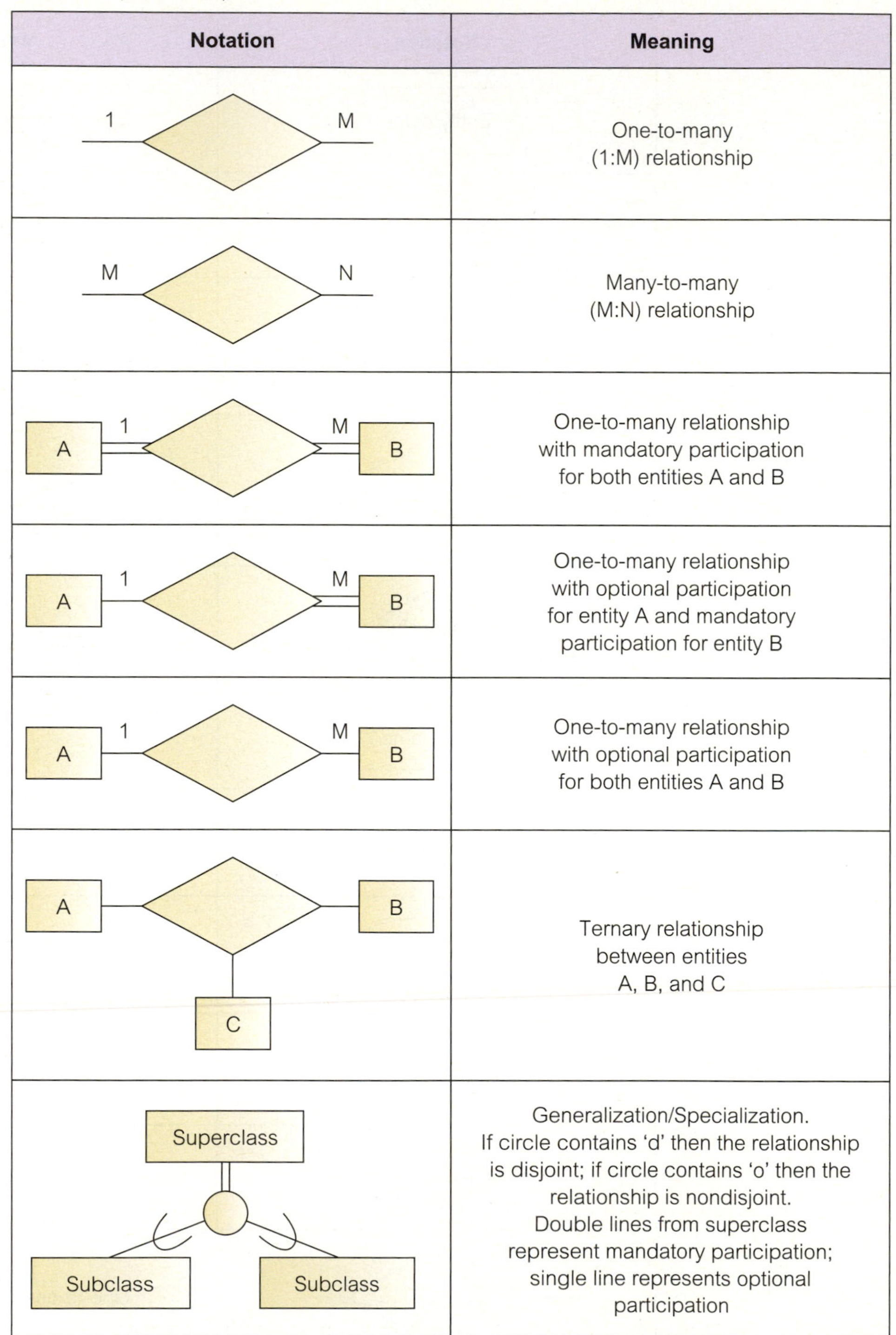

Notation	Meaning
1 M	One-to-many (1:M) relationship
M N	Many-to-many (M:N) relationship
A 1 M B	One-to-many relationship with mandatory participation for both entities A and B
A 1 M B	One-to-many relationship with optional participation for entity A and mandatory participation for entity B
A 1 M B	One-to-many relationship with optional participation for both entities A and B
A B C	Ternary relationship between entities A, B, and C
Superclass Subclass Subclass	Generalization/Specialization. If circle contains 'd' then the relationship is disjoint; if circle contains 'o' then the relationship is nondisjoint. Double lines from superclass represent mandatory participation; single line represents optional participation

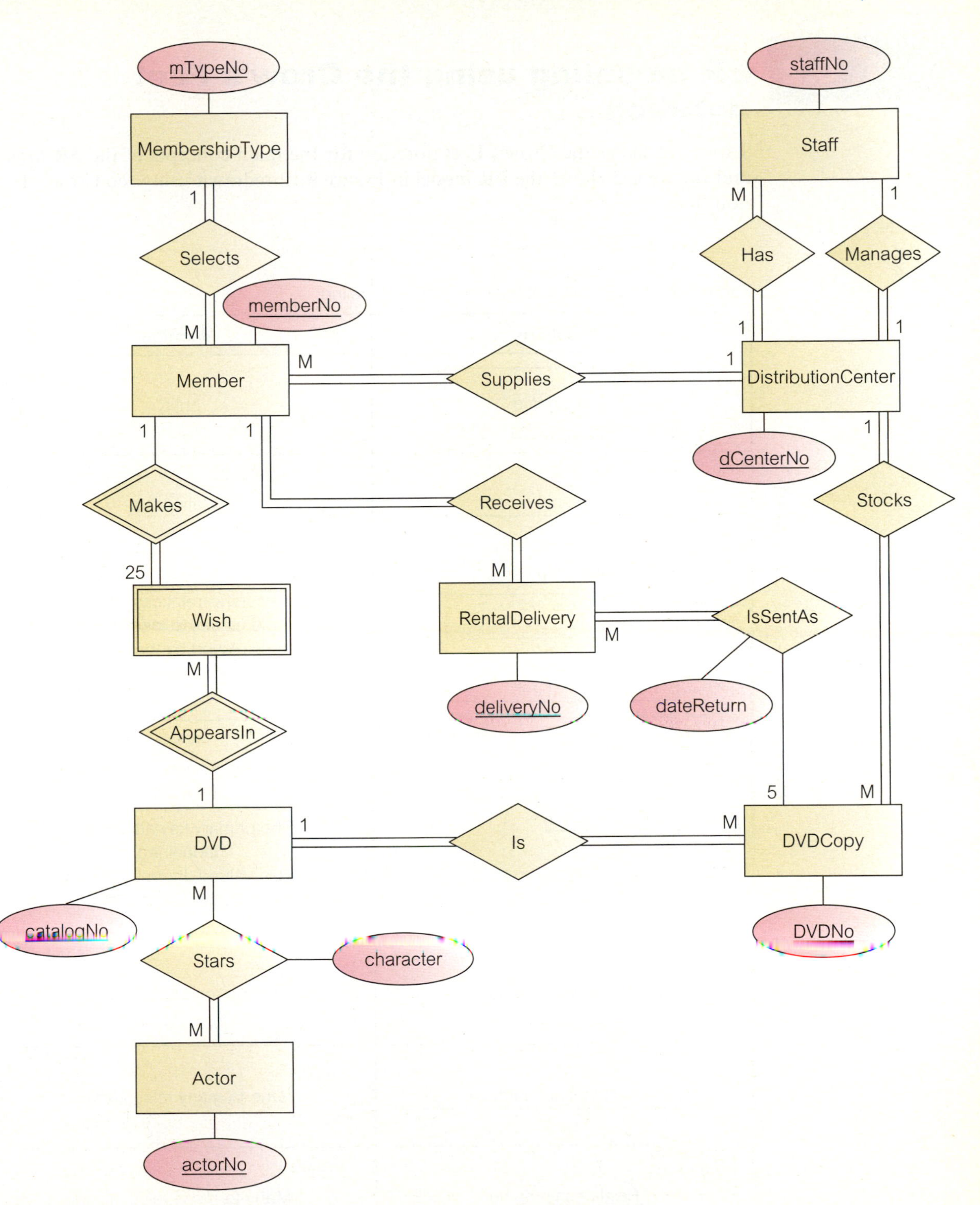

Figure C.1 The ER model shown in Figure 9.12 redrawn using the Chen notation

C.2 ER modeling using the Crow's Feet notation

Table C.2 shows the Crow's Feet notation for the main concepts of the ER model and Figure C.2 shows the ER model in Figure 9.12 redrawn using the Crow's Feet notation.

Table C.2 The Crow's Feet notation for ER modeling

Notation	Meaning
[Box] Entity name	Entity
Relationship name (line)	Relationship
Relationship name; Role name; Role name; [Box] Entity name	Recursive relationship with role names to identify the roles played by the entity in the relationship
[Box] Entity name / Attribute name (underlined) / Attribute 1 / Attribute 2 / Attribute n	Attributes are listed in the lower section of the entity symbol The primary key attribute is underlined Multi-valued attribute placed in curly brackets { }
Relationship name (plain line)	One-to-one relationship
Relationship name (line with crow's foot at one end)	One-to-many relationship
Relationship name (line with crow's feet at both ends)	Many-to-many relationship

Table C.2 *(continued)*

Notation	Meaning
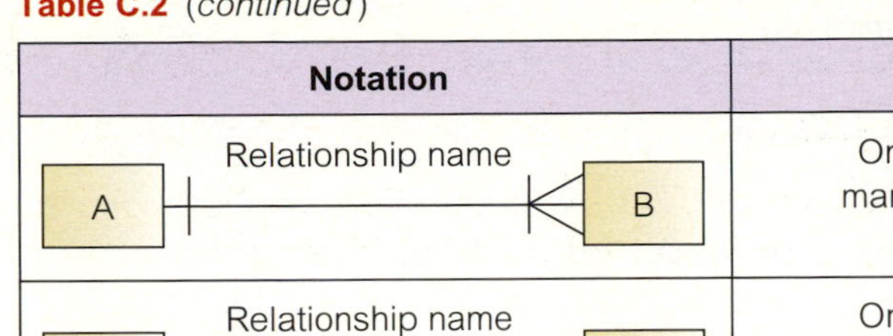 Relationship name A B	One-to-many relationship with mandatory participation for both entities A and B
Relationship name A B	One-to-many relationship with optional participation for entity A and mandatory participation for entity B
Relationship name A B	One-to-many relationship with optional participation for both entities A and B
A B C	Ternary relationship between entities A, B, and C
Superclass Subclass Subclass	'Box-in-box' convention is widely used to represent generalization/specialization, and supported by several CASE tools, including Oracle CASE Designer

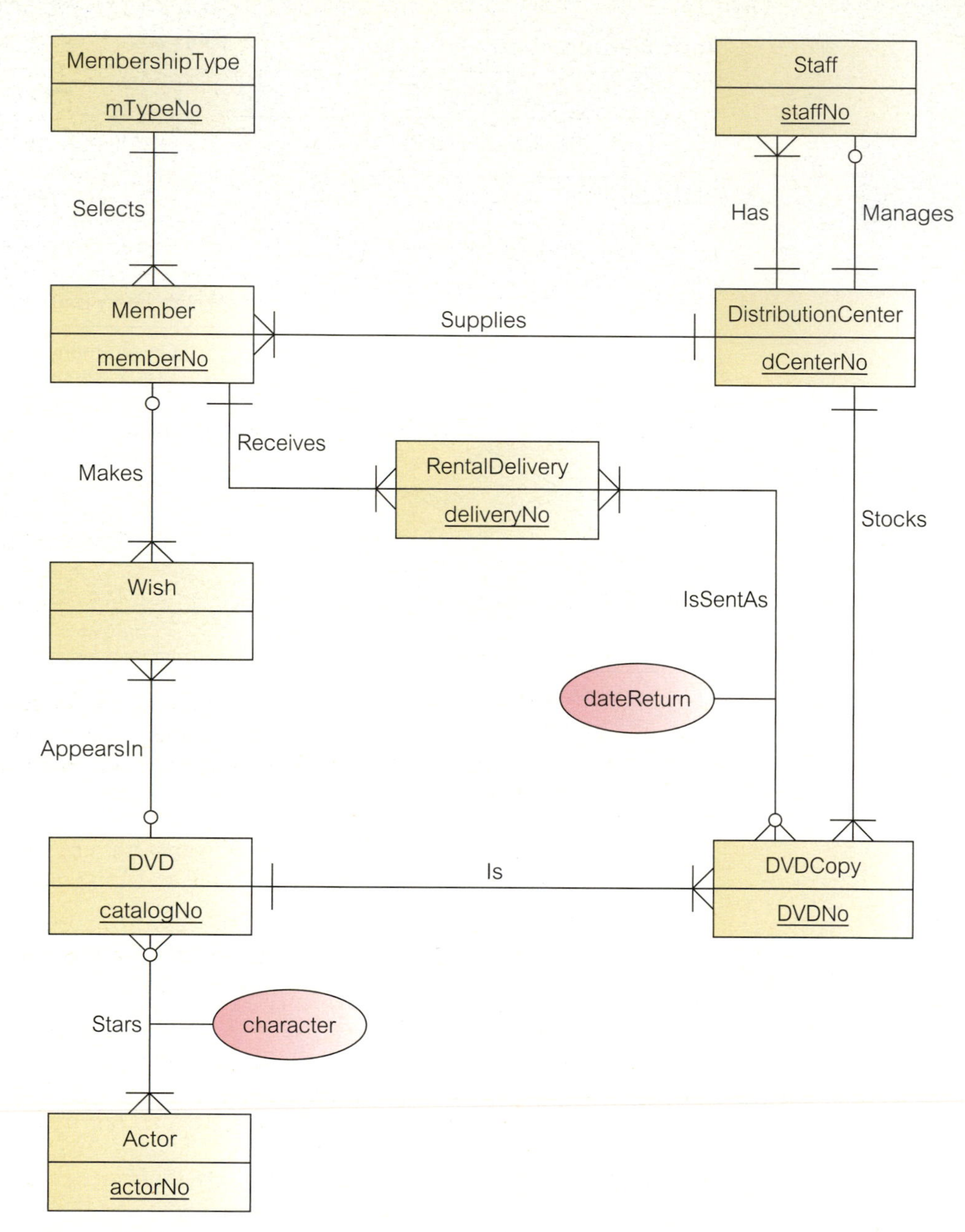

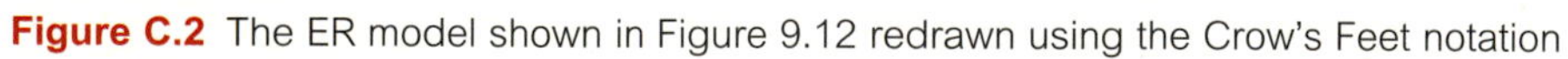
Figure C.2 The ER model shown in Figure 9.12 redrawn using the Crow's Feet notation

APPENDIX

D Summary of the database design methodology

Learning objectives

In this appendix you will learn:

- That database design is composed of three main phases: conceptual, logical, and physical database design.
- The steps involved in the main phases of the database design methodology.

In this book, we present a database design methodology for relational databases. This methodology is made up of three main phases: conceptual database design, logical database design, and physical database design, which are described in detail in Chapters 9, 10, and 11. To summarize:

- **Conceptual database design**: The process of constructing a model of the data used in an organization independent of all physical considerations.
- **Logical database design**: The process of constructing a model of the data used in an organization based on a specific data model, but independent of a particular DBMS and other physical considerations.
- **Physical database design**: The process of producing a description of the implementation of the database on secondary storage; it describes the base tables, file organizations, and indexes used to achieve efficient access to the data, and any associated integrity constraints and security restrictions.

In this appendix, we summarize the steps involved in these phases for those readers who are already familiar with database design.

Step 1 Create and check an ER model

During analysis, you will have identified a number of user views. Depending on the amount of overlap, for manageability you may decide to merge some of these views. The purpose of this step is to build a logical data model of the organization (or part of the organization) for each of these (possibly merged) views.

Step 1.1 Identify entities

Identify and document the main entities in the organization.

Step 1.2 Identify relationships

Identify the important relationships that exist between the entities that you have identified. Determine the multiplicity constraints of the relationships. Document relationships. Use entity–relationship (ER) modeling when necessary.

Step 1.3 Identify and associate attributes with entities or relationships

Associate attributes with the appropriate entities or relationships. Identify simple/composite attributes, single-valued/multi-valued attributes, and derived attributes. Document attributes.

Step 1.4 Determine attribute domains

Determine domains for the attributes in the ER model. Document attribute domains.

Step 1.5 Determine candidate, primary key, and alternate key attributes

Identify the candidate key(s) for each entity and, if there is more than one candidate key, choose one to be the primary key, the others becoming alternate keys. Document candidate, primary, and alternate keys for each strong entity.

Step 1.6 Specialize/generalize entities (optional step)

Identify superclass and subclass entities, where appropriate.

Step 1.7 Check the model for redundancy

Examine the ER model to ensure there is no redundancy. Specifically, re-examine 1:1 relationships and remove redundant relationships.

Step 1.8 Check that the model supports user transactions

Ensure that the ER model supports the transactions required by the users.

Step 1.9 Review conceptual database design with users

Review the conceptual database design with users to ensure that the design is a 'true' representation of the data requirements of the organization.

Step 2 Map the ER model to tables

Map the ER model to a set of tables and check the structure of the tables.

Step 2.1 Create tables

In this step, you produce a set of tables to represent the entities, relationships, attributes, and constraints described in the view of the organization. The structures of the tables are derived from the information that describes the ER model. This information includes the data dictionary and any other documentation that describes the model. Also, document any new primary or candidate keys that have been formed as a result of the process of creating tables for the ER model.

The basic rules for creating tables are as follows:

(a) For each entity, create a table that includes all the entity's simple attributes.

(b) Each relationship is represented by the primary key/foreign key mechanism. In deciding where to post the foreign key, you must identify the 'parent' and 'child' entities in the relationship. The parent entity then posts a copy of its primary key into the child table, to act as the foreign key. Table D.1 gives a summary of how you identify the parent and child entities in a relationship.

A summary of the rules for creating tables from an ER model are shown in Table D.1.

You may use Step 1.6 to introduce specialization/generalization into your ER model. For each superclass/subclass relationship, you identify the superclass as the parent entity and the subclass as the child entity. There are various options on how you may best represent such a relationship as one or more tables. The selection of the most appropriate option is dependent on the participation and disjoint constraints on the superclass/subclass relationship. A summary of how to map tables from your EER model is shown in Table D.2.

Step 2.2 Check table structures using normalization

The purpose of this step is to examine the groupings of columns in each table created in Step 2.1. You check the composition of each table using the rules of normalization. Each table should be in at least third normal form (3NF).

Table D.1 Summary of how to represent entities and relationships as tables

Entity/Relationship	Mapping
Strong or weak entity	Create table that includes all simple attributes.
1:* binary relationship	Post copy of primary key of entity on 'one' side to table representing entity on 'many' side. Any attributes of relationship are also posted to 'many' side.
1:* recursive relationship	As entity on 'one' and 'many' side is the same, the table representing the entity receives a second copy of the primary key, which is renamed, and also any attributes of the relationship.
1:1 binary relationship:	
Mandatory participation on *both* sides	Combine entities into one table.
Mandatory participation on *one* side	Post copy of primary key of entity with optional participation to table representing entity with mandatory participation. Any attributes of relationship are also posted to table representing entity with mandatory participation.
Optional participation on *both* sides	Without further information, post copy of primary key of one entity to the other. However, if information is available, treat entity that is closer to having mandatory participation as being the child entity.
: binary relationship Complex relationship	Create a table to represent the relationship and include any attributes associated with the relationship. Post a copy of the primary key from each parent entity into the new table to act as foreign keys.
Multi-valued attribute	Create a table to represent the multi-valued attribute and post a copy of the primary key of the parent entity into the new table to act as a foreign key.

Table D.2 Options available for the representation of a superclass/subclass relationship based on the participation and disjoint constraints

Participation constraint	Disjoint constraint	Tables required
Mandatory	Nondisjoint {And}	Single table
Optional	Nondisjoint {And}	Two tables: one table for superclass and one table for all subclasses
Mandatory	Disjoint {Or}	Many tables: one table for each combined superclass/subclass
Optional	Disjoint {Or}	Many tables: one table for superclass and one for each subclass

Step 2.3 Check that the tables support user transactions

In this step, you ensure that the tables support the required transactions, as defined in the users' requirements specifications.

Step 2.4 Check integrity constraints

Check that all integrity constraints are represented in the logical database design. These include specifying the required data, attribute domain constraints, entity integrity, multiplicity, referential integrity, and any other constraints. Document all integrity constraints.

Step 2.5 Review logical database design with users

Ensure that the logical database design is a true representation of the data requirements of the organization (or part of the organization) being modeled.

Step 3 Translate the logical database design for the target DBMS

Produce a basic working set of tables from the logical database design.

Step 3.1 Design the base tables

Decide how to represent the base tables you have identified in the logical database design in the target DBMS. Document the design of the tables.

Step 3.2 Design representation of derived data

Consider how derived data will be represented. The choice is to calculate derived data each time it is needed, or to introduce redundancy and store the derived data as a column in a table. Document the design of derived data.

Step 3.3 Design remaining integrity constraints

Design the remaining integrity constraints for the target DBMS. Document the design of the remaining integrity constraints.

Step 4 Choose file organizations and indexes

Determine the file organizations that will be used to store the base tables; that is, the way in which tables and records will be held on secondary storage. Consider the addition of indexes to improve performance.

Step 4.1 Analyze transactions

Analyze the functionality of the transactions that will run on the database to identify those that may impact on performance.

Step 4.2 Choose file organizations

Determine an efficient file organization for each base table.

Step 4.3 Choose indexes

Determine whether adding indexes will improve the performance of the system.

Step 5 Design user views

Design the user views that you identified during the requirements collection and analysis stage.

Step 6 Design security mechanisms

Design the security measures for the database implementation as specified by the users during the requirements collection and analysis stage. Document the design of the security measures and user views.

Step 7 Consider the introduction of controlled redundancy

Determine if introducing redundancy in a controlled manner by relaxing the normalization rules will improve the performance of the system. Consider duplicating columns or joining tables together to achieve improved performance. In particular, consider combining one-to-one (1:1) relationships, duplicating columns in one-to-many (1:*) relationships to reduce joins, duplicating columns in many-to-many (*:*)

relationships to reduce joins, introducing repeating groups, creating extract tables, and partitioning tables.

Step 8 Monitor and tune the operational system

Monitor the operational system and improve the performance of the system to correct inappropriate design decisions or to reflect changing requirements.

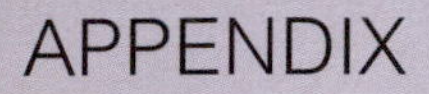

APPENDIX E

Advanced SQL

Preview

In Chapter 3 we provided an extensive tutorial on SQL, covering the SELECT, INSERT, UPDATE, and DELETE statements. In this appendix, we examine some of the more advanced features of SQL, namely:

- creating tables and views using the CREATE TABLE and CREATE VIEW statements;
- the SQL programming language;
- cursors;
- stored procedures and functions;
- database triggers.

Learning objectives

In this appendix you will learn:

- How to create a new table in the database using the CREATE TABLE statement.
- How to create a new view in the database using the CREATE VIEW statement.
- How to use the SQL programming language.
- The purpose and use of cursors.
- How to create and use stored procedures and functions.
- How to create and use database triggers.

E.1 Creating tables

In SQL, base tables are created using the CREATE TABLE statement, which has the following (simplified) format:

```
CREATE TABLE TableName
    {(columnName dataType [NOT NULL] [UNIQUE]
    [DEFAULT defaultOption] [,...]}
    [PRIMARY KEY (listOfColumns),]
    {[UNIQUE (listOfColumns),] [,...]}
    {[FOREIGN KEY (listOfForeignKeyColumns)
    REFERENCES ParentTableName [(listOfCandidateKeyColumns)],
        [[ON UPDATE referentialAction] [ON DELETE
        referentialAction]] [,...]})
```

The full version of the CREATE TABLE statement is rather complex and in this section we provide a simplified version of the statement to illustrate some of its main components. Figure E.1 shows the CREATE TABLE statements to create the `DistributionCenter`, `Staff`, and `DVD` tables. Each statement first defines each column of the table and then has one or two other clauses: one to define the primary key and one to define any foreign keys. We now discuss each of these clauses.

```
CREATE TABLE DistributionCenter (dCenterNo CHAR(4) NOT NULL,
                    dStreet       VARCHAR(60)     NOT NULL,
                    dCity         VARCHAR(20)     NOT NULL,
                    dState        CHAR(2)         NOT NULL,
                    dZipCode      CHAR(5)         NOT NULL UNIQUE,
                    mgrStaffNo    CHAR(5)         NOT NULL,
                    CONSTRAINT pk1 PRIMARY KEY (dCenterNo),
                    CONSTRAINT fk1 FOREIGN KEY (mgrStaffNo) REFERENCES Staff
                      ON UPDATE CASCADE ON DELETE SET NULL);

CREATE TABLE Staff (staffNo     CHAR(5)         NOT NULL,
                    name          VARCHAR(40)     NOT NULL,
                    position      VARCHAR(10)     NOT NULL,
                    salary        DECIMAL(8, 2)   NOT NULL,
                    eMail         CHAR(5)         NOT NULL UNIQUE,
                    dCenterNo     CHAR(4)         NOT NULL,
                    CONSTRAINT pk2 PRIMARY KEY (staffNo),
                    CONSTRAINT fk2 FOREIGN KEY (dCenterNo) REFERENCES DistributionCenter
                      ON UPDATE CASCADE ON DELETE NO ACTION);

CREATE TABLE dvd (catalogNo     CHAR(6)         NOT NULL,
                    title         VARCHAR(40)     NOT NULL,
                    genre         VARCHAR(10)     NOT NULL,
                    rating        VARCHAR(10)     NOT NULL,
                    CONSTRAINT pk3 PRIMARY KEY (catalogNo));
```

Figure E.1 CREATE TABLE statements for the `DistributionCenter`, `Staff`, and `DVD` tables

Table E.1 ISO SQL data types

Data type	Declarations			
boolean	BOOLEAN			
character	CHAR,	VARCHAR		
exact numeric	NUMERIC,	DECIMAL,	INTEGER,	SMALLINT
approximate numeric	FLOAT,	REAL,	DOUBLE PRECISION	
datetime	DATE,	TIME,	TIMESTAMP	
interval	INTERVAL			
large objects	CHARACTER LARGE OBJECT,		BINARY LARGE OBJECT	

Defining a column

The basic format for defining a column of a table is as follows:

columnName dataType [**NOT NULL**] [**UNIQUE**] [**DEFAULT** defaultOption]

where `columnName` is the name of the column and *dataType* defines the type of the column. The ISO standard supports the data types shown in Table E.1. The most widely used data types are:

- CHARACTER(L): (usually abbreviated to CHAR) defines a string of fixed length L. If you enter a string with fewer characters than this length, the string is padded with blanks on the right to make up the required size.
- CHARACTER VARYING(L): (usually abbreviated to VARCHAR) defines a string of varying length L. If you enter a string with fewer characters than this length, only those characters entered are stored, thereby using less space.
- DECIMAL(*precision*, [*scale*]) or NUMERIC(*precision*, [*scale*]): defines a number with an exact representation – *precision* specifies the number of significant digits and *scale* specifies the number of digits after the decimal point. The difference between the types is that for NUMERIC the implementation must provide the precision requested, but for DECIMAL the implementation may provide a precision that is greater than or equal to that requested. For example, DECIMAL(4) can represent numbers between −9999 and +9999; DECIMAL(4, 2) can represent numbers between −99.99 and +99.99.
- INTEGER and SMALLINT: defines numbers where the representation of fractions is not required. Typically SMALLINT would be used to store numbers with a maximum absolute value of 32 767.
- DATE: stores date values in Julian date format as a combination of YEAR (4 digits), MONTH (2 digits), and DAY (2 digits).

In addition, you can define:

- whether the column cannot accept nulls by specifying the keyword NOT NULL;

- whether each value within the column will be unique by specifying the keyword UNIQUE – that is, the column is a candidate key;
- a default value for the column by specifying the keyword DEFAULT followed by a literal value appropriate for the data type – this is, a value that would be used if the value of the column is not specified.

The full version of the ISO standard also allows other conditions to be specified but we refer the interested reader to Connolly and Begg (2005) for further details.

Primary key clause and entity integrity

Entity integrity discussed in Section 2.4.2.

The primary key of a table must contain a unique, non-null value for each row. The ISO standard supports entity integrity (see Section 2.4.2) with the PRIMARY KEY clause in the CREATE TABLE statement. For example, we can define the primary keys for the `DVD` table and the `Wish` table (which has a composite primary key) as follows:

```
CONSTRAINT pk PRIMARY KEY (catalogNo)
CONSTRAINT pk1 PRIMARY KEY (memberNo, catalogNo)
```

Note, the keyword CONSTRAINT followed by a name for the constraint is optional but allows the constraint to be dropped using the SQL statement ALTER TABLE.

Foreign key clause and referential integrity

The ISO standard supports the definition of foreign keys with the FOREIGN KEY clause in the CREATE TABLE statement. The ISO standard supports referential integrity (see Section 2.4.3) by rejecting any INSERT or UPDATE operation that attempts to create a foreign key value in a child table without a matching candidate key value in the parent table. The action SQL takes for any UPDATE or DELETE operation that attempts to update or delete a candidate key value in the parent table that has some matching rows in the child table is dependent on the referential action specified using the ON UPDATE and ON DELETE subclauses of the FOREIGN KEY clause:

- CASCADE: Update/delete the row from the parent table and automatically delete the matching rows in the child table. Since these deleted rows may themselves have a candidate key that is used as a foreign key in another table, the foreign key rules for these tables are triggered, and so on in a cascading manner.
- SET NULL: Update/delete the row from the parent table and set the foreign key value(s) in the child table to NULL. This is valid only if the foreign key columns do not have the NOT NULL qualifier specified.
- SET DEFAULT: Update/delete the row from the parent table and set each component of the foreign key in the child table to the specified default value. This is valid only if the foreign key columns have a DEFAULT value specified.

- NO ACTION: Reject the update/delete operation from the parent table. This is the default setting if the ON UPDATE/ON DELETE rule is omitted.

E.2 Creating views

In SQL, views are created using the CREATE VIEW statement, which has the following (simplified) format:

```
CREATE VIEW ViewName [(newColumnName [,...])]
AS subselect
```

A view is defined by specifying an SQL SELECT statement (known as the *defining query*.) A name may optionally be assigned to each column in the view. If a list of column names is specified, it must have the same number of items as the number of columns produced by the *subselect*. If the list of column names is omitted, each column in the view takes the name of the corresponding column in the *subselect* statement. The list of column names must be specified if there is any ambiguity in the name for a column. This may occur if the *subselect* includes calculated columns and the AS subclause has not been used to name such columns, or it produces two columns with identical names as the result of a join.

For example, we could create a view of staff at distribution center D001 that excludes salary information as follows:

```
CREATE VIEW StaffAtDistributionCenter1
AS SELECT staffNo, name, position, eMail
  FROM Staff
  WHERE dCenterNo = 'D001';
```

E.3 The SQL programming language

The initial versions of the SQL language had no programming constructs; that is, it was not *computationally complete* as we discussed in Section 17.2. However, with the latest release of the standard, SQL is now a full programming language and we discuss some of the constructs in this section. The extensions are known as *SQL/PSM (Persistent Stored Modules)*, however, to make the discussions more concrete we base the presentation on the Oracle programming language, PL/SQL.

PL/SQL is a block-structured language: blocks can be entirely separate or nested within one another. The basic units that comprise a PL/SQL program are procedures, functions, and anonymous (*unnamed*) blocks. As illustrated in Figure E.2, a PL/SQL block has up to three parts:

- an optional declaration part in which variables, constants, cursors, and exceptions are defined and possibly initialized;
- a mandatory executable part, in which the variables are manipulated;
- an optional exception part, to handle any exceptions raised during execution.

```
[DECLARE                              Optional
   --- declarations]
BEGIN                                 Mandatory
   --- executable statements
[EXCEPTION                            Optional
   --- exception handlers
END;                                  Mandatory
```

Figure E.2 General structure of a PL/SQL block

Declarations

Variables and constant variables must be declared before they can be referenced in other statements, including other declarative statements. Examples of declarations are:

```
vStaffNo VARCHAR2(5);
vSalary NUMBER(8, 2) NOT NULL := 30000;
MAX_RENTALS CONSTANT NUMBER := 5;
```

Note that it is possible to declare a variable as NOT NULL, although in this case an initial value must be assigned to the variable. It is also possible to declare a variable to be of the same type as a column in a specified table or another variable using the %TYPE attribute. For example, to declare that the `vStaffNo` variable is the same type as the `staffNo` column of the `Staff` table we could write:

```
vStaffNo Staff.staffNo%TYPE;
vStaffNo1 vStaffNo%TYPE;
```

Similarly, we can declare a variable to be of the same type as an entire row of a table or view using the %ROWTYPE attribute. In this case, the fields in the record take their names and data types from the columns in the table or view. For example, to declare a `vStaffRec` variable to be a row from the `Staff` table we could write:

```
vStaffRec Staff%ROWTYPE;
```

Assignments

In the executable part of a PL/SQL block, variables can be assigned in two ways: using the normal assignment statement (:=), or as the result of an SQL SELECT or FETCH statement. For example:

```
vStaffNo := 'S1500';
vSalary := 48000;
SELECT COUNT (*) INTO x FROM DistributionCenter WHERE mgrStaffNo =
vStaffNo;
```

In the latter case, the variable x is set to the result of the SELECT statement (in this case, equal to the number of centers managed by staff member S1500.)

Control statements

PL/SQL supports the usual conditional, iterative, and sequential flow-of-control mechanisms:

- IF-THEN-ELSE-END IF;
- LOOP-EXIT WHEN-END LOOP; FOR-END LOOP; and WHILE-END LOOP;
- GOTO.

We present examples of these structures shortly.

Exceptions

An *exception* is an identifier in PL/SQL raised during the execution of a block, which terminates its main body of actions. A block always terminates when an exception is raised, although the exception handler can perform some final actions. An exception can be raised automatically – for example, the exception NO_DATA_FOUND is raised whenever no rows are retrieved from the database in a SELECT statement. It is also possible for an exception to be raised explicitly using the RAISE statement. To handle raised exceptions, separate routines called *exception handlers* are specified.

As mentioned earlier, a user-defined exception is defined in the declarative part of a PL/SQL block. In the executable part, a check is made for the exception condition and, if found, the exception is raised. The exception handler itself is defined at the end of the PL/SQL block. An example of exception handling is given in Figure E.3. This example also illustrates the use of the Oracle-supplied package DBMS_OUTPUT, which allows output from PL/SQL blocks and subprograms. The procedure `put_line` outputs information to a buffer in the SGA, which can be displayed by calling the procedure `get_line` or by setting SERVEROUTPUT ON in SQL*Plus.

E.4 Using cursors

A SELECT statement can be used if the query returns *one and only one* row. To handle a query that can return an arbitrary number of rows (that is zero, one, or more rows) SQL uses **cursors** to allow the rows of a query result to be accessed one at a time. In effect, a cursor acts as a pointer to a particular row of the query result. The cursor can be advanced by one to access the next row. A cursor must be *declared* and *opened* before it can be used, and it must be *closed* to deactivate it after it is no longer required. Once the cursor has been opened, the rows of the query result can be retrieved one at a time using a FETCH statement, as opposed to a SELECT statement.

```
DECLARE
  x    NUMBER;
  vMemberNo RentalDelivery.memberNo%TYPE := 'M250178';
-- define an exception for the constraint that prevents a member
-- renting more than 5 DVDs
  e_too_many_properties EXCEPTION;
  PRAGMA EXCEPTION_INIT(e_too_many_DVDs, -20000);
BEGIN
      SELECT COUNT(*) INTO x
      FROM RentalDelivery r , DVDRental d
      WHERE r.memberNo = vMemberNo AND
            r.deliveryNo = d.deliveryNo AND dateReturn IS NULL);
      IF x = 5
  -- raise an exception for the constraint
         RAISE e_too_many_DVDs;
      END IF;
      INSERT INTO RentalDelivery VALUES ('R75346571', vMemberNo, DATE'2-Feb-2008');
      INSERT INTO DVDRental VALUES ('R75346571', '24545663', NULL);
EXCEPTION
  -- handle the exception for the constraint
     WHEN e_too_many_DVDs THEN
       dbms_output.put_line('Member' || memberNo || 'already renting 5 DVDs);
END;
```

Figure E.3 Example of exception handling in PL/SQL

Figure E.4 illustrates the use of a cursor to determine the DVDs rented by member M250178. In this case, the query can return an arbitrary number of rows and so a cursor must be used. The important points to note in this example are:

- In the DECLARE section, the cursor `DVDCursor` is defined.
- In the statements section, the cursor is first opened. Among others, this has the effect of parsing the SELECT statement specified in the CURSOR declaration, identifying the rows that satisfy the search criteria (called the *active set*), and positioning the pointer just before the first row in the active set. Note, if the query returns no rows, SQL does not raise an exception when the cursor is open.
- The code then loops over each row in the active set and retrieves the current row values into output variables using the FETCH INTO statement. Each FETCH statement also advances the pointer to the next row of the active set.
- The code checks if the cursor did not contain a row (`DVDCursor`%NOTFOUND) and exits the loop if no row was found (EXIT WHEN). Otherwise, it displays the property details using the PL/SQL `DBMS_OUTPUT` package and goes round the loop again.
- The cursor is closed on completion of the fetches.
- Finally, the exception block displays any error conditions encountered.

```
DECLARE
   vDVDNo       DVDCopy.DVDNo%TYPE;
   vCatalogNo   DVDCopy.catalogNo %TYPE;
   vTitle       DVD.title%TYPE;
   CURSOR       DVDCursor IS
                SELECT dc.DVDNo, dc.catalogNo, title
                FROM RentalDelivery r, DVDRental dr, DVDCopy dc, DVD d
                WHERE memberNo = 'M250178' AND r.deliveryNo = dr.deliveryNo AND
                   dr.DVDNo = dc.DVDNo AND dc.catalogNo = d.catalogNo
                ORDER BY title;
BEGIN
-- Open the cursor to start of selection, then loop to fetch each row of the result table
   OPEN DVDCursor;
   LOOP
-- Fetch next row of the result table
      FETCH DVDCursor
      INTO vDVDNo, vCatalogNo, vTitle;
   EXIT WHEN DVDCursor%NOTFOUND;
-- Display data
      dbms_output.put_line('DVD number:  ' || vDVDNo);
      dbms_output.put_line('Catalog Number:  ' || vCatalogNo);
      dbms_output.put_line('Title:  ' || vTitle);
   END LOOP;
   IF DVDCursor%ISOPEN THEN CLOSE DVDCursor END IF;

– Error condition
EXCEPTION
   WHEN OTHERS THEN
      dbms_output.put_line('Error detected');
         IF DVDCursor%ISOPEN THEN CLOSE DVDCursor; END IF;
END;
```

Figure E.4 Using cursors in PL/SQL to process a multi-row query

As well as %NOTFOUND, which evaluates to true if the most recent fetch does not return a row, there are some other cursor attributes that are useful:

- %FOUND – evaluates to true if the most recent fetch returns a row (complement of %NOTFOUND);
- %ISOPEN – evaluates to true if the cursor is open;
- %ROWCOUNT – evaluates to the total number of rows returned so far.

Passing parameters to cursors

PL/SQL allows cursors to be parameterized, so that the same cursor definition can be reused with different criteria. For example, we could change the cursor defined in the above example to:

```
CURSOR DVDCursor(vMemberNo VARCHAR2) IS
    SELECT dc.DVDNo, dc.catalogNo, title
    FROM RentalDelivery r, DVDRental dr, DVDCopy dc, DVD d
    WHERE memberNo = 'M250178' AND r.deliveryNo = dr.deliveryNo AND
        dr.DVDNo = dc.DVDNo AND dc.catalogNo = d.catalogNo
    ORDER BY title;
```

and we could open the cursor using the following example statements:

```
vMemberNo1 Member.memberNo%TYPE := 'M250178';
OPEN DVDCursor('M166884');
OPEN DVDCursor('M115656');
OPEN DVDCursor(vMemberNo1);
```

Updating rows through a cursor

It is possible to update and delete a row after it has been fetched through a cursor. In this case, to ensure that rows are not changed between declaring the cursor, opening it, and fetching the rows in the active set, the FOR UPDATE clause is added to the cursor declaration. This has the effect of locking the rows of the active set to prevent any update conflict when the cursor is opened (locking and update conflicts were discussed in Section 14.2).

E.5 Subprograms, stored procedures, and functions

Subprograms are called PL/SQL blocks and can take parameters and be invoked. PL/SQL has two types of subprograms called **(stored) procedures** and **functions**. Procedures and functions can take a set of parameters given to them by the calling program and perform a set of actions. Both can modify and return data passed to them as a parameter. The difference between a procedure and a function is that a function will always return a single value to the caller, whereas a procedure does not. Usually, procedures are used unless only one return value is needed.

Procedures and functions are very similar to those found in most high-level programming languages, and have the same advantages: they provide modularity and extensibility, they promote reusability and maintainability, and they aid abstraction. A parameter has a specified name and data type but can also be designated as:

- IN – parameter is used as an input value only;
- OUT – parameter is used as an output value only;
- IN OUT – parameter is used as both an input and an output value.

For example, we could change the anonymous PL/SQL block given in Figure E.4 into a procedure by adding the following lines at the start:

```
CREATE OR REPLACE PROCEDURE DVDsForMember(IN vMemberNo
  VARCHAR2)
AS . . .
```

The procedure could then be executed in SQL*Plus as:

```
SQL> SET SERVEROUTPUT ON;
SQL> EXECUTE DVDsForMember ('M250178');
```

Packages

A **package** is a collection of procedures, functions, variables, and SQL statements that are grouped together and stored as a single program unit. A package has two parts: a specification and a body. A package's *specification* declares all public constructs of the package, and the *body* defines all constructs (public and private) of the package, and so implements the specification. In this way, packages provide a form of encapsulation. Oracle performs the following steps when a procedure or package is created:

- it compiles the procedure or package;
- it stores the compiled code in memory;
- it stores the procedure or package in the database.

For the previous example, we could create a package specification as follows:

```
CREATE OR REPLACE PACKAGE DVDPackage AS
  procedure DVDsForMember (vMemberNo VARCHAR2);
END DVDPackage;
```

and we could create the package body (that is, the implementation of the package) as:

```
CREATE OR REPLACE PACKAGE BODY DVDPackage
AS
  . . .
END DVDPackage;
```

To reference the items declared within a package specification, we use the dot notation; for example, we could call the DVDsForMember procedure as follows:

```
DVDPackage.DVDsForMember ('M250178');
```

E.6 Database triggers

A **trigger** defines an action that the database should take when some event occurs in the application. A trigger may be used to enforce some referential integrity constraints, to enforce complex integrity constraints, or to audit changes to data. In Oracle, the code within a trigger, called the *trigger body*, is made up of PL/SQL block, Java program, or C callout. Triggers are based on the Event-Condition-Action (ECA) model:

1. The *event* (or *events*) that trigger the rule. In Oracle, this is:
   - an INSERT, UPDATE, or DELETE statement specified on a specific table (or possibly view);
   - a CREATE, ALTER, or DROP statement on any schema object;
   - a database startup or instance shutdown, or a user logon or logoff;
   - a specific error message or any error message.

   It is also possible to specify whether the trigger should fire *before* the event or *after* the event.
2. The *condition* that determines whether the action should be executed. The condition is optional, but if specified the action will only be executed if the condition is true.
3. The *action* to be taken. This block contains the SQL statements and code to be executed when a triggering statement is issued and the trigger condition evaluates to true.

There are two types of triggers: *row-level* triggers that execute for each row of the table that is affected by the triggering event, and *statement-level* triggers that execute only once even if multiple rows are affected by the triggering event. Oracle also supports INSTEAD-OF triggers, which provide a transparent way of modifying views that cannot be modified directly through SQL DML statements (INSERT, UPDATE, and DELETE). These triggers are called INSTEAD-OF triggers because, unlike other types of triggers, Oracle fires the trigger *instead of* executing the original SQL statement. Triggers can also activate themselves one after the other. This can happen when the trigger action makes a change to the database that has the effect of causing another event that has a trigger associated with it.

For example, *StayHome* has a rule that prevents a member from renting more than five DVDs at the same time. We could create the trigger shown in Figure E.5 to enforce this integrity constraint. This trigger is invoked before a row is inserted into the `RentalDelivery` table or an existing row is updated. If the member currently has five DVDs on rent, the system displays a message and aborts the transaction. The following points should be noted:

- The **BEFORE** keyword indicates that the trigger should be executed before an insert or update is applied to the `RentalDelivery` table.
- The **FOR EACH ROW** keyword indicates that this is a row-level trigger, which executes for each row of the `RentalDelivery` table that is updated in the statement.
- The *new* keyword is used to refer to the new value of the column. (Although not used in this example, the *old* keyword can be used to refer to the old value of a column.)

```
CREATE TRIGGER member_not_renting_too_many
BEFORE INSERT OR UPDATE ON RentalDelivery
FOR EACH ROW
DECLARE
 x NUMBER;
BEGIN
    SELECT COUNT(*) INTO x
    FROM RentalDelivery r, DVDRental d
    WHERE r.memberNo = :new.memberNo AND
          r.deliveryNo = d.deliveryNo AND dateReturn IS NULL;
    IF x >= 5 THEN
            raise_application_error(-20000, ('Member ' || :new.memberNo || ' already
renting 5 DVDs');
    END IF;
END;
```

Figure E.5 Trigger to enforce the constraint that member cannot rent more than five DVDs at any one time

Appendix summary

- The **CREATE TABLE** statement creates base tables and supports the specification of the primary key, alternate keys, and foreign keys.
- The **CREATE VIEW** statement allows views to be created by specifying an underlying SELECT statement.
- The initial versions of the SQL language had no programming constructs; that is, it was not *computationally complete*. However, with the latest releases of the standard, SQL is now a full programming language with extensions known as **SQL/PSM** (**Persistent Stored Modules**).
- SQL/PSM supports the declaration of variables and has assignment statements, flow-of-control statements (IF-THEN-ELSE-END IF; LOOP-EXIT WHEN-END LOOP; FOR-END LOOP; and WHILE-END LOOP; GOTO), and exceptions.
- In Oracle PL/SQL SELECT statement can be used if the query returns *one and only one* row. To handle a query that can return an arbitrary number of rows (that is zero, one, or more rows) SQL uses **cursors** to allow the rows of a query result to be accessed one at a time. In effect, a cursor acts as a pointer to a particular row of the query result. The cursor can be advanced by one to access the next row. A cursor must be *declared* and *opened* before it can be used, and it must be *closed* to deactivate it after it is no longer required. Once the cursor has been opened, the rows of the query result can be retrieved one at a time using a FETCH statement, as opposed to a SELECT statement.
- **Subprograms** are called PL/SQL blocks and can take parameters and be invoked. PL/SQL has two types of subprograms called (**stored**) **procedures** and **functions**. Procedures and functions can take a set of parameters given to them by the calling

program and perform a set of actions. Both can modify and return data passed to them as a parameter. The difference between a procedure and a function is that a function will always return a single value to the caller, whereas a procedure does not. Usually, procedures are used unless only one return value is needed.

- A **package** is a collection of procedures, functions, variables, and SQL statements that are grouped together and stored as a single program unit. A package has two parts: a specification and a body. A package's *specification* declares all public constructs of the package and the *body* defines all constructs (public and private) of the package, and so implements the specification. In this way, packages provide a form of encapsulation.
- A **trigger** defines an action that the database should take when some event occurs in the application. A trigger may be used to enforce some referential integrity constraints, to enforce complex integrity constraints, or to audit changes to data. In Oracle, the code within a trigger, called the *trigger body*, is made up of PL/SQL block, Java program, or C callout.

APPENDIX

F

Guidelines for choosing indexes

Preview

Step 4.3 of the physical database design methodology presented in Chapter 11 considers whether adding indexes will improve the performance of the system. In this appendix, we provide a brief overview of indexes and then present guidelines for choosing indexes. To illustrate the process, we show how to select indexes for the *StayHome Online Rentals* case study described in Section 5.4.

Learning objectives

In this appendix you will learn:

- What an index is and how it can be used to speed up database access.
- When to select indexes to improve performance.

F.1 Brief overview of indexes

Index

A data structure that allows the DBMS to locate particular records in a file more quickly, and thereby increase the response to user queries.

An **index** in a database is similar to an index in a book. It is an auxiliary structure associated with a file that can be referred to when searching for an item of information, just like searching the index of a book, in which we look up a keyword and get a list of one or more pages the keyword appears on. An index prevents us from having to scan sequentially through a file each time we want to find an item. In the case of database indexes, the required item will be one or more records in a file. As in the book index analogy, the index is ordered and each index entry contains the item required and one or more locations (record identifiers) where the item can be found.

While indexes are not strictly necessary to use a DBMS, they can have a significant impact on performance. As with the book index, we could find the desired keyword by looking through the entire book, but this would be tedious and time-consuming. Having an index at the back of the book in alphabetical order of keyword allows us to go directly to the page or pages we want.

An index structure is associated with a particular search key, and contains records consisting of the key value and the address of the logical record in the file containing the key value. The file containing the logical records is called the

data file and the file containing the index records is called the **index file**. The values in the index file are ordered according to the **indexing field**, which is usually based on a single column. There are different types of indexes, the main ones being:

- *Primary index*. The **data file** is sequentially ordered by an ordering key field, and the indexing field is built on the ordering key field, which is guaranteed to have a unique value in each record.
- *Clustering index*. The data file is sequentially ordered on a nonkey field, and the indexing field is built on this nonkey field, so that there can be more than one record corresponding to a value of the indexing field. The nonkey field is called a **clustering field**.
- *Secondary index*. An index that is defined on a non-ordering field of the data file.

A file can have *at most* one primary index or one clustering index, and in addition can have several secondary indexes.

F.2 Specifying indexes

Note The initial version of the SQL standard had statements for creating and dropping indexes. However, these statements were removed from the second major release of the standard in 1992 because they were considered to be a physical concept rather than a logical concept. Having said that, most of the major relational DBMSs support these statements in one form or another. The SQL statements we use below are typical of what current products support.

To create an index in SQL, typically the CREATE INDEX statement is used. For example, to create a primary index on the `DVD` table based on the `catalogNo` column, we might use the following SQL statement:

```
CREATE UNIQUE INDEX catalogNoPrimaryIndex
  ON DVD (catalogNo);
```

To create a clustering index on the `DVDCopy` table based on the `catalogNo` column, we might use the following SQL statement:

```
CREATE INDEX catalogNoClusteringIndex
  ON DVDCopy (catalogNo) CLUSTER;
```

To drop an index in SQL, typically the DROP INDEX statement is used. For example, to drop the primary index `catalogNoPrimaryIndex`, we might use the following SQL statement:

```
DROP INDEX catalogNoPrimaryIndex;
```

Note Microsoft Office Access does not support the CREATE INDEX statement. Instead, we create an index through the field properties dialog box. We saw an example of this in Figure 11.4 and we discuss this in more detail shortly.

F.3 Choosing secondary indexes

Secondary indexes provide a mechanism for specifying an additional key for a base table that can be used to retrieve data more efficiently. For example, the `Member` table may be ordered on the member number, `memberNo`, the *primary index*. On the other hand, there may be frequent access to this table based on the `mLName` (last name) column. In this case, we may decide to add `mLName` as a *secondary index*.

However, there is an overhead involved in the maintenance and use of secondary indexes that has to be balanced against the performance improvement gained when retrieving data. This overhead includes:

- adding an index record to every secondary index whenever a record is inserted in the table;
- updating a secondary index when the corresponding record in the table is updated;
- the increase in disk space needed to store the secondary index;
- possible performance degradation during query optimization, as the query optimizer may consider all secondary indexes before selecting an optimal execution strategy.

Step 4.1 of the physical database design methodology presented in Chapter 11 involved a detailed analysis of important transactions. Before we present guidelines for selecting indexes, we discuss the type of information that should be collected from these important transactions that can inform this selection process.

F.3.1 Data usage analysis

For each important transaction identified, we should determine:

(a) The tables and columns accessed by the transaction and the type of access; that is, whether it is an insert, update, delete, or retrieval transaction.

> For an update transaction, note the columns that are updated because these columns may be candidates for avoiding an index.

(b) The columns used in any *search conditions* (in SQL, these are the conditions specified in the WHERE clause). Check whether the conditions involve:

(i) pattern matching; for example: (`mLName` LIKE '%Park%');

(ii) range searches; for example: (`salary` BETWEEN 30000 AND 40000);

(iii) exact-match key retrieval; for example: (`salary` = 30000).

This applies not only to queries but also to update and delete transactions, which can restrict the records to be updated/deleted in a table.

> These columns may be candidates for an index.

(c) For a query, the columns that are involved in the join of two or more tables.

> Again, these columns may be candidates for an index.

(d) The performance goals for the transaction; for example, the transaction must complete within 1 second.

> The columns used in any search conditions for very frequent or critical transactions should have a higher priority for an index.

F.3.2 Guidelines for choosing a 'wish list' of indexes

One approach to determining which secondary indexes are needed is to produce a `wish list` of columns that we think are candidates for indexing, and then to consider the impact of maintaining each of these indexes. We provide the following guidelines to help produce such a 'wish list':

(1) Do not index small tables. It may be more efficient to search the table in memory than to store an additional index structure.

(2) In general, index the primary key of a table if it is not a key of the file organization. Although the SQL standard provides a clause for the specification of primary keys as discussed in Appendix E, note that this does not guarantee that the primary key will be indexed in some RDBMSs.

(3) Add a secondary index to any column that is heavily used for data retrieval. For example, add a secondary index to the `Member` table based on the column `mLName`, as discussed above.

(4) Add a secondary index to a foreign key if there is frequent access based on it. For example, we may frequently join the `DVDCopy` and `DistributionCenter` tables on the column `dCenterNo` (the distribution center number). Therefore, it may be more efficient to add a secondary index to the `DVDCopy` table based on `dCenterNo`.

(5) Add a secondary index on columns that are frequently involved in:
   (a) selection or join criteria;
   (b) ORDER BY;
   (c) GROUP BY;
   (d) other operations involving sorting (such as UNION or DISTINCT).

(6) Add a secondary index on columns involved in built-in functions, along with any columns used to aggregate the built-in functions. For example, to find the average staff salary at each distribution center, we could use the following SQL query:

```
SELECT dCenterNo, AVG(salary)
FROM Staff
GROUP BY dCenterNo;
```

From the previous guideline, we could consider adding an index to the dCenterNo column by virtue of the GROUP BY clause. However, it may be more efficient to consider an index on both the dCenterNo column and the salary column. This may allow the DBMS to perform the entire query from data in the index alone, without having to access the data file. This is sometimes called an *index-only plan*, as the required response can be produced using only data in the index.

(7) As a more general case of the previous guideline, add a secondary index on columns that could result in an index-only plan.

(8) Avoid indexing a column or table that is frequently updated.

(9) Avoid indexing a column if the query will retrieve a significant proportion (for example, 25%) of the records in the table, even if the table is large. In this case, it may be more efficient to search the entire table than to search using an index.

(10) Avoid indexing columns that consist of long character strings.

Key point

If the search criteria involve more than one condition, and one of the terms contains an OR clause, and the term has no index/sort order, then adding indexes for the other columns is not going to help improve the speed of the query, because a linear search of the table is still required. For example, assume that only the genre and rating columns of the DVD table are indexed, and we use the following query:

```
SELECT *
FROM DVD
WHERE (genre = 'Action' OR rating = 'PG' OR title LIKE 'Lord%');
```

Although the two indexes could be used to find the records where (genre = 'Action' **OR** rating = 'PG'), the fact that the title column is not indexed will mean that these indexes cannot be used for the full WHERE clause. Thus, unless there are other queries that would benefit from having the genre and rating columns indexed, there is no benefit gained in indexing them for this query.

If the search conditions in the WHERE clause were AND'ed together, the two indexes on the genre and rating columns could be used to optimize the query.

F.3.3 Removing indexes from the 'wish list'

Having drawn up the 'wish list' of potential indexes, consider the impact of each of these on update transactions. If the maintenance of the index is likely to slow down important update transactions, then consider dropping the index from the list. Note, however, that a particular index may also make update operations more efficient. For example, if we want to update a member of staff's salary given the member's staff number, staffNo, and there is an index on staffNo, then the record to be updated can be found more quickly.

Note It is a good idea to experiment when possible to determine whether an index is improving performance, providing very little improvement, or adversely impacting on performance. In the last case, clearly we should remove this index from the 'wish list.' If there is little observed improvement with the addition of the index, further examination may be necessary to determine under what circumstances the index will be useful, and whether these circumstances are sufficiently important to warrant the implementation of the index.

Some systems allow inspection of the optimizer's strategy for executing a particular query or update, sometimes called the Query Execution Plan (QEP). For example, Oracle has an EXPLAIN PLAN diagnostic utility, Microsoft Office Access has a Performance Analyzer, DB2 has an EXPLAIN utility, and INGRES has an online QEP-viewing facility. When a query runs slower than expected, it is worth using such a facility to determine the reason for the slowness, and to find an alternative strategy that may improve the performance of the query.

Note If a large number of records are being inserted into a table with one or more indexes, it may be more efficient to drop the indexes first, perform the inserts, then re-create the indexes afterwards. As a rule of thumb, if the insert will increase the size of the table by at least 10%, drop the indexes temporarily.

Updating the database statistics

Earlier we mentioned that the query optimizer relies on database statistics held in the system catalog to select the optimal strategy. Whenever we create an index, the DBMS automatically adds the presence of the index to the system catalog. However, we may find that the DBMS requires a utility to be run to update the statistics in the system catalog relating to the table and the index.

F.4 Indexes for *StayHome Online Rentals*

In this section, we demonstrate how to choose indexes when the target DBMS is Microsoft Office Access 2007, and we consider the following queries:

(a) List the name, position, and salary of staff at a given distribution center, ordered by staff name.

(b) List the name of each Manager at each distribution center, ordered by distribution center number.

(c) List the title, genre, and availability of all DVDs at a specified distribution center, ordered by genre.

(d) List the title, genre, and availability of all DVDs for a given actor at a specified distribution center, ordered by title.

(e) List the title, genre, and availability of all DVDs for a given rating at a specified distribution center, ordered by title.

(f) List the details of all DVDs a specified member (first name and last name) currently has on rent.

(g) List the details of copies of a given DVD (title) at a specified distribution center.

(h) List the titles of all DVDs in a specified genre, ordered by title.

(i) List the total number of DVDs in each DVD genre at each distribution center, ordered by distribution center number.

(j) List the total number of DVDs featuring each actor, ordered by actor name.

F.4.1 Guidelines for indexes in Microsoft Office Access 2007

Note When discussing Microsoft Office Access we use the vendor's terminology and use the term 'field' in place of 'column.'

Microsoft Office Access supports indexes as we now briefly discuss. In Access, the primary key of a table is automatically indexed, but a field whose data type is Memo, Hyperlink, or OLE Object cannot be indexed. For other fields, Microsoft advises indexing a field if all the following apply:

- the field's data type is Text, Number, Currency, or Date/Time;
- you anticipate searching for values stored in the field;
- you anticipate sorting values in the field;
- you anticipate storing many different values in the field. (If many of the values in the field are the same, the index may not significantly speed up queries.)

In addition, Microsoft advises that:

- you should consider indexing fields on both sides of a join or create a relationship between these fields, in which case Access will automatically create an index on the foreign key field, if one does not exist already;
- when grouping records by the values in a joined field, you should specify GROUP BY for the field that is in the same table as the field you are calculating the aggregate on.

Microsoft Office Access can optimize simple and complex search conditions (called *expressions* in Access). For certain types of complex expressions, Microsoft Office Access uses a data access technology called Rushmore to achieve a greater level of optimization. A complex expression is formed by combining two simple expressions with the AND or OR operator, such as:

dCenterNo = 'D001' **AND** available = Yes

genre = 'Action' **OR** rating = 'PG'

In Access, a complex expression is fully or partially optimizable depending on whether one or both simple expressions are optimizable, and which operator was used to combine them. A complex expression is *Rushmore-optimizable* if all three of the following conditions are true:

- the expression uses AND or OR to join two conditions;
- both conditions are made up of simple optimizable expressions;
- both expressions contain indexed fields. The fields can be indexed individually or they can be part of a multiple-field index.

Creating indexes in Access

We create an index in Access by setting the Indexed property of a table in the Field Properties section in table Design View. The Indexed property has the following values:

No	No index (the default).
Yes (Duplicates OK)	The index allows duplicates.
Yes (No Duplicates)	The index does not allow duplicates.

We saw an example of setting an index for the `mgrStaffNo` field in Figure 11.3.

F.4.2 *StayHome Online Rentals*

Based on the guidelines provided above, we should ensure that we create the identified primary key for each table, which will cause Access to automatically index this field. Secondly, we should ensure that all relationships are created in the Relationships window, which will cause Access to automatically index the foreign key fields.

From the transactions listed at the start of this section, we may decide to create the additional indexes shown in Table F.1. This figure shows the fields in each table

Table F.1 Additional Indexes for the Member user view of *StayHome*

Table	Field	Transaction	Reason
Staff	name	(a)	ordering
DVD	genre	(c)	ordering
		(h)	search condition
		(i)	grouping
	rating	(e)	search condition
	title	(d), (e), (h)	ordering
		(g)	search condition
Actor	actorName	(d)	search condition
		(j)	grouping, ordering
Member	mFName/mLName	(f)	search condition
DVDRental	dateReturn	(f)	search condition

that should be indexed, the transaction(s) that use the field, and the reason for adding the index (either because the field is used in a *search condition*, as an *ordering* field, or as a *grouping* field). As an exercise, document the indexes for the transactions in the Buyer user view of *StayHome* documented in Appendix A.

> **Note** The `available` field in the `DVDCopy` table is used as a search condition by transaction (e). However, this field can only take two values (Y or N) and so from guideline (9) in F.3.2, it is not worthwhile indexing this field.

Appendix summary

- An **index** is a data structure that allows a DBMS to locate particular records in a file more quickly, and thereby improve the response to user queries
- There are different types of indexes: primary index, clustering index, and secondary index.
- **Secondary indexes** provide a mechanism for specifying an additional key for a base table that can be used to retrieve data more efficiently. However, there is an overhead involved in the maintenance and use of secondary indexes that has to be balanced against the performance improvement gained when retrieving data.
- One approach to determining which secondary indexes are needed is to produce a **wish list** of columns that are candidates for indexing, and then to consider the impact of maintaining each of these indexes.
- Guidelines include: do not index small tables; index the primary key of a table if it is not a key of the file organization; add a secondary index to any column that is heavily used for data retrieval; add a secondary index to a foreign key if there is frequent access based on it; add a secondary index on columns that are frequently involved in selection or join criteria, ORDER BY, or GROUP BY. Avoid indexing a column or table that is frequently updated.

APPENDIX

G

Guidelines for denormalization

Preview

Step 7 of the physical database design methodology presented in Chapter 11 considers whether introducing redundancy in a controlled manner by relaxing the normalization rules will improve the performance of the system. This should be considered only when it is estimated that the system will not be able to meet its performance requirements. In this appendix, we discuss some common situations for considering denormalization to speed up frequent or critical transactions, namely:

- combining one-to-one (1:1) relationships;
- duplicating columns in one-to-many (1:*) relationships to reduce joins;
- duplicating columns in many-to-many (*:*) relationships to reduce joins;
- introducing repeating groups;
- creating extract tables;
- partitioning tables.

The examples in this appendix are drawn from the *StayHome Online Rentals* case study documented in Section 5.4.

Learning objectives

In this appendix you will learn:

- When to denormalize to improve performance.

Key point As a general rule of thumb, if performance is unsatisfactory and a table has a low update rate and a very high query rate, denormalization may be a viable option.

Note We use the term **denormalization** to refer to situations where we combine two tables into one new table, where the new table is in the same normal form but contains more nulls than the original tables.

Combining one-to-one (1:1) relationships

1:1 relationships are defined in Section 6.5.1

Re-examine one-to-one (1:1) relationships to determine the effects of combining the tables into a single table. We should consider this only for tables that are frequently referenced together and infrequently referenced separately. Consider a potential 1:1 relationship between `Staff` and `NOK`, as shown in Figure G.1(a). The `Staff` entity contains information on staff and the `NOK` entity contains information about a member of staff's next of kin.

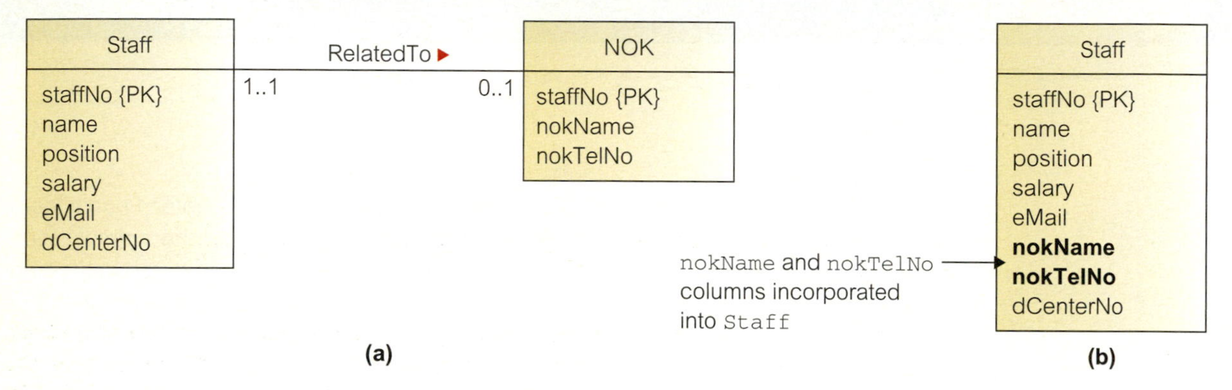

`Staff`

staffNo	name	position	salary	eMail	nokName	nokTelNo	dCenterNo
S1500	Tom Daniels	Manager	48000	tdaniels@stayhome.com	Jane Daniels	207-878-2751	D001
S0003	Sally Adams	Assistant	30000	sadams@stayhome.com	John Adams	518-474-5355	D001
S0010	Mary Martinez	Manager	51000	mmartinez@stayhome.com			D002
S3250	Robert Chin	Assistant	33000	rchin@stayhome.com	Michelle Chin	206-655-9867	D002
S2250	Sally Stern	Manager	48000	sstern@stayhome.com			D004
S0415	Art Peters	Manager	42000	apeters@stayhome.com	Amy Peters	718-507-7923	D003

from original `NOK`

from original `Staff`

(c)

Figure G.1 `Staff` and `NOK`: (a) original table diagram[1]; (b) revised table diagram; (c) resulting table

We can combine the two tables together as shown in Figure G.1(b). The relationship between `Staff` and `NOK` is 1:1 and the participation is optional (see Section 6.5.5). Since the participation is optional, when the two tables are combined together a number of the columns may have nulls appearing within them for some records, as shown in Figure G.1(c). If the `Staff` table is large and the proportion of records involved in the participation is small, there will be a significant amount of wasted space, which has to be balanced against any performance improvements gained by combining the tables.

[1] We use the term 'table diagram' here rather than ER diagram as we want to show foreign keys (which we would not show in an ER diagram.)

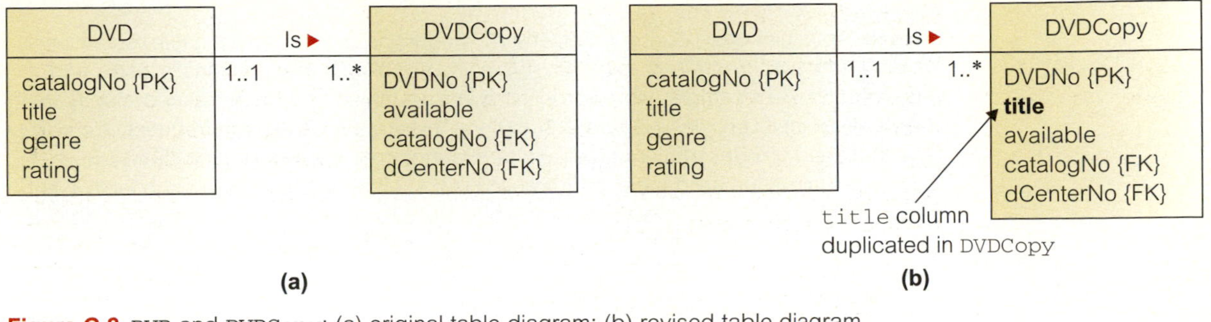

Figure G.2 DVD and DVDCopy: (a) original table diagram; (b) revised table diagram

Duplicating columns in one-to-many (1:) relationships to reduce joins*

With the specific aim of reducing or removing joins from frequent or critical queries, consider the benefits that may result in duplicating one or more columns of the parent table in the child table in a one-to-many (1:*) relationship (see Section 6.5.2). For example, whenever the `DVDCopy` table is accessed, it is very common for the DVD's title to be accessed at the same time. A typical SQL query would be:

```
SELECT dc.*, d.title
FROM DVDCopy dc, DVD d
WHERE dc.catalogNo = d.catalogNo AND dCenterNo = 'D001';
```

based on the original table diagram shown in Figure G.2(a). If we duplicate the `title` column in the `DVDCopy` table, we can remove the `DVD` table from the query, which in SQL is now:

```
SELECT *
FROM DVDCopy
WHERE dCenterNo = 'D001';
```

based on the revised table diagram in Figure G.2(b).

The benefits that result from this change have to be balanced against the problems that may arise. For example, if we change the duplicated data in the parent table, we must also update it in the child table. Further, for a 1:* relationship there may be multiple occurrences of each data item in the child table. Thus, we also have to maintain consistency of the multiple copies. If the update cannot be automated, the potential for loss of integrity is considerable. Even if this process is automated, additional time is required to maintain consistency every time a record is inserted, updated, or deleted. In our case, it is unlikely that the title will change, so the duplication may be warranted. However, another problem to consider is the increase in storage space resulting from the duplication. Again, with the relatively low cost of secondary storage nowadays, this may be less of a problem. However, this is not a justification for arbitrary duplication.

Note A special case of a one-to-many (1:*) relationship is a *lookup table*, sometimes called a *reference table* or *pick list*. Typically, a lookup table contains a code and a description. For example, we may define a lookup table for DVD genre and modify the table diagram as shown in Figure G.3(a). If the lookup table is used in frequent or critical queries, and the description is unlikely to change, consider duplicating the `description` column in the child table, as shown in Figure G.3(b). The original lookup table is not redundant – it can still be used to validate user input. However, by duplicating the `description` column in the child table, we have eliminated the need to join the child table to the lookup table.

The advantages of using a lookup table are:

- Reduction in the size of the child table (in this case, the `DVD` table); the genre number (`genreNo`) occupies 1 byte as opposed to 8 bytes for the genre description.
- If the description can change (which is generally not the case in this particular example), it is easier changing it once in the lookup table (`DVDGenre`) as opposed to changing it many times in the child table (`DVD`).
- The lookup table can be used to validate user input.

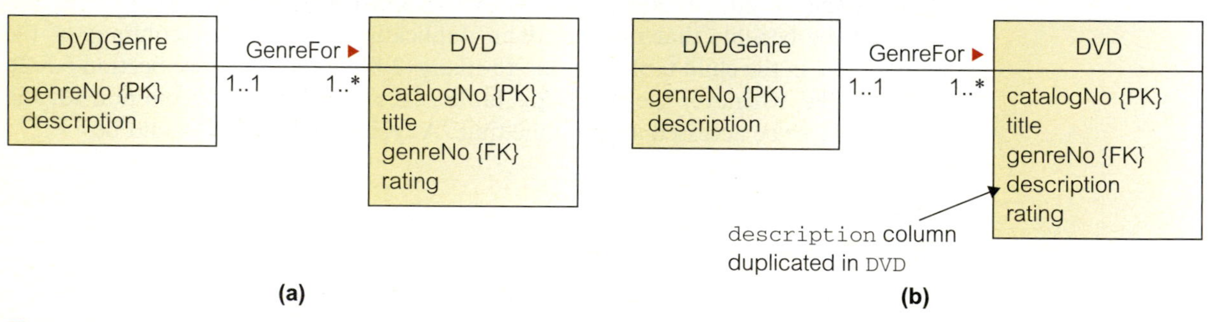

Figure G.3 Lookup table for `DVDgenre`: (a) original table diagram; (b) revised table diagram

Duplicating columns in many-to-many (:*) relationships to reduce joins*

In Step 2.1 of the logical database design methodology presented in Chapter10, we mapped each *:* relationship into three tables: the two tables derived from the original entities and a new table representing the relationship between the two entities. Now, if we wish to retrieve information from the *:* relationship, we have to join these three tables. In some circumstances, we may be able to reduce the number of tables to be joined by duplicating columns from one of the original entities in the intermediate table.

For example, a *:* relationship exists between `DVD` and `Actor`, with `DVDActor` acting as an intermediate entity. Consider the query that lists the DVD titles and roles that each actor has starred in:

```
SELECT d.title, a.*, da.*
FROM DVD d, DVDActor da, Actor a
WHERE d.catalogNo = da.catalogNo AND da.actorNo = a.actorNo;
```

based on the table diagram and tables shown in Figure G.4(a).

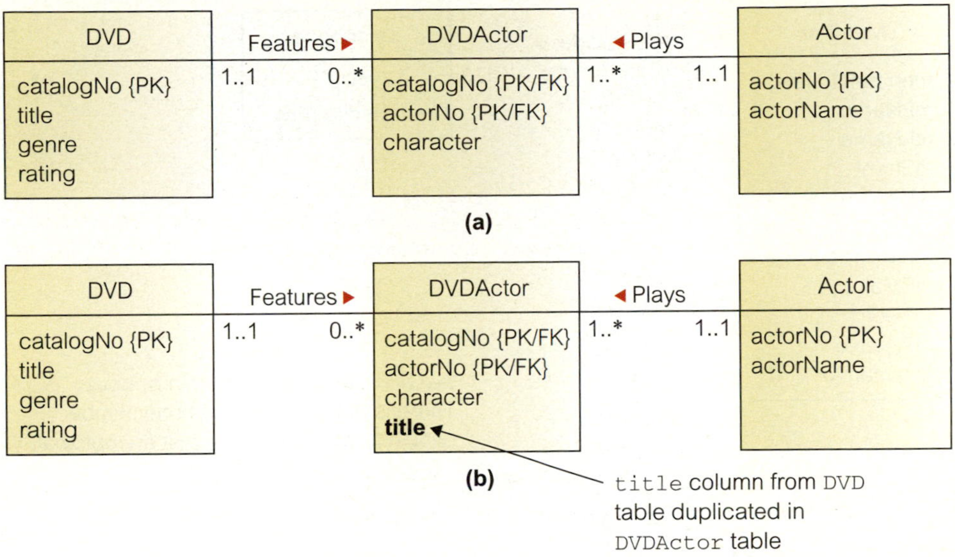

Figure G.4 DVD, Actor, and DVDActor: (a) original table diagram; (b) revised table diagram

If we duplicate the title column in the DVDActor table, we can remove the DVD table from the query, giving the following revised SQL query:

```
SELECT a.*, da.*
FROM DVDActor da, Actor a
WHERE da.actorNo = a.actorNo;
```

based on the revised table diagram shown in Figure G.4(b).

Introducing repeating groups

Repeating groups were eliminated from the logical data model as a result of the requirement that all entities be in first normal form (1NF). Repeating groups were separated out into a new table, forming a 1:* relationship with the original (parent) table. Occasionally, reintroducing repeating groups is an effective way to improve system performance. For example, assume that each *StayHome* member has a minimum of one and a maximum of three telephone numbers, as shown in Figure G.5(a). If access to this information is important or frequent, it may be more efficient to combine the tables and store the telephone details in the original Member table, with one column for each telephone number, as shown in Figure G.5(b).

In general, we should only consider this type of denormalization in the following circumstances:

- The absolute number of items in the repeating group is known (in this example, there is a maximum of three telephone numbers.)
- The number is static and will not change over time (the maximum number of telephone lines for a member is fixed by *StayHome* and is not anticipated to change.)
- The number is not very large, typically not greater than 10, although this is not as important as the first two conditions.

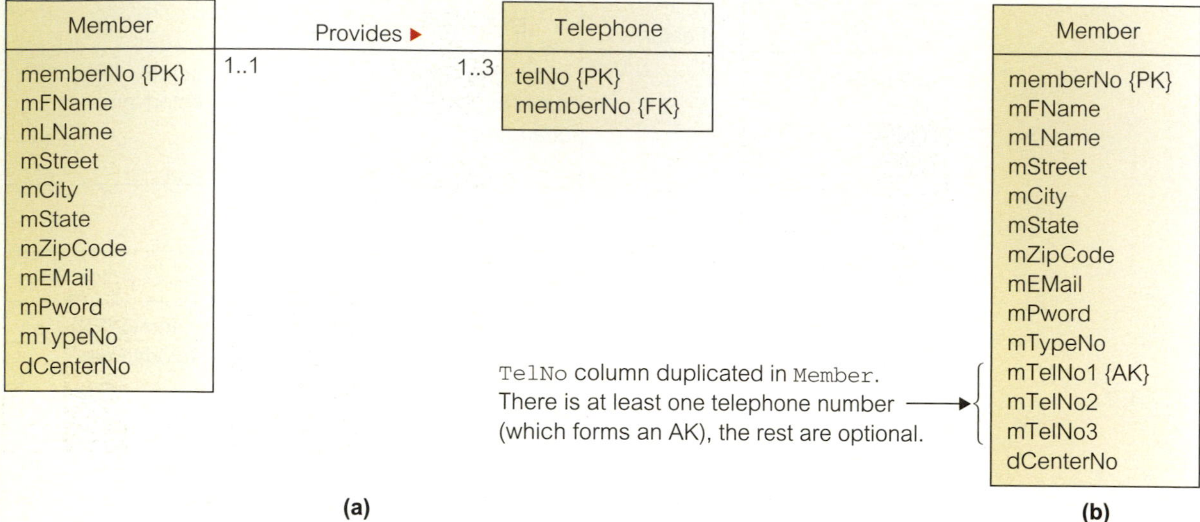

Figure G.5 `Member` and `TelNo`: (a) original table diagram; (b) revised table diagram

Sometimes, it may be only the most recent or current value in a repeating group, or just the fact that there is a repeating group, that is needed most frequently. In the above example, we may choose to store one telephone number in the `Member` table and leave the remaining numbers for the `Telephone` table. This would remove the presence of nulls from the `Member` table, as each member must have at least one telephone number.

Creating extract tables

There may be situations where we have to run certain reports at peak times during the day. These reports access derived data and perform multi-table joins on the same set of base tables. However, the data the report is based on may be relatively static or, in some cases, may not have to be current (that is, if the data was a few hours old, the report would be perfectly acceptable). In this case, it may be possible to create a single, highly denormalized extract table based on the tables required by the reports, and allow the users to access the extract table directly instead of the base tables. The most common technique for producing extract tables is to create and populate the tables in an overnight batch run when the system is lightly loaded.

Horizontal partitioning

Distributing the *records* of a table across a number of (smaller) tables.

Partitioning tables

Vertical partitioning

Distributing the *columns* of a table across a number of (smaller) tables (the primary key is duplicated to allow the original table to be reconstructed.)

Rather than combining tables together, an alternative approach that addresses the key problem with supporting very large tables (and indexes) is to decompose them into a number of smaller and more manageable pieces called **partitions**. As illustrated in Figure G.6, there are two main types: **horizontal** and **vertical partitions**.

Partitions are particularly useful in applications that store and analyze large amounts of data. For example, there are hundreds of thousands of records in the `DVDCopy` table that are held indefinitely for analysis purposes. Searching for a particular DVD copy record at a distribution center could be quite time-consuming,

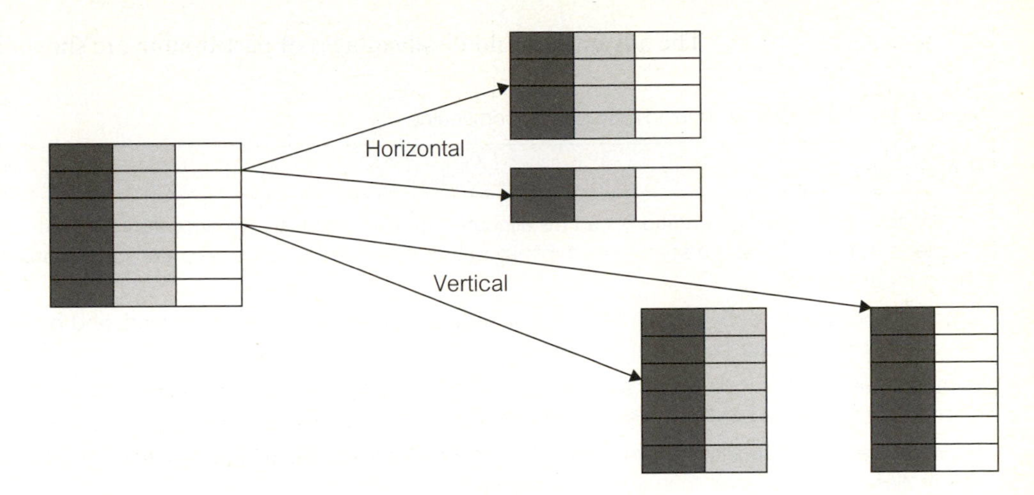

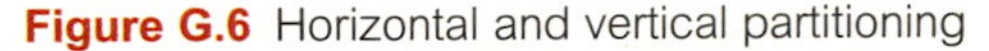
Figure G.6 Horizontal and vertical partitioning

however, we could reduce this time by horizontally partitioning the table, with one partition for each distribution center. We can create a (*hash*) partition for this scenario in Oracle using the following SQL statement:

```
CREATE TABLE DVDCopy_Partition(
            DVDNo       CHAR(6) NOT NULL,
            available   CHAR    NOT NULL,
            catalogNo   CHAR(6) NOT NULL,
            dCenterNo   CHAR(4) NOT NULL,
            PRIMARY KEY DVDNo,
            FOREIGN KEY catalogNo REFERENCES DVD(DVDNo),
            FOREIGN KEY dCenterNo REFERENCES
              DistributionCenter(dCenterNo))
PARTITION BY HASH (dCenterNo)
(PARTITION b1 TABLESPACE TB01,
PARTITION b2 TABLESPACE TB02,
PARTITION b3 TABLESPACE TB03,
PARTITION b4 TABLESPACE TB04);
```

As well as hash partitioning, other common types of partitioning are **range** (each partition is defined by a range of values for one or more columns) and **list** (each partition is defined by a list of values for a column). There are also composite partitions such as range-hash and list-hash (each partition is defined by a range or a list of values and then each partition is further subdivided based on a hash function).

There may also be circumstances where we frequently examine particular columns of a very large table and it may be appropriate to vertically partition the table into those columns that are frequently accessed together, and another vertical partition for the remaining columns (with the primary key replicated in each partition to allow the original table to be reconstructed).

The advantages and disadvantages of partitioning are shown in Table G.1.

Table G.1 Advantages and disadvantages of partitioning

Advantages
Improved load balancing: Partitions can be allocated to different areas of secondary storage thereby permitting parallel access, while at the same time minimizing the contention for access to the same storage area if the table was not partitioned.
Improved performance: By limiting the amount of data to be examined or processed, and by enabling parallel execution, performance can be enhanced.
Increased availability: If partitions are allocated to different storage areas and one storage area becomes unavailable, the other partitions would still be available.
Improved recovery: Smaller partitions can be recovered more efficiently (equally well, the DBA may find backing up smaller partitions easier than very large tables.)
Security: Data in a partition can be restricted to only those users who require access to it, with different partitions having different access restrictions.
Disadvantages
Complexity: Partitioning is not usually transparent to end-users and queries that utilize more than one partition become more complex to write.
Reduced performance: Queries that combine data from more than one partition may be slower than a non-partition approach.
Duplication: Vertical partitioning involves duplication of the primary key. This leads to increased storage requirements but also leads to potential inconsistencies.

Appendix summary

- The term **denormalization** refers to situations where two tables are combined into one new table, where the new table is in the same normal form but contains more nulls than the original tables.
- As a rule of thumb, if performance is unsatisfactory and a table has a low update rate and a very high query rate, denormalization may be a viable option.
- Consider denormalization in the following situations, specifically to speed up frequent or critical transactions: combining 1:1 relationships; duplicating columns in 1:* relationships to reduce joins; duplicating columns in *:* relationships to reduce joins; introducing repeating groups; creating extract tables; partitioning tables that are very large.

APPENDIX H

Object-oriented concepts

Preview

In Chapter 17 we discussed the third generation of database management systems, namely *Object-Oriented Database Management Systems (OODBMSs)* and *Object-Relational Database Management Systems (ORDBMSs)*. In this appendix, we provide an overview to the object-oriented concepts that underlie these systems using examples drawn from the *StayHome Online Rentals* case study documented in Section 5.4.

Learning objectives

In this appendix you will learn:

- The concepts associated with object-orientation:
  - abstraction, encapsulation, and information hiding;
  - objects and attributes;
  - object identity;
  - methods and messages;
  - classes, subclasses, superclasses, and inheritance;
  - overriding and overloading.

Abstraction

The process of identifying the essential aspects of an entity and ignoring the unimportant properties.

H.1 Abstraction, encapsulation, and information hiding

In software engineering, **abstraction** means that we concentrate on what an object is and what it does, before we decide how it should be implemented. In this way, we delay implementation details for as long as possible, thereby avoiding commitments that we may find restrictive at a later stage. There are two fundamental aspects of abstraction: **encapsulation** and **information hiding**.

Encapsulation

An object contains both the data structure and the set of operations that can be used to manipulate it.

Using these concepts, the internal details of an object can be changed without affecting the applications that use it, provided the external details remain the same. This prevents an application becoming so interdependent that a small change has

Information hiding

The external aspects of an object are separated from its internal details, which are hidden from the outside world.

enormous ripple effects. In other words, information hiding provides a form of *data independence* (see Section 1.5.5).

In some object-oriented programming languages, encapsulation is achieved through *abstract data types* (ADTs), in which an object has an interface part and an implementation part. The interface provides a specification of the operations that can be performed on the object; the implementation part consists of the data structure for the ADT and the functions that realize the interface. Only the interface part is visible to other objects or users.

H.2 Objects and attributes

Object

A uniquely identifiable entity that contains the attributes that describe the state of a 'real world' object, and the actions (behavior) that are associated with it.

In the *StayHome* case study, a distribution center, a member of staff, and a DVD are examples of **objects** that we wish to model. The concept of an object is simple but, at the same time, very powerful: each object can be defined and maintained independently of the others. This definition of an object is very similar to the definition of an entity given in Section 6.1. However, an object encapsulates both state and behavior; an entity only models state.

The current *state* of an object is described by one or more *attributes (instance variables)*. For example, the distribution center at 8 Jefferson Way may have the attributes shown in Table H.1. Attributes can be classified as simple or complex. A *simple attribute* can be a primitive type such as integer, string, float, and so on, which takes on literal values; for example, `dCenterNo` in Table H.1 is a simple attribute with the literal value 'D001'. A *complex attribute* can contain collections and/or references. For example, the attribute `Assistants` is a *collection* of `Staff` objects. A *reference attribute* represents a relationship between objects and contains a value, or collection of values, which are themselves objects (`Assistants` is, more precisely, a collection of references to `Staff` objects). A reference attribute is conceptually similar to a foreign key in the relational data model or a pointer in a programming language. An object that contains one or more complex attributes is called a **complex object**.

Attributes are generally referenced using the 'dot' notation. For example, the `dStreet` attribute of a `DistributionCenter` object, `dCenterObject`, is referenced as:

```
dCenterObject.dStreet
```

Table H.1 Object attributes for a distribution center instance

Attribute	Value
dCenterNo	D001
dStreet	8 Jefferson Way
dCity	Portland
dState	OR
dZipCode	97201
Assistants	Sally Adams, John Munro, Mary Keller
Manager	Tom Daniels

H.3 Object identity

Object identifier

A unique identifier for each object in the system.

A key part of the definition of an object is unique identity. In an object-oriented system, each object is assigned an **Object Identifier (OID)** when it is created that is:

- system-generated;
- unique to that object;
- invariant, in the sense that it cannot be altered during its lifetime. Once the object is created, this OID will not be reused for any other object, even after the object has been deleted;
- independent of the values of its attributes (that is, its state) – two objects could have the same state but would have different identities;
- invisible to the user (ideally).

Thus, object identity ensures that an object can always be uniquely identified, thereby automatically providing entity integrity (see Section 2.4.2). In fact, as object identity ensures uniqueness system-wide, it provides a stronger constraint than the relational data model's entity integrity, which only requires uniqueness within a table. In addition, objects can contain, or refer to, other objects using object identity. However, for each referenced OID in the system there should always be an object present that corresponds to the OID; that is, there should be no *dangling references*. For example, in the *StayHome* case study, we have the relationship `DistributionCenter` ***Has*** `Staff`. If we embed each distribution center object in the related staff object then we encounter the problems of information redundancy and update anomalies discussed in Section 8.2. However, if we instead embed the OID of the distribution center object in the related staff object, there continues to be only one instance of each distribution center object in the system and consistency can be maintained more easily. In this way, objects can be *shared* and OIDs can be used to maintain referential integrity (see Section 2.4.3).

H.4 Methods and messages

Method

The implementation of a 'real world' action (behavior) associated with an object.

An object encapsulates both data and functions into a self-contained package. In object-orientation, functions are usually called **methods**. Figure H.1 provides a conceptual representation of an object, with the attributes (*state*) on the inside protected from the outside by the methods. Methods define the *behavior* of the object. They can be used to change the object's state by modifying its attribute values, or to query the values of selected attributes. For example, we may have methods to add a DVD copy for rent at a distribution center, to update a member of staff's salary, or to print out a member of staff's details.

A method consists of a name and a body that performs the behavior associated with the method name. In an object-oriented language, the body consists of a block of code that carries out the required functionality. For example, Figure H.2 represents the method to update a member of staff's salary. The name of the method is `updateSalary`, with an input parameter *increment*, which is added to the *instance* `variable salary` to produce a new salary.

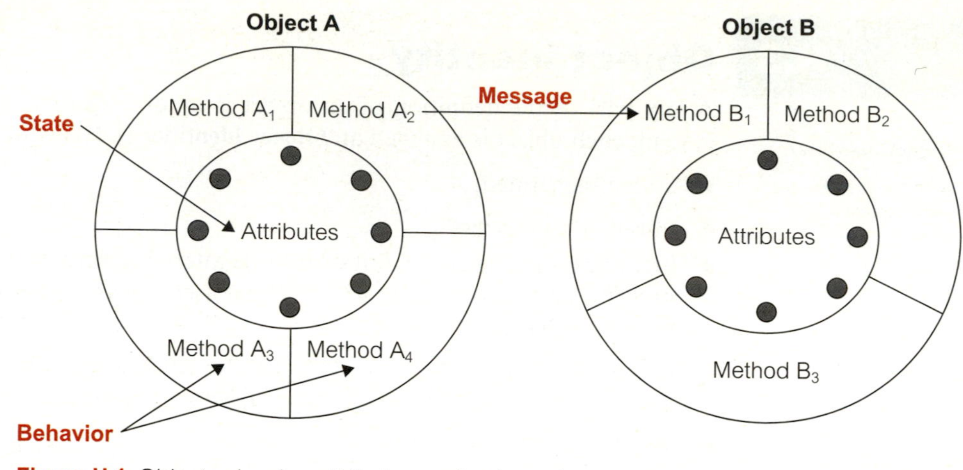

Figure H.1 Objects showing attributes, methods, and messages

```
method updateSalary(float increment)
{
    salary = salary + increment;
}
```

Figure H.2 Example of a method

Message

A request from one object (the sender) to another object (the receiver) asking the second object to execute one of its methods. The sender and receiver may be the same object.

Messages are the means by which objects communicate, as illustrated in Figure H.1. The request may be to change the receiver's state or simply to obtain the value of one of the receiver's instance variables. Again, the dot notation is generally used to access a method. For example, to execute the `updateSalary` method on a `Staff` object and pass the method an increment value of 1000, we write:

```
staffObject.updateSalary(1000)
```

H.5 Classes

Class

A collection of objects that have the same attributes and methods.

Objects that have the same attributes and respond to the same messages can be grouped together to form a **class**. The class encapsulates the object's data representation and methods' implementation. The attributes and associated methods are defined once for the class rather than separately for each object. For example, all distribution center objects would be described by a single `DistributionCenter` class. The objects in a class are called **instances** of the class. Each instance has its own value(s) for each attribute, but shares the same attribute names and methods with other instances of the class, as illustrated in Figure H.3.

In some object-oriented systems, a class is also an object and has its own attributes and methods, referred to as *class attributes* and *class methods*, respectively. Class attributes describe the general characteristics of the class, such as totals or averages; for example, in the class `DistributionCenter` we may have a class

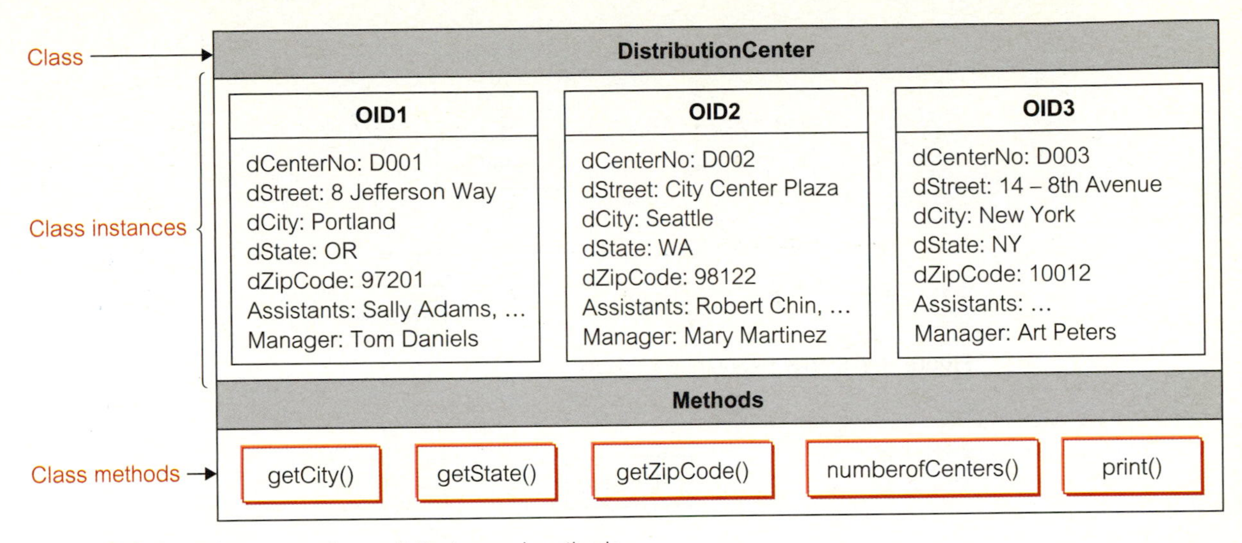

Figure H.3 Class instances share attributes and methods

attribute for the total number of distribution centers. There are special class methods to create new instances of the class and to destroy those that are no longer required. In an object-oriented language, a new instance is normally created by a method called *new*. Such methods are usually called *constructors*. Methods for destroying objects and reclaiming the space occupied are typically called *destructors*. Messages sent to a class method are sent to the class rather than an instance of a class, which implies that the class is an instance of a higher-level class, called a *metaclass*.

H.6 Subclasses, superclasses, and inheritance

Subclass

A distinct grouping of instances of a class, which require to be represented in a data model.

Superclass

A class that includes one or more distinct groupings of its instances, which require to be represented in a data model. See also *Specialization and Generalization*.

Some objects may have similar but not identical attributes and methods. If there is a large degree of similarity, it would be useful to be able to share the common properties (attributes and methods). **Inheritance** allows one class to be defined as a special case of a more general class. These special cases are known as **subclasses** and the more general cases are known as **superclasses**. The process of forming a superclass is referred to as **generalization** and the process of forming a subclass is **specialization**. By default, a subclass inherits all the properties of its superclass(es) and, additionally, defines its own unique properties. However, as we shall see shortly, a subclass can also redefine inherited properties. All instances of the subclass are also instances of the superclass. Further, the *principle of substitutability* states that we can use an instance of the subclass whenever a method or a construct expects an instance of the superclass. The concepts of superclass, subclass, and inheritance are similar to those discussed for the EER model in Chapter 7, except that in the object-oriented paradigm inheritance covers both state and behavior.

The two main forms of inheritance are single inheritance and multiple inheritance. Figure H.4 shows an example of *single inheritance*, where the subclasses `Manager` and `Assistant` inherit the properties of the superclass `Staff`. The term

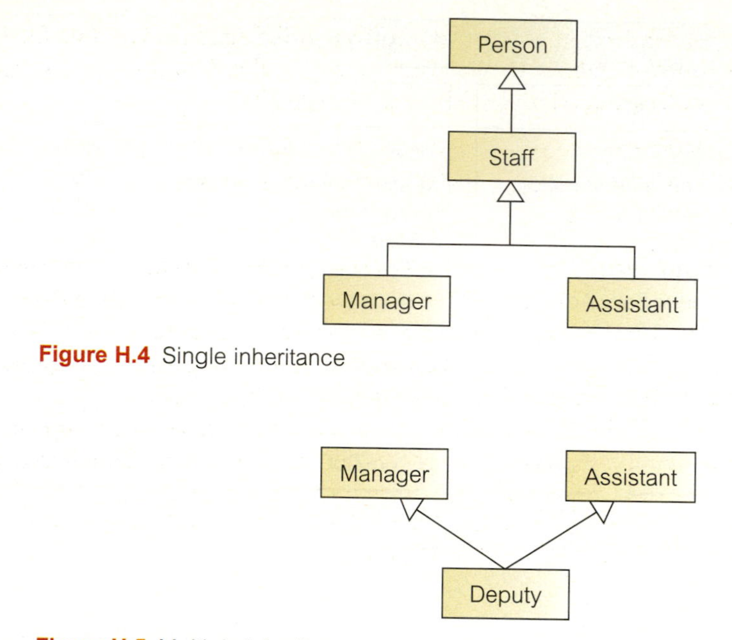

Figure H.4 Single inheritance

Figure H.5 Multiple inheritance

single inheritance refers to the fact that the subclasses inherit from no more than one superclass. The superclass `Staff` could itself be a subclass of a superclass, `Person`, thus forming a *class hierarchy*.

Figure H.5 shows an example of *multiple inheritance* where the subclass `Deputy` inherits properties from both the superclasses `Manager` and `Assistant`. The provision of a mechanism for multiple inheritance can be quite problematic, as it has to provide a way of dealing with conflicts that arise when the superclasses contain the same attributes or methods. Not all object-oriented languages and DBMSs support multiple inheritance as a matter of principle. Some authors claim that multiple inheritance introduces a level of complexity that is hard to manage safely and consistently. Others argue that it is required to model the 'real world.'

H.7 Overriding and overloading

As we have just mentioned, properties (attributes and methods) are automatically inherited by subclasses from their superclasses. However, it is possible to redefine a property in the subclass. In this case, the definition of the property in the subclass is the one used. For example, we might define a method in the `Staff` class to increment salary based on a commission:

```
method void giveCommission(float centerProfit) {
  salary = salary. + 0.02 * centerProfit;
}
```

However, we may wish to perform a different calculation for commission in the `Manager` subclass. We can do this by redefining, or **overriding**, the method `giveCommission` in the `Manager` subclass:

Overriding

The process of redefining a property (attribute or method) inherited from a superclass by a more specific implementation in a subclass.

```
method void giveCommission(float centerProfit) {
  salary = salary. + 0.05 * centerProfit;
}
```

The ability to factor out common properties of several classes and form them into a superclass that can be shared with subclasses can greatly reduce redundancy within systems, and is regarded as one of the main advantages of object-orientation. Overriding is an important feature of inheritance as it allows special cases to be handled easily with minimal impact on the rest of the system.

Overloading

Allowing the name of a method to be reused within a class definition or across class definitions.

Overriding is a special case of the more general concept of **overloading**. This means that a single message can perform different functions depending on which object receives it and, if appropriate, what parameters are passed to the method. For example, many classes will have a `print` method to print out the relevant details for an object, as shown in Figure H.6.

```
method void print () {
  cout << "Center number: " << dCenterNo << endl;
  cout << "Street: " << dStreet << endl;
  cout << "City: " << dCity << endl;
  cout << "State: " << dState << endl;
  cout << "Zipcode: " << dZipcode << endl;
}
```
(a)

```
method void print () {
  cout << "Staff number: " << staffNo << endl;
  cout << "Name: " << name << endl;
  cout << "Position: " << position << endl;
  cout << "Salary: " << salary << endl;
  cout << "eMail: " << eMail << endl;
  cout << "Center number: " << dCenterNo << endl;
}
```
(b)

Figure H.6 Overloading print method: (a) for `DistributionCenter` object; (b) for `Staff` object

Overloading can greatly simplify applications, since it allows the same name to be used for the same operation irrespective of what class it appears in, thereby allowing context to determine which meaning is appropriate at any given moment. This saves having to provide unique names for methods such as `printDistributionCenterDetails` or `printStaffDetails` for what is essentially the same functional operation.

Overriding and overloading are particular forms of a more general concept known as **polymorphism**.

Appendix summary

- The concept of **encapsulation** means that an object contains both a data structure and the set of operations that can be used to manipulate it. The concept of **information hiding** means that the external aspects of an object are separated from its internal details, which are hidden from the outside world.
- An **object** is a uniquely identifiable entity that contains the attributes that describe the **state** of a 'real world' object, and the actions (**behavior**) that are associated with it. A key part of the definition of an object is unique identity. In an object-oriented system, each object has a unique system-wide identifier (the **OID**) that is independent of the values of its attributes and, ideally, invisible to the user.
- **Methods** define the behavior of an object. They can be used to change the object's state by modifying its attribute values or to query the value of selected attributes. **Messages** are the means by which objects communicate. A message is simply a request from one object (the sender) to another object (the receiver) asking the second object to execute one of its methods.
- Objects that have the same attributes and respond to the same messages can be grouped together to form a **class**. The attributes and associated methods can then be defined once for the class rather than separately for each object.
- **Inheritance** allows one class to be defined as a special case of a more general class. These special cases are known as **subclasses** and the more general cases are known as **superclasses**. The process of forming a superclass is referred to as **generalization**; forming a subclass is **specialization**. A subclass inherits all the properties of its superclass and additionally defines its own unique properties (attributes and methods). All instances of the subclass are also instances of the superclass.
- **Overloading** allows the name of a method to be reused within a class definition or across definitions. **Overriding**, a special case of overloading, allows the name of a property to be redefined in a subclass.

APPENDIX

I

Common data models

In this appendix you will learn:

- About common business data models.
- More on building ER models.
- More on creating tables from ER models.

In this appendix, we introduce some common data models that you may find useful. In fact, it has been estimated that one-third of a data model consists of common constructs that are applicable to most companies and the remaining two-thirds are either industry-specific or company-specific. Thus, most data modeling work is recreating constructs that have already been produced many times before in other companies.

The two mains aim of this appendix are to provide you with:

(1) additional knowledge of building ER models and tables;

(2) data model templates that you may find useful in your business. The models featured here may not represent your company exactly, but they may provide a starting point from which you can develop a more suitable model that matches your company's specific requirements.

We provide models for the following common business areas:

- Customer order entry
- Inventory control
- Project management
- Course management
- Human resource management
- Payroll management.

In each case, we provide a short description of the requirements, and show an example of a typical ER model and the mapping of the model to a set of tables. We assume that you are familiar with the modeling notation used throughout the rest of this book. If you are not, look at Chapter 6 on ER modeling and Chapter 7 on enhanced ER modeling, which introduce the main concepts and notations we use in this appendix. You will also find a summary of the database design methodology in Appendix D.

I.1 Customer order entry

A company wishes to create a database for its order entry activities. A customer can place one or more orders, with each order for one or more products. Each order gives rise to one invoice, which can be paid by a number of methods, such as check, credit card, or cash. The name of the employee who initially processes the customer order is recorded.

An employee in the Shipping department is responsible for packaging the order and sending it to the customer. If an ordered product is not in stock, Shipping send out what is in stock, so more than one shipment may be required to fulfill the order. The logical data model is shown in Figure I.1 and the associated tables in Figure I.2.

I.1.1 ER model

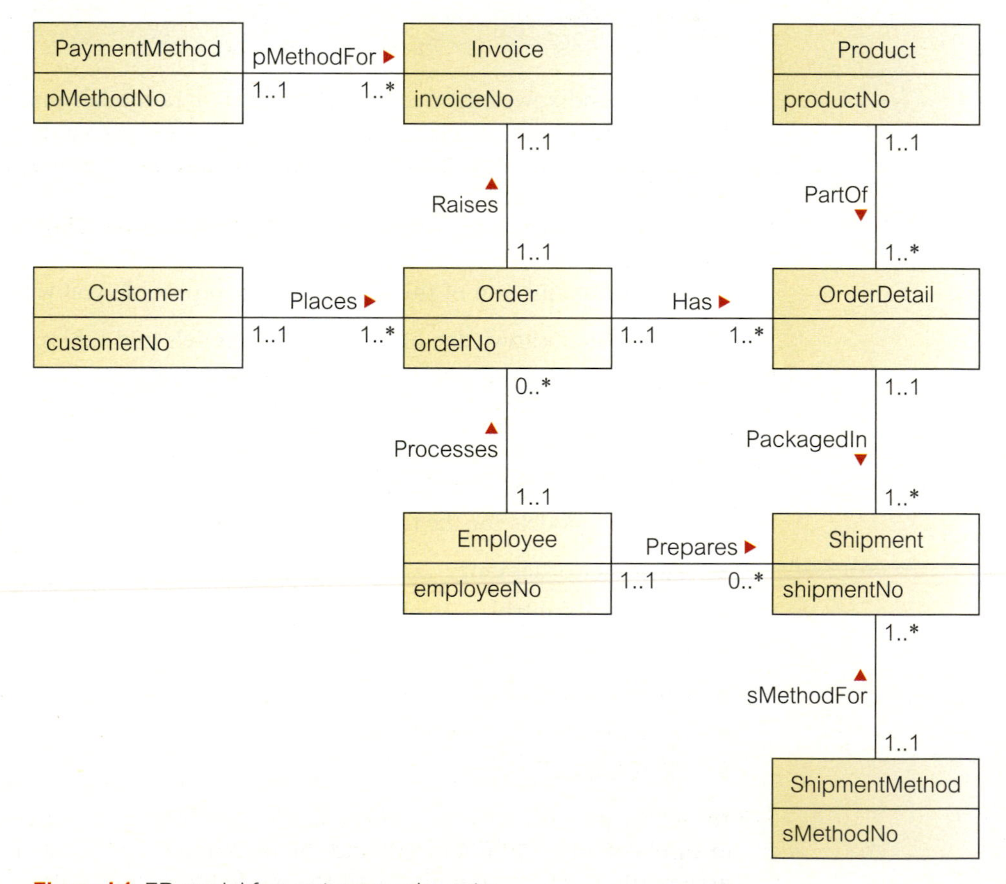

Figure I.1 ER model for customer order entry

I.1.2 Tables

Customer (customerNo, customerName, customerStreet, customerCity, customerState, customerZipCode, custTelNo, custFaxNo, DOB, maritalStatus, creditRating)
Primary key customerNo
Alternate key custTelNo
Alternate key custFaxNo

Employee (employeeNo, title, firstName, middleName, lastName, address, workTelExt, homeTelNo, empEmailAddress, socialSecurityNumber, DOB, position, sex, salary, dateStarted)
Primary key employeeNo
Alternate key socialSecurityNumber

Invoice (invoiceNo, dateRaised, datePaid, creditCardNo, holdersName, expiryDate, orderNo, pMethodNo)
Primary key invoiceNo
Foreign key orderNo references Order(orderNo)
Foreign key pMethodNo references PaymentMethod(pMethodNo)

Order (orderNo, orderDate, billingStreet, billingCity, billingState, billingZipCode, promisedDate, status, customerNo, employeeNo)
Primary key orderNo
Foreign key customerNo references Customer(customerNo)
Foreign key employeeNo references Employee(employeeNo)

OrderDetail (orderNo, productNo, quantityOrdered)
Primary key orderNo, productNo
Foreign key orderNo references Order(orderNo)
Foreign key productNo references Product(ProductNo)

PaymentMethod (pMethodNo, paymentMethod)
Primary key pMethodNo

Product (productNo, productName, serialNo, unitPrice, quantityOnHand, reorderLevel, reorderQuantity, reorderLeadTime)
Primary key productNo
Alternate key serialNo

Shipment (shipmentNo, quantity, shipmentDate, completeStatus, orderNo, productNo, employeeNo, sMethodNo)
Primary key shipmentNo
Foreign key orderNo, productNo references OrderDetail(orderNo, productNo)
Foreign key employeeNo references Employee(employeeNo)
Foreign key sMethodNo references ShipmentMethod(sMethodNo)

ShipmentMethod (sMethodNo, shipmentMethod)
Primary key sMethodNo

Figure I.2 Tables for customer order entry

I.2 Inventory control

A company wishes to create a database to control its inventory, which consists of a number of products divided into a number of categories, such as clothing, food, and stationery. An employee raises a purchase order when a product has to be reordered from the supplier. The tracking records supplies received, units sold, and any wastage. The logical data model is shown in Figure I.3 and the associated tables in Figure I.4.

I.2.1 ER model

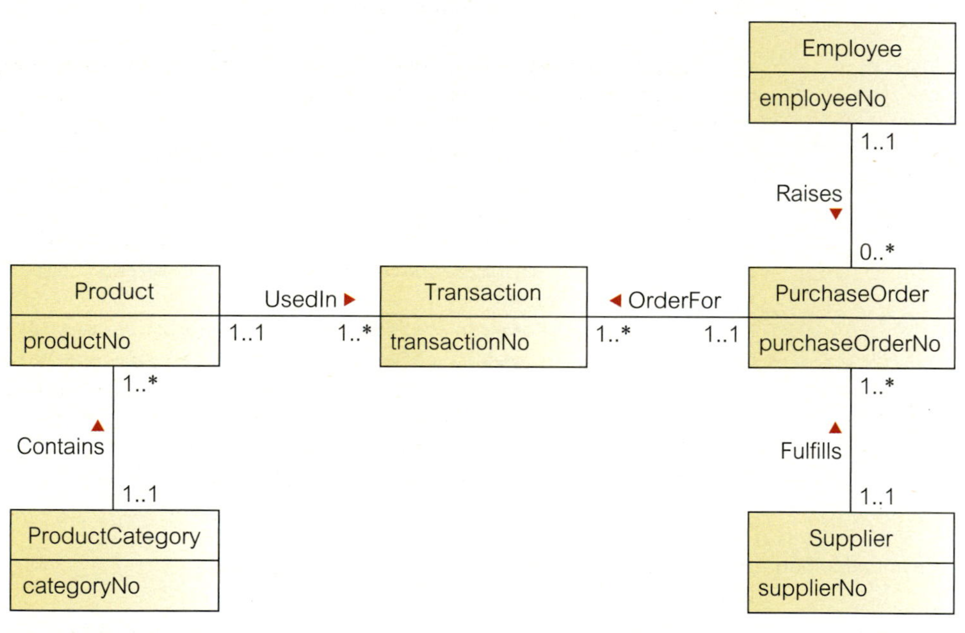

Figure I.3 ER model for inventory control

I.2.2 Tables

Employee	as defined in I.1.2
Product	(productNo, productName, serialNo, unitPrice, quantityOnHand, reorderLevel, reorderQuantity, reorderLeadTime, categoryNo) Primary Key productNo Alternate Key serialNo Foreign Key categoryNo references ProductCategory(categoryNo)
ProductCategory	(categoryNo, categoryDescription) Primary Key categoryNo
PurchaseOrder	(purchaseOrderNo, purchaseOrderDescription, orderDate, dateRequired, shippedDate, freightCharge, supplierNo, employeeNo) Primary Key purchaseOrderNo Foreign Key supplierNo references Supplier(supplierNo) Foreign Key employeeNo references Employee(employeeNo)
Supplier	(supplierNo, supplierName, supplierStreet, supplierCity, supplierState, supplierZipCode, suppTelNo, suppFaxNo, suppEmailAddress, suppWebAddress, contactName, contactTelNo, contactFaxNo, contactEmailAddress, paymentTerms) Primary Key supplierNo Alternate Key supplierName Alternate Key suppTelNo Alternate Key suppFaxNo
Transaction	(transactionNo, transactionDate, transactionDescription, unitPrice, unitsOrdered, unitsReceived, unitsSold, unitsWastage, productNo, purchaseOrderNo) Primary Key transactionNo Foreign Key productNo references Product(productNo) Foreign Key purchaseOrderNo references PurchaseOrder(purchaseOrderNo)

Figure I.4 Tables for inventory control

I.3 Project management

A consultancy company wishes to create a database to help manage its projects. Each project is for a specific client and has a nominated project manager. The project is divided into a number of work packages and employees bill their time and expenses against a work package. Each employee has a specific role, which defines the charging rate for the client. Over time, an employee can work on several work packages associated with the same project. In addition, most, but not all, work packages have a number of associated documents as deliverables, each of which may be written by more than one employee. The logical data model is shown in Figure I.5 and the associated tables in Figure I.6.

I.3.1 ER model

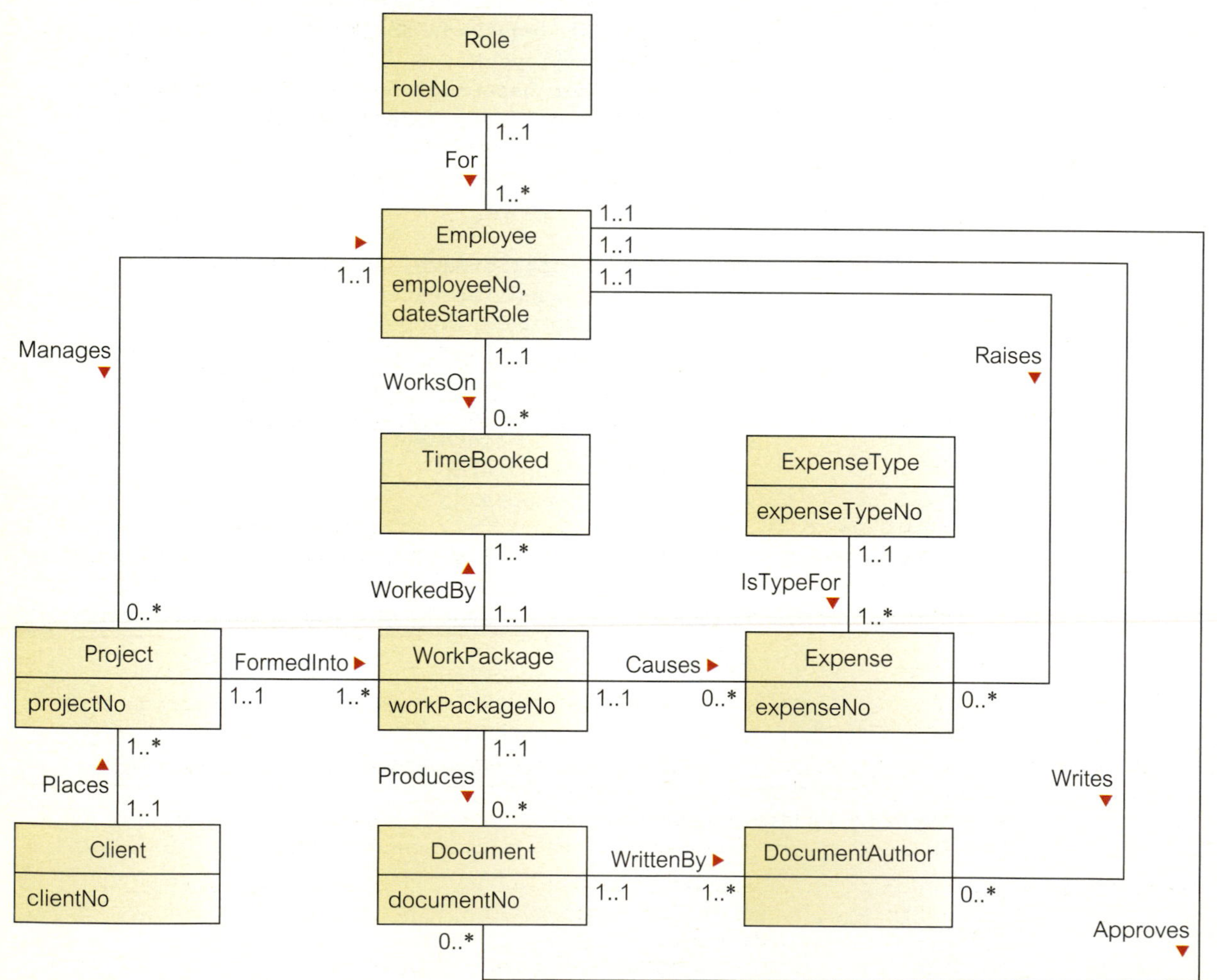

Figure I.5 ER model for project management

I.3.2 Tables

```
Client          (clientNo, clientName, clientStreet, clientCity, clientState,
                clientZipCode, clientTelNo, clientFaxNo, clientWebAddress, contactName,
                contactTelNo, contactFaxNo, contactEmailAddress)
                Primary Key clientNo
                Alternate Key clientName
                Alternate Key clientTelNo
                Alternate Key clientFaxNo

Document        (documentNo, documentTitle, documentDate, versionNo, workPackageNo,
                approvedByEmployeeNo)
                Primary Key documentNo
                Foreign Key workPackageNo references WorkPackage(workPackageNo)
                Foreign Key approvedByEmployeeNo references Employee(employeeNo)

DocumentAuthor  (documentNo, employeeNo)
                Primary Key documentNo, employeeNo
                Foreign Key documentNo references Document(documentNo)
                Foreign Key employeeNo references Employee(employeeNo)

Employee        (employeeNo, dateStartRole, firstName, middleName, lastName, address,
                workTelExt, homeTelNo, empEmailAddress, socialSecurityNumber, DOB,
                position, sex, salary, dateStarted, roleNo)
                Primary Key employeeNo
                Alternate Key socialSecurityNumber
                Foreign Key roleNo references Role(roleNo)

Expense         (expenseNo, expenseDate, expenseDescription, expenseAmount,
                workPackageNo, employeeNo, expenseTypeNo)
                Primary Key expenseNo
                Alternate Key workPackageNo, employeeNo, expenseDate
                Foreign Key workPackageNo references WorkPackage(workPackageNo)
                Foreign Key employeeNo references Employee(employeeNo)
                Foreign Key expenseTypeNo references ExpenseType(expenseTypeNo)

ExpenseType     (expenseTypeNo, expenseTypeDescription)
                Primary Key expenseTypeNo

Project         (projectNo, projectName, plannedStartDate, plannedEndDate,
                actualStartDate, actualEndDate, projectedCost, actualCost, clientNo,
                managerEmployeeNo)
                Primary Key projectNo
                Foreign Key clientNo references Client(clientNo)
                Foreign Key managerEmployeeNo references Employee(employeeNo)

Role            (roleNo, roleDescription, billingRate)
                Primary Key roleNo

TimeBooked      (workPackageNo, employeeNo, dateStartWork, dateStopWork, timeWorked)
                Primary Key workPackageNo, employeeNo
                Foreign Key workPackageNo references WorkPackage(workPackageNo)
                Foreign Key employeeNo references Employee(employeeNo)

WorkPackage     (workPackageNo, plannedStartDate, plannedEndDate, actualStartDate,
                actualEndDate, projectedCost, actualCost, projectNo)
                Primary Key workPackageNo
                Foreign Key projectNo references Project(projectNo)
```

Figure I.6 Tables for project management

I.4 Course management

A training company wishes to create a database of its course information. The company delivers a number of seminars and training courses. Each course is delivered by one member of staff at some location (such as internal seminar room S10, Hilton Hotel Suite 100). The fees vary for each course and on the number of delegates a company sends. For example, if a company sends one person, the charge may be $1000. If the company sends two people, the first may be charged $1000, but the second may be charged $750. The course can be attended by a number of delegates, subject to some upper limit for the course. A delegate can register as an individual or through his/her company. The name of the employee who registers the delegate is recorded. An invoice is either sent to the delegate or to his/her company. The logical data model is shown in Figure I.7 and the associated tables in Figure I.8.

I.4.1 ER model

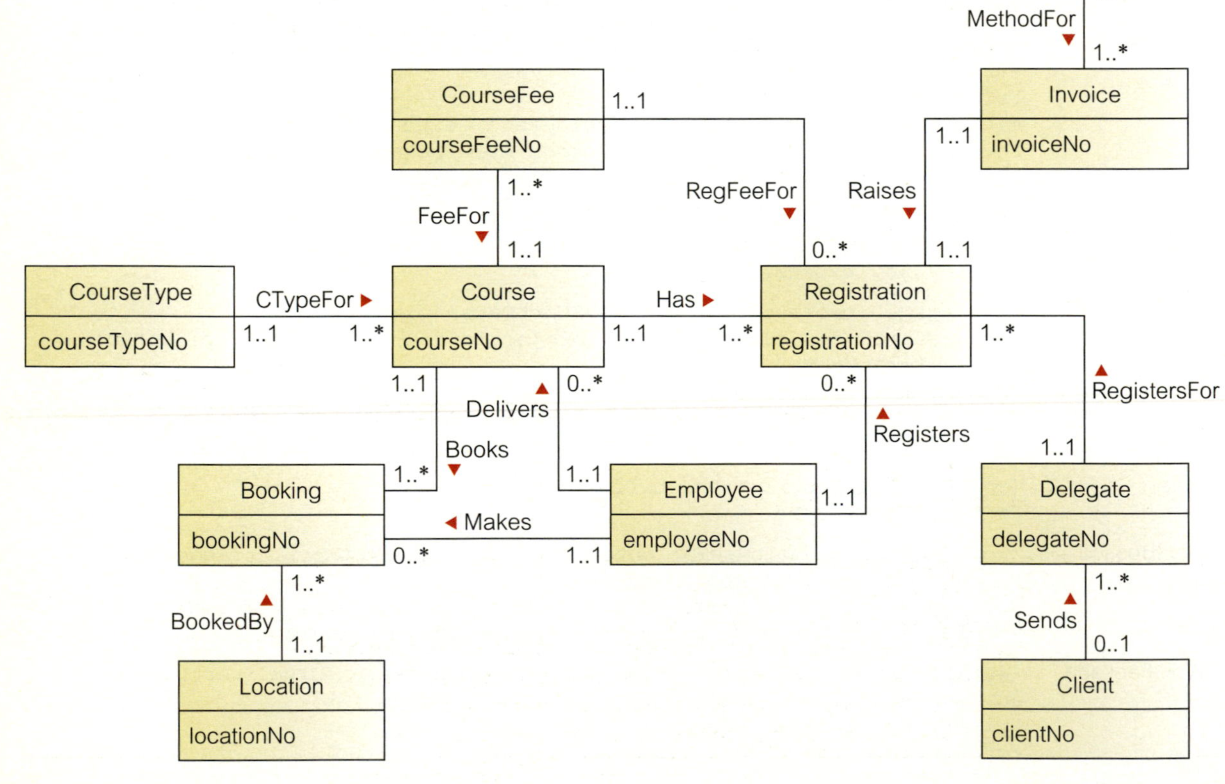

Figure I.7 ER model for course management

I.4.2 Tables

Client	As defined in I.3.2
Employee	As defined in I.1.2
PaymentMethod	As defined in I.1.2
Delegate	(delegateNo, delegateTitle, delegateFName, delegateLName, delegateStreet, delegateCity, delegateState, delegateZipCode, attTelNo, attFaxNo, attEmailAddress, clientNo) Primary Key delegateNo Foreign Key clientNo references Client(clientNo)
Booking	(bookingNo, bookingDate, locationNo, courseNo, bookingEmployeeNo) Primary Key bookingNo Foreign Key locationNo references Location(locationNo) Foreign Key courseNo references Course(courseNo) Foreign Key bookingEmployeeNo references Employee(employeeNo)
Course	(courseNo, courseName, courseDescription, startDate, startTime, endDate, endTime, maxDelegates, confirmed, delivererEmployeeNo, courseTypeNo) Primary Key courseNo Foreign Key delivererEmployeeNo references Employee(employeeNo) Foreign Key courseTypeNo references CourseType(courseTypeNo)
CourseFee	(courseFeeNo, feeDescription, fee, courseNo) Primary Key courseFeeNo Foreign Key courseNo references Course(courseNo)
CourseType	(courseTypeNo, courseTypeDescription) Primary Key courseTypeNo
Invoice	(invoiceNo, dateRaised, datePaid, creditCardNo, holdersName, expiryDate, registrationNo, pMethodNo) Primary Key invoiceNo Foreign Key registrationNo references Registration(registrationNo) Foreign Key pMethodNo references PaymentMethod(pMethodNo)
Location	(locationNo, locationName, maxSize) Primary Key locationNo
Registration	(registrationNo, registrationDate, delegateNo, courseFeeNo, registerEmployeeNo, courseNo) Primary Key registrationNo Foreign Key delegateNo references Delegate(delegateNo) Foreign Key courseFeeNo references CourseFee(courseFeeNo) Foreign Key registerEmployeeNo references Employee(employeeNo) Foreign Key courseNo references Course(courseNo)

Figure I.8 Tables for course management

I.5 Human resource management

An HRM department wishes to create a database to monitor its employees. The company is divided into a number of departments, and employees are assigned to one department. The department has a designated Manager who has overall responsibility for the department and the employees in the department. However, to help manage the department, a number of employees are nominated to supervise groups of staff. When a new employee joins the company, information on previous work history and qualifications are required. On a regular basis, each employee is required to undergo a review, which is normally carried out by the Manager, but may be delegated to a nominated representative.

The company has defined a number of position types, such as Manager, Business Analyst, Salesman, Secretary, and each type has a number of grades associated with it, which for most non-senior positions determines the employee's salary. At a senior level, salary is negotiable. Posts are allocated to a department depending on its workload. For example, a department may be allocated two new Business Analyst posts. A post will be filled by one employee, although over time employees will fill a number of different posts.

The logical data model is shown in Figure I.9 and the associated tables in Figure I.10.

I.5.1 ER model

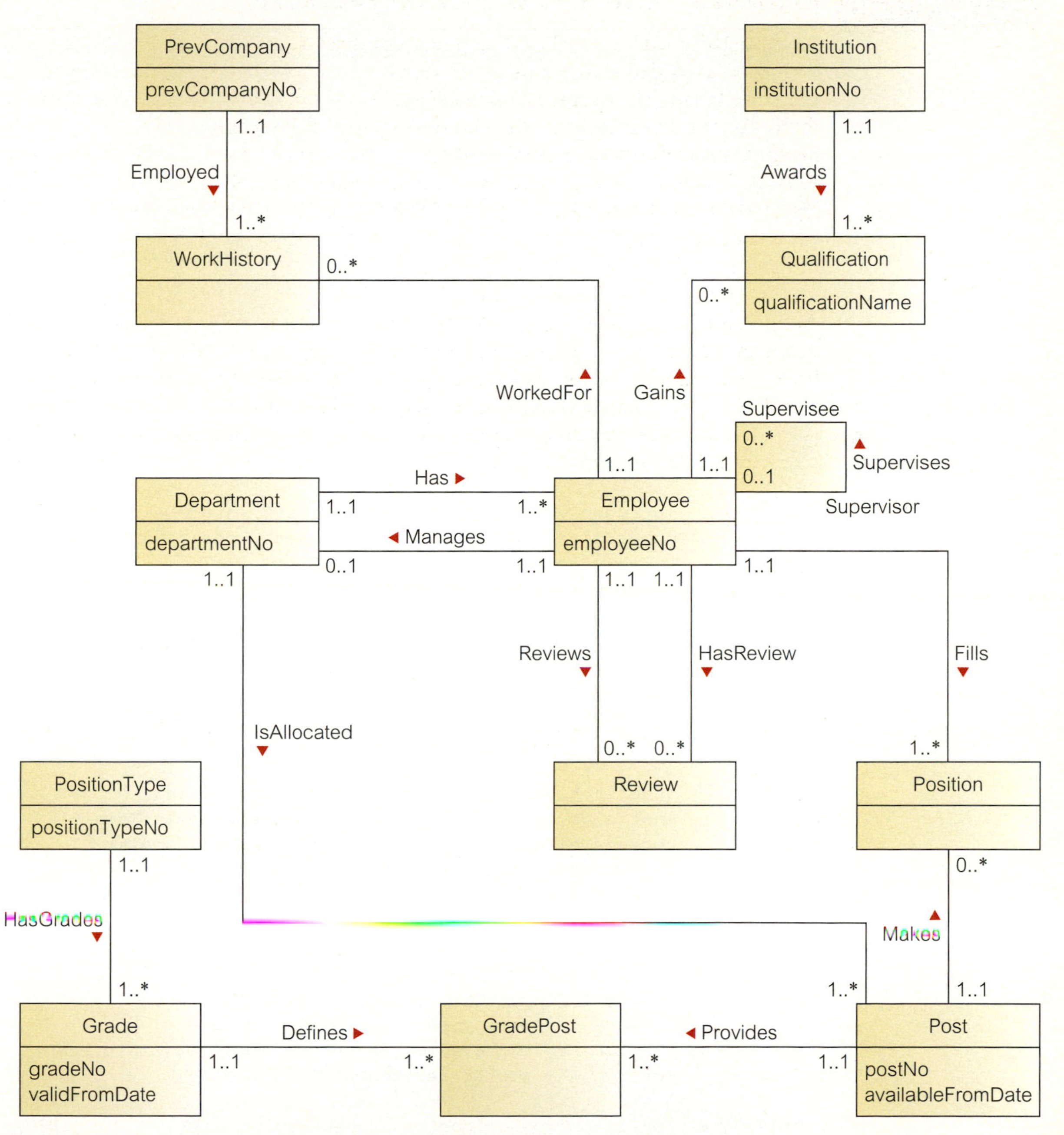

Figure I.9 ER model for human resource management

I.5.2 Tables

Table	Definition
Department	(departmentNo, departmentName, deptLocation, managerEmployeeNo) Primary Key departmentNo Foreign Key managerEmployeeNo references Employee(employeeNo)
Employee	(employeeNo, title, firstName, middleName, lastName, address, workTelExt, homeTelNo, emailAddress, socialSecurityNumber, DOB, position, sex, salary, dateStarted, dateLeft, departmentNo, supervisorEmployeeNo) Primary Key employeeNo Alternate Key socialSecurityNumber Foreign Key departmentNo references Department(departmentNo) Foreign Key supervisorEmployeeNo references Employee(employeeNo)
Grade	(gradeNo, validFromDate, validToDate, gradeDescription, gradeSalary, noDaysLeaveEntitlement, positionTypeNo) Primary Key gradeNo, validFromDate Foreign Key positionTypeNo references PositionType(positionTypeNo)
GradePost	(gradeNo, postNo) Primary Key gradeNo, postNo Foreign Key gradeNo references Grade(gradeNo) Foreign Key postNo references Post(postNo)
Institution	(institutionNo, institutionName, instAddress, instTelNo, instFaxNo, instWebAddress, contactName, contactTelNo, contactFaxNo, contactEmailAddress) Primary Key institutionNo Alternate Key institutionName Alternate Key instTelNo Alternate Key instFaxNo
Position	(employeeNo, postNo, startDate, endDate) Primary Key employeeNo, postNo, startDate Foreign Key employeeNo references Employee(employeeNo) Foreign Key postNo references Post(postNo)
PositionType	(positionTypeNo, positionTypeDescription) Primary Key positionTypeNo

```
Post          (postNo, availableFromDate, availableToDate,
              postDescription, salariedHourly, fullPartTime,
              temporaryPermanent, freeLaborStandardsActExempt,
              departmentNo)
              Primary Key postNo, availableFromDate
              Foreign Key departmentNo references
              Department(departmentNo)

PrevCompany   (prevCompanyNo, pCompanyName, pCompanyStreet,
              pCompanyCity, pCompanyState, pCompanyZipCode,
              pCompanyTelNo, pCompanyFaxNo, pCompanyWebAddress,
              contactName, contactTelNo, contactFaxNo,
              contactEmailAddress)
              Primary Key prevCompanyNo
              Alternate Key pCompanyName
              Alternate Key pCompanyTelNo
              Alternate Key pCompanyFaxNo

Qualification (qualificationName, employeeNo, gradeObtained,
              startQualDate, endQualDate, institutionNo)
              Primary Key qualificationName, employeeNo
              Foreign Key employeeNo references Employee(employeeNo)
              Foreign Key institutionNo references
              Institution(institutionNo)

Review        (revieweeEmployeeNo, reviewerEmployeeNo, reviewDate,
              comments)
              Primary Key revieweeEmployeeNo, reviewerEmployeeNo,
              reviewDate
              Foreign Key revieweeEmployeeNo references
              Employee(employeeNo)
              Foreign Key reviewerEmployeeNo references
              Employee(employeeNo)

WorkHistory   (prevCompanyNo, employeeNo, prevPosition, prevGrade,
              prevSalary, prevLocation, prevResponsibilities)
              Primary Key prevCompanyNo, employeeNo
              Foreign Key prevCompanyNo references
              PrevCompany(prevCompanyNo)
              Foreign Key employeeNo references Employee(employeeNo)
```

Figure I.10 Tables for human resource management

I.6 Payroll management

A Payroll department wishes to create a database to monitor employees' salary payments. To calculate an employee's salary, Payroll need to take into consideration holidays taken against holiday entitlement, number of days sick leave in the pay period, bonuses, and deductions. An employee must specify how his/her salary should be paid, although this may change over time. Most employees are paid by electronic bank transfer, but some types of employees may be paid by cash or check. If payment is electronic, then a routing number and account type are required. Payment can only be made by one method. There are various reasons for deductions being made; for example, federal tax, state tax, medical plan, retirement plan, or cash advance.

The logical data model is shown in Figure I.11 and the associated tables in Figure I.12.

I.6.1 ER model

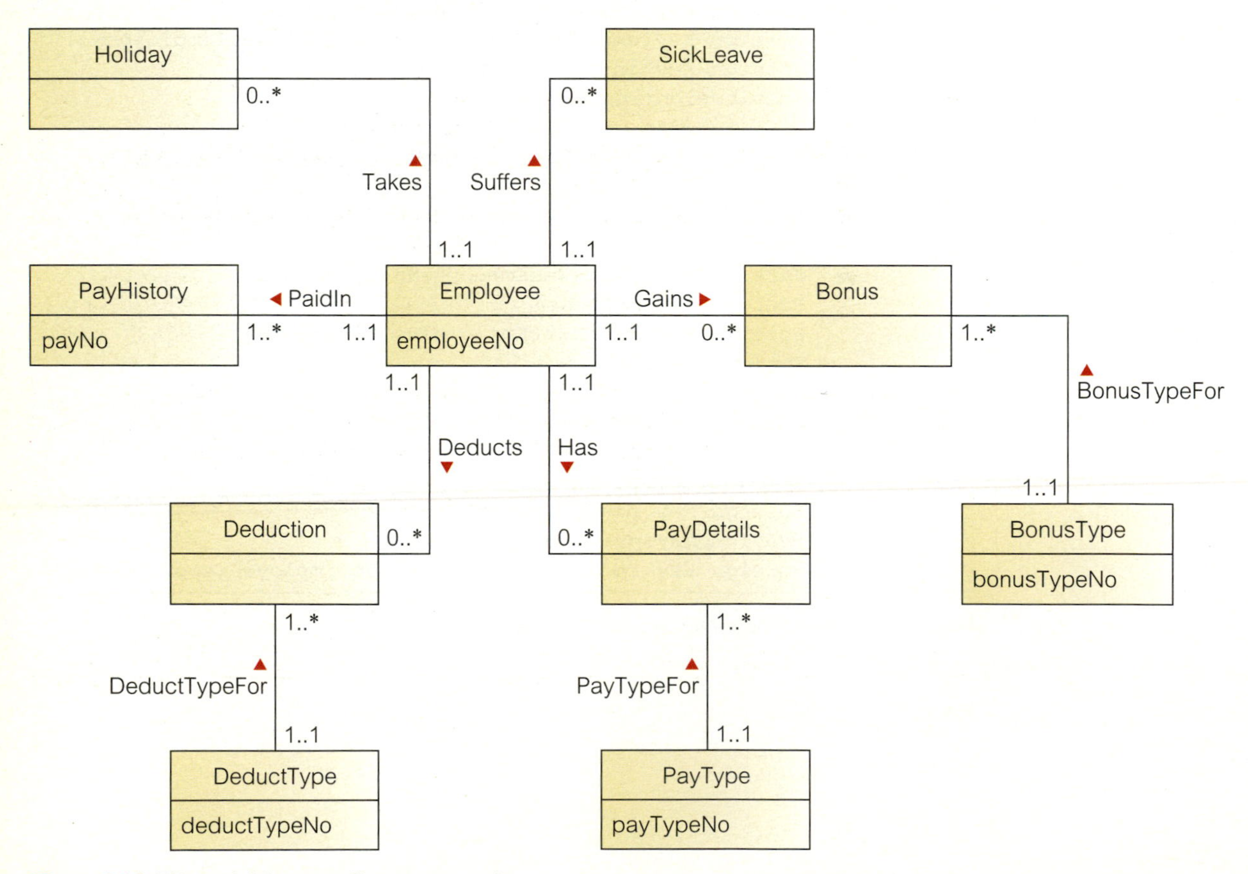

Figure I.11 ER model for payroll management

I.6.2 Tables

Employee	As defined in I.1.2

Bonus	`(employeeNo, bonusDate, bonusAmount, bonusTypeNo)`
	`Primary Key employeeNo, bonusDate`
	`Foreign Key employeeNo references Employee(employeeNo)`
	`Foreign Key bonusTypeNo references`
	`BonusType(bonusTypeNo)`

DeductType	`(bonusTypeNo, bonusDescription)` `Primary Key bonusTypeNo`

Deduction	`(employeeNo, deductDate, deductAmount, deductTypeNo)`
	`Primary Key employeeNo, deductDate`
	`Foreign Key employeeNo references Employee(employeeNo)`
	`Foreign Key deductTypeNo references`
	`DeductType(deductTypeNo)`

DeductType	`(deductTypeNo, deductDescription)` `Primary Key deductTypeNo`

Holiday	`(employeeNo, startDate, endDate)`
	`Primary Key employeeNo, startDate`
	`Foreign Key employeeNo references Employee(employeeNo)`

PayDetails	`(employeeNo, startDate, routingNumber, accountType,`
	`bankName, bankAddress, payTypeNo)`
	`Primary Key employeeNo, startDate`
	`Foreign Key employeeNo references Employee(employeeNo)`
	`Foreign Key payTypeNo references PayType(payTypeNo)`

PayHistory	`(payNo, employeeNo, payDate, checkNumber, payAmount)`
	`Primary Key payNo`
	`Foreign Key employeeNo references Employee(employeeNo)`

PayType	`(payTypeNo, payTypeDescription)` `Primary Key payTypeNo`

SickLeave	`(employeeNo, startDate, endDate, reason)`
	`Primary Key employeeNo, startDate`
	`Foreign Key employeeNo references Employee(employeeNo)`

Figure I.12 Tables for payroll management

Glossary

Abstraction. The process of identifying the essential aspects of an entity and ignoring the unimportant properties.

Access method. The steps involved in storing and retrieving records from a file.

Active Server Pages (ASP). A server-side scripting language developed by Microsoft.

***Ad hoc* query**. 'Spur-of-the-moment' questions that are asked of the database.

Alias. An alternative name given to an attribute. In SQL, you may substitute an alias for an attribute.

Allocation schema. A description of how tables have been allocated about the various sites in a distributed DBMS.

Alternate keys (ER/relational model). The candidate keys that are not selected as the primary key of the entity/table.

Anomalies. See *Update anomalies.*

Application design. A stage of the database system development lifecycle that involves designing the user interface and the application programs that use and process the database.

Application server. Handles the business logic and data processing layer in a three-tier client–server architecture.

Associations discovery. Identifies common sets of items (frequent item sets) and association rules for those sets.

Associative query. A declarative statement with selection based on one or more predicates.

Asynchronous (replication). Replicated data is updated some time after the source data is updated. The delay in regaining consistency may range from a few seconds to several hours or even days.

Atomicity. The 'all or nothing' property. A transaction is an indivisible unit that is either performed in its entirety or it is not performed at all. It is the responsibility of the recovery subsystem of the DBMS to ensure atomicity.

Attribute (ER model). A property of an entity or a relationship.

Attribute (relational model). An attribute is a named column of a relation.

Attribute inheritance. The process by which a member of a subclass may possess subclass-specific attributes, and inherit those attributes associated with the superclass.

Authentication. A mechanism that determines whether a user is who he or she claims to be.

Authorization. The granting of a right or privilege that enables a subject to have legitimate access to a database system or a database system's object.

Availability. Broadly speaking, availability is concerned with whether a system is continuously available during a given time period. See also *reliability*.

Background IP. See *Intellectual property (IP)*.

Backup. The process of periodically taking a copy of the database and log file (and possibly programs) onto offline storage media. A *full backup* is a backup of all of the data in the database; an *incremental backup* is a backup of all of the data that has changed since the last backup; a *differential backup* is a backup of all of the data that has changed since the last full backup.

Backup window. A time period during which the database can be backed up.

Base table. A named table whose records are physically stored in the database.

Binary relationship. An ER term used to describe a relationship between *two* entities. For example, `DistributionCenter` *Has* `Staff`.

Bottom-up approach (to database design). A design philosophy that begins by identifying individual design components and then aggregates these components into larger units. In database design, you start at the bottom level by identifying the attributes and then group the attributes together to form tables that represent entities and relationships.

Browser. See *Web browser*.

Business intelligence (BI). The processes for collecting and analyzing data, the technology used in these processes, and the information obtained from these processes with the purpose of facilitating corporate decision making.

Business-to-business (B2B). Electronic commerce between businesses.

Business-to-consumer (B2C). Electronic commerce between a business and a consumer.

Candidate key (ER/relational model). A superkey that contains only the minimum number of attributes/columns necessary for unique identification.

Cardinality. Describes the number of possible relationships for each participating entity.

Centralized approach (to database design). The requirements for each user view are merged into a single set of requirements for the new database application. A data model representing all user views is created during the database design stage.

Chasm trap. Occurs between related entities that are not directly connected and the indirect pathway that connects them includes partial participation. This means that certain entity occurrences that are related have no means of connection.

Checkpoint. A point of synchronization between the database and the transaction log file. All buffers are force-written to secondary storage.

Class. A collection of objects that have the same attributes and methods.

Click stream. A web or application log that traces where and when a user clicks the links on a web site or application.

Client. A software application that requests services from one or more servers. See also *Two-tier/Three-tier client–server architecture*.

Cluster. A group of one or more tables physically stored together because they share common columns and are often used together. With related records being physically stored together, disk access time is improved. The related columns of the tables in a cluster, called the *cluster key*, is stored only once, and so clusters store a set of tables more efficiently than if the tables were stored individually (not clustered).

Clustering field. Any nonkey field in a record that is used to cluster (group together) the rows that have a common value for this field.

Clustering index. An index defined on a clustering field of a file. A file can have at most one primary index or one clustering index. See also *primary index* and *secondary index*.

Cold fusion. A server-side scripting engine that operates on special tags that extend HTML.

Column (relational model). Same as *attribute*.

Common Gateway Interface (CGI). A Web server interface standard that uses script files to perform specific functions based on the client's parameters.

Complex object. An object that consists of several different objects in complex relationships.

Complex relationship. A relationship where the degree is higher than binary.

Composite attribute. An attribute composed of multiple single components.

Composite key. A primary key that contains more than one column.

Conceptual database design. The process of constructing a model of the data used in an organization independent of *all* physical considerations.

Conceptual level. The community view of the database, as defined in the ANSI-SPARC database architecture. This level describes *what* data is stored in the database and the relationships among the data.

Conceptual schema. A description of the conceptual level of the database. There is one conceptual schema for the entire database. See also *External schema* and *Internal schema*.

Concurrency control. The process of managing simultaneous operations on the database without having them interfere with one another.

Concurrency transparency. Provided by the DDBMS if the results of all concurrent transactions (distributed and non-distributed) execute *independently* and are logically *consistent* with the results that are obtained if the transactions are executed one at a time, in some arbitrary serial order.

Confidentiality. The mechanism for ensuring that data or information is accessible only to those authorized to have access.

Consistency (of transactions). A transaction must transform the database from one consistent state to another consistent state. It is the responsibility of both the DBMS and the application developers to ensure consistency. The DBMS can ensure consistency by enforcing all the integrity constraints that have been specified on the database schema.

Constraint. A consistency rule that the database is not permitted to violate.

Consumer-to-consumer (C2C). Electronic commerce between consumers.

Copyright. Provides an exclusive (legal) right for a set period of time to reproduce and distribute a literary, musical, audiovisual, or other 'work' of authorship.

Cursor (SQL). Allows the rows of a query result to be accessed one at a time. In effect, the cursor acts as a pointer to a particular row of the query result. The cursor can be advanced by one to access the next row. A cursor must be *declared* and *opened* before it can be used, and it must be *closed* to deactivate it after it is no longer required. Once the cursor has been opened, the rows of the query result can be retrieved one at a time using a FETCH statement, as opposed to a SELECT statement.

Data. Raw (unprocessed) facts that have some relevancy to an individual or organization.

Data administration. The management and control of the company data, including database planning, development and maintenance of standards, policies and procedures, and conceptual and logical database design.

Data allocation. The process of deciding where to locate data in a distributed system.

Data conversion and loading. A stage of the database system development lifecycle that involves preparing any data (where applicable) into a form suitable for transferring into the new database.

Data definition language (DDL). The language used to define a database, such as creating, altering, and dropping tables and views.

Data dictionary. See *system catalog*.

Data file. On secondary storage, this is the file that contains the logical records.

Data independence. The separation of data descriptions from the applications that use the data. This means that if new data structures are added to the database or existing structures in the database are modified then the application programs that use the database are unaffected, provided they do not directly depend upon what has been modified.

Data manipulation language (DML). The language used to define, to maintain, and to query a database, including insert, update, delete, and querying commands.

Data mart. A subset of a data warehouse that supports the requirements of a particular department or business area.

Data mining. The process of extracting valid, previously unknown, comprehensible, and actionable information from large databases and using it to make crucial business decisions.

Data model. An integrated collection of concepts for describing data, relationships between data, and constraints on the data used by an organization.

Data ownership. In a distributed system, this relates to which site has the privilege to update replicated data. The main types of ownership are master/slave, workflow, and update-anywhere (sometimes referred to as *peer-to-peer* or *symmetric replication*).

Data redundancy. Same as *redundant data*.

Data replication. The copying and maintenance of data on multiple servers.

Data security. Covers access and use of database objects (such as tables and views) and the actions that users can have on the objects.

Data warehouse. A database system that is designed to support decision-making by presenting an integrated view of corporate data that is copied from disparate operational data sources.

Database. A shared collection of logically related data (and a description of this data) designed to meet the information needs of an organization.

Database administration. The management and control of the physical realization of a database application, including physical database design and implementation, setting security and integrity controls, monitoring system performance and reorganizing the database as necessary.

Database application. A computer program that interacts with the database by issuing an appropriate request (typically one or more SQL statements) to the DBMS.

Database buffers. An area of memory that the DBMS uses to read in data from disk and write data to disk.

Database design. A stage of the database system development lifecycle that involves creating a design for a database that will support the organization's mission statement and mission objectives for the required database.

Data dictionary. See *System catalog*.

Database instance. The data in the database at any particular point in time.

Database integrity. Refers to the correctness and consistency of stored data. Integrity is usually expressed in terms of constraints.

Database Management System (DBMS). A software system that enables users to define, create, and maintain the database, and provides controlled access to this database.

Database planning. The management activities that allow the stages of the database system development lifecycle to be realized as efficiently and effectively as possible.

Database schema. An overall description of a database.

Database security. The mechanisms that protect the database against intentional or accidental threats. RDBMSs generally provide two types of security: *data security* and *system security*.

Database server. Same as server (see *Two-tier/Three-tier client–server architecture*.)

Database system. The collection of database applications that interact with the database along with the DBMS and the database itself.

Database system development lifecycle (DSDL). An ordered list of stages that describe the appropriate techniques and tools to use in the development of a database system. The stages include database planning, systems definition, requirements collection and analysis, database design, DBMS selection, application design, prototyping, implementation, data conversion and loading, testing, and operational maintenance.

DBMS engine. Same as server (see *Two-tier/Three-tier client–server architecture*.)

DBMS selection. A stage of the database system development lifecycle that involves the selection of an appropriate DBMS to support the database system.

DBMS transparency. Hides the knowledge that the local DBMSs in a heterogeneous DDBMS may be different.

Deadlock. An impasse that may result when two (or more) transactions are each waiting for locks to be released that are held by the other.

Degree of a relationship. The number of participating entities in a relationship.

DeMilitarized Zone (DMZ). A special, restricted network that is established between two firewalls.

Denormalization. Formally, the term refers to a change to the structure of a base table, such that the new table is in a lower normal form than the original table. However, the term is also used more loosely to refer to situations where we combine two tables into one new table, where the new table is in the same normal form but contains more nulls than the original tables.

Derived attribute. An attribute that represents a value that is derivable from the value of a related attribute, or a set of attributes, not necessarily in the same entity.

Derived fragment. A horizontal fragment that is based on the horizontal fragmentation of a parent table.

Design methodology. A structured approach that uses procedures, techniques, tools, and documentation aids to support and facilitate the process of design.

Dimension table (dimensional model). Contains the attributes that set the context for the queries on the data held in the fact table. Each dimension table has a simple (non-composite) primary key that corresponds exactly to one of the components of the composite key in the fact table. See also *Fact table*.

Dimensionality modeling. A technique that aims to build a data model that has a consistent and intuitive structure to facilitate efficient multi-dimensional analysis of data.

Disjoint constraint. Describes the relationship between members of subclasses and indicates whether it is possible for a member of a superclass to be a member of one, or more than one, subclass.

Distributed database. A logically interrelated collection of shared data (and a description of this data) physically distributed over a computer network.

Distributed DBMS (DDBMS). A software system that permits the management of a distributed database and makes the distribution transparent to users.

Distributed processing. A centralized database that can be accessed over a computer network.

Distributed request. A database request that allows a single SQL statement to access data at several remote sites in a distributed DBMS.

Distribution transparency. The user perceives the distributed database as a single, logical entity. If a DDBMS exhibits distribution transparency, then the user does not need to know the data is fragmented (*fragmentation transparency*) or the location of data items (*location transparency*).

Distributed unit of work. A database request that allows a transaction (consisting of several SQL statements) to access data at several remote sites in a distributed DBMS.

Document Type Definition (DTD). Defines the valid syntax (rules of the language) of an XML document.

Domain. The set of allowable values for one or more attributes.

Durability (of transaction). The effects of a successfully completed (committed) transaction are permanently recorded in the database and must not be lost because of a subsequent failure.

Dynamic Web page. A Web page that is dynamically constructed when the client requests the page (as opposed to a static Web page, which physically exists at the time of the request).

Electronic commerce (eCommerce). The distribution, buying, selling, and marketing of physical and information goods and services accomplished using computer networks such as the Internet.

Electronic Data Interchange (EDI). The computer-to-computer transfer of business documents over a network using a standard format.

Encapsulation. An object contains both the data structure and the set of operations that can be used to manipulate it.

Encryption. The encoding of data by a special algorithm that renders the data unreadable by any program without the decryption key.

Enhanced entity-relationship (EER). The original ER model with additional semantic concepts such as specialization/generalization.

Enterprise resource planning (ERP) system. An application layer built on top of a DBMS that integrates all the business functions of an organization, such as manufacturing, sales, finance, marketing, shipping, invoicing, and human resources. Popular ERP systems are SAP R/3 from SAP and PeopleSoft from Oracle.

Entity. A set of objects with the same properties that are identified by a user or organization as having an independent existence.

Entity integrity. In a base table, no column of a primary key can be null.

Entity occurrence. A uniquely identifiable object in an entity.

Entity–Relationship model. A detailed representation of entities, attributes, and relationships for an organization.

Ethics. A set of principles of right conduct, or a theory or system of moral values.

Exclusive lock. A lock that is issued when a transaction requests permission to update a data item if no other locks are held on that data item by another transaction. If a transaction has an exclusive lock on a data item, it can both read and update the item.

External level. A users' view of the database, as defined in the ANSI-SPARC database architecture. This level describes that part of a database that is relevant to each user.

External schema. A description of the external level of the database. There is one external schema for each user view. See also *Conceptual schema* and *Internal schema*.

Fact-finding. The formal process of using techniques such as interviews and questionnaires to collect facts about systems, processes, requirements, and preferences.

Fact table (dimensional model). Contains the attributes that hold the facts (measurements) about the events that are being queried. Each fact table has a composite primary key that is made up of the foreign keys of the associated dimension tables. See Dimension table.

Failure transparency. The DDBMS must ensure the atomicity of the global transaction, which means ensuring that subtransactions of the global transaction either all commit or all abort. In addition, the DDBMS must ensure that once a global transaction has committed, the changes are *durable*.

Fan trap. Occurs between related entities that are not directly connected and the indirect pathway that connects them includes two 1:* relationships that fan out from a central entity. This means that certain entity occurrences that are related can only be connected using a pathway that can be ambiguous.

Fat client. A client computer that is responsible for processing the user interface as well as the business and data logic. The processing requirements of a computer can be significant so a high-specification computer is necessary to run the necessary software.

Federated DBMS. A type of DDBMS in which the local DBMSs operate independently but have decided to participate in a federation to make their local data sharable. Each DBMS determines which parts of its database will be made available to other DBMSs. The local DBMSs are not fully autonomous because they need to be modified to allow the exchange of data with each other.

Field (relational model). Same as *attribute*.

File. A named collection of related records stored on secondary storage.

File-based system. A collection of application programs that perform services for the end-users, such as the production of reports. Each program defines and manages its own data.

File organization. A way of arranging the records in a file when the file is stored on disk.

Firewall. A server or router with two or more network interfaces and special software that filters or selectively blocks messages traveling between networks.

First normal form (1NF). A table in which the intersection of every column and record contains only *one* value.

Foreground IP. See *Intellectual property (IP)*.

Foreign key. A column, or set of columns, within one table that matches the candidate key of some (possibly the same) table.

Fourth-generation language (4GL). A nonprocedural language, such as SQL, that only requires the user to define *what* must be done; the 4GL translates the *what* into details of *how* this should be executed.

Fragment. A subset of a table. See *horizontal fragment*, *derived fragment*, *mixed fragment*, and *vertical fragment*.

Fragmentation schema. A description of how tables have been fragmented in a distributed DBMS.

Fragmentation transparency. The user does not need to know that the data in a distributed database is fragmented. As a result, database accesses are based on the global schema, so the user does not need to specify fragment names or data locations.

Full functional dependency. A condition in which a column is functionally dependent on a composite key but not on any subset of that key. If a and b are columns of a table, b is fully determined by a if b is not determined by any subset of a.

Functional dependency. Describes the relationship between columns in a table and indicates how columns relate to one another. For example, consider a table with columns a and b, where column a determines column b (denoted a → b). If we know the value of a, we find only *one* value of b in all the records that has this value for a, at any moment in time. However, for a given value of b there may be several different values of a.

Fuzzy read. See *Nonrepeatable read.*

Gateway. A type of middleware software that is used to convert the language/model of one type of system into the language/model of a different type of system.

Generalization. The process of minimizing the differences between entities by identifying their common features.

Generalization hierarchy. Same as *type hierarchy*.

Global data model. A data model that represents the data requirements of all user views of an organization.

Government-to-business (G2B). Electronic commerce between government and a business.

Government-to-consumer (G2C). Electronic commerce between government and a consumer.

Heterogeneous DDBMS. A DDBMS with sites that run different DBMS products, which need not be based on the same underlying data model, and so the system may be composed of relational, network, hierarchical, and object-oriented DBMSs.

Hierarchical DBMS. A first-generation DBMS that stores records in an inverted tree structure.

Homogeneous DDBMS. A DDBMS where all sites use the identical DBMS product.

Horizontal fragment. Consists of a subset of the records of a table.

Horizontal partitioning. Distributing the records of a table across a number of (smaller) tables.

Hybrid fragment. See *Mixed fragment.*

Hypertext Markup Language (HTML). A document-formatting language used to design Web pages.

Hypertext Transfer Protocol (HTTP). The communication protocol used between a browser and Web server.

Implementation. A stage of the database system development lifecycle that involves the physical realization of the database and application designs.

Index. A data structure that allows a DBMS to locate particular records in a file more quickly, and thereby speed up response to user queries.

Index file. On secondary storage, this is the file that contains the index records.

Index-organized table. The data for a table is held in an associated index. Changes to the table data, such as adding new records, updating records, or deleting records, result only in updating the index. Because data records are stored in the index, index-organized tables provide faster key-based access to table data for queries that involve exact match or range search or both.

Indexing field. The column, or columns, of the table that are used to order the values in the index file.

Information. Data that has been processed or given some structure that brings meaning to an individual or organization.

Information hiding. The external aspects of an object are separated from its internal details, which are hidden from the outside world.

Information system. The resources that enable the collection, management, control, and dissemination of data/information throughout an organization.

Inheritance. See *attribute inheritance*.

Integrity constraints. Rules that define or constrain some aspect of the data used by an organization.

Intellectual property (IP). The product of human creativity in the industrial, scientific, literary, and artistic fields. There are two main types of IP: *background IP* is IP that exists before an activity takes place; *foreground IP* is IP that is generated during an activity.

Internal level. The physical representation of a database on a computer, as defined in the ANSI-SPARC database architecture. This level describes *how* data is stored in a database.

Internal controls. A set of rules an organization adopts to ensure policies and procedures are not violated, data is properly secured and reliable, and operation can be carried out efficiently

Internal schema. A description of the internal level of a database. There is one internal schema for the entire database. See also *Conceptual schema* and *External schema*.

IS-A hierarchy. Same as *type hierarchy*.

Isolation (of transactions). Transactions execute independently of one another. In other words, the partial effects of incomplete transactions should not be visible to other transactions.

Journal file. See *Log file*.

Journaling. The process of keeping and maintaining a log file (or journal) of all changes made to the database to enable recovery to be undertaken effectively in the event of a failure. See also *log file*.

Legacy system. A term used to refer to an older, and usually inferior, system (such as a file-based, hierarchical, or network system).

Local autonomy. The degree of independence for the local DBMSs in a distributed DBMS.

Local data model. A data model that represents the data requirements of one or more, but not all, user views of an organization.

Local mapping transparency. The user needs to specify both fragment names and the location of fragments when accessing data in a distributed database, taking into consideration any replication that may exist.

Location transparency. The user must know how the data in a distributed database has been fragmented but does not have to know the location of the data.

Lock granularity. The level of locking used by a transaction. Locks are requested on a particular data item but the data item can be the entire database, or a particular table, page, row, or an individual field (attribute).

Locking. A procedure used to control concurrent access to data. When one transaction is accessing the database, a lock may deny access to other transactions to prevent incorrect results. See also *exclusive lock* and *shared lock*.

Log file. A file used by a DBMS to recover from failure. The file contains the before-images and after-images of changes made to the database. The before-images can be used to undo changes to the database; the after-images can be used to redo changes to the database.

Logical data independence. Refers to the immunity of the external schemas to changes in the conceptual schema.

Logical database design. The process of constructing a model of the data used in an organization based on a specific data model, but independent of a particular DBMS and other physical considerations.

Message. A request from one object (the sender) to another object (the receiver) asking the second object to execute one of its methods. The sender and receiver may be the same object.

Metadata. Data about data; see *system catalog*.

Method. The implementation of a 'real world' action (behavior) associated with an object.

Micropayment system. Systems that support the transfer of small payment amounts (generally less than US$1.00) with low per transaction costs between parties.

Middleware. Computer software that connects software components or applications. It is used most often in complex distributed applications.

Mission objective. Identifies a particular task that a database system must support.

Mission statement. Defines the major aims of a database system.

Mixed fragment. Consists of a horizontal fragment that is subsequently vertically fragmented, or a vertical fragment that is then horizontally fragmented.

Mobile commerce (mCommerce). Accessing eCommerce products and services using mobile devices.

Mobile database. A database that is portable and physically separate from a centralized database server but is capable of communicating with that server from remote sites allowing the sharing of corporate data.

Multi-database system (MDBS). A distributed DBMS in which each site maintains complete autonomy. An MDBS resides transparently on top of existing database and file systems, and presents a single database to its users.

Multi-dimensional data. Data that can be characterized through many different views. (For example, multi-dimensional data like DVD sales can be viewed in terms of properties associated with DVDs, such as genre, and/or properties associated with buyers, such as home address and so on.)

Multiplicity. Defines the number of occurrences of one entity that may relate to a single occurrence of an associated entity.

Multi-valued attribute. An attribute that holds multiple values for an entity occurrence.

Navigational access. A procedure for processing the records in a file by navigating from one record to another by following the relationships in which the record participates.

Network DBMS. A first-generation DBMS in which data is represented as a collection of *records* and one-to-many relationships are represented as *sets* (one owner, many members). A record may be an owner in any number of sets, and a member in any number of sets. A network DBMS supports *navigational access*.

Network security. Concerned with the protection of servers from intruders by implementing a network security architecture.

Nonkey attribute/column. An attribute/column that is not part of a key.

Nonrepeatable read. A transaction T re-reads a data item it has previously read, but in between another transaction has modified it. Thus, T receives two different values for the same data item.

Normal forms. Stages in the normalization process. The first three normal forms are called *first normal form (1NF)*, *second normal form (2NF)*, and *third normal form (3NF)*.

Normalization. A technique for producing a set of tables with desirable properties that supports the requirements of a user or organization.

Null. Represents a value for a column that is currently unknown or is not applicable for this record.

Object. A uniquely identifiable entity that contains both the attributes that describe the state of a 'real world' object and the actions (behavior) that are associated with it.

Object identifier (OID). A unique identifier for each object in the system. The OID is: system-generated; unique to that object; invariant; independent of the values of its attributes (that is, its state); invisible to the user (ideally).

Object-Oriented Data Model (OODM). A data model that captures the semantics of objects supported in object-oriented programming.

Object-Oriented Database (OODB). A persistent and sharable repository of objects defined in an object-oriented data model.

Object-Oriented DBMS (OODBMS). A manager of an object-oriented database.

Object-Relational DBMS (ORDBMS). A set of extensions to a relational DBMS to incorporate some concept of 'object'. There is no single ORDBMS, rather a number of such systems, whose characteristics depend on the way and the degree to which the extensions have been made.

OnLine Analytical Processing (OLAP). Supports advanced analysis of large volumes of multi-dimensional data that is aggregated (summarized) to various levels of detail.

OnLine Transaction Processing (OLTP). Database systems for business processes such as inventory control, customer invoicing, and point-of-sale. These systems generate operational data that is detailed, current, and subject to change. The OLTP systems are optimized for a high number of transactions that are predictable, repetitive, and update intensive. The OLTP data is organized according to the requirements of the transactions associated with the business applications and supports the day-to-day decisions of a large number of concurrent operational users.

Operational data store (ODS). A repository of current and integrated operational data used for analysis. It is often structured and supplied with data in the same way as the data warehouse, but may in fact act simply as a staging area for data to be moved into the warehouse.

Operational maintenance. A stage of the database system development lifecycle that involves monitoring and maintaining a system following installation.

Overloading. Allowing the name of a method to be reused within a class definition or across class definitions.

Overriding. The process of redefining a property (attribute or method) inherited from a superclass by a more specific implementation in a subclass.

Package (PL/SQL). A collection of procedures, functions, variables, and SQL statements that are grouped together and stored as a single program unit. A package has two parts: a specification and a body. A package's *specification* declares all public constructs of the package and the *body* defines all constructs (public and private) of the package, and so implements the specification. In this way, packages provide a form of encapsulation.

Partial dependency. Describes a relationship between columns in a table and indicates how columns relate to one another. If `a` and `b` are columns of a table, `b` is partially dependent on `a` if `b` is determined by a subset of `a`.

Participation constraint (EER model). Determines whether every occurrence in the superclass must participate as a member of a subclass.

Participation constraint (ER model). Describes whether all or only some entity occurrences participate in a relationship.

Patent. Provides an exclusive (legal) right for a set period of time to make, use, sell or import an invention.

Peer-to-peer (P2P). See *Consumer-to-consumer (C2C)*.

Performance transparency. Requires a DDBMS to perform as if it were a centralized DBMS; in other words, the DDBMS must determine the most cost-effective strategy to execute a transaction.

Phantom read. A transaction executes a query that retrieves a set of records from a table satisfying a certain predicate, re-executes the query at a later time, but finds that the retrieved set contains an additional (*phantom*) record that has been inserted by another transaction in the meantime.

Physical data independence. Refers to the immunity of the conceptual schema to changes in the internal schema.

Physical database design. The process of producing a description of the implementation of the database on secondary storage; it describes the base tables, file organizations, and indexes used to achieve efficient access to the data, and any associated integrity constraints and security restrictions.

Primary index. An index built on the ordering key field of the file, which is guaranteed to have a unique value in each record. A file can have at most one primary index or one clustering index. See also *clustering index* and *secondary index*.

Primary key (ER model). The candidate key that is selected to identify each entity occurrence.

Primary key (relational model). The candidate key that is selected to identify records uniquely within the table.

Privacy. The ability of an individual or group to stop data or information about themselves from becoming known to people other than those to whom they choose to give access.

Privileges. The actions that a user is permitted to carry out on a given base table or view.

Prototyping. A stage of the database system development lifecycle that involves building a working model of a database application.

QBE (Query-By-Example). A nonprocedural database language for relational DBMSs. QBE is a graphical 'point-and-click' way of querying a database.

RAID (Redundant Array of Inexpensive Disks) – a set, or array, of physical disk drives that appear to the database user (and programs) as if they form one large logical storage unit.

RDBMS. Relational DBMS – a DBMS built on the relational data model.

Recommender system. Software that attempts to predict what a user would like based on prior knowledge of the user's profile, or browsing or purchasing activity.

Record (relational model). Same as *tuple*.

Recovery control. The process of restoring the database to a correct state in the event of a failure.

Recursive relationship. A relationship where the same entity participates more than once in *different* roles. For example, `Staff` *`Supervises`* `Staff`.

Redundant data. Duplicated data that is stored in more than one table.

Reference type (SQL:2003). Can be used to define relationships between row types and uniquely identify a row within a table. A reference type value can be stored in one table and used as a direct reference to a specific row in some base table that has been defined to be of this type (similar to the notion of a pointer type in C/C++). In this respect, a reference type provides a similar functionality as the object identifier (OID) of OODBMSs.

Referential integrity. If a foreign key exists in a table, either the foreign key value must match a candidate key value of some record in its home table, or the foreign key value must be wholly null.

Relation. A relation is a table with columns and rows.

Relational algebra. A (high-level) procedural language: it can be used to tell a DBMS how to build a new table from one or more tables in a database.

Relational calculus. A non-procedural language: it can be used to formulate the definition of a table in terms of one or more tables.

Relational database. A collection of normalized tables.

Relational data model. A data model that represents data in the form of tables (or relations).

Relationship. A meaningful association among entities.

Relationship occurrence. A uniquely identifiable association between two entity occurrences.

Reliability. Broadly speaking, reliability is concerned with whether or not a system is running at a certain period in time. See also *availability*.

Remote request. A database request that allows a single SQL statement to access data at a single remote site in a distributed DBMS.

Remote unit of work. A database request that allows a transaction (consisting of several SQL statements) to access data at a single remote site in a distributed DBMS.

Replication. The process of generating and reproducing multiple copies of data at one or more sites.

Replication schema. A description of how fragments have been replicated in a distributed DBMS.

Replication server. A software system that handles the replication of data to remote sites.

Replication transparency. The user is unaware of the replication of fragments in a distributed database.

Requirements collection and analysis. A stage of the database system development lifecycle that involves collecting and analyzing information about the organization to be supported by a database system, and using this information to identify the requirements for the new database system.

Rigorous two-phase locking (2PL). A variation of the 2PL protocol where the release of all locks is left until the end of the transaction.

Ruby on Rails. A framework for creating database-driven web sites using Ruby programming language.

Row (relational model). Same as *tuple*.

Row type (SQL:2003). A sequence of field name/data type pairs that provides a data type to represent the types of rows in tables, so that complete rows can be stored in variables, passed as arguments to routines, and returned as return values from function calls. A row type can also be used to allow a column of a table to contain row values. In essence, the row is a table nested within a table.

Schedule. A particular sequencing of the operations from a set of concurrent transactions. A *serial schedule* is where one transaction must complete before another begins; other schedules are known as *nonserial schedules*.

Script. A small program containing statements written in some programming language (such as Javascript, VBScript, PHP, or Perl.)

Second normal form (2NF). A table that is already in 1NF and in which the values in each non-primary-key column can be worked out from the values in all the columns that make up the primary key.

Secondary index. An index that is defined on a non-ordering field of the data file. See also *primary index* and *clustering index*.

Security. See *Database security*.

Semi-structured data. Data that may be irregular or incomplete and have a structure that may change rapidly or unpredictably.

Serializability. A concurrency control approach that ensures that the selected order of operations in a set of concurrent transactions creates a final database state that would have been produced by some serial execution of the transactions.

Server. A software application that provides services to requesting clients. See also *Two-tier/Three-tier client–server architecture*.

Shared lock. A lock that is issued when a transaction requests permission to read a data item and no exclusive locks are held on that data item by another transaction. If a transaction has a shared lock on a data item, it can read the item but not update it.

Simple attribute. An attribute composed of a single component.

Single-valued attribute. An attribute that holds a single value for an entity occurrence.

Simple Object Access Protocol (SOAP). Based on XML, is used for communication over the Internet.

Specialization. The process of maximizing the differences between members of an entity by identifying their distinguishing characteristics.

Specialization hierarchy. Same as *type hierarchy*.

SQL (Structured Query Language). A nonprocedural database language for RDBMSs. In other words, you specify *what* information you require, rather than *how* to get it. SQL has been standardized by the International Standards Organization (ISO), making it both the formal and *de facto* standard language for defining and manipulating RDBMSs.

Star schema (or star join). A structure that has a fact table containing factual data in the center, surrounded by dimension tables containing reference data (which can be denormalized).

Static Web page. A Web page that physically exists at the time of the client's request (as opposed to a dynamic Web page, which has to be created at the time of the client's request).

Stored procedure and function (PL/SQL). See *Subprogram (PL/SQL)*.

Strong entity. An entity that is not dependent on the existence of another entity for its primary key.

Subclass. A distinct grouping of occurrences of an entity, which require to be represented in a data model. See also *Specialization* and *Generalization*.

Subprogram (PL/SQL). A named PL/SQL blocks that can take parameters and be invoked. PL/SQL has two types of subprograms called (*stored*) *procedures* and *functions*. Procedures and functions can take a set of parameters given to them by the calling program and perform a set of actions. Both can modify and return data passed to them as a parameter. The difference between a procedure and a function is that a function will always return a single value to the caller, whereas a procedure does not. Usually, procedures are used unless only one return value is needed.

Substitutability. In object-orientation, whenever an instance of a supertype is expected an instance of the subtype can be used in its place.

Superclass. An entity that includes one or more distinct groupings of its occurrences, which require to be represented in a data model. See also *Specialization and Generalization*.

Superkey (ER model). An attribute, or set of attributes, that uniquely identifies each entity occurrence.

Superkey (relational model). A column, or set of columns, that uniquely identifies a record within a table.

Supply chain. The flow of raw materials and components from and between suppliers that terminates at a manufacturer.

Synchronous (replication). Replicated data is updated immediately when the source data is updated (that is, as part of the enclosing transaction).

System catalog. Holds data about the structure of a database, users, applications, and so on.

System definition. A stage of the database system development lifecycle that involves defining the scope and boundary of the database system, including its major user views.

System security. Covers access and use of a database at the system level, such as a username and password.

Table (relational model). Same as *relation*.

Ternary relationship. A relationship between *three* entities. For example, the relationship `Registers` between `DistributionCenter`, `Staff`, and `Member`.

Testing. A stage of the database system development lifecycle that involves executing application programs with the intent of finding errors.

Thin client. A client computer that is responsible for processing the user interface and a small amount of business logic. The processing requirements placed on a computer is low so that a low-specification computer is adequate to run the necessary software.

Third-generation language (3GL). A procedural language, such as COBOL, C, C++, that requires the user (usually a programmer) to specify *what* must be done and also *how* it must be done.

Third normal form (3NF). A table that is already in 1NF and 2NF, and in which the values in all non-primary-key columns can be worked out from *only* the primary key (or candidate key) column(s) and no other columns.

Threat. Any situation or event, whether intentional or unintentional, that may adversely affect a system and consequently the organization.

Three-tier client–server architecture. Consists of a *client* that handles the user interface, an *application server* that handles the business logic and data processing layer, and a *database server* that runs the DBMS.

Timestamp. A unique identifier created by a DBMS that indicates the relative starting time of a transaction.

Timestamping. A concurrency control protocol that orders transactions in such a way that older transactions, transactions with *smaller* timestamps, get priority in the event of conflict.

Top-down approach (to database design). A design philosophy that begins by defining the main structures of a system and then moves to smaller units within those structures. In database design, you start at the top level by identifying the entities and relationships between the data, then you add more details, such as the information you want to hold about the entities and relationships (called attributes) and any constraints on the entities, relationships, and attributes.

Trademark. Provides an exclusive (legal) right to use a word, symbol, image, sound, or some other distinctive element that identifies the source of origin in connection with certain goods or services.

Transaction. An action, or series of actions, carried out by a single user or database application that accesses or changes the contents of the database.

Transaction Processing Monitor (TPM). A program that controls data transfer between clients and servers in order to provide a consistent environment for Online Transaction Processing (OLTP).

Transaction throughput. The number of transactions processed in a given time interval.

Transaction transparency. In a DDBMS environment this ensures that all transactions maintain the distributed database's integrity and consistency.

Transitive dependency. Describes a relationship between columns `a`, `b`, and `c`. If `a` determines `b` (`a` → `b`) and `b` determines `c` (`b` → `c`), then `c` is transitively dependent on `a` via `b` (provided that `b` or `c` does not determine `a`). If a transitive dependency exists on a primary key, the table is not in 3NF. The transitive dependency must be removed for a table to achieve 3NF.

Trigger (SQL). Defines an action that a database should take when some event occurs in the application. There are two types of triggers: *row-level* triggers that execute for each row of the table that is affected by the triggering event, and *statement-level* triggers that execute only once even if multiple rows are affected by the triggering event.

Tuple (relational model). A record of a *relation* (*table*).

Two-phase commit (2PC). A recovery protocol for distributed systems. 2PC operates in two phases: a *voting phase* and a *decision phase*. The coordinator of the distributed transaction asks all participant sites whether they are prepared to commit the transaction. If one participant votes to abort, or fails to respond within a timeout period, then the coordinator instructs all participants to abort the transaction. If all vote to commit, then the coordinator instructs all participants to commit the transaction. The global decision must be adopted by all participants.

Two-phase locking (2PL). A transaction follows the two-phase locking protocol if all locking operations precede the first unlock operation in the transaction.

Two-tier client–server architecture. Consists of a *client* program that handles the main business and data processing logic and interfaces with the user, and a *server* program that manages and controls access to the database.

Type hierarchy. The collection of an entity and its subclasses and their subclasses, and so on.

UML (Unified Modeling Language). The successor to a number of object-oriented analysis and design methods introduced in the 1980s and 1990s.

Unary (relationship). A (degree one) relationship that has a single participant (entity). Also known as a *recursive* relationship.

Universal Discovery, Description, and Integration (UDDI). A protocol used to register a Web service for prospective users.

Update anomalies. Inconsistencies that may arise when a user attempts to update a table that contains redundant data. There are three types of anomalies: insertion, deletion, and modification.

User view. Defines what is required of a database application from the perspective of a particular job (such as manager or supervisor) or business application area (such as marketing, personnel, or stock control).

Vertical fragment. Consists of a subset of the columns of a table.

Vertical partitioning. Distributing the columns of a table across a number of (smaller) tables (the primary key is duplicated to allow the original table to be reconstructed).

View. A 'virtual table' that does not actually exist in a database but is generated by the DBMS from the underlying base tables whenever it is accessed.

View integration approach (to database design). Requirements for each user view remain as separate lists. Data models representing each user view are created and then merged later during the database design stage.

Weak entity. An entity that is partially or wholly dependent on the existence of some other entity (or entities) for its primary key.

Web browser. The end-user application used to navigate the Internet. Runs on a client computer and requests services from a Web server.

Web server. The back-end application used to listen for and process client requests and send the requested Web resources back to the client.

Web service. A software system designed to support interoperable machine-to-machine interaction over a network.

Web Services Description Language (WSDL). Based on XML, is used to describe the Web service. WSDL adds a layer of abstraction between the interface and the implementation, providing a loosely-coupled service for future flexibility.

Write-ahead log protocol. Log file records are written *before* the corresponding writes to the database.

XML (eXtensible Markup Language). A meta-language (a language for describing other languages) that enables designers to create their own customized tags to provide functionality not available with HTML.

XML Schema. Defines the specific structure of an XML document including its organization and data types.

XQuery. A query language for XML.

References

ACM (1992). Association for Computing Machinery Code of Ethics and Professional Conduct. 16 October 1992. Available at http://www.acm.org/constitution/code.html

Astrahan M. M., Blasgen M. W., Chamberlin D. D., Eswaran K. P., Gray J. N., Griffith P. P., King W. F., Lorie R. A., McJones P. R., Mehl J. W., Putzolu G. R., Traiger I. L., Wade B. W., and Watson V. (1976). System R: Relational approach to database management. *ACM Trans. Database Systems*, **1**(2), 97–137

BCS (2001). The British Computer Society Code of Conduct. 5 September 2001. Available at http://www.bcs.org/upload/pdf/conduct.pdf

BCS (2004). The British Computer Society Code of Good Practice. 1 September 2004. http://www.bcs.org/upload/pdf/cop.pdf

Bennet S., McRobb S., and Farmer R. (1999). *Object-Oriented Systems Analysis and Design using UML*. London: McGraw-Hill

Bukhres O. A. and Elmagarmid A. K., eds (1996). *Object-Oriented Multidatabase Systems: A Solution for Advanced Applications*. Englewood Cliffs, NJ: Prentice-Hall

Buneman P., Davidson S., Hillebrand G., and Suciu D. (1996). A Query Language and Optimization Techniques for Unstructured Data. *In Proc. ACM SIGMOD Conf.* Montreal, Canada

Buretta M. (1997). *Data Replication: Tools and Techniques for Managing Distributed Information*. New York, NY: Wiley Computer Publishing

Burns E. (2006). Online Retail Sales Grew in 2005. comSource, 5 January 2006. Available at http://www.clickz.com/stats/sectors/retailing/article.php/3575456#table1

Cattell R. G. G., ed. (2000). *The Object Database Standard: ODMG Release 3.0*. San Mateo, CA: Morgan Kaufmann

Chamberlin D., Robie J., and Florescu D. (2000). Quilt: an XML Query Language for Heterogeneous Data Sources. In *Lecture Notes in Computer Science*, Dallas, TX: Springer-Verlag. Also available at http://www.almaden.ibm.com/cs/people/chamberlin/quilt_lncs.pdf

Codd E. F. (1970). A relational model of data for large shared data banks. *Comm. ACM*, **13**(6), 377–387

Codd E. F. (1971). A database sublanguage founded on the relational calculus. In *Proc. ACM SIGFIDET Conf. on Data Description, Access and Control*, San Diego, CA, 35–68

Codd E. F. (1979). Extending the database relational model to capture more meaning. *ACM Trans. Database Systems*, **4**(4), 397–434

Connolly T. M. and Begg C. E. (2005). *Database Systems: A Practical Approach to Design, Implementation, and Management*. Harlow: Addison-Wesley

Date C. J. (1987). Twelve rules for a distributed database. *Computer World*, 8 June, **21**(23), 75–81

Deutsch M., Fernandez M., Florescu D., Levy A., and Suciu D. (1998). XML-QL: A Query Language for XML. Available at: http://www.w3.org/TR/NOTE-xml-ql

Epstein R., Stonebraker M., and Wong E. (1978). Query processing in a distributed relational database system. In *Proc. ACM SIGMOD Int. Conf. Management of Data*, Austin, TX, May 1978, 169–180

Eswaran K. P., Gray J. N., Lorie R. A., and Traiger I. L. (1976). The notion of consistency and predicate locks in a database system. *Comm. ACM*, **19**(11), 624–633

Garcia-Solaco M., Saltor F., and Castellanos M. (1996). Semantic Heterogeneity in Multidatabase Systems. In Bukhres and Elmagarmid (1996), 129–195

Gardarin G. and Valduriez P. (1989). *Relational Databases and Knowledge Bases*. Reading, MA: Addison-Wesley

Inmon W. H. (1993). *Building the Data Warehouse*. New York, NY: John Wiley

Jacobson I., Christerson M., Jonsson P., and Overgaard G. (1992). *Object-Oriented Software Engineering: A Use Case Driven Approach*, Reading, MA: Addison-Wesley

Kim W. (1991). Object-oriented database systems: strengths and weaknesses. *J. Object-Oriented Programming*, **4**(4), 21–29

Kung H. T. and Robinson J. T. (1981). On optimistic methods for concurrency control. *ACM Trans. Database Systems*, **6**(2), 213–226

Lee J. A. N. (2006). Codes of Conduct/Practice/Ethics from Around the world. Available at http://courses.cs.vt.edu/~cs3604/lib/WorldCodes/WorldCodes.html

OASIG (1996). Research report. Available at http://www.it-cortex.com/Stat_Failure_Cause.htm

OJEC (1995). Directive 95/46/EC of the European Parliament and of the Council of 24 October 1995 on the protection of individuals with regard to the processing of personal data and on the free movement of such data. *Official Journal of the European Communities of 23 November*, No L. 281 p. 31. Available at www.cdt.org/privacy/eudirective/EU_Directive_.html

OPSI (1998). Data Protection Act. UK Office of Public Sector Information. Available at http://www.opsi.gov.uk/acts/acts1998/19980029.htm#aofs

Ozsu M. and Valduriez P. (1999). *Principles of Distributed Database Systems* 2nd edn. Englewood Cliffs, NJ: Prentice-Hall

Richardson R. (2007) Computer Security Institute/Federal Bureau of Investigation (CSI/FBI) Computer Crime and Security Survey, pp. 1–25.

Robie J., Lapp J., and Schach D. (1998). XML Query Language (XQL). Available at http://www.w3.org/TandS/QL/QL98/pp/xql.html

Rothnie J. B. and Goodman N. (1977). A survey of research and development in distributed database management. In *Proc. 3rd Int. Conf. Very Large Databases*, Tokyo, Japan, 48–62

Sacco M. S. and Yao S. B. (1982). Query optimization in distributed data base systems. In *Advances in Computers*, **21** (Yovits M.C., ed.), New York: Academic Press, 225–273

Sheth A. and Larson J. L. (1990). Federated databases: architectures and integration. *ACM Computing Surv., Special Issue on Heterogeneous Databases*, **22**(3), 183–236

Shneiderman D. and Plaisant, C. (2004). *Design the User Interface: Strategies for Effective Human–Computer Interaction* 4th edn. Reading, MA: Addison-Wesley

Sommerville I. (2006). *Software Engineering* 8th edn. Reading, MA: Addison-Wesley

Stonebraker M. and Rowe L. (1986). The design of POSTGRES. In *ACM SIGMOD Int. Conf. on Management of Data*, 340–355

Taylor D. (1992). *Object Orientation Information Systems: Planning and Implementation*. New York, NY: John Wiley

Thornberry S. (2002). IT managers face ethical issues from piracy to privacy. *TechRepublic*. 25 September 2002

WC3 (2006). XML 1.1. World Wide Web Consortium. W3C Recommendation 16 August 2006. Available at http://www.w3.org/TR/xml11

W3C (2005). XQuery 1.0 and XPath 2.0 Data Model (XDM). W3C Candidate Recommendation 23 January 2007. Available at http://www.w3.org/TR/xpath-datamodel/

Wiederhold G. (1983). *Database Design* 2nd edn. New York, NY: McGraw-Hill

Index

Note: Entries in **bold** are definitions as given in the text. For further definitions of terms refer to the Glossary